THIS PILGRIM NATION

The Making of the Portuguese Diaspora in Postwar North America

This book tells the transnational history of Portuguese communities in Canada and the United States against the backdrop of the Cold War, the American Civil Rights movement, the Portuguese Colonial War, and Canadian multiculturalism. It considers the ethnic, racial, class, gender, linguistic, regional, and generational permutations of "Portuguese" diaspora from both a transnational and comparative perspective. Besides showing that diasporas and nations can be codependent, *This Pilgrim Nation* counters the common notion that hybrid diasporic identities are largely benign and empowering by revealing how they can perpetuate asymmetrical power relations.

GILBERTO FERNANDES is a post-doctoral visitor at the Robarts Centre for Canadian Studies at York University. Fernandes is an active public historian and documentary filmmaker involved in multiple initiatives in Toronto, including the Portuguese Canadian History Project, of which he is co-founder and president, and the multidimensional project "City Builders: A History of Immigrant Construction Workers in Postwar Toronto," winner of the 2019 Lieutenant Governor's Ontario Heritage Award for Excellence in Conservation.

This Pilgrim Nation

The Making of the Portuguese Diaspora in Postwar North America

GILBERTO FERNANDES

UNIVERSITY OF TORONTO PRESS
Toronto Buffalo London

© University of Toronto Press 2019
Toronto Buffalo London
utorontopress.com

ISBN 978-1-4426-3065-9 (cloth) ISBN 978-1-4426-3068-0 (EPUB)
ISBN 978-1-4426-3066-6 (paper) ISBN 978-1-4426-3067-3 (PDF)

Library and Archives Canada Cataloguing in Publication

Title: This pilgrim nation : the making of the Portuguese diaspora in postwar North America /Gilberto Fernandes.
Names: Fernandes, Gilberto, 1979– author.
Description: Includes bibliographical references and index.
Identifiers: Canadiana (print) 20190218134 | Canadiana (ebook) 20190218193 | ISBN 9781442630666 (softcover) | ISBN 9781442630659 (hardcover) | ISBN 9781442630673 (PDF) | ISBN 9781442630680 (EPUB)
Subjects: LCSH: Portuguese – Canada– History – 20th century. | LCSH: Portuguese – Canada – Social conditions – 20th century. | LCSH: Portuguese – Canada – Social life and customs – 20th century. | LCSH: Portuguese – United States – History – 20th century. | LCSH: Portuguese – United States – Social conditions – 20th century. | LCSH: Portuguese – United States – Social life and customs – 20th century.
Classification: LCC FC106.P8 F47 2019 | DDC 971.0046/91009045–dc23

This book was published with the help of a grant from the Federation for the Humanities and Social Sciences, through the Awards to Scholarly Publications Program, using funds provided by the Social Sciences and Humanities Research Council of Canada.

University of Toronto Press acknowledges the financial assistance to its publishing program of the Canada Council for the Arts and the Ontario Arts Council, an agency of the Government of Ontario.

  Canada Council   Conseil des Arts
for the Arts   du Canada

*For my parents,
my brother,
my wife,
and my children*

Contents

Illustrations and Figures ix

Acknowledgments xi

Abbreviations xv

Introduction 3

1 Portuguese Migration: Numbers, Policies, and Perceptions 25

2 Making Diasporic Souls: Catholic Missionaries, National Parishes, and Transregional Charity 75

3 Making Ethnic Civil Societies: Working-Class Organizations, Community Elites, and Political Federations 111

4 Making Ethnic Culture: Folk Propaganda, Popular Culture, and Language 144

5 Making Imperial Citizens: Lusotropicalism, Public Memory, and the Multiracial Diaspora 183

6 The Radicals' Diaspora: Anti-fascists, War Resisters, and State Surveillance 224

7 New Beginnings, Old Journeys: Multicultural, Generational, and Political Transitions 266

Conclusion 316

Notes 329

Index 381

Illustrations and Figures

Illustrations

1.1	*O Desterrado (The Uprooted)* by Soares dos Reis 31
1.2	New Bedford, MA, Portuguese mother with pictures of her sons in service 36
1.3	Azorean "bulk order" emigrants about to leave for Canada 45
1.4	Portuguese fisherman in Newfoundland 49
2.1	Pilgrims attending outdoor mass in Ludlow, MA 83
2.2	Father Alberto Cunha arriving at the coroner's office 95
2.3	Portuguese congregation in Notre-Dame Basilica, Montreal 98
2.4	Senhor Santo Cristo dos Milagres procession in Toronto 102
3.1	Portuguese-American city fathers of Provincetown, MA 126
3.2	Edmund Dinis campaigning with Senator John F. Kennedy 128
3.3	Portuguese immigrants protesting police violence in Toronto 135
3.4	Booklet for the *Sagres*'s visit to New Jersey 138
4.1	Rancho Lauradinos do Minho from Hartford, CT 150
4.2	Advertisement, *Diário de Notícias* 155
4.3	Mariano Rego playing Portuguese guitar 159
4.4	First Portuguese Canadian Club players celebrating a goal against the Polish-Canadian White Eagles 163
4.5	Banda Açoreana marching band performing in the Azores 165
4.6	Portuguese-American children and a nun in a classroom at a Portuguese-language school in New Bedford, MA 168
5.1	Cape Verdean cranberry bog workers in Falmouth, MA 191
5.2 and 5.3	Bernardo Teixeira with teacher Osceloa Crew and "Portuguese" students in Gaston, NC 194, 195

6.1	Fernando Ciriaco da Cunha 238
6.2	Pro-Salazar demonstrator arrested outside the Portuguese consulate in Toronto 240
6.3	Poster for the 1966 Canadian Conference for Amnesty in Portugal 248
6.4	Protesters outside the Portuguese consulate in Toronto 250
6.5	Front cover of the *Luso-Canadiano* announcing the death of Henrique T. Bello 252
7.1	Clipping from the *Comunidade* introducing the YMCA's Portuguese workers 282
7.2	Crowd gathered for General António Spínola outside Toronto's St Lawrence Centre for the Arts 294
7.3	Portuguese, Canadian, and Azorean flags waving during Toronto's Portugal Day celebrations 305
7.4	Community leaders and Portuguese diplomats posing in front of the padrão monument 310

Figures

Figure 1.1	Portuguese total emigration, 1855–2003 26
Figure 1.2	Portuguese "foreign stock" in the United States, by state, 1870–1990 29
Figure 1.3	Portuguese obtaining legal resident status in the United States, 1820–2009 33
Figure 1.4	Portuguese emigration by destination, 1950–74 37
Figure 1.5	Portuguese foreign revenue (remittances and exports), 1953–74 41
Figure 1.6	Portuguese emigration versus Canadian immigration statistics, 1946–78 48
Figure 1.7	Portuguese emigration to Canada by district of origin, 1955–74 52
Figure 1.8	Portuguese emigration to the United States by district of origin, 1955–74 56
Figure 1.9	Portuguese emigration by destination, 1974–88 57
Figure 1.10	Portuguese expatriate voter turnout in legislative elections, 1976–2011 60
Figure 1.11	Portuguese foreign revenue (remittances and exports), 1974–89 64
Figure 2.1	Madeiran Day total donations, 1934–72 106
Figure 5.1	Casa de Portugal annual expenditures, 1942–63 207

Acknowledgments

As the saying goes, it takes a village to raise a child. The same can be said about books. During the years of research and writing that went into the making of this book, I was able to count on the intellectual, financial, logistic, and emotional support of a large number of people.

I owe a great deal of gratitude to my teacher and dear friend Dr Roberto Perin, who allowed me to be ambitious and trusted that I would complete this project as I had originally envisioned it. His detailed feedback, wise insights, and honest friendliness made my journey as a doctoral student enjoyable. Like Dr Perin, Dr Franca Iacovetta has been a great supporter of my work, including this publication. Her eminent work on postwar immigration and the Italian diaspora has been a major point of reference in my research and public history practice, and I have had the privilege of benefiting from Dr Iacovetta's personal insights. I am also thankful to Dr Adrian Shubert, Dr William Jenkins, Dr José Curto, and Dr Gabriele Scardelatto: their feedback also improved this study. The comments made by the anonymous peer reviewers who read my manuscript were very useful and have greatly enriched this book. Their questions and suggestions helped me take my research in new directions and reach for a wider interdisciplinary audience.

The financial support that I received from various organizations in the form of scholarships, grants, and awards allowed me to work on this research project full time for most of the three and a half years that it took me to write it. I am grateful to the Faculty of Graduate Studies at York University; the Social Sciences and Humanities Research Council; the Ontario Ministry of Training, Colleges and Universities; the Federation of Portuguese Canadian Business & Professionals; and the Canadian Union of Public Employees Local 3903, for having supported my work in this way. I am grateful also to the Federation for the Humanities and Social Sciences for having awarded this book a Scholarly

Publications Program's (ASPP) publication grant. I also owe a great deal of gratitude to York University's Division of Advancement and its Faculty of Liberal Arts and Professional Studies' development officers for the fundraising campaign that they launched in 2015 to support my research and public history work. I am particularly indebted to York's Wade Hall, Mariya Yurukova, and Muneeb Syed, and to the private donors Manuel da Costa and the Laborers' International Union of North America (LIUNA) Local 183 for providing me with the financial means necessary to continue my scholarly work, which included finishing this book. The administrative support that I have enjoyed at York, first as a doctoral student and later as a postdoctoral visitor at the Robarts Centre for Canadian Studies and Department of History, was also very helpful in carrying the project forward.

This book would simply not have been possible if not for the often thankless work of the many archivists and librarians who care for the various collections that I was able to consult in situ and online. I am particularly grateful to the Historical-Diplomatic Archives of the Portuguese Ministry of Foreign Affairs; the Torre do Tombo National Archive in Lisbon; the April 25th Documentation Centre at the University of Coimbra; Library and Archives Canada; the Ferreira-Mendes Portuguese-American Archives at the University of Massachusetts-Dartmouth; and the Clara Thomas Archives and Special Collections at York University. I am especially grateful to the archivists Michael Moir, Anna St Onge, and the rest of the staff at the Clara Thomas Archives for having fully embraced the Portuguese Canadian History Project (PCHP), which I co-founded with Dr Susana Miranda in 2008. By sharing the PCHP's collaborative vision for archival outreach and committing extensive resources to see it come to fruition, they have allowed us to amass, preserve, and make accessible the largest collection of Portuguese historical records in Canada (and the second in North America), reflecting the myriad experiences of these immigrants and their descendants. I am thankful to the archival donors who entrusted their records to the Clara Thomas Archives through the PCHP, including Abílio Cipriano Marques, António Santos (Portuguese Canadian Democratic Association), Cidália Pereira (Portuguese Interagency Network), Professor David Higgs, Domingos Marques, Ilda Januário (Portuguese-Canadian Coalition for Better Education), John Santos, the Canadian Auto Workers(currently Unifor) Local 40, and Professor Wenona Giles. These records were crucial to the writing of this book.

My many friends and colleagues in the faculty and graduate student body of York University's Department of History were also a great source of advice and motivation during this project. I am particularly grateful to Dr Marcel Martel and Dr Craig Heron for championing my work ever since I joined the department as a graduate student. It has also been an absolute privilege and great deal of fun to work closely with my PCHP colleagues and dear friends Dr Susana Miranda, Dr Raphael Costa, Dr Emanuel da Silva, and Anna St Onge, whose personal and professional support system have also helped me write this book.

Every day of my life I am thankful for my parents, Amândio and Elsa, whose generosity, kindness, humour, and curiosity have been my compass. I am thankful also for my older brother, Luis Miguel, for sparking my imagination, showing me how to be creative, and being a willing and cheerful reader of my first adventures in storytelling. Their contributions to my intellectual formation and scholarship, and hence to this publication, are immeasurable, as is my gratitude to them. I dedicate this book to them to atone for my wrongdoing in stealing myself from them when I became an emigrant in 2004. My in-laws (surrogate parents) and my extensive Portuguese-Canadian family, through whom I have the honour of being called son, brother, and uncle, have also contributed to this project by providing me with a comfortable environment where I can step away from my work and not feel guilty about it. My biggest and most heartfelt debt of gratitude is to the very reason why I became an immigrant, Nancy, my wife and mother of my children, who made this book and everything that preceded it possible in far too many ways to list here. This milestone is as much mine as it is hers. Finally, Simão and Vasco, my children, who were not yet born when I completed the first manuscript of this book, I give thanks for making it all worthwhile. This book is also dedicated to them.

Abbreviations

ANI	Agência de Notícias e Informação (News and Information Agency)
AO	Archives of Ontario
APC	Association portugaise du Canada (Portuguese Association of Canada)
APCS	American Portuguese Cultural Society
ARCAT	Archives of the Roman Catholic Archdiocese of Toronto
CCAP	Canadian Committee for Amnesty in Portugal
CDS	Centro Democrata Social (Democratic Social Party)
CD25A	April 25th Documentation Centre (Centro de Documentação 25 de Abril)
CIA	Central Intelligence Agency
COPA	Cambridge Organization of Portuguese-Americans
CPC	Conselho das Comunidades Portuguesas (Council of Portuguese Communities)
CPDP	Committee Pro-Democracy in Portugal
CPRPS	Centre portugais de référence et promotion sociale (Portuguese Centre of Reference and Social Promotion)
CTASC	Clara Thomas Archives and Special Collections
DCI	Department of Citizenship and Immigration
DDS	Directório Democrato-Social (Democrat-Social Directory)
EEC	European Economic Community
EFTA	European Free Trade Association
ESL	English as a Second Language
EU	European Union
FARA	Foreign Agents Registration Act
FBI	Federal Bureau of Investigation
FLA	Frente de Libertação dos Açores (Azorean Liberation Front)

FLAD	Fundação Luso-Americana para o Desenvolvimento (Luso-American Development Foundation)
FPCC	First Portuguese Canadian Club
FPLN	Frente Patriótica de Libertação Nacional (National Liberation Patriotic Front)
HDA	Historical-Diplomatic Archives (Arquivo Histórico-Diplomático do Ministério dos Negócios Estrangeiros)
HGBB	Holy Ghost Beneficial Brotherhood
IAC	Instituto de Alta Cultura (Institute of High Culture)
ICEM	Intergovernmental Committee for European Migration
LAC	Library and Archives Canada
LCA	Luso Canadian Association
MCP	Movimento Comunitário Português (Portuguese Communitarian Movement)
MDP	Mouvement démocratique portugais (Portuguese Democratic Movement)
MFA	Movimento das Forças Armadas (Armed Forces Movement)
MP	Member of Parliament
MPP	Member of Provincial Parliament
NATO	North Atlantic Treaty Organization
NDP	New Democratic Party
OEEC	Organisation for European Economic Cooperation
OCPM	Obra Católica Portuguesa de Migrações (Portuguese Catholic Organization for Migrations)
PACFA	Portuguese-American Committee on Foreign Affairs
PAF	Portuguese American Federation
PAIGC	Partido Africano para a Independência da Guiné e Cabo Verde (African Party for the Independence of Guinea and Cape Verde)
PCC	Portuguese Canadian Congress
PCDA	Portuguese Canadian Democratic Association
PCHP	Portuguese Canadian History Project
PCP	Partido Comunista Português (Portuguese Communist Party)
PCU	Portuguese Continental Union (União Portuguese Continental)
PIDE	Polícia Internacional e de Defesa do Estado (International and State Defense Police)
PMFA	Portuguese Ministry of Foreign Affairs
PPD	Partido Popular Democrata (Popular Democratic Party)
PREC	Processo Revolucionário em Curso (Ongoing Revolutionary Process)
PS	Partido Socialista (Socialist Party)

PSD	Partido Social Democrata (Social Democratic Party)
RCMP	Royal Canadian Mounted Police
SCFR	Senate Committee on Foreign Relations
SCP	Sport Club Portuguese
SEIT	Secretariado de Estado de Informação e Turismo (Secretariat of State of Information and Tourism)
SNE	Secretariado Nacional de Emigração (National Secretariat of Emigration)
SNI	Secretariado Nacional de Informação, Cultura Popular e Turismo (National Secretariat of Information, Popular Culture, and Tourism)
TAP	Transportes Aéreos Portugueses (Portuguese Air Transports)
TTNA	Torre do Tombo National Archive
UN	United Nations
UCP	Union Catholique Portugaise (Portuguese Catholic Union)
UPCC	Union of Portuguese Cultural Communities

THIS PILGRIM NATION

The Making of the Portuguese Diaspora in Postwar North America

Introduction

As of 2014, ninety-eight countries have allowed their expatriated citizens to vote in homeland elections from abroad. Forty-four of them did so in the twenty-first century alone;[1] eighty-four since 1975, when Portugal first introduced external voting rights. Other than the occasional polemic in the news, as when Turkish politicians were banned from campaigning in expatriate communities in Germany in the spring of 2017,[2] the global trend towards enfranchising diasporic constituencies is arguably one of the most underrated political stories of our time. Even among the recent wave of far-right, nativist, and anti-globalist governments, there are those with transnational ambitions. This is the case with the prime minister of Hungary, Viktor Órban, who enfranchised "ethnic Hungarians" living in neighbouring countries, expecting them to vote for him in the 2018 elections.[3] By contrast, some historically liberal-democratic countries, such as Canada and the United States, remain parochial outliers in this global trend. At a time when more countries are harnessing the economic, cultural, and political reach of their diasporas, American and Canadian federal governments in recent years have introduced measures that have strained relations with their emigrants. In 2010, before the election of the anti-globalization and anti-immigration president, Donald Trump, Washington demanded that Americans living abroad file yearly tax returns on their foreign capital, which resulted in their double taxation. This measure generated significant backlash from expatriates, a substantial number of whom responded by renouncing their American citizenship. The tax reform introduced by President Trump in 2018 eliminated this double taxation for transnational corporations, but not for individual emigrants.[4] In Ottawa in recent years, the two ruling parties have characterized expatriated citizens as "Canadians of convenience" and other discrediting epithets, wrongfully believing that they are mostly naturalized immigrants who return to their home countries after a few years in Canada. Such disparaging perceptions were leveraged by Prime Minister Stephen Harper in 2015 to justify significant changes to citizenship and immigration legislation (Bill C-24) along with five-year limits on the external voting rights of Canadian expats.[5] Both countries' self-understanding as "nations of immigrants" have prevented their politicians and intelligentsia from coming to terms with the fact that they too have a long history of transnational emigration. As Michael Collyer would put it, their expatriated citizens have not been embraced as "fully part of the nation, the people."[6] Meanwhile, the world's "emigrant nations" have been busy praising their once embarrassing histories of populational exodus and adapting their national narratives to meet our global era of transnational belongings. This book tells the history of one nation's early efforts towards making its emigrants a national "people" at a time when most countries were primarily concerned with asserting their territorial sovereignty. It is also a history of a relatively small yet surprisingly influential ethnic community in Canada and the United States during a time when ethnic and racial relations were at the heart of those countries' nation-building projects. By interweaving these two, this book ultimately tells the history of the making of Portuguese diaspora in North America.

A "pilgrim nation" of patriotic missionaries, worldly citizens, and pluri-continental communities that included metropolitan residents, colonial settlers, and emigrants in every corner of the world: that was the "ecumenical" vision of Portugal laid out by the Estado Novo's former overseas minister, Adriano Moreira, in 1964 at a meeting in Aveiro that gathered the country's intelligentsia to discuss the beleaguered state of the empire. For Moreira, the need to reclaim expatriates as full citizens of the imperial nation was not simply a "sentimental matter" but a shrewd recognition that their communities were strategic outposts for advancing the government's foreign interests during a time of growing anti-colonialist pressure.[7] Fast forward to the Revolution of the Carnations of 25 April 1974, which put an end to forty-eight years of conservative dictatorship and Portugal's centuries-old colonial empire: diasporic visions now gripped the minds of state officials as never before. In 1977 Ramalho Eanes, the first president of Portugal in the new democratic era, officially proclaimed the dawn of a new diasporic nationhood: "it matters more the man than the ground on which he lives."[8] By replacing imperial with diasporic mythologies, Portuguese intelligentsia found a solution for the "crisis of national identity" into which the country had fallen with the end of the empire.[9] This repositioning allowed the Lisbon government to cling to the old pluri-continental idea of nationhood and maintain some of Portugal's former geopolitical relevance beyond the small corner in

Europe's periphery, which it refused to be restricted to. Once mocked by Portuguese elites, emigrants were now elevated to heroic status, as the flag-bearers of the nation's borderless, entrepreneurial and cosmopolitan spirit, often compared to the explorers of Portugal's "golden age" of seafaring history. They were encouraged to think of themselves as transnational citizens living in a diaspora that the homeland government vowed to nourish and facilitate. Most emigrants welcomed this institutional outreach and saw it as a positive step towards redressing the negligence that they had supposedly been subjected to during the dictatorship and as due recognition for their ongoing contributions to their homeland. Still, this diaspora-building project stood on a foundation that was laid by the imperial dictatorship, built on recycled discourses and methods. Noticing the resemblances between pre- and post-revolutionary strategies, the emigrants grew weary of the homeland's constant appeals to their patriotism and developed a somewhat autonomous diasporic consciousness that sometimes bypassed it altogether.

This book explores the social, cultural, religious, economic, and political processes involved in the making of diaspora in the largest and most concentrated Portuguese communities in North America, located in northeastern United States (New England and the New York metropolitan area) and eastern Canada (Toronto, Ontario, and Montreal, Quebec).[10] It examines the role of the Estado Novo and its opponents in shaping these communities' cultural identities, institutional structures, ruling elites, and political relations and how they set the foundations for the post-imperial reconfiguration of Portuguese "nationhood." Here we will uncover how state diplomats, Catholic missionaries, ethnic entrepreneurs, cultural promoters, political activists, and other transnational agents articulated diaspora at the intersection of home nation, host nation, and migrant communities. The period of study (1950s–70s) encompasses the inauguration of Portuguese mass migration to Canada and its resurgence in the United States; the rise of large international governing bodies, rival Cold War superpowers, and their spheres of influence; the Colonial Wars in Africa and the collapse of traditional settler colonialism; the emergence of cultural pluralism and identity politics in Canada and parts of the United States; the radicalization of the Portuguese "anti-fascist" opposition; and the revolutionary transition to democracy in Portugal. These large processes framed the local, national, and transnational lives of Portuguese immigrants in North America and had a significant impact on their public and private lives.

This study deals primarily with the public, institutional, and political processes of diasporic community formation, not with the immigrants' private "culture of everyday life." As such, I will privilege the actions and motivations of spiritual leaders, community organizers, transnational elites, political activists, and government officials over those of common immigrant workers and their families. The "bottom-up" approach of "new migration historians" such as John Bodnar, Robert Harney, and their intellectual successors has offered valuable insights into the lives of common immigrants and their relationship with the immigrant aristocracy.[11] Notwithstanding their generation's immense contribution to advancing migration history, their efforts to reveal the immigrants' limited yet explicit agency have resulted in an underestimation of the role that middle- and upper-class ethnic leaders played in the process of community and identity formation.[12] Class matters a great deal when it comes to diasporic communities. Migrants with more financial and social capital have easier access to the homeland, which further increases their power as transnational gatekeepers and facilitators.[13] Because of its focus on the public sphere, this study is also largely about patriarchal men. During the postwar period, women were largely removed from the civil society of Portuguese communities – especially in newcomer settlements – or were relegated to "auxiliary" committees, for which there are few surviving records. Furthermore, as Anh Hua argues: "Diasporic women are less likely than diasporic men to have nostalgic memories about their homelands because of their painful recollection of patriarchal attitudes, customs, and traditions found in the 'Old World.'"[14] Although at the same time, as Donna Gabaccia points out: "As long as they could return freely to their hometown, migrant 'men without women' had few reasons to create a national diasporic identity."[15] Still, despite the gender dynamics working to exclude them, some middle-class women participated directly in the diaspora-building processes examined here.

I argue that both diasporas and nations are "imagined communities" with more in common than postcolonial scholars had previously suggested, and that they can reinforce each other when linked by imperial imaginings. The Portuguese example illustrates how nation states can reframe the collective imagination of its domestic and expatriate citizenry along diasporic lines in order to reassert their sovereignty and geopolitical clout in a context of accelerated globalization. While largely successful, this diaspora-building process was not inevitable or without resistance, nor did it follow from a clear long-term plan devised by committed architects, nor was its fragmented outcome foreseen by its original proponents. I will highlight the clumsy and contentious origins of diasporic consciousness as reflected in the emergence of regional, linguistic, racial, and political alternatives to the (trans)national norm. I also contend that hybrid identities produced in the diaspora are not necessarily benign or progressive, as they can perpetuate asymmetrical power relations based on their proximity to the "ancestral homeland." Furthermore, diasporic consciousness, transnational belongings, and dual citizenship are not the products of one particular political ideology. Despite some important differences in approach and rationale, both left- and right-wing political forces in Portugal have served and utilized diaspora. Finally, this study confirms that *international* relations between host and home countries are often assisted by *transnational* agents and networks,[16] and that diplomats sometimes operate in both dimensions, thus muddling them.

The direct intervention of homeland officials in the affairs of emigrant communities and their attempts to create diasporic solidarities for political gains were not unique to the Portuguese dictatorship. Benito Mussolini, Adolf Hitler, Francisco Franco, and Nicholas Horthy all had diaspora-building policies of varied success that sought to mobilize expats through the discreet work of their diplomatic corps.[17] Diasporic communities negotiating national belongings by evoking the intersecting imperial histories of host and home nations are also common to other groups and countries.[18] The transnational support for the Azorean and Cape Verdean independence movements among immigrants in North America was also similar to the much older Irish independence struggle, which mobilized its large diaspora to fight against their homeland's colonial oppressor. While not unique, the Portuguese case is a very instructive one when compared with other diasporas in North America, in large part owing to the fact that it is off-centre from the standard periodization of European immigration history. The Portuguese were one of the last European mass immigrant groups to arrive in Canada and the United States primarily as labourers, whose movement peaked at a time when non-European immigrants with higher skills had become the norm. They emerged from the world's last settler colonial empire and one of the two remaining right-wing dictatorships in Europe after the Second World War, which collapsed roughly at the same time as that migration movement ended. The diasporic-building policies of Lisbon's new democratic government predated by a few decades the similar policies of other "emigrant nations," which started in earnest in the 1990s. The Portuguese are also the only European Latin group other than Spaniards to be commonly referred to as "Latinos" and "Hispanics" in the United States. All these factors complicate the established narratives about European immigration in North America in the postwar period. The Portuguese case allows us to learn more about how diasporas are conceived, what sustains and transforms them, what advantages and disadvantages they offer its stakeholders, and how they relate with other social, cultural, and political constructs.

Before exploring these questions, one must grasp what "diaspora" means and how that meaning has evolved over time. Generally, the term refers to a dispersed group of people that was forcefully or voluntarily displaced from an original "homeland," and it either asserts or is ascribed an identity based on a set of shared geographic factors, a sense of in-group fraternity, and a shared collective memory of migration. In many ways, diasporas are similar to nations, which some aspire to become. This analogy is all the clearer when we consider Benedict Anderson's famous description of nations as "imagined communities": "*imagined* because the members of even the smallest nation [or diaspora] will never know most of their fellow-members, meet them, or even hear of them, yet in the minds of each lives the image of their communion;" "*community*, because, regardless of the actual inequality and exploitation that may prevail in each, nation [or diaspora] is always considered as a deep, horizontal comradeship." The same way that diasporas encompass more than one nation – the one longed for (the homeland) and those where its members reside (the host nation) – nations can host multiple diasporas within their borders, as is the case of Canada and the United States. But, despite juxtaposition, diasporas and nations are said to differ in a fundamental aspect. Unlike diasporas, nations are "*limited* because even the largest of them ... has finite, if elastic, boundaries, beyond which lie other nations. No nation imagines itself coterminous with mankind."[19] Diasporas, on the other hand, are clusters of transnational migrant communities, whose members maintain relationships that span national borders and link distant sites under a shared (though not uncontested) sense of group identity.

Traditionally, "diaspora" referred specifically to the forced and often traumatic displacement and dispersal of a large group of people bound by ties of nationality, ethnicity, race, or religion, such as Jewish exiles, African slaves, and Irish famine and Armenian genocide refugees. For these "refugee" diasporas, the ancient homeland became a largely mythical place. Nonetheless, it remained a pivotal source of "authentic" group identity, to which its members held the vague hope of " returning" one day, motivated by a cultivated sense of victimhood and quest for justice. In the early 1990s, expatriate intellectuals, artists, and politicians began using the term "diaspora" to craft deterritorialized, flexible, and creative hybrid identities to describe and empower large migrant groups that had not been victims of violent dispersal, yet still were marginalized in an increasingly globalized world.[20] This rethinking corresponded with the larger postmodern or postcolonial critique of "nations" and other forms of essentialized belonging as antiquated, reductive, and ultimately harmful paradigms. At this point, "diaspora," "transnationalism," and "globalization" became buzzwords in academia and in the media, used to describe a wide range of human phenomena and states of mind. Because of its overuse, these terms were stretched too thin and lost much of their analytical value. Various scholars set out to pin concrete definitions on the concepts and capture their many variations while limiting their scope. All of them agreed that diasporas are not ethnodemographic or ethnocultural facts, and that they should be studied as cultural and political projects, in much the same way that nations are.[21] I follow this line of thought by treating diasporas as "imagined transnational communities" resulting from mobilization processes, which intersect and/or compete with other identities.

I will try to answer for the Portuguese case some of the research questions proposed by Martin Sökefeld: Who were the agents producing and disseminating transnational community discourses? What were the events, strategies, and practices deployed in this mobilization? What resistance or alternatives were there to these diasporic imaginings? I will also show how nations and diasporas can meld within the same political project when interwoven by a common imperial thread. This approach contradicts the notions that diasporas necessarily decentralize nations and other essentialized belongings, or that cultural hybridity is intrinsically empowering and egalitarian, as proposed by Homi Bhabha.[22] Instead, the making of Portuguese diaspora(s) confirms Vijay Agnew's argument that "not all facets of hybrid identities are equal and symmetrical; rather, they are uneven because they stem from histories that transcend individual intentionality," and that "diasporas construct racialized, sexualized, gendered, and oppositional subjectivities."[23] Furthermore, not all diasporic connections are negotiated through the "ancestral" centre. This study reveals how expatriates often push back, sidestep, or reinterpret the homeland's metanarrative. Anthropologist Edite Noivo reached the same conclusion after doing fieldwork in Toronto's Portuguese community in the late 1990s. She noted that the emigrants' shared sense of estrangement from both home and host societies was as prominent as their sense of belonging to the Portuguese "global nation." In other words, their diasporic solidarity connected them "not only or maybe not even primarily to Portugal, so much as to others who have been similarly forced to leave it."[24]

Although it forms the crux of this study, I will seldom use the term "diaspora" when describing the actions and thoughts of its subjects. Portuguese officials began using that word only in the late 1970s, after which it took some time to percolate into popular parlance. Until the mid-1960s emigrant settlements were often referred to as "colonies."[25] But even then, as today, the term most often used was simply "Portuguese communities." Even the word "emigrant" has been the subject of contentious debate among Portuguese expatriates and politicians. Of course, just because "diaspora" was not used does not mean that there was no diasporic consciousness as we understand it today. But to avoid crowding this study with casual uses of the very expression that I am trying to historicize, I will reserve it for the conclusions, or for when the actors are consciously diasporic, even if they call it something else.

That globalization has not led to the demise of nation states and their borders is today painfully obvious to those who once welcomed that prospect. Yet it remains a powerful call to action for its opponents, who these days are found primarily on the far right; however, much like the far left's "anti-globalization," the hyper-nationalist movement of Nigel Farage, Matteo Salvini, Steve Bannon, and others like them is itself globalized and transnational. Gone for a while, the buzzwords are back. Now that nation states have proven to be more resilient than previously thought, we can examine how these modern political constructs managed to withstand the disintegrating pressures of postcolonial globalization. Faced with international threats to its traditional sovereignty, some nation states resisted their loss of autonomy via macro-regional integration by becoming more rigid and exclusive, while others embraced postmodern notions of nationhood and became more flexible and inclusive. Of course, reality is messier when we look at specific examples. In the Estado Novo's case, both strategies were used simultaneously, sometimes advanced by the same person. However, in the end, the flexible, deterritorialized notion of nationhood prevailed and the colonialist, sovereignty-by-force strategy collapsed.

Setting the Stage: Portugal, Canada, and the United States in the 1950s–1970s

By the end of the Second World War, the Estado Novo was entering its third decade in power. Its origins dated back to 28 May 1926, when a right-wing military coup ousted the democratic republican government, which had been in power since the Republican Revolution of 5 October 1910 (with a brief interruption in 1918). The new authoritarian regime emerged from among various sectors of the right-wing opposition to the First Republic's liberalism, anticlericalism, positivism, and partisan parliamentary system. António Salazar entered the dictatorial government in 1928 as minister of finance and would eliminate Portugal's large deficit through a combination of austerity measures, new taxes, policy tricks, and a tight control over ministerial budgets. His performance raised his profile as a competent and honest statesman, who had "saved" Portugal from bankruptcy, an image that was carefully crafted by the now censored press. Salazar's relatively moderate position within the dictatorship, which included republican conservatives, monarchists, fascists, and other right-wing groups, also raised his influence with President Óscar Carmona, who entrusted him with the task of leading the National Revolution. In 1932, Salazar became dictator-in-chief of the Estado Novo, which was formally inaugurated with its own constitution in the following year.

The Estado Novo was a conservative authoritarian regime headed by an unelected, permanent prime minister, who accumulated various core portfolios and presided over the Ministerial Council (or cabinet), which was supported by a puppet president and an unelected, single-party (União Nacional), consultative National Assembly. To understand the often inconsistent and discretionary actions of its officials, we must keep in mind that the Estado Novo "was not homogeneous, nor coherent, nor strong, nor united around a single man." Today, historians agree that the regime was made up of a diverse hierarchy of institutions and civil servants with different connections, which "competed amongst themselves in order to impose their worldviews, making it difficult for the state to coordinate and direct them."[26]

Inspired by a blend of right-wing ideologies, including integralism, fascism, and Catholic social doctrine, the dictatorship embraced corporatism as its model for social and economic relations, with its vision of harmony between capital and labour and a paternalist ethos marked by traditionalist notions of rural, religious, and patriarchal family life. The regime's corporatist structure abolished free trade unions, strikes, and lockouts and organized labour-capital relations under state-controlled national syndicates, professional guilds, and rural community centres (Casas do Povo or Casas dos Pescadores). Under this anti-capitalist, anti-liberal, anti-socialist ideal, workers and employers were supposed to resolve their differences using the official structures, without resorting to conflict. In reality, the dictatorship's corporatist ideology had little in common with its actual institutions, dominated as they were by large landowners, industrialists, and port authorities, who used them to control labour and wages with the government's consent.

Under the 1933 constitution, all parties except the União Nacional were banned. Youth associations outside the Moçidade Portuguesa (Portuguese Youth) – a paramilitary scout organization inspired by the fascist Opera Nazionale Balilla and the Nazi Hitler Youth – were also prohibited, except for those connected with the Catholic Church. The right of association for political, social, cultural, recreational, or any other collective activity was subject to state approval. Public gatherings considered to be of a political or social nature also had to be sanctioned and monitored by the authorities. Some civic organizations were tolerated by the regime, especially those of a seemingly folk communitarian character. In rural settings, the Casas do Povo were also important secular public spaces, where people could participate in collective organizations, such as sports and other recreational programs. These community houses also offered limited social assistance and job training. However, most working families could not access their services, since they could not afford the membership fees.

State welfare was practically non-existent until the late 1960s. Until then, the responsibility to assist seniors, the sick, unemployed, and poor lay primarily with the extended family and the charity of Catholic organizations, such as Caritas[27] and the Society of St Vincent de Paul.[28] In Salazar's view, public welfare discouraged individuals from being self-reliant, threatened family bonds, and embraced "socialist principles repelled by the Christian concept of life."[29] The rural background of the industrial workforce was thought to function as a social insurance policy, since the unemployed could always return to the fields and live off the land.

This rural social pacification was most pronounced in the northern mainland and in the Azores,[30] where most emigrants departed from. Here, small-scale subsistence farming predominated and the Church regulated much of public and private life. In the Azores, individual families owned the vast majority of the land (nearly 80 per cent in 1965); though very few of these holdings were capable of providing a living income (only 7 per cent that year). The situation was even worse in São Miguel, the largest and most populated island, where most of the land was owned by a few landowners, who rented small plots to farming families or hired farmhands to work their fields. While the high rents made it difficult for tenant farmers to subsist, the high population density produced chronic unemployment and kept wages low. The concentration of land, wealth, and industry in the hands of a few *Micaelense* (of São Miguel) families made up a powerful conservative force opposing economic reform or meaningful social mobility.[31] By contrast, farmland in the southern mainland was concentrated in large estates owned by a few landholders, who relied on a large mass of rural proletarians. It was common for these farmhands to sojourn or settle in the greater Lisbon area, where they became urban proletarians and developed a working-class consciousness; many of them joined the ranks of the clandestine labour movement and the underground Portuguese Communist Party (PCP). Conversely, the minifundia in the north worked as a divisive force among rural workers, who were protective of their small properties, since it heightened intraclass competition over interclass conflict. Nonetheless, independent family farming often required extra help to perform time-sensitive tasks, and the best way to undertake them was through neighbourly cooperation and reciprocity – a practice that Portuguese emigrants took with them to North America.

The regime's conservative views on social security prevailed after the inauguration of the Ministry of Corporations and Social Welfare in 1950. Essentially a ministry of labour, this government branch was staffed with socially minded Catholics, who were later inspired by the progressive ideas coming out of the Second Vatican Council (or Vatican II) of 1962–5. Their push for more economic redistribution policies and greater social equality gained some traction during the rule of Marcello Caetano – Salazar's successor after 1968. Seeking political legitimacy, the new "modern" dictator introduced various social programs aimed at appeasing a workforce that was increasingly destitute, restless and, because of the emigrants, more aware of government welfare in other countries.

Before the war, public education in Portugal was valued for its proselytizing and indoctrinating role and little more. Its emphasis on Catholic morals and corporatist doctrine taught individuals to accept their place in society and renounce aspirations of social mobility. This was a clear departure from the First Republic's positivist program that sought to eliminate Portugal's soaring illiteracy rate and secularize society. Instead, the dictatorship reduced mandatory schooling, increased the Catholic Church's grip on the public school curriculum, and reduced the professional credentials required of educators, the vast majority of whom were women. Salazar feared the disruptive effects that intellectual culture and higher education could produce if made available to the general population. The regime's propaganda and popular culture institutions were designed to avoid "altering an individual's capacity for knowledge, perfecting intellectual faculties, developing a critical spirit, [or] sharpening aesthetic taste."[32]

Three central features of the Estado Novo were its widespread propaganda, censorship, and political repression. Together, they ensured the government's views were widely disseminated and unchallenged. The National Secretariat of Propaganda – which changed its name to National Secretariat of Information, Popular Culture, and Tourism (SNI) in 1944, then dropped Popular Culture (SEIT) in 1968 – was responsible for crafting the regime's messages, running its censorship services, developing popular cultural policies, and regenerating the Portuguese "national spirit." Although most active in the 1930s, when it developed large propaganda productions and events inspired by its fascist and Nazi peers, this agency continued to play a central role in the formation of Portuguese cultural identity until 1974, including among the emigrants. The dictatorship's most infamous and violent tool of repression was the International and State Defense Police (PIDE), which operated under the Ministry of the Interior and was supervised by Salazar himself. This secret police was dedicated to eliminating political threats in Portugal and its colonies, targeting especially PCP militants. The PIDE's eyes and ears reached all sectors of Portuguese society through a vast network of paid informants, resulting in a panopticon of fear and suspicion, where it was common for neighbours, co-workers, and acquaintances, at home and abroad, to denounce those whose loyalty was deemed questionable.

Along with being citizens of an impoverished, antiquated, uneducated, pious, patriarchal, and undemocratic European nation, Portuguese emigrants also were proud members of one of the world's oldest colonial empires,[33] which the Estado Novo reasserted as a sacrosanct part of the nation. After the Colonial Act of 1930, which reasserted Lisbon's unilateral rule over its colonies and Portugal's "historic function" to "colonize its overseas domains and to civilize the native populations contained therein," the regime actively tried to impress an "imperial mentality" on its citizens. Portuguese people were told that theirs was "not a small country," since it extended "from Minho to Timor."[34] This imperial self-understanding was central to the articulation of Portuguese identity in North America, especially in the United States.

The actions of Portuguese officials towards emigrant communities, their reception, and consequences were in no small part determined by the international context in which they unfolded. At the end of the Second World War, the United States and the Soviet Union emerged as the world's new superpowers, each with its own all-encompassing ideology and geopolitical sphere of influence. Both sides indirectly battled each other in a protracted Cold War that engaged many of the world's nations over four decades. As tensions escalated between the communist East and the liberal-democratic West, underlined by the threat of nuclear Armageddon, a group of non-aligned countries composed initially of recently emancipated colonies in Africa and Asia, formed a third bloc that demanded an end to all forms of colonialism. The main stage for their diplomatic battles was the United Nations, founded in 1945 to prevent competing national interests from escalating into military conflicts and to promote international legal standards on a number of issues, including universal human rights and the right of national "peoples" to self-determination. Also aiming to create the political conditions for a lasting peace in Europe, the United States began distributing massive financial stimulus and other forms of aid to those countries affected by the war, so they could rebuild their economies. Launched in 1948, this European Recovery Program (known as the Marshall Plan) was supervised by the Organisation for European Economic Cooperation (OEEC), which laid the foundations for other international trade organizations, such as the European Economic Community (EEC) – launched by the continent's strongest national economies in 1957 – and the European Free Trade Association (EFTA) – founded in 1960 by some of the EEC's outlying countries. In the meantime, the Cold War's rival factions congealed into two large international military alliances: the Washington-led North Atlantic Treaty Organization (NATO), founded in 1949, and the Moscow-led Warsaw Pact, created in 1955.

In a world dominated by the vanquishers of far-right dictatorships and opponents of settler colonialism, the Estado Novo found itself in an awkward position, as an authoritarian colonial empire torn between its ideological affinities with the former Axis nations and its historical alliance with Great Britain. But Salazar's "collaborative neutrality" with the Allied forces during the war, together with his staunch anti-communism, earned him an invitation to become a founding member of the OEEC and NATO. At the same time, Salazar despised American capitalism and its liberal world view and was averse to the rise of the United States as the West's champion. But by the 1950s American Atlantic supremacy was an unavoidable fact that the dictator was forced to engage with in order to ensure the survival of his regime and empire. The key to this unfolding alliance was the Lajes Air Base on the Azorean island of Terceira. The Americans, who were first granted access to the base in 1944, considered Lajes's location in the mid-Atlantic to be of high strategic value and an absolute necessity for their Cold War military plans. In 1948, Salazar agreed to a renewable long-term lease, turning Lajes into the most important bargaining chip in Portugal's diplomatic relations with the United States.

Lisbon's diplomacy expanded in the 1950s when its foreign missions intensified their activities in NATO countries. The number of embassies and consulates multiplied as the number of emigrants in North America and Europe grew. In addition to its embassy in Washington, Portugal had a diplomatic delegation at the UN General Assembly in New York City and consulates in Boston, Fall River, New Bedford, Providence, New York City, Waterbury (after 1964), and Newark (after 1968). Though not a diplomatic mission, the Casa de Portugal, Lisbon's tourism and trade information bureau in Manhattan, also kept links with the Portuguese-American communities. In addition, Portugal increased its diplomatic presence in Canada after the war, when the former British colony fashioned a role for itself as an independent international player. In 1955, Portugal elevated its legation in Ottawa to full embassy status, and during the following year it replaced the previously honorary consuls in Montreal and Toronto with career diplomats; it also opened a new consulate in Vancouver in 1959.

Despite Portugal's good relations with its NATO allies, pressures on Salazar to democratize and forgo his colonial empire mounted at the United Nations. The dictator recognized the need to improve the Estado Novo's international image and updated core pieces of legislation and government agencies. One of the most significant democratic overtures in this period was to allow the opposition to run their presidential candidates against the regime's nominee, albeit with severe restrictions on their ability to campaign. This move gave the opposition a platform to openly criticize the regime and mobilize people in the cause of democracy. The regime's political crackdown following the widespread popularity of the opposition's candidate, General Humberto Delgado, during the bogus presidential elections of 1958 would radicalize the democratic opposition and swell the ranks of political exiles, many of whom would help shape the institutional life of emigrant communities.

Most of the internal reforms after 1945 were purely cosmetic, involving little more than renaming controversial government agencies. In some cases the dictatorship's repressive means were extended, as was the case with the PIDE, which was granted the power to arrest anyone deemed "subversive" for purposes of "interrogation" without the need for a warrant, pressing charges, or providing access to a lawyer for up to six months. The regime also purged dissenting civil servants, deported political opponents and labour organizers, or sent them to the brutal Tarrafal prison camp in Cape Verde; sometimes to die. In 1954 the PIDE saw its powers increase once again, being given the legal means to invoke preventive "security measures" to suspend an individual's entitlement to habeas corpus for up to a year. This authorization effectively allowed the political police to detain "suspects" perpetually without a trial, since they could simply be re-arrested the moment they stepped out of prison.

Another important transformation in the 1950s was the modernization and industrialization of Portugal's economy, a long-term plan that became part of the Estado Novo's basis of legitimacy in the postwar period. These new economic objectives also raised Lisbon's concern for the educational levels of its population, as the growing industrial sector demanded more qualified labour. During this time, the dictatorship introduced measures to reduce the very high rate of illiteracy in the country – nearly half of the total population (a significantly higher proportion among women) were illiterate in the 1950s.[35] Tied to this industrial investment was a new commitment to assert and expand Portugal's presence in Angola and Mozambique, in an attempt to enlarge colonial markets. The imperial regime framed its "Portuguese economic space" with various protectionist policies that privileged the metropolis, built large public infrastructures, and actively encouraged Portuguese emigrants to settle in Africa.

These and other investments did not stop with the outbreak of the Colonial Wars in 1961, when Portuguese armed forces began a protracted military conflict with African national armies, first in Angola, then in Portuguese Guinea (present day Guinea Bissau) in 1963, and Mozambique in 1964. The defence of the empire became Lisbon's chief priority at this point, which spent the lion's share of its Treasury in the war effort – much of it being indirectly financed by the emigrants' remittances. The dictatorship conscripted all men of military age, initially for a two-year period, then for four years after 1968. By the time the wars ended in 1974, hundreds of thousands of young men had been drafted to fight in the bloody conflicts. A large number of them (20 per cent of all those eligible to be drafted by 1972) and those families with male children approaching military age avoided conscription by leaving the country, often clandestinely.[36] The Colonial Wars provoked a major increase in emigration, which reached record levels in the 1960s–70s.

The North American societies encountered by Portuguese emigrants also underwent deep transformations in this period. Mainstream public opinion and policymakers in Canada and the United States converged in a growing liberal consensus that gradually accommodated cultural diversity, as long as it fit within the tenets of free enterprise, individualism, national loyalty, and middle-class gender norms. At the same time, various social progressive movements pushed for radical transformations and achieved important reforms in their countries' legal and political structures. Following the landmark Civil Rights Act of 1964, black, feminist, and some ethnic minority activists were able to challenge the laissez-faire dogmas of American free-market capitalism with "affirmative action" legislation, which brought employment, education, housing, and other social and economic benefits to these historically marginalized groups. These programs met opposition by American conservatives, who considered them "reverse discrimination" and a corruption of liberal-capitalist principles. Less anticipated was the resentment of white ethnic minorities, particularly those less privileged, who faced social and economic problems similar to those of their inner-city black neighbours. Old European immigrants complained that they had worked their way out of poverty without government aid and had been told that economic success and full citizenship were available only to those who shed their ethnic heritage and draped themselves in American (white) skin. They were not amused when race and ethnicity became key for accessing government aid.

By the late 1960s, the legislative gains made by the civil rights movement clearly had failed to improve the socio-economic situation of most African Americans. Urban centres in northern American states had received a steady flow of black migrants from the segregated South since the 1940s, who settled in low-income neighbourhoods, often alongside European immigrants. These inner-city black communities grew at the same time as middle-class whites began moving to the suburbs, leaving behind working-class European ethnics. By the mid-1960s, African Americans had become the demographic majority in many of these cities, yet municipal governments failed to represent them. Such discrimination was made clear by their disproportionately high rates of unemployment, crumbling and insufficient housing, poor schools, and other evidences of prolonged government neglect. Adding to these social problems was a sense of disillusionment with the civil rights movement's legal achievements. The sense of desperation among urban blacks, especially youth, climaxed in the late 1960s, when various radical black liberation organizations were formed, many of them involved in the over 300 racial riots that erupted across the United States after 1964.

The Civil Rights language of group rights and Black Power's reclaiming of African "roots" and cultural identity proved useful for European ethnics to voice their own historical grievances against WASP America, reject the assimilationist "melting pot" ideology, and distance themselves from white supremacy. This European ethnic revival turned into orthodoxy with publication of the book, *A Nation of Immigrants* (1958), a narrative of America as imagined by its first hyphenated president, John F. Kennedy. Its popular cultural appeal and mass media dissemination also captured the imagination of many white Canadians. At the heart of this new national paradigm was an epic "bootstraps" narrative based on a romantic archetype of the European immigrant story as "downtrodden, hard-working, self-reliant, [and] triumphant." However, the replacing of Plymouth Rock for Ellis Island as the stepping-stone to a more pluralist national identity, merely reinforced whiteness as "the key to American belonging and power relations" by relocating its normative source to a post-slavery moment. As Matthew Jacobson argued, white ethnicity was born to ease "the conscience of a nation that had just barely begun to reckon with the harshest contours of its history forged in white supremacism."[37]

The growing nostalgia for the Old World and the "ethnic ghetto" eased the reopening of mass immigration to the United States in 1965, now without blatant racist restrictions. Old and new ethnic clubs, schools, businesses, and other community institutions flourished at this point, revitalized by European newcomers. But contrary to the experts' predictions, most immigrants now arrived from Asia, South America, and other "coloured" parts of the world. In Canada, immigration reforms in 1967 also made way for a large influx of newcomers from Asia, Africa, and other regions outside Europe. These ethnically and racially diverse immigrants encountered a maturing pluralist society, to which they added their distinct contributions. Most would applaud Prime Minister Pierre E. Trudeau's multiculturalism policy statement of 1971 – largely motivated by the rise of Quebec separatism – which celebrated the fact that Canada was made up of multiple cultures. It also committed its federal government to promoting ethnic diversity and eliminating cultural discrimination through various forms of aid. Some provinces followed suit with their own multiculturalist policies. However, these policies were largely symbolic, as they lacked the resources and mechanisms necessary to advance pluralism beyond a superficial dialogue and failed to address the more pressing socio-economic and legal obstacles facing immigrants, especially "visible minorities." Although increasingly celebratory of cultural diversity, Washington had no comprehensive multiculturalism policy structuring access to government resources or streamlining relations between ethnic representatives and public officials beyond a racial framework. Still, some states, such as New England, launched narrow multiculturalist programs addressing primarily the educational needs of ethnic communities. One important deterrent to introducing a federal multiculturalism policy in the United States was the white ethnic pluralism behind the "nation of immigrants" paradigm, which shifted further to the right in the 1970s. Conservative politicians such as President Richard M. Nixon regularly deployed the European immigrant "bootstraps" mythology of triumph through "hard work" and "self-reliance" to criticize the "welfare dependency" of black Americans and decry the "insularity" of non-European immigrants arriving in greater numbers since 1965.[38]

Around this time, the Estado Novo launched a new series of reforms after Caetano replaced the aging Salazar, who stepped down on 23 September 1968, injured by a fall that resulted in a brain haemorrhage (he would die as a result two years later). Initially acclaimed as a moderate reformist, Caetano was expected to usher in the regime's gradual liberalization, modernization, and Europeanization. To do so, he counted on the reserved support of a new generation of civil servants and parliamentarians known as the "Liberal Wing" and public opinion that was tired of the Colonial Wars and the regime's old-fashioned conservatism and repression. However, their hopes were short-lived, since the new dictator soon conceded to pressures from the regime's far-right wing and compromised on the extent of his liberal reforms in order to continue fighting in Africa.

The 1970s saw the resurgence and radicalization of the Portuguese opposition, with various Maoist and Marxist-Leninist parties and armed groups appearing on the scene, some of them pulling militants away from the Moscow-friendly PCP. The labour movement too gained new life with the inauguration of the clandestine Intersindical in 1970, which organized various illegal strikes. Some sectors that had previously served as bulwarks of the regime, such as the Catholic Church, also saw a rise in oppositional voices. In addition, threats to Caetano's rule emerged from the far right, where there was talk of a military coup. In 1974, the conservative vice-chief of the armed forces, General António Spínola, publicly stated that the Colonial Wars were lost and that the only solution to end the conflicts was for Portugal to grant independence to its African colonies.

Caetano's commitment to continuing the Colonial Wars ultimately sealed the fate of the Estado Novo. The final blow was dealt by a group of military officers organized as the Armed Forces Movement (MFA). Originally coming together to advocate their professional interests, they soon became politicized, many of its leaders embracing radical forms of socialism. On 25 April 1974, the MFA's forces advanced into Lisbon and arrested Caetano, putting an end to the dictatorship that had ruled Portugal since 1926. The revolutionaries were cheered effusively by thousands of Lisboners, who mingled with the MFA's soldiers as they carried on their largely peaceful Revolution of the Carnations – named after the flowers distributed amongst the crowd and decorating the soldiers' rifles that day. Support for the MFA remained strong in the urban centres and in the southern regions of Portugal – regions of low emigration – during what became known as the Ongoing Revolutionary Process (or PREC), which lasted until the first constitutional election of 25 April 1976. This transition process was marked by intense political turmoil, taking the country to the brink of civil war, as various factions fought for control over the revolutionary institutions, with support from large sectors of the now heavily politicized population. In the days following the revolution, the military conflicts in Africa came to a halt; political prisoners were freed, leading members of the opposition arrived from exile, and new political parties emerged. Pressed by the departing rulers, the revolutionaries invited General Spínola to preside over the interim National Salvation Junta. But soon, ideological differences and disagreements over which path of decolonization to follow caused a rift. Spínola resigned as interim minister after the MFA and its left-wing allies barricaded Lisbon, preventing a conservative "silent majority" rally from taking place, which the general had called as a show of support for his rule. This opened the way for the PCP to take hold of important positions in the revolutionary government. On 11 March 1975, after rumours spread that the PCP and the MFA's radical wing had compiled a list of right-wing leaders to be assassinated, Spínola attempted a military coup, which was foiled. Subsequently, Spínola and his group fled the country.

With the removal of Spínola and his conservative allies, the MFA veered farther to the left and began implementing its socialist vision in collaboration with the PCP and other radical Marxists. Under the leadership of General Vasco Gonçalves, who presided over four short-lived provisional governments until 25 September 1975, the state nationalized various industries central to the Portuguese economy – including the banks – and supervised the occupation of vacant houses and farmland across the country. Gonçalves also initiated the decolonization process, leading to the formal independence of Portugal's African territories and the massive "return" movement of former colonial settlers. The first democratic elections in almost fifty years were also held during this period, on 25 April 1975, when voters were asked to select their representatives in the constitutive assembly that would draft a new democratic constitution.

A large portion of the population was vehemently opposed to Gonçalves's policies and the communist parties that supported him. Tensions between far-left and centre-right supporters escalated in the "hot summer" of 1975, when the offices of communist parties were ransacked or burnt in the northern and central regions of the mainland and on the Atlantic islands. New radical armed groups emerged on both sides of the political spectrum and a large number of rallies, strikes, occupations, and other civil unrest occurred at this point. By September 1975, a group of democratic socialists denounced the MFA's Soviet tendencies and raised fears of a violent clash between the two leftist political factions within the military. After this episode, a moderate provisional government (the sixth) was formed, with support from the centre-left Socialist Party and the centre-right Social Democratic Party. The moderates' victory was cemented on 25 November 1975 after General Ramalho Eanes – who later became president – foiled an attempted coup by a military unit affiliated with the PCP. On 25 April 1976, Portuguese citizens at home and abroad elected the first government of the new democratic era and inaugurated a new constitution. Marked by the socialist ideals of its architects, the new constitution enshrined a long list of individual and collective rights and founded a social-democratic system that assigned welfare responsibilities to the government. At this point, Lisbon began pursuing a new foreign policy, increasingly oriented towards Europe and away from the Atlantic.

Chapter Structure

The past is a mess. By trying to make it intelligible and accurate, historians unavoidably betray their commitment to representing the past "as it was" and are forced to settle for well-founded plausibility. Making sense of complex interplays of social, cultural, economic, political and other local, national, and international factors shaping the lives of large groups of people, along with their individual motivations, actions, words and silences, is never a casual or innocent task. This is even more the case when three different countries are being considered, each with multiple governments, regions, communities, languages, and histories. The chapter structure I chose to tell this history is my attempt at making sense of the mess. I will start each chapter with a comprehensive introduction to the topic in question to familiarize readers with the various intersecting contexts at play. Chapter 1 does so for the whole book, by placing our period of study within the larger history of Portuguese modern emigration and offering an overview of its cycles, policies, and cultural perceptions from the first half of the nineteenth century to the present day. In order to address the questions I set out to answer, I will examine each major realm of Portuguese diasporic activity – religion, civil society, ethnic and national culture, race and empire, and transnational politics – somewhat separately in chapters 2 to 6, which cover only the 1950s and 1960s. These meandering realms and processes intersected regularly, but their dynamics were distinct enough to warrant separate attention.

Chapter 2 begins the book's central examination of the goals and methods of Estado Novo officials in their efforts to shape the emigrants' identities and community lives, focusing on their relationship with Catholic missionaries in North America, who were usually the first homeland envoys and community organizers. Here I will discuss the joint efforts of the Portuguese government and Catholic Church to prevent the emigrants' assimilation into Canadian and American mainstream societies; the intersection of nationalist, imperialist, and ecumenical discourses in their spiritual and social work; and the role of lay parishioners in resisting or facilitating these processes. Besides creating and maintaining transnational connections essential to diasporas, Portuguese Catholicism, which was deeply entwined with regional, national, and imperial identities, offered an important spiritual and universalist (yet markedly European) quality to the "pilgrim nation." However, it also became one of the chief catalysts for the emergence of a separate Azorean diaspora.

Chapter 3 shifts the reader's attention to the secular civil society – mutual aid societies, hometown fraternities, sports clubs, trade unions, and media – and examines how homeland diplomats influenced ethnic leaders through their patronage. While class relations are considered throughout the book, this chapter delves into that topic with greater attention. Here I will pay particular attention to those middle-class businessmen and professionals who improved their social status, wealth, and political influence by acting as both patrons and brokers for their less privileged countrymen. The organizations they led became the institutional infrastructure on which Lisbon's diplomats surreptitiously established powerful ethnic confederations, which the dictatorship tried to influence for political gain, citing diasporic notions of transnational group solidarity and self-interest.

Chapter 4 moves into the realm of culture and language, or specifically how the Estado Novo's evolving traditionalist propaganda helped Portuguese emigrants develop an ethnic identity that met the folksy expectations of North America's proto-multiculturalism. I will examine the ambiguous coexistence of tradition and modernity in Lisbon's cultural policies, in the tourism and trade marketing of peasant life by upper-class diplomats and in the embrace of an idealized rurality by ethnics who traded Portugal's countryside for North America's industrial cities. This chapter also discusses the efforts of predominantly mainland emigrants to preserve and bequeath their language by building Portuguese schools and libraries and Lisbon's inconsistent response to their requests for aid. The discussion highlights important regional distinctions when it came to the articulation of Portuguese ethnic or diasporic identity in Canada and the United States and how the mainlander minority was able to advance a homogenized self-serving ethnicity to the detriment of the Azorean majority's distinct language and culture.

Chapter 5 explores the imperial and foreign policy dimension of the Estado Novo's expatriate outreach and the origins of its diaspora-building strategy. Although a prevalent theme throughout this book, the behind-the-scenes manipulation of ethnic institutions by homeland diplomats is highlighted in this chapter, along with their efforts to rally the support of Portuguese emigrants and descendants for the homeland's foreign political interests. I will shed light on the diplomats' influence over the editorial rooms of ethnic media and their use of Portuguese-American lobbyists to sway the views of American politicians. This chapter also examines the complex racial identities of various "Portuguese" groups in the United States and how the Estado Novo's multiracial imperial propaganda (*lusotropicalismo*) affected the way in which white and black "Portuguese" (i.e., Cape Verdeans) referred to themselves and to "others." Unpacking these racial dynamics is essential to our understanding of the specific ways in which Portuguese diasporic identities were constructed in the United States.

Chapter 6 is dedicated to the Estado Novo's opponents, namely, those political "exiles" and other pro-democratic emigrants who fought the dictatorship and its colonial empire from North America, as part of a wide transnational network. I will examine the local and transnational political activities of the small groups of "anti-fascists" operating in Toronto, Montreal, and the greater New York City area and how they developed an alternative diasporic consciousness based on shared memories of poverty, persecution, and exile. I will also reveal the surveillance methods used by American, Canadian, and Portuguese secret services to gather and exchange intelligence on these "radicals." Despite their home and host governments' attempts to undermine their pro-democratic and anti-colonialist activities, these émigrés would ultimately play a leading role in negotiating a new relationship between the Portuguese government and its emigrant communities immediately after the revolution.

The period of the 1970s deserves its own chapter (7) for being distinctively transitional, when the various processes of diasporic formation developing in the 1950s–60s culminated in multiple consciously diasporic identities, each with its institutional supports. Here, I will return to the topics discussed in previous chapters and discuss them in light of the intersecting transformations unfolding in this period, including the emergence of a new generation of ethnic activists, the introduction of multiculturalist policies in Canada and parts of the United States, the rise of Azorean and Cape Verdean ethnicity and political autonomy, and the deep political, social, and cultural changes caused by the "April 25th" revolution. All of these changes affected the self-understanding of "Portuguese" or lusophone people(s) in North America and cemented their diverse collective identities and political solidarities. I will explore these relationships while discussing the reactions to the narratives, reforms, and promises of Portugal's revolutionary governments and their efforts to involve diasporic citizens in the homeland's affairs.

1 Portuguese Migration: Numbers, Policies, and Perceptions

A Portuguese who is only a Portuguese is not a Portuguese.
Consul Eduardo de Carvalho,
Os Portugueses da Nova Inglaterra (1932).[1]

In a country with a long history of population movement, dating back to its maritime expansion starting in the fifteenth century, romanticized notions of travelling, exploring new lands, and seeking fortune abroad have been an integral part of the national psyche. This history has provided the ideological fodder by which Portuguese modern emigration has been interpreted, which in turn replenished national mythologies with new references and meanings.[2] In order to gauge the Estado Novo's contribution to developing diasporic communities in North America, we must situate it within the larger history of Portuguese modern emigration (figure 1.1).

Historians often divide this long-standing phenomenon into three large cycles: (1) the long classic cycle, beginning with Brazil's independence in 1822 and continuing to the Great Depression of the 1930s; (2) the postwar cycle, beginning in the aftermath of the Second World War and ending with the global economic crisis of the mid-1970s; and (3) the post-imperial cycle, starting with the revolutionary transition in Portugal and ending in the late 1990s. Portuguese emigration has risen during the 2000s, soaring to new heights in recent years. Its distinct characteristics make this a new cycle, but it is still too soon to comprehend its full historical significance. Special attention will be given to the movements to Canada and the United States and to the Portuguese government's emigration policies of the 1950s–80s. By considering the long-term history of Portuguese emigration, we can better identify its prevalent threads and themes and how they factored in the diasporic-building processes discussed in subsequent chapters.

Figure 1.1 Portuguese total emigration, 1855–2003.

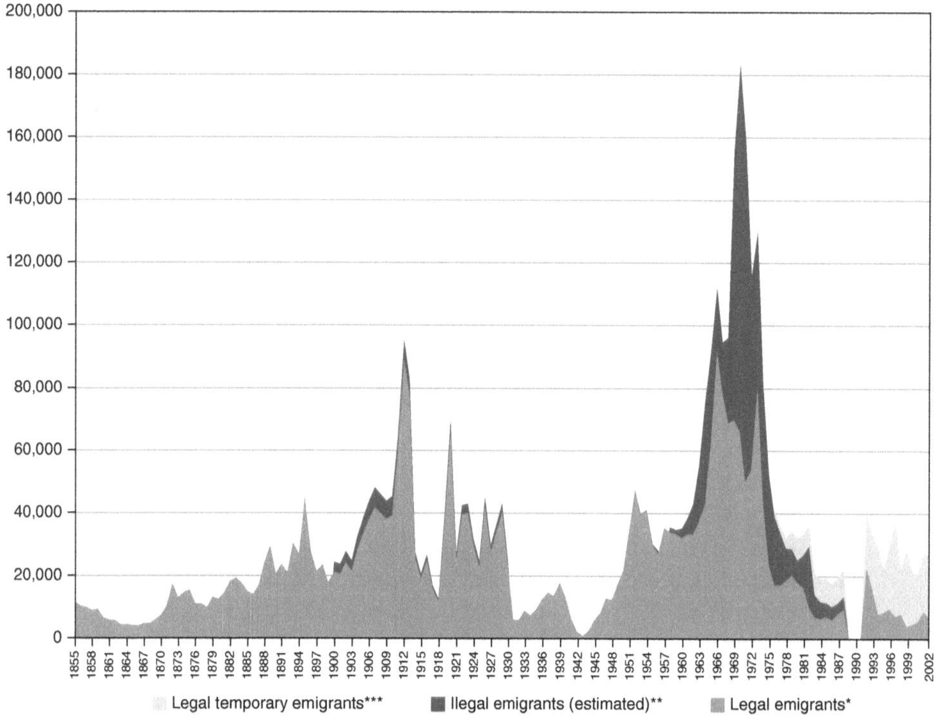

Legal temporary emigrants*** ■ Illegal emigrants (estimated)** ■ Legal emigrants*

Notes: There are no data for total emigration in 1989–92.
*It is not clear from sources if values up to 1976 include temporary emigration.
**Estimated values for illegal emigration are available only for 1900–30 and 1950–88.
***The break-up of legal emigration data between permanent and temporary is available only for 1976–2003. They are represented in the graph as cumulative not juxtaposed values.
Sources: Joel Serrão (A Emigração, 1982); Baganha ("As Correntes," 1994); Humberto Moreira, "Emigração Portuguesa ("Estatísticas retrospectivas e reflexões temáticas," *Revista de Estudos Demográficos* 38 (2006): 56)

Traversing these distinct periods is the persistent ambivalence of cultural, economic, and political elites towards emigration, to which they attached unresolved dichotomies. Their ambivalence often resulted in timid, contradictory, and largely ineffective policies that never fully satisfied those ruling classes with conflicting views on emigration. This overview also allows us to detect the gradual changes in policies and perceptions, such as the shift from an apprehensive, restrictive, and paternalistic view of "emigration" to the more favourable, liberal, and glorifying view of "diaspora."

The Early History of Portuguese Modern Emigration

Throughout the nineteenth and well into the twentieth centuries, the overwhelming majority of Portuguese emigrants went to Brazil. The United States was a distant second choice, followed by Argentina, British Guyana, and Hawaii. Most emigrants hailed from the rural regions of the northern mainland, except for those America bound, the majority of whom came from the Azorean islands. The economic reasons driving emigration from these regions were largely the same as those in other southern European countries: the predominance of small-plot subsistence farming rarely with marketable surplus; population growth resulting from lowering death and increasing birth rates; little arable land available to be divided between descendants; no significant industrialization capable of absorbing excess rural populations; a long tradition of intra-European and transatlantic labour migration; and the introduction of new, faster means of transportation. For most of the nineteenth century, Portuguese migrants were almost exclusively single male sojourners. A great number of them were unaccompanied minors sent by their families to work in Brazilian plantations and escape military service. Many were indentured servants effectively sold to plantation owners by recruiters and ship's captains as payment for their transportation. By the mid-nineteenth century, a significant number of these early migrants had turned to commercial activities in the urban areas of Brazil. A large minority of these *brasileiros* (Brazilians), as they became known, achieved considerable fortunes and returned to Portugal, where they invested their newly acquired wealth. The "myth of fortune" embodied by these prosperous returnees was the Portuguese rural equivalent of the myth of the "self-made man" in industrial societies. The popular belief that one could become rich abroad almost instantly placed great social and psychological pressures on the emigrants to meet expectations; in turn, they exaggerated their success in letters home, further inflating the myth. This desire for social ascension upset the ruling classes, who criticized the emigrants' supposed greed, leading some to suggest that poverty was morally right and uplifting.[3] The over-representation of urban success stories obscured the fact that many more emigrants returned to Portugal in conditions of dire poverty and illness or perished anonymously in the unforgiving Brazilian hinterland.[4]

In the United States, the expansion of the Massachusetts whaling industry in the mid-nineteenth century raised the demand for labour.

Crewmen had become harder to find as more Americans projected their future towards the expanding western frontier. At this point, it became common practice for whalers to hire officers in the United States then fill their crews at the various ports where they stopped to restock. Located two thousand miles off the coast of Massachusetts, the Azores were inside the area covered by New England whalers, who scoured its waters looking for sperm whales and stopped at Horta's and Ponta Delgada's ports of call to replenish supplies. Many young Azorean men joined these whaling crews hoping to make the journey to the United States without paying for passage while earning wages during the voyage, which could take up to three years and a great deal of hard and dangerous toil. Another important source of labour for the Massachusetts whaling fleet was the Cape Verde archipelago. Discovered by Portuguese explorers in the sixteenth century, these islands located off the coast of West Africa were colonized by white Europeans and black African slaves, who would later produce a large Creole population. While lacking fertile land or significant natural resources, Cape Verde profited from its strategic location, thriving as a centre for the transatlantic slave trade. After slavery declined in the nineteenth century, the islands' geographic location and good harbour conditions continued to offer economic returns to the colonial empire, which invested almost exclusively in Cape Verde's maritime and commercial infrastructures to the detriment of social, cultural, and other economic areas. With limited opportunities to earn a living, Cape Verdeans began emigrating in large numbers in the late nineteenth century, the vast majority of them going to the United States.

Once there, these early immigrants settled in New England's coastal cities (mainly New Bedford), where they found ample employment in whaling and its derivative industries. Many were able to supplement their income by working as farmhands in the outskirts of New Bedford and Providence or as cranberry pickers in Cape Cod (particularly Cape Verdeans). Other harbour cities, such as Boston and New York, also attracted a significant number of migrant seamen, who found waged work in the merchant navy. California and Hawaii also began receiving large flows of Portuguese immigration from the beginning of the "gold rush." In the 1850s–60s, California was the main destination for Portuguese immigrant families, many of whom made large fortunes in the dairy-farming and tuna-fishing industries (figure 1.2).

Massachusetts became the centre of American industrialization in the early nineteenth century, when places such as Fall River and New Bedford evolved into factory towns, attracting many thousands of native and European migrant workers of various nationalities into its cotton mills. By the 1870s, the textile industry had replaced whaling as New England's main economic driver. The mills, which had a very high demand

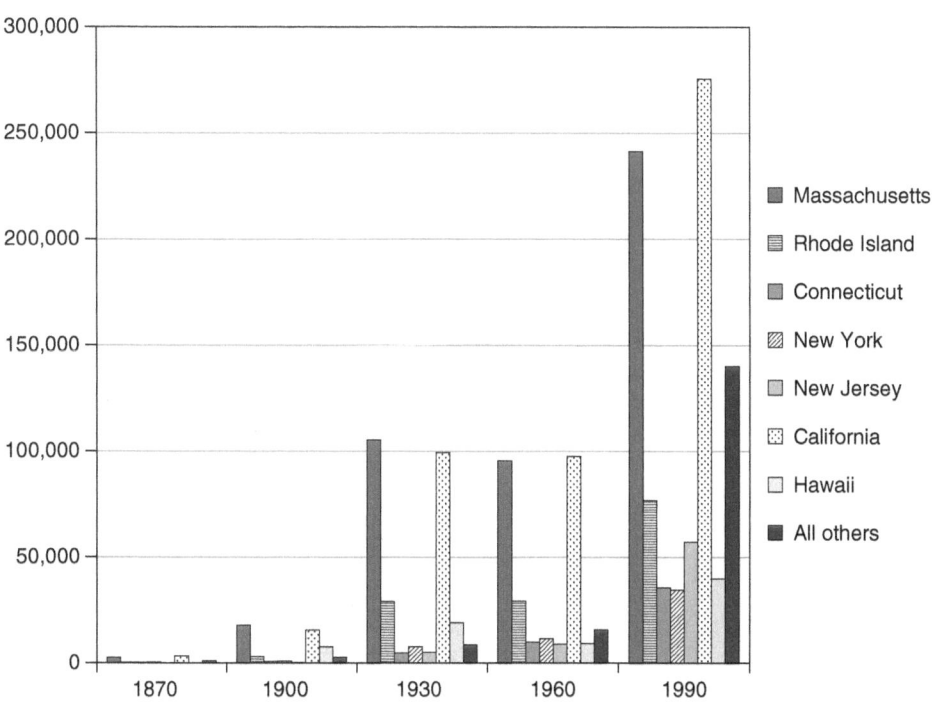

Figure 1.2 Portuguese "foreign stock" in the United States, by state, 1870–1990.

Source: Williams (2005).

for low-skilled labourers willing to work long, tedious hours for low pay, actively recruited workers in Europe and eastern Canada. Entire families migrated to these factory towns, attracted by the fact that textile mills employed every able-bodied family member, including women and children. The early Portuguese fishermen who had settled in these cities were instrumental in determining the settlement and occupational patterns of the larger immigrant cohort that followed, most of them linked by kinship ties and hometown connections. By 1900, Massachusetts had surpassed California as the American state with the largest Portuguese population. Rhode Island had attractive factors similar to those of its eastern neighbour and also drew a significant flow of Portuguese immigrants, who converged in Providence, the state's capital and industrial heart.

Emigration was a regular topic of discussion in Portugal's public sphere, engaged by some of the country's most influential thinkers, politicians, and artists, who debated its virtues and vices along with its benefits and disadvantages relative to national interests. Exile was also familiar to Portugal's political class, going back to 1807, when Maria I and her court of 15,000 people escaped to Brazil to avoid capitulating to Napolean's invading army, making Rio de Janeiro the effective capital of Portugal for over thirteen years. The Crown eventually returned to Lisbon after the liberal revolution of 1820, which introduced constitutional rule. Subsequently, Portuguese governments had a difficult time reconciling their respect for individual freedom of mobility with their national economic and defence interests. Moreover, following reports of Portuguese workers living miserably in Brazil, Lisbon was compelled to assume a more interventionist role in emigration in order to protect its expatriate citizens. This constituted the most persistent conundrum in Portuguese emigration policy: every new restriction triggered an increase of illegal departures by labourers determined to improve their economic situation abroad, thus making it even harder for Lisbon to control their movement and ensure their well-being.

While sympathetic to the "plight" of those forced to seek a better life elsewhere, Portuguese political commentators in this period saw emigration as a structural problem with profound detrimental effects for national morale, economic development, and military manpower. The celebrated writer-politician-historian Alexandre Herculano pointed to the exodus of his countrymen as a sign of Portugal's "collective misery," providing justification for the economic reforms proposed by his liberal caucus. "Out goes the energy, in stay the inert and mendicant arms," lamented Oliveira Martins, one of Portugal's pioneer socialist theoreticians and historians of the late nineteenth century. Martins praised emigrants for their "gifted" initiative and "money-making aptitudes," yet urged them to stay for the sake of developing their country.[5] Other important figures of Portugal's liberal, socialist, and republican intelligentsia studied this phenomenon and invariably concluded that it was a national problem that ought to be fixed through deep reforms. Theirs was an ambivalent perception, which saw emigrants as victims of both want and greed.

The "emigrant" was a recurrent character in Portuguese literature, explored by several of the country's most celebrated authors, some of them with personal histories of displacement. The *brasileiro* figured prominently in various nineteenth-century romanticist novels, commonly portrayed in an unflattering light, mocked as a moneyed, uneducated rustic obsessed with social climbing. The twentieth-century neorealist generation would redeem this character by describing the hardships faced by expatriate labourers and paying tribute to their courage and survival spirit. Representations of emigration in the visual arts were scarce at this point. However, one piece captured the

1.1 *O Desterrado (The Uprooted)* by Soares dos Reis, 1872–4. Photograph by Manuel V. Botelho, 2013, Wikimedia Commons.

imagination of Portuguese intellectuals in 1872: Soares dos Reis's sculpture *O Desterrado* (*The Uprooted*).

Considered by experts to be one of Portugal's masterpieces in that medium, the sculpture was inspired by Herculano's poem "Sorrows of Exile," about the poet's own political exile and bitter longing for his homeland. Other artists drew inspiration from this piece, including the poet-philosopher Teixeira de Pascoaes, founder of the nostalgic *saudosismo* doctrine,[6] who considered *O Desterrado* to be the ultimate plastic representation of Portugal's national soul. A century after the sculpture's unveiling, in 1972, the social historian Joel Serrão projected onto *O Desterrado* the dominant leftist perception of emigrants at the time, as "innocent victim[s] of an unfair society that boycotts [their] joy of being, [searching for] reasons to confirm [their] resolve to return to [their] lost paradise."[7]

The concerns of government officials and landowning elites regarding the impact of emigration on the country's economy were aggravated at the turn of the century when more families began to leave, leading to serious depopulation in some regions and demographic stagnation at the national level. But while the large agriculturalists complained about the nation's dwindling labour pool and subsequent increase in wages, they were happy to see the economic status quo be maintained by the exodus of a potentially disruptive, impoverished population. Another factor placating public condemnation of emigration was the growing size of remittances. On this topic, Fernando Silva, an early emigration scholar, commented in 1917: "It is from misery that comes our best riches: it is from the nostalgic pariah, the atavistic adventurer who leaves the inhospitable beaches of a land that failed to give him bread, in a tormented demand for better yet unsure destinations, that the gold comes."[8] Curiously, Silva would become a Bank of Portugal administrator two years after making this statement.

Emigration dropped drastically during the First World War but would recover much of its previous momentum after 1918, except to the United States (figure 1.3).

Two main factors contributed to a drastic reduction in the number of Portuguese arrivals in that country. First, the dwindling economic conditions leading to the closure of New England's textile mills and the introduction of automated looms downsized their labour force. In the meantime, New York City's garment industry tried to contain rising labour costs prompted by federal immigration restrictions that disrupted the steady flow of cheap, unskilled workers. Garment factories relocated to New Jersey and Connecticut, where production costs remained low, and began attracting labour from the pool of unemployed in southern New England. A substantial number of these internal migrants were Portuguese families whose members had been laid off from Massachusetts textile mills. The majority moved to Newark, New Jersey's largest

Figure 1.3 Portuguese obtaining legal resident status in the United States, 1820–2009. Cape Verdeans were recorded as "Portuguese" from 1892 to 1952.

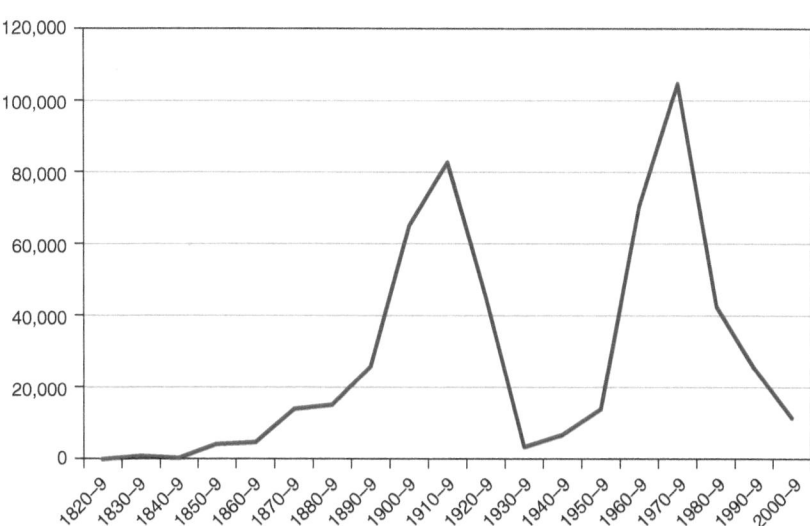

Source: Yearbook of Immigration Statistics: 2013 (Washington, DC: US Department of Homeland Security, Office of Immigration Statistics, 2014).

city, where they found work in unskilled, low-paying, factory jobs. In the state of New York, the Long Island counties of Nassau and Queens were the most common destinations for Portuguese migrants. In Connecticut, the fast-growing Portuguese population settled primarily in the cities of New Haven and Hartford. Second, the slew of immigration restrictions introduced since 1917 greatly curtailed the Portuguese transatlantic movement. The most draconian was the annual national quota system, first introduced in 1921, which limited the number of migrants allowed into the country to 3 per cent of the population of the same nationality living in the United States in 1910. In 1924, this cap was reduced to 2 per cent of the resident population in 1890. Despite the tiny quota assigned to Portugal (503 arrivals per year in 1924 and 440 after 1929), special provisions allowed for thousands of Portuguese immigrants to enter the country before the discriminatory quota system was abolished in 1965. Nonetheless, between 1922 and 1932, more Portuguese returned home than entered the United States.[9]

In the 1920s–40s, Portuguese emigration dropped to its lowest level, as a result of the economic and political effects of the Great Depression and the Second World War. Since 1929, the Estado Novo had tried to control emigration through various legislative and bureaucratic measures, seeking to ban the departure of labourers under the pretext of national interest, social protection, and crime prevention. Salazar never envisioned a Portuguese diaspora or considered the cultural and political value of emigration in the concerted way that other European dictators did. However, he did express interest in the Portuguese communities in the United States during his tenure as foreign affairs minister in 1936–47, mostly out of concern for the political actions of a vocal group of republican exiles.[10] Like his predecessors, Salazar held ambivalent views on emigration. While he sought to reduce Portugal's dependence on foreign powers and referred to emigration as "a problem," he also acknowledged the importance of its massive remittances towards balancing the government's finances and maintaining the country's liquidity. On the other hand, the uncoordinated and largely unlawful population exodus was something the authoritarian regime simply could not tolerate. This was especially the case once the government began directing emigrants to the African colonies, in an attempt to expand their incipient European settler population and unleash their economic potential as colonial markets. The colonialist push also was motivated by Lisbon's desire to replace Brazil as a major source of remittances, which came to a sudden halt in 1931, after that country restricted European immigration and the outflow of capital.

Simultaneously with the ending of Portuguese emigration to Brazil, New England's economic woes worsened, as the Great Depression brought about the ultimate collapse of its textile industry. Once bustling factory towns, Fall River and New Bedford became economically depressed cities with a long-term systemic problem of unemployment. Those in low-skilled occupations, like the overwhelming majority of Portuguese workers, were most affected by the massive lay-offs: in New Bedford, nearly half were unemployed in the 1930s. Even before this collapse, the economic situation of Portuguese mill workers was bleak, which reflected on their social, cultural, and personal well-being. Portuguese families in Fall River and New Bedford had one of the highest infant mortality rates in the country with 200 deaths for every 1,000 births (more than double the national average).[11] In these economically depressed cities, "being Portuguese" became associated with chronic unemployment and other social ills, which had negative implications for the group's collective pride and identity. Many Portuguese immigrants and descendants disassociated themselves from their ethnic group and hid their cultural and linguistic heritage during this time. This cultural shaming was reinforced in public schools, where immigrant children were taught to deplore their ancestral nation and customs and to become "American." The lack of a significant immigration flow that could sustain a regular connection with the homeland also contributed to this cultural breakdown.

However, among middle- and upper-class emigrants, public expressions of Portuguese patriotism and homeland loyalty grew after 1933 and until the Second World War. Much of it resulted from the interest prompted by the creation of the Estado Novo and the propaganda surrounding Salazar and his regenerative vision for the imperial nation. For those community elites who had long complained about Lisbon's lack of interest in their efforts towards maintaining Portuguese culture in the United States, this was a welcome new tone, even if the regime's anti-liberal ideology was at odds with their liberal-democratic American views. The transnational political opposition by the relatively small yet vocal group of republican émigrés in New Bedford and New York City also intensified public debate about homeland affairs in the community press and civic organizations. But the main factor rekindling the homeland patriotism of Portuguese-American elites was the Estado Novo's response to the growing influence of these exiled political opponents. The outreach work of new and more skillful diplomats, the visits by high-ranking government officials, and the creation of agencies dedicated to dissiminating pro-Estado Novo propaganda all contributed to strengthening Lisbon's relations with Portuguese-American communities and curbing dissenting voices within them – at least until the start of the war. Once Western liberal democracies came under attack by the Axis forces, with which the Estado Novo was ideologically aligned, and especially after the United States entered the war on the side of the Allies, relations between the Lisbon government and the Portuguese-American communities sharply declined.[12]

Many of the economic problems in the United States were temporarily resolved by wartime industrial demands, which introduced an abundance of new jobs in northeastern factory cities. The "total war" mentality, pervasive in all areas of American life, also heightened patriotism, which censored the "dual loyalties" that ethnics were believed to espouse. A new generation of Portuguese descendants was raised amidst this patriotic fervour, many of them fighting with the US army overseas or joining in the war effort on the "home front."

Their sense of ethnicity, when not entirely consumed by American conformity, became dormant or diluted. Still, the high residential concentration of Portuguese families in New England mitigated assimilationist pressures and maintained spaces where these ethnics could use their heritage language, observe endogamous marriages, and partake in cultural and religious traditions away from mainstream scrutiny. Transnational immigrants also kept in contact with their families back home by sending money and other gifts regularly. These introverted links

1.2 New Bedford, Massachusetts, Portuguese mother with pictures of her sons, who are all in service, spring 1942. Photograph by John Collier, retrieved from LOC, www.loc.gov/item/owi2001046697/pp/.

with the homeland would be reactivated with the return of Portuguese mass migration and served as a footing for Portuguese Americans to reassert their ethnicity in the postwar period.

The Postwar Cycle: 1950s–1970s

Peacetime reconstruction efforts prompted a large intra-European migratory flow, as the countries of the south met the large demand for labour in those northern and western countries most affected by the war. With little capacity to retain its excess population, which had been spared the war's tragic death toll, Portugal became one of the largest providers of migrant labour for this reconstruction. In the 1950s, the transatlantic movement was still dominant, representing 93 per cent of all emigration, until the European movement finally surpassed it in 1963 (figure 1.4).

Figure 1.4 Portuguese emigration by destination, 1950–74.

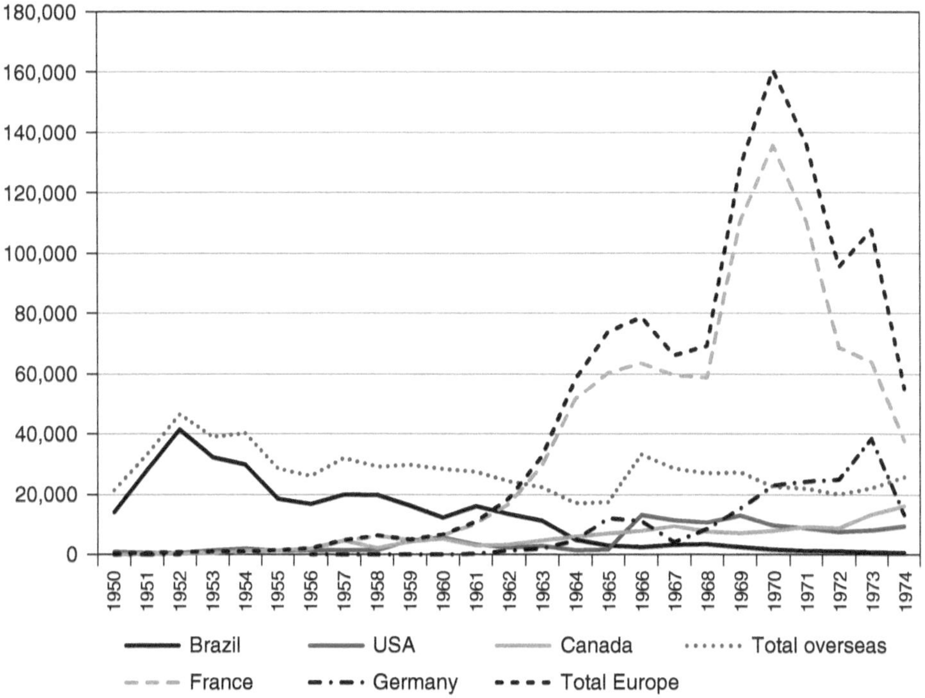

Source: Baganha ("Portuguese Emigration," 1998) for emigration statistics; Marques and Medeiros (*Portuguese Immigrants*, 1980) for Canadian immigration statistics.

Although decreasing in relative importance, overseas emigration was still sizable in this period. Brazil gradually lost its prominence as new transatlantic destinations emerged, such as South Africa, Venezuela, Canada, and Australia; old ones, such as the United States, also reopened. Between 1950 and 1988, an estimated 36 per cent of all departures were clandestine. Many emigrants crossed the Spanish border covertly through the mountainous regions in the north with the help of hired smugglers, making the long journey on foot or hidden in cargo vehicles in what was known as *o salto* (the jump). The bulk of the European movement went to France (59 per cent of all emigrants in the 1960s), particularly to Paris's metropolitan area, where Portuguese migrants built large shanty towns (*bidonvilles*). In the largest of these suburban slums, Champigny-sur-Marne, over 12,000 residents lived in dismal conditions in the mid-1960s. As Victor Pereira aptly noted, there were more Portuguese living in France in 1974 than in all of Portugal's African colonies "after 450 years of colonization."[13]

Compared with transatlantic emigrants, who came predominantly from rural areas in the Atlantic islands and the northern mainland, the European movement had a larger portion of urban and industrial workers. As in the past, the majority of emigrants from the mainland planned to return and spend their earnings in their hometowns after a period of intense work abroad, while those from the Azores were keener on settling permanently in North America, where many of their family members had been transplanted. Most of these mobile workers focused almost exclusively on accumulating savings quickly by working long hours at multiple jobs and reducing living costs to a minimum, often at the expense of their personal rights, comfort, and dignity. In Europe, the geographic proximity with Portugal allowed these sojourners to visit their families more regularly than their transatlantic peers could, which helped them endure long stretches of intensive labour and mitigate the emotional toll and personal sacrifices. Over time, European sojourners too began settling in their host countries and calling for their families to join them.

The rampant clandestine migration endangered the traditional clientelism that dominated class relations in Portugal's countryside. Local elites saw their power diminished every time a cheap labourer left their fiefdom without their personal assent, mediation, paid services, or high-interest loans. Those successful emigrants who returned and their families who stayed behind also jeopardized this hierarchical system by elevating their own social, cultural, and financial capital and becoming less dependent on local bosses. This class of rural elites, from which many of the Estado Novo's civil servants were recruited (some of them landowners), were a vigorous and influential social force opposing emigration. In March 1947, in an early attempt to assert its authority over the rural exodus, the dictatorship suspended emigration altogether, except for candidates with a foreign work contract. Lisbon soon acknowledged that it was incapable of upholding the ban and seven months later replaced it with a system of annual emigration quotas, determined by the country's labour needs.

To better control this exodus, the regime created the Emigration Junta, which it tasked with coordinating the recruitment, transportation, and settlement of emigrants and "protecting" them from smugglers. The task of policing illegal migration and screening passport applicants remained with the PIDE, which, like the Junta, operated under the Interior Ministry. The new agency was also responsible for overseeing international migration agreements; defining the terms and duration of the emigrants' labour contracts, conditions for repatriation, and access to welfare and health benefits; facilitating remittances and the transfer of wages to Portugal; and advising the government on emigration matters. However, its perennial lack of funding and staff prevented it from fulfilling much of its mandate beyond processing applications and supervising emigrant movements. The Junta reflected the regime's paternalistic view of emigrants as humble people who had to be escorted away from miserable lives abroad and towards a destination more suitable for national interests. It also upheld or tried to appease the negative views on emigration held by rural bosses, which its president António Baptista was able to do with significant discretion by leveraging his unrivalled command of the muddled emigration legislation.[14] Regardless of its paternalistic and restrictive ways, the Junta was one of the earliest government agencies among "emigrant nations" to operate under the notion that the homeland state had ongoing responsibilities towards its expatriated citizens.[15]

Salazar's lack of diasporic vision is evident in the 1959 Nationality Law, which drew the boundaries within which individuals could claim or renounce their citizenship. From then on, those who voluntarily took up citizenship in a foreign country automatically lost their Portuguese nationality. The new law followed the principle of *jus solis*, meaning that territory determined the assigning of citizenship. There were exceptions to this rule. Emigrant descendants born abroad to a Portuguese father could be granted citizenship if they, or their father, declared an interest in obtaining it. Portuguese mothers could also pass on their citizenship to their children as long as the father's nationality was unknown. Foreign women automatically obtained citizenship when they married a Portuguese man, unless they requested otherwise. Portuguese women who married foreigners were allowed to hold dual nationality as long as they expressed a desire to maintain their citizenship.

In the 1950s, Salazar shifted his focus away from the traditional labour-intensive industries and into the modern industrial sector emerging in Lisbon's metropolitan area. At this point, the Foreign Affairs Ministry called for the modernization and liberalization of emigration in line with the principles of international labour mobility promoted by emerging continental trade organizations. The Ministry of Corporations and Social Welfare, in turn, believed that emigration should be under its purview, seeing it primarily as a matter of labour and social policy rather than sovereignty and criminality. As Pereira noted, both ministries challenged the Emigration Junta's traditional "mercantilist model" that saw clandestine emigrants as "selfish [people] who place [their] ambition and personal interests above [those] of the nation," instead of as "creator[s] of wealth who contributed to the country's prosperity," or even as "hero[es]," as the supporters of modernization began to see them.[16] Still, the negative and restrictive view of the Interior Ministry and its Junta prevailed until the mid-1960s. In 1962, Lisbon banned the emigration of skilled workers in strategic occupations, introduced a special "emigration passport," and announced a maximum annual quota of 30,000 departures. Once again, this quota was dropped in the following year, after the government recognized that the exodus continued to grow and inflate the ranks of illegal emigrants. With the start of the Colonial Wars in 1961, the regime criminalized clandestine emigration and escalated the PIDE's efforts to prevent the massive outflow of draft dodgers. However, the dictatorship's authoritative emigration policies contrasted with their lackadaisical enforcement measures.

In addition to Salazar's own ambivalence, the regime's disjointed nature led it to make conflicting pronouncements and take contradictory actions. Emigration continued to be seen largely as a convenient "safety valve" for releasing social and political pressures arising from a large, unemployed, and impoverished population. For dissatisfied workers living under a violent repressive state, clandestine emigration was seen to be a more immediate and safer (though not without peril) alternative to political activism, much to the exasperation of communist organizers. At the same time, the state's softness on illegal emigration upset northern industrialists and major landowners, who repeatedly expressed concern over the serious labour shortages and rising wages precipitated by mass emigration. Employers complained about the feebleness and lack of docility of those workers who stayed, characteristics they invoked to argue against increasing wages. Salazar's general indifference to their pleas reflected his belief that the country's labour structure would be reshaped by the modern industry emerging in the south and its high demand for skilled workers and professionals, who traditionally did not emigrate in large numbers.

Another reason for the Estado Novo's ambivalent stance on emigration was its increasing dependence on remittances, which became indispensable for Portugal's balance of payments in this period and a major source of indirect funding for its Colonial Wars (figure 1.5).

The volume of remittances more than doubled in the 1950s, growing at an even faster rate by the mid-1960s. Emigration officials deliberately separated families by allowing men to leave while making it hard for women to follow, thus guaranteeing a steady inflow of remittances.[17] Whereas scholars disagree on the impact that emigration had on Portugal's macroeconomic development, there is general consensus on the negative net effect of remittances, which led to a rise in inflation and a large trade deficit.[18] The cash inflow also subsidized and perpetuated

Figure 1.5 Portuguese foreign revenue (remittances and exports), 1953–74. Values in thousands of US$, converted from Portuguese escudos through fxtop.com historical currency converter.

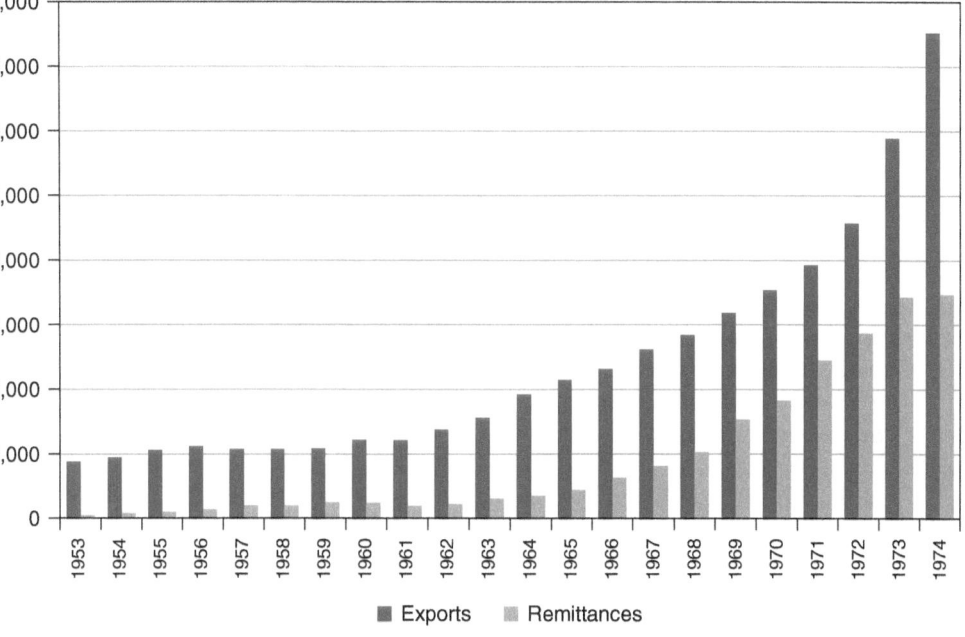

Source: Baganha ("As Correntes," 1994).

the otherwise unviable agrarian system in those rural regions where the emigrants came from. But at the micro level, remittances were a lifeline for many Portuguese families, who used that money to pay for their increasing costs of living and in some cases to modernize their consumer habits. Emigrants also sent news of the latest fashions and luxury products, which they sometimes brought or sent home. This was especially true in the Azores, where the majority of the population had little money and news from the wider world, other than what their relatives in North America provided.

The Estado Novo's emigration policies began to change in the second half of the 1960s, forced by the uncontainable surge of the European movement; the international coverage of the emigrants' poor living conditions; the large increase in remittances; the modernization of the industrial sector and its decreasing reliance on cheap labour; the intensification of diplomatic relations and international propaganda in defence of the colonial empire; and the increasing liberalization of some sectors of the regime, influenced by their working relations with allied Western democracies and by Vatican II's social doctrine. Once dominated by notions of displacement, estrangement, and distant transatlantic settlement, the perception of emigration – especially European – was increasingly as a temporary "cycle," where emigrants and their children were expected and encouraged to return. The paradigm shift prompted Lisbon to invest more in preventing the emigrants' "denationalization" – generally defined as the loss of Catholic spirituality, family ties, language, and cultural practices, and the embrace of oppositional political views – by providing greater social, cultural, and economic aid to its expatriate communities. This was especially the case after a Ministerial Council meeting in 1965, when the modernists' views on emigration gained momentum inside the regime; Salazar, however, remained largely disinterested. The Foreign Affairs Ministry also cemented its increasingly diasporic approach in 1966 by making its embassies responsible for "protecting and defending the rights and interests" of expats; by promoting the "progressive organization of Portuguese communities"; and by guiding "the activities of individuals and collectivities, in order to make them active elements in the defence of Portuguese interests and the expansion of [its] commerce and trade."[19]

Still, this new approach competed with the minister of the interior's traditional treatment of emigration as a national "problem." In fact, after 1964, the censorship of news alluding to clandestine emigration intensified, not so much to discourage restless workers (many of them illiterate) but to hide the scope of the exodus from the ruling classes who opposed it. In the press, churches, and other public forums, people were reminded of the dangers of illegal emigration and learned that emigrants undermined the nation and empire, traded peaceful rural havens for wretched and immoral foreign industrial cities, were contaminated by radical political ideas that they later disseminated in Portugal, and risked living forever mired in *saudade* (nostalgia).[20]

When the international press drew the world's attention to the miserable living conditions of Portuguese emigrants in France, Lisbon officials and the ruling classes considered it a national embarrassment. Even Salazar was moved by media reports about Paris's bidonvilles.[21] The Estado Novo was pressured into signing social welfare agreements with various European countries home to large Portuguese populations. In 1968, close to 69,000 Portuguese families with at least one member working in France, West Germany, Luxembourg, or the Netherlands received free medical assistance and drugs from foreign health organizations as a result of these accords. Another 181,303 emigrant families in

France and Luxembourg received an allowance from Portugal.[22] Many more failed to take advantage of these international welfare systems because they ignored their existence, had little experience in handling state bureaucracy, or were undocumented and therefore avoided interacting with government officials. Another less public objective of these bilateral agreements was to curb the movement of skilled workers, political exiles, and war resisters.[23]

With Caetano at the helm, the Estado Novo's public views on emigration became more articulate and pivotal. In fact, this was one of the few issues where the new dictator openly departed from Salazar, who, unlike his successor, rarely addressed the emigrants directly. Portuguese media started discussing Lisbon's views more openly, which increasingly described emigration as a normal factor of modernization and social progress across southern European countries, resulting from the continent's economic integration; yet publications calling emigration the outcome of economic and political failures were still censored. Caetano stated his intention to prevent the emigrants' "denationalization" through greater cultural investments in their communities. Nonetheless, he maintained that mass emigration was a "cancer" that ought to be eradicated – not through repressive means that merely boosted clandestine migration, labour exploitation, and loss of national prestige, but by Portugal's economic modernization, which he believed would generate employment and better living conditions for rural workers.[24]

In 1969, Lisbon stopped prosecuting clandestine economic emigration as a crime and began treating it as a lesser violation penalized with heavy fines; the penalty for smuggling undocumented emigrants, however, increased. The next year, the Ministerial Council again debated the emigration question and developed a comprehensive plan for providing more social services to emigrants and greater protection for their labour and other individual rights, and also for strengthening the cultural ties of Portuguese descendants with their "homeland."[25] To implement this plan, the regime replaced the Emigration Junta with the National Secretariat of Emigration (SNE), operating under the Ministry of Corporations and Social Welfare. At the same time, the responsibility for supervising emigration was transferred from the PIDE to other police forces. The new agency, run by socially progressive Catholics, provided greater aid to Portuguese schools and cultural associations abroad, created summer camps for emigrant children and youth, and ran welcoming programs for expats vacationing in Portugal. Lisbon officials also began visiting the emigrant "colonies" regularly in the early 1970s. On the eve of the 1974 revolution, the Estado Novo was preparing what some have called "the most liberal law of this period."[26] Ironically, at that point, the emigration "cancer" had already begun to dwindle.

Canada[27]

Portuguese workers have landed on Canada's Atlantic shores since the sixteenth century, when they began fishing for cod off the coast of Newfoundland. After declining in the seventeenth century, Portuguese cod fishing in the Grand Banks revived in the twentieth century, at which point St John's was large enough to attract and retain those fishermen who jumped ship. Estimates suggest there may have been as many as 6,000 Portuguese in Newfoundland in 1935. During the Second World War, their cod-fishing convoy earned the famous "White Fleet" nickname, in reference to the colour of its ships' hulls, painted white so that German U-boats could easily identify the neutral Portuguese out at sea. By 1941, close to 3,000 fishermen, most of them from fishing villages in the northern mainland, made the annual trip to the Grand Banks.[28] Despite the ancient link to Newfoundland and the gradual accumulating of runaway fishermen in the region, no identifiable Portuguese community or migration chains emerged as a result.

During the time that Portugal tried to limit the exodus of its workers in the postwar period, Canada shifted to a more liberal immigration policy in order to meet the increasing labour demands of its rapidly expanding economy. Responding to moral imperatives, capitalist interests, international commitments, and nation-building goals, Ottawa introduced a "bulk order" labour migration program in 1947 that allowed employers to place orders for foreign workers with the Department of Citizenship and Immigration (DCI), which then recruited in Europe's refugee camps. Between 1947 and 1952, over 100,000 "displaced persons" were admitted to Canada under this scheme. Once the refugee camps were emptied, Canada's leading industries pressured Ottawa into recruiting labourers from the "less desirable" southern European countries. After extensive negotiations, Ottawa and Lisbon finally agreed to a small pilot group of skilled male workers in 1952. The positive experiences of this first group gave officials on both sides reasons to be optimistic about a larger bulk order movement in the future.

With unemployment soaring in the mainland and nearing crisis proportions in the Azores, the Estado Novo once again turned to emigration as a temporary solution. Lisbon saw in this labour migration scheme an opportunity to open a lasting transatlantic movement to Canada; especially among Azoreans, who had a long tradition of settlement and migration chains in North America. Despite initial reservations from DCI gatekeepers about the supposed inability of Azorean workers to adapt to Canada's farming conditions, Portuguese officials convinced their counterparts to include a sizable number of islanders in these bulk orders.

1.3 Group photo of Azorean "bulk order" emigrants about to leave for Canada, 1956. Photographer unknown. Ponta Delgada. York University Libraries, CTASC, David Higgs fonds.

Eventually, the Canadians recognized the value of Azorean workers, whom they deemed more reliable than mainlanders when it came to fulfilling their contracts. The first group of Portuguese bulk order labourers arrived on Pier 21, in Halifax, aboard the *Saturnia* on 13 May 1953. By 1961, when this official movement ended, 6,875 male workers had been requested, 88 per cent of whom were destined for unskilled occupations on farms and in railway-track building, mining, logging, and other toiling jobs shunned by native Canadians. A large minority of these "labourers" were, in fact, tradesmen and small-business owners, who pretended to be common workers in order to meet the criteria of Portuguese and Canadian bureaucrats. After a few years of working as labourers, many were able to return to their trades and businesses, some achieving great professional success and building sizable companies, especially in food importing and wholesaling, construction, and electronics. Together with the 800 skilled workers included in the bulk orders and others sponsored by their kin, these educated migrants would assume leadership positions in the ethnic communities that later emerged in Toronto, Montreal, Vancouver, and other urban centres.

In 1956, when the number of Portuguese contract "skippers" became alarming, DCI officials proposed that male workers be allowed to bring their families, hoping such a change would check their mobility. That year, Ottawa broadened its family migration provisions by allowing landed immigrants to sponsor their spouses, children, and siblings, along with the sponsored individual's own nuclear families. These changes greatly affected the volume of Portuguese migration to Canada, which nearly doubled in 1957 outside the bulk order movement. In the following year, Ottawa's new Conservative government promised to restrict the entry of unskilled workers and focus on extending family sponsorship. Despite its interest in developing migration chains to Canada, Lisbon still raised barriers for women wanting to emigrate. The Emigration Junta first declined Ottawa's request for female domestic workers, citing paternalist concerns over their isolation in a foreign environment. Then, when family reunification began, it delayed the process, claiming it first had to confirm the financial security of the male sponsor. Most of the women who eventually moved to Canada were either married or engaged, and they joined their partners in the cities. Contrary to the dictatorship's rationale, it was their multi-faceted contributions to the immigrant household that improved their financial welfare and that of their budding ethnic communities.[29]

Before settling in the cities, many of these sojourners had a common experience of isolation, exploitation, and hardship in the Canadian hinterland, resulting in large part from their lack of English- or French-language skills, but also from their employers' prejudicial views on "Latin" immigrants. Together with injuries to their personal dignity, these workers' bodies often carried the marks of their dangerous jobs, including the loss of limbs and life. Portuguese farmhands in Ontario and Quebec were the most aggrieved, making multiple complaints to homeland officials about their isolation, overwork, malnutrition, underpayment, and general mistreatment. The consul in Montreal and the Emigration Junta's inspector supervising the movement tried to appease these migrants by paying them occasional visits, shifting them between farms, or speaking to their employers, ultimately trying to manage the perceptions of Canadian immigration authorities about the quality of Portuguese workers. As was common among other bulk order groups, the number of Portuguese sojourners breaking their one-year contracts to look for better jobs elsewhere was high. Despite the efforts of government officials on both sides, the number of contract skippers increased exponentially with every new migrant cohort arriving in Canada. As their co-national support networks in Canada expanded, information about jobs in different parts of the country circulated with greater ease and newcomers wasted less time before chasing them. Ottawa usually tolerated the high rates of absconding hired farmhands, since they filled important labour shortages in the cities, especially in construction and factory work. This phenomenon became unacceptable only when it coincided with periods of high unemployment and the slowing down of British immigration. Reacting to one such moment, Ottawa finally ended the bulk order agreement with Lisbon in 1961 and moved to limit the entrance of more unskilled migrants into Canada.

By the time the bulk order movement ended, a critical mass of Portuguese emigrants had settled in Canada. As Lisbon intended, they would generate large autonomous migration chains from the Azores capable of sustaining that movement, despite Ottawa's attempts to curb southern European immigration. The termination of the labour migration agreement coincided with the beginning of the Portuguese Colonial Wars, which provided a strong incentive for young families and military-aged men to leave Portugal. By 1965, the now Liberal government in Ottawa saw family sponsorship as "one of the most serious immigration problems," since it provided a means for large numbers of labourers to enter Canada without undergoing occupational selection, the Portuguese being one of the main culprits.[30] The "point system" immigration selection process introduced in 1967, which privileged highly skilled and well-educated applicants, raised a significant barrier to Portuguese mass immigration, which owed its existence to Canada's high demand for lower-skilled labourers. Still, their numbers continued to grow, not only through family sponsorship, but also through extensive clandestine migration streams that developed alongside official channels.

Before the first Portuguese bulk order cohort arrived in 1953, a small but pivotal stream of "re-emigrant" men from Venezuela, Brazil, the United States, and other countries had begun to make their way into Canada illegally, heeding the call for foreign labourers. The discrepancy between recorded departures from Portugal and arrivals in Canada indicates a parallel movement in the 1950s of a few hundred migrants every year, a number that grew considerably after 1961 (figure 1.6).

However, the total number of Portuguese emigrants from other countries was undoubtedly higher, since official statisticians did not capture clandestine migration. One commonly acknowledged clandestine movement, on which there are few quantitative data, was that of cod fishermen who jumped ship in Atlantic Canada and made their way west.

After the Second World War, demand for cod again increased in Portugal and Brazil, leading to an upturn in Portuguese fishermen working in the Grand Banks. Unlike other European fleets, the White Fleet combined modern trawlers with traditional, single-manned dories, where solitary fishermen caught fish through the strength of their arms. This was a very labour-intensive and risky occupation with a high rate of injuries and deaths, due not only to the many dangers of the sea but

Figure 1.6 Portuguese emigration versus Canadian immigration statistics, 1946–78.

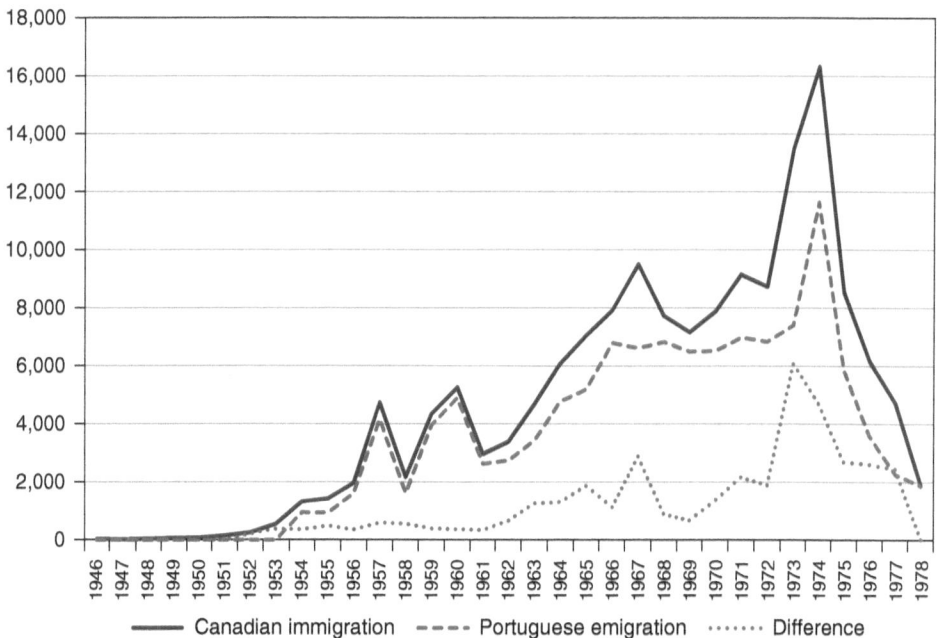

Sources: Marques and Medeiros (*Portuguese Immigrants*, 1980); Baganha ("Portuguese Emigration," 1998).

to the propensity of the larger ships to catch fire. It is no surprise that so many of these men abandoned this hard life once their ships docked.

A more common way for undocumented migrants to enter Canada was to pass as tourists, overstay their visas, and later apply for landed status. They often did so with the help of illegal migration rackets run by travel agents in various countries, sometimes aided by Portugal's consular staff. For instance, in 1957, the Portuguese consulate in Montreal was implicated in two illicit migration schemes, resulting in public scandals. The first involved a scam orchestrated by a Paraguayan travel agent in Montreal, who defrauded Portuguese migrants in British Columbia, then ran away with over CA$3,000 collected from prospective emigrants in the Azores – all with the implicit help of consular staff. The second case implicated two travel agencies in Montreal and Caracas, which together brought Portuguese "tourists" to Canada via Brazil and other South American countries. Once in Canada, the Montreal agency helped these undocumented migrants apply for landed

1.4 Portuguese fisherman standing on the dock, Newfoundland, 1961. Photograph by Bob Brooks. Library and Archives Canada, Mikan, 4314204.

status. An investigator sent by Lisbon to audit the consulate's involvement in these illegal schemes discovered that one of its staff members was a former general manager of the offending agency. After this case became public, the travel agency changed ownership, yet the new manager (a Portuguese American) continued to operate an illegal migration racket, this time catering only to those wanting to move to the United States. In October 1958, the Emigration Junta called for a stop to the issuance of ordinary passports for common workers wishing to visit Canada, arguing that they were, "by norm, in no condition to do tourism." Three months later, the dictatorship amnestied those undocumented emigrants who returned to Portugal and regularized their status.[31]

Canada's membership in the Organisation for Economic Co-operation and Development, which promoted freedom of mobility among member countries, limited Ottawa's power to curtail the influx of undocumented migrants from Portugal – one of the international body's founding nations. After September 1963, Portuguese citizens visiting Canada for a period of up to three months were no longer required to obtain tourist visas, which resulted in a surge of applications for landed status from within the country. The number of those entering Canada with a non-immigrant visa jumped from 650 in 1958–63 to over 3,000 in 1963–4. By the end of 1965, fewer than 25 per cent of these individuals were known to have left the country after their visas expired. Canadian officials saw this situation as a "complete breakdown" of its immigration system and the Portuguese as its worst offenders.[32] Hoping to clear its application backlog, Ottawa made it easier to apply for landed status from within Canada in 1966. The next year, it created the independent Immigration Appeal Board to hear appeals from individuals facing deportation, who could base their arguments on humanitarian and compassionate grounds. These two pieces of legislation were greatly misused by prospective migrants and their informal facilitators. The right to apply for landed status from within Canada encouraged more "visitors" to try their luck, while the lengthy appeal process allowed them to stall a deportation order if their applications were unsuccessful, during which time they would continue to work for wages. Counselled by cunning immigration consultants, these "visitors" appealed their deportation even when they lacked legal merit, hoping to receive amnesty on compassionate grounds, based on the fact they had established roots in Canada. Such tactics led to an enormous backlog at the Appeal Board, where cases could take up to seven years to resolve, further aggravating the problem. Under Prime Minister Pierre Trudeau, Ottawa took decisive action to fix the problem by revoking the right of visitors to apply for landed status and the right of undocumented residents from countries without visa requirements to appeal a deportation order. To clear the outstanding backlog, Ottawa granted undocumented migrants a period of sixty days to regularize their status. About 39,000 people were amnestied as a result of this Adjustment of Status Program.[33] However, at this point, Portuguese migration had already begun to decline as a result of the global recession of 1973–4 and the deep transformations that followed the 1974 revolution.

Over 150,000 Portuguese arrived in Canada between the 1950s and 1970s. Despite the introduction of the "point system," more of them landed in the first half of the 1970s than before. During 1966–75, they represented 8 per cent of the annual number of arrivals, ranking fourth among newcomer groups. By 1981, 68 per cent of all ethnic Portuguese in Canada (188,100) lived in Ontario (129,000) and 14 per cent in Quebec (27,370), followed by smaller settlements in British Columbia, Manitoba, and Alberta. Toronto's metropolitan area had the largest Portuguese population in the country (88,885), which included the suburban city of Mississauga, the third-largest Portuguese settlement (8,875) after Montreal's metropolitan area (23,250).[34] Against Ottawa's original wishes, over 60 per cent of all Portuguese immigrants came from the Azores (nearly 80 per cent from São Miguel) (figure 1.7).

As the Estado Novo intended, they made a concerted effort to transplant their extended families to North America. While close relatives often settled near each other, some family members lived in other parts of North America. It was normal for Azoreans in Canada to visit their relatives in the United States and vice-versa. Though there are few data on the volume of this cross-border traffic, anecdotal evidence suggests that those in central and eastern Canada were likely to have relatives in New England, while those in western Canada extended their families to California.

United States

Over 400,000 European war refugees entered the United States under the Displaced Persons Acts of 1948–52. Unlike the situation in Canada, this large influx was not accompanied by a liberalization of American immigration laws, despite President Harry S. Truman's efforts in that direction. Citing concerns over national security and communist infiltration, conservative senators from both parties ensured that the admission of displaced persons was limited by national quotas and other discriminatory restrictions working against Jewish refugees. The 1952 Immigration and Nationality Act followed this restrictive Cold War rationale by narrowing the formula used to calculate immigration quotas,

Figure 1.7 Portuguese emigration to Canada by district of origin, 1955–74.

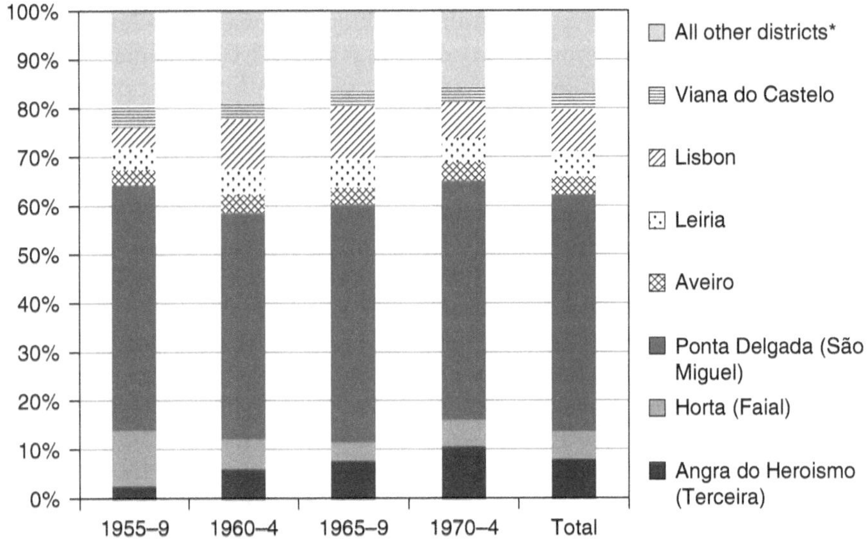

Legend:
- All other districts*
- Viana do Castelo
- Lisbon
- Leiria
- Aveiro
- Ponta Delgada (São Miguel)
- Horta (Faial)
- Angra do Heroismo (Terceira)

Categories on x-axis: 1955–9, 1960–4, 1965–9, 1970–4, Total

Source: Arroteia (*A Emigração Portuguesa*, 1983).

which continued to privilege northern and western Europeans; Portugal was allotted a mere 438 immigrants per year. Like Truman, President Dwight D. Eisenhower opposed this discriminatory immigration act and urged Congress to pass legislation admitting a larger number of southern Europeans.[35] Eisenhower's calls for reform led to the 1953 Refugee Relief Act, which authorized the admission of over 214,000 non-quota refugees, defined under this law as: "any person in a country or area which is either Communist or Communist-dominated who because of persecution, fear of persecution, natural calamity or military operations is out of his usual place of abode and unable to return thereto."[36] As this bill was being debated in the House of Representatives, the Portuguese ambassador in Washington Luis E. Fernandes (1950–61)[37] lobbied Republican Minority Leader Joseph W. Martin – the representative for New Bedford, Fall River, and other towns in Bristol County with large Portuguese-American populations – to include 2,000 Portuguese immigrants in the proposed non-quota visas. While interested, Martin lamented that the Portuguese did not qualify as "refugees."[38]

It took a "natural calamity" to reopen America's doors to Portuguese mass immigration. On the morning of 27 September 1957, the Capelinhos underwater volcano on the shore of Faial Island erupted for the first time in nearly four centuries. Over the next seven months, lava, toxic gas, and giant clouds of ash destroyed close to 4,200 acres of pasture and arable land. In May of the next year, a spate of seismic activity destroyed over 600 buildings, leaving several thousand Azoreans homeless.[39] The first organized reaction from Lisbon came in June 1958, when it introduced an emergency plan for recovering the island's economy, rebuilding its infrastructure, and providing food, clothing, and medical assistance to those affected.[40] Efforts were also made to move displaced families to the African colonies, though with poor results.[41] No calls for international aid were made.

Azorean communities in the United States organized aid relief committees and asked Congress to pass legislation allowing for the admission of the volcano's victims. State Representative Joseph Perry, whose parents had emigrated from Faial, brought this matter to the attention of Rhode Island's and Massachusetts's congressional delegations. One of its members was Senator John Pastore (the son of Italian immigrants), who introduced Bill S. 3942 allocating non-quota visas to "heads of families" affected by the Capelinhos eruption. The bill gained greater political weight after Senator John F. Kennedy endorsed it. On 2 September 1958, President Eisenhower signed it into law, opening America's gates to 1,500 Azorean "heads of families" and their "dependents" (wives and unmarried children under the age of twenty-one) until 1 December 1959. Only those who had been forced "out of their usual place of abode" and were "unable to return thereto," or were "in urgent need of assistance for the essentials of life" were eligible to apply for a refugee visa.[42] American officials initially interpreted this definition to mean only Faial residents directly affected by the volcano. Many Azorean Americans were disappointed by this circumscribed interpretation of the natural disaster's impact in the archipelago and lost their initial enthusiasm for the refugee program. This posed a challenge for relief organizers, since prospective Azorean refugees were required to prove they had offers of employment and housing in the United States, for which they needed the assistance of Portuguese Americans. The Catholic Welfare Conference, which canvassed New England's Portuguese communities under instructions from the State Department, had trouble mobilizing Azorean Americans, largely because few were able to hire or find employment for their fellow islanders. Still, there were some who sponsored a large number of refugees, such as the Azorean priest Augusto Furtado, who sheltered many of the displaced islanders at his St John of God Church in Somerset.[43]

The Estado Novo's reaction to Washington's humanitarian gesture was lukewarm at best. Besides his aversion to foreigners meddling in

Portugal's domestic affairs, Salazar worried about the Americans' increasing influence over Azoreans. Unsurprisingly, Lisbon rejected Washington's suggestion that it seek the help of the Intergovernmental Committee for European Migration (ICEM) to facilitate this refugee movement. Created in 1952 to coordinate the movement of refugees and other immigrants in western Europe, the ICEM was often criticized by its member states for infringing on their national sovereignty. Portuguese officials, who had refused to join the ICEM, declined its offer to cover transportation costs and use its vast institutional network to resettle Azorean refugees. Though looking more favourably on the International Catholic Migration Commission, Lisbon also declined an offer from this lay organization to pay for the costs of transportation and help find jobs and housing in Portuguese-American settlements, since one of its conditions was that Washington's funding be channelled through the ICEM. At this point, the governor of Faial, António Pimentel, repudiated the "alarmist" tone used in reports describing the widespread misery caused by the volcano and claimed that there was no reason for an Azorean exodus. According to him, the aid from the national government and Caritas was enough to address any outstanding issues. Lisbon too considered the term "refugees" to be an inapt description of those displaced by the volcano. The records do not explain why, but one can assume that the regime rejected the term's connotation of abandonment and its suggestion that the government was incapable of rescuing its own people.[44]

Once the extent of the volcano's destruction became undeniable and the plight of those affected lingered, Lisbon finally agreed to opening a temporary American vice-consulate in Faial that could process visa applications and expedite the "refugee" movement. Governor Pimentel changed his position on the scale of the crisis and tried to convince American officials to broaden their criteria for issuing non-quota visas. Eventually they yielded and began accepting applications from Azoreans living outside the most damaged areas. In 1959, over the course of nine months, 1,500 non-quota Azorean families arrived in the United States. Building on this largely successful experience, Congress approved another 2,000 non-quota visas the following year, coinciding with the UN World Refugee Year. Overall, 4,811 people were admitted into the country through what became known as the Azorean Refugee Acts.[45]

The 1965 Immigration and Nationality Act, which privileged family sponsorship and skilled workers, eliminated the national origins formula, allotted a 20,000 annual quota to every sending country, and a total of 120,000 visas to the western hemisphere and 170,000 to the eastern hemisphere. Inspired by the civil rights movement and John F.

Kennedy's "nation of immigrants" vision, the act enshrined by President Lyndon B. Johnson ended racist restrictions and opened "the gates" to immigrants from every part of the world. Still, the authors of the bill had southern and eastern Europeans in mind when they proposed a redress of past injustices and assumed that it would lead to a new wave of Italian, Greek, and Polish immigrants. However, the only significant increase in European immigration after 1965 came from Portugal and Greece. The majority of newcomers now arrived from Asia and Latin America, which came as a shock to many of the act's proponents and strained their Ellis Island mythology.[46]

The 1965 act opened a new chapter in Portuguese-American history by revitalizing old migration chains and re-establishing links with the homeland. The number of Portuguese arrivals jumped from 13,928 in the 1950s to 70,568 in the 1960s, peaking at 104,754 in the 1970s (then the third-largest source of European immigrants, behind Italy and the United Kingdom). About 57 per cent of those arriving between 1955 and 1974 were Azorean, the majority of them sponsored by relatives (figure 1.8).[47]

By then, most of their extended families lived in the United States, as reflected in the fact that return migration to the Azores practically ended after 1965. Newcomers tended to settle with or near their relatives, which furthered Portuguese residential concentration in New Bedford, Fall River, and various other cities and towns in the southeastern region of Massachusetts popularly known as "The Portuguese Archipelago."[48] While Massachusetts, Rhode Island, and California continued to host the largest communities, Bridgeport in Connecticut and Newark in New Jersey (both in New York City's metropolitan area) saw a sizable increase in Portuguese population (figure 1.2). Besides its rapid growth, the Newark settlement was remarkable for its high number of mainlander newcomers, the majority of them coming from the Aveiro district.

The Post-Imperial Cycle: 1970s–1980s

Two events inaugurated this migratory cycle: the 1973–4 global "oil crisis" and the 1974 Revolution of the Carnations. The first generated a worldwide economic recession that shrank job markets everywhere and led to widespread anti-immigration policies in Europe, and the second led to a massive return movement of former emigrant workers, political and intellectual exiles, and colonial settlers. France, which had already introduced tough immigration restrictions in the early 1970s, decided in 1974 to halt the incoming flow of foreign workers. As

Figure 1.8 Portuguese emigration to the United States by district of origin, 1955–74.

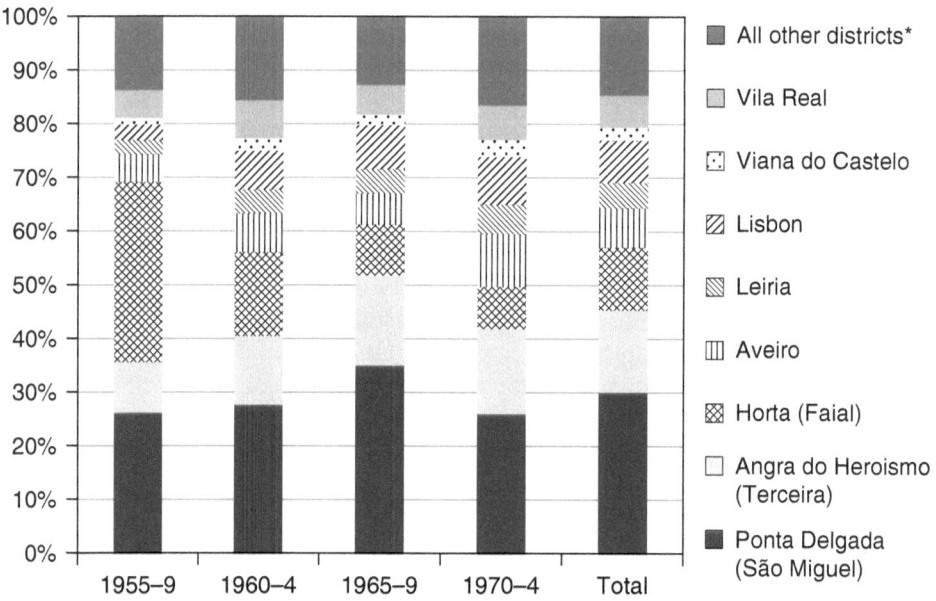

Source: Arroteia (*A Emigração Portuguesa*, 1983).

a result, Portuguese emigration fell sharply by the end of that decade (figure 1.9).

This drop was particularly noticeable in the European movement, which dropped from 83 per cent of total emigration in 1973 to 63 per cent in 1975, then to 39 per cent in 1979. The overseas movement became dominant once again after 1978 (except for the years 1982–4), accounting for 51 per cent of total emigration in 1980–8. The number of returned migrants – not including the colonial "returnees" forced to leave Africa in 1975 – increased significantly during this period, from close to 7,000 in the 1960s to 13,000 in the 1970s, then to 52,000 in the 1980s. Over a quarter were children and youth under the age of nineteen who had never lived in Portugal. Close to 90 per cent of former emigrants settled in the same rural communities they had left. The majority still had few formal qualifications: 12 per cent were illiterate, 24 per cent had no formal schooling, and 56 per cent had attended only primary school. They often found it difficult to transfer the skills learned abroad or were simply not interested in resuming the same occupations they had had as emigrants. Furthermore, 41 per cent removed themselves

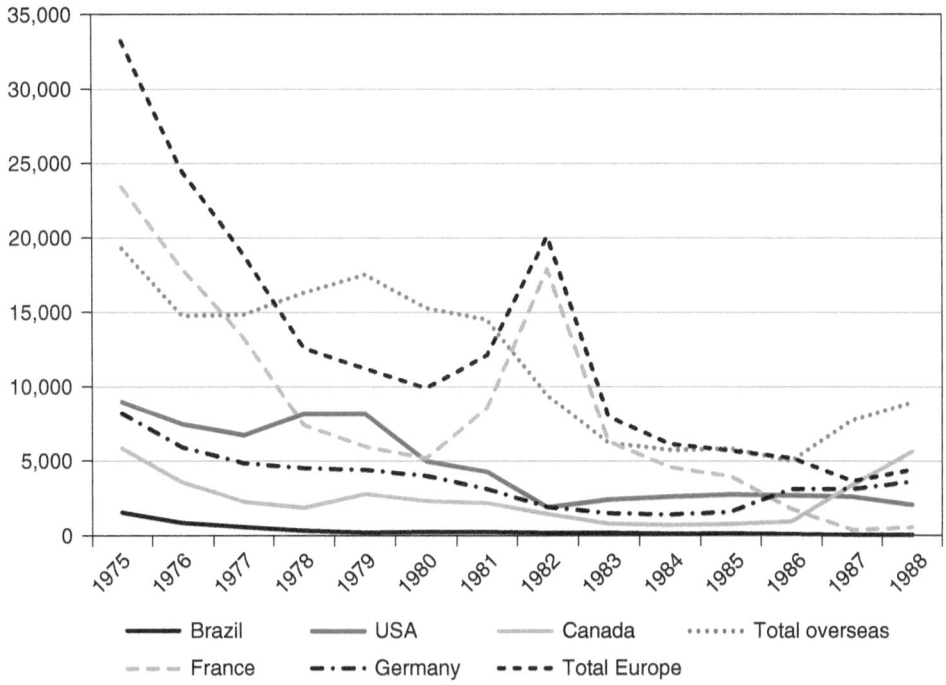

Figure 1.9 Portuguese emigration by destination, 1974–88.

Source: Baganha ("Portuguese Emigration," 1998).

from the workforce altogether. Those who remained active tended to open their own small businesses or turned to farming. Overall, their stories of emigration were triumphant, as reflected in their new wealth, property, consumer habits, and the ability to stop working for wages.[49]

Political exiles returning to Portugal in the aftermath of the revolution contributed towards building a new democratic country. Some of the politicians who determined the fate of the Third Republic, including Álvaro Cunhal and Mário Soares, leaders of the Portuguese Communist Party (PCP) and Socialist Party (PS), respectively, returned to Portugal at this point. This cohort also included a significant number of intellectuals, artists, and professionals, who were now celebrated as heroes for their contributions in the fight against "fascism," which had led to their exile. Many would assume leadership positions in their respective fields and political organizations and would contribute to the modernization of Portugal's outdated ways. Their heroic homecoming contrasted with the hasty return of over half a million imperial *retornados* (returnees), as they became known, hurried out of Angola and Mozambique in 1975–6, after civil wars broke out between opposing nationalist forces immediately following independence. The situation in the former African colonies became desperate so quickly that an international airlift had to be organized to fly these so-called refugees back to Portugal, many of them leaving with nothing more than the clothes on their bodies and the few belongings they could carry. These former settlers faced hostility from Portuguese civil society, now dominated by the far left, which saw them as reactionary colonialists who had lived luxuriously in Africa thanks to the racist exploitation of the black populations. While in many cases this perception corresponded with the truth at some level, in many others it did not. In any case, Portuguese nationals were reluctant to aid them and resented the programs introduced by Lisbon to assist in their reintegration, often accusing retornados of "stealing" their housing and jobs. Contrary to the expectations of the day, a spike in re-emigration did not follow from this mass repatriation. Still, a significant number did re-emigrate to countries with large Portuguese expatriate populations, including Canada and the United States, and became active members in these communities. Only 60 per cent of the African retornados had been born in Portugal. The vast majority were white, although a significant minority were black or of mixed race (mostly Cape Verdeans).[50] Along with their skin colour, the latter also stood out for their deepening poverty and harsh living conditions in shanty towns around Portugal's largest cities. Unlike white retornados, they had no kinship networks in Portugal who could offer them temporary aid. Making matters worse was the Nationality Law of 1975. While this legislation maintained the principle of *jus soli* (including former colonial territories), those born in Africa had to trace their European-Portuguese ancestry back three generations in order to be eligible for citizenship, which effectively excluded the majority of black colonials.

Some scholars have argued that emigration was "the main form of resistance used by the Portuguese popular classes."[51] The future prime minister and president, Mário Soares, reached a similar conclusion during his exile in France: all emigrants had been moved by a rejection of economic and political oppression, even if they were not initially aware of that fact.[52] This perception was not shared by labour organizers or the PCP, who partly blamed emigration and its remittances for supporting the dictatorship and for undermining their own organizational efforts at collective mobilization. After the revolution, the far left's view on emigrants became more sympathetic to their personal sacrifices and remittances, which the revolutionaries now solicited in order to build the country's future. Helping this rapprochement was a rally held in Lisbon on 11 August 1974, attended by thousands of emigrants who came to show their support for the MFA. After marching down one of the city's main avenues, they gathered at the May 1st stadium, where they were treated to concerts from some of the most popular leftist songwriters and poets. Speaking to reporters at the festival, the communist writer Modesto Navarro noted how the emigrants' contributions to class warfare in Portugal's most isolated regions, where they introduced new ideas about labour rights and organization, were undervalued. He also explained how those same remittances that once sustained the dictatorship were now essential to ensuring the revolution's survival in the face of an international capitalist boycott. Still, parties to the left of the PS worried about granting external voting rights to emigrants, whom they considered to be largely "reactionary," and sent representatives to their communities so to "explain" what was happening at home. Portuguese left-wing media also insisted on the emigrants' victimhood by focusing on the exploitation and privations they faced as workers abroad, which contrasted with the latter's own narrative of triumph and liberation. For instance, in June 1975, a popular left-wing magazine published an article titled "Emigrant: The Revolution Needs You," where it questioned whether "leaving [was] a more courageous act than staying."[53]

Expatriate citizens were first allowed to vote for their own political representatives in Portugal's constitutive assembly elections of 25 April 1975. Overall, 21,934 expats in thirty countries joined their fellow national citizens in electing the group of deputies that would write Portugal's new democratic constitution, introduced in 1976. Dominated by left-wing parties, the assembly guaranteed external voting rights to citizens living abroad, provided that they registered with their nearest Portuguese consulate or embassy. The constitution also created two external electoral districts, one for "Europe" another for "Outside of Europe," each electing two members of parliament. Voter turnout increased in the 1976 government elections: 51,693 votes were cast in Europe and 40,047 in the rest of the world, representing 87.6 per cent of all registered expat voters (figure 1.10). While the number of voters registered abroad continued to grow until the mid-1990s, their actual turnout dropped sharply in the 1980s, stagnating at the 20–30 percentile since 1987.[54]

The first two constitutional governments (1976–8), led by the socialist Soares, continued on the same track as its provisional predecessors had in negotiating social security accords with various countries (including Canada) and ensuring that emigrant workers were guaranteed the same labour rights as the citizens of their host countries were. They also pledged to advance expatriate interests in Portugal, boost their investments in the home country, protect their private property, facilitate their

Figure 1.10 Portuguese expatriate voter turnout in legislative elections, 1976–2011.

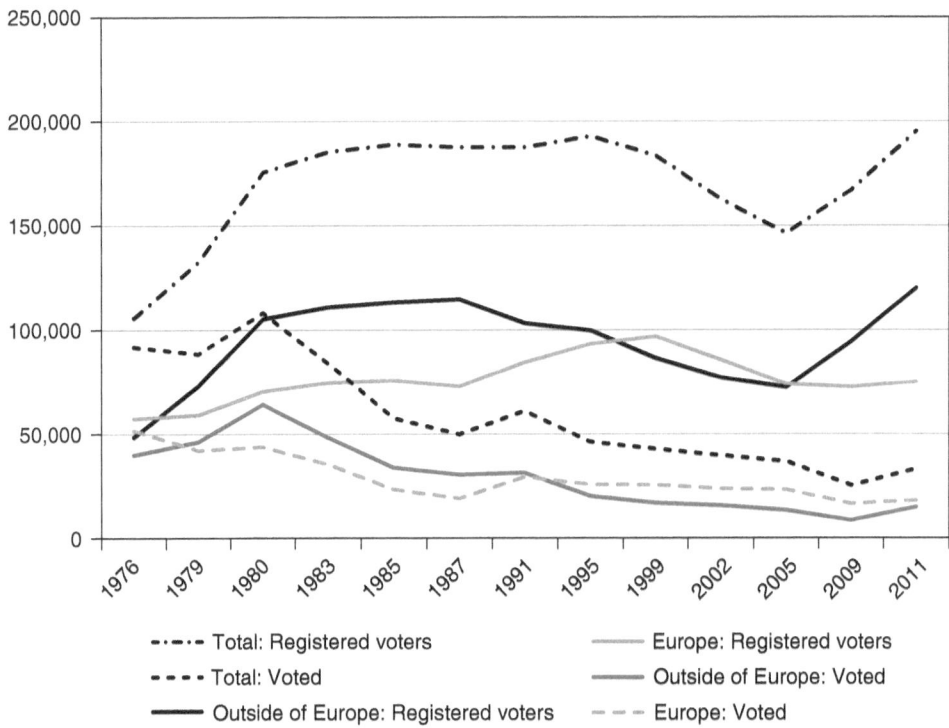

Source: Comissão Nacional de Eleições website.

return, defend the emigrants' and their children's constitutional right to education in Portuguese by equipping and subsidizing their community schools, and train instructors to teach abroad. Their declared aim was to boost the national consciousness of emigrant children by teaching them the language, history, and geography of their ancestral homeland – but "without chauvinism."[55] Like many before them, the socialists saw emigration as a national "problem" resulting from decades of poor economic management and deep-seated social inequality. But while economic development was the obvious solution in the eyes of the government, high unemployment rates forced it, once again, to open the emigration "valve" as a short-term solution for the labour surplus. Interviewed by a Portuguese-Canadian newspaper during a visit to Toronto in 1977, the secretary of state for emigration, João Lima, expressed his own ambivalence towards his role: "When systematic, the policy of emigration is extremely reproachable; it blocks the country from performing its most precious function, which is that of apportioning work. However, the present realities impose that some emigration be encouraged ... I've been battling with myself, but I must develop that policy, hoping and trusting that in the medium term the country's overall development will impact its underdeveloped regions."[56]

After 1977, the cultural identity of Portuguese expatriate communities and their position within the post-imperial nation was amplified in Lisbon's official discourse. Emigrants were described no longer as "uprooted" folk in need of rescuing by their homeland state, but as national "ambassadors" praised and valued for their integration in their host societies. Portuguese officials now promoted a new collective imagination that could reassert the nation's former greatness, reinvigorate a sense of patriotism among its people, and reclaim some of its geopolitical relevance. But the discourse and tropes used to elaborate this globalized national identity were largely the same as those deployed by the old colonialist regime. The romantic notion of the explorer as the "adventurous," "industrious," "cultural broker" was recycled and redeployed, no longer identifying the "civilizing colonizer" but the "entrepreneurial emigrant." As the anthropologist Caroline Brettell noted: "it is in this desire for unboundedness, this desire to escape the ever prevalent thought that Portugal is [a small country] that one can find an explanation for the symbolic transformation from *navegador*, to *colono*, to *emigrante*."[57] Like most nationalist projects, it was a highly gendered process, where the nation's flag-bearer was always a man. This is clear in President Eanes's national address during the 1977 Portugal Day celebrations:

> What distinguishes the Portuguese from other men is his exceptional capacity for making the whole world his land and every human being his brother, without ever losing the traces of his Lusiad roots.
>
> Today, as yesterday, greatness lies in the universal dimension of our people ... They have a right to the title of "strong" men, which Camões reserved for the great performers of Lusitanian diaspora. And decolonization, far from meaning that Portugal has lost its ecumenical perspective, has, on the contrary, reclaimed its historical vocation in a purer state. The country that we are today does not look at men as instruments of territorial exploration, but instead considers them links of an indestructible community of sentiment and culture ...
>
> Thus, a new concept of Fatherland emerges from our authentic national tradition: it matters more the man than the ground on which he lives.[58]

At this point, the terms "Portuguese communities," "diaspora" and "citizens residing abroad" entered official parlance, while "emigrant" was avoided along with the unflattering memories it conjured in Portuguese psyche, associated as it was with poverty, illiteracy, and other ignoble stereotypes. This semantic sensibility was reflected in the renaming of the national holiday, known since 1977 as the Day of Portugal, Camões and the Portuguese *Communities* (changed from the previous "Race").[59]

The Azorean and Madeiran regional governments, which obtained political autonomy from Lisbon in 1976, following growing calls for independence, also took measures to connect and consolidate their expatriate communities. In June–July 1977, the first Congress of Madeiran Communities brought together representatives from various emigrant organizations to discuss their expectations regarding their relationship with the regional government. Their advisory capacity was institutionalized in 1984 with the creation of the Permanent Council of Madeiran Communities. The Azorean government organized a similar congress in August 1978, where its delegates discussed how best to serve its emigrants and develop intercommunity connections.[60] Azorean officials did not create their own diasporic council but held annual meetings with emigrant representatives, launched agencies dedicated to fostering transnational ties with its expatriate communities, and sponsored cultural initiatives advancing *Açorianidade* (Azoreanness) abroad.[61] Some mainland regions also organized their own diasporic congresses, for example, the emigrants from the central Beiras, who met in Fundão in 1977 and Fermentelos in 1980; however, no autonomous diasporic institutions resulted from these meetings.

It was in Fermentelos that the Social Democratic (liberal) prime minister, Francisco Sá Carneiro (1980–1), first articulated his PSD party's diasporic version of the nation, with its deterritorialized, transnational, and flexible communitarian structure. A leading member of the short-lived "Liberal Wing" during Caetano's rule, Carneiro was the PSD's chief founder and the first prime minister of the centre-right governments that would dominate Portuguese politics for most of the 1980s and early 1990s. Carneiro saw the emigrant communities as guarantors of Portugal's independence in the post-imperial era and a solution to the country's (presumably financial) problems. Taking on the emigrants' problems as the nation's own, he proposed to change the constitution to reflect this new version of nationhood and increase the expats' political representation in Lisbon.[62] Prime Minister Pinto Balsemão, who succeeded Carneiro after he died in a plane crash in December 1980, continued the PSD's courting of the emigrant electorate, whose votes he personally solicited when touring the emigrant communities during his 1981 campaign. More than votes, what justified Lisbon's investment in multiple agencies and programs serving emigrants was the continuous rise in remittances, which grew by a massive 2,106 per cent between 1974 (US$173,600) and 1989 (US$3,656,025).[63] Their relative value to the Gross Domestic Product also increased, from 8 per cent in 1973–9 to 10 per cent in 1980–9 (figure 1.11).[64]

Another important driver behind the government's increased activity on emigration was Maria Manuela Aguiar, the secretary of state for emigration for most of the 1980s (serving under both right- and left-wing governments) and a member of parliament for "outside of Europe" and "Europe" throughout the 1980s–2000s period. A pioneer feminist politician, Aguiar was a dynamic advocate of emigrant causes in parliament and within her own cabinets. Her ideas and dedication shaped not only Lisbon's emigration policies but also the expectations placed on homeland politicians by the expatriate communities. One of Aguiar's most important contributions was advocating for women's issues in the diaspora, which she realized early on in her tenure was a male-dominated domain. In her own words: "I could rarely speak to the women, 'locked' in the associations' restaurant kitchens or seated in the second and third rows of the audience, attentive and discreetly silent."[65]

The 1980s saw the entrenching of diasporic consciousness in the minds of Portuguese politicians, who now readily acknowledged that emigrants had been historically marginalized from their nation's decision-making centres, despite having played an important role in its development. The vision of a borderless citizenship led the centre-right coalition government to create the Council of Portuguese Communities (CPC) in 1980, one of the world's first diasporic councils. Inspired by the Conséil supérieur des Français de l'étranger founded by the Paris government in 1948, the CPC was designed to advise Lisbon on expatriate matters and safeguard "the cultural values alive in the Lusiad communities across the World and [reinforce] the ties that bind them to Portugal." This council was expected to consolidate these communities into a recognizable diaspora by providing "a platform for dialogue and better mutual understanding that reflects the union of Portuguese organizations and of their descendants living abroad."[66] Among its members were the state secretary for emigration, the parliamentarians representing the emigration districts, representatives from expatriate organizations, delegates from Portugal's labour unions and employers' associations, and a group of experts on emigration affairs. Countries with a "justifiable" number of emigrants were invited to form their own local committees responsible for representing their communities at the CPC and vice versa.[67] As Aguiar later recalled, Lisbon expected the CPC to become a "100% civil society!"[68] Three hundred delegates

Figure 1.11 Portuguese foreign revenue (remittances and exports), 1974–89. Values in thousands of US$, converted from Portuguese escudos through fxtop.com historical currency converter.

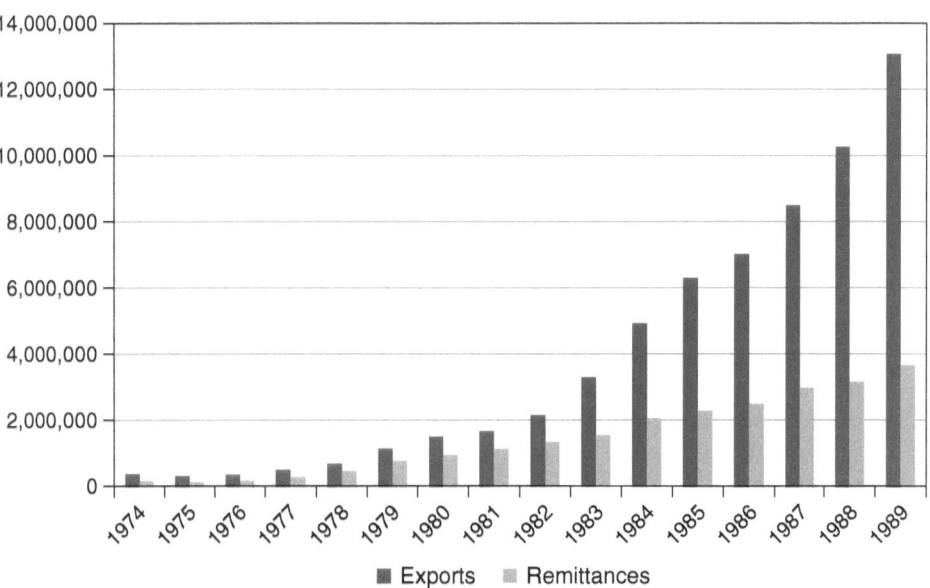

Source: Baganha ("As Correntes," 1994).

from various emigrant communities attended the CPC's inaugural meeting in Lisbon, 6–10 April 1981, to discuss a range of social, cultural, legal, professional, political, and other issues important to emigrants. Contrary to the organizers' unifying objectives, the meeting uncovered the myriad viewpoints and political disharmony within expatriate communities, which were riddled with personal rivalries and factions. Those delegates on the left accused the organizers of turning the CPC into a partisan platform for the ruling PSD and complained about the undemocratic ways by which some delegates had been selected. The Lisbon government was also criticized for its political instability and lack of continuity in its policies.[69] This precarious start would set the tone for much of the CPC's tenure – interrupted between 1988 and 1996 – which has been marked by controversies pitting delegates from different factions and by succeeding attempts from the national government to reform its functioning.

Another critical step towards asserting the nation's global reach was the introduction of a new Nationality Law in 1981, which replaced the previous ruling principle of *jus soli* (determined by place of birth) with that of *jus sanguinis* (determined by lineage). Both father and mother could now bequeath their Portuguese nationality to their children born outside the country. The new law also recognized the dual nationality of emigrant descendants, along with those former citizens whose nationalities had been stripped by the Estado Novo for taking up citizenship in their host countries. In contrast to the dictatorship, Portuguese officials, such as President Mário Soares and his successors, began encouraging biculturalism and dual citizenship at this point, arguing that the best way for expats to serve their homeland was to become fully integrated members of their host societies. Lisbon further instrumentalized dual citizenship by helping create private diasporic institutions dedicated to fostering international cooperation between Portugal and the host countries, as is the case with the Luso-American Development Foundation (FLAD), created in 1985 under a diplomatic agreement with the United States and endowed by the Portuguese government with the equivalent of $85 million euros.[70]

After Portugal's entry into the EEC in 1986, migrant workers were able to travel within that labour market with greater ease and pursue higher wages in the same northern and western European countries as their predecessors. Now, however, the number of sojourners was much higher. Lisbon was finally able to secure the comprehensive legal protections it had previously sought to implement through bilateral agreements with individual countries, as the rights of Portuguese expatriates living in EEC countries increased to match those of their host countries' citizens. At this point, Portuguese expatriate elites began refusing the term "emigrants," not only because they now saw themselves as European citizens but also because they rejected the foreignness associated with it. Recognizing the need for a more inclusive language of nationality, Lisbon adopted the term "non-resident Portuguese" in 1987.

Perceptions about emigrants evolved as more of them returned to their hometowns in the countryside, where they were most noticeable. Generally, Portuguese residents held sympathetic views about emigrants, especially when referring to the sacrifices that the latter had had to make during the dictatorship in order to find a better life for themselves and their families. It also became common for national residents to praise the emigrants' work ethic, especially when criticizing their own. As in North America, Portugal's centre-right used the conservative "bootstraps" narrative of self-reliance as an ideological prop. In Carneiro's words: "Wherever there is a Portuguese, there is a will ... to grow by our own work and to have increasing self-respect."[71]

Nonetheless, some disparaging notions about emigrants persisted, echoing those of nineteenth-century commentators. Although the returned *francês* (Frenchmen) never amassed the kind of legendary fortune that their *brasileiro* predecessors were known for, relative economic success was common. For the most part, these returnees were able to improve their socio-economic status, invest in their children's education, refurbish old houses, build new ones, and open small businesses. Their newer and often luxurious houses, their imported cars, their large tips at the local café, or their foreign accents and mixed vernacular stood out in the otherwise dull countryside. These traits did not go unnoticed by urban people, who tended to see emigrants as a mixture of "nouveau riche yokels" and by-products of a ruralist and traditionalist past that they wished never to return. At the same time, some emigrants found it difficult to reconcile their sometimes hyper-Portuguese identity with the anti-chauvinism of post-revolutionary nationals. It was also common for those visiting Portugal to note how they no longer recognized their "home." Still, many working-class emigrants now wondered whether their lives would have been better had they stayed in Portugal, where citizens benefited from free higher education, public health care, and other generous social welfare programs.

A "Country of Immigrants": 1990s–2000s

As a member of the community of modern European nations, Portugal began shedding its reputation as a have-not nation of "emigrants" and reimagining itself as a desirable country of "immigrants." Lisbon changed its national discourse from the previous emphasis on diaspora to one that presented Portugal as a modern European country at the centre of an international linguistic commonwealth. Once again, emigration became primarily a labour issue, removed from the government's foreign policy. Still, those national (and regional) institutions serving emigrants remained in operation and new services continued to be created, including the Azorean government's Regional Directorate of Communities, launched in 1998. External voting rights were also widened to include European parliamentary elections in 1986 and presidential elections in 1997. Emigration officials remained dedicated to the idea of diaspora. However, their work was no longer a government priority and fewer resources were allocated to it.

This reinvention was consolidated when a larger number of immigrants began arriving in Portugal in the 1980s–90s, initially from the former African colonies, then later from Brazil, eastern Europe, and Asia.[72] The growing presence of "other" racial and linguistic communities stirred dormant nativist prejudices, although many welcomed the cultural diversity introduced by these immigrants. The rise of new hybrid cultural habits and forms of expression resulting from the fusion of different cultures, especially those sharing the same linguistic background, was most apparent in urban contexts where the immigrants settled in greater numbers. Gradually, this hybridism percolated into the mainstream without great resistance from traditionalist cultural forces. These developments were supported by the Lisbon government, which introduced programs promoting pluralism and highlighting the multiracial make-up of Portuguese society. However, the immigrants' modest cultural integration had few corresponding social, political, and economic equivalents, areas where they continued to fall behind white nationals. Furthermore, as various anthropologists have argued, behind Lisbon's official cultural hybridity is an imbalance of power favouring the old imperial metropolis's version of Portuguese culture, from which "other" lusophone cultural and linguistic traditions supposedly descended or took inspiration.[73]

Also behind this emphasis on pluralism was the Portuguese government's attempt to legitimize its claim to be a broker nation occupying a "privileged" intermediary position between developed Europe and developing Africa. Despite having shifted its foreign policy focus from the Atlantic to Europe after 1974, Portugal maintained close diplomatic ties with its former colonies. In 1987, the state secretary of foreign affairs and cooperation, José M. Barroso (who later became prime minister of Portugal, president of the EU Commission, and chairman of Goldman Sachs International), explained this "special situation":

> Portugal ... is one of the least developed countries in the European community and at the same time a former colonial power ... We are, therefore, in a rather original position. On one hand, Portugal still receives some international aid, while on the other, it is itself a provider of international aid ... For that reason, along with our participation in the EEC and NATO, one of our priorities is to maintain a special relation with those Portuguese-speaking African countries.[74]

Central to this political program was *Lusofonia* (Lusophony), a broad concept adopted by the governments of Portuguese-speaking countries to amalgamate a diverse group of people from different nations, regions, and diasporic communities, who shared a linguistic background and its associated cultural traits. The term is often used interchangeably to refer to the common international interests of lusophone countries and the body of literary and artistic work drawn from Portuguese linguistic traditions and the intersection of its various cultures. Since 1996, this postcolonial commonwealth has been organized under the Community of Portuguese Language Countries.[75] Lusofonia has had many supporters and detractors, including among advocates of cultural pluralism. The latter's criticism focused on what they claim are the "underlying asymmetries" of Lisbon's postcolonial transnational discourse, which repurposes old imperialist tropes to articulate a Portugal-centric version of lusophone multiculturalism; one that reinvents the past through a process of "selective remembering and forgetting."[76] Nonetheless, Lusofonia's top-down message of pluralism has seeped into the collective psyche of Portuguese nationals through multiple public and private channels, in turn encouraging its civil society to measure government officials against their own pluralist standards. In fact, before the 2008 financial crisis, various signs indicated that Lisbon had taken significant steps towards fulfilling its own vision of an inclusive citizenship and was recognized by the international community as a leader on that front.[77]

Though superseded, the emigrants were not forgotten in this shift towards immigration and Lusofonia. Political candidates running in emigration ridings, hometown politicians fundraising for public projects, and homeland dignitaries visiting expatriate communities on ceremonial occasions – all continued to praise the diaspora, now said to be "five million"[78] strong (equivalent to nearly half of the country's residents). As in the past, these visitors extolled the many virtues of their "hard-working" brethren and commended their continued patriotism. Doing so was made easier in 1992 with the launch of Portuguese international public television station RTPi. Since then, emigrants have had the opportunity to follow daily occurrences in Portugal more intensely than ever before. Originally intended as a tool for reinforcing and disseminating Portuguese culture in the lusophone world, RTPi quickly became the diaspora's television channel. Its typical programming has consisted of news, talk, variety, and game shows; sports broadcasts; soap operas and other fictional series; and some educational content. Among RTP's most popular shows, on both national and international stations, are the daily variety talk shows that cater to both resident and emigrant audiences, where local, national, and transnational themes are seamessly woven. It is common in these live broadcasts for the guests, members of the audience, or viewers calling in to send messages to loved ones abroad and vice-versa. In the summer, these shows travel around the country, broadcasting live from town squares, where they are surrounded by crowds of cheerful local spectators. They showcase the people, landscapes, food, arts and crafts, and folk traditions of the region, along with recent infrastructural developments and other modernizing initiatives, often introduced by local politicians and businessmen. Until recently, the modern expressions of Portuguese culture favoured by the urban and younger populations, including those multicultural expressions lauded in the government's lusophone discourse, were largely absent from RTPi's programming. In 2015, the international public broadcaster launched a roster of shows and documentaries produced in partnership with expatriate communities around the world. One of them was the daily show *Hora dos Portugueses*, which features the work of correspondents in more than twenty countries, showcasing the activities, views, and achievements of both high-profile and everyday Portuguese immigrants and descendants in all sectors of society. I was one of the producers and reporters for the Canadian part of the show until the end of 2017. Some of my interviews for this show are cited in this book.[79]

Many emigrant descendants (*luso-descendentes*) have produced artistic works in their host countries reflecting on their immigrant and ethnic background. In recent years, a growing number of authors have published novels and memoirs based on their experiences growing up in Portuguese migrant families and their personal struggles trying to reconcile their ethnic and national identities.[80] While most of these literary works are relatively unknown in Portugal, homeland residents are quick to claim the ancestry of musicians, actors, and athletes of Portuguese descent who achieve international recognition. This national appropriation is completed when these celebrities publically embrace their Portuguese roots. The most notable example is that of Portuguese-Canadian singer Nelly Furtado. Born in Victoria, British Columbia, to a family of emigrants from São Miguel, Furtado became an international pop star in 2000 with the release of her album *Whoa Nelly!* which sold millions of copies worldwide. In her songs, videos, and live performances she often includes references to her Portuguese (and Azorean) heritage. Following her international success, the Portuguese government invited her to record the official song of the UEFA Euro Cup football tournament, one of the largest sport competitions in the world, which Portugal hosted in 2004. Furtado was also invited to sing at the closing ceremony in Lisbon's Luz Stadium, where she performed on a stage made to look like a futuristic caravel, representing Portugal's past and future, surrounded by a group of folk dancers from the northern mainland. More recently, the Portuguese-Canadian multiple award-winning and global pop star Shawn Mendes, the son of an immigrant from the Algarve region, recorded the official song of the Portuguese Football Federation's men's national team for the 2018

FIFA World Cup Tournament. This version of his massive hit song "In My Blood" includes the lyrics (in Portuguese): "We are Portugal. One single voice and one heart." This marriage of diasporic (ethnic) and national pride through football reflects the centrality that the global sport has had in the lives of Portuguese immigrants and descendants, who have come to celebrate the accomplishments of the homeland's national men's team as their own. Since the 1990s, the worldwide popularity of Luis Figo and Cristiano Ronaldo, two of the sports' all-time greatest players, have provided diasporic youth with mainstream representations of Portuguese talent, success, flair, and other desirable traits to which they become associated by virtue of their common ethincity. Football is also one of the key elements in Portugal's growing "soft power," ranked among the top ten nations of the world in 2018–19.[81]

For an immigrant group that has long been under-represented in mainstream North American media, and that historically has been associated with demeaning stereotypes in their host societies, Portugal's recent international recognition as one of Europe's most peaceful, friendly, democratic, progressive, cosmopolitan, and fashionable countries is a powerful tonic – especially when contrasted with the authoritarian far-right movements ascending to power throughout that continent. Much of this recent positive attention follows from that comparison, one that is made more stark by Portugal's success story as a country that climbed out of massive debt and achieved significant economic growth after a governing left-wing coalition rejected the draconian austerity measures dictated by the International Monetary Fund, the European Central Bank, and the European Committee (the troika) in the terms outlined for the 2010–14 financial bailout. The global financial crisis of 2008 had a devastating impact on Portugal's economy, which caused emigration rates to rise to levels not seen since the 1960s, placing the old phenomenon back at the centre of public debate. This time, a larger number of new emigrants were highly qualified professionals, creative workers, scientists, and academics with little hope of finding decent employment in the country that had invested heavily in their education. The PSD government of Prime Minister Pedro Passos Coelho, which zealously implemented the troika's neo-liberal agenda, told the large numbers of the unemployed that they should see their situation as an opportunity for personal growth – if only they could "abandon their comfort zone" – and consider emigration as a viable economic strategy, a proposition that prompted much public outcry.[82]

It is true, nonetheless, that many recent emigrants have gained recognition in their professional fields fairly quickly and joined the growing number of luso-descendants rising to international fame in recent years, which has boosted national pride. Reflecting this return to the emigrant "success stories" is the creation in December 2012 of the Council of the Portuguese Diaspora by President Cavaco Silva. This advisory body, chaired by the president and vice-chaired by the foreign affairs minister, is composed of 300 appointed expats, all of them highly accomplished and influential individuals in the fields of business and finance, civics, art, and science. The re-emergence of mass emigration has also been reflected in the growing body of scholarship, fictional and documentary filmmaking, radio and television programming, and various artistic expressions dedicated to that topic. In these recent works, the old emigrants, forebears of a reality that many young middle-class Portuguese have recently begun to experience, are portrayed in a largely positive light.[83] Evidence of Lisbon's return to a national diasporic imagination is the fact that President Marcelo R. de Sousa celebrated Portugal Day in Paris in 2016, then Rio de Janeiro and São Paulo in the following year along with Prime Minister António Costa. This return has also gone the other way, with the mass arrival of former emigrants and their descendants escaping Venezuela's political and economic crisis, and in some cases persecution. Reminiscent of the successful reintegration programs for the imperial retornados, the socialist government of Prime Minister Costa has announced the launch of a €50 million line of credit for entrepreneurs and an online employment service with 18,000 available jobs for those Portuguese who return from Venezuela – a decision supported by the right-wing opposition parties.[84] This national diaspora consensus, with its ever-ambivalent admiration for the emigrants and condemnation for the long-standing causes of emigration, will be further memorialized, celebrated, and studied in the Museum of Diaspora and Portuguese Language announced in 2016.[85] Once built, this institution might confirm the homeland's centrality in the diaspora as the chief steward of its public memory and the official meeting place of national and diasporic Portuguese.

Conclusion

Few phenomena have been as persistent in Portugal's history as the exodus of its people. Whether for economic or political reasons, emigration has been a normal and sometimes expected part of life, especially for rural and fishing populations in the northern mainland and Atlantic islands. It has also been a constant concern for Portuguese governments since the early nineteenth century, which repeatedly had to concede to the exodus's overwhelming strength, given their inability to control its flow in any predictable way. Every restriction meant to prevent workers and soldiers from leaving the country often resulted in a surge of clandestine departures, which further increased the vulnerability of undocumented expatriate citizens. This was particularly true of the postwar movements to Europe, where several thousands of Portuguese crossed the borders on foot, away from the state's gaze. Transatlantic migrants had fewer opportunities to avoid American and Canadian border authorities, who nonetheless were confronted with high Portuguese clandestine immigration in the 1960s–70s. That movement has had a strong, furtive, and autonomous dynamic since the first Portuguese fishermen began jumping ship on North American shores in the nineteenth century.

The extent to which government restrictions determined the volume of Portuguese migration is difficult to know, since most were introduced in periods of economic downturn or war, which were arguably more important in determining migratory movements. In times of prosperity, Portuguese workers jumped ship, broke contracts, overstayed their visas, and did whatever they had to do in order to leave their chronically impoverished and repressive country. In Canada, once they reached a critical mass, immigrants were able to thwart Ottawa's efforts at curbing their inflow by way of lawful or illegal migration chains. However, it would be wrong to suggest that government officials were never able to affect the movement of people determined to cross national borders. A clear example was the restrictions introduced by American lawmakers since the late 1910s, which ended Portuguese mass immigration. Another was the role played by Lisbon officials in shaping the size, provenance, and characteristics of the bulk order migrant labour movement to Canada.[86] While not entirely powerless, Lisbon's emigration policies were undermined by the porousness of its borders and the limitations of its state apparatus. This was especially the case during the repressive yet largely impotent Estado Novo.

Portuguese political, economic, and intellectual elites since the nineteenth century have considered mass emigration to be a reflection of the nation's past mistakes and a threat to its future. At the same time, the desire to maintain the status quo moderated the protests of those in power. As was common among "emigration nations," Portugal's early response to its populational exodus was to "erect barriers against exit, switching after some time to a position of 'benign neglect,' [reflecting] a transition from mercantilism to *laissez-faire* in the ruling class' political outlook."[87] This transition was less than smooth during the tenure of the Estado Novo, which entertained both approaches in its ambivalent emigration policy. Since the 1930s, Portuguese officials had occasionally contemplated the diasporic potential of expatriate communities.

But other than the ever-growing flow of remittances and the radicalization of migrant workers, emigration occupied little space in Salazar's mind. The decisive shift towards a more favourable, comprehensive, and engaged emigration policy started in the regime's international sectors, that is, foreign and colonial affairs, then gradually expanded to its domestic branches. This movement paralleled important internal and external changes happening in Portugal's economic and political reality in the 1960s, a time when the empire faced serious threats. After Salazar's many failed attempts – some arguably by design – at limiting the massive populational exodus, the dictatorship eventually assumed a more positive view of emigration under Caetano, who acknowledged the benefits of the growing diaspora.

Listing emigrants (i.e., workers, exiles, war resisters) among the victims of the Estado Novo, the post-1974 democratic governments vowed to correct the supposed wrongs done to expats by the dictatorship. The interim revolutionary cabinet saw emigration largely as a labour issue resulting from Portugal's long-standing structural inequalities, which they sought to end through various reforms. However, even the socialists quickly realized that the country's economy could not handle a massive repatriation and came to rely on the profitable trade-off of surplus population and remittances. Under Soares, the democratic government began shifting its emigration policy from a socio-economic to a cultural and political paradigm. At this point, the previously circumspect diasporic vision re-emerged, although this time it was at the centre of national politics.[88] Still, it was the centre-right governments of the 1980s that translated the diasporic discourse into actual institutions and legislation, such as the right to dual citizenship. Emigrant elites took advantage of these diasporic mechanisms to press their agendas and demand a more extensive and inclusive national membership. Common emigrants, in turn, benefited from new social, cultural, and economic aid programs, which they saw not as generous gifts from the homeland but as due recognition for their large financial contributions to Portugal's Treasury. By then, emigrants had come a long way in the nation's collective imagination, from the "miserable rustics" obsessed with social climbing, to the "global ambassadors" of an adventurous, cosmopolitan, and industrious homeland. Portuguese national residents also revised their own unflattering perceptions of emigrants, less informed by Lisbon's official narrative than by their interactions with returnees. The term "emigrant" became only one of various designations used to identify a range of migrant categories, from the esteemed "political exiles" to the unwelcomed "reactionary" retornados, all of which had different meanings depending on the region of the country.

After joining the club of modern industrial European nations, Lisbon shed much of its celebratory tone when referring to the country's long-time population exodus, along with its associated stereotypes. Instead, it embraced a future where Portugal would become a desirable, multicultural country of immigrants. Just as the "emigrant" replaced the "colonizer," language replaced territory as the crux of a national identity that continued to aspire to global greatness, now at the centre of a lusophone commonwealth that included the "five million" diaspora. That reality changed, once again, in recent years, when emigration soared to heights not seen since the 1960s. This time, however, the story has different characters and scenarios, involving the exodus of Portugal's most highly qualified generation in history, many of them urban youth, who will once again push emigration perceptions and policies in new directions.

2 Making Diasporic Souls: Catholic Missionaries, National Parishes, and Transregional Charity

> Separated by the sea and the continents, the secret of our union is our Faith, the foundation of our Portugality, and the spirit of the Portuguese Christian family.
>
> D. José Maria Neves,
> OCPM director, 13 December 1962[1]

Despite the ambition, daring, and other brave personality traits that voluntary immigrants identified with, leaving home and loved ones to start a new life abroad was a daunting prospect. Building a better life in an unfamiliar land, where they were expected to sacrifice their bodies for meagre wages, had problems communicating, and were ostracized simply because they looked, sounded, or acted the way they always had, was a taxing experience. These challenges were greater for those pioneering cohorts without long-settled relatives or well-established ethnic communities to rely on, as was the case in 1950s Canada. Coming from deeply Catholic societies, where the Church interpreted and regulated much of their lives and often served as the state's proxy and only viable institution of authority in remote villages, it is no surprise that the majority of Portuguese immigrants sought solace in their spiritual beliefs and social aid from their clerics. Early sojourners made long treks from their isolated farms to attend Sunday mass in the nearest towns and seek counsel from travelling priests visiting their work camps. When families began arriving in the 1960s, they chose to settle near their kin and work sites, but also near churches with Portuguese services, which became gravitational nodes in their ethnolinguistic maps. First in the basements, then later on the main floors, these typically large, working-class families filled their parishes to capacity, forcing their archdioceses to meet the growing demand for Portuguese priests and sites of worship. For the first time, these devout Catholics had to press their prelates in order to secure dignified spaces in which to celebrate their faith as they knew how. Despite the resemblances, unfamiliar rites and languages in the new country made immigrants feel like strangers in their own Catholic faith. Their religious ways, supreme and undisputed in Portugal, became a matter of national tradition and a marker of ethnicity in North America.

The difficult socio-economic situation faced by newcomer families in the 1950s and early 1960s presented Protestant social workers with the opportunity to proselytize when offering services. Fearing the "denationalization" of its emigrant flock through assimilation into Protestant or Irish/French Catholic denominations, Portuguese ecclesiastical authorities saw the need to send missionaries to these expatriate communities. Founded on a Christian interpretation of national identity and imperial mission, the Estado Novo recognized the Church's importance in maintaining the emigrants' ties with their homeland and facilitated this exchange. The marriage of Catholic ecumenical doctrine and the regime's Christian imperialism folded religious and national identities together even further and made one a refuge for the other. Raised in this ideological environment, Portuguese missionaries often were devoted to their homeland's self-proclaimed Christianizing mission in the world and fervently championed Lisbon's imperialist agenda. Immigrant laity, prelates, and government officials worked together, with the Vatican's backing, to create their own national parishes[2] in North America, often against the will of Irish and French bishops. Given their low number and the very high demand for social and spiritual services, immigrant priests worked much harder than their peers at home, who lived fairly comfortable lives with undisputed moral authority over their parishioners. Their greater activity and impact in creating the foundations of community life meant that some priests became nuisances for the regime, particularly when their personal ambitions interfered with the diplomats' own plans for controlling the emigrant communities. Rogue missionaries were common during the years of immigrant settlement, when American and Canadian prelates scrambled to find priests willing to care for their ethnolinguistic congregations. These clergymen sometimes clashed with each other as they competed to expand their "clientele" in a context where larger flocks meant "more money, more power, more prestige."[3] Parishioners in North America were not always keen on following the clergy's instructions. Battles sometimes broke out between priests and laity over the financing of parish activities and the organizing of religious celebrations. Eventually, immigrant priests realized that their success in carrying out their pastoral duties and meeting their personal goals depended largely on the laity's support, which they won by catering to the regional traditions of their parishioners. Ethnic processions, feasts, charities, and other religious pursuits belied the worldly politics of their organizers. They also became important sites for transnational exchange with the immigrants' hometowns and fellow communities across North America and for the articulation of distinct regional diasporic identities, especially Azorean.

This chapter will examine how Estado Novo officials, Catholic clergymen, and immigrant laity worked together to maintain religious customs, meet social welfare needs, and develop a diasporic spirituality based on regional, national, and imperial ideas. While important for understanding the anthropological content of Portuguese ethnicity, the focus will be not on the formal features of religious celebrations and how they adapted to North American contexts,[4] but on their role in shaping diasporic networks among geographically distant communities.

The Estado Novo, the Vatican, and the Portuguese Catholic Organization for Migrations

One of Salazar's hallmarks was his piety. His corporatist ideology was heavily predicated on the ideas of Popes Leo XIII and Pius XI and other Catholic ideologues who critiqued both capitalism and its radical alternatives. The dictator also understood Catholicism to be a unifying thread throughout Portugal's history and took measures to ensure it remained an omnipresent force in Portuguese society. For most of the Estado Novo's tenure, especially in moments of crisis, the Catholic Church had an important "legitimating function," coming to its aid in matters of moral ambiguity.[5] Another of Salazar's spiritual legacies was his copious use of the Fátima apparitions[6] in state propaganda and of the anti-communist Marian cult as a national treasure. After studying in a Catholic seminary for eight years, Salazar enrolled at the University of Coimbra, where he became one of the chief opponents of the anticlerical Republican regime, alongside his personal friend Manuel G. Cerejeira, the future cardinal of Lisbon and head of the Catholic Church in Portugal (1929–72). In the 1933 constitution, Salazar officially recognized Roman Catholicism as Portugal's national religion. In that year, Cardinal Cerejeira founded the Portuguese Catholic Action, a group that aimed to rekindle religious devotion in post-Republican Portugal, increase the laity's participation in Church affairs, and be the Church's wing in civil society. In 1940, the Estado Novo signed a concordat with the Vatican granting the Catholic Church administrative powers over Portugal's public education system and marital laws, along with fiscal benefits. At this point, Salazar renewed Portugal's missionary accords with Rome, guaranteeing state funding and logistic support for missionary work. Under the aegis of the imperial regime, missionaries were charged with fulfilling Portugal's "civilizing mission" in the world and turning native Africans into good "Catholic-Portuguese."[7] Missionaries were also assigned to the emigrant "colonies," especially in the United States, which in the 1950s hosted the second-largest Portuguese expatriate population, behind the lusophone and largely Catholic Brazil, where "denationalization" concerns were less prominent.

Rome had started to address the specific needs of migrant flocks in 1887, when it created the Scalabrinian missionaries.[8] But it was only in 1952 that Pope Pius XII articulated the Catholic Church's doctrine on migrant flocks in his apostolic constitution, *Exsul Familia*, which outlined procedures for the provision of spiritual care and social welfare to migrants and refugees. The Vatican urged national governments to open their doors to the millions of people displaced by the war – equating their forced exile with that of the Holy Family fleeing Egypt – and instructed the host countries' dioceses to provide appropriate pastoral care to these foreign nationals. This document placed migrant missionaries under the jurisdiction of the dioceses they were sent to and ruled that new "national" parishes had to first be approved by the Holy See. Pius XII also created the Higher Council for Emigration, which met for the first time in 1957. That year, the council tasked national bishops with creating and directing Catholic organizations in their countries responsible for overseeing emigration. In Portugal, that responsibility fell on Bishop José Silva, who became the Catholic Organization of Portuguese Emigration's first director. Following the council's instructions, the Portuguese episcopacy also launched the Day of the Emigrant, celebrated annually in every diocese in the country, in order to raise awareness of emigration matters and unite "the great Catholic family through prayer."[9]

At around this time, a growing number of dissenting voices emerged within the Catholic Church's ranks in Portugal, criticizing the Estado Novo's neglect of the poor, its brutal methods of political repression, and its violent colonialism. Many clerics were punished for voicing their negative views of the government and some were forced into exile. These dissenters were invigorated by the progressive changes taking place in the Catholic Church after 1962, when Pope John XXIII convened the Second Vatican Council, which ushered in the modernization of the Church's internal structures, increased lay participation in parish affairs, and promoted greater interdenominational dialogue.

Proponents of Liberation Theology, who believed Rome should be more assertive in advancing the rights of workers and other marginalized peoples and call for an end to capitalist and colonialist exploitation, also used Vatican II to advocate for their political views.

The Portuguese Catholic Organization for Migrations (OCPM), founded in 1962, carried out Rome's new directives on the migrants' pastoral care by producing studies on emigrant communities, cooperating with Church officials in host countries, and sending priests to expatriate congregations. Despite the growing anti-colonialist sentiment within the Catholic Church, the OCPM assisted the regime's processing of colonial settlers leaving for Africa. Families waiting to embark in Lisbon were given tutorials about life in the colonies delivered by Emigration Junta agents and religion and morality lessons by OCPM clergymen. The priests heard confessions and gave clothing, crucifixes, images of Our Lady of Fátima, rosaries, prayer books, and Catholic identity cards to those about to depart. The OCPM offered such generous send-off tokens only to colonial emigrants, since the Junta did not share information on non-colonial departures. In any case, the OCPM's imperial duties were in accordance with its "ecumenical" view of missionary work, as expressed by its first director, Bishop José Neves, in 1962:

> It was the will of God and of our Betters not to limit our Motherland to a territory in one continent or one island. She covers lands and peoples from the whole World and all the races. The ideal that guided us then and guides us still today is that of the Christian apostolate – "Go and teach all peoples," "Go and make Christendom" ... Thus, we became a people of essentially emigrants and missionaries. We formed a Motherland different from the other Motherlands because we brought all peoples in brotherhood under the principles of the Christian doctrine we profess.[10]

Ensuring that Portuguese emigrants were provided with spiritual care from their own national priests was a serious challenge for the OCPM, which was never able to recruit enough clergymen to meet the demands of all expatriate communities. According to Bishop Silva, who inaugurated fourteen Portuguese missions abroad (six of them in Canada)[11] during his time as director of the OCPM's predecessor, there were only ninety Portuguese priests for over 350,000 emigrants (outside Brazil and the American east coast) in 1961. After 1966, under Bishop António Rodrigues, the OCPM launched training programs for prospective missionaries that were partially run by the regime. Only in 1971 did the Portuguese episcopate invite the Scalabrinians to set up a permanent mission in Portugal, in the hope of expanding the pool of missionaries.

In the mid-1960s, the Estado Novo again turned to Catholic organizations to deliver its promised social assistance to expatriate citizens. In France, for instance, Caritas provided the Portuguese embassy with three social workers who dealt with the ever-growing queues at its Paris consulate doors. Another expressed intent of these Catholic social workers was to ward off the penetration of "communist" ideas in emigrant communities.[12] During the 1960s, the main focus of Catholic emigration workers, like most government officials, was the European movement. Only in the early 1970s did the OCPM begin focusing more on North America, which is not to say it was previously forgotten. Portuguese Americans had "jubilantly" received visits from homeland bishops since the 1920s, including Cardinal Cerejeira, who had travelled to California in 1936. In turn, Portuguese government and Catholic Church officials received American prelates visiting Fátima with great honour, including Francis Cardinal Spellman of New York and Archbishop Richard Cushing of Boston. After 1974, the OCPM shifted its attention to domestic realities and, like the revolutionaries, started focusing on "fixing" the causes of emigration.[13] During this period, the OCPM concerned itself primarily with assisting returned emigrants, initially colonial retornados and later voluntary returnees from Europe and other parts of the world. As the number of African immigrants grew in the following decades, the OCPM became increasingly concerned with their social integration and combating racial discrimination. Still, it has continued to coordinate the work of missionaries abroad and advocate for the rights and overall advancement of Portuguese emigrant communities.

National Parishes, the Cult of Fátima, and the Portuguese Clergy in the United States

One of the first things that Portuguese immigrants did once they had settled in the United States in the nineteenth century was to found their own churches.[14] By 1941, they had inaugurated thirty parishes in New England alone.[15] However, the shortage of Portuguese priests prevented the creation of more national parishes and sometimes led to the denationalization of existing ones. Twenty years later, there were seventy-five Portuguese clerics for twenty-nine national parishes, at a time when the estimated Portuguese "foreign stock" population in the United States neared 280,000.[16] Those in California were especially underserved, which alarmed church and government officials in Portugal, who worried that these emigrants would fall prey to religious and cultural assimilation. After mass migration restarted in the 1960s, similar concerns grew on the east coast, especially in newcomer communities in New York City's metropolitan area.

Portuguese immigrants had to become accustomed to their minority status in North America's Irish-dominated Catholic Church (or the French-Canadian Catholic Church in Quebec). Much has been written about the ways in which these dominant Catholic groups acted as gatekeepers of their Church and host nations.[17] As was true of other Catholic groups, the relation between Portuguese congregations and their Irish-American bishops was characterized by the latter's resistance to recognizing the former's distinct devotional practices or approve their national parishes and related infrastructures, often contravening Rome's instructions. Portuguese diplomats saw this opposition as a serious obstacle to preventing the emigrants' denationalization. One of the tactics used by the regime to sway Irish-American bishops into meeting the requests of Portuguese parishioners was to placate them with honorific titles for their supposed contributions to Portugal and its expatriate citizens. For instance, in 1955, Lisbon asked its ambassador in Washington to assess whether Bishop James Connolly of Fall River merited a medal. After surveying the community, the ambassador found that Connolly had done positive things for the Portuguese in his diocese and had publicly expressed admiration for the Estado Novo. Still, he added, the bishop's primary loyalty rested with his fellow Irish Americans, with whom Connolly shared misgivings about "foreign" congregations. In conclusion, the ambassador believed it would be "useful to ingratiate [Connolly], even if just to neutralize him." In 1957, Lisbon bestowed on Bishop Connolly the Portuguese Order of Christ.[18]

Portuguese-American priests and laity often recruited the help of homeland officials to pressure Irish-American bishops. That was the case in 1951, when a group of immigrants in Newark asked the Portuguese ambassador to write to Archbishop Thomas Walsh endorsing their efforts to build a national parish; he did so, but to little effect. Two years later, the new archbishop, Thomas Boland, continued to ignore the requests of his Portuguese congregation. Frustrated by the archbishop's unresponsiveness, the ambassador asked the foreign affairs minister to take matters directly to the Vatican. In early 1954, after meeting with a committee of Newark's Portuguese, which included the local consul, Boland finally allowed construction to start on the new national church and permitted a priest to be sent from Portugal to lead this initiative; his only stipulation was that he speak English. Reporting to Lisbon, the ambassador attributed the archbishop's sudden change of heart to the minister's direct appeal to Rome.[19] Contrary to the wishes of Newark's congregation, their new priest was not sent from the homeland but from another Portuguese parish in Cambridge, Massachusetts. Still, they were likely pleased with the choice of Fr José Capote, as he was a native of Aveiro, where most of Newark's Portuguese were from. In 1956, after an eight-year campaign, Capote and his congregation finally opened the Our Lady of Fatima chapel.

Learning from Newark's example, Portuguese Catholics in Connecticut bypassed the American bishops by making their pleas directly to the Holy See with the help of homeland diplomats. The cities of Hartford, Bridgeport, and Waterbury inaugurated their own Our Lady of Fatima parishes in 1958, 1962, and 1971, respectively. Following the successes of their Connecticut peers, the Portuguese of Peabody, Massachusetts, asked Lisbon to forward their request for a national parish to Rome. A positive response led to the creation of Peabody's Portuguese Catholic mission in 1965, which inaugurated their own Our Lady of Fatima church ten years later. Another national parish dedicated to Fátima opened in Cumberland, Rhode Island, in 1967, this one decorated with nationalist motifs, including the Portuguese Order of Christ Cross and details inspired by the Padrão dos Descobrimentos monument in Lisbon. In 1973, Archbishop Boland approved the creation of yet another Our Lady of Fatima church, this time in Elizabeth, New Jersey, where a Portuguese Catholic mission had existed since 1923. Altogether, seven out of the eight Portuguese parishes founded in the United States between 1948 and 1973 were named Our Lady of Fatima, and more in subsequent years.

One of the *Exsul Familia*'s chief advocates and most dedicated champions of the cult of Fátima in the United States[20] was the Azorean Manuel Rocha, a well-educated and respected cleric with connections to the upper echelons of the Catholic Church in Portugal and the Vatican. Before migrating, he founded the Portuguese wing of the international Jocist movement (Young Christian Workers), which he led for seventeen years. Rocha also served as the first religious director of the Moçidade Portuguesa and was an aide to the Portuguese Catholic Action's secretary general. In the 1930s, he travelled to the United States, hoping to convince a Hollywood film studio to produce a movie on the Fátima apparitions.[21] It is unclear what resulted from this attempt or what happened to Rocha before he became an aide to Fr Augusto Furtado in Somerset in the 1940s. In 1948, he was transferred to Ludlow, Massachusetts, to tend to the growing Portuguese congregation in that town, where they would become one of the largest ethnic groups in the 1950s.

Since the 1910s, Ludlow's Portuguese had celebrated mass at various temporary sites, until they raised enough money to build their own church, which they hoped to name "St Anthony's." In 1948, Bishop

2.1 Pilgrims attending outdoor mass at the Our Lady of Fatima shrine in Ludlow, Massachusetts. HDA, PEA M251, *Fatima Review*, 1963(?).

Thomas O'Leary finally granted them permission to build a national parish. Under Fr Rocha's direction, the congregation bought a large plot of land and erected the new church, which he convinced parishioners to name Our Lady of Fatima – the first church of that name in the United States. In the ample church grounds, Rocha planted an arboretum and built a replica of the Cova da Iria chapel and a shrine to the Fátima apparitions. The site later became a pilgrimage destination for several thousands of Portuguese from eastern North America.

Rocha's rectory hosted many Church dignitaries from Portugal and Rome during their visits to New England. He also maintained personal friendships with Ambassadors Luis Fernandes and Pedro Teotónio Pereira (1947–9, 1961–3), with whom he corresponded regularly. Rocha's dedication to the cult of Fátima was matched by his patriotism and unconditional support for the Estado Novo and the empire. His political outlook, which conflated Catholicism, Portuguese nationalism, and imperialism, corresponded with the regime's own message on Fátima, as stated by Consul Jorge Freitas during the twenty-first anniversary of Ludlow's Our Lady of Fatima parish:

> Perhaps no other nation on earth has ... demonstrated such an inseparable relationship between its history and the strength of its religious ideals, as manifested by its missionary spirit and what might be called a national raison d'être, which embraced the dissemination of Christianity ... By consecrating the name of Fátima in this manner, one might say that [Mary] was paying tribute to the faith of the Portuguese people and was thus contributing towards the glory of Portugal.[22]

Rocha was not shy about advocating for the Estado Novo and its empire with American politicians. In 1960, he wrote to Senator John F. Kennedy expressing his happiness about the fact that a Catholic was running for the White House and addressing the Democratic Party nominee's anti-colonialist views. He invited Kennedy to publicly acknowledge that the Portuguese empire was exceptional, for it was a Catholic empire. The following year, Rocha received direct instructions from Ambassador Fernandes to "guide the Catholic population in this country into supporting the policies of the Portuguese Government." After meeting in the same hall where on 31 December 1941 a group of Ludlow's Portuguese-American associations passed a resolution asking the Lisbon regime to support the allied forces during the Second World War, Rocha and other community leaders appealed to President Kennedy to declare his "friendship for Portugal."[23] Rocha's patriotic advocacy was both cause and consequence of his privileged relationship with Portuguese officials, who were often amenable to his requests. On various occasions, the priest used Ambassador Fernandes's diplomatic influence to push for the creation of new national parishes in the United States, to expedite visa applications for Portuguese clergymen, to host visiting Church dignitaries at the embassy, and to confer other favours. One of the projects that Rocha and the Washington embassy collaborated on was the creation of a Portuguese-American apostolic vicariate[24] separate from the Irish-American purview. This idea had been first proposed in 1955 by Fr Henrique Rocha (Manuel Rocha's cousin) of St Elizabeth's church in Bristol, Rhode Island, and endorsed by a member of the Roman Curia. Five new Portuguese national parishes resulted from this collaboration; yet, for reasons unknown, the plan for the vicariate itself never came to fruition.[25]

Another outcome of this initiative was the launching of the Lusitania Institute, a non-sectarian Portuguese language centre in Ludlow, open to students of all nationalities. This was Rocha's pet project, whose underlying goal – supposedly suggested to him by the Holy See – was to identify those students with a pastoral vocation and convince them to study for priesthood in Portugal or in Rome and thus increase the pool of Portuguese-speaking priests in the Americas. With support from Portugal's national education minister, a team of architects drew plans to build a university college for 800 students. To propel this project forwards, Rocha was able to collect major sponsors, such as Cardinal Cerejeira, the União Nacional party and its parliamentarians, and some of the Estado Novo's most prominent ministers, including then minister of the presidency, Marcello Caetano. He was also able to secure a total of US$28,500 in subsidies from the finance and foreign affairs ministers; according to Rocha, the latter had promised him additional funds should he obtain Francis Cardinal Spellman's public support for Portugal's right to defend its African territories. In 1955, Rocha convinced the education minister to grant a scholarship to his assistant, Fr Joaquim Lourenço, to research and write the history of the Portuguese in North America, which would allow him to tour the communities of the United States and Canada and raise interest for the new institute.[26] With the money he raised, Rocha bought the land for the future college and began construction in sections. The first building opened in 1962, where Rocha and other priests taught high school classes. The institute also hosted distinguished visiting lecturers from Portugal, including the former overseas minister, Adriano Moreira. Two years later, it received a large grant (US$20,500) from the American branch of the Gulbenkian Foundation,[27] which paid for a language laboratory, allowing it to offer an intensive Portuguese-language course. Later, Gulbenkian also funded English-language classes for newcomer children. Among the institute's Portuguese-language students were clergymen, businessmen, and professionals looking to work in Brazil instead of in the Portuguese immigrant communities of North and South America. Noticing this demand, Rocha began searching for bulk clients interested in working in or with Brazil. Among his prospective clients were the Port of New York, through which much of the American trade with that country came, and the US Peace Corps, the international development volunteer organization founded by President Kennedy in 1961.[28]

Rocha's new business strategy displeased Ambassador Vasco V. Garin (1963–71), particularly his lobbying of the Peace Corps. In the ambassador's view, those initiatives fell outside the Lusitania's mission, and he began to question the institute's ability to disseminate Portuguese language and culture in the United States. We can only speculate as to why the Portuguese government urged Rocha not to become involved with the Peace Corps, although it is clear from the records that both parties made sure they kept it confidential. Whatever the reasons, Rocha obliged the ambassador's wishes and stopped pursuing that contract. However, doing so curbed the institute's options to boost its stagnant enrolment numbers. Unimpressed with the college's enrolment (an average of ten students per year), Gulbenkian finally suspended its funding in 1969. At this point, Portuguese diplomats were convinced that Rocha had failed to deliver on his promises and were prepared to instruct him to reimburse the Lisbon government and Gulbenkian by selling the unused land parcel he had bought with their money. Somehow, Rocha convinced them not to sell the property and to continue subsidizing its mortgage payments. Subsequently, the Lusitania Institute continued to operate as a private, non-profit, language school with what seemed to be largely symbolic ties to the Portuguese government.[29]

Around the same time as Portuguese officials started losing interest in Rocha's projects, another Azorean priest began climbing the ranks of the American Catholic Church, eventually becoming one of the most prominent and influential Portuguese immigrants ever in the United States. Born in São Miguel, Humberto Medeiros moved with his working-class parents to Fall River in 1931 at age fifteen. Once the family had settled there, his father took him out of school and found him a job as a sweeper in a textile mill. Medeiros eventually returned to his studies after his two younger brothers were old enough to replace him at the mill. A talented student, he gained his high school diploma with the best academic score in his school's history, contradicting the low expectations for "Portagee" students held by prejudiced American educators. Thanks to financial support from various benefactors, Medeiros went on to complete four degrees at the Catholic University of America and the Pontifical North American College in Rome. During the two decades after he was ordained into the priesthood (1946), Medeiros worked at various Portuguese parishes in Massachusetts, eventually directing Fall River's St Michael's church. After he had moved up the ranks in the Fall River diocese, Pope Paul VI named him bishop of Brownsville, Texas, in 1966. Four years later, he became archbishop of Boston, then finally cardinal in 1973. In Brownsville, Medeiros earned the epithet "the poor man's bishop" because of his affinity with Mexican migrant labourers, whom he followed throughout the midwest during harvest season. As one of his aides noted: "He eats with them; he lives with them; he shares everything with them." Soon after arriving in Texas, Medeiros became an ally of César Chavez's United Farm Workers during the fruit pickers' struggle for minimum wage, as one of the five members of an ad hoc committee established by the National Conference of Catholic Bishops, which helped Chavez secure his victory. Medeiros also publically criticized capitalism as an exploitative and irresponsible system, made critical remarks on controversial topics such as the Vietnam War, and fraternized with contentious "radical" groups, for instance, the Mexican American Youth Organization and the Black Panthers.[30] In 1970, Medeiros left the country's smallest and poorest diocese to run its second largest, replacing the popular Richard Cardinal Cushing, a close friend of the Kennedy family and a politically influential figure. The elevation of a Portuguese immigrant to archbishop of a historically Irish-American archdiocese – the first non-Irishman to occupy that position in 124 years – shocked and infuriated many Bostonians. After the pope's announcement, protesters expressed their discontent by destroying church property, setting a cross on fire on the chancery lawn, planting an unexploded pipe bomb at its front door, and burning and raiding other sites. Defiant priests also sometimes were heard hurling bigoted remarks at their "Portagee" superior.[31] Medeiros's "radical tendencies" also disconcerted right-wing commentators, who nonetheless appreciated his staunch opposition to abortion and other forms of birth control.

Despite his "liberal" and "radical" political views, and his relations with African- and Latinx-American movements, Medeiros's new, powerful role within the American Catholic Church was too alluring for the Estado Novo not to harness. Portuguese diplomats looked for ways to lay claim to Medeiros's Portuguese identity while deflecting his impoverished emigrant background and American liberal education. The consul in Boston warned Lisbon that the way in which the American media reported Medeiros's life story, as a poor immigrant who had developed his intellect in the United States, made celebrating his Portuguese background "somewhat delicate" yet "no less convenient." Upon meeting Medeiros, Ambassador João Hall Themido (1971–81) was pleased to report to his superiors that the archbishop spoke Portuguese fluently and maintained personal attachments with his homeland. Two years after his consecration, Medeiros was awarded the Great Cross of the Order of Christ, the highest distinction bestowed by the Portuguese government. Meanwhile, a group of students picketed Boston's Harvard Club, where the ceremony was held, protesting Medeiros's implicit endorsement of Portugal's imperial dictatorship.[32]

In 1973, the now Cardinal Medeiros took a very public trip to São Miguel, sponsored by Portuguese-American businessmen from New Bedford and Fall River. With him went an entourage of American clergymen, Portuguese-American leaders, and US$40,000 in donations to be disbursed among charity organizations and a seminary on the island. Medeiros's "homecoming" falls within the "roots" trip tradition started by Kennedy's visit to Ireland in 1963 and later followed by Nixon, Reagan, and other Euro-American politicians, who "returned" to their ancestors' homelands in order to assert their Old World pedigree in the now sovereign "nation of immigrants." Like the Irish crowds in New Ross and Dublin, which had hailed their favourite Bostonian "son" a decade earlier, Micaelenses cheered their own famous emigrant as he returned to the sites of his childhood and addressed the crowds of onlookers. Those who could not see the cardinal in person were able to follow his tour in the Azorean and Bostonian media. Familiar with this type of coverage, American audiences were introduced to another rags-to-riches immigrant story that reinforced their nation's self-understanding as a beacon of liberty for the world's oppressed. But unlike the "freedom-loving" people of Ireland, whose colonial oppression was in the past, the Portuguese still suffered under dictatorship. The reporter sent by Boston's WBZ-TV noted the Azores's "backward nature" and its "oppressive, indifferent" government, from which many of its people escaped. Others mentioned the islands' poor infrastructure, extensive poverty, and lack of educational opportunities. Besides this political and economic backdrop, the American coverage focused primarily on the cardinal's personal "pilgrimage" to his native land and how enthusiastically the locals embraced him. His many interactions with Portuguese officials were given passing mention, except for Medeiros's remarks at a formal dinner where he celebrated the bonds of friendship between Portugal and the United States. In his speech he claimed that both nations were a "powerful force for the betterment of the condition of mankind" and "the development of peoples around the world," despite their many cultural dissimilarities. Reinforcing this different-but-equal coexistence, Medeiros added: "I have love for both my native land and my adopted land."[33] The local *Diário dos Açores* offered a more positive narrative of Medeiros's journey, as voiced by a local official: "Here with you returns, entering the people's city grounds and our hearts' silent emotion, that great and sometimes tragic figure, though always beautiful in his tenacious and redemptive hope for the future, the Portuguese Emigrant." Medeiros reciprocated by confirming the patriotism of Portuguese Americans and reciting the regime's imperialist mantra:

> Being a small country, we don't rely on armed forces to conquer the world, but instead, we rely on spiritual forces to install in all the world the Truth that sets us free, the Truth that our missionaries spread yesterday and

today, making Portugal known and loved, esteemed by foreigners. Every Portuguese, be it priest or not ... be it religious or not ... has been and continues to be a missionary of Portuguese culture, which ... integrates in itself a Catholic faith.[34]

Medeiros's tribute to his homeland contrasted with Kennedy's in 1963. Whereas the hyphenated president had extolled the kindred independent spirit of his fellow Irishmen as allies of America's fight against colonialism and communism, Medeiros aligned himself with Lisbon's interpretation of Portugal's colonialism, seen as a peaceful, Christian, liberating, civilizing mission, of which he was an agent. The cardinal's denial of Portugal's military intervention in Africa – then in its twelfth year – would have been especially jarring to anti-Vietnam War activists, who once saw him as an ally, had his statements been reported in the American media. Unlike Kennedy's, Medeiros's nostalgia for his humble origins was based on his personal boyhood memories. Still, commentators used the opportunity to attach their own narratives to Medeiros's migration story in line with their respective national mythologies. Indeed, throughout his ecclesiastic career, Medeiros agreed to become a representative for various conflicting groups and causes. Though he tried to harmonize his competing loyalties, others would frame his public identity, leading to myriad characterizations about his position on important issues and the subsequent disaffection of his supporters. The allure of a simpler and anonymous past in São Miguel may have stayed with the priest, as he failed to solve his archdiocese's high debt crisis and live up to the expectations of civil rights activists, who were disappointed by his general inaction during Boston's bussing crisis. Medeiros's "homecoming" would be one of his last major public appearances. Lacking the charisma, the fundraising skills, the political acumen, and the right kind of ethnicity of his popular predecessor, the humble cardinal retreated from the public eye for much of his remaining tenure, which lasted until 1983, when he died.

Newcomer Families, Social Services, and Covetous Priests in Canada

Most immigrant families were able to improve their financial situation after living for a few years in Canada, where they were able to adapt tested economic strategies to their new context, including their aptitude for stretching household budgets and minimizing expenses; a willingness to trade personal short-term comfort for long-term economic gains; and pulling the waged contributions of every able-bodied household member towards building the family's savings and buying property. Nonetheless, their relative economic success often was realized at a heavy cost to their mental and physical health and led to severe strains on the family structure. Seasonal unemployment, work-related injuries and fatalities, domestic violence following threats to patriarchal norms, high rates of school dropout, and youth criminality were some of the most common social problems encountered in Portuguese immigrant households.[35] Eager to address these problems were an army of Canadian social workers and settlement agencies, most of them informed by social reform values or directly associated with Protestant Churches. One of the new economic strategies that Portuguese immigrants adopted in Canada was to take advantage of the material aid offered by these service agencies. Those early sojourners who settled in Toronto accessed the programs of mainstream agencies, such as the secular International Institute of Metropolitan Toronto, the Protestant (United Church) St Christopher House, or the Catholic Pro Aliis Club; in Montreal, they could access the Catholic Centre d'Assistance aux Immigrants de Bon-Conseil and the Service d'Acceuil aux Voyageurs et aux Immigrants. When their wives and children joined them in Canada they too used these organizations' nursery schools, youth programs, and other services, where they were taught how to be "good citizens."

Much has been written about the role played by Canadian settlement agencies in assisting newcomers and their attempts to assimilate immigrants into a Cold War, middle-class, liberal-democratic version of citizenship. Yet, as historians have demonstrated, postwar immigrants were usually able to use the resources offered by these agencies without relinquishing their autonomy and cultural practices, thus thwarting the disciplining efforts of ethnocentric social workers.[36] Less known is the fact that early migrants also benefited from social aid (albeit meagre) from the homeland. Before joining the programs of urban settlement agencies, the first experience of Portuguese immigrants with social aid in Canada was through their consulates. In his reports to Lisbon, the vice-consul in Montreal, Fr Manuel Almeida, mentioned multiple trips around Quebec to meet isolated migrant farmhands who requested his help in resolving conflicts with employers, dealing with injuries, connecting with fellow countrymen, finding employment, or simply uplifting their spirits. Almeida also gave close to CA$3,000 from his own pocket to help these men, of which a third had not been reimbursed by Lisbon months after he left his consular post.[37] In 1955, his successor, Consul Vital Gomes, alerted Lisbon to the overwhelming number of aid requests received from emigrants across Quebec and how his office had helped them find employment and obtain free medical assistance. Regrettably, he had not been able to satisfy requests for money or "avail them of the most basic food, clothing and housing needs," given that consular regulations allowed it only in cases of repatriation. Gomes also reported that his limited staff assisted newcomers at Montreal's airport on a regular basis, sometimes late into the night, without additional pay.[38]

The first bulk order migrant workers in Toronto found the honorary consul – a Danish insurance broker with business ties to Portugal – to be less generous. According to a subsequent consulate worker, the businessman took advantage of his position to sell insurance policies to those he was supposed to serve. Consular services expanded in 1956 after Lisbon sent a career diplomat to Toronto, who increased his staff. The first consulate workers were hired from among immigrants with higher education and English skills. For instance, the Madeiran Crescêncio Ferreira was hired shortly after arriving, in 1955, when he went to register at the consulate; he ended up working there for over thirty years. The Micaelense Marcelino Moniz, a former teacher, also was hired after visiting the consulate to register a Portuguese club; he later became vice-consul. According to Moniz, consular staff were "a kind of clergymen, bosses, friends, [and] counsellors" for the immigrants.[39]

In 1955, Portuguese foreign officials expressed concern over the well-being of sojourners in Canada in light of the fact that these workers sent most of their earnings to their families back home, placing themselves in difficult financial situations in their new country. The embassy in Ottawa proposed that its consulates be equipped with an emergency aid fund for emigrants in distress, and that the Canadian Catholic clergy be approached for help. In the diplomats' view, the best people to provide "moral assistance" to these isolated workers and broker relations between farmers and their migrant labourers were Canadian Catholic priests, who were familiar with the region and its inhabitants and had their own newcomer settlement services.[40] Heeding that call, the Emigration Junta initiated contacts with Catholic aid organizations and bishops in Quebec, Ontario, and the Azores. Two of them, the Immigrant Aid Society and the Rural Settlement Society of Canada, provided Portuguese sojourners with various kinds of assistance, including transit fares, clothing, job information, and loans to pay for their families' emigration to Canada. Meanwhile, the Portuguese Foreign Affairs Ministry paid CA$100 per month into a fund to be disbursed by the consulates to those emigrants in need.[41]

In the 1960s, Canadian settlement agencies started hiring lusophone workers to better serve the growing Portuguese communities in their cities. Many were former United Church missionaries who learned the language while serving in Portuguese Africa. As the decade progressed, these mainstream agencies faced increasing competition from the growing number of social services providers emerging within the immigrant community. The first such services were offered by travel agencies, which multiplied in this period. Newcomers, the vast majority of whom could not speak English or French or were illiterate, sought Portuguese travel agents for their bilingualism and higher education, which they marketed in the form of interpreting, translating, accounting, legal counselling, and other paid services. While these intermediaries helped other newcomers at a time when there were few Portuguese-speaking services available, their motivations were hardly altruistic. In fact, immigrants came to resent them once they learned that many of the services they had paid for were freely available at Canadian government agencies, social service centres, and the consulates. In 1962, a diverse group of mainlander and islander men and women in Toronto launched the Luso Canadian Association (LCA), the first secular community organization committed to offering social work and childcare to Portuguese children, along with a school, a library, a newspaper, and radio and TV programs. A subsidiary committee was formed in Montreal the following year, with support from immigration aid agencies and Catholic prelates. Led by the Azorean-Bermudan lawyer David Botelho and the Lisboner journalist Maria Alice Ribeiro, this ambitious organization had the official support of the Portuguese consulates and the SNI. That backing, however, was not enough to guarantee its success, since the organization folded shortly after being launched.[42]

By the mid-1960s, Portuguese clergymen had become the main sources of social aid in their communities, which they now dispensed through social centres set up in their churches. As one social worker at Toronto's Our Lady of Mount Carmel church explained to a reporter, Portuguese immigrants preferred the parish services to Canadian government agencies because they were "suspicious of bureaucratic Anglo-Saxon departments" and found it "easier to confide in a parish-oriented community worker."[43] The first Catholic welfare organization set up by a Portuguese priest in Canada was a St Vincent de Paul Society branch at Toronto's St Mary's church, launched in 1958 by the Madeiran Alfredo Camacho, who had arrived that year to lead the new congregation.[44] For the next two years, Camacho earned the esteem of his countrymen by finding them jobs, enrolling their children in Catholic schools, counselling estranged couples, and visiting the sick in hospitals, among other deeds. However, the Toronto community did not yet have the financial capacity to support the priest, who found himself in a precarious situation and was forced to leave. After Camacho was reassigned to Buenos Aires, in 1960, Archbishop

James Cardinal McGuigan called Fr Joaquim Lourenço from Ludlow to replace him at St Mary's. He would be joined in 1965 by three other Portuguese priests, Frederico Fatela, Antero de Melo, and Manuel de Freitas Leite, who consolidated St Mary's as Toronto's "Portuguese" church – officially, it remained a territorial parish until 1973, when it became a national parish. Before the year was over, that group of priests parted ways after clashing over their pastoral roles, community plans, and parish finances. Their conflicts also divided the congregation, of which over 500 parishioners sent a petition to Archbishop McGuigan requesting the creation of a new Portuguese parish. Instead of the congregation's favoured Fr Melo, McGuigan assigned a former missionary in Brazil to the Italian parish of Our Lady of Mount Carmel, where he offered pastoral services in Portuguese.[45]

After this split, Fr Leite, who had spent the previous two years travelling in New England and Canada upon instructions from the papal nuncio in Lisbon, sent his assessment of the Toronto community to the Portuguese foreign affairs minister. He described the prototypical emigrant as illiterate, obsessed with money, prone to slander and intrigue, and having no schools, daycare centres, or entertainment venues such as Portuguese Americans had. He also warned of the pernicious presence of anti-Salazar exiles and "communist Protestants" who took advantage of the community's supposed disarray to recruit followers. The United Church was, in fact, a vocal critic of Portugal's violent colonial rule, which many of its missionaries had experienced or seen first-hand.[46] For example, George Kimball, the United Church minister responsible for Toronto's small Protestant Portuguese congregation, had spent a year in Lisbon learning the language and another three years in Angola, from which he was banned in 1961 for supposedly aiding African nationalist rebels. Kimball's outspoken criticism of Portugal's colonialism earned him the respect of anti-Salazarists in Toronto, with whom he collaborated regularly. But despite the concerns of Church and government officials, the few Portuguese Protestant congregations in Canada and the United States never managed to convert a significant number of souls.[47]

To improve the community's poor social and cultural conditions, Leite urged Lisbon to send "moral and material" support and deploy "means of propaganda and penetration," such as launching a local newspaper, providing broadcast content to lusophone radio stations, or creating a tourism centre that could organize arts festivals. The priest then informed the minister of his plans to build a pastoral centre separate from Toronto's diocese and requested the embassy's support.[48] Together with Fr Lourenço, Leite set up a fundraising cooperative to buy a large enough building to host a chapel, a travel agency, a health clinic, a library, a credit union, and other educational, recreational, legal, and sports programs. To their surprise, Ambassador Eduardo Brazão (1962–7) decided not to endorse their initiative. The diplomat questioned the appropriateness of having a pastoral centre offering credit services, especially when its by-laws stated that it would "always be run by a Portuguese priest," and that membership was conditional on a capital deposit yielding a generous 6 per cent interest rate. In Brazão's view, the average emigrant was "suspicious by nature" and hardly understood the concept of credit.[49] Contributing to his suspicion may have been the reports arriving from the Paris embassy about a local Portuguese Catholic mission that had become a profiteering "employment agency for clandestine emigrants."[50] Another reason behind his reluctance was Leite's criticism of the Toronto newspaper *Correio Português* and its co-founders, the couple Maria Alice and António Ribeiro. According to the priest, the latter had previously approached Lourenço with the idea of launching a Portuguese periodical in Toronto. Leite's colleague eventually bought the necessary equipment to produce the newspaper and invited António to be its editor. However, while working on the first issue, the two men had a disagreement and the partnership fell through. The Ribeiros moved ahead with the project and launched the *Correio* in 1963. In Leite's version of events, the couple had stolen Lourenço's idea and placed it at the service of "communist Protestants." Unfortunately for Leite, he was unaware that Maria Ribeiro was a personal friend of Brazão (a former SNI director), who had encouraged her to launch the *Correio*, which was funded by Lisbon.

Reporting this interaction, Ambassador Brazão commented that secular community initiatives should be launched by the emigrants and only afterwards be steered by the diplomats and clergy, who ought to be careful not to subject them to "direct or indirect tutelage" in order to avoid backlash. Brazão considered the clergy's role in this discreet manipulation as "an indispensable complement to consular action." Yet, the ambassador saw Leite's organizational efforts as a power grab over the Toronto community, intent on "destroying what has already been accomplished with much effort and sacrifice."[51] Despite the embassy's distancing, Leite and Lourenço managed to raise enough money to secure a lease on a building. But soon afterwards, in 1966, a displeased Archbishop McGuigan removed the two priests from St Mary's and replaced them with Alberto Cunha and Cândido Nogueira, the former taking over that parish.[52]

Before moving to Canada, Cunha had served in the northern mainland diocese of Braga, in a parish with a long tradition of migration

2.2 Father Alberto Cunha arriving at the coroner's office during the coroner's inquest on Ângelo Nóbrega, 26 May 1969. Photograph by Leo Harrison. CTASC, Toronto Telegram fonds, ASC56079.

to South America. He had helped screen applicants for the bulk order labour migration movement to Canada, which was when the bishops of Kingston and Hamilton invited him and his brother, Fr António Cunha, to tend to that immigrant flock arriving in their cities. In doing so, the Canadian episcopate bypassed their Portuguese counterparts and went directly to Rome for permission. Ambassador Brazão was upset with the circumvention, since it granted these priests considerable autonomy from Portugal's ecclesiastic authorities and by extension his government's control. Still, Brazão praised the services to the community and "national fervour" of the Cunha brothers, whom Portuguese officials had "always been able to count on," enough to secure each of them a CA$200 monthly subvention from the Emigration Junta.[53] Over time, Portuguese diplomats grew concerned about what they perceived was Alberto Cunha's controversial personality, questionable ethics, and hunger for power. Like his St Mary's predecessors, Cunha had launched a fundraising cooperative in Ottawa-Hull to build a large community centre. Local volunteers bought and renovated the building, which was unveiled in 1964. For reasons unknown, the plans for the centre fell through shortly after. According to Portuguese officials, Cunha retained ownership of the property and leased it to a new tenant while refusing to return the money donated by the community. Years later, the embassy became aware of another incident, in which Cunha was taken to trial for allegedly assaulting a fellow immigrant in Toronto.[54] The regime's officials in Canada tried to submit the rogue priest to their will by way of Lisbon, urging the Portuguese episcopacy to exert their authority over Cunha and send a strong-willed priest who could challenge his dominance. However, there was little the OCPM could do to control the priest, since he was under the jurisdiction of Toronto's archdiocese and was now a Canadian citizen.[55]

Despite his polemical behaviour, Cunha was very popular with the St Mary's parishioners, many of whom felt indebted to him for having found them employment and providing other meaningful social services through the parish community centre, which by 1971 had two full-time secretaries. Azoreans in particular thanked Cunha for introducing to Toronto their *Senhor Santo Cristo dos Milagres* (Holy Christ of Miracles) procession, a Catholic tradition specific to the island of São Miguel. Besides using the pulpit and the parish's weekly newsletter to sway his flock and intimidate his detractors (and sell ad space), Cunha also had his own newspaper, *O Jornal Português*, where he disseminated his political views and diatribes against perceived enemies.[56] The priest's antagonizing ways were such that in 1970 a furious António Ribeiro, of the rival *Correio* newspaper, wrote to Ambassador Alfredo Veiga (1967–70) requesting Lisbon's "decisive" intervention to rid the community of the "odious" priest, after the latter had sent him and his wife a threatening letter.[57] Once again, there was little the ambassador could do to stop Cunha's "venomous" exploitation of Toronto's Portuguese. He simply kept his distance from the pastor and declined invitations to participate in the Santo Cristo procession, to the disappointment of its Azorean followers. Portuguese consuls in Toronto, in turn, could not ignore Cunha, given his popularity and influence over the community. Instead, they tried to maintain good relations with the clergyman and keep him as an ally. After all, Cunha was a staunch supporter of the dictatorship and its colonial empire and a fierce enemy of its vocal political opponents in Toronto, whom he indiscriminately vilified as "communists."

While still commanding, Cunha's influence over Toronto's Portuguese diffused as the community began spreading to other parts of the city, drawing in more lusophone priests, who opened other social centres in their own parishes. In 1967, the Italian-Canadian Fr Roberto Marino opened the Portuguese Social Service Centre at Our Lady of Mount Carmel church, offering a wide range of language, employment, immigration, health, housing, youth, and other services free of charge. Such was its success that Ambassador Veiga endorsed Marino's request for funding from Lisbon, though nothing seems to have come of it. Marino retired the following year and was replaced by the Azorean Fr Melo, who was able to secure funding from the municipal and federal governments to hire a young social worker from Portugal. In 1970, that worker was released, owing to lack of funds, and Melo was transferred to a third lusophone parish, St Agnes, replacing the Brazilian Fr Alexandre Neves. Together with two other Portuguese priests, he launched another social service centre in that parish's basement. Neves in turn moved to St Helen's church and opened yet another lusophone social service centre in 1973, financed by the Canadian episcopate plus the city and the federal governments. By 1975, there were thirteen Portuguese priests serving in Toronto.[58]

In Montreal, Portuguese-language masses were first offered in 1959, thanks to the efforts of Manuel Teixeira and his Union Catholique Portugaise (UCP). Before emigrating from the northern mainland, Teixeira, who spoke English and French, worked as an interpreter in the Fátima sanctuary. There he met the French-Canadian priest Raoul Gagnon, who tended to the growing Portuguese congregation at the Notre-Dame Basilica and encouraged him to move to Montreal, which he did in 1955. Three years later, Teixeira offered a statuette of Virgin Mary to the Basilica, which Paul-Émile Cardinal Léger, archbishop of Montreal, blessed in a small unveiling ceremony covered by Radio-Canada.

In the eyes of the Portuguese consul, this had been a significant event from both a religious and a political standpoint, since it gave the

2.3 Portuguese congregation at Notre-Dame Basilica, Montreal, 1958. Manuel Teixeira stands in the front row, second from the right. Photographer unknown. CTASC, Domingos Marques fonds, ASC17696.

impression that the Portuguese were well connected with Quebec's Catholic hierarchy. Still, he argued, such a ceremony would have had greater impact had it been hosted by a Portuguese priest, who could have warded off "the political intonation" of French-Canadian priests and their attempts to "integrate foreign colonies into 'French Canada.'"[59]

The Portuguese in Montreal were aware of Fr Camacho's pastoral services in Toronto and began requesting a missionary of their own. They had a chance to do so personally with the OCPM's Bishop José Silva during his visit to Montreal in 1960.[60] To organize their efforts, Teixeira and a group of laymen founded the UCP. This organization arranged for monthly Portuguese masses to be held in the basement of the Notre-Dame Basilica, led by Fr Gagnon and assisted by a Brazilian priest.

Consul Artur Nogueira, who attended these services, was pleased with Teixeira's initiative. However, he found the "well-meaning dynamic man" to be "irksome," "insincere," "pretentious," and "boldly impertinent" (Teixeira had sent a letter to Salazar asking to be reimbursed for the statuette that he had offered the Basilica, a request the dictator agreed to). Nogueira was especially vexed by what he saw as Teixeira's vanity, which contrasted with the fact that he was, according to the consul, "hardly literate" and nonsensical. Such was the man's potential for embarrassing Nogueira that he once dissuaded Teixeira from giving an interview to the CBC, afraid he would make all Portuguese look bad. In fact, one of the motivations behind the consul's appeal to the Portuguese episcopate, asking them to send a priest to Montreal, was so that he could silence Teixeira. Regardless of Nogueira's disparaging assessment, Teixeira would become one of the most respected Portuguese leaders in Montreal, responsible for launching professional and business associations; teaching in community schools; serving on school boards; counselling Quebec's immigration ministry; administrating provincial and national ethnic press federations; and achieving many educational and civic accolades, including the Order of Canada in 1983.[61]

In December 1960, the Franciscan António Janeiro was sent to Montreal from Lisbon in response to Gagnon's request. But to the exasperation of those who had looked forward to the arrival of a Portuguese priest, Janeiro proved to be a tremendous nuisance. At this point, the UCP had become a respected organization offering a variety of liturgical activities, now under a largely Azorean administration. Its new director, Domingos Vieira, pleaded with the Portuguese consul to intervene in what he described was Janeiro's "insane and insensate" campaign of destruction and subjugation. Vieira accused the priest of seeking to ridicule and destroy his organization, vilify its directors, take over its sources of income, and transform it into "a submissive instrument for his hate and avarice." Most egregious to Janeiro's flock was his rapaciousness, to the point of transforming the pulpit into "a scandalous flea market tribune," where he made commercial announcements "paid by top dollars." Vieira described various examples of Janeiro's cupidity, such as refusing in-kind gifts from the UCP and scolding its members for not giving him cash. In another incident, the greedy priest tried to "violently" take possession of the proceeds from a feast before Gagnon managed to stop him.Vieira was convinced that Janeiro's behaviour stemmed from the fact that the UCP had introduced him to the congregation as a humble Franciscan, for whom money was a "vile object" that would never stand in the way of "his spiritual action" in the community. Janeiro also tried to take over the Montreal newspaper

Voz de Portugal. After failing to do so, he began publishing a parish bulletin attacking the local Portuguese press and drawing their sources of advertising revenue. He was also accused of being arrogant to his parishioners and constantly invoking his supposed friendship with Salazar and Cardinal Léger in order to legitimize his acts and threaten those who crossed him. Finally, Janeiro made a habit of commenting publically about his enemies' private lives. He was even brazen enough to visit the foreign affairs minister in Lisbon to denounce the supposed licentious conduct of the vice-consul in Montreal.[62]

Portuguese diplomats feared that Canadian media might get word of the scandalous priest and hurt the community's reputation. Cardinal Léger too was concerned with the allegations against Janeiro and ordered an inquest into his activities. However, Léger delayed this investigation for a month to avoid the impression that he had ceded to the community's pressure. During this period, Janeiro ramped up his attacks and nearly got into a physical confrontation with the UCP's executives. After this, Léger immediately ousted the belligerent priest, who left for Portugal in July 1961. The following month, the defiant Janeiro was back in Montreal, threatening to resume his pastoral duties. At this point, UCP members warned they would resort to violence should Janeiro showed up to say mass. This seems to have scared the priest, since he moved to New Bedford the next month, from where he continued to write to Portuguese officials – including Salazar – complaining about the vice-consul's personal conduct.[63]

To replace the erratic priest, Cardinal Léger chose the French-Canadian Thomas Leblanc, who had lived for many years in a convent in Fátima and spoke Portuguese fluently. Unlike his predecessor, Leblanc was well liked in the community and made efforts to have Montreal's archdiocese recognize the Portuguese as a formal national congregation. Backed by a group of laymen, Leblanc finally convinced Léger to authorize the creation of the Santa Cruz Mission, which opened in December 1964 in a former Jewish "gymnasium" bought by the diocese and refurbished by its new tenants. As the mission's director, Leblanc launched a St Vincent de Paul Society branch, a Sunday school, and various youth programs. He also led a committee that brought together the two largest Portuguese organizations and newspapers in Montreal, DCI officials, and settlement workers, collaborating towards achieving Portuguese "integration" into Canadian society.[64] Ambassador Brazão reported the positive developments to Lisbon and commended Léger's and Leblanc's community work. However, he noted that the latter had not once sought the support of the Portuguese consulate, "certainly following instructions from his superiors," he added.[65] Brazão believed that only a Portuguese priest could truly meet the emigrants' spiritual and psychological needs, connect them to their homeland's traditions, and unite them. Doing so, he added, was "the missionary's job more than the consulate's." The ambassador recommended that his government arrange for the sending of an assistant priest with the purpose of gaining control of the parish centre.[66] The foreign affairs minister followed up on this recommendation and alerted Cardinal Cerejeira's office to the fact that a large Portuguese congregation in Quebec was at risk of losing its national characteristics, which led to negotiations between Catholic officials on both sides.[67] But at this point, Leblanc found a replacement in Fr Fatela, whom he recruited in Toronto. After a few months working as an assistant, Fatela took over as the mission's director in August 1965.[68] Under the new priest, the parish launched two Portuguese schools, a boy scout troop, and Montreal's own Senhor Santo Cristo procession.

Religious *Festas*, Laity, and Transregional Charity

The Portuguese liturgical calendar in North America has been filled with annual events of various shapes and sizes, of diverse cultural meanings and organizational structures, and of specific regional attachments. There were also common elements in this devotional diversity, such as the popular *festas* (fêtes), lay governance, and charity. While eager to perform their distinct Catholic identity publicly, many patrons looked forwards to the festas not so much for spiritual reasons but for their worldly entertainment, which usually included food, dances, marching bands, and sports competitions, along with profane recreations such as drinking, kissing, and the occasional brawl. They were also opportunities to bring family members together from across North America, renew friendship bonds, and make new acquaintances. This blend of devotional and social functions was common to the way in which people in Portugal engaged with their church. The same juxtaposition existed in parish community centres, which attracted more people than the ethnic clubs, especially among Azoreans. However, this marriage of spiritual and worldly pursuits was not without tensions between the clergy and laity. Given the somewhat mystical and profane characteristics of lay religious festas, Portuguese priests were generally uneasy about their doctrinal propriety. As anthropologist Stephen Cabral noted after studying Portuguese feasting in New Bedford: "These rituals of status reversal enabled villagers to affirm their popular religious sentiment against the formalism of the Catholic Church. For one weekend, the *festeiros* publicly challenge the priest's authority and control over church activities."[69]

2.4 Senhor Santo Cristo dos Milagres (Holy Christ of Miracles) procession marching down Bathurst Street, Toronto, May 1970. Photo by David Cooper. CTASC, Toronto Telegram fonds, ASC08248.

The idiosyncratic rituals introduced by Portuguese and other Catholic groups complicated the relatively monolithic versions of Catholicism in North America. Irish Catholics, in particular, saw them as injurious to their hard-earned respectability in their Protestant-dominated countries and a challenge to their monopoly over the articulation of Catholic identity, and hence of their own. However, Portuguese clerics knew better than to upset their ethnic parishioners by standing in the way of their traditional customs, and they quickly recognized the financial and political benefits that such large gatherings could bring them. Reluctantly or not, Portuguese priests facilitated these "unsavoury" manifestations of Catholic faith even if they did not share their parishioners' festive traditions, as was the case with the northern mainlander Alberto Cunha, who launched the Azorean Santo Cristo procession in Toronto in 1966.

Specific to the island of São Miguel, the Senhor Santo Cristo procession in May, on the fifth Sunday of Easter, is devoted to a wooden statue of *Ecce Homo*, whose legend claims it as evidence of divine intervention during an earthquake that hit the island in the eighteenth century. Around their necks, inside their suitcases, and in their prayers, Azorean immigrants – especially Micaelenses – brought their favourite image of Christ's tortured body with them to North America, which they displayed in small tiles on the front of their houses, inside dedicated shrines in their churches, and on the streets of their adopted cities. In Toronto, the procession grew into a weekend-long program of street festivities involving dances, carnival rides, and food vendors, consistently drawing several thousand participants from various parts of Canada, the United States, and Bermuda. They gathered in St Mary's churchyard, which was baptized Portugal Square in the 1960s in recognition of the ethnic community that grew around it. In 1973, the *Toronto Star* reported the arrival of twenty-five buses from Fall River carrying Portuguese-American devotees, who joined the 55,000 participants in that year's festa – the attendance record sits at an estimated 100,000 in 1974. According to Portuguese diplomats, the event brought Fr Cunha around CA$20,000 every year.[70] Like other "respectable" Catholics, Ambassador Veiga was uncomfortable with the "painful spectacle"[71] offered by the Azorean faithful, with their passionate and sometimes gory displays of devotion during the procession. Canadian politicians and bureaucrats cared less about ritual peculiarities and regional specificities and recognized the usefulness of these large gatherings for making electoral gains by marching alongside Cunha and other ethnic notables or advertising their services with information booths.

Although the Santo Cristo festival attracted large crowds in Toronto, Montreal, Fall River, and other cities, the most widespread Azorean religious festival was the *Festa do Divino Espírito Santo* (Feast of the Holy Ghost). A highlight in the liturgical calendar of every Azorean island, celebrated in May and June, the Holy Ghost is one of the oldest Portuguese festivals in the United States, most common in the older settlements of New England and California. The cult is dedicated to Christian charity, as exemplified by Queen Elizabeth, a thirteenth-century Portuguese monarch canonized in 1625 for her dedication to feeding the poor. One of the highest points of this celebration is the communal meal of soup, meat, bread, and wine, meant as a gift to the poor and infirm though open to everybody who wishes to join. And join they did, in the thousands, to relish the work of generous parishioners who volunteered their time and money to preparing the feast. Formally independent of the Church, the Holy Ghost Feast was organized by local lay fraternities known as *Irmandades* (Brotherhoods). Despite being heavily dependent on the work of women, who were responsible for cooking the Holy Ghost meal and other important tasks, these fraternities were traditionally exclusive to men, regardless of social class.

Mainlanders had their own, smaller religious celebrations. Two of the largest were the Feast of Our Lady of Fatima in Ludlow, launched in 1948, and Montreal's candlelight procession dedicated to the Virgin Mary's apparitions at Cova da Iria, launched on 13 May 1961. The only Portuguese-American procession centred on the Virgin Mary that rivalled the islanders'celebration in size was the Blessing of the Fleet, celebrated in various New England fishing towns. At the beginning of each fishing season, the archbishop of Boston visited the coastal town of Gloucester – where the largest of these events took place – and blessed the fleet, around which other festivities were organized. Part of the ceremony was the procession from Our Lady of Good Voyage church to the town harbour, where fishermen carried a statuette of Virgin Mary that had been blessed by Cardinal Cerejeira and brought to the United States by the White Fleet.[72] Of note is that, even in the 1950s, this annual celebration attracted hundreds of New England clergymen, including Irish-Americans. That this was an American-born ritual may explain why so many non-Portuguese clerics endorsed it.

Though a minority, Madeirans were quite visible in the public life of North America's emigrant communities. In fact, they organized what became the largest annual Portuguese gathering in the United States: New Bedford's Feast of the Blessed Sacrament. Created by four immigrants in 1915, the feast grew into one of the largest public events in that city and one of its few tourist attractions. In the mid-1970s, it attracted an average of 150,000 people every year and generated around US$100,000, about half of which was profit.[73] The three-day festival celebrated in August was originally associated with Our Lady of Immaculate Conception parish. But over the years, it became a secular, Americanized, commercial affair, centring more on its social and entertainment functions than on its religious purpose. This was especially the case in the postwar period, when more immigrant descendants took over its organizational duties and began catering to non-Portuguese patrons. The American-born generations introduced "Yankee" staples such as carnival rides, drum and bugle parades, baton twirlers, and "gaily clad" majorettes, along with pizzas, hot dogs, and other mass-produced foods that competed with the ethnic *linguiça*, lupine beans, and grilled codfish. Such Americanization of homeland traditions was an issue of contention for Portuguese priests, such as Manuel Rocha, who complained about the introduction of queens and majorettes to the Holy Ghost cast, with dresses that were "far from 'liturgical.'"[74]

In the mid-1950s, the organizers used the feast's earnings to buy half a city block and build its permanent grounds: the Madeira Field. This investment marked a clear shift in the feast's orientation, which had previously donated all its earnings to the parish and charitable institutions in Madeira. The local Portuguese parish, which depended on the feast's donations to remain solvent, now received a lower percentage of the profits (though larger total amounts). This change strained relations between the lay organizers and the parish priests. Displeased by the clergy's attempts at interfering in the feast's business, the organizers distanced themselves from the parish even further, keeping to a merely formal association. As a result of this rift, the parish, led by a mainlander, eventually shifted its patronage to an Azorean festival, the *Senhor da Pedra* (Lord of the Stone), which had been revived in 1959 by Micaelense "refugees" recently arrived in New Bedford. While he preserved the liturgical characteristics and pecuniary duties of the Azorean festival, the priest also fanned the rivalry with the secularized Madeiran feast.

The extensive volunteer teamwork and donations that went into organizing these large events made them important religious, ethnic, and regional community-building moments. However, this process was heavily gendered. For instance, membership in the Clube Madeirense S.S. Sacramento, which took on the responsibility of organizing the Feast of the Blessed Sacrament, Madeiran Day, and St John's Night Feast in 1953, was exclusive to male "heads of family" born in Madeira or with a Madeira-born father. The sons of Madeiran women and non-Madeiran men were excluded. This gender discrimination was also reflected in the Feast of the Blessed Sacrament parade, where until 1976 women marched behind the men.[75] Despite being premised on the benevolent deeds of a queen, the chief sponsors and organizers of the Feast of the Holy Ghost were also male "heads of families." Assisted by a troop of aides, usually children, these men were responsible for covering about half of the festival's costs – the rest being covered by the Brotherhoods – and in turn received various accolades for their generosity.

Women played essential roles in organizing these festivities, by preparing food, crafting decorations and costumes, and organizing bazaars and other fundraisers, to name just a few. However, their contributions were considered "auxiliary" to the central and more ritualized role of "virtuous" men. The only time women were individually honoured was in the crowning of the Holy Ghost queen and her maids of honour – another American innovation – a title often reserved to young Azorean girls. Nonetheless, Catholic parishes and charity organizations were more accepting of women's leadership and community work than the secular, male-dominated, ethnic civil society, with

Figure 2.1 Madeiran Day total donations, 1934–72, United States. Values in US$.

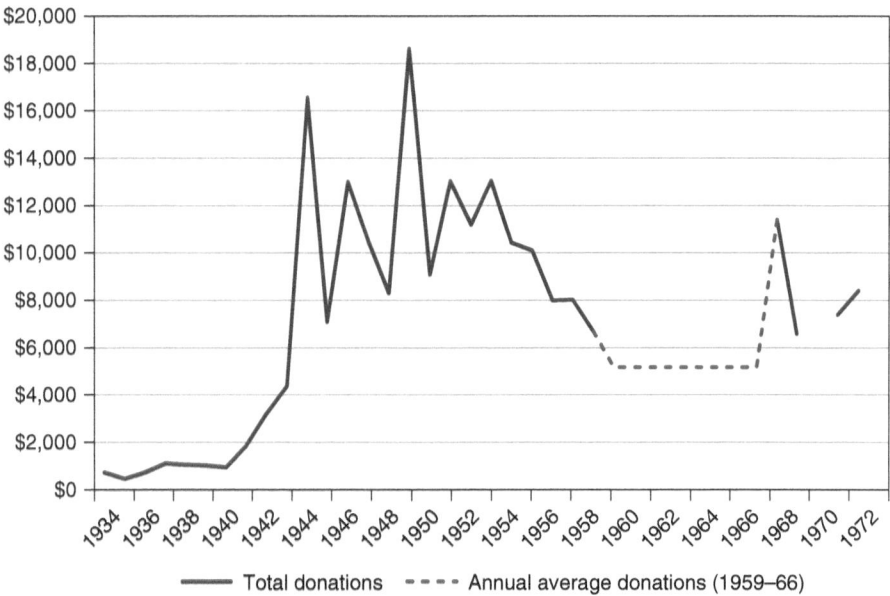

Note: Figures for 1959–66 and 1969 are missing; we do know that donations for 1959–66 totalled $41,500 (averaging $5,187 per year).
Sources: HDA, PEA M183, Madeiran Day annual booklets, 1951, 1953, 1955–8.

some important exceptions.[76] This attitude was consistent with the gender-prescribed role of women as care providers with innate nurturing skills. Still, women contributed greatly to the survival and growth of secular clubs by organizing fundraisers and family-oriented activities that helped recruit new members and pay for the club's bills. This was common to all ethnic communities in North America, which maintained somewhat separate yet crucial female public spheres, much of which centred on charity work.

Whereas the Feast of the Blessed Sacrament became a largely commercial enterprise, the Madeiran Day[77] maintained its traditional charitable function. Launched in 1934, at the height of the Great Depression, the Madeiran Day was how New England's islanders chose to answer a call for help from an orphanage in Funchal. Starting as a small community picnic in New Bedford, the event grew into a large annual festival celebrated across New England and California, raising donations to support charitable institutions in the Madeira islands (figure 2.1).

Curiously, donations rose quickly after 1941 – the year the United States entered the Second World War – and remained high during the conflict, a time when Americans were urged to invest their earnings in government bonds, and displays of "foreignness" and "dual-loyalty" were less tolerated. At this point, most public celebrations of ethnic identity were interrupted or hidden. Yet faith and devotion were private matters, pertaining to the realm of personal beliefs, which could be shared and celebrated away from the gaze of mainstream nativists. During the war, Portuguese priests continued to celebrate the traditional rites of their congregations inside their parishes and in other private settings. Ironically, patriotic propaganda promoting public-spiritedness among American citizens in support of their country's war effort may have also inspired Madeiran Americans to be more altruistic towards their own non-aligned homeland. By 1967, Madeiran Day organizers had sent over US$230,000 in cash and in-kind donations to hospitals, sanatoriums, orphanages, colleges, trade schools, seminaries, St Vincent de Paul Society branches, and other institutions in the islands.[78] While it subsidized religious organizations, the festival was not officially associated with the Church and was arguably profane, since the majority of donations were raised at the beer tent. Women raised another large portion of the funds through auctions, bazaars, picnics, banquets, dances, concerts, and other paid activities.

Similar transregional charity "Days" existed for different Azorean islands and northern mainland towns, which altogether sent "millions of dollars" in charity to Portugal.[79] This response was disconcerting for some Portuguese officials, such as Armando Medeiros, an Azorean parliamentarian in Lisbon's National Assembly, who in 1950 drew Salazar's attention to the islanders' deep poverty and how they relied on the large donations of second-hand clothing sent by relatives in the United States (37,000 bags that year alone). He added: "'Were it not for America, we would have nothing to wear': one hears this said frequently. What such a lament could produce in the political and social arenas, Your Excellency can guess better than anyone else."[80] Portuguese immigrants were also quick to send humanitarian aid to their homeland in moments of crisis, such as in the aftermath of natural disasters. The most generous donations usually came from the wealthy communities of California, for example, the US$43,000 sent to the victims of the Capelinhos volcano in 1958 or the US$70,000 to the victims of the São Jorge earthquake in 1964. In contrast, a public petition by Rhode Island's Portuguese parishes was able to raise only US$2,800 for the Capelinhos victims, although there were other smaller petitions across New England.[81] Lisboners affected by the massive floods of 1967 received three tons of clothing from Portuguese immigrants in New Jersey and New York, along with CA$18,000 from those in Ontario.[82] The largely mainlander First Portuguese Canadian Club of Toronto also sent a large amount of clothing and food to the victims of an earthquake in the Azores in 1973, which was transported by Canadian air force planes.[83]

Non-profit organizations in Portugal sometimes asked the emigrants for help with financing civic projects, as was the case during the construction of the Christ the King Monument.[84] However, these requests did not seem to muster the same goodwill among emigrants living in North America as did their own community-run charitable initiatives. Lisbon waived taxes on humanitarian aid to facilitate this transnational charity and encouraged emigrants to channel their donations through its relief agencies. However, some feared the dictatorship would misappropriate their contributions and preferred to channel them through international relief organizations, such as Caritas and Oxfam, or have their own charity committees distribute their gifts directly to families in Portugal, which sometimes delayed the process.[85]

Conclusion

Catholic devotion was a primary concern for Portuguese immigrants from the moment they settled in North America. Their homeland government and Catholic Church officials understood the importance of spirituality for preserving the emigrants' national identity in the face of assimilationist pressures from both Protestant and Irish/French Catholic societies. Diplomats acknowledged the gravity of the priests' work, not only for the social and spiritual welfare they provided but also as a means to indirectly intervene in community affairs and influence the collective views of distant citizens. This was a natural extension of the role that clergymen played in rural Portugal as proxies of the controlling yet deficient state. But despite their best efforts, the lack of missionaries willing to move to North America made this a difficult task. At the same time, their shortage empowered migrant priests already in these communities, where the high residential concentration made for large ethnic congregations. This was particularly true in Canada, where there were fewer Portuguese clergymen serving congregations with arguably greater social demands. Portuguese Americans already had ordained their own pastors at this point – the first Portuguese priest to be ordained in Canada was in 1979 – and had longer roots in the American Catholic Church. Their battles focused less on warding off Protestant proselytizers or setting up social service centres and more on establishing their own national parishes and elevating their position within the Irish-dominated Church hierarchy. Accordingly, Estado Novo officials invested more in the American context, where rewards were higher. This is not to say they ignored the needs of Catholic emigrants in Canada. In fact, requests for social aid nearly overwhelmed the consulates in the early years of settlement, urging Portuguese officials to seek the help of priests.

Although intrinsically boundless and universal, the spiritual realm was not immune to nationalist sentiments and the promotion of political borders. In the Portuguese case, that boundlessness and parochialism came together in the "ecumenical" understanding of the colonial empire and associated "pilgrim nation," as I will discuss further in chapter 5. Most Portuguese missionaries were keen on swaying their parishioners towards their political views, which in most cases meant fostering homeland patriotism and support for the Catholic, anti-communist dictatorship and its Christian empire. Their hyper-nationalism convinced Lisbon to grant them subsidies and other logistical support. However, this collaboration was not immune to the sometimes conflicting priorities of the Church and the Portuguese state. Moreover, relationships between homeland officials and Catholic missionaries were sometimes counterproductive, especially when the latter's personal ambitions and idiosyncrasies collided with the diplomats' plans or risked damaging the congregation's reputation.

In the 1950s–60s, parishes were at the centre of community life for arguably the majority of Portuguese immigrants. But the Catholic Church in North America lacked the overwhelming authority it had in Portugal. In the United States and Canada, the laity's support was crucial for priests to carry out their missions and meet their goals, meaning that parishioners had greater leverage when it came to determining church activities and rites. This fact gave rise to influential lay organizations and leaders, who mixed their religious activities with more secular community initiatives. Nonetheless, their bottom-up organization and advocacy relied on the top-down support of the homeland government and Church officials, who pulled many strings to make their wishes come true, often against those of Irish-American/Canadian and French-Canadian bishops.

Judging from the sustained Catholic faith of Portuguese immigrants and their descendants in North America today, a large number of whom continue to frequent national parishes, engage in ethnic religious celebrations, and enrol their children in Catholic schools, efforts to prevent their spiritual assimilation into mainstream host societies were largely successful. The Americanization of the 1910s–40s convinced many

Portuguese Americans – those who were able – to assimilate into the dominant white society. However, many others remained mentally or materially connected with kin across the ocean and in other parts of North America through their church activities and religious rites. More than imperial imaginings, what drove the diasporic spirituality of Catholic Portuguese were their shared religious festivities and charitable obligation towards the destitute, particularly their homeland's poor. Besides transplanting traditions from Portugal, religious feasts were an opportunity for emigrants from specific towns and regions to come together and for transnational families to reconnect. Their transregional charity, in turn, helped maintain meaningful links to the impoverished places where they or their ancestors had come from, which in turn served as a pretext for these ethnic gatherings to take place. While nationalist priests did manage to bolster the emigrants' loyalty for their homeland and empire, they also inadvertently helped their parishioners consolidate regional solidarities at the expense of a single national or diasporic identity. Portuguese immigrants of various backgrounds mingled inside their Catholic churches. But religious festivals, charity campaigns, and the lay organizations that ran them were largely regional. More than mainlanders, who were most active in secular organizations, islanders made their religious traditions bastions of regional pride and diasporic identity.

3 Making Ethnic Civil Societies: Working-Class Organizations, Community Elites, and Political Federations

Of course, the "philanthropists" who reign in the ethnic communities always take advantage of and exploit the immigrant. They are supported by Canadian governmental authorities as well as those from the old country; and they serve both countries as watchdogs.

Unknown author,
"Segregation Canadian Style,"
Novo Mundo 15 (November 1973)[1]

Portuguese immigrants have shown remarkable capacity for civic engagement since the early decades of settlement in the United States, where they joined labour unions, created mutual aid fraternities, and launched newspapers and other secular institutions around which their ethnic identities were formed. This civic momentum withered after the immigration restrictions of the 1920s and the wartime emphasis on Americanization. Nonetheless, when mass immigration from Portugal resumed in the 1960s, there were plenty of Portuguese-American organizations left for these newcomers to revitalize. In Canada, postwar immigrants had to build their institutions from the ground. Their civic dynamism, especially when contrasted with Portugal's stifled civil society, was enabled by their high residential concentration in inner-city neighbourhoods, such as Toronto's Kensington Market and Montreal's Mile End, where the Portuguese quickly became the dominant group. In these and other postwar settlements, the Portuguese were credited with transforming once "squalid ghettoes" into thriving commercial districts, whose restaurants, bakeries, cafés, and other businesses attracted patrons from across the city. They also launched clubs and associations that increased their ethnic group's profile in Canada's proto-multiculturalist polity. In its typical ambivalent fashion, the Estado Novo, which repressed civic and political engagement at home, encouraged it among emigrant and ethnic "elites" in North America, hoping to steer them towards Lisbon's foreign interests. It was these individuals and their organizations that the Portuguese government counted on to build the diaspora's institutional framework.

As migration historians have repeatedly noted, most working-class immigrants prioritized economic concerns over civic and political ones. Indeed, organizational efforts were usually left to a minority of educated, bilingual, middle-class businessmen and professionals, who arrived with the mass of immigrant workers, or in the case of Portuguese Americans in the postwar period, left to those older established immigrants and descendants with long-standing commercial and political interests in their ethnic communities. Still, after their initial sojourning and settlement period, ordinary immigrant men also began forming new or joining existing ethnic clubs in considerable numbers, reinforcing the working-class masculinity of their community's secular public spaces. In many cases, their civil societies were dominated by self-appointed leaders, who cemented their positions by forging relationships with mainstream local politicians, host government officials, and homeland diplomats. However, not all of these men were cultural or economic "elites," especially in Canada, where there were fewer upper-class immigrants. To understand the formation of Portuguese civil societies in North America and the methods used by homeland diplomats to affect this process, we must account for the different class dynamics in each context. The term "ethnic entrepreneurs" is useful here. As Caroline Brettell proposed, these were intermediaries who combined the roles of *brokers* – "attracting followers who believe [them] able to influence the persons who control the favors" – and *patrons* – "recruit[ing] followers by [their] power to dispense favors" – when distributing cultural, economic, and political resources.[2] In order to guarantee their positions of influence, these ethnic entrepreneurs maintained the linguistic and cultural boundaries separating immigrants from mainstream society, as was the case with travel agents, who were both patrons building their clientele and brokers connecting host and home societies. Using Brettell's classification, we will examine how homeland diplomats, too, combined the roles of broker and patron in their dealings with transnational ethnic entrepreneurs. This chapter examines the differences in the institutional and class make-up of Portuguese secular civil societies in Canada and the United States and the Estado Novo's role in forming them. I will reveal how Portuguese diplomats empowered amenable community leaders and helped create ethnic confederations in North America that they hoped to control surreptitiously. Their joint community-building efforts advanced notions of ethnic unity, transnational solidarity, and political self-interest, bolstered by homeland-sponsored celebrations of national pride. These initiatives created the conditions for a group of "elites" to claim spokesperson status and monopolize relations with home and host nation officials. The growing dominance of middle- and upper-class, liberal and conservative, mainlander men in their ethnic civil society, and the resulting marginalization of other Portuguese solidarities, will also be discussed.

Working-Class Organizations: Labour Unions, Mutual Aid Societies, and Social Clubs

Portuguese Americans had a long history of labour organization, a living memory of large-scale strike actions, and their own union champions. Men and women from both the mainland and the islands had been involved in New England's labour movement as both rank-and-file workers and union leaders prior to the Second World War. But despite making up the majority of the workforce, Portuguese and other unskilled immigrants had been largely neglected by mainstream textile unions. As a result, they tended to organize in smaller, more radical unions, which attracted a few anarcho-syndicalists and other experienced labour organizers from mainland Portugal. In the 1930s, when President Franklin D. Roosevelt's New Deal stimulated union membership, a new generation of Portuguese-American labour leaders emerged. One of them was the Micaelense Mariano Bishop, who in 1934 led Fall River's textile workers into one of the largest labour strikes in American history, involving close to 400,000 workers across many states. The long process of labour "deradicalization" that ensued after the war reinforced the dominance of the conservative faction within the American labour movement, which was traditionally anti-immigration. Immigrant labour activists were further repressed by the 1952 Immigration Act, which gave American officials the legal means to deport those they considered to be "subversive aliens." Eula Mendes, a former member of the American Communist Party, who had helped organize Portuguese workers in the New Bedford strike of 1928, was issued a deportation order in 1953 for her return to Portugal, where she had no family left. As she later recalled, her deportation made many Portuguese immigrants afraid of suffering the same fate.[3]

The urban centres where Portuguese postwar newcomers settled saw an important economic shift away from manufacturing and into service industries, which raised the demand for qualified workers. The temporary boost provided by wartime industrial demand was over by the 1960s, and some New England cities returned to their economically depressed condition. In New Bedford and Fall River, unemployment remained high and per capita income was among the lowest in the country,[4] an ignoble record matched by its very low schooling rates.[5] However, these low educational levels, combined with the abundant supply of unskilled immigrant workers, kept labour costs down, which delayed the complete end of manufacturing in these cities. As a result, there were still enough unskilled jobs available to attract newcomers to New England's "Portuguese Archipelago." Here, Portuguese women made up the majority of the garment industry's workforce, while the men were concentrated in different factory and construction work. Other pockets of manufacturing also pulled Portuguese immigrants to the Boston suburbs of Somerville and Cambridge, where a moderate number of low-paying jobs in electronic equipment factories were available. In Newark, the southern area of the Ironbound district, where most Portuguese immigrants settled, continued to host a significant industrial complex capable of attracting new factories after the war. In the 1960s, the nearby Port Newark-Elizabeth Marine Terminal – one of the busiest cargo ports in the United States – became another large employer. As a result, the Ironbound's Portuguese were one of the most affluent ethnic groups in Newark.

The rapid postwar economic development in Canada generated a very large demand for heavy industrial and residential construction workers, who were needed to build the necessary transportation and utilities infrastructures and the sprawling subdivisions and high-rise apartment buildings for the fast-growing urban population and economy. This was especially the case in Toronto, Canada's new chief financial centre, whose ever-expanding suburbs would later become some of the country's largest cities. Montreal too launched large public works projects in the 1960s, driven by Quebec's Quiet Revolution and economic development, which led to the modernization of its cities' built environment. As one of the last groups of primarily low-skilled workers to settle in Canada, the Portuguese were ready to grab hold of these construction jobs, particularly in the immigrant-dominated, poorly unionized, and dangerous residential construction sector. Portuguese female wage earners were largely restricted to factory and janitorial work or other low-paid manual labour. In a growing service economy, where more office buildings were built and more middle-class women worked outside their homes, cleaning offices and private residences became one of the few expanding unskilled occupations available to these immigrants. As different scholars have noted, the fact that mainlanders predominated in construction and Azoreans in janitorial work had significant consequences for the socio-economic development of each group. In short, mainlanders had greater access to a range of construction jobs, trades, and unions, which brought them more wealth, security, benefits, and career advancement opportunities than their Azorean counterparts had in the low-paying and largely non-unionized office-cleaning industry.[6] Still, Portuguese workers in Canada did not join labour unions in large numbers until the late 1970s. In addition to their early sojourning mentality (a willingness to endure undue hardship and make personal sacrifices abroad over a short period of time for the sake of bettering their lives in the homeland), their predominantly rural backgrounds, and their previous experiences under a repressive anti-union dictatorship, the employment conditions that these immigrants found in Canada also determined their initially low unionization rates. For example, residential construction workers in concrete forming, house basement, and concrete and drain, where many Portuguese immigrant men in Toronto found employment, were not fully organized until the mid-1970s and the 1980s.[7] Organizing the janitorial workforce was also difficult. Domestic cleaning was nearly impossible to unionize because of its isolated and informal nature, while building cleaners had to contend with the common practice of contracting out jobs to private companies without observing successor rights, thus allowing contractors to free themselves of previous concessions achieved through collective bargaining.[8]

Popular alternatives to labour unions were the male-dominated ethnic fraternities. As was true of other immigrant groups, mutual aid societies were one of the earliest forms of collective organization among Portuguese immigrants in the United States. In the nineteenth and early twentieth centuries, when state welfare was virtually non-existent, immigrants had to rely on traditional mutualistic strategies in order to guarantee some financial protection in the event of unemployment, sickness, or death.[9] Their multiple lodges also became important social spaces for co-nationals seeking companionship, support, news, and information in their native tongue. During annual conventions, lodge representatives from around the country shared their local experiences and expectations with their distant peers. Over time, these meetings took on more pomp and pageantry, instilling a sense of ethnic pride in members. Lodges also began offering recreational activities and festivities based on homeland cultural practices, seeking to expand their membership and endowments. These fraternities helped develop and disseminate a sense of shared Portuguese-American working-class identity across the country.

The first Portuguese-American mutual aid societies were founded in New Orleans (1847), Boston (1866), and California (1868). Subsequently, a long list of similar societies emerged throughout the United States, some of them with lodges in several states. This movement was particularly strong in California, where the largest fraternities were based. For instance, the Portuguese Union of the State of California, founded in San Leandro in 1880, had 150 lodges by 1918. While not as high, the number of mutual aid societies on the east coast was also significant. In New England alone, there were thirty-five such fraternities (including lodges) in 1912. However, many of them did not survive past the 1920s–40s. The only eastern multistate mutual aid society to remain open after the Second World War was the Portuguese Continental Union (PCU). Founded in 1925 by a group of *continentais* (mainlanders) in Plymouth and Cambridge, the fraternity was closed to Azoreans and Madeirans until 1931 and to Cape Verdeans until 1959. By 1970, its headquarters were located in a large building in downtown Boston, connecting sixty-eight lodges across Massachusetts (twenty-three), New York (nine), Connecticut (seven), Pennsylvania (seven), New Jersey (six), Rhode Island (five), New Hampshire (one), and Ontario (one). Altogether, they comprised 7,540 members and over US$1.5 million in assets. For some time, the PCU also tried to open a lodge in Lisbon to serve those members who had returned to Portugal.[10] With its extensive membership and capital, the PCU commanded considerable attention from American and Portuguese officials. However, the outwardly cordial relations between Lisbon's diplomats and the PCU's executives hid underlying political tensions. For instance, Aníbal Branco, the PCU secretary-general (1934–68) and former chancellor in the Portuguese consulate in Boston, endorsed General Norton de Matos's presidential bid in 1949, during which he voiced his pro-democratic criticism of Salazar's dictatorship. Still, Branco's prominent position guaranteed him an invitation to any event organized by the regime's diplomats in New England. The Portuguese ambassador was also a regular guest at PCU functions, sometimes against the advice of his staff. For example, in 1950, the consul in Boston counselled the newly arrived ambassador Luis Fernandes to keep the PCU's founders at arm's length, since they were hostile to the Estado Novo and known to be "communists." This advice, however, did not stop the ambassador from attending the PCU's twenty-fifth anniversary celebrations and praising the organization and its founders for their benevolent services to Portuguese immigrants.[11]

In the postwar period, ethnically based mutual aid societies began losing relevance and power as the American state welfare system expanded, gradually removing incentives for workers to join private social insurance fraternities. Starting in the 1950s, the PCU had a difficult time signing new members, and by 1963 its total membership had begun decreasing.[12] To strengthen its position in this new context, the PCU merged with California's Portuguese Benefit Association in 1957, creating the Luso-American Fraternal Federation / United National Life Insurance Society, the largest Portuguese-American organization at the time. By 1968, it had close to 14,000 members and over US$5 million in assets.[13] Despite the merger, the PCU, which continued operating under its name on the east coast, kept losing members (although its funds grew), reflecting its failure to connect with postwar immigrants.

Newcomers settling in Portuguese-American communities were not always well received by the older generations, as tensions flared over social, cultural, and political differences, and the fact that they competed for the same scarce jobs. Older immigrants and their descendants begrudged what they perceived to be the excessive facilities offered to "greenhorns," who were provided with housing and jobs by their sponsoring relatives and with government entitlements, to which they contrasted their own settlement experiences in a less hospitable American society. Older Portuguese Americans also resented the fact that newcomers did not face the same assimilationist pressures that they had, as workplaces, businesses, social agencies, and even mainstream newspapers began catering to Portuguese speakers in the 1960s–70s. While causing real psychological and sometimes bodily harm, the discrimination that Portuguese newcomers suffered from their Americanized predecessors had limited consequences for their material and civic advancement. Postwar immigrants were able to join the few surviving ethnic clubs – often sponsored by their relatives or friends – in such large numbers that by the late 1960s they came to dominate these organizations. This development, in turn, expedited the exodus of older Portuguese Americans from ethnic civic life.

Most Portuguese fraternities served specific regional groups and were inspired by parochial rivalries. Even within the larger regional divisions (i.e., mainlanders, Azoreans, Madeirans, and Cape Verdeans) there were rifts based on island and hometown origins. These rivalries were constant throughout the history of Portuguese civic life in North America, though were most intense during the communities' formative years. In the United States, newcomers rekindled these parochial divisions, although some have argued that this cohort had a more acute sense of shared nationality than their predecessors.[14] The intensity of these regional rivalries waned among following generations, who either renounced their ancestors' national or ethnic identities or associated themselves with a more comprehensive – though not fully inclusive – pan-Portuguese or pan-lusophone one. In smaller settlements outside the larger cities, where more immigrants began to resettle in the 1970s, these divisions were less accentuated and more Azoreans were involved in secular organizations. That said, Azorean fraternities usually made no clear distinction between secular and religious life, as even those dedicated to spiritual traditions sometimes served as mutual aid societies, recreational clubs, and political organizations. This was the case with the Holy Ghost Beneficial Brotherhood (HGBB) of East Providence, which organized the Holy Ghost annual procession and feast; ran a mutual aid society; operated a baseball team; and arranged boxing matches, carnivals, and other events that attracted large crowds. Its Philip Street Hall also hosted the St Francis Xavier parish, where lusophone Catholics congregated until they inaugurated their own church building in 1931.

In Canada, until the late 1960s, the Portuguese community of Montreal was considered by the regime's diplomats to be the most important, since it was where most professionals, intellectuals, and political exiles settled. Besides being Canada's chief metropolis at the time, many of these educated emigrants could speak French and were familiar with francophone societies. Toronto's Portuguese community, on the other hand, was believed to be almost exclusively working class. But once Toronto replaced Montreal as Canada's corporate capital following the rise of Quebec separatism, a larger number of higher-educated Portuguese moved west and joined or created ethnic associations in that growing anglophone metropolis. Of the various Portuguese ethnic organizations launched in Canada in the postwar period, the Association portugaise du Canada (APC) in Montreal and the First Portuguese Canadian Club (FPCC) in Toronto deserve special attention for their longevity and popularity.

Founded by consular staff on 7 January 1956, following a well-attended Christmas movie screening at the Montreal consulate, the APC was the first Portuguese association to open in Canada. Although led by businessmen and professionals, the APC's membership included common workers, most of them men from the mainland. Women were allowed to join only as "conjugal members" without voting rights and relegated to auxiliary committees. From the outset, the APC's executives clashed with Consul Vital Gomes, who wanted them to align themselves with the Estado Novo, keep him involved in the association's affairs, and report on the political activities of its members. When they declined, Gomes tried to discredit the APC as being a "communist haven" and ordered its closure. The APC's executive retaliated by denouncing the consulate's participation in a migration racket that defrauded prospective emigrants in Canada and the Azores (as mentioned in chapter 1), which resulted in Gomes's removal by Lisbon.[15] The new consul, Artur Nogueira, tried to mend his office's relations with the APC and offered them a small subsidy, which led to conflicts between those members who favoured this funding and those who refused to associate themselves with the dictatorship. This prompted the APC's founding administration to resign.[16] At this point, Henrique Tavares Bello, a former consulate worker who had arrived in Canada with his wife in 1955, became the APC's new president. During his time at the consulate, Bello had been a vocal critic of the way Canadian employers treated Portuguese farmhands, which provoked a reprimand from Consul Gomes. In the APC, Bello continued to denounce the exploitation of immigrants at the hands of travel agents and other immigration racketeers, some of whom were members of the association. He was also critical of some Portuguese businessmen in the city and of Salazar, which upset many within the APC – nonetheless, he approved of Consul Nogueira's subsidy. These conflicts resulted in yet another split within the membership and prompted Bello's resignation. This time the APC also lost its official organ, the *Luso-Canadiano*, which Bello owned and transferred to the anti-fascist social club, Maison des Portugais, which he founded in 1961. Another consulate staff member replaced Bello at the APC's helm, but he failed to prevent its closure several months later. In the consul's eyes, the main reasons why the organization struggled to stay open were twofold: the absence of "associational spirit among the immigrant masses, who prefer to live in isolation ... in order to better amass a few dollars" and the small number of available "elites," which prevented "leadership renewal."[17] The APC would reopen in 1961 with a new set of by-laws that prohibited its members from using the organization for political purposes. Still, the APC and its new organ, *Voz de Portugal*, turned to Lisbon for funding and resumed their political rivalry with Bello's organization and its newspaper.

In Toronto, mainlanders and Madeirans led most secular ethnic organizations. Except for the LCA and another similar, short-lived organization,[18] Azorean secular civic participation was low before the 1970s. This was the case with the FPCC, the largest and longest-running Portuguese club in Toronto, founded in September 1956. Most of the club members were workers, as reflected in its 1964 incorporation papers, which listed the occupations of its executives, among which were mechanic, chauffeur, assembler, painter, plasterer, welder, foreman, and labourer.[19] Despite the regional divide, the FPCC had the distinction of bringing together individuals from opposing political factions without falling victim to the schisms that splintered other clubs. The reason was likely the fact that its main focus was sports, including football, basketball, and cycling, whose teams enjoyed competitive success and had a relatively large following. The LCA's early civic efforts, along with some of its members, transferred to the FPCC, which launched a wide range of social, educational, recreational, financial, and travelling services in the 1960s–70s. Still, its main attraction and source of revenue remained the men's football team, whose roster included construction workers, factory workers, and professional musicians, some of whom had played competitively in Portugal. As the club grew, the FPCC hired a few players directly from the homeland, such as the Mozambican-Portuguese international football star Matateu, who helped the club win the Canadian National Soccer League championship in 1969 – a feat they repeated in 1979. The club's other major program since 1964 was its Portuguese-language Saturday school, which was also dominated by mainlanders, as I will discuss in the next chapter.

The Ethnic Elites: Businessmen, Newsmen, Professionals, and Politicians

Hoping to escape the drudgery of waged labour, become their own bosses, or continue the self-employed occupations they had in Portugal, many immigrants opened businesses catering to their countrymen in the highly concentrated Portuguese settlements. It was common for these entrepreneurs to have landed as labourers and spent their first years working for wages before amassing enough capital to start their businesses. Rural immigrants, some never having worked for another person before, opened food markets and sold groceries, while others ran boarding houses, cafés, restaurants, and other commercial establishments. The most business savvy recognized the growing demand for homeland products and began importing goods from Portugal. Tailors, bakers, butchers, barbers, mechanics, typographers, and other tradesmen set up their own shops as well. Those with more education and fluency in English or French opened travel agencies, driving schools, notarial services, and other service-oriented businesses.

A few cultured immigrants with a penchant for writing and an interest in journalism launched newspapers, while others more loquacious and entertaining opened radio stations. Together they quickly gave rise to lively and often polemicist local community media. The Portuguese-language newspapers published in eastern North America in the postwar period were the *Diário de Notícias*[20] (1919–73) of New Bedford; *A Luta* (1926–?) of New York; the *Luso-Americano* (1928–) and *Novos Rumos* (1961–?) of Newark; the *Luso-Canadiano* (1958–71), *Voz de*

Portugal (1961–), and *Lusitano* (1964–74) of Montreal; and the *Correio Português* (1963–90s), and *O Jornal Português* (1968–75) of Toronto.[21] Most of them were small operations with limited and sometimes irregular circulation, often struggling to stay open. In 1936, one Portuguese diplomat in the United States described these "rags" as "speculative little businesses, often of opportunity, run by three distinct people – publisher, redactor and editor – rolled into one individual who solicits, adulates, intrigues and threatens in order to obtain a few ads and subscriptions, and ... is able to obtain some provisions, objects, groceries and services [in return]."[22] The exception was the *Diário* of New Bedford, the oldest, most circulated (10,000 copies per issue in 1966), and only daily Portuguese-language newspaper in North America. Besides having a sizable readership, it also counted on a wide range of contributors in various locations, who reflected the diversity of political views espoused by Portuguese-Americans, including monarchists, republicans, socialists, liberals, and fascists. But more than the political commentary, its success relied on the fact that it was the most readily available, news-based Portuguese-language paper, covering daily affairs from the host and home countries, at a time when newspapers from Portugal arrived weeks late. The *Diário*'s popularity and liberal inclination was cause for concern among Lisbon officials, including Salazar himself, who in 1935 instructed his ambassador to keep him informed about every single communication that attacked his government circulating in the Portuguese-American communities. Subsequently, the Estado Novo's diplomats and propaganda agencies made efforts to bring the *Diário* and other media outlets in line with their views and foreign messaging (see chapter 5).[23] There were many other smaller newsletters published by ethnic associations and parishes as well as publications from other parts of the lusophone world distributed in Canada and the United States. Considering the high rates of illiteracy among the Portuguese, the large number of lusophone publications circulating in North America was remarkable.

Those with little access to print media and who lived near the major communities could enjoy Portuguese radio and television. The first daily (later weekly) radio show in the United States was *The Voice of Portugal*, serving Rhode Island and southeastern Massachusetts since 1933. Launched by the mainlander Ferreira Mendes, this broadcast introduced listeners to Portuguese artists, announced community events, delivered the news, and ran charitable campaigns aimed at helping fellow immigrants and homeland residents in distress. Mendes is credited with raising over US$500,000 in donations for various humanitarian causes though his show. He also directed East Providence's WRIB, the first Portuguese radio station on the American east coast, between 1952 and 1967. The few lusophone radio broadcasts in New England – one daily and twelve weekly shows in 1959[24] – offered by stations such as Boston's WLYN and WUNR and New Bedford-Fall River's WBSM/WGCY, which had broadcasted exclusively in Portuguese since 1969 – were enough to cover its concentrated population. Those in New Jersey could tune in to WHBI for their first lusophone broadcast starting in 1964. In Canada, the first Portuguese radio shows began in 1958 with *Voices of Portugal* on Toronto's CKFH, followed by *The Portuguese Hour* on Montreal's CFMB in 1962; many more followed. In 1968, a group of immigrants in Kensington Market launched the Rádio Clube Português, the first Portuguese-owned radio station in Canada, which broadcast fifteen hours of daily programming. A similar closed-circuit station, Ecos de Portugal, opened in 1969 in Montreal.[25] In addition to these community-based broadcasts, after 1962 Portuguese in North America could also tune into *Radio Voice of Freedom*, transmitted biweekly from Algiers by anti-fascist exiles, who sometimes relayed messages from fellow democrats in Toronto and Montreal.

In close proximity to each other, Portuguese businesses, service providers, media outlets, and civic associations imparted a dense ethnic character to those heavily populated working-class neighbourhoods with bustling commercial strips. Arguably the most famous was Toronto's Kensington Market, or "Augusta," as it was known to its patrons, who named it after the Portuguese-sounding avenue where most ethnic businesses were located. Its fame as a Portuguese immigrant hub even reached France, prompting some expats there to try their luck in Toronto.[26] The prevailing notion among outsiders was that ethnic "enclaves" were places where it was "entirely possible to work, shop, eat, worship, bank, marry, live, and die without ever speaking English or leaving the neighborhood except to travel [to] Portugal."[27] Mainstream commentators, and some within the community, criticized the insularity provided by the "institutional completeness"[28] of these neighbourhoods and blamed it for reinforcing the immigrants' marginality. However, most critics either exaggerated or underestimated the psychological, social, and economic necessity of these ethnolinguistic spaces. Here, immigrant workers who did not speak English or French well enough, who were weary of interacting with government agencies given their experience with Portugal's repressive state, or whose status was undocumented, could access otherwise inaccessible information and services essential for interacting with their host societies. Besides offering homeland products and services in the immigrants' native language, ethnic markets also welcomed consumer practices common in Portugal, such as bartering and keeping store credits, which increased their buying power. Most ethnic stores were family owned, which made for a more personable commercial exchange, where relationships between businesses and consumers relied on personal reputation and mutual trust, unlike the anonymous interactions of mainstream shopping.

The same was true of ethnic credit unions. These were membership-run, financial cooperatives, traditionally affiliated with ethnic clubs or parishes, dedicated to providing affordable credit to its members; to investing in community projects, organizations, and local businesses; and to facilitating remittances. Besides their willingness to lend money to newcomers with little financial credit, these institutions appealed to their Portuguese clientele by being located in their neighbourhoods and employing lusophone staff, with whom customers could rely on personal reputation as much as on their credit rating. Earning the community's trust, however, was not easy. For instance, Montreal's Caisse d'économie des Portugais, founded in a humble building in January 1969, carried on an outreach campaign that involved door-to-door visits, offering matrimonial advice, lending bail money to a Portuguese inmate, and other unorthodox services. The credit union's efforts were largely unsuccessful until the Micaelense Celestino Andrade led the team in 1971 and managed to convince the predominantly Azorean community to entrust him with their savings. Between 1971 and 1978, the Caisse's funds grew from CA$21,300 to CA$6 million. By 1980, it had enough money to build its own two-storey building on Saint Laurent Boulevard.[29]

One of the most famous Portuguese-Canadian success stories is that of António Sousa, who opened the first community business in Toronto in 1956, three years after arriving in Halifax aboard the *Saturnia*. A certified businessman by formal education and family tradition, Sousa left behind a fishing supplies store in his hometown of Nazaré and migrated to Canada as a bogus carpenter. His decision was motivated by his fear of the PIDE, which had taken notice of him since he had supported the Norton de Matos presidential bid in 1949.[30] Sousa's first job in Canada was on a chicken farm in Sarnia, Ontario, which he quickly left for Montreal, where a fellow countryman found him a job as a kitchen helper at an airbase in Goose Bay, Labrador. There he learned English from a Russian cook and made extra money by selling first snacks and beverages to his fellow workers in the evening, then clothing, jewellery, and other luxury goods ordered from the Eaton's catalogue and retailers in Montreal. In 1954, Sousa moved to Toronto and sent for his wife and son to join him; then they bought a property in Kensington Market and opened a restaurant and boarding house. As the only Portuguese landmark in the city, their business became a focal point for newcomers looking to settle in the city and contributed towards making Kensington the hub of the Portuguese community. In 1958, he sold the restaurant to the same friend who had found him work in Labrador and opened a food-importing company, which he later complemented with fish stores and bakeries in Toronto and Winnipeg, along with other businesses. Sousa was involved in various community initiatives, including the LCA, FPCC, and the Rancho da Nazaré folk dance troupe, which he co-founded and directed. Sousa's civic activity also extended to his hometown, where he helped build a sheltering harbour, unveiled in 1983 by his brother, the town's mayor.[31] Later in life, the Sousas moved to the city of Mississauga in the Greater Toronto Area and, like other wealthy Portuguese Canadians, began spending their summers in Palm Beach, Florida, where a community club was founded in the 1980s. In 2007, their youngest son, Charles Sousa, who was raised in Kensington Market, became a member of the provincial Parliament (MPP) for Mississauga. In 2013, after having held the Ontario ministries of labour, and of citizenship and immigration, Charles was appointed minister of finance by Premier Kathleen Wynne, becoming the highest-ranking Portuguese-Canadian politician to date.

Like those of the Sousas, other Portuguese businesses opened shortly after the first sojourners settled in Toronto and Montreal.[32] Many of these businessmen were ethnic entrepreneurs, known for folding multiple roles into one person as multiservice providers. As Brettell argued, rural emigrants had been used to dealing with a single person for a range of services, usually the priest or the local *cacique* (boss), who performed a variety of roles. In many ways, ethnic entrepreneurs fit this "preconceived image of a man of many parts."[33] A clear example was José Rafael. Having learned English at the US airbase in Terceira, where he had worked as a janitor, Rafael moved to Toronto in 1957. Starting as a downtown office cleaner, he soon became a travel agent, to which he added the roles of real estate agent, immigration consultant, radio announcer, and community organizer. Besides advertising his services on the Rádio Clube Português, Rafael twice used Toronto's airwaves to mobilize his community to protest the murder of two of its young members, in 1969 and 1977. He also used it to fight Fr Cunha's dominance, who in turn used his pulpit to attack Rafael's businesses and community involvement. Canadian authorities also took an interest in Rafael's immigration consulting activities, leading to charges of racketeering and fraud in 1971, which he successfully defended in the Supreme Court of Ontario the next year.

While material rewards were an important motivation, it was certainly not the only one for these ethnic entrepreneurs. Some expected personal recognition and a respectable social status from their organizing efforts or were genuinely interested in developing their community for its own sake. Those few businessmen and professionals whose economic success did not rely on the ethnic market normally distanced themselves from the civic initiatives of their less privileged co-nationals or engaged only from a distance. Not only were their middle-class ways at odds with the experiences and interests of the working-class majority, they also avoided being associated with an ethnic group to which the host society assigned various unflattering stereotypes. There were exceptions, such as the millionaire supermarket chain operator Joseph Fernandes in the United States or the electronic telecommunications manufacturer Manuel Mira in Canada, both of whom were actively involved in the civic and political life of their Portuguese communities.

The same intersection of ethnic entrepreneurship, civic engagement, and political ambition existed in Portuguese-American civil society, although with important differences. Here, the older immigrant generation and their descendants controlled most positions of influence. Postwar newcomers hoping to establish themselves in the ethnic marketplace had to compete with their experienced and well-connected predecessors. Portuguese Americans also made up a larger and more established political constituency than their fellow ethnics in Canada. Since the early twentieth century, Democrats and Republicans in Massachusetts and Rhode Island consistently included Portuguese Americans in their party nominations, although only a few were elected before the Second World War.

In the postwar period, the number of Portuguese-American elected officials increased, especially in East Providence, where a combination of demographic and legislative factors made them favourable political arenas for these ethnic politicians.[34] Many of these Rhode Island politicians attributed their electoral success to their membership in the HGBB, which became an incubator for political careers after its president was state representative in 1945.[35] Political aspirants – mostly businessmen and professionals, but also a significant number of skilled workers and union leaders – joined this popular Azorean fraternity to network and raise their profiles in the Portuguese-American community. They also developed public-speaking and decision-making skills, learned how to raise votes, and discovered other governing practices while serving as HGBB administrators. But more than civic tutoring, it was the fact that, in the 1960s, the HGBB became an unofficial nomination pool for the Democratic Party that propelled so many of its members into a political career.

3.1 City fathers of Provincetown, Massachusetts, all of Portuguese descent, gathered in council, April 1942, before a painting representing the signing of the Mayflower Compact in Provincetown Harbor upon the first landing of the Pilgrims on American soil. Photograph by John Collier, Library of Congress.

Other prominent organizations promoting political engagement were the Portuguese American Civic League of Massachusetts, founded in 1913 (relaunched in 1928), and its Rhode Island namesake, founded in the 1930s. The main purpose of these "non-partisan" leagues was to raise interest in American politics, organize citizenship drives, and encourage Portuguese Americans to run for public office. Over time, these civic leagues became political organizations in their own right, advocating on policy matters affecting their ethnic group, campaigning on behalf of Portuguese-American candidates, and raising support for heritage projects memorializing co-ethnic war veterans and other notables. Arguably, their most active sections were the women's "auxiliaries," which organized dances, pageants, street parades, and other recreational activities attracting large crowds and new members. The leagues' annual conventions also brought together hundreds of delegates from multiple branches, along with various American dignitaries. According to one consul, its organizers were mostly "humble folk" with considerable political influence in their community. The same diplomat reported in 1964 that the Massachusetts civic league had close connections with the Kennedys, who saw this organization as "the most effective vehicle of penetration in the Portuguese colony." In hindsight, he lamented how unfortunate it had been for Lisbon not to "follow in the footsteps ... of these crafty politicians" instead of "wasting its time" with less prestigious community leaders. It was the consul's opinion that, with time, these civic leagues could be swayed into doing the Estado Novo's bidding.[36]

Nonetheless, the Estado Novo's diplomats tried to cultivate relations with Portuguese-American politicians, including high-ranking Democrats such as the Massachusetts state senators Mary L. Fonseca – the first female majority whip in that legislature – and Edmund Dinis, and cultivate their favour with honorary titles and other forms of flattery. Many of these politicians were unapologetically proud of their cultural heritage and made use of the "ethnic vote" to get elected. The Micaelense Dinis, for instance, dedicated much of his political career (1948–70) as state representative, senator, and district attorney to promoting Portuguese-American causes, especially the heritage-praising kind. Besides his Portuguese patriotism, conservative views, and influence in the ethnic community, his personal ties to the Kennedy family made him a highly desirable asset to Lisbon's American strategy.[37]

Like other community leaders, Dinis was an "ethnic entrepreneur," who recognized the persuasive power of ethnic media when he bought the Portuguese-language station WGCY in 1975, just before he ran for Congress. In Canada, Portuguese businessmen and professionals too were involved in local party riding associations since the 1960s – mainly with the Progressive Conservative Party in Toronto and the Liberal Party in Montreal – but it was not until the late 1970s that Portuguese Canadians began running for political office.

Surveying the most prominent Portuguese civic leaders in the United States and Canada, one immediately notices the almost absolute absence of women in positions of power. This was especially the case in Canada, where Maria Alice Ribeiro, a trained nurse and journalist with professional ties to Portuguese and Brazilian foreign officials in North America, was the only prominent female civic leader, as the editor of the *Correio Português* and executive member of various community organizations.[38] Club halls, with their games rooms, bars, and other traditional homosocial spaces, were considered disreputable places for

3.2 Edmund Dinis campaigning with Senator John F. Kennedy in Hyannis, Massachusetts, 1958. Claire T. Carney, Library Archives and Special Collections, Ferreira-Mendes Portuguese-American Archives, MC94.23.

women, who were welcomed only on special occasions, such as dances, picnics, and other events geared towards families. This despite the fact that women's volunteer "auxiliary" work was often essential to the survival and development of these organizations. In both countries, ethnic leaders tended to be skilled workers, business owners, company managers, and professionals, although the Americans had a larger pool of individuals in prestigious occupations and public offices. This difference reflected the longer time that the Portuguese had lived in the United States, where they had been able to move up the social ladder and generate a larger intelligentsia. In the American case, mainlanders and Azoreans were nearly evenly split in leadership roles, followed by Madeirans and Cape Verdeans. While Azoreans predominated slightly, their leadership representation still fell short of their overwhelming majority in total population. Mainlander over-representation in secular civic life was most pronounced in Canada, where few Azoreans occupied positions of leadership. Moreover, despite being a minority in the overall migration movement, a significant number of community leaders in Canada came from Lisbon and the surrounding area.

Besides accumulating executive positions in predominantly working-class clubs, these ethnic elites also formed separate professional and businessmen associations, like those founded in Montreal in 1967 and in Toronto in 1969. Another elitist organization was the Pro-Culture Society, founded in Toronto in 1972 by the Micaelense Humberto Carvalho, a former teacher turned bank manager turned construction materials importer, who was also an amateur stage director and Progressive Conservative Party grass-roots organizer. This organization had the distinct goals of introducing Canadians to more sophisticated Portuguese culture and consolidating the ethnic community's political leverage. Speaking to a *Toronto Star* reporter, Carvalho bemoaned the divisive and belligerent attitudes of "so-called leaders," which he blamed for keeping those "few Portuguese who are qualified to 'direct' the community [from] offer[ing] their services to their people."[39] Some time after this interview, a disgruntled reader named Eurico Nunes, a member of the leftist Portuguese Canadian Democratic Association (PCDA), wrote a letter to the editor berating Carvalho and his club and criticizing the *Star* for regularly "wasting time" with "phony" leaders and their plans to unite Toronto's Portuguese. According to Nunes, all the really important issues affecting the community, such as ethnic discrimination, unemployment, education, immigration laws, and exploitation remained unresolved. "After all," he added, "what culture can they get from businessmen who are only interested in promoting themselves? Culture happens naturally, it doesn't come out of board rooms, wrapped in plastic, as some kind of detergent."[40] Despite its initial success – about 200 people attended its first monthly meetings – Carvalho's Society failed to have his desired impact in the Toronto community and soon became a "black tie" club for the immigrant aristocracy.

The Quest for Unity: Diplomatic Patronage, Ethnic Confederations, and Portugal Day

Multiple efforts were made in the mid-1960s and early 1970s towards uniting Portuguese organizations in the United States and Canada under large umbrella organizations and presenting their ethnic constituencies as cohesive political forces to their host nation's decision-makers. The ethnic confederations created in this period were heavily influenced by homeland politics, in large part following the backstage guidance of Lisbon's diplomats. Together with their traditional diplomatic responsibilities, ambassadors and consuls were expected to maintain positive relations with the emigrant communities and foster their loyalty to Portugal by supporting their organizations and participating in their events. This expectation was first set by Ambassador João António de Bianchi (1933–47), whose regular visits to the emigrant communities and personal communications through their media outlets had a very positive impact in improving Portuguese-Americans views about and relations with the Estado Novo.[41] In the postwar period, Portuguese ambassadors were persistently invited to attend community events. Most of the time they sent their regrets or their consuls or other embassy staff did so on their behalf, which occasionally provoked grumblings from community organizers. Besides being unwilling or unable to attend every "card game and family feast," as one newspaper put it, ambassadors also avoided been perceived to favour one organization or population over another, and they declined invitations from organizations that seemed interested in boosting their own profile versus that of their rivals.[42] Despite this selective approach, a significant amount of the diplomats' time was spent attending community events. A constant theme throughout their reports to Lisbon, especially among newly arrived diplomats, was their amazement at the emigrants' dedication to Portugal, its symbols, language, and traditions and their enthusiastic reception of homeland officials. In their correspondence, it is apparent that many diplomats were moved and inspired by the intense displays of patriotism, to which, some argued, Lisbon did not do justice. For instance, in Ambassador Fernandes's report after the PCU's anniversary event, in 1950 (his first community visit), he mentioned how it had "far exceeded his expectations," particularly the great enthusiasm shown by Portuguese Americans towards their homeland. Inspired by their warm welcome, he instructed his consuls to maintain regular contact with the emigrant "colonies" and increase efforts to coordinate their organizational initiatives. Some consuls, however, continued to treat emigrants with derision and ignored Fernandes's instructions. This insubordination became a public affront when none of the consuls in New England showed up for an important scholarship fundraising dinner, organized in 1955 by the American Portuguese Loyalty Association (APLA) of Fall River, which brought together the governors of Rhode Island and Massachusetts, Congressman Joseph Martin, two Portuguese-American state senators, the mayor of Fall River, and a crowd of 900 people. According to Fernandes, the consuls had refused to pay for their own dinner. He would be embarrassed again later that year when none of the consuls came to receive him at Gloucester's Blessing of the Fleet, which caused consternation among organizers and ethnic media. In Fernandes's opinion, these insubordinate consuls only went to community events where they were guaranteed to be the highest-ranking homeland dignitaries in attendance.[43]

At the same time, Ambassador Fernandes found the incessant invitations from small community clubs irritating. In his view, the only organizations of interest to Lisbon were the PCU and APLA. He also sometimes chided Portuguese-American elites for their pretentiousness and questionable loyalty to Portugal. In 1953, he wrote to the foreign affairs minister about the occasional testimonies of Portuguese-American travellers in the American press, in which they expressed condescending views about Portugal. As he put it, he despised their "airs of importance as cultivated and well-traveled people," and their "constant preoccupation in showing that they are true 'Yankees,' with such attenuated bonds to Portuguese stock ... as if they were worthy descendants of the first Nordic settlers, from a race 'above' the Latin."[44] These paternalistic views were sometimes repeated by Portuguese Americans themselves, as was the case with the PCU's secretary-general Anibal Branco, who thanked the ambassador for his visit and apologized for the humble manners of his fraternity's members. As Branco described them, they were "simple workers" with "modest" intellect, who were, nonetheless, proud to assert "their place alongside the world's most civilized peoples."[45] In another instance, the Feast of the Blessed Sacrament's organizers tried to convince the ambassador to accept their invitation after learning of his attendance at the Blessing of the Fleet and assured him that theirs would be an exquisite reception, since, unlike Gloucester's Portuguese, they were no lowly "fishermen."[46]

The general perception among Portuguese Americans was that Lisbon's officials despised and dismissed average working emigrants. One patriotic Portuguese from New Bedford wrote Ambassador Fernandes alerting him to this widespread negative view in the community, which he claimed was spread by the regime's enemies, "who are busy night and day sowing suspicion of its acts and aims." This sentiment, he added, was supported by the fact that "no 'average' citizen, no 'poor' man" had ever been awarded an honorary title by the Portuguese government – only politicians, clergymen, media personalities, and other notables. As a way of refuting this elitism, he suggested that Fernandes award a medal to Johnny Furtado, an "honourable," destitute, physically disabled "ardent Catholic," who had worked for thirty years as a newspaper vendor on a street corner, come rain or sunshine, out of "love for the people he meets." Many in New Bedford shared this admiration for Furtado, including some of its most eminent citizens, who were among the 375 guests at a banquet held in his honour in 1950. The distinguished guests toasted Furtado's "virtuous" work ethic, which they considered especially commendable given "his humble profession," and they reminded the audience that, "in this world of cynics," Furtado was a clear example of how there was "more to life than earning money."[47] The ambassador sent Furtado a private letter praising his perseverance, social contributions, and Catholic "virtue," adding: "we feel proud that the blood running in your veins is of the same nationality as ours."[48] Still, despite the accolades, no medal or other tangible award was bestowed on the "humble" man.

By the mid-1960s, the disharmony between higher and lower classes, whites and blacks, mainlanders and islanders, east and west coasters, pro- and anti-Estado Novo camps, and other rifts splintering Portuguese Americans had become intolerable for the regime's diplomats. In 1965, the new consul in New York, Pedro Corte-Real Pinto, assessed the state of government relations with Portuguese Americans and made recommendations on how to improve them. He argued that, in the absence of a prominent and well-established Lisbon-backed institution in the United States, the task of "diffusing our viewpoints in this country" fell principally to the expatriates. According to Pinto, previous outreach methods had been limited to delivering speeches at community events and providing aid to clergymen and the PCU. Support for the latter, the consul argued, had resulted in the exclusion of other mutual aid societies for fear of the PCU's reactions, "which is said to be very powerful." This strategy, he believed, failed to produce lasting results, especially when contrasted with Madrid's approach, which was capable of mobilizing its diaspora on matters of importance to Spain though its government-backed institutions in the United States. In Pinto's view, Portuguese officials should abandon their traditional passive attitude, as "advocated by the [PCU] for their own self-interest," and engage in "almost daily intensive action" with the emigrant communities. This tactic was particularly important when selecting community allies. The consul believed that his government should collaborate with "economic-focused" individuals and organizations, which could "gradually upstage certain dangerous groups that have for a long time frightened the [communities'] hierarchy" and regularly attacked the Estado Novo in the press.[49] Pinto also urged the creation of institutional hubs that could unite the various community factions. To achieve this result, he proposed that committees be formed in every settlement, with members drawn from among the local elites and given instructions from Lisbon, with the goal of integrating them in a larger Portuguese-American federation. In this way, Pinto argued, they "could easily influence the American administration to ease some of its anti-Portuguese positions" without being seen to be meddling in its domestic affairs.[50]

The old mutual aid societies, civic leagues, and other fraternities continued to open new lodges in the 1960s and claimed to speak for large numbers of Portuguese Americans. But at that point, new ethnic confederations began emerging in the United States and Canada, bringing together various community associations under large umbrella organizations, claiming the title of spokespersons for their ethnic group. In July 1965, 150 delegates from various parts of the northeastern United States met in Bristol, Rhode Island, for the Congress of the Communities. Its organizers were inspired by the Congress of the Portuguese Communities held in Lisbon during the previous year, where hundreds of expatriate delegates from around the world discussed ways to improve the relationship between the homeland government and the diaspora (discussed at length in chapter 5). Consul Pinto claimed to have been able to sway the discussion in various committees through a loyal and influential community member who did his bidding; this individual would be appointed vice-consul in Connecticut later that year. Pinto was able to persuade delegates to reject a proposal that called for the amalgamation of various mutual aid societies into one large bank in New York and to convince them instead to create a large ethnic confederation, which became the Portuguese American Federation (PAF). To chair the steering committee tasked with creating this umbrella organization, the delegates nominated the millionaire businessman Joseph Fernandes. In Pinto's opinion, this choice was a welcome departure from the "political type of men on which our diplomatic actions in America have been based" towards recruiting "individuals with real significance in the American world."[51]

The PAF was officially launched in September 1966 with its first general congress in North Easton, Massachusetts. Attended by "a broad cross-section of Portuguese-Americans representing practically every major profession and interest," the meeting broached a wide range of topics, including politics, citizenship, education, media, youth, the "social advancement" of newcomers, the creation of a radio station and museum, and the meaning of "being Portuguese." As the federation grew, the traditional power holders, such as the mutual aid societies and the clergy, saw their dominance dissipate. In 1972, the PCU's secretary reminded Portuguese immigrants and descendants in the eastern United States and Canada that there was no need to organize new ethnic confederations, since the Boston-based fraternity had been representing their interests, "above any regionalism," for forty-five years. Moreover, they were considering merging all mutual aid societies under "one sole and gigantic Portuguese Fraternity." The secretary's confidence turned to lament when he appealed for his arguments to be heeded by "those we so badly need."[52]

In Canada, the first Portuguese confederation was launched in Toronto in September 1969. Founded by a group of prominent individuals and associations in Toronto and Hamilton, the Portuguese Canadian Congress (PCC) claimed to act as the spokesman for all Portuguese Canadians in their collective dealings with host and home nation government officials and with the representatives of other ethnic groups.[53] Canadian officials welcomed this umbrella organization, since it suited their "top-down" approach to ethnic groups by way of community elites. The need for such an advocacy organization was first felt after the death of the young Madeiran immigrant Ângelo Nóbrega on 5 May 1969 at the hands of a Toronto police detective. The controversial circumstances surrounding Nóbrega's death and the polemical enquiry that resulted in the detective's acquittal, heightened the sense of powerlessness shared by many non-"white" immigrant groups in a city dominated by Anglo-Celtic conservative forces. This episode upset Toronto's Portuguese, of which around 500 demonstrated outside City Hall to express their frustration with the too frequent police violence against immigrants. The PCC emerged from the community leaders' efforts to organize a collective response to this incident.[54]

The initiative originally came from the community's left wing, which called on their conservative peers – led by St Mary's Fr Alberto Cunha – to unite with them. The PCC's founding president was the mainlander Domingos Costa Gomes, a former communist organizer and lawyer representing political prisoners in Portugal who escaped to Montreal in 1966 via Belgium after being charged with "subversive activities," then later moved to Toronto, where he worked as a janitor. During his time in Canada he became a leading member of the Portuguese anti-fascist organizations in both cities. Despite the oppositional credentials of some of the PCC's architects, the Estado Novo's consul in Toronto backed this organization and hosted its inaugural meeting in July 1969. However, peace between the rival factions lasted only three months, as those organizations close to the consulate and St Mary's splintered from the PCC and created their own federation. This rival organization, which vowed to "stay out of Portuguese domestic politics," wrote to Premier John P. Robarts, claiming that the PCC had made false claims regarding the size of its membership, and that it lacked legitimacy to

3.3 Portuguese immigrants protesting police violence at Nathan Phillips Square, Toronto, 17 May 1969. Photograph by Jim Kennedy. CTASC, Toronto Telegram fonds, ASC08235.

represent Ontario's Portuguese. After this split, the PCC elected a new executive, led by the wealthy industrialist Manuel Mira. The departing president, Gomes, accused Cunha and his allies of running a smear campaign against him and his associates and of using "divide and rule" tactics. He would return to Portugal later that year. Subsequently, Cunha's dissident federation virtually disappeared.[55]

By late 1970, another PCC executive was elected, this time led by Fernando Costa, a chemical engineer of Goan descent, who was also a riding organizer for the governing Progressive Conservative Party of Ontario. One of Costa's first actions as president was to request financial aid from various Ontario ministers, warning them that "closed communities" excluded from their host countries' political life were potentially a "danger for peaceful and democratic life," as proven by the recent American racial riots and the black student uprising at Montreal's Sir George Williams University. Federal and provincial officials agreed to assist the Portuguese community, which, as they saw, needed "all the help it can get." However, upon further investigation prompted by Costa's grant requests, Ontario officials became concerned over that community's divisive and "competitive nature." As one bureaucrat later put it, "we probably could not work with or help any group without getting some flak from the others."[56] In March 1971, Minister of Citizenship John Yaremko – the MPP for the increasingly Portuguese riding of Bellwoods in Toronto – announced he would provide the PCC with a CA$1,000 grant. But before the month was over, Costa would resign following an internal dispute with those executive members affiliated with the PCDA – known in the community as a "communist" organization – over the organization of that year's Portugal Day festivities.

In the 1940s, The Estado Novo turned the Portugal Day holiday into a major propaganda event, which later became an important annual celebration across the Portuguese diaspora. Its first large official commemorations in North America happened in New York City in 1957. The Casa de Portugal organized the festivities, assisted by the consuls in California and on the east coast. The high point of the program was a parade down Fifth Avenue of Portuguese-American organizations from New England, New York, New Jersey, Pennsylvania, and California.[57] The following year, two Portuguese navy frigates carrying hundreds of sailors visited New England, coinciding with the Portugal Day celebrations. Their presence adorned the streets and community halls of coastal cities and some interior towns with large Portuguese-American settlements. For instance, in Pawtucket, Massachusetts, feast organizers called on community members to volunteer their vehicles and assemble a caravan to drive the sailors into town. The *Diário*'s local correspondent reported enthusiastically:"It's consoling to see how Portugueseness takes over our people when they are given an opportunity of this nature. Even if Portuguese patriotism is hazy ... among some ... it immediately manifests itself ardently and real before people of their own race."[58]

While there have been other smaller Portugal Day celebrations in the United States since then, it was not until the late 1960s that Lisbon began celebrating its national holiday in North America in a consistent and coordinated manner. At this point, the regime's diplomats started seeing Portugal Day as an opportunity to unite all emigrants and rally their diverse organizations and leaders around a single cultural heritage, ethnic identity, and, it was hoped, political solidarity. As Consul Pinto had recommended, his colleagues in the United States began sponsoring the formation of Portugal Day organizing committees that involved the largest possible number of associations. Their coordinated efforts resulted in richer and lengthier programs capable of attracting large crowds, as was the case in 1969, when close to 30,000 people participated in Providence's Portugal Day celebrations – one of the largest Portuguese-American gatherings up to that point.[59]

Lisbon's most effective method of boosting homeland pride and patriotism among Portuguese Americans was to send warships to visit their coastal settlements. Community organizers requested that these visits coincide with their events, since they guaranteed large turnouts. Behind this enthusiasm was the fact that, in contrast to visits from homeland dignitaries, emigrants and their descendants were able to interact personally with the young sailors, who were "real" people from the same towns and cities that they or their ancestors had left. During their stay ashore, the sailors were treated to various kinds of receptions, such as dinners, dances, soccer matches, and church masses. Sometimes they were given shelter overnight in Portuguese-American family homes. Of all the vessels in the Portuguese navy fleet, the school ship *Sagres* was the most popular and romanticized. The tall, three-mast vessel, with a white hull and sails bearing the Order of Christ Cross, evoked not only the memory of the caravels of Portugal's seafaring past but also New England's old whalers. That was surely in the mind of Ambassador Pereira, a sailing enthusiast and co-founder of the Tall Ships' Race, when he convinced his government to acquire the *Sagres* for its navy. Afterward, the respective ministry received numerous requests for the famed school ship to participate in various naval events in North America. In 1967, the Portugal Day celebrations coincided with the *Sagres*'s visit to Norfolk, Virginia. After multiple requests, navy officers decided to include stops at various northeastern port cities with large Portuguese settlements. Choosing which ones, however, was a delicate task, as they had to take into account potential rivalries and jealousies. Community organizers solicited the endorsement of American dignitaries in order to convince Lisbon of the worthiness and prestige of their receptions. At the same time, it was the promise of diplomatic and military pageantry that lured governors, senators, state representatives, admirals, and other powerful Americans to the events of an otherwise humble immigrant community. Once again, Portuguese diplomats took advantage of these visits to try to unite and leverage the ethnic community. For example, in preparation for *Sagres*'s visit to Newark, the local consul called a meeting with prominent community leaders, where he stressed the need to project an image of unity and showing American politicians that New Jersey's Portuguese Americans were "a potential force not to be neglected." Following the consul's suggestion, the

3.4 Booklet for the *Sagres*'s visit to New Jersey, 16–22 June 1967. HDA, PEA M425.

leaders agreed to organize the event through a committee representing every Portuguese-American organization in that state.[60]

Visits from the Estado Novo's warships to NATO-allied Canada and the United States were also used by exiled activists to distribute political literature among visiting Portuguese sailors, as they did in Providence in 1964 and Montreal in 1967. Besides alerting their young seafaring countrymen to the undemocratic ways of the dictatorship and its warring empire, these immigrant activists encouraged the sailors to desert the imperial navy and join them in their host countries, where groups of exiles and war resisters were prepared to help them. While aware of Portugal Day's propagandistic nature, some political exiles, who themselves were dedicated patriots, were drawn to the holiday's civic spiritedness and appreciated the opportunity to celebrate their heritage alongside their countrymen. Sometimes this led to unlikely collaborations, as was the case of Newark's Portugal Day committee of 1970, sponsored by the Portuguese consul and Casa de Portugal, and chaired by Eduardo Covas, the secretary of the most active anti-Estado Novo organization in the United States – the Committee Pro-Democracy in Portugal (CPDP). Anti-fascist exiles in Canada also held their own 10 June events, which usually consisted of politically conscious cultural activities. That year, after hosting a conference and poetry session, the Portuguese Democratic Movement in Montreal released a communiqué justifying their national holiday commemorations: "we want to affirm our people's *unity* beyond the political manoeuvres with which they want to divide us, and pay testimony to the fact that it is possible to bring peace to the Portuguese family even if the people do not have the material means to defeat the anti-democratic forces."[61]

Portugal Day festivities in Canada were originally co-organized by the consul and a small cast of community elites, who decided how their countrymen should celebrate their homeland. Their programs typically started with an official proclamation by the local mayor and a flag-raising ceremony at City Hall, followed by speeches from political dignitaries and homeland diplomats, a dedicated mass at a Portuguese parish, a parade with nationalistic and religious overtones, folk dance performances, and a football match. The first large Portugal Day celebration in Canada was organized in 1966 by then recently arrived Fr Alberto Cunha and attracted several thousand people to Toronto's Exhibition Coliseum. The following year, coinciding with Canada's centennial commemorations and the fiftieth anniversary of the Fátima apparitions, Cunha arranged another momentous Portugal Day celebration. It included a parade with eleven floats representing different homeland cities and a small army of children dressed in white knight- and nun-like outfits and bearing the Portuguese Order of Christ Cross, who marched through Toronto's downtown. The event ended with a large open-air mass at Maple Leaf Stadium, where 10,000 people were said to be in attendance. In 1968, the Ontario government recognized Cunha's civic efforts by officially proclaiming the week of 10 June as Portuguese Week.[62]

As the national holiday grew in popularity, those working-class organizations previously excluded from the elitist organizing committees began demanding a seat at the table or tried to circumvent Lisbon's diplomats and their community clients, as was the case with Toronto's 1971 celebrations. That year, Toronto Mayor William Dennison invited the PCC to organize the city's Portugal Day festivities. In an attempt to avoid the sure rejection by the PCC's leftist executive members, who detested Cunha's group, President Costa tried to covertly include the controversial priest and consul in the program without respecting proper decision-making procedures. Once discovered, Costa resigned as president following the left-wing faction's outrage and refusal to recognize the dictatorship's diplomats as Portugal's rightful representatives and to include religious ceremonies, arguing that doing so contravened the PCC's secular by-laws.[63] Subsequently, the PCC fell into disarray and failed to deliver on Mayor Dennison's request. Meanwhile, Cunha and his allies moved ahead with their own Portuguese Week program, as they had done in previous years. This time, however, the PCDA was not ready to see yet another official endorsement to the Estado Novo go unchallenged and held a public rally during the flag-raising event. About sixty democrats chanted anti-fascist and anti-colonial slogans at City Hall as the consul performed his ceremonial duties. During this debacle, Mayor Dennison, himself a member of the transnational and highly sectarian Orange Order,[64] whose electoral bid had been endorsed by the PCDA, tried to appease the crowd of proud Portuguese patriots with a typical assimilationist mantra: "Leave your differences behind you ... Start out afresh to do something for yourselves." This was a message that political exiles would hear more frequently from Canadian officials as the liberal discourse of multiculturalism began taking hold in the 1970s, with its emphasis on apolitical expressions of ethnicity. Offended by the mayor's paternalism, the PCDA released "An Open Letter to the 'New World,'" stating:

> Is it not sufficient proof [of] our participation in the life of this hospitable country that received us ... the fact that we use the democratic laws we now enjoy to express our contempt for the Caetano Regime? ... Our

Portuguese democratic members do not intend to be only recognized as hard working, honest and law-abiding people. We intend to participate in a world where all are able to live freely and democratically.[65]

After Costa's resignation, another PCC administration was elected, the fourth in less than two years, though this time without a strong PCDA presence. Minister Yaremko decided to proceed with the grant despite the PCC's internal turmoil and Cunha's relentless attacks through his newspaper. Ontario officials were aware of Cunha's "rather negative attitudes towards any new agencies or development which might detract from his own position in the Portuguese community." Some in the ministry were also keener on funding the PCC after its purportedly communist members had left the administration. According to one official, their departure had removed "the final obstacle [for] proceeding with the grant."[66] Yaremko's cheque was finally presented to the PCC after the Portuguese Week celebrations.

Conclusion

Ethnolinguistic markets in highly concentrated Portuguese neighbourhoods allowed the smaller group of immigrant tradesmen, businessmen, and professionals to sell their skills and services soon after arriving in the new country and average workers to aspire to middle-class status. In Canada, it was these "elites" who became ethnic entrepreneurs and profited from their intermediary role between immigrant and host societies, by linking economic interests to their civic volunteerism. Their grip on the communities' civic life was compounded by their group's recent arrival in Canada and their relative educational advantage over their rural countrymen. In the United States, ethnic brokers and patrons operated at a higher level, since a considerable number of Portuguese Americans occupied positions of power in mainstream institutions by the time their co-ethnic newcomers had arrived. Thus, the term "elites" is more suitable to describe Portuguese leaders in the United States than in Canada, since the former featured a larger body of older, upper-middle-class, highly educated, distinguished professionals and public officials, while the latter included many younger, lower-middle-class, moderately educated small businessmen, who were, for the most part, only relatively better off economically than their working-class peers. Lisbon and its diplomats recognized this important difference when dispensing patronage to community leaders, who in turn sought to strengthen their status as transnational brokers and improve the collective profile of their ethnic group. At the same time, Portuguese officials empowered these leaders in order to increase their leverage with host nation authorities and make use of their political influence. In this sense, diplomats also played the dual role of brokers and patrons, not only between the emigrants and the homeland government, but between ethnic leaders and their host nation as well.

In Canada, the communities' nascent character and limited elite pool increased the relative value of the homeland's patronage. Here, diplomats were better positioned to affect the organizational efforts and public opinion of Portuguese emigrants. In the United States, diplomats also commanded a fair amount of influence over community affairs and were regularly approached for "favours." However, they were also clients of powerful Portuguese-American ethnic leaders, including the heads of large mutual aid fraternities and others who could sway their communities' oscillating views on the Estado Novo. Moreover, the expatriate "colonies" in Canada were not as strategic to Lisbon as those in the United States, which were more numerous, more powerful, and ultimately more useful for the colonialist regime, as they were better positioned to influence American and by extension international public opinion.

Whereas newcomers revived the civic life of old Portuguese-American settlements, the once powerful ethnic fraternities saw their influence drop as they failed to attract "greenhorns." At this point, Portuguese diplomats saw the need to change their outreach strategies and focus on creating ethnic confederations with more reliable leaders. Despite renewed efforts, Lisbon still depended on the limited pool of community elites available to carry out their consolidation projects, which included individuals who had been problematic in the past or were actively opposed to the dictatorship, especially in Canada. Unsurprisingly, old personal and political rivalries continued to plague these ethnic confederations, sometimes overpowering their members' shared patriotism and civic goals.

Like other ethnic groups in North America, the Portuguese were not a homogeneous bunch. Although riddled with conflicts between opposing factions, their civil society still failed to represent the extent of their communities' diversity. Generational, regional, political, class, gender, and racial identities all dampened calls for ethnic unity. Still, this did not stop those white, middle- and upper-class, liberal and conservative, mainlander men, who secured most of the leadership positions in their immigrant communities, from claiming to speak for all Portuguese in their respective polities. These elites and their ethnic confederations would become the agents and the foundations on which Portuguese officials tried to build a loyal diaspora, many of them ready to advance the Estado Novo's political agenda in a concealed manner. But collaborations between homeland officials and ethnic elites did not always follow the diplomats' plans or produce their desired results. Nonetheless, by preferring to deal with obsequious spokespersons in place of the incoherent masses, home and host nation officials granted official legitimacy to these individuals' claims to leadership. With such leverage, the small ethnic aristocracies would shape the institutional boundaries of Portuguese civil societies, with increasingly real material implications in the developing multicultural polities of Canada and the United States.

Regardless of the distinct motivations of community leaders, homeland diplomats, and host nation officials for using ethnicity as a political force, its currency relied on the immigrant's cultural distinction, especially after multiculturalism became the new framework for official interactions between immigrant and host governments. Hence, the promotion of Portuguese cultural values and traditions in Canadian and American public life carried with it underlying political agendas, which I will reveal next.

4 Making Ethnic Culture: Folk Propaganda, Popular Culture, and Language

It matters little if from the Azores, Madeira, or the Mainland.
What matters is that we be good folk.
                                                  Song performed by the
Rancho Folclórico das Províncias e Ilhas de Portugal.[1]

Views on the authenticity of ethnic cultures, their survival over multiple generations, their role in distributing material resources and political capital, and other social and cultural significances, have evolved since the 1960s, when study on this topic began in earnest. Scholars have long moved away from essentialist understandings of ethnic cultures as crystalized versions of Old World traditions transplanted to the New World, or as evidence of the immigrant's refusal to fully integrate in their host societies. The consensus among scholars today is that ethnic cultures are situational formations that evolve according to the challenges and opportunities confronted by immigrant groups in a deeply contextual process that involves constant negotiation with mainstream societies. This constructionist view perceives diaspora as "a special case of ethnicity," since it acknowledges that both ethnicity and diaspora are generated, attributed, and deployed via social and political mobilization. Hence, processes of ethnic culture formation are not always, if ever, spontaneous, informal, or uninhibited. They result from conscious exchanges between immigrant leaders, host principals, and homeland officials pursuing corresponding local and transnational agendas. In other words, ethnic culture is not simply inherited but is made. Thus, the survival of ethnic identities over multiple generations is determined not only by the temporal distance from the pre-migration experience, or by the receptiveness of host societies, but also by the extent to which the homeland has the will and the means to nurture them.

To be sure, ethnic and diasporic identities are not the same, though they are often juxtaposed. The latter presupposes a self-identification with an "imagined transnational community," in which there can be multiple conversing cultural (or ethnic) identities.[2] In this chapter, I will examine the extent to which Portuguese ethnic and diasporic consciousness in North America corresponded.

Often deemed "folk" or "traditional" during multiculturalist celebrations, ethnic cultures are the hybrid result of adapting pre-migrant customs (mostly rural) to immigrant contexts (often urban) in a state of constant flux. These notions are usually underpinned by traditional/ modern dichotomies that do not fully correspond with the immigrants' conciliatory world view. The idea that ethnicity represented "a haven of authenticity" removed from "the bloodless, homogenizing forces of mass productions and consumption, mass media, commodification, bureaucratization, and suburbanization," as Jacobson described it, appealed to both progressive and conservative anti-establishment movements of the 1960s.[3] For the immigrants, who went looking for a prosperous future in North America's industrial cities, this rejection of modernity was more problematic, although not inconceivable. Ironically, the anti-modernist undercurrent in North American political movements was compatible with Salazar's own traditionalist ethos and propaganda, which became increasingly conflicted as Portugal industrialized. These evolving contexts and ideological tensions shaped the regime's cultural policies and their messy implementation in the emigrant communities.

More than a shared national identity, it was linguistic kinship that led sojourners in an unfamiliar and often inhospitable land to seek the company of their countrymen. The linguistic interdependence of the pioneering generation, who for the most part could not speak English or French, led to the high residential concentration that later generated ethnic neighbourhoods, where immigrant parents made extensive efforts to bequeath their native language to their children.[4] However, Portuguese language was not the anodyne common denominator that one might expect from a nation that prides itself on having been linguistically homogeneous since the thirteenth century. The making of Portuguese ethnicity and diaspora in North America was premised, to a great extent, on the linguistic domination of one regional variation over the rest. As the sociolinguist Emanuel da Silva noted, "the dominant discourse recognizes that 'standard' Portuguese is spoken in the regions of Lisbon and Coimbra in Mainland Portugal. All the other regional and international varieties of Portuguese are made to fall in the line behind it."[5] Particularly significant in the American and Canadian contexts was the relation between the minority of "standard"-speaking mainlanders and the Azorean majority, who spoke the Micaelense variety and whose accent is considered impenetrable by other lusophones, who often mock it.[6] This linguistic division heightened larger social, economic, religious, and other cultural tensions between Azoreans and mainlanders. As da Silva argued, host and home nation officials legitimized the mainlanders' "cultural and linguistic capital" by promoting a homogeneous view of ethnicity and diaspora that corresponded with their respective multiculturalist and imperialist nation-building projects. However, there were important differences between the American and Canadian communities. In this chapter I will examine the Estado Novo's role in shaping the ethnic and diasporic identities of Portuguese immigrants and descendants in North America's increasingly pluralist postwar societies and how the cultural expressions embraced by the emigrants related to the national culture "invented"[7] by the conservative dictatorship. I will also discuss the homogenizing propensity of this state-sponsored ethnicity and diaspora and the heterogeneous cultural expressions it alienated as a result.

Tradition versus Modernity: The Estado Novo's Cultural and Educational Policies

In a country where political engagement was forcefully discouraged and civil society highly restricted, national culture was the only avenue available to the Estado Novo to mobilize its citizens. Portuguese people everywhere were invited to participate in the affairs of the nation by assuming their role as agents of its "spiritual mission" in the world. Salazar's doctrine was simple: "We need to convince the people that happiness is achievable not by modern life and its artifices, but by each one seeking to adapt to the characteristics of his external environment."[8] The dictator rejected modernity for what he saw were its ill effects on western societies, namely, the progressive secularization of life, the proletarianization and politicization of labour, the competitiveness and individualism of liberalism, and the relentless material accumulation of capitalism. Instead, Salazar envisioned Portugal as a peaceful and orderly country and an exemplary conservative alternative to the modern ideologies that recurrently plunged the West into crisis and war. In short, "the message was that simple peasant living was superior to modern, materialist dominated culture."[9] This was the paradigm under which Portuguese ethnic leaders dealt with the Lisbon government.

The dictatorship's corporatist, nationalist, and imperialist ideology was disseminated via an extensive propaganda apparatus grounded on a "nationalist-ruralist-traditionalist model of popular culture."[10] The *política do espírito* (politics of the spirit), as formulated by the regime's inspired propagandist António Ferro, was expected to produce the moral regeneration of Portuguese people by inculcating in them a national identity based on Christianity, family, historical consciousness, rurality, and its popular traditions. Ferro aestheticized this conservative ethos by skillfully recovering and reinventing traditional forms of popular culture (e.g., folk dances), and combining them with erudite conventions (e.g., ethnographic museums). Despite Salazar's aversion to modernity, Ferro also relied heavily on modern mass media, such as radio and cinema, to engage a population that was largely illiterate.

This vanguardist traditionalism was on full display in the 1939 World's Fair in New York and the 1940 Golden Gate International Exposition in San Francisco, where the Estado Novo's propagandists presented Salazar as a charismatic "national saviour." As the regime's general commissioner for these two events, Ferro stayed in the United States for nearly three months, where he carried on an extensive and widely successful propaganda campaign in the Portuguese American communities on the east and west coasts. Community leaders were delighted to hear from Ferro that, unlike the previous republican regime, the Estado Novo would shift its attention towards the *portugueses da saudade* (the nostalgic Portuguese) in the United States once it finished fixing the national economy. Proof of that was the inauguration of a Casa de Portugal in New York City in 1941.[11]

In 1949, Ferro resigned as SNI director, disappointed with the agency's rigid bureaucratic structure and lack of funding. Without him, the SNI lost much of its cohesive vision and became more pragmatic and reactive, concerned primarily with controlling information, selling tourism and trade, and monitoring cultural activities. Nonetheless, it remained one of the regime's core instruments of indoctrination and public relations, incorporating popular culture in its programming. Its international front was made up of a network of information bureaus called Casas de Portugal, whose oversight was transferred from the Foreign Affairs Ministry to the SNI in 1944. Curiously, three of the SNI/SEIT's administrators held diplomatic positions in North America: Eduardo Brazão, who directed it in 1956–8; Pedro Pereira, who was minister of the presidency in 1958–61 (under which the agency operated); and Pedro Corte-Real Pinto, who directed it in 1973–4.

As Portugal's industry expanded after the war, a new collective imagination emerged in some sectors of society, where material progress and modernity came before social conservatism and spiritual values. To counterbalance this economic modernization, the regime renewed its promotion of ethnographic forms of popular culture, particularly *ranchos* (folk dances), which flourished in the 1950s. By linking the state with the nation's past, this traditionalist policy, with its focus on cultural and historical continuity, claimed for the government the stewardship over the collective memory and identity of Portuguese people. At the same time, Lisbon introduced measures to abate Portugal's high illiteracy rates in order to meet growing industrial demands for qualified labour. Mandatory schooling was introduced to fourth grade for boys and third grade for girls in 1956, and then raised to sixth grade for both sexes in 1964. The results of this public education investment were apparent by the 1960s, when the illiteracy rate dropped below 30 per cent of the total population – still one of the highest rates in Europe. Lower-class families still could not afford university education for their children. The only viable alternative for lower-class boys to pursue advanced studies was to enrol in a seminary, which still involved considerable personal and financial costs. Also, since 1952, individuals between the ages of fourteen and thirty-five had to finish at least third grade before being allowed to emigrate. Besides encouraging greater school enrolment, the regime wanted to guarantee that its emigrants did not become a national embarrassment abroad. However, this rule merely contributed to increase clandestine emigration among illiterate workers. As a result, in the mid-1960s the Emigration Junta and various ministers recommended that this literacy rule be dropped, but Salazar refused to do so.[12]

Despite his suspicion of public education, the dictator, who was a former university professor, valued intellectual pursuits and scholarship but reserved them for the elites. Salazar considered the formation of professional elites to be of greater urgency to the welfare of the nation "than to teach everyone how to read," since he believed that "national problems [ought to] be resolved not by the people but by the elites framing the masses."[13] In the absence of a dynamic civil society, universities played a central role as talent pools for the regime's cadres. Compared with other sectors of Portuguese society, universities enjoyed a greater yet limited degree of intellectual freedom and were important windows on the world, where information circulated with greater ease. An unintended result of this relative freedom was the emergence of militant groups of student activists who organized high-profile protests in the 1960s. The number of university students increased steadily during the life of the regime, growing rapidly in the 1970s after Caetano – a former dean of the University of Lisbon – created new universities and renovated old ones in some of Portugal's largest mainland cities.

The Estado Novo rejected the secular and positivist ideals behind the First Republic's plan for advancing scientific research and scholarship. But despite its censorship, faculty purges, and other measures inhibiting critical thinking and scientific output, the dictatorship assimilated some of the previous republican initiatives and supporters and created agencies dedicated to subsidizing research centres, scholarships, international scholar exchanges, and promoting Portuguese scholarly and literary achievements internationally. In 1952, the regime placed these responsibilities under the Institute of High Culture (IAC), which was to coordinate Lisbon's increased promotion of Portuguese erudite culture and language abroad – especially after 1961 – although with very limited funding. After 1967, when the advancement of scientific research was transferred to another agency, the IAC was able to concentrate solely on disseminating language and literate culture. While it targeted academic and other highly educated audiences, some of the IAC's programs would also benefit the educational initiatives of common emigrants.

Popular Culture and Rurality: The *Ranchos Folclóricos*

One of the most popular representations of Portuguese rurality and peasant traditions in Portugal and abroad were the *ranchos folclóricos* (folk dance troupes). Originating in the northern mainland region of Minho in the early decades of the twentieth century, ranchos were disseminated across the country by the Estado Novo as bona fide national culture. This propagation transformed the original local characteristics of its songs, choreographies, and outfits and introduced new universal references to an idealized Portuguese rurality. To a large degree, one can say that the regime invented ranchos as we know them today. Despite being part of the SNI's repertoire since its early days, it was only in the 1950s that ranchos proliferated in Portugal and became regular features at official ceremonies. The growing size of the tourism industry in this period was another important venue for popularizing ranchos, as their performances were a regular feature in its marketing events.

Ranchos became one of the most popular manifestations of Portuguese culture among immigrants and one of the default expressions of ethnic identity at multicultural venues across North America.

For those parents hoping to ward off the host society's assimilationist pressures, they were also seen as appropriate supervised venues for social interaction, where their children were to practise their home language and develop their ethnic consciousness, and older youths could seek endogamous partners. These folk-dancing descendants, who, like their audiences, ignored the ethnography and politics behind these practices, in turn became agents in the formation and dissemination of Portuguese ethnic identity through their performances. Emigrant

4.1 Group photo of the Rancho Lauradinos do Minho from Hartford, Connecticut (n.d.). Ventura, UMass Dartmouth Archives Digital Collections, accessed 14 November 2018.

ranchos departed from their homeland counterparts not only because they took on social and cultural purposes specific to their North American contexts, but also because they rearranged their regional ethnographic characteristics into a somewhat improvised amalgam of costumes and repertoire, recreated from the few resources available to them.[14]

The ethnic pluralism emerging in postwar Canada and the United States was a fertile ground for folk expressions of national culture to thrive in, where even old "gatekeeper" settlement agencies showcased the colourful traditions of the immigrant groups in their catchment areas. However, this liberal cosmopolitanism was not egalitarian. As Franca Iacovetta argued, the success of this proto-multiculturalist programming relied on "the established Canadians' enjoyment and approval," for whom the newcomers were "expected to perform their role as pleasing, decorative symbols of Canadian tolerance and pluralism, and to perform an ethnicity that was a carefully contained presentation of music, costumes, dances, handicrafts, and food." While reflecting a growing appetite for cultural diversity, this "folklorization of immigrants" was never meant to threaten the privileges of the dominant Anglo-Celtic group or decentralize it from Canada's postwar nation-building project, but to "co-opt the cultures of racial minorities as a way of strengthening their power and privilege."[15]

Portuguese diplomats followed these cultural debates with great interest, carefully considering how such growing pluralism could help them nurture the emigrants' ties to their homeland. They particularly appreciated the folklorist type of multiculturalism developing in Canada, since it fit the regime's propagandistic uses of popular culture. In 1962, a rancho of Montreal performed at a folklore festival organized by that city's Catholic School Commission. The local consul reported to Lisbon that the troupe had made a good impression, despite not being able to secure authentic costumes or a knowledgeable choreographer. He noted that there was great enthusiasm among the Québécois for folkloric activities, and that Canadian authorities did not pursue a "melting pot" type of policy but instead sought to preserve "the sociological individuality" of ethnic groups. Considering this approach, he saw an "urgent necessity" for Lisbon to provide aid to these emigrant ranchos so they could "dignify the traditions and the art of our people." In 1964, Toronto's Rancho da Nazaré – the first in Canada, founded in 1958 – won first prize in a local festival showcasing folk dances from around the world. In attendance was Prime Minister Lester B. Pearson, who presented the victors with the award. According to the local consul, this success had a considerable impact in the Portuguese community, given that it was the first time it had achieved "such publicity and appreciation in the social life of this city." He was also impressed with the size of the event, which included forty representations from Toronto's largest ethnic groups. The consul noted that the Portuguese rancho had received no subsidy from Lisbon, unlike other national troupes who had been aided by their homeland governments.[16]

Other ranchos appeared in Ontario, Quebec, Manitoba, and British Columbia in the 1960s. Many of them visited Portuguese settlements across North America to perform at local events, including Montreal's First Festival of Portuguese Folklore in 1966. Some also performed for mainstream audiences on Canadian and American television shows. Yet, despite the consuls' repeated appeals, no one in Lisbon made consistent efforts to assist the emigrants' cultural initiatives beyond reacting to occasional requests for costumes, music records, and decorative materials. When that help came, it was usually minimal and restricted, as was the case when the SNI sent the consul in Montreal a collection of music records and a single traditional *lavadeira* (laundry woman) costume, which were to be kept at the consulate and lent to community associations. Before meeting the emigrants' requests, SNI officials asked their diplomatic colleagues to comment on the merits of each initiative, its benefits to Portugal's interests, and the "political suitability" of its organizers. Even when requests were approved, it could take months before Lisbon came through with its support; that is, when it did not fail to deliver altogether, which sometimes happened.

Although prepared to advocate for their local ranchos, most diplomats felt a deep-seated disdain for the emigrants' unsophisticated cultural expressions, stemming from their uncomfortable relationship as members of the Portuguese monarchal and bourgeois aristocracy with the peasant traditions of the expatriate workers they were supposed to represent. Part of the diplomats' duties was to monitor public opinion in their host countries and the ways in which Portugal and its government were portrayed in the international media. They were upset to find that Portugal was commonly perceived as a backward country stuck in antiquated traditions.[17] Moving in the sophisticated, high-society circles of the cities where they were posted, Portuguese diplomats resented being associated with the unflattering rural imagery projected by their own government.[18] For example, in 1958, the consul in Montreal complained to Lisbon about a Disney documentary screening in that city that focused exclusively on Portugal's rural life, which according to him was "leaving a bad impression" in the community. The scene that most irritated him showed the grape harvest in the Douro region – where port wine is produced – which culminated in the traditional pressing of the grapes by a dozen barefoot men, with their pants rolled up to their knees, stomping the fruit to the sound of an accordion. The consul was unaware if this was still a common practice, but he knew that "such a spectacle" was "unpleasant," and that he had "personally heard complaints from the audience ... that translated into true repugnance for that scene." He added: "People will think twice before drinking another glass [of port wine]." Middle- and upper-class immigrants and their descendants shared a similar unease about their ancestral home's prevalent representation as a land of peasants. During preparations for the Prince Henry quincentennial celebrations in 1960, the consul in New York communicated to Lisbon that there was a general desire in the community for images of modern Portugal. While forwarding a request from community organizers for photos of their homeland, the consul asked that they show the large-scale public works projects in progress in the mainland and colonies instead of the "same old" images of natural landscapes and traditional customs. According to him, Portuguese Americans were anxious to see their homeland's modern developments "instead of folkloric Portugal," which not only failed to impress but frustrated "those – and there are many! – who for better or for worse, have allowed themselves to be won over by their surrounding obsession for material progress."[19]

Exporting Portugal: Tourism, Trade, and Fado

The propagandist António Ferro understood Portugal's potential for becoming a popular tourist destination for western travellers wishing to escape their stressful industrial societies and enjoy the simple bucolic pleasures of beautiful natural landscapes, Mediterranean climate, long coastline, and romantic historic sites. He also recognized the importance of tourism for delivering Salazar's national regeneration project and improving the dictatorship's image abroad. Aware that Portugal could not compete with Europe's cosmopolitan capitals and their sophisticated cultural attractions, the SNI marketed Portuguese tourism by highlighting its pleasant, colourful, generous, hospitable, folksy rural features. Patriotic citizens were asked to play their part in selling tourism by performing their "Portugueseness" for visiting travellers. A great number of these were Americans, who in the 1950s surpassed the British in becoming the second-largest source of tourists to Portugal – Spaniards being the first. Canadians also began spending their holidays in Portugal in greater numbers after Canadian Pacific Air Lines inaugurated a flight connecting Toronto, Montreal, Santa Maria, and Lisbon in 1958.

A driving force behind this increased tourist interest was the Casa de Portugal, located in Manhattan's Rockefeller Center. One of its regular functions was to lend photographs and films to immigrant associations and mainstream institutions. In 1964, it lent 1,814 photos and 363 films. Also much solicited by the ethnic media were its subsidies in the form of advertisement contracts, which were as much about selling Portugal as they were about controlling editorial boards – as I will discuss in the next chapter. The Casa also sponsored visits from newspaper owners, journalists, and travel agents to Portugal, where they were offered the regime's favoured view of the country. In 1964, a year that saw American tourism to Portugal grow more quickly than the European average, the Casa sponsored the visits of thirty-four journalists, eleven travel agents, and twenty-three airline staff.[20] Lisbon also hired American public relations firms, which published newsletters, articles, and other forms of tourism marketing in popular publications. Aimed at the mainstream American public, this marketing strategy made no special efforts to target Portuguese Americans, much to the despair of ethnic newspaper owners, such as João Rocha of New Bedford's *Diário de Notícias*. Interviewed by Rocha in 1954, Ambassador Fernandes contended that, in his "unofficial" opinion, the "spiritual link attracting Luso-Americans to their original *pátria* ... is so sincere that it should not be adulterated by 'propaganda.'"[21] However, in the 1960s, the Casa regularly bought advertisement space in the American and Canadian Portuguese-language press.

Starting in that decade, a significant number of visitors from North America were emigrants returning to their hometowns for the holidays, who now took advantage of more frequent and cheaper flights. This was the beginning of what is today called *turismo de saudade* (nostalgia tourism), a recent concept used by Portugal's tourism industry to refer to the emigrants' annual vacation trips and the marketing strategies targeting them. While the expression is recent, the practice certainly is not, as evidenced by a 1961 Casa de Portugal ad:

Remember the old olive tree at your parents' home ...
the old trunk where you played ...
where you searched for the sparrows' nests?
So go, remembering, evoking the time that has passed
and will never come back ...
The old olive tree, in its hurt,
calls for you, dreaming, every night
in that little corner of OUR PORTUGAL![22]

Pilgrimages to Fátima also became common in the 1960s, organized by Portuguese clergymen in collaboration with travel agencies and airline companies, who advertised directly to pilgrims though church bulletins.[23]

Portuguese immigrants were often reminded of their patriotic obligation to consume and promote homeland products. Even American companies with business ties to Portugal fanned the patriotism of its Portuguese-American customers. In 1954, an American freight company that transported goods between Portugal and its colonies, published an ad reminding all Portuguese in the United States of their "duty ... to contribute by any means at his disposal to divulge and increase the consumption of products coming from Portugal." Ethnic associations in Canada, such as Montreal's APC, also reminded their communities that consuming and divulging homeland products was a way of "improving the living conditions of those who toil and suffer

4.2 "Always have in your home to toast your family and friends, in 1970, Brandies of Portugal. Table, Port and Madeira Wines and other Portuguese Products. Available in every fine establishment." Advertisement, *Diário de Notícias*, 8 April 1970. Claire T. Carney, Library Archives and Special Collections, Ferreira-Mendes Portuguese-American Archives.

in our Country." However, as was true of emigrant tourism, consistent advertisement of Portuguese products in the ethnic press did not start until the 1960s. Again, João Rocha asked Ambassador Fernandes in 1955: why not launch a "patriotic campaign" calling on emigrants to consume homeland products as a way of nurturing their connection to Portugal and prevent their assimilation? To which the ambassador replied that it was up to Portuguese Americans to spontaneously import their favourite homeland products, as the Italians, Spaniards, and Greeks did, according to him.[24]

The regime's lackadaisical attitude towards emigrant markets changed in the 1960s. Proof was the new SNI director's visit to New England and California in 1960, where he inspected the Casa de Portugal's work; met with travel agencies, transportation companies, and specialty press; and heard from Portuguese Americans about what they needed to better sell Portugal's brand in the United States. Interviewed by a reporter upon returning to Lisbon, the regime's chief propagandist noted that the most common request from Portuguese Americans was that he "make Portugal's presence in the U.S. more frequent and more visible" by providing lecturers, ranchos, music bands, and theatre and ballet companies and creating "cultural embassies." While he admitted that such activities fell under the SNI's purview, its limited budget forced him to be strategic with spending, especially in the face of a country "so rich, so vast, and so demanding as the United States, which attracts the very best in the world in the areas of culture and art."[25] The Casa de Portugal's ads in the ethnic press instructing readers to buy homeland food products subsequently became more common. This was especially the case during festive seasons, when families were keen to prepare traditional meals. Portuguese Americans seemed to have responded positively to this call, since annual exports to the United States increased 10 per cent in 1954–64. The majority were household consumer products, such as tapestries, copperware, glassware, embroideries, china, clothing, and food products, such as wines, tea, coffee, canned food, chestnuts, and olive oil. Canada also saw a significant increase in Portuguese imports in the 1960s, eventually tipping the balance of trade in Portugal's favour in the early 1970s. In Toronto alone, there were three Portuguese food importers (est. 1958), one of wine and marble (est. 1963), one of cigarettes (est. 1965), and one of chocolate (est. 1967).[26]

Although the Casa's scope of action extended to Canada, it limited itself there to subsidizing the Portuguese-language press and occasionally providing the consulates with marketing materials. In the diplomats' view, the affluent lifestyle of middle-class Canadians, combined with the country's long, cold winters, was favourable for selling sunny Portugal. However, Lisbon was slow to recognize Canada's potential as a tourist market and left the advertising work to the consuls themselves, some of whom had to create their own marketing showcases with materials requested from the SNI. Individual government agencies wishing to conduct their own marketing events, such as the Portuguese Wine Junta, which had hosted annual wine-tasting events in various Canadian cities since 1955, also recruited the consuls and their staff. They in turn invited Portuguese-Canadian dignitaries, whose smiling faces, well-groomed suits, and evening gowns plastered the pages of the *Correio Português*.[27]

By 1963, 73 per cent of all music records exported by Portugal went to the United States. The main portion, it is safe to say, was *fado* music. Of all Portugal's cultural exports, fado, with its brooding melancholia, tales of sorrow and longing, and other themes associated with saudade, arguably made the greatest impression on North Americans. Although some songs refer to the rural lives of peasants and fishermen, fado is primarily an urban music, filled with images of working-class life in Lisbon and student musings in the university city of Coimbra. While descending from musical traditions of different parts of the world, fado is essentially a mainland cultural expression that later reached other regions of Portugal through mass media. Like other forms of popular culture, its status was elevated during the Estado Novo, which turned it into Portugal's official "national song." Starting in the 1930s, the regime's propagandists took fado from its seedy working-class city venues and moved it onto radio, cinema and theatre stages, making it accessible to the masses. Tourists in Lisbon and Coimbra were given access to live performances at Casas de Fado, which became the formally designated spaces for that bohemian yet increasingly respectable music. With fado's commercialization and professionalization, the state also began policing its lyrics and licensing the musician's careers, thus restricting their creativity and subversiveness.

The rising interest in Portugal among North American travellers was in part stimulated by the international success of fado singer Amália Rodrigues, and the popularity of the song "April in Portugal." Amália's rise to stardom started in the mid-1940s, when she performed at some of the most distinguished music halls in Rio de Janeiro, London, and Paris and made her movie debut in *Capas Negras* (1947). Her international career was propelled further in 1950, when she was invited to tour Europe with other artists as part of a series of shows sponsored by the Marshall Plan. In one of these concerts, the French singer Yvette Giraud heard Amália perform "Coimbra," a song that paid homage to that city and its student life. Giraud later recorded a version of the song under the title "Avril au Portugal," which was later adapted by various popular American musicians, including Les Baxter, Vic Damone, Tony Martin, Louis Armstrong, Bing Crosby, and others. "April in Portugal," whose English lyrics were written by the Irish songwriter Jimmy Kennedy, spoke of finding love in Portugal, where spring, music, and wine inspired a fleeting romance between two lovers that ended on a rainy morning. By 1953, there were nine different recorded versions of "April in Portugal" in the United States; five of them made it to the *Billboard* magazine chart. Following the song's success, Amália performed a Portuguese and English medley on NBC's *The Eddie Fisher Show* while promenading on a set resembling an idyllic European town. Other popular American television shows broadcast similar performances, such as *The Dinah Shore Show*, where the famous Hollywood hostess sang in a setting also made to look like a typical Portuguese town.

Professional migrant musicians in North America also promoted fado as Portugal's national song. Initially, the fado songs in their eclectic repertoires were adapted to meet the popular tastes of mainstream audiences, who swooned at the time over Italian-American crooners and French romantic singers. For instance, the Lisbon composer Frederico Valério, who wrote various songs for Amália, moved to the United States in 1948 and met considerable success on Broadway with his two 1954 musicals *On with the Show* and *Hit the Trail*. While there, he saw his fados "Partir, Partir" and "Ai Mouraria" adapted to "Don't Say Goodbye" and "Star of the Night" by Damone and Fisher. In another case, the Micaelense Mariano Rego, who had captivated Azorean radio listeners with his guitar-playing virtuosity since the age of five, started touring the United States and Canada in 1953. Four years later he settled in Toronto, where he formed the first professional ensemble of Portuguese immigrant musicians in Canada. They became the house band in El Mocambo, one of the city's most famed venues, and played in Portuguese and Spanish restaurants, where they performed traditional Iberian tunes.

Similarly, the Porto native Rui Mascarenhas toured North America and other parts of the world before settling in Toronto in the 1960s. Better known as a romantic crooner, he incorporated more fado into his act as mainstream audiences became more familiar with that genre. Like ethnic businessmen and professionals, immigrant musicians participated in community life in multiple ways. For instance, Rego was a devout Catholic, who donated the Santo Cristo statue that is carried around St Mary's every year. Like some of his fellow immigrant musicians, he was also a football player with the local Portuguese United

4.3 Mariano Rego playing Portuguese guitar, 1980. Courtesy of photographer Gilberto Prioste.

Club. Another example is Francisco Gomes, or "Chico Alentejano," who arrived on the *Saturnia* in 1953. While working as a welder, tunneller, and food vendor, Gomes found time to be one of the FPCC's founders and a member of the anti-fascist PCDA, who used his fado performances to raise funds for people in need.[28]

Fado's acceptance in the United States as the quintessential music of the Portuguese is reflected in the inclusion of performers from Fall River in the 1970 edition of the Smithsonian Festival of American Folklife.[29] These types of recognition bolstered the ethnic pride of Portuguese Americans, who welcomed the prestige attached to their homeland's cultural heritage, which now figured alongside other "Yankee"-approved foreign genres, such as polka, samba, and pasodoble.[30] Building on this popularity, airliners selling flights to Portugal bolstered their marketing campaigns by bringing Portuguese musicians, actors, and radio and television celebrities to do promotional events in North America. On one such occasion, a famous Portuguese radio and television hostess brought by Canadian Pacific Air Lines to Toronto in 1963, complained that she had received no help from the SNI to promote Portugal in Canada.[31] These visits became more regular after Transportes Aéreos Portugueses (TAP) inaugurated flights connecting Lisbon, Ponta Delgada, and New York City in 1968, Boston in 1970, and Montreal in 1971.

Ethnic communities also generated their own impresarios, such as the mainlander Amadeu Vaz in Toronto. Before opening a radio station and record store dedicated to Portuguese music in 1968, Vaz had a typical sojourner experience in the first years after his arrival in Canada in 1955, when he worked as a farmhand, railway builder, hotel worker, and construction worker. In the 1970s, he furthered his role as a transnational cultural agent by bringing some of Portugal's most popular artists to Toronto and other North American cities. His shows sometimes catered to larger lusophone audiences, as was the case with Roberto Carlos's concert at Toronto's Varsity Arena in 1970, which drew around 3,800 to see one of Brazil's most popular singers. Another common cultural import from Portugal were the *revistas* (revues), a form of theatrical entertainment characterized by a mix of comedy sketches, musical acts, folk dances, and some female nudity that was popular among the lower classes. Some of these touring ensembles travelled long distances, such as the *Vedetas Show*, which visited Montreal, Oakville, Toronto, Winnipeg, Edmonton, and Vancouver in 1969.[32] While appreciative of the wide array of performers brought by impresarios like Vaz, who kept expatriate communities up to date with the latest acts in Portugal's show business, immigrant audiences were not shy of criticizing their choices and demanding better value for their money. A *Correio Português* editorial in 1969 echoed what it reported was a common complaint heard from the audience at a *Vedetas Show* about its non-Portuguese finale, where the performers, dressed in tropical outfits, sang the Brazilian song "Cidade Maravilhosa":

> We must not lose sight of the fact that the artists who visit us from Portugal are like ambassadors ... For the final apotheosis of a show for Portuguese living outside the Pátria, it pains us to say that there should have been room for only Portuguese performances, with or without folklore, where the public could partake.[33]

The People's Kind of Popular: Football and Marching Bands

More than ranchos and fado, football (or soccer) was the most consensual form of popular entertainment during the Estado Novo, attracting the most followers across generations, social classes, and regions of the empire. After 1974, it became commonplace to accuse the regime of promoting "the three Fs" – Fátima, fado, and football – as alienating cultural forces or escapist pastimes meant to distract the "masses" from their country's poverty and political repression. This notion has recently been disproved when it comes to football, whose mass appeal predated and was in fact disliked by Salazar. In the 1940s, the regime tried to obstruct football's massive popularity by preventing its professionalization. But by the 1960s, when Portuguese clubs and the national team achieved international fame, the social and cultural power of football as a source of interclass solidarity and national pride became too big for the Estado Novo to alienate.[34] Many of Salazar's opponents were fans of the game, and even Sport Lisbon Benfica – the most popular international football club at the time – had avowed communists in its administration. The same was true in the immigrant communities. For example, Jaime Monteiro, a former factory worker and PCP member from the greater Lisbon area, who became one of the most active opponents of the dictatorship in Montreal and Toronto, wrote for the Lisbon sports weekly *A Bola*, the most circulated Portuguese newspaper in Canada – and likely the United States. Together with other anti-fascists in Montreal, he co-founded a football club in 1965, which was meant to rival the APC's team.[35] In contrast, Portuguese leftists despised ranchos, which they saw as SNI propaganda fuelled by Salazar's ruralist fetish.

In the immigrant communities, football was the raison d'être for many working-class clubs. Since the 1920s, when soccer experienced a "golden era" in the United States, there have been many successful Portuguese-American teams and players competing in state- and nation-wide leagues. One of the all-time best American footballers was the Madeiran descendant Adelino "Billy" Gonçalves, who played for various prominent Massachusetts clubs and the US national team in the 1930 and 1934 FIFA World Cup tournaments. One of the effects of wartime "Americanization" was the decreasing popularity of the immigrant-favoured soccer over "Yankee" sports such as baseball and boxing. Regardless of their cultural specificity, sports remained central for community gathering and civic engagement among Portuguese-American men. For instance, in 1953, the PCU invited the Italian-American boxing champion Rocky Marciano to attend its annual convention in Fall River as a way to attract younger members. In Rhode Island, Portuguese Americans hailed the Cape Verdean boxing champion George Araujo at fights organized by the HGBB and cheered its baseball team in the local rivalry with East Providence's Portuguese-American Athletic Club. With the return of mass immigration in the 1960s, the number of football fans grew once again and old rivals replaced the baseball diamond for the soccer pitch. In New Bedford alone, there were ten

Portuguese-American football clubs competing in 1965. In 1973, nine teams across New England formed the Luso American Soccer Association, which grew to twenty-eight clubs a few years later, all of them made up of Portuguese immigrants and descendants.[36]

As social scientists have noted, for current generations of Portuguese descendants football has been the most popular rallying point for immigrant youth (especially male) to connect with their ancestral homeland and maintain a regular transnational relation with it. This is in large part because it allows immigrant descendants to affirm their ethnic pride regardless of their Portuguese-language competency or cultural knowledge. As Pereira noted, for the Portuguese in France, football has been instrumental in creating bonds between fathers and sons, the first passing their love of the game to their offspring, who are expected to be loyal to their families' favourite club and by extension to the family itself.[37] In North America, where soccer has not been a mainstream sport, such dedication to Portugal's national pastime was a greater and more deliberate marker of ethnicity than in parts of the world where the game was popular. Football also served as an excuse for transnational families to visit relatives in other North American cities, as fans sometimes followed their teams across the border to play their Canadian or American counterparts. Ads like the one in *Correio*, in July 1964, about a friendly match between the Madeira Club of Toronto and the hosting Portuguese United of New Bedford, invited readers to register for group trips to that Massachusetts city and support their local team on the road, reminding them of the opportunity to visit loved ones south of the border.[38]

Football was one of the most cherished and sustained links between emigrants and their homeland. On weekends, men gathered in their community clubs and cafés to listen to broadcasts of matches in Portugal. Torontonians recall the crowds of football fans outside the Portuguese Bookstore in Kensington Market every Sunday afternoon, where the men listened to broadcasts blasted from the store's speakers. The same bookstore was also the principal vendor of Portuguese newspapers – the most popular being the sports titles – and the main ticket office for FPCC's games.

Some emigrant associations were affiliated with major football clubs in Portugal as part of their expanding international network. Toronto's Benfica House, founded in 1969, was the first such official branch to open overseas and one of the earliest social clubs in the community. Occasionally, homeland football teams played exhibition matches for their loyal fans in North America. While sanctioned by government officials, the organization of these visits fell largely on

4.4 First Portuguese Canadian Club players celebrating a goal against the Polish-Canadian White Eagles, 26 April 1970. Photograph by Leo Harrison. CTASC, Toronto Telegram fonds, ASC12877.

the expatriate fans. In 1957, Benfica became the first Portuguese club to play a series of exhibition matches in Newark, Fall River, and New York City. In 1966, already with the Mozambican-Portuguese Eusébio in its roster – one of the sport's all-time greatest and earliest international superstars – Benfica played in Toronto. In 1972 it treated fans in Massachusetts to Portugal's biggest derby, with two exhibition matches against their Lisbon rivals, Sporting Club Portugal. Sometimes these tours were co-organized by ethnic clubs on both sides of the border, as was the case in 1973, when the FPCC facilitated a visit from the Lisboners *Os Belenenses* to Newark and New Bedford after hosting them in Toronto.[39]

In the same way it tried to contain football at home, the dictatorship also intervened in the visits by Portuguese teams to the emigrant communities. In 1955, a group of Portuguese Americans in Ludlow asked the ambassador about the possibility of bringing *Os Belenenses* to play an exhibition match in New England. The embassy responded that the government allowed teams to play abroad only "in circumstances where they are assured a positive result or that they will not embarrass Portuguese sports." Given that North American soccer was "not the strongest," they saw no inconvenience in allowing the match to happen. *Os Belenenses* eventually played in New York City in 1962. The ambassador saw this occasion as a good photo opportunity and accepted the invitation to perform the ceremonial kick-off. Unforeseen by him was the fact that anti-Salazar protesters seized the opportunity to stage a demonstration and embarrass the ambassador, which they did by booing him from the stands during the national anthem and kick-off, while flashing a placard that read: "Godspeed *Os Belenenses*. Portugal yes, Salazar no."[40]

Azoreans too enjoyed football, fado, and to a lesser extent ranchos. But there were other forms of popular culture more meaningful to them that did not figure in the dictatorship's folk propaganda or receive its formal support. Arguably the most popular musical expression in the islands was the philharmonic (or marching) bands. Usually born into band families going back to the nineteenth century, the hundreds of amateur musicians in the islands were taught to read and play music – mostly brass and percussion instruments – in one of the Azores's many ensembles. Outside of dedicated music festivals, where rival bands competed, their main stage was the various outdoors religious celebrations with which Azorean marching bands became associated. Azorean immigrants, many of them trained musicians, brought the islands' love of philharmonics to North America, where they founded new bands. Coincidently, John Philip Sousa, the most famous bandleader and composer of American marching music in the late nineteenth and early twentieth centuries, was a Portuguese descendant. His musical education, however, did not stem from Azorean traditions.[41] Nonetheless, he was another "American" reference that Portuguese ethnic leaders would claim as theirs. But even this cultural icon could not prevent the disappearance of Azorean philharmonic bands by the 1950s, except for a few in Fall River. In the 1960s, Azorean marching bands reappeared in North America, founded by the newcomers. The earliest were Toronto's Senhor Santo Cristo Band, founded at St Mary's Church in 1966, followed by Oakville's Filarmónica Lira Bom Jesus and Fall River's Our Lady of Light Band, both launched in 1969. Fifteen other bands sprouted throughout Canada (five) and the United States (ten) in the 1970s, each starting with about twenty to thirty members.[42] The high costs of starting a philharmonic band, with its dozens of expensive instruments and outfits, led many of them to become formally

4.5 Banda Açoreana marching band of Fall River performing at a procession in the Azores (1980s). *Portuguese Times* photographer, UMass Dartmouth Archives Digital Collections.

associated with local churches, which hosted band practices and music schools in their parish halls. In return, those churches had their own marching band to enliven their religious celebrations and attract more parishioners.[43] Despite their financial and logistic challenges, which explain their relatively tardy emergence in postwar communities, these ensembles, like football teams, travelled to Portuguese settlements on both sides of the border.

I found no evidence of the Portuguese government or its individual diplomats providing or soliciting any kind of support for these bands.

Portuguese-Language Instruction and Community Schools

Heritage-language instruction was the cultural pursuit that most appealed to common immigrants, civic leaders, and ethnic entrepreneurs alike, as it was deemed critical for strengthening the affective bonds between generations and ensuring the ethnic community's survival. The linguistic disconnect between the immigrant generation and its descendants was felt most acutely within family relations. The majority of newcomers encountered English or French for the first time in North America. While English as a Second Language (ESL) classes were readily available in urban centres, working immigrants did not always find time to attend them or lacked the inclination to return to school. The many illiterate were unable to enrol in these classes, since they required basic reading and writing skills. Furthermore, in Canada, government-sponsored ESL classes were available only to "breadwinners," which excluded the majority of immigrant women, who were considered "dependents." Those who attended ESL classes did find them useful for improving their employability and empowering them in various ways. However, they did not provide a level of linguistic proficiency that allowed them to express complex thoughts and emotions. Their children, on the other hand, raised and schooled in the new country, could speak the dominant language(s) fluently but often had difficulty conversing in their parents' tongue. It was also common for children to translate and interpret for their immigrant parents, helping them with doctors' appointments, dealing with financial matters, filling government forms, and taking on other adult responsibilities. In their recollections, Portuguese descendants often lament having been forced to become adults sooner than other children because of their linguistic burden.[44]

Different families had different views and strategies on language retention and acquisition. Some strove to pass on their native language to their children by speaking it at home, usually motivated by a desire to return to Portugal in the future – this was particularly true for mainlanders. Others chose to repress it, seeking instead to assimilate voluntarily, convinced that this would improve their children's chances of success in the new society – an outlook more common among Azoreans. Census data suggest that the latter was not the norm among postwar immigrants. In 1971, 87 per cent of the 85,845 people who answered "Portuguese" as their "mother tongue" in the Canadian census also said that Portuguese was the "language most often spoken at home"; in 1981, the number of native Portuguese-speakers had nearly doubled to 164,615 (24,850 born outside Portugal), though the ratio of home use had dropped to 74 per cent.[45] American census data do not allow us to calculate this ratio, but judging from the growing number of people who answered "Portuguese" as their mother tongue in 1960 (91,592) and 1970 (140,299), and those "foreign-born" who answered "Portuguese" (including Creole) as the "language spoken at home" in 1980 (232,794), that ratio was likely high among newcomers.[46]

As discussed in the previous chapter, one important difference between the two countries was the fact that the majority of Portuguese civic leaders in Canada were mainlanders, while in the United States their over-representation vis-à-vis Azoreans was less pronounced. This led to mainlander dominance over the process of ethnic formation in Canada's homogenizing, multiculturalism policy. It was also true for Portuguese language teachers, among whom there were more islanders in the United States than in Canada. Another significant difference was the fact that newcomers in the United States settled in multigenerational communities, where Portuguese Americans had gradually lost contact with native speakers, and those who remained involved in ethnic civic life increasingly conducted their business in English. That is not to say that Portuguese-American organizations had stopped using their heritage language altogether, or that the old guard had no interest in preserving it. In 1950, the PCU's president expressed concern over what he saw was the youth's apathy at branch meetings, which he attributed to their lack of Portuguese language skills.[47] His concern for language instruction among immigrant descendants may have been more material than affective, since ethnic mutual aid societies depended on the contributions of young, healthy, working members in order to guarantee their survival. However, conducting meetings solely in English seems to have been out of the question, presumably not to marginalize those older members with poor English skills.

Language was also of critical importance when it came to religious services. Portuguese-speaking priests were among the first needs identified by the immigrants. Parishes were also the community spaces where Portuguese linguistic diversity was best represented, given that churchgoers and their priests came from various lusophone backgrounds. Not surprisingly, Portuguese clergymen set up the first community schools in their parishes, starting in Fall River in 1912. By the early 1940s, there were over a dozen Portuguese-language schools in New England, New York, and New Jersey. They ranged from a single teacher dedicating a couple of hours per week at the local club to larger parish schools with buildings and resources fully dedicated to that purpose. One of the largest was run by New Bedford's Our Lady of Mount Carmel parish, comprising twelve classrooms, a hall for 700 people, and a gym.

Inaugurated in 1941, this parish school was the brainchild of the Micaelense priest António Vieira who dedicated much of his time to convincing Irish-American prelates to allow its construction. Bishop James Cassidy of Fall River finally consented to the school after receiving an honorific title from Lisbon in a ceremony prepared by the

4.6 Portuguese-American children and a nun in a classroom at Our Lady of Mount Carmel's Portuguese-language school, New Bedford, Massachusetts, April 1942. Photograph by John Collier. Roman Catholic Portuguese School. Library of Congress.

Portuguese priests in his diocese. The cost of building the school was covered in large part by community donations, to which the IAC later added its own occasional contributions. Although dependent on financial and in-kind community donations, some schools were able to offer free classes, removing what was potentially a prohibitive expense for some working-class families. That was the case with the Luís de Camões School of Newark, founded in 1939 by the Sport Club Portuguese (SCP) and fully financed by the contributions of its members and other community donations. The school's directors often complained about the lack of interest shown by Lisbon, which constantly reneged on its promises to send textbooks and provide legal accreditation. Notwithstanding the paucity of support from the homeland government at this time, some diplomats took a personal interest in the immigrants' efforts to teach Portuguese to their descendants and appealed to Lisbon to dedicate more resources to this cause. They knew that the number of immigrant families with school-age children that actually returned to Portugal was very small, and that the trend was for descendants to stay in North America. Still, the diplomats were supportive of language instruction as a way of guaranteeing the immigrants' national and ethnic identity. For instance, in 1940, the Portuguese ambassador in Washington convinced the IAC to cover the teacher's salary (US$40 a month) at the Portuguese Official School of New Bedford and led a group of "gentlemen" to make a significant donation of school furniture.[48] In the same year, the consul in New York started a community petition requesting Lisbon to grant official status to the Portuguese-language schools in his consular area; this initiative would lead nowhere, owing to the absence of certified teachers. Two decades later, another consul recalled that only two of the "seven or eight" Portuguese schools in New York and New Jersey had survived his government's inaction.[49]

The official accreditation of community schools by the Portuguese government was a priority for those parents who wished to return to Portugal eventually, since it ensured that their children's diplomas were recognized there. Accreditation was also paramount to these schools' survival, as it granted them access to funds from Lisbon and gave them a competitive advantage over non-official schools. In order for community schools to be granted official status, they had to be in operation for at least three years prior to the request, have a minimum of forty students in each of those years, and employ educators with teaching certificates from Portugal. These requirements excluded the majority of immigrant schools in North America, since their inconsistent enrolment numbers did not meet the requirements and certified Portuguese teachers were hard to find.

The lack of interest of Portuguese and American officials for heritage-language education was a source of much disappointment in ethnic communities in the 1940s–50s. Critics repeatedly lamented the absence of Portuguese studies in American colleges and universities and wondered why such a flagrant oversight existed, given Portugal's historical contributions to western civilization. The *Diário* of 24 October 1950, published on its front page a lengthy essay, "The Crisis of Portuguese Language in the US," which resulted in the banning of that issue in Portugal. The author related a conversation he had had with an American professor, who explained that this gap in the curricula was not a dismissal of Portugal's "magnificent language" and "noble people," but a reflection of Americans' "invincible, instinctive repugnance" for the Estado Novo, which the writer compared to a new Portuguese Inquisition.[50]

The situation of Portuguese-language instruction abroad began improving in the 1950s, and more rapidly in the 1960s, when Lisbon started granting more subsidies and textbooks and accrediting more community schools. Portuguese Americans in New England also pressured Congress into changing the policy regarding the immigration of foreign-language teachers in 1951, when they were added to the list of skilled workers allowed to immigrate outside the national quota system.[51] One of the leading advocates of Portuguese-language instruction in the United States was the Azorean immigrant Laurinda Andrade, who, at age seventeen, landed in New Bedford in 1917, where she would find work at a cotton mill. Despite financial difficulties, Andrade completed a master's degree, which would lead her to become an "Americanization" teacher. Later she became editor and director of an ethnic weekly in Newark and secretary in the embassy in Washington, where she contributed towards advancing Portuguese ethnic identity. Determined to introduce the Portuguese language into the American public school curriculum, Andrade returned to New Bedford in 1942, where she began teaching English and French in high school. Two years later she co-founded the Portuguese Educational Society of New Bedford, whose goal was to stimulate cultural exchange between the United States, Portugal, and Brazil. In 1955, Andrade opened a Portuguese Department at New Bedford High School – the first such department in the United States – which she directed until her retirement in 1966.[52]

Interest in Portuguese as a language of business grew among American officials in the postwar period, driven by Brazil's rising political and economic significance. Over five days in October 1950, the Library of Congress hosted the International Colloquium of Luso-Brazilian Studies, bringing together close to 260 delegates from various parts of the world. The main recommendations coming out of this meeting were that Portuguese-language and lusophone literature be taught in American secondary and post-secondary public schools; that Portuguese and Brazilian cultural institutions join efforts to increase lusophone collections in American libraries; that faculty and student exchange programs be established between universities; and that international seminaries and intellectual missions be promoted. Curiously, the Library of Congress, which agreed to collect and disseminate data on lusophone studies in the United States, delegated this task to its Hispanic Foundation.[53] The 1958 National Defense Education Act identified Portugal as one of the countries whose study had been most neglected in the United States and encouraged scholars to advance Washington's knowledge of it. Two years later, after returning from a trip to South America, President Eisenhower stated that relations between the United States and its southern neighbours were at an "all time high," and urged "millions of Americans" to learn Spanish and Portuguese. At around the same time, the State Department designated Portuguese a "critical language." These political incentives led to the inclusion of Portuguese in the curricula of some American schools and universities, which Lisbon saw as an opportunity to improve its influence in the United States. Since the continuation of Portuguese studies in American universities depended on student enrolment, it became imperative for Lisbon to interest Portuguese Americans in learning their heritage language.[54]

Portuguese Americans did not need the homeland's orientation to launch their own language programs. Various ethnic organizations offered scholarships and ran summer exchange programs for youth wanting to study at the University of Coimbra. In 1957, at the founding meeting of the Luso-American Fraternal Federation, the PCU and the Portuguese Benefit Association of California created an Education Committee with that purpose. In 1963, after drawing a positive response from students, the committee launched a comprehensive Portuguese studies program with the University of Coimbra, coordinated by the San Francisco-based Luso-American Education Foundation. Besides awarding scholarships, coordinating student exchanges, and promoting Portuguese-language instruction in California, the Foundation also took on the responsibility of organizing San Francisco's Portugal Day celebrations, beginning in 1966.[55]

In Newark, the Luis de Camões School continued to plead with Lisbon for accreditation. In 1958, its only teacher – a former principal in Funchal – told the ambassador she would be happy to obtain the required teaching certificate but her current situation did not allow her to travel to Lisbon, where the exams were held. Portuguese officials were steadfast in their requisites and withheld accreditation for the school. Nevertheless, the IAC gave the school a US$519 annual subsidy to help with maintenance costs. About a year later, the local consul reported that the school had enrolled seventy students in two classes, a remarkable number in his view, considering that students attended these classes in addition to their regular schooling without receiving extra credits. The consul also noted that Newark's Portuguese were grateful for the subsidy and were enthusiastic about their school. After visiting it during his 1960 tour of the United States, the SNI's director acknowledged that his government should study how to best support Portuguese-language instruction in the emigrant communities in a "realistic" manner. Following the director's advice, the Camões School hired a certified teacher from Portugal. Still, another eight months passed before Lisbon granted it official status, in July 1961. Afterwards, enrolment grew to over 100 students per year, nearly doubling in the late 1960s. In 1970, the SCP received another subsidy, US$7,000, from the IAC to cover part of the expenses of expanding the school.[56]

Other community schools also benefited from Lisbon's new-found interest in its expats, even if its aid remained inadequate. For instance, the Official School of New Bedford received hundreds of textbooks in 1960 and 1962. In the latter year, it also started receiving a US$519 annual subsidy from the IAC. However, by 1963, its building was in such disrepair that it faced the prospect of closing, and in 1966, it reported that some of its students had been forced to drop out because they lacked textbooks. The maintenance costs of its second site, located in a different part of the city, had to be partly covered by the teacher's meagre salary. Worried that the school's potential closure would hurt the regime's "prestige" in the eyes of the emigrants and their fellow Americans, Ambassador Pereira reminded Lisbon that, in the so-called Portuguese capital of America, smaller ethnic groups were capable of maintaining their own schools. Following this dire assessment, in 1964, the IAC increased the school's annual subsidy to US$1,730.[57]

In Canada, Portuguese-language classes were first offered in 1959 to the children of the APC's members in partnership with the Montreal Catholic School Commission, starting with close to fifty students on Saturday mornings. Toronto's PCDA followed in 1960, driven by concerns over the separation of immigrant families, given that some parents sent their children to Portugal to study the language. One of the largest and most successful Portuguese schools in Canada was that of Toronto's FPCC, which opened in 1964. The idea for it came to the club's president, Lourenço Gonçalves, while volunteering with St Mary's St Vincent de Paul Society. There he learned about the social ills affecting the Portuguese in the city and was struck by the lack of communication between parents and their children. Gonçalves then asked for the local consul's assistance in setting up the school and convinced the Gulbenkian Foundation to provide the textbooks. The school opened with eighteen students, one certified teacher from mainland Portugal, and a Micaelense director. The next year, enrolment jumped to ninety-four students, a second teacher was hired, and classes were extended from one to three days a week, held after regular school hours. Four years after it opened, Lisbon accredited the school and granted it a CA$1,882 (50,000 escudos) annual subsidy, while the Toronto District School Board gave it free access to classrooms from Monday to Friday.[58]

With or without funding, the lifeline of these community schools was the teachers who ran them, often at great personal sacrifice. They were mostly women who had been educators in Portugal and they usually took on teaching in North America as a second job. Additional income, however, does not fully account for their dedication to these community schools, since their wages were meagre and often inconsistent. Maria Luz, who had taught at New Bedford's official school since 1950, saw her IAC salary for 1962 delayed for over a year, to the point that the embassy had to advance her money while she waited. In the next year she was entitled to a US$87 monthly wage, which was considerably less than American primary-school teachers received in a week; in addition, part of her wages was used to pay for school expenses. With her husband sick at home, Luz decided to quit that year and move to California, where she was offered a better job. The consul in New Bedford alerted his superiors that no one in that community wanted to take her job because of the low pay. Eventually, he was able to hire Carolina Moniz, a teacher from Funchal, Madeira, where she had been a school principal for over three decades. Shortly after she was hired, Moniz realized that her salary fell well short of the amount of work she was asked to do, and she threatened to quit; she eventually decided to continue, despite the low pay. As the consul later reported, the teacher had a hard time dealing with the students and their parents, which resulted in conflicts where he had to intervene. The main reason behind these conflicts was the fact that Moniz often arrived late to class and showed no interest in teaching at both school sites, as stipulated in her contract. According to the consul, this was because she was "not young and finds herself tired at the end of the day, given that she has to work in a factory." The situation deteriorated as more newcomers arrived, increasing demand for Portuguese classes. In 1965, Moniz asked the ambassador to intercede with Lisbon officials, given that she had not received wages for seven months and her situation was becoming desperate. She added that her pay at the factory was so little that she was forced to ask for aid from people in the community. Following this report, the IAC sent Moniz a cheque for US$893 to cover the first semester of that year. Unfortunately for her, the inconsistency of payments remained unresolved, since by October 1968 she was owed her monthly wage (US$144) for fourteen months straight. The Portuguese ambassador scolded the IAC for its continuing failure to honour its commitments and forcing Moniz to repeatedly ask the local consul for cash advances, which he lent from his own pocket, and for tarnishing the government's reputation among Portuguese Americans.[59]

Various diplomats expressed their criticism of the IAC's funding delays, irregular textbook deliveries, and limited aid for community schools. Similar condemnation of the government's failure to preserve the emigrants' "Portugueseness" was heard at the National Assembly. The IAC in turn restated its commitment to promote Portuguese-language instruction in the United States and reminded its critics that the agency's limited funding prevented it from doing more. The 1965 Ministerial Council finally decreed that diplomatic offices be provided with education counsellors tasked with helping emigrant schools obtain accreditation and pedagogic support from the minister of national education. Momentum was stalled over concerns about the high costs of funding language instruction abroad, but it would take off again in 1968, after an IAC representative had visited the Portuguese communities in France.[60] During the year before, the IAC had begun compiling information on the various Portuguese communities around the world, aiming to draw a comprehensive plan to aid their schools. The consuls were asked to fill out a survey asking for the different kinds of lusophone groups in their jurisdiction, their estimated population, the strength of their Portuguese traditions, how they promoted "Portuguese influences" in their milieu, and the kind of assistance the local institutions had received from the consulates in the past.[61] Responses varied most when it came to each community's cultural and linguistic practices. The consuls in New Bedford and New York City noted that the emigrants largely retained their native language and traditions and had a strong sense of patriotism, regardless of what part of the empire they came from. The consul in Boston, on the other hand, noted that Portuguese Americans in his area spoke very limited Portuguese and most of the traditions they adhered to were tied to the Church. He also noted that Azorean newcomers had very limited "cultural education" and their language was riddled with regional variations. When it came to assessing the communities' needs and priorities, nearly all consuls referred to their efforts at preventing the emigrants' assimilation, which typically amounted to attending social functions and celebrations, assisting in the creation of new associations, and consolidating existing ones. Every consul pointed to the lack of infrastructure needed to meet the high demand for language classes and other cultural services and also how the growing number of newcomer families exacerbated this problem. Finally, they all urged government officials and philanthropists to invest in the expatriate communities and provide them with more resources, schools, libraries, and cultural centres.

At this point, the lusophone scholar community also began pressuring the dictatorship to recognize language as an internationally valuable resource deserving of greater investment. The Luso-Brazilian Symposium on Contemporary Portuguese Language, organized by the IAC in Coimbra in 1968, proved that Lisbon was open to do more on this matter. One of the participants presented a paper on the state of Portuguese-language instruction in the United States, England, and Canada, arguing: "It matters little whether Portuguese is being taught with an Azorean accent (as in the secondary schools of New Bedford, Fall River, Providence) or Brazilian; what is summarily important is that we raise greater enthusiasm for the Portuguese language." For the presenter, there were more reasons to be optimistic about the future of Portuguese studies in North American universities than in high schools. While there were only 8 "official schools" in Massachusetts and Rhode Island and another 2,802 students in Catholic parish schools, 117 American universities accepted Portuguese-language proficiency as an admission prerequisite, 100 offered Portuguese courses at the elementary level and 84 offered them at the intermediate level; 11 offered doctoral programs in Portuguese. In Canada, only 4 universities offered Portuguese-language courses. Altogether, there were an estimated 9,000 students enrolled in Portuguese-language classes at all school levels in North America in 1968. Overall, lusophone scholars were confident that Portuguese-language instruction had a promising future, since the international profile of Brazil continued to grow.[62]

In March 1969, a new law reaffirmed the regime's commitment to educating emigrant children about Portuguese language, history, and geography, and creating primary schools in foreign territory. This initiative was in line with Caetano's mission to "valorize men through education, making them more valuable and productive."[63] However, this policy failed to produce meaningful results in some emigration countries, such as France and Germany. The recently created SNE blamed the IAC's lack of motivation more than a lack of financial resources for this inaction. In March 1972, after the SNE assumed control over this portfolio, Lisbon announced the creation of 200 Portuguese classes abroad.[64] The renewed interest in language instruction among Portuguese officials paralleled the growing trend in the United States towards accommodating linguistic minorities in the public school system and enshrining their rights to "bilingual education." In 1968, Congress passed its first bilingual-education law, included in President Johnson's Elementary and Secondary Education Act, which recognized the need for special programs aimed at immigrant children with limited English skills and provided funding for school districts to run them. Additional legislation promoting the instruction of heritage languages followed in the 1970s, in both American states and Canadian provinces. Because of the organizational efforts of community educators and the meagre yet essential funding from Lisbon, Portuguese immigrants were well placed to benefit from the emerging multiculturalist policies of North American legislators.

Literate Culture: Cultural Societies, Ethnic Media, and Literature

Ironically, efforts to promote Portuguese literate culture in North America received more direct aid from the Estado Novo than did performances of popular culture. In the 1960s, the IAC, the Gulbenkian Foundation, and other government agencies increased their support for Portuguese "high culture" in North America by sponsoring visiting lecturers at foreign universities, offering scholarships to emigrants and their descendants, among other initiatives. A few elitist societies also contributed to disseminating Portugal's erudite culture in the United States, such as the American Portuguese Cultural Society (APCS). Founded in 1962 (though most active after 1966), the APCS was made up of powerful individuals with political and commercial ties to Portugal and its colonies, including heads of banks and major corporations, performing-arts promoters, lawyers, university professors, and a few Portuguese-American leaders. Its funds came from oil companies, banks, business associations, multinational corporations, the Gulbenkian Foundation, and TAP. In the 1970s, Admiral George W. Anderson Jr, chief of naval operations in the American blockade during the Cuban missile crisis and ambassador to Portugal in 1963–6, combined his position as president of the APCS with that of chairman of Nixon's President's Foreign Intelligence Advisory Board. This organization sponsored art exhibits, concerts, lecture tours, and luncheons with illustrious Portuguese guests at distinguished American venues, with the goal of promoting greater understanding of Portugal's education, science, literature, fine arts, and commerce. Although nominally open to the general public, the events made no effort to connect with working-class Portuguese Americans. The APCS was particularly keen on educating American investors about Portugal's ongoing industrial and financial modernization. This aspect pleased Foreign Affairs Minister Rui Patrício, who met with its members in 1971 and to whom he communicated the need to reshape the "defamed" image of Portugal in American universities, emphasize its modernity, and avoid the tendency to focus solely on its past. The minister confirmed his government's commitment to the APCS by granting it a US$3,600 subsidy and appointing a liaison officer at the Portuguese embassy to deal directly with their requests.[65]

A more important venue for preserving and articulating national, linguistic, and ethnic cultures among Portuguese communities was the lusophone media. The community press and radio met the linguistic needs of its immigrant audiences, many of whom had difficulty understanding English or French. They also allowed native Portuguese speakers to engage with the local, national, and international news of the day by use of common expressions, stylistic characteristics, and literary and popular references particular to their linguistic culture. For the most part, that meant linguistic culture from the mainland. Except for the *Voz*, founded by a Micaelense, all of the Portuguese-language press in Canada prior to the 1970s were operated by mainlanders. At the same time, this linguistic bulwark excluded those descendants who did not speak Portuguese, further alienating them from the very communities that ethnic gatekeepers hoped to keep alive. This barrier was aggravated by the grandiloquent style of some newspapers, which often published pretentious editorials on abstract topics, using pompous and sometimes cryptic vocabulary incomprehensible to even the most educated reader. Unsurprisingly, lusophone newspapers incentivized Portuguese-language education in order to maintain their readership, especially in the United States, where mass immigration from Portugal did not re-start until the mid-1960s. For instance, the *Diário* of New Bedford placed a small note on the top-right corner of its front pages, from 1942 until 1959, informing its readers that "Portuguese [was] not a foreign language," since it was spoken by "47 million" people in the Americas (1942), as well as by "65 million" around the world (1948), which made it "a cultural and economic tool of tremendous value" that they should learn and read.

Ethnic newspapers also published sections on arts and literature, including poems and short stories from some of Portugal's most illustrious authors as well as local community writers. There was no shortage of immigrants pouring out their thoughts and emotions in poetry and prose about the country they had left behind and the one they had adopted. For example, Toronto's *Novo Mundo* newspaper published *Os Bastardos das Pátrias* by Lourenço (Gonçalves) Rodrigues – an aircraft mechanic – which became the first novel by a Portuguese writer in Canada about the author's immigrant experience. The same newspaper organized a tour of eastern Canada's Portuguese communities by the distinguished neo-realist author Fernando Namora in 1972. Other works by Portuguese immigrants – almost all mainlanders – appeared in the late 1970s, although a body of Portuguese-Canadian literature began to take form only in the 1990s.[66] South of the border, works by Portuguese-American authors started garnering critical acclaim and commercial success after the Second World War. Not all of them reflected on their Portuguese heritage, for instance, the Trinidad-born Olga Cabral. Others did so at a later stage in their careers, as was the case with the celebrated Madeira-descendant John Dos Passos in his *The Best Times: An Informal Memoir* (1966) and *The Portugal Story* (1969). Yet others made their cultural background the main focus of their writing, such as Alfred Lewis, whose bestseller *Home Is an Island* (1951), about his childhood memories on the island of Flores, and the sequel, *Sixty Acres and a Barn* (unpublished until 2005), about an Azorean immigrant's coming of age in rural California, are forerunners of the 1960s ethnic revivalism in American literature. Still others wrote primarily for lusophone readers about Portuguese topics, such as the Lisboners Jorge de Sena in California and José Rodrigues Miguéis in New York City. Considered one of the most prolific and influential Portuguese authors in the United States, Miguéis self-exiled in New York in 1935 after Salazar's rise to power.There he contributed to various publications, including the journal *Seara Nova*, Portugal's most influential dissident periodical. Outside the grasp of the dictatorship's censorship, Miguéis published a large body of work in the 1950s–80s, much of which dealt with social inequality, the exploitation of migrant workers, uprootedness, and the emigrant's hopeless desire to return to the homeland. He was responsible for introducing various American authors to the lusophone world with his translations and as assistant editor of the Portuguese *Readers Digest*. Miguéis was also involved in Portuguese-American civic and political life as a member of the republican opposition in exile and a community organizer in New York, where he championed the rights of Portuguese and Spanish migrant workers in the press, in public lectures, and through the Portuguese Workers Club, which he founded in East Harlem in 1940.[67]

The Estado Novo also tried to commission works of literature in the United States for propaganda purposes. In 1968, the Casa de Portugal approached Dos Passos to write a book about Portuguese-American communities, which led nowhere; it is unclear why. At the same time, António Eça de Queiroz, the son of José Eça de Queiroz – one of Portugal's most illustrious writers – and former deputy director of the National Secretariat of Propaganda (the SNI's predecesor), was working on a travel narrative on the same topic. After meeting with Queiroz in April, the Portuguese consul in New York expressed concern over the nature of the author's work, since he proposed to "destroy the concept of luso-tropicalism," "a strange idea" in the consul's eyes. Queiroz never finished his work on Portuguese Americans, as he died in May of that year.[68]

These authors could be found in the libraries of ethnic clubs, whose shelves were stocked with book donations from the IAC, Ministry of Overseas, Gulbenkian Foundation, and other homeland institutions, which typically sent national and imperial histories and geographies along with foundational works of Portuguese literature. Curiously, sometimes among the IAC's donations were titles by authors who openly opposed the regime and whose works had been censored in Portugal, such as Miguel Torga (arrested by the PIDE in 1939), José Régio (Delgado's supporter), and Manuel da Fonseca (PCP militant). Subversive Portuguese literature also found its way to Toronto, Montreal, and Newark, circulated by local anti-fascist groups. These activists distributed books, newspapers, communiqués, and other political literature received from fellow exiles around the world, especially from the *Portugal Democrático* newspaper published in São Paulo, Brazil. The chief organ of the leftist opposition in exile, this newspaper had a sizable circulation in North America, thanks largely to the efforts of its agents in Canada, who sold subscriptions to readers across the continent, and even in Africa. In 1960, less than a year after its founding, Toronto's PCDA informed their São Paulo providers that demand for publications in Portuguese and English extended throughout Canada, where "many hundreds of books" had been distributed. Most of the money from these book sales went to support the costs of publishing the *Portugal Democrático*. Those in Toronto and Montreal had greater success distributing subversive literature than their fellow anti-fascists in Newark, who failed to connect with Portuguese Americans.[69]

Conclusion

Forming and performing ethnic or diasporic identities were not priorities for most working-class immigrants, who cared first and foremost about improving their economic situation. But as their children grew up in a different culture and language, as their socio-economic condition improved, as they realized their lives were permanently bound to the new country, as they sought the company of fellow countrymen in community social spaces, as their cultural "otherness" was increasingly rewarded by the host society, and as their homeland encouraged them to preserve their national identity, common immigrants began to acknowledge the need and seek the means to assert their cultural heritage and pass it on to their children. Portuguese diplomats had long believed that emigrants could play an important role in spreading Portugal's linguistic influence in the world and tried to convince Lisbon of the same. But it was only in the 1960s that the dictatorship began taking larger steps towards disseminating Portuguese language and literate culture abroad, even if it fell short of the rising expectations of the growing expatriate communities. Not only did the regime's deficient interdepartmental cooperation hinder a comprehensive, planned approach, the limited resources available to its agencies made it impossible for them to make a sustained commitment to the emigrants' cultural initiatives, even when they met Lisbon's populist criteria. The Estado Novo's stark distinction between "low" and "high" culture was apparent in its cultural investments, which gave more attention to elitist initiatives than those popular ones preferred by the lower-class majority. Still, in some cases, the distinction between popular and literate culture was muddled in the diaspora, since the IAC's mandate to disseminate Portuguese language sometimes led it to partner with working-class organizations in their efforts to build community schools and libraries.

As transnational intermediaries, diplomats were both the lightning rods for the emigrants' criticism and their most adept advocates in Lisbon. Some were genuinely dedicated to the communities they served and undertook tasks that went beyond their expected duties. Most foreign officials admired the emigrants' efforts to preserve their cultural and linguistic heritage and occasionally rebuked their own government for not reciprocating. But despite delivering the Estado Novo's traditionalist propaganda, diplomats were embarrassed by the "peasant" character of ethnic performances and found it at times inappropriate for modern North American audiences. Still, the type of white ethnic pluralism celebrated in North America in the 1960s, which focused on the performative, consumable, and iconic aspects of the immigrant's national cultures or what critics of multiculturalism call "the three-Ds approach" (dress, diet, and dance), was receptive to the SNI's cultural engineering and propaganda. This budding European multiculturalism was convenient for the regime's diplomats, as they strived to unite the expatriate communities, nurture their national identity, and subsequently increase exports. For Portuguese officials and ethnic entrepreneurs, commerce and culture were mutually reinforcing ventures. Nurturing the emigrants' cultural connections with the homeland and celebrating their quaint ethnicity brought economic benefits to these agents, since they promoted a vision of Portugal that corresponded with Lisbon's tourism marketing and cultural exports and buttressed the ethnic markets where they sold their products and services.

The Portuguese case confirms that ethnicity is situational and that primordialism can be a "very powerful *political* device."[70] For the Estado

Novo, primordialism took the form of "invented traditions," such as ranchos. But even these were supported by modern infrastructure such as mass media. This coexistence of traditional and modern was not new to emigrants, who had traded Portugal's rural countryside for North America's industrial cities since the nineteenth century. The tension between modern and traditional customs, material progress and spiritual nurturing, and urban and rural lifestyles was intrinsic to the Janus-like character of most immigrants. On one hand, the vast majority shared a rural background that greatly shaped their world views and whose symbols they cherished when articulating their ethnicity. The rural world, associated with notions of collectivism and spirituality, contrasted with the individualism and materialism of North America's capitalist culture and accentuated the ethnic group's social and cultural distinctiveness. The difficult living and working conditions that most immigrants faced in the host country, paired with the nostalgia for the land they grew up in, often gave rise to romanticized memories of a simpler and more meaningful rural life, to which many hoped to return one day. Their descendants, raised in some of the most modern and urbanized societies on the planet, may not have had the same desire to "return" to the land, but they too were prone to mythologize their rural heritage, which they knew indirectly through their ancestors. This nostalgia, coupled with their host nation's emerging cultural pluralism, made Portuguese ethnic communities fertile soil in which to cultivate Ferro's "politics of the spirit." On the other hand, immigrants were the antithesis of Salazar's traditionalist and ruralist ethos. They chose to abandon their peasant lives, even if temporarily, and pursue their material advancement in foreign modern industrial societies. Those who were less romantic about the past could still remember the difficult living conditions and asphyxiating political culture they had left behind. At the same time, those who were born and raised in the United States but whose ethnic identity remained associated with Portugal – a poor, "backward," undemocratic country in the eyes of the world – welcomed the representation of their "homeland" as a modern and industrializing nation, since that improved their own status as hyphenated Americans.

Portuguese immigrants were able to follow popular culture trends in their homeland. However, they were not empty vessels waiting to be filled with cultural symbols by government agencies and their intermediaries. Indeed, their ethnic performances imitated what was done in Portugal. Yet, the immigrants' ability to improvise with few available resources, and their willingness to borrow from and meet the expectations of host societies, gave a hybrid quality to their cultural expressions. They also produced and circulated a diverse array of literature, including works forbidden in the homeland; drew a significant number of modern artists to their community stages; nurtured their love of football and developed transnational ties with homeland and other diasporic clubs; and generated an impressive number of marching bands and musicians, all with little help from the Lisbon government. The regime's passivity towards the last two reflected its narrow cultural policy, which neglected the mobilizing and unifying (though competitive) power of football and marching bands as presenting opportunities for ethnic and diasporic activity. While the most visible elements of Portuguese ethnic culture in postwar North America largely corresponded with the Estado Novo's propaganda, other cultural expressions, each with its diasporic connections, developed alongside it. All of these attempts to preserve Portuguese language and culture in the diaspora, including those endorsed by Lisbon, relied primarily on the immigrants' volunteer work. Still, the regime's lack of support for Azorean philharmonic bands was symptomatic of its mainland-centric propaganda, which made no mention of island-specific cultural expressions as "national," as it had done for ranchos and fado. In the eyes of host and homeland officials, this omission granted further legitimacy to the supposed representative status of mainlander ethnic leaders. Linguistic standards in mainlander-dominated communities, such as those in Toronto and Montreal, also consolidated the social and cultural exclusion of other regional groups, particularly the Micaelense majority. While mainlanders were over-represented in the United States, their dominance was less apparent, since regional linguistic variations were better represented in secular and parish community schools, where more of its teachers and directors were islanders. Ultimately, immigrants could access the massively attractive cultural offerings of North American mainstream society and ignore or relinquish their ethnic group and its derivative cultural expressions. Nonetheless, there were plenty of Portuguese ethnic leaders willing to drape themselves in the cultural flags waved by the Estado Novo's propaganda. Far from being innocuous, these cultural references were filled with political messages supporting the dictatorship's increasingly imperial-diasporic vision, which I will discuss next.

5 Making Imperial Citizens: Lusotropicalism, Public Memory, and the Multiracial Diaspora

> This pilgrim Nation on foreign land that are our emigrants.
> Adriano Moreira, president of the Lisbon
> Geographic Society, 9 May 1964.[1]

When the Portuguese emigrated to North America they left not only their hometowns, islands, and country but their imperial space as well. Even those who emigrated in the nineteenth century were aware of their nation's global geography. Their schools, churches, press, their very homes in the middle of the Atlantic, all reminded them of Portugal's seafaring history. Moreover, since the 1930s, emigrants were urged by their government to choose Portugal's African colonies as their destination. As metropolitan citizens of a European empire with colonies in Africa, Asia, and once South America, Portuguese emigrants were aware of their "whiteness." But because it was unchallenged, their racial identity was not important to their daily lives in Portugal and therefore never fully articulated. That changed when they arrived in North America and were confronted with an extremely racialized society, where Anglo-Saxons were at the top of a ranking that privileged northern Europeans. Portuguese Americans were one of what James Barrett and David Roediger called the "inbetween" races.[2] Given their physical characteristics, geographic origins, national history, and low-entry status in the labour market, Portuguese immigrants did not fit in the neat, hegemonic white/black framework of American society. This was also true for other southern European groups, such as the Italians (particularly those from the south), whose "full-blooded Caucasian" pedigree was occasionally questioned by white American commentators.[3] Still, their "whiteness" was less ambiguous than that of the Portuguese, given the presence of a sizable mixed-race Cape Verdean community in New

England that self-identified as "Portuguese," hence "European," hence "white." Those who could pass as white tended to avoid racial prejudice by concealing their "Portagee" background and avoiding ethnic identifiers. Like other racialized European groups, those who failed to pass as WASP Americans or wished to retain their heritage culture, engaged in a "process of adaptation and legitimization" through which they became "white" by contrasting themselves with "black" Cape Verdeans and excluding the latter from their ethnic communities.[4] Their historical identity as white European colonizers complicated the racial identity of Portuguese Americans in ways that are perhaps unique among "inbetween" immigrants in the United States. This complexity was reflected in their embrace of imperial myths and tropes and their public support for the Estado Novo's foreign policy whenever it promoted their identity as European, Western, and white ethnic Americans.

After the Second World War, this imperial strand in Portuguese-American identity was roused by a growing anti-colonialist consensus in American public opinion and the international siege on the Estado Novo. In some cases, the political reverberations of Salazar's anti-American stance unravelled the hyphenated identity of Portuguese Americans, pulling them farther away from their heritage. In other cases, Lisbon's propaganda and diplomatic influence heightened the immigrant's pride in their imperial heritage and generated a Portuguese hyper-nationalism not seen before in the United States. The regime was able to shape the political views of a large swathe of Portuguese civic leaders in North America and win their hearts and minds by elevating them to the status of cultural and political "ambassadors" of their homeland's global "imagined community." At the same time, the imperial government's international propaganda now affirmed the mixed racial origins of the Portuguese and their supposed pro-miscegenation brand of colonialism. Gaining momentum at the same time as the civil rights movement, this new multiracial discourse cancelled the earlier attempts of Portuguese Americans to "become white" and prompted them to (re)connect with their "fellow" Cape Verdean Americans. It also urged them to somehow reconcile their colonialist heritage with an endorsement of African-Americans' struggle for racial equality.

Collective memory and historicity are integral parts of diasporic consciousness. From classic to postmodern understandings of diaspora, memories of the "ancestral homeland" have been a central source of "authentic" group identity. Diaspora scholars are aware of this fact but have written largely about memory making from the point of view of private individuals (even if in groups), as opposed to the public institutions that support personal narratives.[5] In order to understand how

"Portuguese" diasporic identities evolved in the United States, it is essential that we unpack the complex intersections of ethnicity, race, and empire and the ways in which public memory framed them. In this chapter I will reveal how the Estado Novo's imperial propaganda helped Portuguese Americans articulate their fluid racial identities as both "white" and "multiracial" citizens and assert their "itinerant" ethnicity as being "rooted" in the New World. Conveniently for the Lisbon government, Portuguese Americans in the 1960s regained interest in their ethnic roots and were therefore more willing to promote the regime's view of empire as an inextricable part of the pluri-continental homeland. Many of its ethnic representatives welcomed the homeland government's attention and accepted the new "ambassador" roles attributed to them. This chapter discusses how this transnational outreach gained momentum within the regime and in the emigrant "colonies" leading to the creation of deliberately diasporic networks with ties to homeland institutions.

Protecting the Empire: Lusotropicalism, International Relations, and the Colonial Wars

After the UN Charter's ratification in 1945, pressure on Portugal to surrender its colonies became more vigorous. Confronted with an increasingly hostile international community, Salazar made changes to the empire's institutional and juridical structures and adopted a new nationalist discourse that eschewed the colonialist terminology of his detractors. The new vision was enshrined in 1951 through a constitutional reform that replaced the term "colonies" with "overseas provinces," now considered parts of a single pluri-continental and multiracial nation. Central to this legal revision was the *lusotropicalismo* thesis proposed by Brazilian anthropologist Gilberto Freyre. In *Casa-Grande & Sanzala* (1933; *The Masters and the Slaves*, 1946), Freyre argued that the racial, geographic, and socio-economic characteristics of Portuguese culture and society made for an exceptional brand of imperialism, which was more humane and adaptable to tropical cultures. As Gerald Bender synthesized, lusotropicalism proposed: "The Portuguese colonizer, basically poor and humble, did not have the exploitative motivations of his counterpart from the more industrialized countries in Europe." Proof of this supposed absence of racism among the Portuguese were their pro-miscegenation tendencies, as seen in Brazil's "large and socially prominent *mestiço* population" and in the fact that Portugal had no segregationist legislation, as South Africa and the United States did.[6] Salazar recognized the usefulness of Freyre's thesis for making his imperial government more palatable to the international community, and he turned lusotropicalism into official doctrine, constantly alluded to in the regime's propaganda and diplomatic relations. More than ever, "being Portuguese" was said to be a universalist vocation, which included a natural aptitude for cultural brokerage and a historical imperative to spread Christian civilization.

The first signs of crumbling within the empire emerged in the 1950s, when nationalist liberation movements, some of them linked to the Soviet Union, appeared in the Portuguese territories in Africa and India. At this point, Salazar began characterizing Portugal's presence in Africa as "Europe's rear" in the battle against international communism. Meanwhile, calls for decolonization increased at the United Nations, the loudest coming from the African-Asian bloc, which in 1960 became the voting majority in the General Assembly – the same year it passed the Declaration on the Granting of Independence to Colonial Countries and Peoples. Despite the growing international opposition, Salazar could still count on the "collaborative neutrality" of important Western allies, such as France, the United Kingdom, West Germany, Spain, Brazil, and the United States. In fact, one of Salazar's most productive friendships was with President Eisenhower, during whose administration the dictator enjoyed his most amicable diplomatic relations. In 1961, Portugal's Western entente began to disintegrate. The election of liberal John F. Kennedy in the United States and of socialist Jânio Quadros in Brazil, both anti-colonialists, removed important support for Salazar. British Prime Minister Harold Macmillan also changed his country's position on European colonialism in Africa, now believing "the winds of change" would inevitably bring the independence of its colonized peoples. Canada and the Scandinavian countries also escalated their criticism of Salazar's dictatorship and colonial policies, introducing moratoria on arms sales to Portugal and calling for its removal from NATO. Salazar's intransigent position on Portugal's feeble empire became even less tenable with the outbreak of the Colonial Wars in Africa following the massacre of 15 March 1961. On that day, nationalist rebels affiliated with Holden Roberto's Union of Peoples of Angola unleashed a series of attacks in the north of Angola, killing a large number of white settlers and their "loyal" black (Ovimbundu) servants. The counter-offensive began soon afterwards with equally senseless violence in the jungles and cities, much of which was carried out by Portuguese civilians, who engaged in horrible atrocities against non-combatant African natives.[7] By mid-1963, the Portuguese army had managed to contain the rebels in Angola, although two new fronts had opened in Portuguese Guinea and later in Mozambique.

With the start of the Colonial Wars, protecting the empire became the chief mission of Portuguese diplomacy, led by the "Africanist" Foreign Affairs Minister Franco Nogueira (1961–9). That task became harder once President Kennedy took office on January 1961, having promised to usher in a new liberal era in American foreign policy, less tolerant of authoritarian regimes and settler colonialism. At this point, the American ambassador to the United Nations was instructed to vote in favour of any Security Council resolution advocating the self-determination of African nations, while the Central Intelligence Agency (CIA) began secretly funding Holden Roberto's pro-Western party – and later the Mozambican leader Eduardo Mondlane – after the African leader met with Kennedy in Washington. In March 1961, after the United States approved a UN resolution calling on Portugal to move towards the self-determination of Angola, a wave of anti-American rallies took place throughout Portugal and some of its colonies with the regime's tacit support; the largest bringing together 15,000–20,000 protesters outside the American embassy in Lisbon. Salazar's supporters accused the Americans of treachery, demanded they be evicted from the Lajes Air Base, and, curiously, called for the emancipation of African Americans. Public anger was amplified by the arrival of disturbing news and images of massacres from the north of Angola. Also fuelling this anti-American sentiment was Washington's collaboration with known opponents of the regime, starting with Captain Henrique Galvão and his Iberian "pirates." In January 1961, a squad of Portuguese and Spanish armed rebels led by Galvão, seized the cruise liner *Santa Maria* off the coast of Curaçao, along with its 600 passengers and crew. Their plan was to sail to Angola to join a group of anti-Salazar settlers and African nationalists and launch an uprising that they hoped would trigger a revolution in Lisbon. For twelve days, Galvão and his men avoided capture by Portuguese, British, and American navy vessels. Three days into the pursuit, the world learned of their freedom-fighting goals and their association with then leader of the opposition Humberto Delgado. To the dictatorship's despair, the British navy subseqently withdrew, while the Americans treated Galvão as a legitimate political representative instead of an "international criminal." The Americans also helped negotiate Galvão's asylum in Brazil, where they safely escorted the ship.

Kennedy also exploited the fissures that had developed within Portugal's military since the start of the colonial wars. Many high-ranking officers had grown fond of the liberal democracies of their NATO allies. In April 1961, the US government enticed the Portuguese minister of national defense and former military attaché in Washington, General Júlio Botelho Moniz – an apologist of decolonization and democratic reform – to lead a putsch from inside the regime. However, their plan failed. In the cabinet reshuffle that followed this attempted coup, Salazar appointed the thirty-eight-year-old Adriano Moreira as the new overseas minister. Moreira's political trajectory had been the reverse of many democratic dissidents, since he started as a moderate opponent of the regime and later became one of its rising stars. Despite being a champion of lusotropicalism and other imperialist myths, Moreira was a conservative reformist who believed the colonies should gradually become autonomous from Lisbon. He removed legal barriers preventing indigenous Africans from becoming citizens, abolished rules allowing the forced labour of black rural workers, and promoted public education, among other changes. Still, these social reforms were secondary to the military defence of Angola, where the efforts to crush African nationalist rebels intensified. Moreira also reopened the Tarrafal prison camp, where many of the Estado Novo's enemies had previously been sent to die and now dedicated to incarcerating African liberation leaders. Salazar originally endorsed Moreira's policies, since they improved the empire's international image and somewhat normalized the political situation in the colonies. Having raised his profile within the regime, the young minister was now seen as a legitimate contender to succeed the aging Salazar, the other candidates being Pedro Teotónio Pereira and Marcello Caetano. However, by the end of 1962, the dictator had ordered Moreira to reverse his policies, which the minister refused to do. Moreira then resigned and dedicated himself to academia, promoting higher education in Portugal and presiding over the Lisbon Geographic Society – a scientific society primarily concerned with providing an intellectual basis for the colonial empire.

Meanwhile, after a ten-year-long diplomatic battle with an unyielding Salazar, India's Prime Minister Jawaharlal Nehru finally abandoned Gandhi's non-violent methods and ordered his army to occupy the poorly defended Portuguese territories of Goa, Daman, and Diu, in December 1961. Despite the Estado Novo's repeated appeals to the United Nations and the United States, there was no resolute international condemnation of India's attack. In fact, Kennedy banned the sale of arms to Portugal and ensured that military equipment sent through NATO was not deployed in its colonies. In January 1962, Salazar expressed his frustration with the United States and threatened to leave the United Nations, and his supporters responded with another wave of anti-American protests in Lisbon. The deterioration of Portugal-United States relations jeopardized the Americans' hold on the Lajes Air Base, whose leasing agreement was up for renewal in 1962. However, after the Cuban Missile Crisis of October 1962, during which Portugal remained steadfastly on the side of its NATO ally, Kennedy's anti-colonialist agenda was superseded by national defence concerns. The conservative-dominated Congress, particularly those congressmen from heavily Portuguese-American districts in Massachusetts, such as Republicans Joseph Martin and Hastings Keith and Democrats John W. McCormack and Thomas "Tip" O'Neill Jr, also pressured Kennedy to reassess his policy towards Angola and improve relations with Portugal. The rapprochement began in late 1962, with the two countries inaugurating a new period of "collaborative neutrality." Afterwards, Kennedy's administration offered Portugal substantial military aid, reduced its conspicuous contacts with African nationalist rebels, and became silent on matters related to Portuguese colonialism. In exchange, Salazar granted provisional access to the Lajes Air Base, until a new lease was finally signed in 1971. Washington's tolerance of its Atlantic ally increased as the American military presence in Vietnam grew in 1961–2, which further reduced the already limited media coverage of Portugal's wars in Africa. Relations with Lisbon improved during the administrations of Presidents Johnson and, especially, Nixon. Henry Kissinger, Nixon's influential national security advisor, stopped supporting African nationalists, partially lifted the arms embargo on Portugal, and embraced that NATO ally as a stalwart defender of the West engaged in a fight against communism on "the African flank."

As for Canada, Portuguese diplomats realized that its foreign policy was now determined more by Washington than by London. Still, despite the Americans' change of heart, Ottawa continued to publicly oppose Portugal's wars in Africa and refused to sell arms to the colonial regime. Nonetheless, according to Stephen Lewis, the leader of the left-wing New Democratic Party (NDP) in Ontario, in the late 1960s over a third of Canadian exports to Portugal were industrial supplies that could be used in war production, along with firearms, ammunition, and explosives. Furthermore, the jet fighters used by the Portuguese air force to drop napalm bombs on Angola, Mozambique, and Portuguese Guinea were made in Canada.[8]

The short-lived "liberal spring" that followed Caetano's ascension to power in 1968 failed to democratize the regime at the same time as it fought its wars in Africa. When Caetano backtracked from his reformist project in 1970, the many malcontents inside and outside the regime recognized that they had lost their last chance for a peaceful political resolution to the Estado Novo's antiquated rule. The colonial wars would last until 1974. In the end, it was the dictatorship's resolute defence of the empire that precipitated its fall, though not without first claiming the lives, limbs, and sanity of tens of thousands of soldiers and civilians on both sides of the conflict – in addition to the many landmine victims in its aftermath – and leaving a legacy of political turmoil in its former African colonies.

"Black Europeans" or "White Africans": The Racial Complexities of Portuguese and Cape Verdean Americans

In the United States, where race touched every aspect of society and only "whiteness" granted full access to the so-called merit-based economy, the notion that the Portuguese favoured miscegenation and were historically of mixed race initially was not advantageous. Like other Europeans, Portuguese immigrants had long learned to assert their whiteness and shed their ethnicity as a form of self-preservation and self-promotion. One common strategy was to Anglicize their names, "Perry" replacing "Pereira," "Silver," "Sylvia," or "Wood" replacing "Silva," among other examples. Southern and eastern European immigrants occupied an ambivalent position in America's racial hierarchy, as defined by policymakers, the courts, employers, labour unions, and overall popular opinion. Pseudo-scientific studies validated these popular prejudices, for example, Donald Taft's 1923 doctoral thesis at Columbia University, which attributed the many social ills afflicting Portuguese families in New England to their "Negroid blood." While Taft concluded that the Portuguese were hardly suited to America's urban industrial society, they were still better equipped than the more "negroid" proletarians.[9] This "inbetweenness" was also reflected in the recurrent stereotypes ascribed to the "Portagee," including in American literature – as in Herman Melville's *Moby Dick* and John Steinbeck's *Tortilla Flat*[10] – ranging from the well-meaning "honest," "hard-working," "law-abiding," and "family-oriented," to the demeaning "dull," "docile," "temperamental," and "reluctant to change."[11]

The racial identity of Portuguese Americans was complicated further by the presence of Cape Verdeans in New England.

A people of mixed-race descent, Cape Verdeans were the Portuguese empire's own "inbetween" people: neither fully African nor fully European. Educated in Catholic seminaries and Protestant missions, many Cape Verdeans occupied intermediary roles in the Portuguese colonial administration, which further distinguished them from continental Africans. This racial and ethnic "inbetweenness" continued in the United States, where Cape Verdeans migrated not as "black Portuguese" or even necessarily as "Cape Verdean," but as Catholic, lusophone, Portuguese nationals. Regardless of racial perceptions, Cape Verdeans landed in the United States holding Portuguese passports, under Portugal's immigration quota, and were therefore legally

Making Imperial Citizens 191

5.1 Cape Verdean cranberry bog workers in Falmouth, Massachusetts, September 1911. The photographer, Lewis W. Hines, noted: "Housing 7 Portuguese in bunks. Dirty clothes and garbage on the floor. There were bunks for 12 persons. The shack was 10 × 12 feet and 8 or 9 feet high." Library of Congress, nclc 00154.

"Portuguese."[12] However, their movement became a small stream after the restrictive immigration policies of the 1920s and would remain limited after the 1965 act, since Portuguese colonial bureaucracy made it nearly impossible for average Cape Verdeans to obtain emigration visas. Still, the legal status of those who made it across the Atlantic not only confounded American authorities but also thwarted some of their racist policies, such as the ban on African immigrants from becoming US citizens (lifted in 1952).

Whether moved by a cultural affinity for their European colonizers or by a strategic interest in joining a "racially fluid" group that allowed for "the greatest malleability in their racial classification,"[13] Cape Verdean immigrants presented themselves as Portuguese Americans (a similar assertion of whiteness existed among Portuguese-Goan immigrants in Australia).[14] At the same time, like other European immigrants, Cape Verdeans distanced themselves from *pretos* (black Americans), realizing that their easy association with "blackness" was detrimental. Following the same logic, European Portuguese excluded Cape Verdeans from their neighbourhoods, churches, clubs, and workplaces in order to protect their own whiteness.[15] Over time, Cape Verdeans formed associations and parishes where they practised their Kriolu (Creole) language and Catholic faith and maintained transnational ties with their homeland. Still, until the 1960s–70s, their organizations' chief concern was asserting their "Portugueseness." For instance, Brooklyn's Society for the Perpetuation of Portuguese Heritage, a Cape Verdean association restricted to "individuals of Portuguese descent" with no less than high school education, strove to "cement closer relationships, preserve customs, culture and traditions, promote activities and cultural development of people of Portuguese heritage" and "acquaint [them]selves with the achievements of the people of Cape Verdean descent, both here and abroad."[16]

State bureaucrats in the 1950s remained unsure about how to categorize Portuguese Americans in their rigid racial matrix. In the American south, where segregation was most virulent, this confusion resulted in curious legal compromises. In January 1958, the *Virginian-Pilot* reported that "Portuguese" children in the small township of Gaston in Northampton County, North Carolina, were being segregated based on a "century-old stigma." As the press described it, there were sixteen destitute rural families in Gaston thought to be descendants of white migrants from the north, Native Americans, and free blacks, who had mixed at some time in the antebellum period. Their relation to Portugal, however, was a mystery, as their ancestors had left no written records. Despite being Caucasian, Methodist, and having Anglo surnames, these "Portuguese" had long been ostracized by the county's "pure whites," who banned "Portuguese" children from attending white-only schools in 1923. Because "Portuguese" parents refused to send their children to black-only schools, the state allowed them to build a Portuguese-only primary school in Gaston, which provided classes only up to the eighth grade. The *Pilot*'s reporter interviewed the school's teacher, Miss Osceloa Crew, a "pure white" Northampton resident, who tried to instil in her students a sense of pride in their supposed heritage by teaching them about Vasco da Gama, Ferdinand Magellan, and other heroes of Portugal's maritime explorations.[17] The press in Portugal and the *Diário de Notícias* in New Bedford ran this story for months, expressing outrage over the ignorance of North Carolina's legislators and the "misuse" of the label "Portuguese." The *Diário*'s director, João Rocha, suspected these families had no real connection with his own ethnic and religious ancestry and were "simply an unfortunate group of people, without roots or history, living adrift in a hostile world."[18] In a letter to the *Pilot*'s editor, he asked:

> Are they really Portuguese? And, if they are, they certainly belong to some racial segment. If they came from continental Portugal, the Azores or Madeira and their fathers were Portuguese, they are Caucasians – WHITE ...
>
> However, there are Portuguese CITIZENS who might well be negroes. They came from Portugal's African territories ... There are, too, Portuguese CITIZENS who [are] Mongolians (the "yellow" race). They obviously must come from Portugal's Asiatic colonies
>
> ...
>
> What may be difficult for [North Carolina's legislators] to comprehend is that Portugal and the Portuguese are proud of them all.
>
> That is why Portugal gives to all its colonials – whether it be native of Asia or the negro from Africa – the same rights and privileges that the white enjoys in his own native mother country.[19]

This was not yet an "evasion of whiteness,"[20] since Rocha pointed to the supposed multiracial make-up of Portugal's imperial citizenship, not the mixed-race origins of "white" Portuguese, as celebrated by lusotropicalism. In Rocha's view, all the schoolteacher had to do to boost her students' ethnic pride was tell them about the feats of "Caucasian Portuguese mariners" and the contributions of famous Portuguese Americans to their nation's history, such as the Revolutionary War hero Peter Francisco or the composer John Philip Sousa. Meanwhile, scholars gathered at the Lisbon Geographic Society debated the origins of these Gaston families and arrived at the simplistic conclusion that, because they were born in North Carolina, they were not Portuguese but American.[21]

Infuriated Portuguese Americans in the north sent letters to their political representatives complaining about the abusive and demeaning use of their ancestry for segregationist purposes in the south. In Ambassador Fernandes's opinion, Lisbon should not falter in the face of this "insult." He proposed referring the case to the State Department and lobbying congressmen from North Carolina and Northampton County to fix this problem.[22] To learn more about these "Portuguese" families, the ambassador sent his press officer, Bernardo Teixeira, to

5.2 and 5.3 (above and opposite) Bernardo Teixeira with teacher Osceloa Crew and "Portuguese" students in Gaston, North Carolina, March 1958. Photographer unknown. HDA, PEA 71.

Gaston to investigate. After spending a week there, Teixeira described his interaction with the children as an "unforgettable experience," noting with irony that some had light blond hair and blue eyes, and looked "whiter" than their "pure white" teacher, who had brown eyes and darker skin.

The county school's superintendent prohibited Ms Crew from speaking to the press and did not permit photos being taken of her students. Still, she agreed to speak with Teixeira and that the children could be photographed for the embassy's records. According to Teixeira, some of the children refused to have their photos taken, while others timidly accepted on the tacit understanding that doing so could help them improve their situation somehow. As Ms Crew explained, the *Pilot*'s story had hurt the students, as did anything that drew attention to their "Portuguese" label, since it reminded them of their supposed "inferiority and isolation." In fact, every time she tried to teach the children about Portuguese history, they recoiled in their seats. She once invited a former missionary in Brazil to give a presentation on Portuguese architecture in that country, but many of the children cried in shame and some even skipped class the next day. The teacher added that the press coverage "horrified" the parents, who worried that those relatives who had managed to escape the "Northampton siege" and were now living as "normal whites" in other states might be exposed.

According to the "semi-legendary" memories of local elders, these families descended from crew members of a Portuguese merchant ship wrecked on North Carolina's shores sometime before the Civil War, who later settled in Northampton County and had sexual relations with black slave women and the Creole daughters of white plantation owners. Teixeira believed instead that they were descendants of Portuguese labourers who migrated from Pennsylvania in the early twentieth century to work on the building of a nearby canal.[23] Whatever the case, none of these individuals had a connection to Portugal, which they knew little about. Teixeira's report was very critical of the "stupidity" of American southerners, who forced the "Portuguese" of Northampton to live in constant fear and suspicion, and to abhor that national label that "isolates them from the world like lepers in the Middle Ages."[24]

Following Ambassador Fernandes's appeals, the State Department official Charles Elbrick – who became the American ambassador to Lisbon soon after – pressured Northampton's state representatives to remove the term "Portuguese" from their segregationist legislation and use some other designation to discriminate against those Gaston families. The State Department alerted the governor of North Carolina to the negative international implications of legally discriminating against a group of people on the grounds of their national heritage. The governor replied by noting that the old legislation barring "Portuguese" from white-only schools had been revoked, and that efforts were underway in North Carolina's legislature to include this group in the same electoral lists as whites, which finally happened on 19 June 1959.[25]

While more Portuguese-American leaders asserted their ethnicity in the 1950s, their communities were still fairly reluctant to follow suit. This situation changed after the Capelinhos volcano crisis and the return of Portuguese mass migration, which coincided with the rise of African-American cultural nationalism and white ethnic revivalism. According to the Portuguese studies scholar Francis M. Rogers, the arrival of these newcomers created two camps in these ethnic communities: the *orgulhosos* (proud), those who held a positive view of their national heritage and racial identity; and the *envergonhados* (ashamed), those older generations who had learned to hide their ancestry and its questionable whiteness. He argued that newcomers and their predecessors differed further in that the first had more formal education – though still below the American average – and came from a modern Portugal, where racial diversity was part of the official discourse. Rogers claimed that these *orgulhosos* were appalled by the extent of racial segregation in the United States and were offended by the assimilationist proclivity of older immigrants.[26] As one newcomer, who arrived in 1966, told a reporter from Cambridge's *Harvard Crimson* in 1974: "I have learned [since coming] here that sometimes people have been ashamed that they are not from the U.S ... The 'mixing pot' ideal is not good. We can gain from living in the U.S., but we have something to offer too." Another immigrant who had lived in the United States since the age of nine said: "If I'm going to be called anything, I'd like to be called Portuguese, because I don't believe in giving up a nationality and taking on another one. There is no American heritage. I felt that I would be giving up something by becoming American."[27]

Since the nineteenth century, European immigrant elites had promoted a sense of pride in their group's historical roots and articulated a distinct ethnic identity integrated in American nationhood. Portuguese-American intelligentsia had been engaged in various memorialization campaigns since the 1940s, seeking official heritage status for those Portuguese navigators who explored the Pacific and Atlantic coasts of North America in the sixteenth century. By weaving their national narratives into Euro-American and Euro-Canadian foundational myths, ethnic leaders sought to free themselves from the stigmas of "foreignness" and "dual loyalty," and to secure their group's full membership in their colonialist host nations. One of the most prominent of these ethnic heritage champions was Manuel Luciano da Silva of Bristol, Rhode Island. A spirited and polemical proponent of the Portuguese pre-Mayflower settlement thesis, Silva dedicated his life to preserving and commemorating the Dighton Rock's inscriptions and obtaining official assent from politicians and scholars of the supposed discovery of the American northeastern Atlantic coast by the Azorean navigator Miguel Corte-Real.[28] Silva was a divisive figure in the Portuguese-American community because of not only his flamboyant personality and conceit, but also his regular tirades against the Estado Novo and its diplomats, whom he accused of incompetence, discrimination, and lack of concern for the emigrants – even though Silva regularly requested and occasionally received support from Lisbon. Like other Portuguese-American leaders, Silva reconciled his fervent Portuguese patriotism and support for the lusotropicalist empire with his equally proud commitment to the foundational American values of liberty and democracy. Throughout his life he was heavily involved in Portuguese-American affairs and spearheaded a number of social causes, including curbing Cape Verdean discrimination. Under his presidency, Rhode Island's Portuguese American Civic League first opened its membership to "non-white" individuals in 1966. Four years later, as the Portuguese American Federation's president, Silva launched a campaign in the lusophone media calling for Lisbon to abolish the costly visa requirement for Americans travelling to Cape Verde. According to him, this requirement unfairly targeted Cape Verdean immigrants who were "as much if not more Portuguese than those immigrants from the Mainland, Madeira or the Azores."[29]

Portuguese heritage advocates in North America benefited from the imperialist discourse and political capital provided by the Estado Novo's propaganda and pushed by the diplomatic corps. For instance, in 1963, Ambassador Brazão, a prolific historian of Portuguese diplomacy and maritime explorations – including the explorations of navigator Gaspar Corte-Real, said to have reached the coast of Labrador in 1501 – was received with exceptional honours by Newfoundland's Premier Joseph Smallwood and his recently confederated provincial government. Speaking at St John's Rotary Club, Brazão educated his audience about the "true" history of Canada's "discovery" and Portugal's role in it, adding:

> [The Portuguese empire is] the crowning of our sociological ideal ... a multi-racial formation of homogeneous groups of different colours but interrelated in a way analogous to the colours of the rainbow. This approach did not imply ... compulsion, nor imposition under duress or otherwise, of the will of one power or nation over other ethnical [sic] groups, but was done with open arms, it was the moral and physical elevation of the aborigines whom we found ... in the primitive state. This is the WORK of Portugal, a great enterprise of social equality in the approximation of races.

He then asked Canadians to endorse Portugal's historical mission, which depended on

> the comprehension and understanding of the Western world, which must realize that the ... labels – colony, colonization, anti-colonization – do not rightly apply to us ... We are preparing a new chapter in the History of the World ... Everything depends on us. The winds of history must not make us drift off the true course.[30]

In Brazão's view, to be ignorant of Portuguese history was not only to be ignorant of Canadian history but also to jeopardize Western civilization, of which both countries were stakeholders. Two years later, in 1965, accompanied by Toronto's Rancho da Nazaré, Portuguese ethnic leaders from Canada and the United States, a group of White Fleet fishermen, and various Canadian dignitaries, Brazão unveiled a statue of Corte-Real in front of Newfoundland's new legislative assembly, as a gift from Portugal to the people of St John's. Smallwood, whom Brazão commended for having the courage to publicly declare his admiration for Salazar, accepted the gift from Britain's "famous old ally," asserting Newfoundland's ancient link with continental Europe.[31]

On another occasion, Ambassador Garin delivered a speech during the 1964 Cabrillo Day festivities[32] in Sacramento, celebrating the "discovery" of California by the supposedly Portuguese navigator João Rodrigues Cabrilho in 1542. Garin offered a warped Cold War interpretation of Cabrilho's landing, arguing that, since "Russia's sinister expansionist designs were later witnessed in the north, in Alaska, rather than on California's shores, one can say that we owe to Cabrilho the securing of California for the Western World ... and that he came to serve well the future cause of free men with his superhuman exploit." According to Garin, the Portuguese empire was defined by a deep respect for "human dignity and social justice and for equal rights for all, regardless of race, creed or colour," and was "a fountain of inspiration to those countries who criticize us and are looking for solutions for some of the problems besetting them." This indirect reference to America's racial conflicts certainly caught the crowd's attention, which had seen the Civil Rights Act introduced only a few months before.[33]

Most Portuguese immigrants and their descendants welcomed celebrations of their homeland's Western heritage, which inflated their ethnic identities. The largest such commemoration was the quincentennial of Prince Henry the Navigator in 1960, which involved a large number of events across the United States, backed by the Portuguese government. Some of these memorials were held outside the immigrant communities, which testifies to Henry's historical significance in the eyes of Americans. Still, the main celebrations took place in the Portuguese settlements in New England and Greater New York City, where local committees were tasked with organizing the festivities, supported by Lisbon and its diplomats. In Boston, the week-long commemorations in October started with a pontifical high mass celebrated by Bishop Thomas J. Riley at the Cathedral of the Holy Cross. On the final day, a parade of Portuguese-American marching bands, fraternities, parish groups, and various American civic organizations marched towards Park Square in downtown Boston, attracting an estimated 50,000 people. The festivities ended with a banquet attended by 800 patrons at the Sheraton Plaza, among whom were various Portuguese and American dignitaries. Similar events happened throughout October and November, in Newark, New York City, Providence, New Bedford, and Fall River. The celebrations concluded in the latter with a parade that ended at the Prince Henry statue, which had been unveiled in 1940 by Congressman Joseph Martin Jr, who now attended this event alongside his personal secretary, Ernesto Ladeira, Fall River's quincentennial committee chair.[34]

But the most popular celebrations of Portuguese seafaring heritage in North America were the many visits of Portugal's navy ships to northeastern city ports. For instance, in 1967, thousands of Portuguese Americans in New York City, Boston, Bristol, Fall River, New Bedford, and Newark took the time to see the *Sagres*, one of Portugal's most esteemed symbols of nautical might. As Newark's *Novos Rumos* newspaper noted, it was the chance to mingle with the young sailors that made these visits memorable:

> The brief stay of the school-ship SAGRES ... was not a mere courteous visit, like those of diplomats and their stiff, ironed shirts, which muffle the pulsating heart in their chests. It was a visit of brothers, of people we know, or that we came to know for a few moments, and from which affinity, friendship, caring, and even love was born. Because of this, at the sight of this handful of youth ... departing, we feel in our soul the sweet and hurtful sting of saudade.[35]

The ancestral identity said to be conveyed by these young bachelors and the process by which they aroused patriotism among young Portuguese Americans was highly gendered, as was made clear by the *Diário*'s story on the *Sagres*'s visit to New Bedford:

> Needless to say, a vast percentage of those waiting for the arrival of the ship were young Luso-American ladies, in which an ancient instinct seemed to have awakened the same feelings that agitated the chests of their great-great-grandmothers, when the rugged sailors of bygone times returned from India.
>
> The "Sagres's" farewell ... was a "sorrowful" one for those "teenagers" of Luso blood who, hugging their Manel or João Marinheiro, whom they met only hours before, cried copiously, as their ancestors must have cried at the departure of the Gamas and the Cabrals.
>
> It is known that Portuguese women have always had a special "crush" for the sailor's uniform, and the tanned and athletic boys of the "Sagres" proved, in the few hours they spent ashore, that they remain the worthy

descendants of the "valiant little Portuguese," who have parented and loved in the four corners of the known earth.[36]

To the delight of Estado Novo officials, illustrious American guests addressing the crowds at Portuguese-American heritage celebrations often regurgitated Lisbon's imperialist mantra by referring to Portugal's contributions towards advancing Western civilization. During the proclamation of Taunton's "Dighton Rock Day" in 1951, Joseph E. Warner, a Massachusetts Superior Court judge of mixed Portuguese descent, contended that Portugal had "never subjected the inhabitants of those [imperial] regions to its political or military system against their will," and that "the ideals of Prince Henry [the Navigator] demonstrated the superiority of the spiritual over the material power," in his efforts to promote Christianity and human science against the "weight of the mahometans against our civilization." He went on to say that the Corte-Reals carried this civilizing mission to North America, 140 years before the arrival of the first white settlers.[37] The California government also indirectly endorsed Lisbon's imperial administration by appointing Sarmento Rodrigues, the former governor of Portuguese Guinea and Mozambique, and former minister of the colonies, as the 1970 Cabrillo Festival's commissioner general. The state legislature acknowledged that California's prominent position in the country was "attributable in great measure to the strength and continuing contributions of Californians from many foreign lands ... The oldest and most significant of these contributions [being] those of the Portuguese people and their great nation."[38] To mark the state's bicentennial anniversary, Lisbon sent two navy frigates to be part of a commemorative flotilla. Governor Ronald Reagan expressed his appreciation for Portugal's contribution and the opportunity provided by their "mutual interest" in Cabrilho to engage in "an exchange of dialogue and ideas in the name of friendship."[39] Lisbon was all too happy to maintain an open dialogue with such powerful American politicians, especially when they shared the Estado Novo's views on colonialism, as was the case with Reagan.[40]

In the 1960s, black activists, such as Stokely Carmichael and Malcolm X, urged their brethren to look to their African roots as a source of cultural pride, identity, and political strength that would help them overcome their historical anonymity and sense of inferiority and redefine their place in American society. Their calls for an African-American ethnicity were embraced primarily by black youth, who strove for more than just integration into the inherently racist liberal capitalist society, and wished instead to change its political and economic structures. Ironically, the voluntary assimilation into black America by Cape Verdean youth occurred at the same time as white ethnic youth began to de-assimilate from WASP America. The emergence of African-American cultural pride and the struggles for independence in Portuguese Africa further complicated the racial consciousness of Cape Verdean Americans. While the majority of Portuguese immigrants and descendants had deliberately joined "white America" during the Second World War, Cape Verdeans had been subsumed into "black America." Those fighting in the US armed forces were often placed in segregated regiments, where they interacted with black Americans from across the country and experienced racism from "a wider society that did not know or care about their ethnic identity," as Marilyn Halter noted. In the 1960s, despite having little contact with their homeland, the Africanist message of the anti-colonial and socialist leader Amílcar Cabral and his African Party for the Independence of Guinea and Cape Verde (PAIGC) was particularly powerful for American-born Cape Verdeans, who had little affinity with the *yambob* (white Portuguese) – their former colonizers and current labour market rivals. Intergenerational conflicts between those "staunchly Portuguese" Cape Verdean immigrants and their increasingly African-American children intensified in this period.[41]

Portuguese diplomats had to tread carefully in this racial minefield when dealing with New England's two "Portuguese" communities. Still, the racial sensitivities of European Portuguese did not stop Lisbon officials from harnessing the assertive "Portugueseness" of Cape Verdeans and obtaining their support for the empire. In 1960, Cape Verdeans in Bridgeport, Fall River, and Brooklyn joined in the Prince Henry quincentennial commemorations, which also celebrated the discovery of the Cape Verdean islands.[42] The event gave the Portuguese consulate in New York the opportunity to reconnect with that community, from which it had grown apart over the years. Helping negotiate this rapprochement was the president of the Society for the Perpetuation of Portuguese Heritage, José Monte, who in turn recruited the consul's help in securing the Gulbenkian Foundation's aid for building libraries in Cape Verdean-American community halls. Along with sponsoring libraries, the Lisbon government also sent a photography exhibit and films showcasing its colonial territories, produced bilingual booklets about the islands, and promoted nostalgia tourism among its emigrants. The Cape Verdean Society also sought the regime's help celebrating Kriolu culture, as was the case in 1967, when the SNI covered the costs of shipping a monument to the poet and composer Francisco X. Cruz (or B. Leza) – paid for by Cape Verdeans in the United States – destined for his gravesite in São Vicente island.[43] Another example of collaboration with Lisbon was the Cape Verdean Beneficent

Association's annual debutante ball in New Bedford. Portuguese diplomats attending it often noted the heightened "Portugueseness" of Cape Verdeans. As was common with other Portuguese-American beauty pageants, the "Queen of the Ball" and her mother were awarded tickets for free flights to mainland Portugal by the Lisbon government, which they received from the diplomats' hands.[44]

Despite the amicable relations between Portuguese officials and Cape Verdean immigrants, this connection became increasingly ambivalent after 1961, as reflected in the ambiguous solidarities of its most prominent leader, Massachusetts Assistant Attorney General Roy F. Teixeira. Portuguese diplomats believed him to be "very easy to influence" and regularly sought his collaboration.[45] In July 1961, Teixeira joined a Portuguese-American delegation to Washington that was organized by the American public relations firm Selvage & Lee with Lisbon's support. They met with three Massachusetts congressmen and had a very brief audience with President Kennedy, to whom they expressed their opposition to the White House's position on Portugal's "overseas provinces." Following this visit, the delegation released a press statement prepared by Selvage & Lee criticizing Kennedy's administration for voting with the Soviet Union at the United Nations on the Angola issue and denouncing the communist international propaganda that characterized Portuguese colonizers as being racist. The communiqué highlighted the fact that one of the individuals in the delegation was "a Portuguese of Negro extraction," which supposedly testified to Portugal's racial equality – a reference to the lawyer António Cardozo, another prominent Cape Verdean American.[46] At the same time as he endorsed the regime's colonialist project, Teixeira tried to mobilize support for the PAIGC in New England. However, unlike Amílcar Cabral, he believed that Cape Verde should remain within Portugal's political sphere after its independence, in a kind of postcolonial commonwealth, where each member nation would have "the same citizenship, interdependence, common commerce and defense, so we can maintain our culture in a free regime."[47] Simultaneously, Teixeira was affiliated with Newark's Committee Pro-Democracy in Portugal, and was a personal friend of its chairman Abilio Águas, who believed, like Henrique Galvão, that the "tribal peoples" of Portuguese Africa would not be prepared for self-rule until democracy was reinstated in Lisbon. In December 1962, Teixeira was able to discuss his views with Cabral during the latter's visit to the United Nations and tried to convince the PAIGC's leader to lend his support to the Portuguese liberal opposition. Teixeira was disappointed to learn of Cabral's re-Africanization program and his party's intention to cut ties with Portugal altogether.[48]

Whether inspired by the Civil Rights movement or lusotropicalist propaganda, Portuguese Americans began changing their racial attitudes in the 1950s–60s. Various ethnic organizations dropped their exclusionary membership policies and allowed non-whites to join in. This overture was not always volunteer, as was made clear by the PCU secretary general's remarks on a bill tabled at the Massachusetts legislature in 1955, forcing mutual aid societies to abolish membership restrictions based on race or religion: "If such law is approved ... we will be forced to accept as members any individuals who want to be part of the [PCU], be they black or yellow, Greeks or Australian, Catholic or Muslim ... And help us God, they could also force us to accept the blind and crippled!" Despite its initial resistance, the struggling PCU finally allowed Cape Verdeans to become members in 1959.[49] The reluctance of "white" Portuguese Americans to welcome the "black" Cape Verdean counterparts in their midst was hard to reconcile with lusotropicalism's profession of racial equality. American journalists noticed this ambiguity, along with the "civil rights limbo" in which "mixed-blood" Cape Verdeans found themselves. In 1968, the *Washington Post* interviewed Manuel (Manny) Costa, a fifty-year-old Cape Verdean descendant and civil rights advocate in New Bedford, who commented: "The Cape Verdean has a pathological fear of being associated with blacks ... so that the bulk of his life, his energies and resources are spent defending his 'white' origins." However, he had no doubts: "I'm black and I know it." Costa recognized that Cape Verdean culture, with its Catholic faith, pidgin dialect, and island cuisine, was distinct from other black minorities. Still, they all had one thing in common: "low incomes and a high number from each group on the city's welfare rolls."[50] Indeed, the poor living conditions that black residents were subjected to was one of the main catalysts of the wave of "race riots" that assailed various American cities, including Newark in July 1967 and New Bedford in July 1970.

Newark was the stage for one of the most intense American "race riots" of the 1960s, resulting in twenty-three deaths (the majority killed by state police and the National Guard), over 700 injured, and close to 1,500 arrests over a period of five days. The Portuguese and Italian neighbourhoods were the least affected by the massive street clashes between the city's black population and the state police and military, protected as they were by armed citizen patrols and the National Guard. After the riots, the "white flight" to the suburbs accelerated, leaving Portuguese and Italians as the only two large European communities in inner Newark. Later, the city's Portuguese became the target of anti-colonial campaigns led by local black activists, such as the writer Imamu A. Baraka (formerly LeRoi Jones), founder of the Congress of African People. In 1970, Baraka called for a boycott of Portuguese products as a way of protesting that country's Colonial Wars in Africa. This campaign involved small protests outside the Portuguese consulates in Newark (including a bomb threat) and Boston, and at the Casa de Portugal in New York City.[51] Responding to these "insults," Portuguese-American leaders in Newark called a meeting at Our Lady of Fatima's parish hall, attended by 800–1,000 community members. As reported by the *Newark Evening News*, the message that came out of that meeting was clear: "We are Americans and we want to be respected as Americans."[52]

New Bedford's 1970 riots were marked by various incidents of arson, looting, shootings, and street confrontations with police. Hundreds of people were arrested and one seventeen-year-old Cape Verdean boy, Lester Lima, was murdered by a group of three white civilians in a drive-by shooting. The riots involved a large number of Cape Verdean Americans, including the Vietnam War veteran and Black Panther Party activist Frank "Parky" Grace.[53] Notably absent from the *Diário*'s limited reporting on the riots was any mention of the Portuguese or Cape Verdean backgrounds of those involved. Protesters were simply referred to as "blacks" (*pretos*), even though most had Portuguese surnames. The paper also made no mention of Lima's background, despite the fact that a Portuguese priest celebrated his funeral in a Portuguese parish. The *Diário* also chose not to mention Mayor George Rogers's ethnicity – the first Portuguese American to occupy that office – who was criticized by the Massachusetts governor's office for his lack of leadership during the riots.[54] This would not be a glaring omission had the *Diário* not had a habit of emphasizing the heritage of successful Portuguese Americans recognized by mainstream society, as was the case when Rogers was elected mayor in January 1970. Other American newspapers, such as the *Harvard Crimson*, did allude to the Portuguese heritage of Cape Verdean Americans and reported that Lima's killing had "contributed to a growing sense of solidarity" between the two groups. According to that newspaper, this unity was reinforced by their common demand for jobs and affordable housing.[55]

Smaller episodes of violence flared throughout the summer, affecting the Feast of the Blessed Sacrament, New Bedford's largest annual public gathering. On the night of 29 July, two days before the start of the Madeiran feast, a group of protesters set fire to vehicles and buildings and engaged in a gunfight with the police. To prevent further violence, Mayor Rogers declared an evening curfew over a week-long period and cancelled the feast. The organizers eventually convinced him to allow a smaller two-day event to take place in order to recover some of the costs already incurred in its preparation. Following the mayor's request and the example of local politicians, the Portuguese consul decided not to attend the shorter celebrations. This decision irritated Lisbon's foreign affairs minister, who reminded his subordinate that his obligations to the Portuguese community prevailed over "local circumstances."[56]

Rallying for Empire: Shaping the Imperial Consciousness of Portuguese Immigrants

Portuguese Americans came to the defence of their imperial homeland on multiple occasions in the 1950s. Their readiness to do so proves once again that the Americanization of European immigrants was not a fait accompli by the end of the Second World War. In 1950, when Nehru first threatened to annex Portugal's territories, Portuguese Americans held public rallies in New Bedford, Fall River, and East Providence to show solidarity with their fellow countrymen in India. They sent telegrams to Salazar, Goa's governor general, India's ambassador in Washington, and the United Nation's secretary general expressing their repudiation of Nehru's hostile demands. Led by the Madeiran Day's president, Carlos Morais, this movement was joined by various Portuguese-American civic and religious leaders, who were able to mobilize sizable crowds at a series of public meetings in these three New England cities. They were large enough to draw the attention of Republican Minority Leader Joseph Martin, then Salazar's chief ally in the US Congress. Writing on behalf of Portuguese Americans in his Fall River district, Martin appealed to Secretary of State Dean Acheson to take into account the historical presence of Portugal – according to him a nation of "bold seaman who took ... the light of civilization to all parts of the world" – in Goa, and persuade Nehru to desist from his territorial pretensions.[57]

Since the 1950s, the Estado Novo had tried to shape American public opinion by hiring public relations firms to push their propaganda in the mainstream press. Between 1950 and 1963, it worked with the Manhattan-based George Peabody & Associates, contracted for a median annual payment of US$48,300. The Casa de Portugal's funding also quadrupled between 1951 (US$44,895) and 1961 ($191,514) (figure 5.1). Yet the SNI's limited resources, networks, and know-how were unable to deliver an effective public relations campaign in the United States. That may be why Lisbon decided to hire the New York firm Heyward Associates in 1963; the Portuguese government would retain its services until 1989.[58] Another disseminator of Salazar's propaganda in Bristol County was Basil Brewer, the president of E. Anthony & Sons, whose newspapers

Figure 5.1 Casa de Portugal annual expenditures, 1942–63. Values in US$.

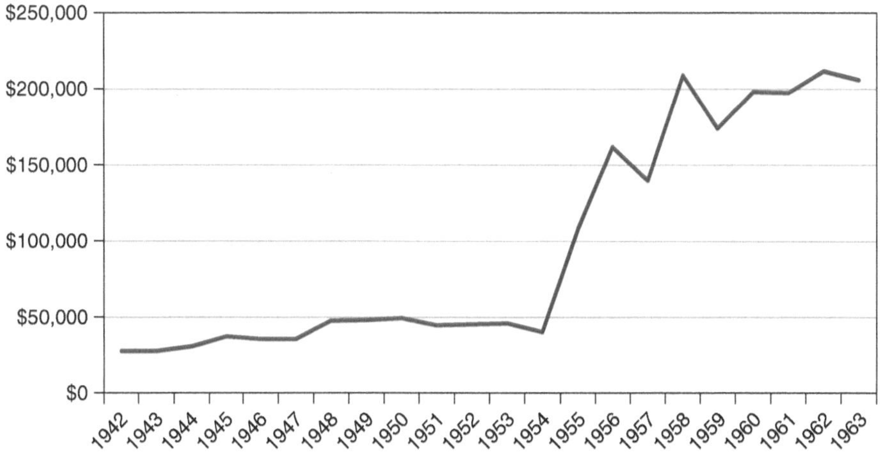

Sources: TTNA, AOS/CO/PC-81B Pt 10, Casa de Portugal annual reports, 1964.

and radio and television stations routinely praised the Portuguese empire – he was a member of New Bedford's Prince Henry quincentennial committee.[59] Such were his contributions that, in 1947, he was awarded a Portuguese Order of Christ for his work in "promoting better understanding" between the two countries.[60] According to the *Diário*, Brewer helped raise the profile and "Lusitanian" pride of Portuguese Americans in New Bedford. Also useful was Brewer's influence over congressman Hastings Keith, who often backed Salazar's interests in Washington.[61]

These large public relations contracts did not include Portuguese ethnic media, much to the frustration of their directors. However, those media outlets that endorsed the regime or were uncritical towards it (as most were) received advertising contracts from the Casa de Portugal, which were often vital for their commercial viability. Occasionally, their editors also expressed frustration with North Americans' ignorance about or disdain for Portugal and tried to improve their homeland's profile. Their mixture of patriotism and self-interest often led them to publish wholehearted defences of Lisbon's actions, even if that meant going against Washington's views. Ethnic newspapers focused a great deal on homeland affairs, especially in newcomer communities like those in Canada. Much of its content was taken from publications in Portugal or was sent by Lisbon's official news agency, ANI, and the SNI/SEIT. Portuguese radio stations in North America also used content provided by the Emissora Nacional – the regime's national broadcaster – and featured addresses by local consuls. As for the coverage of community affairs, most ethnic media focused primarily on the activities of social clubs and national parishes, the finances of mutual aid societies, social and religious events, charity fundraising campaigns, the successes of co-ethnic entrepreneurs and politicians, and the *fait divers* of the bourgeoisie. Largely absent from their pages were the everyday realities of common immigrants and their many socio-economic problems. Editorials and letters to the editor sometimes delved into political commentary of some consequence to their communities' civic life, although they often descended into public spats and diatribes.

But there were exceptions, such as the *Diário de Notícias* of New Bedford. The intense political discussions between pro- and anti-Salazar contributors published in its pages, which had first caught the Portuguese government's attention in the 1930s, were mostly gone after the war. Under João Rocha, who became the editor (and later publisher) in 1943, the *Diário* had become a largely moderate liberal newspaper that occasionally attacked the Estado Novo on narrow issues of concern to its emigrants. Initially critical of the Casa de Portugal's disappointing work, Rocha moderated his commentary in the late 1950s when his newspaper began publishing ads from that tourism bureau. Another important sponsor was the PCU, whose mutual aid services, social activities, and financial reports were extensively advertised in the paper, along with its directors' occasional opinion pieces. The PCU's president, Luis Gomes, who was also a Casa staff member, was the linchpin in this relationship. His accumulation of roles displeased Portuguese diplomats, who believed he used his insider status in these organizations and their access to confidential information regarding Lisbon's interests in the United States to advance the PCU's agenda.[62]

After the war, the *Diário* gradually came under the Estado Novo's influence. While they regularly considered it a nuisance, Portuguese ambassadors in Washington refused to see the daily newspaper as a lost cause, believing it could become a major asset if only they could control its director. Despite Rocha's nagging criticism, the *Diário*'s patriotism contributed to disseminating Portuguese language and culture in a way that served the regime's interests. Portuguese consuls, including those attacked by Rocha, were told to ingratiate themselves with him as much as possible and avoid engaging in open discussion, limiting their responses to "clarification" letters. Nonetheless, in November 1950 (and briefly in 1948), the minister of the interior banned the *Diário*. Before that, only single issues were occasionally barred. Fearing that this interdiction would aggravate Rocha's hostility and have negative repercussions among Portuguese Americans, Ambassador Pereira and the foreign affairs minister expressed their objections to the moratorium. In turn, the minister overseeing state censorship argued he had been "benevolent" with the *Diário* multiple times, yet the paper insisted on challenging his authority; so the ban continued. In 1952, the SNI joined those calling for the ban to be lifted, but to no avail. At this point, Lisbon's censors suggested that the government create another newspaper in New Bedford and staff it with pro-Salazar supporters.[63]

As expected, Rocha increased his attacks on the dictatorship following the ban, publishing damning statements by public figures in Portugal, articles by former Protestant missionaries denouncing the racist oppression of black Africans in the colonies, and warning emigrants of growing suspicions about public employees in Portugal opening their correspondence and sometimes stealing their contents.[64] By the end of 1953, Rocha began accusing Lisbon of squandering money on Peabody's firm, which he argued would be better invested in the Portuguese-American press. Around this time, Ambassador Fernandes learned that the *Diário* was in dire financial straits and had asked the US State Department for an annual subsidy. Rocha's political motivations were, it seems, more material than ideological. As he confessed to the consul in Boston years later, the *Diário*'s financial situation prevented it from alienating any potential readers, which was why it published content that appealed to both sides of the political spectrum.[65] The ambassador understood Rocha's attacks to be a call for the embassy to "buy [his] silence." The Interior Ministry finally decided to lift its ban in 1954.[66] However, this olive branch did not stop the *Diário* from attacking the regime. In 1957, the PIDE opened a file on Rocha's political activities and asked the local consul to relay information on him. The next year, a PIDE agent received instructions to follow Rocha during his family trip to Portugal and record where he stayed and with whom he met – he met with members of the Portuguese press, the SNI, and the Lisbon Geographic Society. Perhaps awkward for the agent was reporting Rocha's interview with Salazar at the dictator's official residence. As the *Diário*'s director described in the article that ensued, Salazar praised his onerous efforts to run a Portuguese daily in the United States, and thanked Portuguese Americans for their patriotic reaction to the Goa crisis: "They were admirable," said the dictator. Rocha in turn described Salazar as a "great" and "simple man, affable, a profoundly human creature."[67]

In 1961, Lisbon abandoned its laissez-faire approach to Portuguese ethnic media and took measures to control it. That decision was prompted by the wide international coverage of the *Santa Maria* highjacking, which exposed Salazar's dictatorship to the world and propelled the Portuguese opposition into the American and Canadian mainstream. The consul in Montreal, for instance, was displeased with the lack of a quick and organized response from the city's Portuguese to the unfavourable coverage of the *Santa Maria* episode in the Canadian media and in the pages of the anti-Salazarist *Luso-Canadiano*. In his estimation, this reluctance was due to the community leaders' disappointment with Lisbon's unreliability when it came to supporting their projects, including the SNI's delay in helping launch the *Voz de Portugal* newspaper. The consul warned Lisbon about the impending danger of its allies in Montreal's Portuguese community breaking ranks and urged his superiors to increase aid to these "uneducated" yet keen emigrants.[68]

Like the *Voz de Portugal*, various Portuguese-American publications were founded in 1961 with the SNI's support. Among them were Newark's *Novos Rumos*, created by Fr José Capote and endorsed by the local consul. To the latter's disappointment, this periodical soon became an outlet for progressive Catholics and other moderate critics of the dictatorship, which led the Casa de Portugal to cancel its advertisement contract. But as they had in the case of the the *Diário*, Portuguese foreign officials recognized the overall usefulness of Capote's paper and feared that cutting its subsidy would make him more hostile.[69] New York City's *A Luta* and *Our Lady of Fatima*, both published by the founding director of St Anthony's Mission in the Bronx, Fr José Cacella, were less ambiguous about touting the Estado Novo's message, validation for which they were compensated. Another champion of Salazar in the United States was Gil Stone,[70] a former Casa director and *Diário* reporter, who was dedicated to fighting the "red infiltration" in the Portuguese community. With a meagre and short-lived SNI subsidy, Stone launched the *New York Bulletin* in December 1961, which he circulated by mail to American journalists, congressmen, civil servants, UN delegates, and various national embassies, and the monthly *Vidalusa*, mailed to about 1,000 Portuguese-American subscribers.[71]

In May 1961, the Overseas Companies of Portugal, a consortium of petroleum, hydropower, railway, mining, shipping, agricultural, and other corporations with large investments in Angola (and later Mozambique), some of them partially owned by the Portuguese government, hired the Manhattan-based public relations firm Selvage & Lee to push Lisbon's imperial propaganda in the United States. Their three-year contract, worth US$0.5 million per year, was among the largest of its kind at the time.[72] It paid for editorials, articles, letters to editors, pamphlets, speeches, "study trips" overseas, lobbying activities, and other means of propaganda in the press, radio, and television.

Leading this campaign were staunch conservatives with deep ties to the Republican Party, big business, the military, the civil service, and the press. Among its contributors were both far-right white supremacists and respected African-American conservatives. To carry out its lobbying activities, Selvage & Lee spent about $200,000 on the Portuguese-American Committee on Foreign Affairs (PACFA), a front organization launched in September 1961, chaired by the Boston lawyer Martin T. Camacho.

Born in Madeira, Camacho migrated to the United States as a child in 1917, where he would become a trade unionist and a Harvard-educated labour lawyer. Camacho was an active member of the Massachusetts Portuguese-American community, where he held executive positions in various ethnic fraternities, including the influential Portuguese American Civic League of Massachusetts. One of his achievements, in the eyes of Portuguese diplomats, was convincing the League, which had traditionally shunned the Estado Novo, to send a letter to President Kennedy and his brother Senator Ted Kennedy asking them to publicly support Portugal's claims in Africa. Camacho had some social capital with the Kennedys, having chaired a Portuguese-American committee that campaigned for John during his bid for senator in 1952 and later helping organize a campaign rally during Ted's senate run in 1961. Camacho also chaired the Prince Henry quincentennial organizing committee in Boston, when he worked closely with Portuguese officials. Since then, he had become a vocal defender of the empire, delivering speeches on radio and releasing his own pamphlets, especially during the *Santa Maria* hijacking. His relationship with Selvage & Lee started after a Portuguese official at the United Nations asked him to organize a petition calling for the improvement of Portugal-United States relations and to deliver it to congressmen during the Portugal Day celebrations of 10 June 1961. The following month, he led the Portuguese-American delegation to Washington mentioned above. The PACFA was launched a few months after this trip.[73]

On paper, the PACFA had seventy-one members in June 1963. But in reality, it was only Camacho and his secretary Ida Pimenta, a Portuguese-American woman who had lost five relatives in the 15 March massacre. Still, it introduced itself as an independent civil society organization made up of American citizens. But under the Foreign Agents Registration Act, Camacho was clearly an "agent of a foreign principal" and was required to register as such, which he failed to do until January 1962, when the Department of Justice instructed him to do so. Until then, Camacho corresponded with congressmen, produced pamphlets, gave several speeches, and was interviewed by news media outlets without ever disclosing his affiliation with the Overseas Companies. During that period, the PACFA also distributed a Selvage & Lee pamphlet titled *On the Morning of March 15*, containing graphic images of the victims' mangled bodies and the lines: "Are those who inspired and order these acts fit to govern? ... Are they fit to enlist the support of the United States?" Over 20,000 copies were distributed to private citizens, media outlets, and congressmen, with the help of right-wing (including white-supremacist) organizations. Camacho was also invited to speak at colleges, churches, and large gatherings, including the 1962 Christian Crusade Convention in Tulsa, Oklahoma, organized by pro-segregation evangelist minister and broadcaster Billy Hargis.[74]

In his communications, Camacho likened Portugal's relationship with its "overseas provinces" to that of the United States with Hawaii or Alaska and described the Portuguese empire as a multiracial haven that sharply contrasted with American racial segregation and the "plight of the American Negro." He accused those "Negro leaders" who criticized Portugal's colonial policies and supported what he described as Soviet extremists in Africa of "practicing racism in reverse," given that "most of the leaders in the new African states are frankly racist," whose actions would lead to "race war" with that continent's whites. In Camacho's eyes, this confirmed that "[American Negroes] are not, in fact, ready for equality in the United States." Selvage & Lee amplified the message that Portugal stood "in the way of black racism and rabid nationalism, which seek to drive the whites from Africa," as Ambassador Pereira stated at the Commonwealth Club of California; the public relations firm circulated a press release with quotes from Pereira's speech after they had "cleared it" with him. Other accusations of American hypocrisy on race relations and colonialism were regularly made by Portuguese officials, including Overseas Minister Adriano Moreira, who liked to point out that the United States was founded by colonizers who did not extend its founding principles of liberty and democracy to Indigenous peoples.[75]

Other community groups organized their own initiatives in defence of their homeland government. In the spring of 1961, Ludlow's Portuguese associations called on President Kennedy to improve relations with Portugal (as mentioned in chapter 2, above). That summer, a group of concerned patriots, organized in committees in Massachusetts, Rhode Island, Connecticut, New York, New Jersey, Pennsylvania, California, and Ontario, launched the Portuguese-American Fund, which raised donations to aid "victims of strife in Angola." By the end of its campaign, in January 1962, they had raised over US$14,000, which they sent to the Red Cross in Angola. In May 1963, a crowd of over 1,000 immigrants in Toronto and about 3,000 in Galt, Ontario, waved small

Portuguese flags outside their local churches, greeting Ambassador Brazão, who reported his astonishment at the welcome.[76]

While Camacho tried to mobilize his fellow Portuguese Americans, none of the Overseas Companies' investment went to the ethnic media. As expected, João Rocha criticized Selvage & Lee's campaign. However, at this point, the *Diário* had reduced its attacks on the dictatorship and much of its content now came from the regime's news agency.[77] By December 1961, Camacho believed: "The entire South ... if properly handled, could easily be persuaded to side with Portugal. In fact, I think the whole country could be persuaded to side with Portugal." Ambassador Pereira's letters to Salazar also mentioned with increasing regularity and enthusiasm a positive turn in the American press coverage of Portuguese Africa. Even Secretary of State Dean Rusk commented to Minister Nogueira that Portugal's propaganda was having an impact on American public opinion.[78] In 1962, Camacho visited Capitol Hill twice, where he met with over twenty congressmen (or their assistants) from both parties, most of them from districts in California, New England, and New Jersey with large Portuguese-American constituencies. One of them was the representative for Kennedy's former Boston district, Thomas "Tip" O'Neill Jr, a personal friend of Camacho for twenty-five years, who placed his office and staff at the lobbyist's disposal and introduced him to other congressmen. Camacho's efforts bore fruit on 5 October 1962, when the House of Representatives held a round of speeches on Portugal-United States relations at Congressman O'Neill's request. For one hour, fourteen Republican and Democratic representatives criticized Kennedy's policy towards its NATO ally's "overseas provinces" while citing the "proud heritage" of Portuguese Americans, using talking points provided by Selvage & Lee. Over 900 copies of O'Neill's speech were later sent to the PACFA's mailing list using the representative's franked envelopes.[79]

In April and May 1963, the illicit activities of Selvage & Lee and its associates were exposed by the Senate Committee on Foreign Relations, which investigated the lobbying activities of unregistered non-diplomatic agents acting on behalf of foreign governments in the United States. After interviewing the public relations firm's managers and staff, including Camacho, the committee found the connections between Selvage & Lee, the Overseas Companies of Portugal, and the Portuguese government. Documents subpoenaed during this investigation revealed that the Manhattan firm had cooperated "fully" and worked "closely" with Portugal's ambassadors in Washington and New York City; reviewed or translated the regime's English communications; arranged for press coverage of Portuguese diplomatic affairs in the United States; advised Lisbon officials about the granting of travel visas to American newsmen; and met with the dictatorship's ministers, among other actions that went beyond their stated relationship with the Overseas Companies. The committee hearings also revealed that the embassy's press officer, Bernardo Teixeira, was on Selvage & Lee's payroll with Ambassador Pereira's consent, where he was tasked with assisting Camacho, doing translations, delivering speeches, and transmitting to that firm information received at the Portuguese embassy from the US State Department.[80] Some major American newspapers reported this story following the publication of the committee's proceedings on 24 July 1963, prompting those representatives who had spoken in favour of Portugal's "overseas provinces" to quickly claim that they were simply representing the views of their large Portuguese-American constituencies. This scandal was among the few cases that informed the amendments to the Foreign Agent Registration Act passed in July 1966.[81]

Despite the public controversy, the Overseas Companies continued to push Lisbon's colonialist propaganda in the United States until 1974. In April 1964, they dropped Selvage & Lee, along with its PACFA, and hired the Washington-based Downs & Roosevelt, whose administration and personnel was largely the same as those of the Manhattan firm. That year, the Casa de Portugal reported that Americans were becoming more favourable to Lisbon's position and that the ethnic media had been "extremely valuable" in influencing the views of Portuguese Americans regarding their homeland. As the Casa's director argued: "As long as [the emigrants] speak Portuguese at home and show interest for news from their homeland, we can count on the colony in periods of emergency." Its limited resources, however, forced the Casa to turn away the many requests it received for advertising contracts not foreseen in its budget.[82] In 1966, its new director informed the embassy that the relationship between Lisbon and the Portuguese-American media had never been better: the *Diário* had largely stopped its attacks, thanks to the Casa's advertising contract and efforts to pacify João Rocha, who had been awarded an honorific title from the Estado Novo earlier that year; the *Luso-Americano* continued to provide valuable services in Newark, which was deemed the most difficult community, owing to the presence of "communists"; the Portuguese press in California was also falling in line with the regime; and thirty radio shows had received content from the Casa. The only newspaper in the United States that continued to be a nuisance was Newark's *Novos Rumos*, but even that publication curbed its critical tone after Portuguese officials appealed to New Jersey's Catholic episcopacy to restrain the political conduct of its director, Fr Capote. The Casa director was also happy to report that, in the previous year, the television stations ABC, NBC, CBS, and WBR (broadcasting in the United States and Canada) all had shown films provided by his bureau. Furthermore, over 1 million Americans had reportedly attended the 1,377 Portuguese film screenings, including the travel documentary *Bravo Portugal*, seen by over 100,000 people in sixty-five of "the most important cultural centers in North America."[83] Support for the Estado Novo continued under Caetano's rule. In 1968, a coalition of Portuguese-American Catholic priests, ethnic associations, newspapers, and radio broadcasters in California, New York, and New Jersey, sent a group letter to the UN Security Council stating their allegiance to the Lisbon government and countering another letter sent to that international body by a group of Portuguese exiles in São Paulo. The same group of patriots later invited Caetano to visit the Portuguese-American communities of California, but he declined.[84]

The Imperial Diaspora: Adriano Moreira and the Union of Portuguese Cultural Communities

When Estado Novo officials first called for the integration of emigrant "colonies" into Lisbon's purview and its imperial self-understanding, they did so in reference to North America. In 1944, Luis Câmara Pina, then a Portuguese army major and professor at a military studies institute, delivered a paper at the União Nacional's second congress, titled "The Duty of Portugal towards the Lusiad Communities of North America"; it would be published the following year with a preface by Cardinal Cerejeira. In it he praised the emigrants' ability to resist cultural assimilation even after financial success; their commitment to preserve religious traditions; their "rare" and impressive capacity for associational life; their ability to generate and redistribute capital through large mutual aid societies; their great fortunes in California's dairy industry; and the proliferation of their schools, newspapers, and radio shows. Pina urged his fellow party members to ensure that the national "sentiment" and language of these expats be not only preserved but expanded. He added: "It is not possible [or] admissible to cut spiritual ties with those Portuguese who one day left for America ... It is not right, fair, or rational to lose moral interest [and] the material advantage of possessing on the Atlantic's [western] margin ... half a million ambassadors." Pina made three recommendations for retaining these communities in the "Portuguese spiritual empire": remove barriers to emigration and convince the United States to raise Portugal's immigration quota; intensify cultural exchanges by sending news content, books, newspapers, and sponsoring student exchange programs; and send Portuguese instructors to teach in its community schools. He also called for the creation of two cultural and linguistic institutes, one on each coast, with the help of missionary priests. In Pina's estimation, it was these "heroic" missionaries who prevented the extinction of Portuguese language in the United States.[85] However, it is unclear whether Pina's vision inspired those diplomats, priests, and ethnic leaders who would actualize some of its elements decades later.

Surely, Lisbon officials followed General Franco's efforts at mobilizing the Spanish diaspora since founding the Council of Hispanidad in 1940. But the notion of using state resources to engineer a Portuguese diaspora had little traction within the Estado Novo's upper echelons before the 1960s. Still, some officials occasionally mused about the untapped potential of the emigrant communities and what responsibilities Lisbon had towards them. In 1955, while endorsing a proposed tour of Portuguese-American communities by the former archbishop of Goa and Daman, the overseas minister noted: "These days, when there is so much talk about Goa ... where we still have half a million Portuguese, half of them Catholic ... it is perhaps pertinent to remember that we have almost a million practising Portuguese Catholics in North America."[86] Pina's vision of an "ecumenical" Portugal that encompassed national, colonial, and emigrant communities re-emerged in 1964, this time spearheaded by the former overseas minister and now president of the Lisbon Geographic Society, Adriano Moreira. The latter believed the regime should change its negative views on emigration and acknowledge its potential benefits. In Moreira's words:

> The Portuguese presence in foreign lands can and must be utilized as an instrument for defending and strengthening our interests in this epoch of internationalization
>
> ...
>
> This is not just a sentimental matter ... but also a cold evaluation of our immediate interests. Whenever we feel the need to mobilize world opinion against an aggressor ... we can count on the Portuguese communities, Portuguese descendants, and those aligned with Portugueseness to rise up and fight, more than we can on public relations techniques ... This institutionalization is within our reach more immediately than a remedy for economic growth that can halt our increasing emigration rate, which is a necessary phenomenon that can be mitigated but never extinguished.[87]

To fulfil and sustain this triad of nation, empire, and diaspora, Moreira envisioned the creation of an advisory body through which emigrants would be able to intervene in the domestic and foreign affairs of their homeland government whenever they were of mutual interest. Like those politicians who would create the CPC in the 1980s, Moreira cautioned against this body becoming a government-run, top-down, "bureaucratic organism," as opposed to "a corporation that lived from the contributions and interventions of Portuguese communities."[88] Moreira spent months visiting emigrant communities around the world, where he generated momentum for the first Congress of Portuguese Communities, held in Lisbon on 8–16 December 1964. Portuguese leaders in Massachusetts, Rhode Island, Connecticut, California, Hawaii, Ontario, and Quebec welcomed the former minister at various receptions attended by illustrious guests and ethnic reporters, who heard Moreira's thoughts on diaspora and empire. Each time, Moreira reminded his audience: "The Portuguese who are today engaged in armed conflict against terrorism in Angola and Guinea are exactly the same as those who ... are integrated in the collective efforts of the American people, as exemplary citizens ... [who] actually respect all their neighbors irrespective of color, race or creed."[89]

Given Salazar's increasingly narrow focus on colonial matters, those hoping to discuss emigration issues with the aging dictator had to frame it as matter of international prestige and diplomacy.[90] This might explain why a diasporic congress led by an ejected minister was able to count on the Estado Novo's support. Some of the regime's most prominent officials and supporters were part of the congress's organizing committee, including the then head of state for the army, General Luis Pina; the railway, oil, and financial capitalist, and Overseas Companies' chair, Alexandre P. Basto; the Gulbenkian Foundation's president; along with former ministers, navy officers, bureaucrats, and civic professionals. There were 192 delegates present – only twenty-two of whom were women – representing emigrant communities on all continents. The majority came from Brazil (eighty-four) and the United States (fifty-eight), followed by Spain (nine), Canada, France (six each), Argentina, Japan, Venezuela (four each), Hong Kong, Malaysia, Pakistan, South Africa, Uruguay (two each), Australia, Malawi, South Rhodesia, Singapore, Sweden, and Turkey (one each). The delegates were received with state honours from the ministers of foreign affairs and of overseas, the mayor of Lisbon, and the SNI director. The event opened with an afternoon mass at the grandiose Monastery of the Hieronymites – a symbol of Portugal's nautical explorations since the fifteenth century, which houses the tombs of Vasco da Gama and Luis Vaz de Camões – accompanied by the choir of the Portuguese Community of China. Salazar himself chaired the congress's inaugural session that evening. The rest of the proceedings took place at the Lisbon Geographic Society's hall and were divided among social, religious, economic, cultural, and technological sessions.

The papers included pseudo-scientific lectures on lusotropicalism-related topics, such as "The Bio-Social Expansion of the Portuguese Man" and the "Scientific and Historically Humanist Roots of the Spiritual Unity of the Portuguese World"; overviews on the emigrants' social, demographic, geographic, and religious characteristics; technical presentations on telecommunications and transportation; assessments of the expatriate communities' financial, economic, and political potential; and unabashed professions of patriotism and eternal loyalty to the homeland. Almost every communication made heroic references to Portugal's seafaring history, usually followed by a comparison with the emigrant's own courageous journey, framed by lusotropicalist references. Also extolled repeatedly were the contributions of migrant priests to preserving the emigrant's cultural heritage and language.

Sometimes, wrapped in these celebratory messages were allusions to the structural socio-economic problems prompting emigration, its negative impact on rural economies, and the deep poverty that many emigrants were subjected to abroad. While this viewpoint was in line with the regime's traditional anti-emigration rhetoric, some of the speakers' commentary and recommendations were in direct opposition to the dictatorship's conservative ways. One delegate cautioned the participants not to live "in the permanent contemplation of the past while turning [their] backs to the future," and alerted them to the "great crisis" in which Portuguese language and literary arts were in, suffocated as they were by censorship. The same speaker pointed to Spain's Institute of Hispanic Culture as an example of the "spiritual integration" that Portugal should follow, noting how the cultural power of Hispanidad was such that even Portugal and Brazil had been swept under its umbrella in the eyes of the world – a perception that the concept *Lusitanidade* had not yet vanquished.[91] The most caustic communication was that of Anibal Branco, the PCU's veteran secretary general and former chancellor in Boston's Portuguese consulate. After praising his fellow Portuguese Americans as "honest" and "hard-working," Branco criticized Lisbon's lack of interest in filling the bookshelves of community libraries – a common request made by delegates from various countries. He was particularly incensed by the poor quality of the consuls and their staff, who occasionally hurled insults at those emigrants who traded their Portuguese nationality for American citizenship. Besides being rude and unfair, their attitude was shortsighted, Branco argued, since these Portuguese Americans could offer "better services to Portugal with the American authorities than those who never naturalized." Other participants contested traditional definitions of Portuguese nationality and proposed a broader, more inclusive interpretation. In the absence of dual citizenship, they argued that foreign naturalization and subsequent loss of Portuguese citizenship should be seen as a purely legal process without cultural implications, motivated by the emigrants' desire to access all the rights available to them in their host countries. According to Lisbon's *Diário da Manhã*, the delegates at this congress resolved: "Being Portuguese has, therefore, a predominantly spiritual content that does not prevent the perfect exercise of citizenship in another country."[92]

Other delegates proposed progressive policy changes, such as reducing legal restrictions on emigration that resulted in massive clandestine departures, creating a repatriation fund for emigrants who failed to adapt to their host countries, appointing social attachés in diplomatic offices tasked with providing social assistance to emigrants, and appointing expatriated citizens to the National Assembly in representation of the largest emigrant communities, as was done for the "overseas provinces." Other suggestions, such as creating confederations uniting all ethnic Portuguese organizations in their adopted countries, raising the IAC's investment to community schools and libraries, increasing the number of visits by Portuguese scholars and artists, sending more books and films, and establishing more flight connections with popular emigration destinations were later implemented with varied success, as discussed in previous chapters.[93] The congress also gave birth to the Union of Portuguese Cultural Communities (UPCC), associated with the Lisbon Geographic Society. It was supposed to be "a private international apolitical institution, the purposes of which are to promote and assure the relations and cooperation among those associations, groups or individuals connected with, or interested in, the conservation and propagation of Portuguese traditions." Its membership was limited to expatriate individuals born in Portugal, their descendants, and those "affiliated with Portuguese culture," along with their organizations. The title "cultural communities" resolved some of the ambiguities surrounding Portuguese nationality, since it included foreign citizens and racialized groups such as the Cape Verdeans.[94]

Overall, the delegates reacted favourably to the congress and seemed convinced of Lisbon's genuine interest in connecting with the diaspora, thus improving the relationship between community leaders and Portuguese officials. The PAF's founders, for example, cited this meeting as their inspiration for the 1966 congress in Bristol and their resulting confederation. Even Branco noted in the PCU's annual report that, despite his initial reservations about what he expected would be a highly "political" event, the Lisbon congress had been a triumph of fraternity and goodwill with few political discussions.[95] Portuguese exiles, on the other hand, saw this meeting as a propaganda affair orchestrated by Moreira and his fellow imperialists to mobilize the emigrants' support for the colonialist government. Washington shared this view, as was communicated by the American cultural attaché in Lisbon to a group of Portuguese Americans attending the congress. The American official reminded his guests that the Johnson administration still defended the right of self-determination of all colonized peoples, and that US relations with Lisbon were not the friendliest. He argued that the congress's objectives were clearly political and warned the delegates about the organizers' intent to pass a motion supporting the imperial government and its wars. Indeed, such motion was proposed by a Portuguese-American delegate not present at the meeting. The cultural attaché also advised this group to avoid the next congress should it be held in one of the African colonies.[96]

As expected, the second Congress of Portuguese Cultural Communities was held in Mozambique on 13–23 July 1967. This time there were 200 participants – one of them Gilberto Freyre – but a smaller Portuguese-American delegation. The ten-day meeting took place aboard the luxury liner *S.S. Príncipe Perfeito*, which cruised the Mozambican coast, stopping at various ports, including the Fort of São Sebastião, as Vasco da Gama had done on his way to India. The themes of this meeting were similar to those of the first, although its imperialist overtones were even more pronounced and the links to Brazil emphasized. As the *New York Times* reported, some delegates were uncomfortable with the meeting's political tone: "They felt they were being pressed to support Portuguese policy in Africa."[97] Also on the agenda were the circulation of literary works in the Americas' vast lusophone market and the preservation and international standardization of the Portuguese language. The definition of *Lusiad* – "community" and "nation" – was also discussed at length, with arguments made for their separation from the political concepts of "state" or "territory."[98] This would be the last congress organized by the UPCC, which would fizzle out in the early 1970s. It is not clear what role, if any, Moreira, the UPCC, and the two congresses played in the Estado Novo's decision to create the SNE in 1970. Nonetheless, it is evident that their efforts contributed to improving the diaspora's profile in the eyes of Lisbon officials.[99]

Conclusion

The history of race relations in the United States is enormously complex, especially when accounting for the particular characteristics of different ethnic or national groups – nuances too often lost in popular discussions about race. Introducing an imperial perspective to this discussion admittedly complicates matters further. But it also reveals an important strand in this historical mesh that helps us understand the specific experiences of "inbetween" immigrant groups such as the Portuguese and Cape Verdeans and uncover new transnational agents behind the historical (re)constructions of American racial identities. Homeland officials helped shape the racial identities, political views, and diasporic consciousness of Portuguese communities in North America in line with Lisbon's increasingly cultural and linguistic imperial narrative. Most ethnic leaders found ways to reconcile their support for the dictatorial and colonialist regime with adherence to their host nations' anti-authoritarian and anti-colonialist stance, finding common ground in their shared anti-communism and Western heritage.

Similarly ambivalent were those Italian Americans who endorsed Mussolini's invasion of Ethiopia in 1935, when fascist propaganda stimulated the emigrant's "sense of pride in their home country." They too had supporters in the American conservative press, which wrote of the Ethiopians' "savage" attacks against Mussolini's troops, who were supposedly fighting to "replace barbarism with civilization." There were also conservative and liberal detractors who condemned the fascists' "imperialist aggression," among whom were those who refuted the Italians' so-called civilizational drive by pointing to their willingness to "lower themselves" to the level of natives, with whom they fraternized and miscegenated. Curiously, after the Second World War, the same social and cultural proximity between Portuguese settlers and African natives, proposed in the Estado Novo's lusotropicalism, was deployed as a tactic to appease the anti-colonialist liberal consensus.[100] In both Portuguese and Italian cases, celebrating the homeland's empire "constituted a kind of ransom for [the immigrants'] own lives, so full of sacrifice."[101] Like the Portuguese, Italian *prominenti* asserted their long-standing "roots" in the United States and Canada by obtaining official recognition of Christopher Colombus and John Cabot (or Giovanni Caboto) as "discoverers" of the New World. After examining the Italian-Canadian efforts to memorialize Caboto – launched by Mussolini's diplomats in the 1920s – Anne-Marie Fortier concluded that "memory, rather than territory, are the principle grounds of identity formation."[102] But unlike the Italian case, the centuries-old empire was much further ingrained in the Portuguese national and ethnic psyche and was a contemporary political and territorial reality, one that was under threat, along with the "glorious" memory attached to it. That seafaring history of itinerancy and adaptability provided Portuguese Americans with a stock of useful metaphors for articulating their personal and collective narratives of belonging to both home and host nations. At the same time, the imperialist mantras woven into those narratives were hard at work reinforcing the political borders of Portugal's colonial territories. By elevating their status within the Eurocentric foundational myths of North America, which perpetuated the historical erasure of North America's Indigenous peoples and of the Atlantic slave trade, Portuguese-American heritage champions were involved in a less violent yet still exclusionary project similar to that of other European immigrant groups who managed to "become American" by asserting their own "whiteness" as a condition for full citizenship.[103]

The Portuguese case offers clear examples of how racial identities are historically constructed and deeply contextual. The ethnic elites' patriotic embrace of their glorious imperial history contrasted with the abhorrence felt by the "Portuguese" of North Carolina at the mention of that racial label and its supposed heritage. The promotion of a Portuguese-American founding mythology of North America in the context of New England's emerging ethnic pluralism worked to legitimize that group's historical whiteness. At the same time, the visible whiteness of Gaston's "Portuguese" was tainted by local historical hearsay, which was enough to justify their segregation. The racial "stupidity" of the "backward" American South further vindicated the heritage campaigns of Portuguese Americans in the "advanced" North, since it allowed them to rise above their host nation's racial divide and preach their homeland's supposed racial pluralism. At the same time, Portuguese intellectuals were quick to dismiss the supposed ancestry of Gaston's "unfortunate people" and demand that American officials stop "misusing" their national identity to describe these poor, illiterate, isolated, rural, mixed-race, and somehow assimilated families, whose association with their much vaunted pro-miscegenation and versatile "Portugueseness" they deemed insulting.

The ethnic revivalism of Portuguese-American elites and their heritage champions was largely conservative; especially when compared with the cultural nationalism of African Americans, who sought to change the political and economic structures oppressing non-whites in the United States rather than improving their status within them. However, in the 1960s, Portuguese immigrants, who shared some of the same socio-economic problems as their black neighbours, seemed more willing to identify with the latter's demands for increasing government investment in public housing, employment, and other social programs. As Barrett and Roediger argued, this convenient flexibility between seeking distance from and finding common ground with non-whites was a common characteristic of "inbetween" immigrants.[104] However, when African-American activists turned their attention to Portugal's colonialism and boycotted Portuguese-American businesses, the latter were quick to conceal their ancestry, seen once again as a liability, and declared themselves as just "Americans."

While more explicit in the United States than in Canada, this racial dimension was central to the creation or emboldening of a Portuguese diasporic consciousness in North America, fuelled as it was by imperialist notions of lusotropicalist miscegenation and pluri-continental nationhood. The threats to Portugal's sacrosanct empire and the resources mobilized to protect it provided the impetus for Lisbon officials to re-imagine the nation's geography and its people's deterritorialized identity. In Sökefeld's terms, the colonial wars were a "triggering event" for mobilizing "imagined transnational community" discourses. A by-product of this discursive bulwark was the annexation of diasporic "colonies" as outposts of the imperial nation in foreign hostile polities. By conflating colonial and emigrant settlements as equal parts of the same imperial nation, the Estado Novo's overseas officials laid the building blocks of the diaspora-building policies that re-emerged triumphantly after the fall of empire – but not without first prompting the creation of an alternative diaspora of anti-fascist radical exiles.

6 The Radicals' Diaspora: Anti-fascists, War Resisters, and State Surveillance

Sons of the PEOPLE OF PORTUGAL, in this country there are hundreds of political exiles and young men who had the nobility of deserting the colonialist army. Join us ...
                                             Movimento Democrático Português, Montreal, 1967.[1]

After the Second World War, a new wave of political exiles[2] left Portugal to preserve their personal and intellectual freedom. Most of them went to Brazil, Algeria, and France, although their networks extended throughout Europe, Africa, and South and North America. A significant number went to Montreal, Toronto, and the Greater New York City Area, where they organized pro-democratic committees dedicated to fighting the Estado Novo from abroad. Many of them would spend a great part of their lives outside Portugal, yet remain intensively dedicated to it. Among them were leftist radicals who opposed not only Lisbon's conservative and colonialist dictatorship but also their host nation's capitalist system. Others were moderate democrats, who identified with the liberal-democratic ideals of Canada and the United States. All believed that the dictatorship could be defeated only through a coup or revolution, especially after 1958. In light of this conviction, American and Canadian authorities saw these transnational activists as "subversives" working to overthrow a NATO-allied government, which happened to be undemocratic.

"New migration" historians have written extensively on radical activists and their interactions with their immigrant communities and host nation officials. Many underscored John Bodnar's claim that, while common immigrants were prepared to "deal with capitalism, albeit on their own terms," they paid little attention to the rallying cries of radical militants.[3] Other social historians, such as Roberto Perin, wondered if the significance accorded to radical immigrant "intellectuals" was justified, given that they were "atypical immigrants" who, for the most part, disassociated themselves from or condescended to their humbler countryman, who were "after all rooted in a Canadian reality."[4] Bodnar's and Perin's cautions are important reminders of the resistance that radicals encountered when trying to politicize their fellow immigrants and how we should not assume that the disproportional presence of these atypical individuals in the archival record corresponds with their overall impact within their communities. However, not all political exiles were upper- or middle-class intellectuals detached from their working-class communities, which is not to say they were incapable of condescending to their less literate countrymen. Furthermore, the supposed disengagement of common immigrants from homeland or host nation politics was not entirely rooted in their local everyday reality; it was also in part fuelled by their fear of reprisal from the Estado Novo's political police.

Other migration historians have described a more engaged relationship between activist and common immigrants that went beyond local realities. As Carmela Patrias noted, the efforts of Hungarian nationalist and communist militants to raise the political consciousness of their fellow immigrants in Canada would not have been successful "had their ideologies, and the institutions that they created and supported, not responded to the needs of the immigrants." Even international-minded communists relied on "aspects of shared culture and fellow-feeling" and infused their radicalization programs with an "ethnic component."[5] Indeed, the extent to which Portuguese anti-fascists were involved in ethnic community life helps explain the differing successes of their mobilization efforts. Elisabetta Vezzosi's "radical ethnic brokers" is a useful concept for understanding the liminal role played by political exiles in their immigrant communities. As she put it: "In the lives of [radical ethnic brokers], protest and accommodation were not counterposed but merged in the same figures, who thus became leaders of 'passage' or 'transition'... between immigrant communities and the larger society."[6] This notion will resonate as we examine the political activities of Portuguese radicals in North America; how they linked home and host nation polities; how they effectively created an alternative diasporic consciousness and networks; and how American, Canadian, and Portuguese secret services reacted to the "subversive" activities of these pro-democratic "radical ethnic brokers" in the context of the Cold War.

The "External Front": Humberto Delgado, Henrique Galvão, and the National Liberation Patriotic Front

Although the 1926 military coup forced many republicans and other opponents into exile, it was not until General Humberto Delgado's failed presidential bid that the opposition's "external front" began to take shape. As in the past, Salazar expected the 1958 presidential elections to be a formality, a way to assess the opposition and reinforce the regime's political legitimacy. However, Delgado's charismatic, Eisenhower-style campaign rallied an unprecedented and unexpected surge of popular support, as reflected in the large public gatherings at his events, which caught the dictatorship unprepared to deal with such mass defiance. Delgado's campaign followed a period of intense political repression known as the "led years" (1949–58), when many left-wing leaders were sent to prison or exiled, throwing the rank and file into disarray. At this point, the split in the opposition became more pronounced, with communists on one side and social democrats, liberals, and democratic conservatives on the other. In the first camp were primarily factory workers, tradesmen, and other urban labourers, along with farm workers from the south, organized by the PCP, a clandestine yet robust political party with ties to Moscow. The second camp was more fluid. In 1958, it was represented by the somewhat amorphous Democrat-Social Directory (DDS), whose leaders (mostly intellectuals and middle-class professionals) were inspired by Western democracies. There were ideological cleavages within the DDS, but in the early 1950s its members agreed that "peaceful evolution" rather than revolution was the most feasible path for political change. After Josef Stalin's death in 1953, even the PCP recognized the benefits of coalescing the various anti-Salazar factions into a united "national reconciliation" front, and engaged in legal, electoral, reformist political action. The 1958 presidential election was an opportunity to test this united front's strength.

Believing the best nominee to be someone from within the regime's own ranks who could eventually lead an internal putsch, the centrist opposition camp selected Delgado as their "independent candidate." Initially excluded from this nomination process, the PCP eventually withdrew their own candidate's bid and threw their support behind Delgado. Before becoming the opposition's candidate, Delgado had been an officer in the Portuguese air force and a supporter of the Estado Novo, which he represented in Montreal at the International Civil Aviation Organization (1947–50) and in Washington, first as the Portuguese military attaché and later as the mission chief with NATO (1952–7). During his time in North America, Delgado developed a liberal consciousness and began repudiating Salazar's dictatorship. But more than his ideas, it was Delgado's novel brand of politics, characterized by his bravado and public theatrics, that rallied so many behind "the fearless General" – a nickname he earned after telling a reporter he would "obviously fire" Salazar once he became president. The charismatic general shunned the republican opposition's traditional political methods, with its "chronic legalism, its moderation, its attachment to republican shibboleths," replacing them with "mass politics and bold, direct action."[7] Less than a week into the campaign, the regime reverted to its traditional methods of intimidation and invaded Delgado's campaign offices, beating and imprisoning his supporters at public rallies, and deploying other repressive tactics. In the end, the elections were rigged. However, this time it was obvious to everyone the official ballot results did not reflect the popular mood. After the phony elections, the PIDE clamped down on Delgado's supporters, forcing many to flee the country. The general himself was granted asylum in the Brazilian embassy until he managed to leave for Brazil in April 1959.

Delgado's campaign inaugurated a period of crisis for the Estado Novo that would include the beginning of the colonial wars and a series of high-profile revolutionary actions that captured the attention of media around the world, opening the regime to an unprecedented level of international scrutiny. The most dramatic of these actions was the highjacking of the *Santa Maria* liner on 22 January 1961, which Henrique Galvão had planned in Venezuela with Delgado's assent. After a long pursuit, the "freedom fighting pirates" docked safely on 2 February in Recife, where recently elected President Jânio Quadros granted them asylum. While Galvão's original plan failed, his action was seen as a massive success, since it tore down the decades-long "curtain of silence" that had kept Portugal hidden from the world's gaze, and it exposed the existence of widespread opposition to a regime that had been accepted by the West as "a patriarchal entity, benevolent, and even adequate, to the lowly politics of the Portuguese."[8]

Once in Brazil, Galvão and his men joined the group of Portuguese exiles in São Paulo. In March 1961, about 100 political émigrés led by a small group of socialists gathered in that city to discuss how to organize the exiled diaspora (the "external front"), and how best to support the opposition in Portugal (the "internal front"), led largely by the PCP; they also agreed the latter should remain the primary field of battle. The participants concluded that they could benefit from the international attention garnered by the Colonial Wars, as long as they clearly stated their support for the African liberation movements and worked together despite ideological differences.[9] But this was not Galvão's view or style. Months after arriving in Brazil, the rogue captain became estranged from Delgado and his left-wing allies. In large part this falling-out was due to Galvão's pro-colonialist views, which he developed during his long career as an imperial officer, including being the director of the 1934 colonial exhibit in Oporto, district governor in Angola, National Assembly deputy for Angola, and inspector-general of the Overseas Territories. Galvão believed that Angolan "tribes" had no sense of nationhood and would not be ready for self-determination until a democratic government in Lisbon prepared them for it. His views became untenable for the left-wing opposition after April 1961, when it agreed to share resources and coordinate actions with the African liberation parties. Galvão also had pretensions to become the leader of the democratic opposition in Brazil, which placed him on a collision course with Delgado. The two men found themselves in Morocco at the same time later in 1961, each preparing his own revolutionary actions. Galvão helped Hermínio Palma Inácio plan the first ever highjack of a passenger airplane. On 10 November 1961, Inácio seized a TAP aircraft mid-flight from Casablanca to Lisbon, dropped anti-Salazar and anti-communist pamphlets over the capital, then returned safely to Morocco. Delgado in turn entered Portugal with fake papers in anticipation of a popular insurrection that he hoped to lead following an assault on Beja's military barracks, which unfolded on New Year's Eve 1961. After the attack was foiled, the regime launched a widespread manhunt for the escaped assailants; Delgado managed to leave the country upon hearing of the mission's failure. In the general's eyes, it had been Galvão's earlier action and public boasting that alerted Portuguese authorities and ultimately compromised the Beja assault. The schism between the two liberal leaders grew in the following years, fuelled by their spirited and tenacious personalities. But while Delgado remained a central figure in the leftist-dominated opposition, Galvão became increasingly isolated.

After 1958, the opposition became more radicalized, as reflected in the various high-profile political actions that followed, including Álvaro Cunhal's prison break in January 1960 and the PCP's return to its revolutionary ethos, the Washington-backed attempted coup by General Botelho Moniz in April 1961, the student strikes in the universities of Coimbra and Lisbon in 1962, along with various workers' strikes throughout the country. The dictatorship responded to this increasing defiance by beating and sometimes shooting at protesters, making sweeping political arrests, intensifying its use of torture, and reopening the Tarrafal prison camp. The escalation of political repression and military conscription generated one of the largest departures of political exiles and war resisters – including draft-dodgers and deserters – most of them going to western Europe, North Africa, or South America. The call from São Paulo for a united "external front" became more pressing as the exiled diaspora grew. In December 1962, their efforts finally materialized with the founding of the Frente Patriótica de Libertação Nacional (FPLN; National Liberation Patriotic Front) in Rome, becoming the largest Portuguese revolutionary organization among exiles. Still, its founders agreed the FPLN should always defer to the "internal front." The new transnational network, which set up its base in Algiers in 1963, connected exiled groups in Algeria, Belgium, Brazil, Canada, France, England, Morocco, Switzerland, Uruguay, and Venezuela and kept ties with African nationalist movements. In that year, the liberal Delgado and the communist Cunhal agreed to work together and seek a common revolutionary solution to overthrow Salazar. A new FPLN executive committee was formed, with Delgado as president, Cunhal as vice-president – though he often delegated that role to another PCP representative – and Fernando Piteira Santos and other socialists as supporting executive members.

By the fall of 1964, ideological disagreements and competing revolutionary strategies had given rise to intense factionalism within the FPLN, culminating in Delgado's divorce from the organization and the creation of his short-lived National Liberation Portuguese Front in Rabat. True to his reputation, the "fearless General" continued to plot wild revolutionary plans, until 13 February 1965, when he was lured into an ambush on the Spanish-Portuguese border and assassinated, together with his secretary. Because the murder happened soon after Delgado's falling-out with the FPLN, speculation about his death became rampant. One conspiracy theory, proposed by Henrique Cerqueira, Delgado's aide in Rabat, accused the FPLN and the PCP of betraying the general and enabling his assassination. Cerqueira's controversial thesis captured the media's attention and was conveniently endorsed by the regime – years later it was confirmed that PIDE agents had murdered Delgado. This scandal damaged the international reputation of the Portuguese opposition and deepened the many fissures breaking apart the once united anti-Salazar front. Afterwards, the FPLN continued to operate despite the opposition's internal turmoil, but lost much of its early impetus and assumed a more intermediary role in the exiled diaspora. Still, the FPLN continued to attract new socialist leaders, who came to dominate the organization under Piteira Santos's leadership. In 1970, yet another ideological split culminated in the PCP's leaving the FPLN, after which the latter lost much of its influence.[10]

Abilio Oliveira Águas and the Committee Pro-Democracy in Portugal of Newark

The republican exiles that moved to the United States after the 1926 coup introduced a transnational dimension to the political life of Portuguese-American communities. This was especially true on the east coast, where the former minister of education, João Camoesas,[11] the priest Joaquim Correia,[12] the author José Rodrigues Miguéis, and the former consul and businessman, Abilio Águas, were active and articulate critics of the Estado Novo. These republicans maintained ties with the leading members of the opposition in Portugal, contributed regularly to their publications, and shared their political views with Portuguese Americans through their Clube Republicano Português (Portuguese Republican Club), the Aliança Liberal Portuguesa (Portuguese Liberal Alliance), and in the pages of New Bedford's *Diário de Notícias*. As was often the case with Salazar's enemies, Portuguese diplomats and their community allies branded these liberals and social-democrats as "communists," convincing American authorities to police their activities and limit their freedom of speech. However, after Camoesas and Correia died in 1951, the republican opposition in the United States lost much of its vitality. Following the *Santa Maria* episode, some of the old republicans sprang back into action and joined the growing exiled community in the United States, as was the case with Águas. Born in the mainland city of Figueira da Foz in 1890, Águas was educated in Lisbon and London, where he met some of Portugal's most distinguished republican thinkers. After working as a colonial administrator in Mozambique, he became a manager with the Brazilian office of a British investment company, which took him on business trips across South America, Africa, and Canada. In 1925, he was appointed vice-consul of Portugal in Providence, where he earned the reputation of being a friend of the downtrodden for his solicitude in helping newcomers deal with American officials. Four years later, Águas was relieved of his diplomatic duties after having denounced the French shipping company Fabre Line for transporting Cape Verdean immigrants in their ships' cargo holds. Afterwards, he became an outspoken critic of the regime and its neglect of emigrants, voicing his opinions in the pages of Providence's *News-Tribune* and lecturing in community halls. Águas also helped found Rhode Island's Portuguese American Civic League and was involved in various civic initiatives and heritage campaigns; he was one of the original advocates of Professor Edmund Delabarre's (his father-in-law) thesis about the Dighton Rock's petroglyphs as evidence of early Portuguese presence in New England.

Águas was one of the most respected and well-connected Portuguese immigrants in Washington's circles, with illustrious friends such as President Harry Truman. After the war, he became the president of the Portuguese section of the Democratic Party's nationalities directory, and ran as a municipal candidate in Berkley, Massachusetts, where he lived; he also secured some of the first Portuguese-American public appointments in Rhode Island.[13]

By 1960, a small group of exiles, predominantly from urban mainland Portugal, had converged in the Greater New York City Area, where they formed a political nucleus. One of its leaders was Eduardo Covas, a former accountant from the suburbs of Lisbon with connections to "well-known and active communists," according to the PIDE, who landed clandestinely in New York in 1950 aboard a merchant ship.[14] Covas had various factory jobs in New Jersey before starting his own business making guitar strings, while remaining an "illegal alien." Another leading member was António Dias, a fishing-trawler pilot from the outskirts of Oporto, who had been deported from the United States six times before 1954 until he married an American citizen and became a permanent resident. Other members were sojourners turned immigrants in the 1950s, most of them labourers, although a few were white-collar workers and small-business owners. Their early activities consisted primarily of distributing political literature, including the *Portugal Democrático* – much as the Portuguese Liberal Alliance in the 1930s had distributed the *Portugal Republicano*, also published in Brazil. It was the editors of the São Paulo newspaper who connected them with Águas, with whom they founded the Committee Pro-Democracy in Portugal (CPDP) in April 1961.[15] With Águas as chairman, Covas as secretary-general, and about sixty members spread across New Jersey, New York, Massachusetts, and Connecticut, the Newark-based CPDP advocated the restoration of the republican regime under the principles of the 1910 revolution.[16]

The CPDP's membership consisted largely of immigrant workers with few material resources and some Portuguese-American descendants with more financial means; according to Águas, the latter were less committed to their transnational cause. Much of Águas's sizable wealth, amassed through business ventures, was locked in bad investments in Portugal, which he was unable to oversee in person for fear of being arrested. Still, he enjoyed ample political capital and was able to find help from many influential Americans. After witnessing the rise of the postwar generation of Portuguese-American civic leaders, the veteran republican decided to stay away from them and their ethnic activities – including the heritage-making kind – given their association with Lisbon's diplomats, and he instructed the CPDP's operatives to follow suit. However, this withdrawal furthered the group's disconnect with the larger ethnic community, which paid little attention to the CPDP's calls for mobilization.[17] In fact, various civic leaders, clergymen, journalists, and ethnic organizations countered the CPDP's message with political action of their own. Still, there were enough influential and resourceful individuals in the lusophone communities willing to aid Águas and his group on a regular basis.

Contrary to the dominant perception in the Portuguese-American community, Águas and his group were firmly opposed to communism and made sure they stayed clear of any association with the far left. This distancing was in large part moved by Águas's concern for the optics of the CPDP among those Americans whose cooperation they depended on. In 1962 it led Águas to cut ties with the increasingly "philo-communist" newspaper *Portugal Democrático* and withdraw support for all actions carried by the "totalitarian" camp. True to his pre-Delgado political roots, he also advised his followers not to engage in public demonstrations, since he believed they eroded their organization's prestige. For instance, Águas rejected his secretary's suggestion of distributing political literature to the *Sagres* crew during their visit to New England in 1964, fearing that doing so would cause "adverse reactions;" although Covas and his men did it regardless.[18] Furthermore, Águas shared Galvão's colonialist views, as reflected in the CPDP's inaugural communiqué, which stated: "We do not collaborate with those who want independence for Angola, and we would place ourselves on the side of the government, even the Dictatorship, if a foreign power, whichever it may be, tried to take possession of any parcel of territory under Portugal's flag."[19] With the help of Cape Verdean-American leader Roy Teixeira, Águas tried to convince the Cape Verdean community to join in the CPDP's struggle for democracy in Portugal and subsequent self-rule (not independence) in Cape Verde. In his assessment, only a democratic coup in Lisbon could prevent the Africanization of Cape Verdeans and guarantee their ongoing link to Portugal, "where, after all, they have always been considered our equals ... well above the savages of the African Continent."[20] Soon after its founding, the CPDP connected with the FPLN and other leaders of the opposition. However, their primary loyalty rested with Galvão, whose trust Águas earned when he raised funds for the *Santa Maria* operation. By August 1961, the rebel captain was sending his mail to Portugal through his friends in Newark. Galvão also accepted the CPDP's invitation to visit Newark and address Portuguese democrats in that city, but he was unable to secure a visa to enter the country.[21] Not until December 1963 did the CPDP finally managed to bring Galvão to New York, where he spoke at the United Nations.

The UN's Special Committee on Territories under Portuguese Administration first invited Galvão to make a deputation in March 1962. To secure the cooperation of American officials, Águas and Teixeira set up a delegation representing close to forty organizations and went to Washington to speak to Secretary of State Dean Rusk, who declined to receive them. The politically astute Águas realized he would not be granted access to the State Department, nor would Galvão be issued an entry visa while negotiations over the Lajes Air Base lease extension were ongoing.[22] What Águas did not predict was the extent to which Washington's interests in the Azorean airstrip allowed Salazar to co-opt the Kennedy administration into accepting many of the dictator's terms. Once they learned of the UN's invitation to Galvão, the Portuguese foreign affairs minister began pressuring American officials to deny entry to the international "terrorist," warning of "grave consequences" otherwise. The Americans recognized the diplomatic risks of allowing Galvão into the country and took discreet actions to prevent him from doing so. Facing a bureaucratic blockade from the US border services, Galvão's visa applications were repeatedly delayed, until the UN invitation finally expired in July 1962. Resistance to Galvão's presence at the United Nations also came from some sectors of the Portuguese opposition, especially Delgado, who criticized the CPDP for its allegiance to his revolutionary rival, for labelling Galvão's detractors as "communists," and for failing to communicate with fellow anti-Salazarists in Brazil. Delgado was especially concerned with Águas's influential connections in Washington, where the CPDP's manoeuvres could do more harm than good.[23]

The Newark committee continued to plead with the United Nations to renew its invitation to Galvão and secure his safe passage to New York. Águas sought the favour of his powerful American friends, some of them actively involved in the international fight against Salazar's dictatorship and colonial empire.[24] Squeezed between the UN African-Asian bloc's demands that Galvão be allowed into the United States and Lisbon's assurance that it would seek his extradition once he landed, American officials decided to delay Galvão's arrest until after his address. After many months of negotiation, Galvão finally arrived in New York on 9 December 1963 and immediately delivered his speech to the UN Trusteeship Council. For two and a half hours, the former colonial officer expressed his controversial views on Portuguese imperialism, arguing that African "tribal peoples" were not prepared for peaceful democratic self-rule, mostly because Salazar had corrupted

Portugal's emancipatory humanist mission. He also contended that African nationalist rebels were harbingers of Soviet neo-colonialism, and that the only way to end the wars and bring independence to Portugal's colonies was for democracy to return to Lisbon. While consistent with his previous statements, well known to the Portuguese opposition, Galvão's testimony infuriated the African delegation, which voted to strike it from the record. An Algerian UN delegate, speaking to the press afterwards, described Galvão's appearance as "a mountain giving birth to a mouse," a headline repeated in the pro-Salazar press. As American officials had hoped, Galvão returned to Brazil the next day, before the courts could process a warrant for his arrest.

The CPDP continued to endorse Galvão after his deputation, Águas translating and forwarding the captain's essays to American politicians and press. However, in the mid-1960s, the older liberal-republican opposition, now gathered around the Social-Democratic Action, was beginning to lose momentum as their former socialist allies achieved greater public attention with their new Portuguese Socialist Action led by former DDS and FPLN members, including future Prime Minister Mário Soares. Around the same time, the deteriorating health of the CPDP's seventy-two-year-old leader began worrying his supporters. Poor returns from Águas's investments in Portugal also began to take a toll on his personal finances. At this point he asked Galvão to convince his associates in Lisbon to send funds to the CPDP so they could continue their work. The veteran politician also began resenting what he saw was the ingratitude of former business partners and fellow republican exiles, along with Portuguese Americans in general, who, according to him, "know and feel that Portugal is a pawn of the so-called Democratic powers and feel nothing but indifference or disdain for our People." Águas was equally disillusioned with Portuguese immigrants and their supposed unshakable apathy. This frustration informed his views on Adriano Moreira's "flirting" with the Portuguese-American communities, whose efforts Águas believed would yield minimal results. According to him, the immigrants were "entirely indifferent to the overseas question and even less to Portugal." Having predicted that no more than ten Portuguese-American delegates would attend the 1964 diaspora congress in Lisbon, Águas's sense of defeat was likely aggravated once he learned that over fifty had participated.[25] Referring to the *Sagres* visit that year, he wrote to Covas: "I went to Providence to see the ship, but from afar."[26] Águas's Portuguese seafaring heritage advocacy too had been sidelined by the regime's propagandists and its Portuguese-American clients, whose campaigns for preserving the Dighton Rock were able to draw the support of Massachusetts officials, who created a dedicated state park in 1963. Finally, in 1965, the US Department of Justice forced the CPDP to close its doors after a long investigation by the Federal Bureau of Investigation (FBI), which I discuss later in this chapter. The CPDP reopened some time afterwards but they would never again achieve the same publicity as when they brought Galvão to New York.[27]

Anti-fascists in Canada: The Portuguese Canadian Democratic Association and the Mouvement Démocratique Portugais

Founded on 15 September 1959 by a group of twenty immigrants, the Portuguese Canadian Democratic Association (PCDA; Canadian Portuguese Democratic Committee until 1962) was the second Portuguese association to open in Toronto and one of its most enduring, lasting until 2007. For nearly fifty years, its various executives reshaped its political orientation and activities while remaining faithful to its anti-fascist roots. The majority of its members were migrant labourers from the mainland, almost all men,[28] some having gone into exile after Delgado's campaign. There were a few professionals among them, including the founding president, Fernando Ciriaco Cunha, an agricultural engineer and former bureaucrat, who arrived in Canada with his wife and children in 1957. In an open letter to Salazar, in which he criticized the dictator and announced his support for Delgado, Ciriaco described his life growing up under the Estado Novo. He recalled joining the Moçidade Portuguesa as a child in Lisbon, marching in parades and shouting at the top of his lungs with his arm raised in fascist salute. He had praised Salazar for sparing Portugal the horrors of the Second World War and joined the União Nacional. But once the world learned the full extent of Hitler's and Mussolini's barbarities, Ciriaco noticed similarities between them and Salazar and saw the dictatorship as a "caricature" of the nazi and fascist regimes.[29] In 1943, at age twenty-two, Ciriaco left Portugal along with his job in a municipal government and, according to DCI officials, joined the Belgian Armed Forces, with which he served in various parts of the world. Acording to Ciriaco, he worked as a technocrat in the Belgian Congo, where he learned about the independence struggles of Africa's colonized peoples. Four year later, Ciriaco left for Colombia, where he worked for Rojas Pinilla's authoritarian government and, according to him, became one of the dictator's "closest advisors" on matters of agriculture and colonization. Here again he saw glimpses of Salazar's "rotten" rule as he learned "how dictatorships were installed and maintained." After a short period in Brazil, Ciriaco moved to Canada, where he became an office administrator at the T. Eaton Company.[30] Once in Toronto, he organized the few Portuguese exiles in that city and began corresponding with Delgado, Galvão, and other leaders of the exiled opposition.

Unlike their president, most of the PCDA's members were labourers without a steady income. As Ciriaco explained to Galvão, justifying the modest donation sent to the captain's recently inaugurated radio broadcast in Caracas: "it's on those [sojourners] that we count to raise funds for our activities, but only when they return at the end of summer. Here it's like the African hinterland; money is earned when isolation is greater and saved because there is nowhere to spend it." Nonetheless, these migrant workers were generous with their money and more often than not satisfied requests for aid from fellow exiles around the world. The majority of them lived in the working-class, inner-city neighbourhoods of Kensington Market and Alexandra Park or in suburban Scarborough. Ciriaco, who was a Protestant, preferred to keep a distance from his countrymen. In his eyes, Portuguese immigrants were "trained to follow others, not think for themselves," and were led by incompetent leaders who spent their time and energy fighting each other. He concluded that the best way to consolidate his committee was to avoid appearing in public and live far from the "colony," with which he remained connected through his collaborators: "This way I maintain my personal prestige and prevent the possibility of them trying to involve me in hearsay and gossip."[31]

The PCDA sought to expand its membership beyond Toronto early on. In 1960, it ran a membership drive in northern Ontario, Manitoba, and Saskatchewan. That year, Ciriaco encouraged fellow anti-Salazarists in Montreal to create their own committee and sought potential leaders among his contacts in that city. In his view, the Estado Novo's fall was imminent and there was urgent need to launch a "democratic instruction" campaign among Portuguese emigrants, to prepare them for the post-dictatorial future.[32] In 1961, Henrique Bello founded the social club Maison des Portugais, which, according to the consul in Montreal, was composed primarily of former Portuguese civil servants.[33] In 1964, Bello revamped this organization, now called the Mouvement démocratique portugais (MDP), attracting political exiles and war resisters arriving in that city in increasing numbers. Like the PCDA, most of its members (about thirty in total in 1964)[34] were mainlander men. Many had considerable experience with political activism in Portugal, for instance, the Lisboner Maximino Serra and the Madeiran Mavílio Mendes, who had escaped to Morocco after participating in the failed Beja assault;[35] or Eugénio Vargas, a former member of Delgado's renegade Front in Rabat, who arrived in Montreal in 1965.[36] Others were PCP militants, such as the lawyer Domingos Gomes and the factory worker turned merchant Jaime Monteiro; both men later moved to Toronto and joined the PCDA. Still others were liberal professionals, including Rui Cunha Viana, a journalist and former newspaper owner from Lisbon, who arrived in Montreal with his family in 1965, where he became a librarian.

Ciriaco began corresponding with Delgado and Galvão a few months before the *Santa Maria* highjacking, which would put him and his fellow anti-fascists on the front pages of Canada's mainstream press. Canadians were thrilled to read about "freedom-fighting pirates" eluding American, British, and Portuguese warships, planes, and submarines: as a reporter called it, a "real-life Errol Flynn drama." The *Toronto Daily Star* and the *Globe and Mail* ran the story for sixteen days, dedicating many cover pages, editorials, and illustrations to it. At one point, the *Star* had seven reporters stationed in Portugal, Brazil, Angola, St Lucia, Trinidad and Tobago, and Puerto Rico, covering what one of the journalists described was "one of the biggest [stories] of the decade."[37] Another reporter from the conservative *Toronto Telegram*, who had recently been arrested in Lisbon for taking photos of Portugal's crumbling air force equipment, wished "good luck to the pirates."[38] Audiences were drawn by emphatic headlines such as "Pirates Capture Liner," "Atom Sub in Chase. Still Won't Surrender," "The Pirate Captain Says: 'Salazar's a Portuguese Hitler,'" and oddities such as "8-Year-Old Has Plan for Capture" and "Newsmen 'Chute to Ship, Land in Ocean." Torontonians were reeled further into the drama when reading "Toronto Man's Brother in Crew of Santa Maria," "Pirate Chief Has Friends in Toronto," or "Pirate War Reaches Our Bay St."

Anti-Salazarists in Toronto and Montreal received major exposure, as they became the spokespersons for Delgado and Galvão in Canada. In an interview in the *Star*, Delgado saluted his "loyal followers" in Montreal. A few days later, the same newspaper published an exclusive message from the general to all Canadians: "This is the first step for Liberation of the slavery which dominates our beloved Portugal." The *Telegram* mentioned the fact that Delgado had been a supporter of Salazar until he worked in Montreal and Washington, during which time he learnt what "true democracy" was. Another article reported that Delgado's message had been read to about 100 Portuguese supporters gathered at a joint meeting of the PCDA and the FPCC.

Reporters at this event interviewed Ciriaco, whom they introduced as "a long-time personal friend" of Delgado and Galvão, and the only man in Canada who knew the rebels' real objectives and destination, "but he's not telling." Ciriaco did tell the reporter he had been informed of Galvão's plan in a telephone conversation with Ciriaco's brother in

6.1 Fernando Ciriaco da Cunha, 27 February 1961. Photograph by Jim Kennedy. CTASC, Toronto Telegram fonds, ASC54673.

São Paulo. He also explained that the PCDA's mission was to prepare Portuguese immigrants in Canada for their transition to democracy.[39]

In Montreal, a small group of demonstrators organized by Bello picketed the American consulate on 25 January to protest the US navy's pursuit of the *Santa Maria*; they rallied again three days later outside the Portuguese consulate. Interviewed by the *Montreal Gazette*, the Portuguese consul dismissed the "negligible" number of protesters (fifteen in the first rally and forty in the second), most of whom, he claimed, included "intellectuals," no Azoreans, and some Spanish exiles. Some of the consul's allies in the city publicly dismissed Bello's legitimacy, noting that the vast majority in the Portuguese community did not share his views; Artur Ribeiro of the *Voz de Portugal* even argued that Bello had lost the right to debate Portugal's domestic politics because he was now a Canadian citizen.[40] The PCDA organized similar although larger rallies in Toronto, including a drive-by protest in front of the consul's residence in the upmarket suburb of Forest Hill and an evening one outside the consulate on Bay Street, in the heart of Toronto's financial district. The latter was scheduled to coincide with the arrival of a pro-Salazar delegation delivering a petition to the consul, signed by 714 people pledging their support for the regime. The number of Salazar's loyalists reported to be present varied drastically, from 1,000 in the *Star*, 700 in the *Telegram*, and only 200 in the *Globe*. The organizers, among whom were various Portuguese priests, mobilized immigrants from Hamilton, Galt, Oshawa, and Toronto, who arrived carrying placards reading: "Delgado and Galvão are vampires" and "Send pirates to Russia where they belong." One of the leaders, a thirty-year-old immigrant from Hamilton, deplored the media's slanted coverage of the *Santa Maria* crisis, which he believed made it seem as if the majority of Portuguese opposed Salazar. Touched by the large turnout, he added: "This shows the Canadian press Portugal has freedom. It shows the government has support." Their display of patriotism climaxed when the consul descended to the lobby, stood on a chair, and waved to the crowd, which responded with loud cheers.[41] But contrary to the organizers' intentions, the main story in the newspapers the next day was not the arguments of the pro-Salazar camp but their violent reaction to their pro-democratic fellow countrymen.

The PCDA's motorcade consisted of seventeen cars draped in anti-Salazar signs and flags, drivers honking their horns as they passed the consulate. When they came around a second time, a large number of Salazar supporters, "many of them women carrying babies," exited to the street and engulfed the cars, blocking their passage. Some loyalists kicked, rocked, and eventually flipped over one of the vehicles. One of the democrats was punched through his open car window, others were poked with their own flagpoles, and yet others jumped out of their vehicles and got into fistfights. Leading the motorcade was Ciriaco's car, which carried his wife and children, who shouted "*Polícia! Polícia!*" as he drove away through a dodging crowd. Meanwhile, as a *Star* reporter noted: "100 feet away, in an elegant restaurant, diners quietly continued eating as the battle raged outside."

After ten minutes, the Toronto police arrived and dispersed the crowd, arresting two pro-Salazar supporters, who were released shortly after; Lisbon would pay for their court expenses. According to the consul, the police later failed to identify who had damaged the cars, "thanks to the spirit of national solidarity in the colony"; in his eyes, this was a tremendous defeat for the PCDA.[42]

The "Bay St. riot," as the press called it, gave Canadians a clear example of how foreign politics of apparently no direct concern to them could have an impact on their cities through their immigrant communities. But judging from the absence of letters to the editor and opinion columns dealing with this incident, Torontonians, much like the undisturbed diners on that night, did not seem greatly upset about this transplantation of foreign political conflicts onto their streets. The reason may have been the fact that they had had a chance to learn

240   This Pilgrim Nation

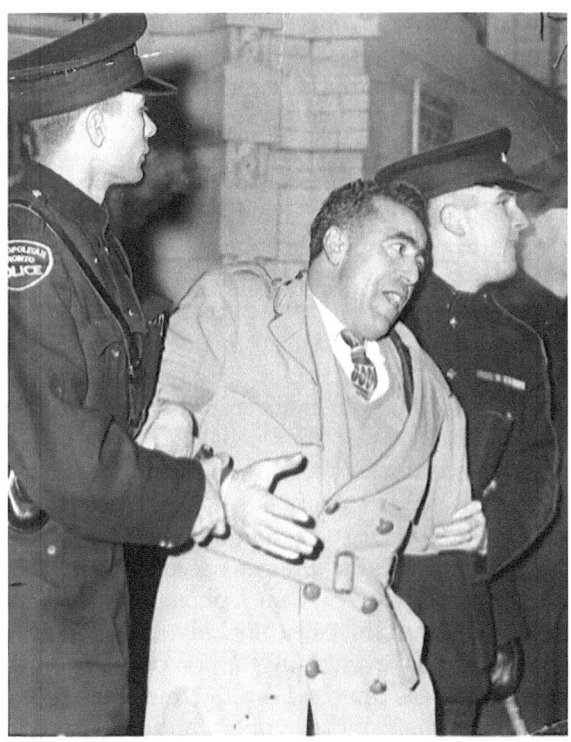

6.2 Pro-Salazar demonstrator arrested by Metropolitan Toronto Police outside the Portuguese consulate on Bay Street, 30 January 1961. Photograph by Proulx. CTASC, Toronto Telegram fonds, ASC27215.

about Portuguese politics and the anti-fascists' struggle for democracy through the *Santa Maria* coverage. Because they could identify the camps and comprehend the issues in a familiar "democracy versus fascism" framework, they were invited into what would otherwise be an entirely alien conflict. Moreover, for those enthralled with the modern buccaneer saga, the "riot" may simply have spiced up a story that kept rewarding those who followed it. The only negative reaction in the press to this violent incident and its foreignness was a small piece in the *Star* section "The Newcomers," which asked: "Why a riot over Portuguese politics on lower Bay St.?" and "Why don't they get this excited over Diefenbaker versus Pearson?" The reporter quoted a DCI officer who remarked: "They chose this country. They came here, but they refuse to look upon it as a home. We try to stress Canada is their new home during occasional lectures at the International Institute."

The piece failed to mention that the PCDA had worked in collaboration with the DCI and the International Institute to promote Canadian naturalization among Portuguese immigrants in Toronto and Montreal; in fact, it was one of the first Portuguese-Canadian organizations to do so. The journalist then asked Ciriaco and António Vaz (also in the motorcade) to explain why there was a demonstration over Portuguese politics on Toronto's streets and what the protesters had meant by "our country." Both men argued that their commitment to democracy was borderless and rejected the implication that a concern for homeland politics precluded a sense of belonging to Canada. Instead, they maintained that their fight against Salazar's dictatorship was a tribute to Canada's values and citizenship, which allowed them the freedom to protest; something they did not have in Portugal. Indeed, Vaz, a tool and die maker who had emigrated to Toronto from mainland Portugal in 1955, later became an active community worker, civic leader, school board trustee, and advocate with various ethnic and mainstream organizations, including sitting on the boards of various prominent Toronto institutions and in a Progressive Conservative Party's riding association. As a member of the community's right-wing faction and a devout Catholic, Vaz also became an opponent of the PCDA alongside Fr Alberto Cunha.[43]

The *Santa Maria* saga was the catalyst that led Portuguese anti-fascists in Montreal to create their own organization. Around the same time, Henrique Bello also created the Canada Movement for Freedom in Portugal and Colonies, an organization that convened influential Canadian individuals and organizations, including the Co-operative Commonwealth Federation (CCF) national leader Hazen Argue, the Canadian Labour Congress (CLC) President Claude Jodoin, along with journalists, authors, student leaders, and other left-wing activists. Its goal was to muster interest for the Portuguese struggle among Canadians and counter the Estado Novo's propaganda. In August 1961, Bello attended the founding convention of the New Democratic Party (NDP; formed from a merger of the CCF and the CLC) in Ottawa and secured the new party's commitment to join the fight against Lisbon's dictatorship and its colonial empire, particularly its suppression of free trade unionism.[44]

After splitting from the APC in 1959, Bello's *Luso-Canadiano* became the first commercial lusophone newspaper in Canada and one of the most circulated anti-Salazar publications in the country, along with São Paulo's *Portugal Democrático*. Until October 1960, the paper was printed in mainland Portugal (Montijo), where it was subjected to the regime's censorship, during which time it was largely apolitical. To escape the "blue pencil," Bello called his typographer José Neves Rodrigues from Portugal and began printing the now bi-weekly in Montreal. To the diplomats' dismay, the *Luso-Canadiano* (re)inaugural editorial introduced itself as an "anti-fascist," "anti-Bolshevik," and "independent" newspaper that strove for a return to democracy in Portugal. Bello recruited correspondents from large and small Portuguese settlements in Canada, especially from among fellow anti-Salazarists in Toronto, who lent him money, wrote content, distributed the newspaper, and connected it with the Portuguese exile community around the world.[45] When the *Luso-Canadiano* became associated with the *Maison*/MDP in 1961, the SNI helped launch its local rival and new APC organ, *Voz de Portugal*, which was first printed at the Salesian College in Lisbon before moving to a Portuguese-American press in Newark a few months later. In a letter to Montreal's *La Presse*, the director of the *Voz*, Artur Ribeiro, repudiated Bello's tirades during the *Santa Maria* episode and affirmed that the latter had only began opposing Salazar after Lisbon denied the *Luso-Canadiano* a subsidy, something Ribeiro claimed the *Voz* would never request. Bello, whose reputation in the transnational exile community was injured following this and previous allegations, took legal action for defamation against the rival title and its director. After being served a notice to appear in court as a result of this libel suit, the publishers of Newark's *Luso-Americano* stopped producing the *Voz*. Once it found a new press in Montreal, in 1962, the newspaper was back in circulation, this time with content cut and pasted from New Bedford's *Diário de Notícias*. The courts eventually ruled in Bello's favour and ordered Ribeiro to pay him damages and legal costs. In 1964, the splintering continued when dissidents from the *Voz* founded a third newspaper, *O Lusitano*. The following year, a new administration led by the newly arrived mainlander Armando Barqueiro – an accountant by training who worked in Montreal as a landscaper, waiter, and hotel worker before opening a furniture store and travel agency – ended the *Voz*'s open confrontation with Bello and his anti-fascists and moved politically towards the centre, no longer being the "consulate's sheet."[46]

In 1963, Ambassador Brazão was happy to report to Lisbon that Bello had written him a "lengthy and pleasant" reply to a letter he had published in the *Luso-Canadiano*. The ambassador interpreted this as a gesture of reconciliation and an attempt by Bello to reconnect with the Portuguese government. Brazão instructed the consul in Montreal to approach Bello and carefully offer a grant for his newspaper, which the latter declined, arguing it infringed on his journalistic principles. However, he was willing to accept ads from Casa de Portugal, in the same way that the Canadian government published its public announcements in the ethnic press. Bello also revealed that he did not belong to any particular ideological camp other than being a democrat, and that his paper's "extremist" leftist bent stemmed from the "anarchist" tendencies of its former typographer and editor Neves Rodrigues. In fact, Bello said that he had refused various requests to place the *Luso-Canadiano* at the disposal of opposition leaders, arguing that, as a democratic newspaper, he wished to keep it open to various political viewpoints. Moreover, he wanted to focus more on immigrant issues than on homeland affairs. The consul here saw an opportunity to neutralize the "nefarious" newspaper, although cautiously, in order not to "give the impression we want to buy it." Brazão informed Lisbon about the arrangement and recommended that the advertisement contract offered to the *Luso-Canadiano* match the direct subsidy given to its rival *Voz*. A few days later, to the diplomat's exasperation, the dissident newspaper published a rebuttal to Brazão's previous letter to the editor by the PCDA's president. Spats between rival Portuguese-Canadian newspapers soon extended to Toronto, where the *Correio Português*'s editor, Maria Alice Ribeiro, accused Bello of accepting a subsidy from Lisbon, while the PCDA criticized Ribeiro for receiving SNI funds to spread lies "on the backs of Portugal's famished." While the *Luso-Canadiano* continued to be an important platform for anti-Salazar activists in Canada, by 1963 it also carried Casa de Portugal ads.[47]

That year, Ciriaco started a job in the federal government and moved to Ottawa, after which he disconnected from the PCDA. According to the Portuguese consul in Toronto, a DCI senior officer had warned Ciriaco after the *Santa Maria* protests that it was "in his best interest" to refrain from getting involved in Portuguese politics.[48] Replacing Ciriaco at the helm of the PCDA was its co-founder, Firmino Oliveira. The new leader had escaped to Canada in 1959 after an acquaintance reported him to the PIDE for supporting Delgado's presidential bid. Oliveira was committed to expanding the PCDA's social services in partnership with the International Institute and the DCI, and he changed its by-laws to reflect a more social, educational, and cultural role, while keeping its pro-democratic spirit. Under his leadership, the PCDA continued to picket the Portuguese consulate and attract the press's attention. However, Oliveira tried to improve relations with the consul, even warning him of upcoming demonstrations and asking him not to take them personally. In 1964, Oliveira yielded his presidency to Guilherme Santos, a recent immigrant who impressed the PCDA's membership at community events with his articulate Marxist critique of the Estado Novo. That year, Oliveira and the consul co-organized the screening of a Lisbon-sponsored film about Angola. At the end of the show,

Santos delivered a lengthy attack on the dictatorship, during which the consul and Oliveira left the room. The latter's solidarity with the diplomat caused a rift with the other PCDA members, leading the former president to sever ties with the association.[49] Afterwards, Oliveira became the FPCC's president and opened a travel agency with business dealings with the SNI/SEIT.

Under Santos, the PCDA shifted farther to the left and became affiliated with the FPLN, although it continued to correspond with Delgado and Galvão. In November 1964, the PCDA launched its bulletin *The Truth / A Verdade*, distributed across Canada, the United States, and other Portuguese emigrant communities; its December 1964 issue mentioned a circulation of "close to a thousand" copies per issue and anticipated an increase in the near future. The newsletter published communiqués from the FPLN, African liberation movements, and other anti-Salazar organizations around the world; news about the plight of political prisoners in Portugal; transcriptions of critical articles published in the mainstream press; and commentary from PCDA members, many of them with a clear Marxist bent.[50] From its pages we learn that these anti-fascists considered their political struggle in the "unsuitable terrain" of emigration to be "an arduous one" and believed their countrymen had forgotten about the social and political ills experienced in Portugal after achieving some financial comfort in Canada, a complaint repeated by other Portuguese exiles in North America.

While the PCDA hoped to raise immigrants' political consciousness, their tone was patronizing, judgmental, and ultimately alienating. This was especially the case when it came to the Azorean majority, seen by Portuguese exiles in North America as a major reactionary force. In a letter to Delgado, Oliveira blamed the "Bay St. riot" on the "ignorance of the Micaelense majority." When anti-Salazarists in Canada invited Galvão to visit Toronto and Montreal in 1964, his associates in the United States convinced the captain to decline, given the organizers' socialist tendencies and the predominance of "hostile" Azoreans in their communities.[51] In an attempt to reach out to that section of the community, *A Verdade* published an "Open Letter to a Portuguese of the Azores." In it, the PCDA invited Azoreans to join in their fight for democracy in Portugal and integrate into Canadian life, where men with "a solid Christian moral foundation" knew real freedom. To remove any misgivings, the author added:

> I know that when I speak to you about "integrating into Canadian life" you confuse it with "Portuguese denationalization" and when you speak of "Salazar" you believe you are speaking of "Portugal" ....

> The bad formation of your mentality, in respect to the interpretation of these two words, is no fault of your own, but that of ... the mainland fascists, who ... introduced in the humble milieu in which you lived an absurd and false mystical [belief] that Portugal is Salazar.[52]

The author also stated that Azoreans were as "good Portuguese" as those in the mainland and promised to "come out swinging, fighting the deprecators, seeking to elucidate them on anything pertaining to the Azores." On another occasion, *A Verdade* published a note from a disgruntled immigrant asking to have his name removed from the subscription list, who observed: "If you don't have anything better to do, go work with a pick and shovel as I do. Please wipe your [?] with the papers." The editors took offence and criticized the man's rudeness while asserting their own intellectual superiority over Salazar's "illiterate" supporters. Another person circulated an open letter in the community criticizing the PCDA for their harsh response to the "poor illiterate" immigrant. *A Verdade* responded by warning of "heavy costs" awaiting anyone who criticized the PCDA, followed by a lengthy essay teasing every grammatical and semantic imprecision in the "fascist" detractor's letter. Despite their condescension, the editors liked to point out that *A Verdade* was written by miners, peasants, construction workers, and other proletarians.[53]

The PCDA was preparing to receive Delgado, who had accepted their invitation to visit Toronto in May 1965, when news of his disappearance emerged. Believing the general had been incarcerated in Spain, they sent a representative to Europe and North Africa to learn what had happened. In the meantime, the MDP and PCDA picketed Portugal's and Spain's diplomatic offices in Montreal, Toronto, and Ottawa, demanding Delgado's release. The rallies gathered hundreds of demonstrators, including Spanish exiles and Canadian university students, and attracted the media's attention. By May, it was apparent that Delgado was, in fact, dead. Instead of cheering the expected arrival of "Portugal's legitimate president" in Toronto, the PCDA once again took their anger to the Portuguese consulate on Bay Street.[54]

The pro-democratic movement in Toronto, which had expanded significantly, began splintering along ideological lines as the PCDA became increasingly associated with the far left. The PCDA continued to advocate the unity of all anti-fascists while criticizing democratic actions of the "Platonic kind," believing that only an armed revolt could defeat the dictatorship.[55] In June 1965, Henrique Cerqueira (Delgado's polemical aide) visited Toronto on a mission to reveal information on the general's murder and raise funds to carry out his revolutionary plans.

That summer, Cerqueira was able to convince various Portuguese immigrants in the city to donate close to CA$3,000 for a supposed revolutionary action in the works. Seeing that the PCDA's leaders were unconvinced by his promises and conspiracy allegations, Cerqueira and a group of dissident members he had met in Morocco attacked the association's executives, accusing them of being communist and therefore being involved in Delgado's death.[56] In President Santos's eyes, Cerqueira took advantage of the PCDA's community outreach and wrecked the revolutionary spirit they had patiently cultivated among the immigrants. After reporting these incidents to the FPLN and asking for their help in exposing Cerqueira as an "agent provocateur," Piteira Santos concluded the two organizations should tighten their relationship in order to ensure the PCDA did not "fall into the hands of dubious elements."[57] The MDP had its own problems with members arrived from Rabat, such as its President Vargas, who preferred to be not "too active" so its members' identities would not be exposed. Under his leadership, the MDP stopped communicating with Toronto and Algiers for about a year, until the *Luso-Canadiano*'s former editor Neves Rodrigues took the helm of that organization in July 1966.[58]

In January 1966, Júlio Félix, a cabinetmaker and PCP militant from mainland Portugal, became the PCDA's new president, after Guilherme Santos left the association for somewhat obscure reasons.[59] It is not clear what happened to Santos between then and 28 July 1968, when he was arrested at the Lisbon airport for "activities against the security of the State;" he was released eight days later. Félix reinforced ties with the FPLN, which expressed interest in intensifying its presence in Canada, one of the few NATO countries to assume "critical and reserved attitudes" towards Salazar. This renewed partnership led to the PCDA's hosting he fourth international conference on Portuguese political prisoners in Toronto, on 28–30 October 1966, following São Paulo (1960), Montevideo (1961), and Paris (1962).[60]

After Portugal's colonialism, the PIDE's civil and human rights abuses over political dissidents was what drew most international condemnation of the dictatorship, as reflected in Peter Benenson's decision to create Amnesty International in 1960 after reading about two Coimbra university students who were sentenced to seven years in jail for toasting "liberty." When a large number of students were arrested and sent to fight in Africa following the 1962 university strikes in Coimbra and Lisbon, fellow academics around the world held solidarity rallies. The expulsion and occasional arrest of Canadian Protestant missionaries in Portugal and Angola, who criticized the colonial government or associated with nationalist rebels, was another issue enraging Canadian public opinion.[61] In 1966–7, Canadians were also upset about the arrest of forty-nine Jehovah's Witnesses (thirty-six of them women), who were charged with "subversive activity" for proselytizing among Portuguese youth a religion that called for their refusal to serve in the army or swear allegiance to the national flag. In October 1966, the Portuguese embassy in Ottawa reported having received an average of twenty letters per day from across Canada protesting their imprisonment.[62]

The three-day Canadian Conference for Amnesty in Portugal tapped into this growing international opposition to Salazar's rule. While the PCDA and FPLN were the conference's organizers, they chose to work behind the scenes and leave the spotlight on a Canadian committee chaired by United Church minister George Kimball. By presenting it as a "Canadian" event, they hoped to avoid a purely "ethnic" connotation. They also tried to deflect the partisan and ideological labels ascribed by the Portuguese consul and his allies in Toronto by emphasizing that the PIDE imprisoned individuals of all political stripes, including Catholic activists. The organizers stressed this was not a "political" conference but one that dealt with human rights violations, which "interests all citizens of any country." As the organizers explained: "It's precisely because it is a Canadian Conference, with important Canadian personalities, that it has more value and projection and can compel authorities in Portugal to free political prisoners."[63]

Still, the PCDA tried to muster the support of like-minded Portuguese in Canada, including 142 immigrants who contributed CA$720, many anonymously. The MDP offered logistical support and sent a delegation to participate in the conference, while the *Luso-Canadiano* acted as its official media outlet. Other Portuguese exile organizations around the world sent funding, delegates, and propaganda material, the largest contribution coming from the FPLN. Describing its membership as workers with little more than primary education, the PCDA requested its allies in Algiers to send someone more experienced to oversee the conference's organization. The FPLN sent Silas Cerqueira, an exiled PCP militant and research assistant at Sorbonne University in Paris, who spent a month and a half coordinating media outreach and connecting with Canadian politicians and activists in Toronto. Cerqueira was able to count on the prestige of Paris's own pro-amnesty conference, which he also co-organized, attracting distinguished personalities such as the philosopher Bertrand Russell and France's former President Vincent Auriol. Newark's CPDP, which had eschewed the Paris conference, owing to its organizer's affiliation with the far left, initially abstained from supporting the PCDA's efforts. Águas had begun exchanging

6.3 Poster for the 1966 Canadian Conference for Amnesty in Portugal in Toronto. CTASC, PCDA fonds.

correspondence with anti-Salazarists in Canada in July 1961, but some time later he concluded that his fellow exiles to the north were poor allies, since they sided with São Paulo's "philo-communists" and had not lived in North America long enough to fully understand its politics. Still, Silas Cerqueira, who visited New York City to study a potential visit by a pro-amnesty delegation to the United Nations, convinced the CPDP to send financial aid (a meagre US$45) to the conference organizers. However, he was unable to dispel Águas's misgivings about the FPLN and its associates in Canada.[64]

The many months of preparation paid off when a large number of Canadian dignitaries endorsed the conference, including federal and provincial party leaders and members of Parliament (MPs), distinguished civil servants, union leaders, activists, journalists, authors, intellectuals, and artists. The popular Canadian journalist and author Pierre Berton chaired the conference, which was officially inaugurated by Toronto mayoral candidate William Dennison. Federal MPs Andrew Brewin and David MacDonald spoke of their recent visit to Portugal, where they had secretly met with various opposition lawyers, students, doctors, journalists, and the families of political prisoners. The FPLN delegation, composed by representatives from Algiers and São Paulo, reminded the audience that the tacit support of leading Western nations enabled Salazar's "fascist" dictatorship to carry on its human rights abuses in Portugal and Africa.[65] One after another, the speakers denounced the lack of civil liberties, the PIDE's repressive "security measures," the brutality of Tarrafal's prison camp, Delgado's assassination, the Colonial Wars, NATO's provision of weapons to Portugal, and Canada's collaboration as a Western ally. Various individuals and organizations in Canada and abroad sent messages of support that were read at the event, including former Prime Minister John G. Diefenbaker, Bertrand Russell, the anti-apartheid activist Bishop Trevor Huddleston of Masani (Tanzania), along with student organizations, labour unions, and exiled groups around the world.

Conference participants approved various resolutions condemning the Estado Novo. They also resolved that the conference's organizing team remain in operation as the Canadian Committee for Amnesty in Portugal (CCAP), which would assume responsibility for coordinating material aid for the families of political prisoners in Portugal, inform Ottawa about human rights abuses in that country, and collaborate with similar organizations around the world. The conference also launched a public campaign asking Canadians to write to the Portuguese ambassador in Ottawa and his superiors in Lisbon demanding amnesty for

6.4 Protesters demanding the release of political prisoners outside the Portuguese consulate on Bay Street, Toronto, 1967. Photograph by Reed. CTASC, Toronto Telegram fonds, ASC08256.

political prisoners; a month later, over 1,000 people had signed a petition demanding the release of four prisoners.[66]

Ten Liberal, NDP, and Progressive Conservative MPs met with an FPLN representative to discuss potential collaborations with that leftist, exile organization. Law Professor Mark MacGuigan edited a documented outlining the different ways in which Lisbon had violated the UN Charter, which was submitted to that body's Human Rights Commission and to Prime Minister Pearson. This action was followed by a visit by a CCAP delegation to the UN headquarters in New York City. Finally, Brewin and MacDonald presented their findings to the Canadian Department of External Affairs after the conference, drawing Ambassador Brazão's condemnation, who accused them of meddling in Portugal's domestic affairs. These Canadian parliamentarians defended their actions by pointing to the human rights standards outlined by various international documents, "the breach of which transcend matters of merely domestic concern and justify ... appropriate protest." Reporting to Lisbon, Brazão commented that the tables could be easily turned if Portugal's "National Assembly deputies contacted Indians [and] Eskimos in their 'reserves' under the guise of those same [international] principles."[67]

According to the PCDA, the conference was a "resounding success," as it generated great interest among Portuguese Canadians, many of whom became involved with the association afterwards. But while the *Luso-Canadiano* and the exile press in Brazil gave it extensive coverage, the mainstream Canadian media did not. The *Globe* and the *Star* made brief mention of Brewin's and MacDonald's visit to Portugal, of the conference's resolutions, and of a protest letter sent to Lisbon signed by 118 "Portuguese leaders." A francophone television station aired an interview with two FPLN delegates a month after the conference. Attendance over the three days of the conference was also lower than anticipated, with an average of sixty people per day. Portuguese diplomats, who had expected to do much damage control after the event, were relatively satisfied. Even right-wing democrats such as António Vaz, who had participated in the PCDA's *Santa Maria* motorcade, criticized the FPLN-dominated conference, whose humanitarian agenda he accused of having been highjacked by communists to advance their ideology and "bring discredit on the Portuguese government." Encouraged by the Portuguese consul in Toronto, Vaz wrote to Prime Minister Pearson to share his views on the conference and caution him against endorsing its resolutions. Despite the diplomats' relatively favourable assessment, the conference clearly irritated Lisbon officials, since in February 1967, all Canadian citizens who had endorsed it were banned from entering Portugal; this interdiction would be lifted in January 1968, except for that against MPs Brewin and MacDonald.[68]

The pro-amnesty conference was the last high-profile action organized by Portuguese anti-fascists in Canada until 1974. Afterwards, the CCAP continued to run its "adopt a prisoner" campaign with relative success, raising funds for political prisoners and their families in Portugal. The PCDA also ran its own campaigns, raising a modest CA$385 (from 125 donors) in 1961 and CA$611 in 1973. Some donations came from remote places such as Kitimat and Louis Creek in British Columbia's interior. These were small but heartfelt contributions, as indicated by an immigrant in Griffith, Ontario, who wrote: "Me and another friend send five dolas each with our best intentions. I apologize for it being so little. I ask that my name is not mentioned to avoid complications with my wife."[69]

No dia 3 de Dezembro, às 12,30 horas, faleceu em Montreal, no hospital Jean Talon, o director do Luso-Canadiano, Henrique Tavares Bello.

Semanário independente em lingua portuguesa fundado por Henrique Tavares Bello

CANADA'S PORTUGUESE WEEKLY ● L'HEBDO PORTUGAIS DU CANADA

MORREU HENRIQUE TAVARES BELLO

Amaram-no os que o conheceram intimamente. Respeitaram-no os adversários. Detestaram-no os medíocres. Caluniaram-no os vermes da existência. Eis o mais que se pode dizer dum Homem que viveu no fogo das ideias sem nunca se deixar abrasar pelo ódio ou pela intolerância.

Henrique Tavares Bello atravessou a existência com um sorriso de bondade no rosto sereno. Amou todos os o compreenderam. Compreendeu e desculpou todos os que o hostilizaram. Simples como uma criança nas horas lazer. Firme como um rochedo nas horas de luta. Sereno sempre. Sempre terno. Sempre superior.

Podem os fracos ser brutais ou agressivos. Podem os mediocres ser altivos ou arrogantes. Podem os que nada têm para dar exigir tudo dos outros. Ele foi suave, humilde e deu-se inteiramente. Deixou uma obra de jornalismo e de combate que se prolongará para além da sua morte. Deixou uma dor profunda em todos os que o amam e querem ainda a sua presença. Deixou uma perplexidade cáustica em todos os que o combateram, porque esses nunca compreenderam o mistério da sua mão sempre a estreitar fraternalmente todas as mãos, mesmo aquelas que a traição humedecia. Deixou um rastro de esperança e uma mensagem de força que, como uma comunhão de místicas certezas, agita agora o sangue de todos os seus companheiros de ideal.

Eu que não acredito na morte, sei-te presente nesta ausência amarga. Falo contigo Companheiro Henrique e saúdo-te na tua nova existência, Proletário da Esperança. Cá estamos todos para continuar a luta que interrompeste, pedreiros do Templo onde o Homem será, um dia, o único Deus. Pedreiros de instrumentos fracos alguns de nós, mais fortes outros, mais ou menos hábeis, todos pondo a nossa complexidade humana ao serviço do futuro, para maior glória do Homem.

Serão por vezes duras as nossas palavras. Serão muitas vezes desvastadoras as nossas acções. Para que o futuro que sonhaste irrompa deste ressequido terreno onde vicejam ainda os exploradores, os tiranos, os assassinos e os traidores, tard o nosso amor que se converter em raiva e a nossa alegria soluçar pragas — possam os nossos rostos permanecerem serenos como o teu, e os nossos corações bater os dois compassos da indignação no tempo e do absolvição no espaço.

Proletário da Esperança repousa agora! Nós tudo faremos para merecer a tua Vida.

CUNHA VIANA

HENRIQUE TAVARES BELLO
— PRESENTE!

POR DR. COSTA GOMES

Estava frio no cemitério de Côte des Neiges. Os amigos tristes, à volta do caixão que descia lentamente para a terra-mãe, olhavam e pareciam não compreender a brutalidade do acontecimento.

E vier...-me umas saudades imensas do sol do meu país, do mesmo sol que aqueceu os dias da infância e da adolescência de Henrique Tavares Bello.

E vieram-me umas saudades imensas do mar, do mar tépido de Portugal a beijar docemente as praias.

E vieram-me umas saudades imensas de amigos queridos que por lá penam nas cadeias para presos políticos ou na incerteza do dia a dia.

E vieram-me umas saudades imensas do cheiro a rosmaninho e do chilrear dos pássaros.

Cerrei os dentes e uma raiva surda subiu em mim. Henrique Tavares Bello, desterrado como a maioria dos portugueses na própria

(Continua na página 2)

AGRADECIMENTO

Tornamos pública por esta forma a nossa imensa gratidão por todos aqueles que nesta hora de sofrimento nos deram a sua solidariedade.

A FAMÍLIA DE H. TAVARES BELLO

A REDACÇÃO

6.5 Front cover of the *Luso-Canadiano* issue of 15 January 1967, announcing the death of its founder, Henrique T. Bello. CTASC, Domingos Marques fonds.

The PCDA and MDP changed executives in 1967 and started dedicating greater attention to local affairs. The Montreal group, especially, assumed a more comprehensive role in its immigrant community: opening a library; offering French-, English-, and Portuguese-language classes; gym classes; music lessons; a choir; and a café bar, among other social and cultural programs.[70] In December of that year, its founder, Henrique Bello, died of cancer.

His wife, Maria Bello, continued publishing the *Luso-Canadiano* with help from MDP members, until it finally closed in May 1971. In September and November 1968, the "Portuguese Antifascists in Canada" came together in two meetings held in Toronto and Montreal, where they agreed to coordinate activities. They encouraged Portuguese exiles around the world to follow their example and called for an international meeting of the "external front" to discuss its future in the Caetano era and to form a government in exile, for which they endorsed the PCP's former presidential candidate Ruy Gomes as its head.[71] At this point, however, the FPLN had lost much of its original impetus and the "external front" was increasingly fragmented. At the same time, the PCDA's and MDP's members increasingly lacked the means, energy, and enthusiasm of its early years. Membership dwindled, while their meeting places gradually became social spaces similar to those of other ethnic clubs.

Cold War Surveillance and Deportation: The PIDE, FBI, and RCMP

Fear of infiltration by the PIDE and its wide informant network in North America was prevalent and played a critical role in ensuring that most Portuguese immigrants remained politically passive. For those hoping to return to Portugal or whose families remained there, it seemed wise not to participate in activities that might haunt them later. As Bello explained in a letter to Immigration Minister Ellen Fairclough, fear was a "general sickness" that plagued Portuguese immigrants, who believed that the PIDE had infiltrated "this democratic Canada of ours, to train and place ... spies and villains capable of making depositions and accusations that can menace our jobs."[72] By pointing to real and imagined PIDE agents at every corner, political exiles inadvertently helped the dictatorship, which instrumentalized these fears to repress political activity. Nonetheless, while mostly based on rumours, fear of political surveillance was justified. It was common for the PIDE to act on intelligence received from expatriate civilian informers, diplomats, and host-nation intelligence services, which sometimes led to arrests of political emigrants returning home, searches of their residences abroad, and harassment of their families in Portugal. This was one aspect of emigration that Salazar kept well informed about through his almost daily conversations with the PIDE's director.[73]

As a member of NATO, the PIDE had privileged access to the Western powers' intelligence networks and was able to develop partnerships with various national agencies under the guise of fighting "common criminality."[74] One of the most productive collaborations, formalized in 1956, was with the CIA, which helped modernize the PIDE's database and introduce its agents to various spying and counter-intelligence techniques useful for infiltrating the PCP.[75] The PIDE's interaction with the Canadian secret services was less intense. Nonetheless, as Reg Whitaker noted, Canadian officials had few qualms about engaging with "dubious elements in repressive dictatorships that happened to proclaim their strong anti-Communism," such as Lisbon's, whose police services they deemed "more or less efficient ... liaison with whom was left to the [Royal Canadian Mounted Police (RCMP)]'s discretion."[76] In fact, throughout its history, the RCMP had consistently sought to "identify, intrusively observe, and even actively counter 'subversive' organizations formed among minority communities."[77] Moreover, since the beginning of Portuguese mass migration to Canada, the RCMP had sought the PIDE's assistance in screening the political leanings of migrant candidates and prevented the entry of individuals with "political ideas contrary to the established Order." In 1951, Ottawa and Lisbon had agreed to alert each other whenever a communist national attempted to "infiltrate" the other's territory, giving border officials the option of denying entry visas while agreeing not to disclose their information source.[78] Still, it was possible for political dissidents to slip through this security screening or perhaps be allowed to leave with the PIDE's tacit consent, as was the case of António Sousa, who was allowed to board the *Saturnia* in 1953 despite being, according to him, a known opponent of Salazar.

I found no evidence of Canadian officials deporting Portuguese immigrants on the basis of their political affiliation, as they did with other migrant groups.[79] However, this lack of evidence may stem from the fact that the 1952 Immigration Act granted immigration officials wide discretion to reject and deport immigrants without disclosing the reasons or the source of the information. Another possible explanation is the fact that Portuguese mass immigration began in the 1960s and 1970s, when Canadian public opinion demanded greater checks and oversight on the RCMP's power and influence. Still, Canadian authorities deported various undocumented Portuguese migrants, some of them young men escaping military duty in Africa. The PCDA and MDP pleaded with immigration officials on behalf of war resisters and other clandestine migrants seeking political asylum in Canada and warned them about the violent reprisals these men would face if repatriated. Canada's immigration ministers were reluctant to overrule deportation orders issued on these émigrés, when appealed to by Portuguese exiles, although sometimes they allowed the clandestine migrants to leave by their own means to a country of their choosing. However, once released, these undocumented exiles often evaded the authorities and became fugitives.[80]

The PCDA and MDP received various requests for aid from fellow exiles and war resisters around the world (particularly from North Africa) and helped some enter the country illegally. In Montreal, the Portuguese consul turned to *La Presse* and the *Voz* to characterize these facilitators as "agitators" and the migrants they helped as bogus refugees. This led Canadian authorities, working with information provided by the consul, to raid Montreal's Portuguese community in 1961, including the meeting places of the MDP. The latter complained to Minister Fairclough about the arrest of one of its members (a former University of Lisbon student) and the constant threats and insults hurled at them by the *Voz* and its "vice-editor" the Portuguese consul, whom they tried to have declared persona non grata.[81] In May 1967, Rev. A.S. Murray, a representative of the World Council of Churches refugee aid, published a letter in various Canadian newspapers recounting his frustrating attempt to convince immigration officials not to deport a Portuguese asylum-seeker to Salazar's country. The young student, who had been detained in Quebec for three months after travelling clandestinely to Canada aboard a ship, feared being shot by the PIDE if repatriated. So he sought the help of the MDP, which in turned contacted Murray. The latter found an organization in France willing to assist the boy, while the MDP offered to pay for his trip there. Despite these efforts, Canadian authorities, according to Murray, did not budge and the boy was deported to Portugal. Following the allegations, Canadian immigration officials looked into their files and found no record of such a case, although the search was admittedly made difficult by the fact that they lacked the boy's name. Responding to this case, the deputy minister of immigration reassured his boss that it was not their policy to repatriate undocumented migrants when there were credible indications that they would be punished for political offences.[82] Nonetheless, the saga of Portuguese undocumented war resisters took a tragic turn on 7 December 1967, when twenty-three-year-old Gomes Rosa jumped to his death from the eighth-floor window of a federal building in Montreal after being informed that his refugee application had been declined and that he had to return to Portugal. After this incident, the MDP sent a letter signed by various Portuguese organizations to Minister of Manpower and Immigration Jean Marchand, pleading for a more "humane attitude" whenever deciding the fate of clandestine migrants fleeing the Colonial Wars, a message they underlined with a rally outside Montreal's immigration office.[83] According to Jaime Monteiro, an MDP delegation later met with the minister, who assured them that no other Portuguese migrant would be deported without first seeking their counsel.[84] The MDP and PCDA continued to encourage Portuguese war resisters to seek asylum in Canada, including those sailors who occasionally docked in Montreal, who were told: "When you serve under a banner of crime and treason, desertion is honourable."[85]

Deportations of Portuguese clandestine migrants, including political exiles, were also common in the United States. The most prominent anti-Salazarist to be detained by American immigration officials was Palma Inácio. As a mechanic, Inácio sabotaged twenty aircraft in a Portuguese airbase during a failed republican coup in 1947, for which he was incarcerated. Two years later he escaped prison and absconded to Morocco. In 1951, he travelled from Casablanca to California as a table waiter on a cruise ship. Eventually Inácio made his way east, settling in Windsor Locks, Connecticut, and he worked as a mechanic and flight instructor in Northampton, Massachusetts. In March 1954, immigration authorities arrested Inácio and were preparing to repatriate him, following Lisbon's request. However, Abílio Águas and the Portuguese-Brazilian industrialist Lúcio Feteira convinced American officials to let Inácio leave for Brazil, where he connected with Delgado and Galvão, and planned his infamous 1961 airplane highjack.[86] That year, the PIDE created a file on the CPDP, after the consul in New York forwarded their communiqué published in the *Diário*, where its founders revealed their identities. From this information, the PIDE would learn about the lives of these individuals and their families in Portugal, with the help of diplomats, community informants, and the FBI.[87] In May 1964, they started a file on the PCDA after receiving one of its communiqués from a Toronto informant. The MDP also became a target of investigation in December of that year after its members revealed their identities by signing an FPLN protest letter to the United Nations.[88]

In the aftermath of the "Bay St. riot," Ciriaco told the *Star* he had recognized three members of "the Portuguese Gestapo" whom he had met in Portugal. According to him, these agents settled in the expatriate communities and posed as regular emigrants for a couple of years, then reported anti-government activities back to Portugal, where the police pressured the families of subversive emigrants to urge them to keep quiet. Ciriaco said he was aware of cases where Portuguese emigrants in other countries had been arrested upon returning home for the holidays based on information provided by these infiltrated agents. On a CBC TV show later that year, Oliveira reaffirmed that the PIDE had infiltrated Toronto and Montreal and mentioned that a man was arrested in Portugal, owing to his brother's anti-Salazar activities in Canada. Curiously, two years later, Oliveira wrote an article in the *Luso-Canadiano* dispelling "rumours" about the PIDE's infiltration, arguing that the political police knew that Portuguese emigrants were "protected by the democratic institutions of Canada."[89]

On 4 July 1970, twenty-nine-year-old Eurico Nunes, a landed immigrant in Canada, was arrested when crossing the border into Vilar Formoso in northern Portugal, where he had travelled with his American wife to visit his ailing father. A communist, Nunes had been a political prisoner in Portugal before travelling to Syria, Turkey, and Egypt, from where he moved to Canada two years prior. Since then, he had become an executive member of the PCDA; enrolled in Ryerson Institute of Technology, where he led its Students for Democratic Society chapter; and worked as a government translator at the Toronto international airport and as a freelance journalist for the *Luso-Canadiano* and CBC Radio. As to the reasons for his arrest, the PIDE cited two interviews with a miner and fado singer that he had written for the *Luso-Canadiano*, his translation into Portuguese of articles from *Le Monde* and other French publications about the 1968 crisis, three UN petitions that he had signed, and letters to a friend in Portugal, all of which were critical of the regime. Canadian foreign officials, partially prompted by MP Andrew Brewin, quickly began monitoring his situation. They agreed that, despite having no legal obligation to intervene on Nunes's behalf, as he was not a Canadian citizen, they had a "moral obligation" to seek his release, since his arrest resulted from legal activities done in Canada. During his time in prison, Nunes was subjected to the PIDE's infamous "statue" torture technique, where he had to stand motionless for twelve hours straight – what a Canadian security official considered "low-key" interrogation. He was let go four days after his arrest and allowed to return to Canada, which he did about a month later. Earlier, Nunes explained to Canadian officials at the Lisbon embassy that he owed his freedom to his wife, whose American citizenship allowed her to make representations on his behalf without fear of reprisal. Also of help were the appeals made to the police by a friend of the family who was a National Assembly deputy. Nunes alerted the Canadians to the fact that "several landed immigrants" visiting Portugal had been arrested and released on condition that they become PIDE informants in Canada; however, when prompted, he failed to offer examples. After returning to Toronto, Nunes's PCDA associates noted that he had withdrawn from the Portuguese community altogether out of fear of further reprisal.[90]

I found no direct evidence of PIDE agents being sent to North America to spy on Portuguese emigrants, as was the case in France, where they were informally allowed to operate discreetly.[91] The same is unlikely to have happened in Canada or the United States, given that the PIDE's budget and personnel were limited, especially after 1961, when its overseas attention shifted to Africa. However, there were plenty of civilian informants, whose identities and personal motivations are for the most part unknown. In one known case, a Toronto informant was a family relative of a PIDE inspector.[92] In New York, the newsletter publisher Gil Stone began relaying information to Lisbon in August 1963. The PIDE and the Foreign Affairs Ministry agreed that payments for Stone's information should be made outside the official channels, so they decided to send the money through his friend Henrique Medina (the Estado Novo's official portraitist). In typical fashion, it took over three years for Stone to receive these payments.[93] Even the public relations agent George Peabody shared sensitive information with Lisbon. According to Peabody, American intelligence agencies approached him regularly to obtain information on Portuguese subversives in the country. In 1963, he was asked about the CPDP's activities and its relations with Galvão and Delgado. Following this enquiry, Peabody approached his contacts in Brazil and obtained the names of the exiles' connections in Newark. He then relayed that information to the SNI's director and requested that his identity be concealed.[94]

Exiled organizations were cautious when accepting new members, as they feared infiltration by informants and agent provocateurs. They organized their own intelligence network through the FPLN, with whom they exchanged information about known Salazar supporters, PIDE collaborators, and other suspicious individuals amidst their communities. For instance, candidates for MDP membership (*amigos*) underwent a six-month probation period before becoming full members (*companheiros*), where they had to prove their pro-democratic convictions and integrity and carry themselves with "a social, familial or professional conduct [worthy of] dignified Man."[95] Despite the exiles' carefulness, Portuguese authorities were able to collect information from sources inside or very close to their organizations. In fact, one of the PCDA's founders, whom we will call Xavier, volunteered information on his former comrades to the PIDE. In November 1967, after being denied entry into Portugal and ordered to return to Canada, Xavier contacted Portuguese authorities trying to ascertain why he was barred, and offered to clear his name with the PIDE by sharing information on "agitators" in Toronto. In his request for a travel visa, Xavier explained that, despite having become a Canadian national, he felt "as Portuguese as those who defend it in our Land with arms in hand" and refused to work with "leftist elements and others foreigners who sought to embarrass Portugal." The Portuguese ambassador in Ottawa endorsed Xavier's visa application and confirmed he had relinquished his previous subversive activities, on which the PIDE had gathered information since 1963; that year they had issued an arrest order for him, which was replaced with a prohibition to enter the country in 1967. In January 1968, with a visa in hand, Xavier was finally allowed into Portugal. Once there, he walked into the PIDE's headquarters in Lisbon and offered his testimony about the activities of his former PCDA comrades.[96]

This was not the first time Xavier had shared information on the PCDA's members. According to him, in the early 1960s, two RCMP undercover agents began frequenting the PCDA pretending to be NDP organizers. They approached Xavier – a Canadian citizen since 1964 – and asked that he provide information on two members affiliated with Canada's "Communist Trotskyist Party" (likely the League for Socialist Action), who had recently applied for citizenship. According to Xavier, the RCMP consulted him every time a "suspicious" Portuguese immigrant applied for naturalization; the use of citizenship security screenings to recruit ethnic informants was a common practice of the RCMP during the Cold War.[97] He also mentioned the RCMP had made similar requests of Ciriaco after he accepted a job with the federal government. With Xavier's insight, Canadian officials rejected the citizenship bids of the two Trotskyists. At this point, the PCDA's membership began suspecting there was an informant in their midst. That suspicion fell primarily on Xavier after he opposed the sending of funds to African nationalist forces. To erase doubts about his loyalty, Xavier became more active in the PCDA's rallies, communications, and administration. In 1964, the RCMP convinced Xavier not to abandon the association after Guilherme Santos's arrival and asked him to obtain information on the new president, which he was unable to do. Xavier eventually left the PCDA against the RCMP's wishes, but kept abreast of its internal dynamics, which he revealed to the PIDE.

While they suspected the PIDE's presence, political exiles, many of whom had become Canadian or American citizens, hardly expected to be under surveillance by their democratic hosts, much less that their agencies would share intelligence with Portuguese authorities. But that was what happened after June 1961, when the Portuguese consul in New York asked the FBI to gather information on the CPDP. The FBI's reports to the PIDE indicate that they consulted with known registered informants; interviewed community members; and searched the records of the Immigration and Naturalization Services, Newark's public gas and electric power supplier, motor vehicle registration, and a local credit bureau. The FBI also kept notes on those individuals who picketed the Portuguese consulate, including during the *Santa Maria* protests. The RCMP too shared information on Portuguese anti-fascists with the PIDE. For instance, in September 1967, the director of security and intelligence, William Higgitt (RCMP commissioner after 1969), relayed information to Inspector Agostinho Barbieri Cardoso (one of the PIDE's leading agents, who planned Delgado's assassination) on the PCDA, MDP, and CCAP. In turn, Higgitt requested intelligence on these groups' connections with communists in Portugal.[98] In February 1968, the Department of External Affairs also opened a file on the activities of "Portuguese foreign nationals" in Canada and alerted the RCMP about the MDP, following a letter sent by that "pressure group" to Prime Minister Pearson congratulating him on refusing to sell arms to Portugal.[99]

After learning the identities and addresses of these subversive expatriates and their families in Portugal, the PIDE was able to intercept their correspondence, monitor their movements, and unravel their networks. To avoid this incursion, the exiles developed complex mailing systems to conceal their communications. For instance, while in Brazil, Galvão corresponded with his contacts in Lisbon by way of Newark so to avoid detection. The CPDP set up a system by which Galvão's letters were mailed under a fake identity to Eduardo Covas's teenage son in Portugal.[100] For large packages the Newark committee relied on trusted steamship crew members. According to Águas, these were "humble people ... experienced with handling customs officers," who supplement their meagre income with contraband. CPDP operatives visiting Portugal sometimes personally handed mail to the DDS leaders. However, in March 1964, after identifying Covas's family in Portugal with help from the FBI, the PIDE installed a wiretap on their home phone and listened in on their conversations. Afterwards, the PIDE was able to intercept most correspondence between Águas, Galvão, and the DDS.[101] The PIDE also intercepted correspondence to Portugal from exiles in Canada. For example, in February 1967, the MDP sent to the publishers of Lisbon's *República* newspaper a cheque, the product of a Christmas fundraiser for the families of political prisoners in Portugal.

The PIDE had intercepted the letters arranging this transaction and confiscated the cheque, for which they were publicly shamed in the opposition's media. Besides intercepting mail, the PIDE also sent letters to exile organizations passing as fellow anti-fascists and spreading damning rumours about individual members. According to Ciriaco, the majority of requests for information and funds received in the PCDA's mail turned out to be "exploiters, swindlers, and even people tied to the PIDE."[102]

Portuguese authorities issued arrest warrants on these exiles for when they visited home. For instance, in March 1963, the PIDE intercepted a letter from Águas to a DDS leader raising concerns about a planned family trip to Portugal by one of the CPDP's operatives. The PIDE obtained an arrest warrant for this man on the grounds of his distributing anti-Salazar propaganda and escorting Galvão during his visit to New York, information they had received from the FBI, which interviewed this CPDP operative (and American citizen) in November 1962. In this case, the PIDE decided to cancel the warrant and discreetly watch the man's movements while he was in Portugal, something they repeated when he returned in 1965 and 1968.[103]

Although upset about the FBI's inquiries, Águas believed that no harm could come from them and welcomed the opportunity to clarify the CPDP's pro-democratic position. In his assessment, the orders for their surveillance had likely come from the State Department as part of its ongoing efforts to appease Lisbon during the Lajes Air Base negotiations. Anticipating trouble, the CPDP's founders had pre-emptively informed the State Department in May 1960 about their intentions and asked if their proposed actions contravened any laws or conduct expected of American citizens – the PCDA had done the same with the RCMP soon after they were formed.[104] Still, the FBI carried on its investigation until 1964, at which point the US Foreign Services had their own file on the CPDP, which they too shared with the PIDE. In November of that year, FBI agents questioned Covas – his undocumented status was not mentioned in their report – about the CPDP's relationship with Galvão and the Social-Democratic Action, and whether their committee planned to overthrow Salazar by force, to which Covas replied that the CPDP was merely a point of contact between the Action and Washington.[105] In March 1965, the Department of Justice instructed the CPDP and its members to abide by the Foreign Agents Registration Act – the same legislation that had plagued Camacho and his PACFA – and register as spokespersons for the Social-Democratic Action, which American officials understood to be a political party. Águas rejected this interpretation and stressed that the CPDP was made up of American citizens and long-term residents who neither received nor solicited funding from foreign sources, but to no avail. Refusing to accept that legal imposition, along with the increased scrutiny that such official status would force upon them, Águas and his companions decided to close the CPDP, although they vowed to continue working unofficially. However, a few months later they were back in operation, after a former US attorney general and "old friend" of Águas convinced the Department of Justice to drop the case against them. Still, Washington's harassment and effective rejection of their anti-Salazar message was a major blow to the morale of these pro-Western activists. As Covas remarked, his faith in the "so-called mentors of the Free World" had been broken to the point that he was "absolutely convinced that the communists are right ... in that the much praised American democracy is nothing more than a farce."[106]

Conclusion

Social scientists have traditionally measured the "political participation" of immigrant groups by looking at their electoral turnout and number of candidates, basing their conclusions on their samples' socio-economic characteristics. Their national and liberal-democratic bias has misconstrued the political profiles of immigrant communities by excluding non-citizens, transnational politics, and a range of direct forms of political action and grass-roots activism outside formal electoral representation. Seen through this prism, Portuguese immigrants in the United States and Canada have long been perceived as politically apathetic, resulting from a combination of historical, sociological, and even anthropological factors.[107] These arguments are consistent with those of early social historians who argued that common immigrants paid little attention to the abstract promises of radical activists. Yet, as we have seen, Portuguese immigrant workers organized rallies, petitions, humanitarian campaigns, and other informal political actions that addressed specific causes and sought tangible results. To be sure, "new migration" historians did not suggest that common immigrants were docile or that politics played no role in the formation of their communities. Still, their focus on the immigrants' "local realities" missed a fundamental part of their experience, ideologies, and solidarities as transnational beings. Both the civic and the religious lives of Portuguese communities were indeed infused with intense political battles that straddled home and host nation politics. Their political history confirms Patrias's argument that "even immigrant communities comprised largely of semi-literate peasants and rural labourers should not necessarily be seen as enclaves, cut off from outside influences," and that "a handful of better-educated immigrants can exert a crucial influence on community development by infusing it with ideological content and by linking the group to political concerns in the homeland and in the receiving society."[108]

As Gabaccia noted concerning Italian republicans abroad, radical transnational immigrants were equally interested "in changing the world and the countries where they lived and worked" as they were in the politics of their homeland.[109] The active engagement of "radical ethnic brokers" with American and Canadian political parties and other civic institutions contradicted the nativist view of homeland politics as something that prevented or delayed the immigrants' integration in their host societies. The fact that these activists educated their fellow immigrants on their host nation's liberal-democratic processes, promoted naturalization, and opposed an authoritarian colonialist regime criticized by their own host governments mattered little to North American authorities, which saw them primarily as transnational "subversives" and "communists" bent on overthrowing an allied government. The exiles' foreignness prevailed when it came to sharing damning information with the Estado Novo's political police, even when they were American or Canadian citizens. Such blatant disregard of the principles of liberal-democratic citizenship, which Western nations claimed to protect, was common in the Cold War period. While sanctioned by elected officials, North American secret services carried out these investigations with a great deal of autonomy in a manner that disregarded national sovereignty conventions in order to meet the transnational threat of international communism.[110]

Reluctance to acknowledge homeland politics as legitimate forms of civic engagement in the host country continued in the multiculturalist 1970s. As Harold Troper and Morton Weinfeld argued, Prime Minister Pierre Trudeau "believed Old World antipathies should be discarded when immigrants entered Canada," since they did not serve the country's needs.[111] This was a message that Portuguese exiles heard more frequently after 1971, as official multiculturalism privileged innocuous expressions of ethnic culture over more politicized identities and solidarities. As we saw in previous chapters, American and Canadian officials regularly endorsed the proud testimonials of dual patriotism voiced by Portuguese ethnic revivalists and heritage champions and rarely coaxed them to forgo their homeland affinities. However, this tolerance for homeland solidarities was not always extended to leftist exiles, seen to be dangerous. Furthermore, the fact that Portuguese anti-fascists refused to embrace the Estado Novo's folksy cultural expressions placed them at a disadvantage in North America's emerging multiculturalist polity. Nonetheless, despite lacking ample resources, these exiles were able to disrupt Lisbon's foreign agenda in North America with the help of their transnational networks. They circulated "subversive" literature, raised funds and organized high-profile political actions that tarnished the dictatorship's carefully crafted image of consensus. They also mustered substantial support from progressive politicians, activists, and public figures in their host countries, along with the mainstream media's consistent attention (particularly in Canada), thus increasing their political leverage. In the CPDP's case, endorsements from American dignitaries were possible, owing to Águas's political capital and wide personal network. In turn, the PCDA and MDP, whose members and some executives had little formal education or financial means, were able to count on the FPLN's network, through which they exchanged resources, information, know-how and credibility. To some extent, the exiles' reliance on external allies to raise their political profile in North America resembled the exchanges between conservative ethnic brokers and Portuguese government officials.

Middle- and upper-class "radicals" tended to distance themselves from their working-class countrymen and their ethnic affairs. This isolation was more pronounced in the CPDP, whose members, spread around the Greater New York City Area, followed Águas's example and avoided the community's social activities. In contrast, the PCDA's and MDP's members were active in other popular community clubs and lived in or frequented their cities' Portuguese neighbourhoods. This difference helps explain why the latter were more successful at politicizing their fellow immigrants than their American peers, despite the arguably greater resistance from conservative forces in Toronto and Montreal. Another important distinction explaining this relative success was the fact that their organizations operated in newcomer settlements, where the memories of poverty and persecution in the homeland were sharper than in the multigenerational Portuguese-American communities. Furthermore, political exiles in Canada, most of whom were staunch anti-colonialists, did not have (yet) to contend with an ethnic elite that was preoccupied with ethnic heritage campaigns, as their Portuguese American counterparts did. Águas and his associates, on the other hand, held the untenable position of being both anti-Estado Novo and pro-empire, which further alienated them from both the ethnic and the radical exile communities. While he capitulated to the Estado Novo on the heritage front, Águas shared its celebratory imperialist version of itinerant "Portugueseness." However, most political exiles (including the CPDP's rank and file) traced their itinerancy to a more recent past of forced displacement from their beloved country. Besides their commitment to bringing down the dictatorship, their transnational solidarity was based on these shared painful memories. As the Portuguese opposition moved further to the left and more war resisters filled their ranks, their networks narrowed their political affiliations and became more radical, anti-colonial, and anti-capitalist. Though they never engaged directly with Moreira's "pilgrim nation" ideal, the FPLN and the opposition's "external front" facilitated the creation of a transnational network that resembled an alternative diaspora. Despite professing very different goals and ideals, the two diasporic imaginings shared discursive similarities. In both cases, expatriates were urged never to forget their fellow countrymen back home and to strive to advance their well-being and advocate for Portugal's national interests from within their host countries. In short, both the regime's emigrant "colonies" and the FPLN's "external front" were subsidiaries of the homeland, where the future of Portuguese nationhood was ultimately decided.

7 New Beginnings, Old Journeys: Multicultural, Generational, and Political Transitions

I came from afar, from very far. What I've trekked to get here!
I will travel afar, so very far, where we will find ourselves, with what we have to give us.

Chorus for the song *Eu Vim de Longe,
P'ra Muito Longe* (1982) by José Mário Branco.[1]

News of the Estado Novo's fall on 25 April 1974 was initially greeted with hope and euphoria by most emigrants outside the colonies. But in the turbulent revolutionary transition period that followed, Portuguese expatriates grew apprehensive about their kin and property in the homeland, as they watched tensions between opposing political factions escalate into near civil war. This political shift intersected with other transformations unfolding in the 1970s that were equally important in shaping the future of Portuguese communities, including the "minority rights revolution" in the United States, the advent of multiculturalism in Canada, and the emergence of a new generation of young ethnic activists in both countries. This convergence of momentous transitions warrants the 1970s a special place in the history of the Portuguese in North America. In this final chapter, we will revisit some of the topics previously discussed and highlight their changes and continuities in this period. We will also join in the debate on whether North American identity politics, framed by multiculturalist and civil rights ideologies, limited or stimulated political activity among immigrant communities. Specifically, we will engage with Wenona Giles's and Irene Bloemraad's assessments on how multiculturalism affected the political attitudes of Portuguese immigrants in Canada and the northeastern United States.[2]

After studying the settlement and labour experiences of Portuguese women in Toronto, Giles concluded that Canada's official multiculturalism was a patriarchal, consensus-building policy that rewarded ethnicity over other forms of political identity, such as class or gender, and deliberately empowered self-appointed middle-class ethnic leaders whose personal agendas were out of touch with the needs of those immigrant workers they claimed to speak for. In her view, by limiting state funding criteria to "ethnic" activities, Canadian governments effectively restricted the range of issues that immigrant activists could advocate for, thereby curbing their activism in other critical areas. Bloemraad, on the other hand, has a more positive outlook on multiculturalism and its effect in promoting civic and political engagement. After comparing the Portuguese of Toronto and Boston, she found that naturalization rates in Canada increased rapidly after 1971, departing from its historical parity with the United States, despite greater rewards for citizenship in the latter; while permanent residents in Canada could sponsor immigration applications, in the United States that privilege was reserved to citizens. Bloemraad attributed this difference to Canada's multiculturalism policy introduced in that year, since it helped create ethnic organizations where immigrants could develop an interest in public life and learn about their host country's decision-making processes.

In contrast, David Colburn and George Pozzetta argued that, in the United States, European ethnics seeking group recognition in the 1960s could not go as far as to challenge "the basic belief in the rationality of individuals and markets, which elites had long held to be the essence of the American capitalist system."[3] In other words, white ethnics stopped short of demanding access to affirmative action programs. Still, women of all backgrounds benefited from equity programs created after the 1965 Equal Employment Opportunity Commission; in Canada, they had to wait until the 1986 Employment Equity Act. It was only able-bodied white males, comprising the vast majority of Euro-American ethnic leaders, who were excluded from affirmative action programs. Many "inbetween" white ethnics began mobilizing in large numbers in the late 1960s and early 1970s to demand inclusion in the "minority rights revolution" and benefit from equity programs redressing their historical marginalization.[4] This was the case with the new generation of Portuguese ethnic activists in North America, who used the language and resources provided by civil rights and multiculturalist policies to advance progressive causes that went beyond cultural identity. However, their growing civic and political engagement was not the result of one "revolution" but a combination of intersecting processes taking place in their local, national, and transnational contexts.

Multicultural Societies: Portuguese Communities in the Early 1970s

Once avoided by white, middle-class, city residents and neglected by municipal officials, some of the inner-city immigrant "ghettos" of yesteryear became quaint multicultural destinations in the 1970s, as North American urbanites developed their pluralist world views. Cosmopolitan city-dwellers hoping to experience the sights, sounds, and flavours of different world cultures began seeking them in these neighbourhoods, where ethnic entrepreneurs were ready to cater to them. These commercial interactions were at the genesis of the multicultural tourism described by a *New York Times* reporter in 1982, who wrote of his visit to Newark's Ironbound, where "April in Portugal" was "waiting just across the Hudson":

> The Saturday stroller along almost a mile of Ferry Street ... is plunged into a Lusitanian world, where signs and talk on the street are in Portuguese, where loudspeakers on stores or on automobiles blare soccer recaps and melodies from Portugal, where the stores are jammed with shoppers seeking Portuguese groceries, pastries, wine, clothing and household gift items. At night, the visitor can sit in restaurants and absorb the keening of the fado ... or join in hearty simple-stepped but colorful dances that bring back memories of home, even if the dancers have never been to the old country.[5]

Municipal officials also recognized the economic and electoral potential of these communities and began supporting the development of their cities' multicultural landscapes as profitable tourist venues, sometimes even enhancing their "ethnic" features.[6] Streets and squares were renamed to reflect the foreign origin of its local residents, while city maps identified their ethnic neighbourhoods as miniature homelands, for instance, "Little Portugal" or "Portugal Village." By the 1980s, these ethnic spaces had become the quintessential material and geographic expressions of multiculturalism, by then a well-established public ideology in Canada and in those northeastern American states where the Portuguese had settled. However, the fixity of these geographic markers contrasted with the immigrants' mobility and transnational lives. The imagined boundaries did not prevent them from leaving their original working-class settlements in search of better housing, usually in areas of the city occupied by older ethnic groups or middle-class suburbs. In Toronto, the Portuguese were gradually "pushed out" of Kensington Market by Caribbean and East Asian newcomers arriving in the 1970s, and they moved to neighbourhoods predominantly occupied by Italians or to the suburbs. In Montreal's Plateau Mont-Royal, the home renovations done by the Portuguese, recognized with an award from the Ordre des architectes du Québec in 1975, were partially responsible for the neighbourhoods' gentrification and the immigrants' subsequent flight. In Fall River, it was Portuguese newcomers who prompted older Portuguese Americans to leave their historical quarters; by 1972, the city's population was roughly evenly split between American and foreign born. In 1980, 74 per cent of the Portuguese in Massachusetts and 73 per cent of those in Rhode Island had arrived in the country after 1965.[7]

While many of the earlier immigrants had improved their living conditions and become homeowners – an important symbol of status and rootedness in the new country – thanks in large part to their families' intensive labour and meticulous saving strategies,[8] they still faced considerable social and economic challenges. At this point, the American and Canadian labour movements started shifting their attention away from the declining manufacturing industries and onto white-collar sectors. Portuguese women, who began moving out of the vanishing needle trades and other manufacturing jobs and moving into service work, benefited from this labour shift, since they began organizing in higher numbers and made strides towards achieving greater pay equity. This was especially the case among immigrant descendant women with higher education, who moved into traditionally female-gendered professions, such as social work, health care, and teaching. Portuguese men, on the other hand, tended to stay in the construction industry, where they could pursue its many skilled trades and entrepreneurial opportunities. In Toronto, and surely other North American jurisdictions, construction workers in those residential sectors where Portuguese immigrants predominated had little union protection until the mid-1970s and the 1980s, which left them vulnerable to the many greedy (sub)contractors, who subjected them to various kinds of exploitation and highly unsafe working conditions. It was particularly true of the numerous undocumented migrant workers arriving during those decades.[9]

Part of the relative economic success of Portuguese working-class families resulted from the economic contributions of their children, who often worked part time after school or helped in family-owned businesses. Some parents, especially those with little schooling themselves, took their children out of school as soon as they were legally allowed to or simply did not encourage them to pursue higher education. At the same time, Portuguese youth, especially boys, were often eager to drop out of school and work for wages, following their parents' example of achieving relative material comfort with little formal education – a prospect made more attractive as the number of unionized construction workers grew, along with their employment opportunities, wages, benefits, and pension plans. By abandoning school, Portuguese youth also forsook the repeated assaults on their personal dignity and sense of self-worth that many suffered under bigoted teachers in Anglocentric public school systems. Furthermore, in areas with few highly skilled jobs, as was the case in Fall River and New Bedford, there were few economic incentives for educational advancement. In such cases, as Dorothy Gilbert noted, "individuals who go to college run the risk of educating themselves out of the city's capacity to employ them."[10] To this day, Portuguese youth in Canada and the northeastern United States continue to register high dropout rates and rank among the lowest in academic achievement. This phenomenon has attracted a great deal of attention from educators, activists, politicians, social workers, and researchers inside and outside Portuguese communities.[11]

In Massachusetts, various ethnic communities (including the Portuguese) experiencing high dropout rates among its students, joined the movement led by Hispanic educators to pressure the state legislature into addressing the cultural and linguistic needs of their children in the public school system. After a two-year campaign, Massachusetts became the first state to pass its own bilingual education law, the 1971 Transitional Bilingual Education Act (Chapter 71A), which mandated bilingual education in any school district with twenty or more non-English-speaking students and earmarked funds for implementing these programs. Besides offering classes in the immigrants' native languages, the act also called for classes on the history of their "home" countries. However, the fact that immigration from Europe began declining after 1965 (except for Portuguese and Greeks) meant that fewer European immigrant children used these bilingual school programs. As a result, most of the funding disbursed by federal and state governments was channelled to Spanish speakers. For instance, in 1973, only four Portuguese bilingual programs received federal funding, compared with 165 Spanish equivalents. The Ethnic Heritage Studies Program introduced in 1972 also authorized Washington to assist in "planning, developing, establishing, and operating" programs providing ethnic students with opportunities "to learn about the nature of their own cultural heritage, and to study the contributions of the cultural heritages of other ethnic groups of the Nation."[12] However, it was never meant to be more than a token program, as was made clear by the meagre funding of US$2 million per year. As John Skrentny argued, "multicultural education developed in a way that completely ignored [European] ethnics."[13]

In the meantime, Portuguese consulates were overwhelmed by the growing number of newcomer families with school-aged children settling outside traditional Portuguese-American centres. Some consuls pleaded for help from Lisbon, while others took more direct approaches to resolving the problem; for example, in 1971 the consul in Waterbury led fifty teachers and club directors into creating an organization dedicated to introducing Portuguese classes in Connecticut's public school system. Fortunately for community organizers, there were plenty of certified teachers (including Micaelenses) among the newcomers, who joined the staff of existing schools or founded new ones in Canada and the United States. For instance, Montreal inaugurated one secondary and two primary Portuguese schools in the 1970s, one of them being named after its sponsoring Portuguese bank, Atlântico. The largest of these schools, founded in 1971, was run by the Santa Cruz Mission and had nearly 500 students and fifteen teachers in its opening year. Its creation resulted from the combined efforts of Fr Fatela and the Portuguese consul, who secured the IAC's accreditation along with funds from the Canadian Ministry of Immigration.[14] The FPCC's school in Toronto also grew, offering classes up to sixth grade in 1970, thanks in part to a subsidy from another Portuguese bank. The following year, twenty-one full-time teachers and five supply teachers taught a complete preparatory curriculum to nearly 400 students. These teachers received only CA$4 for travel and meal expenses, subsidized by a nominal enrolment fee and Lisbon's annual grant of CA$1,900. Like his predecessors, the Portuguese consul was a strong advocate for the FPCC's school, in part because his wife was a kindergarten teacher there. Also worthy of note was the fact that the FPCC did not ask for classrooms from Toronto's Catholic school board – where most Portuguese children were enrolled – as it had done with its public counterpart. One DCI researcher suggested that this choice was made in order to avoid dealing with Portuguese clerics, particularly Fr Cunha, who had plans to open a St Mary's Separate School, for which he failed to obtain Lisbon's support. Meanwhile, in 1971, Ottawa rejected a request from the FPCC for a CA$57,800 subsidy, meant to pay teachers' salaries and expand the school to the suburbs, where a growing demand was unmet. Still, they managed to increase enrolment to a peak 762 students in 1974, after which the student population began to drop.[15] This declining enrolment was due not only to the lower immigration flow but also to the growing competition from other Portuguese schools opening in Toronto, which now obtained accreditation from Lisbon faster than before. Notably, one of the FPCC's leading teachers in the 1970s–90s was from Rabo de Peixe, in São Miguel, where the Micaelense accent is thickest. Still, the majority of Portuguese teachers in Canada were mainlander women, which reflected the composition of their classrooms, populated predominantly by mainlander girls.[16] Though a sizable goup, the numbers of teachers and students in Portuguese community schools in Canada and the United States were well bellow those in France and Germany in the same period.[17]

Besides availing themselves of the aid coming from the homeland, Portuguese Americans also pressed local politicians to commit more resources towards building community libraries. In 1971, the radio host António Alberto Costa rallied hundreds of listeners to crowd New Bedford's Municipal Council offices and demand that city councillors reverse an earlier decision not to cover the US$6,000 monthly salary required to hire a new librarian, its approval by the city being a condition for securing a US$56,000 grant from Washington, earmarked for purchasing books and equipment to build a Portuguese library. As a result of the community's demands, the council reversed its decision and apologized for having made it in the first place.[18] The Portuguese in Canada also advocated for their native language to be included in public schools serving areas with large lusophone populations. Some of these demands were organized by the students themselves, as was the case in Toronto's Harbord Collegiate Institute, where in 1973 the student representative body circulated a petition asking for the introduction of a Portuguese-language class. Two years later their wish came true. The students involved in this initiative also instructed the Toronto Board of Education on which Portuguese publications to subscribe to and which books and music records to buy for their school's library. According to one student: "At Harbord there is a Portuguese culture but one that is typically Torontonian. That culture results from the fusion of not just the North, South, and Centre of Portugal, but also the Mainland and the Adjacent Islands. All sit in one room and discover by themselves that they are all equal, all Portuguese."[19]

In the 1970s, more Azoreans in Canada started creating their own secular organizations, many of them splintered along island or town solidarities, as was the case of the Toronto sports clubs Angrense and Lusitania, both founded by immigrants from Terceira in 1974 and 1976, respectively. In Mississauga, where Micaelense workers first settled in 1954, Azoreans founded one of the largest and most active pan-Portuguese clubs in Toronto's metropolitan area. Launched in 1974, the Portuguese Club of Mississauga drew middle-class members from various regions of Portugal, who had begun relocating to that suburb.[20] Marching bands also proliferated in the 1970s, each involving a few dozen members, weekly practices, administrative teams, and social activities similar to those of other ethnic clubs. While often connected with parishes, these organizations were effectively secular.

Ethnic media too expanded during this decade, with television now offering immigrants more diverse and accessible lusophone content. Between 1973 and 1975, at least one Portuguese television station and seven programs on different channels were launched in New England, Ontario, and Quebec. Through shows such as *Passport to Portugal*, launched by New Bedford-Providence's WTEV (Channel 6) in 1970 and broadcast in California in 1971–3; *Reflections of Portugal*, shown on Montreal's National Cablevision in 1971; and others that followed, immigrants of varying literacy skills were able to see the sights and hear the sounds of their home country and revisit the places and customs of their youth from their living rooms in a way that no other media could provide. The number of Portuguese publications in North America also increased rapidly. In Toronto and Montreal alone, twenty-two new periodicals were launched in the 1970s.[21] New sources of advertising revenue became available to Portuguese ethnic media, as American and Canadian governments began publishing more public announcements in the immigrants' native languages, and more community businesses sought to promote their products and services to their co-ethnics. This change reduced their dependence on Lisbon's subsidies, thus increasing their editorial freedom. While still publishing pre-approved content from the Estado Novo's propaganda and news agencies, the ethnic press now focused more on host society issues, especially those affecting their local communities. However, these new sources of revenue were not enough to sustain the struggling *Diário de Notícias*, which published its last issue on 19 October 1973, marking the end of a fifty-four-year era in the history of the Portuguese-American press.

Meanwhile, the Lisbon weekly *O Emigrante* (renamed *Mundo Português* after 1974), founded in January 1970 and distributed in various parts of the world, sought to connect with the Portuguese diaspora as a platform to "inform, discuss, denounce, and demand" concerning matters of importance to emigrants.[22] Because it was published in Portugal, *O Emigrante* was subject to the regime's censorship. Most of its content was discreet and reflected the views of liberal reformists, including Adriano Moreira and his diasporic vision of Portuguese nationhood. Still, the censors cut various articles deemed problematic: those dealing with the emigrants' miserable living conditions, the horrors of the colonial wars, and Christian appeals for peace. Among them were opinion pieces by a Portuguese-American correspondent, who argued in favour of American naturalization and encouraged emigrants to vote in their adopted countries. In one of his texts, the expat criticized Lisbon for sponsoring the visits only of business delegations and having only profits in mind when dealing with emigrants, and he wondered: "Do they think we all have great fortunes in banks or hidden under our mattresses?" The author contrasted this attitude with the fact that community organizations had to cover the costs of bringing artists, football teams, ranchos, and other entertainers from Portugal out of their own pockets.[23] He added:

> We have the right to benefit from Portugal's cultural evolution through aid, which ought to be sent [to us] by government agencies whose mission is to educate and transmit the richness of luso culture, of which every emigrant is proud, even if they have little knowledge of it ... We seriously need to face our rights and obligations with the Mother Country and create a distinct and indissoluble personality, capable of imposing and demanding from Portuguese society the place that is ours by justice.[24]

Similar complaints were made to Portuguese diplomats by community organizers, such as the president of New Bedford's Feast of the Blessed Sacrament, who in 1973 requested financial aid to pay for the trip of a rancho from Madeira. After having his request denied by the Casa de Portugal and other government agencies, the organizer shared his frustration with the ambassador:

> Here we are trying to expose Portuguese Culture to thousands of people and no one cares to help. Please realize Mr. Ambassador that many in the [organizing] committee are American born and yet we have an inner warmth and pride of being of Portuguese descent, that we are sacrificing our time, money and hard work to be part of this great traditional Feast. Yet we are having difficulty in convencing [sic] the Portuguese themselves.[25]

The diplomat explained that the embassy had no budget for cultural expenses of "that kind" and suggested they seek TAP's representative in the United States; the prospects of future charter business might convince him to sponsor the feast.

Ranchos continued to grow in popularity in the Portuguese communities, galvanized by their host societies' ethnic revivalism and multiculturalist ideology. Even long-standing Portuguese-American mutual aid societies such as the PCU, now struggling in the age of the welfare state, tried to harness the ranchos' popular appeal to attract new members. In 1971, the PCU sponsored a tour by a rancho from mainland Portugal, which performed at its lodges in New England, New York, New Jersey, and Pennsylvania. This initiative followed from a resolution passed by the PCU's general membership calling on it to become more involved in "Portuguese activities" as a way of promoting its financial services.[26] It was the first time the old fraternity had organized a tour with so many performers (forty in total), which was a major undertaking. To cut costs, the PCU's directors asked lodge members to host the performers in their homes and in those of their friends and relatives. In the end, the tour was a success, with every performance attracting large crowds of potential new members. In Newark, the interest was such that they scheduled a second show, where the rancho performed for 1,500 people.[27]

Visits by artists and celebrities from Portugal also increased in the 1970s. Sometimes these tours prompted them to return as immigrants, as was the case with the young fado singer Natércia Conceição. After touring New England with the Vedetas ensemble, Conceição, who was considered a potential successor to Amália Rodrigues, decided to abandon her promising career in Lisbon's fado scene and settle in Massachusetts. In 1970, together with Valentina Félix – another fado singer who had settled in the United States after performing at the PCU's 1969 annual convention – Conceição opened what was possibly the first fado house in North America, in Acushnet, Massachusetts. She later made a career as a radio hostess with New England's Portuguese stations. More fado singers appeared in various Portuguese settlements at this point, attracting patrons to its club halls and restaurants, as was the case of Dina Maria, who moved from Paris to Montreal in 1970 and then to Toronto the following year, where she spent most of her career.[28] Immigrant musicians also created their own travelling ensembles, for instance, the Azorean Caravan, co-founded by the Micaelense António Câmara "Tabico" and his future wife Lourdes Faria. Tabico moved to Canada clandestinely after being invited to perform his *desgarradas* (a form of improvised and humorous fado singing battles) in Montreal in 1970. While working in various menial jobs, he and Lourdes decided to pursue their passion for singing and invited two other Azorean musicians in Toronto to form a troupe. In 1971, they toured Winnipeg, Calgary, Edmonton, Vancouver, and various New England locations. Their Caravan would tour North America and the Azorean islands many times more and produce several records.[29]

Portugal Day celebrations also grew in popularity during this decade, emerging in new locations and drawing a wider range of organizers. Montreal (and Vancouver) celebrated the national holiday for the first time in 1970, including the participation of Quebec's Premier Robert Bourassa, his ministers of cultural affairs and immigration, various members of the federal and provincial parliaments, the archbishop of Montreal, and other dignitaries. During the preparations for this celebration, a group of community organizations offered the city a bust of Camões and asked Mayor Jean Drapeau to rename a street after the epic poet. Drapeau went further and promised to name a public square scheduled for construction in the next year; it was not until 1975 that the city built the Parc du Portugal in Le Plateau Mont-Royal, an area later known as "Little Portugal." Other more cynical views about the 10 June celebrations also became common in the ethnic media in this period. For instance, in its 1973 Portugal Day edition, the once pro-Salazar *Voz de Portugal* subverted the national symbolism of Camões, who had spent a large part of his life overseas and eventually died poor and ignored in his home country, as a metaphor for the modern emigrant.[30]

Although Portuguese communities became more independent of Lisbon in the early 1970s, homeland diplomats still had significant pull over the emigrants' public affairs and commanded considerable deference from its expatriate citizens. For example, a crowd of over 600 bystanders greeted Foreign Affairs Minister Rui Patrício as he walked the streets of Newark's Ironbound neighbourhood in 1970 on an official visit. Diplomats continued disbursing patronage to cooperative community leaders and guiding them towards political unity, while ethnic organizations kept inviting homeland officials to their functions and bestowed on them various honours. Also invited to these receptions were host politicians who tried to ingratiate themselves with this growing ethnic constituency. Sometimes this led to awkward (even if inadvertent) endorsements, as was the case in 1971, when Ontario Minister of Trade and Development Allan Grossman attended a FPCC dinner for the departing Portuguese consul in Toronto and sat at a head table draped in the fascist-like Moçidade Portuguesa (Portuguese Youth) flag.[31]

Furthering trade became a higher priority on the agenda of Lisbon's diplomats, as Portugal's trade surplus with Canada and the United States continued to grow. Portuguese exporters recognized the capacity of emigrant markets for buying and selling their products abroad and increased their presence in these communities. Canadian officials, such as Minister Grossman – whose electoral riding included Kensington Market – were also interested in developing trade with the EFTA member. During his trade visit to Portugal in 1971, Grossman claimed that Ontario's largely working-class Portuguese community had become an "elite" for whom Canadians had "the most respect and consideration." This increased respect for the immigrants' transnational economic power was shared by Portuguese banks, which began opening offices in immigrant settlements in the 1970s in order to capture the ever-growing remittances. While reliant on these funds, Lisbon left the channelling and pooling of remittances in the hands of private banks, despite recommendations from different ministers calling for greater government intervention in this financial sector. Some banks had fleets that travelled the Portuguese countryside collecting deposits from recipient families; in France they also collected money transfers in immigrant settlements. In Canada, Portuguese banks sought to win the favour of their customers primarily by funding community schools, sports clubs, and events and advertising their services in the ethnic media.[32] Political exiles, much like their comrades in the homeland, opposed this transnational financial activity, which they believed propped up the regime. On 5 October 1971, the MDP issued a communiqué calling on Ottawa to prevent the proliferation of Portuguese banks in Canada and curb the growing outflow of remittances. In their eyes, these transactions were a "double treason," since they drained capital from Canada while financing Portugal's dictatorship and Colonial Wars. Curiously, in 1970, the PCDA accepted an invitation from the consul to attend the inauguration of a Portuguese bank office in Toronto.[33]

By the early 1970s, political factions in Canada's Portuguese communities were well defined and its representatives had made inroads into mainstream political parties. The PCDA and MDP continued raising the immigrants' democratic consciousness, denouncing the dictatorship and its colonial empire, and advocating on behalf of political prisoners in Portugal and war resisters in Canada. They also restated their support for the now socialist-dominated FPLN and their commitment to "an armed revolution seeking the radical destruction of Portugal's current socio-political structures and their restoration on the basis of socialism by the Portuguese people, for the Portuguese people."[34] These anti-fascists began collaborating more closely with political exiles from other countries, such as Brazil, Chile, Greece, and Spain,[35] and were regularly asked for financial and logistic support by newer leftist Canadian organizations. In late 1969, the PCDA welcomed one of its most prestigious members, the Portuguese-Brazilian sociologist Florestan Fernandes, who taught at the University of Toronto until 1975.[36] In 1970, the MDP co-founded the Anti-Torture International Front together with the Committee Solidarity-Brazil and a group of Greek, Haitian, and Vietnamese activists.[37] At the same time, these groups intensified relations with Canadian political parties, labour unions, ethnic federations, and other progressive organizations. Some PCDA members joined the ranks of the Communist Party of Canada, while others continued to help NDP candidates running in Portuguese-heavy ridings.[38] In the MDP, there were some who supported Quebec's sovereignty movement (unlike most immigrants) and joined the progressive Parti Québecois. Premier René Lévesque would appoint some of them to public office, for instance, Amadeu Moura and Arlindo Vieira. However, the MDP's support weakened after Lévesque introduced Bill 101 in 1977, enforcing the use of French language in commercial signage and restricting access to English-language instruction (in 1974, 70 per cent of Portuguese students in Quebec attended anglophone Catholic schools).[39]

Despite their ambitious aspirations, the PCDA's executives now dealt with an aging, frustrated, and increasingly disengaged membership, most of whom had little memory of their association's history and founders. The new managers tried to dispel the pervasive notion that theirs was a communist organization, strictly interested in politics and virtually dead. So they organized picnics, children's parties, dances, created a library, hosted lectures, organized trips to the Azores with "non-official" Portuguese travel agencies, and participated in various kinds of community events.[40] However, the PCDA's financial constraints continued to narrow the scope of its actions. In response, two of its members, both small-business owners, launched the non-profit Portugal Investment Corporation in 1970, 90 per cent of whose shareholders were PCDA members. The next year, both men were expelled from the PCDA because their corporation refused to lend it money at zero interest.[41] Around the same time, the MDP's Neves Rodrigues spearheaded the creation of a housing cooperative, which evolved into the Caisse d'Économie des Portugais de Montréal. While constraining, the MDP's financial woes were less severe than the PCDA's, since in the 1970s it received funds from the Quebec government.[42] Still, its membership dwindled. To reverse this tendency, the MDP's new director Rui Viana changed tactics. Instead of organizing poorly attended rallies, he focused on developing consciousness-raising cultural programming, including a workers' theatre company and choir, poetry recitals, film screenings, debates, and performances by political singer/songwriters. Many of the latter were exiled in France, like Luis Cília, who performed in Montreal in 1967, the same year he wrote the PCP's unofficial anthem "Avante Camarada." In Viana's view, "only culture or hunger can make revolutions, and with our fridges full and our books closed we are a magnificent ground for all kinds of servitude."[43] The same shift in strategy was happening in France, where political exiles also began focusing on cultural programming to surreptitiously convey their messages to otherwise indifferent emigrants.[44] This programming was also meant to contrast with the folksy performances idealized by the Estado Novo and embraced by the ethnic clubs and to showcase more sophisticated and politicized arts.

In 1971, upon Viana's invitation, the PCDA joined the MDP in setting up a Portuguese anti-fascist confederation, which sought to mobilize various local committees across North America in order to increase their collective leverage with political officials and mainstream media. Among its goals were sending financial aid to the PCP's armed revolutionary wing, along with clothing, medicine, and money to those colonial regions "freed" by African rebels. At this point, a group of young, educated activists appeared in New England, most of them recently arrived from Portugal. Two of them were the Micaelense Onésimo Almeida, who later became a prominent Portuguese scholar at Brown University and a respected public intellectual in the Azorean diaspora; and the mainlander José Aica, a war resister who moved to Toronto in 1971, where he joined the PCDA before resettling in East Providence the following year. In October 1973, Portuguese exiles in Canada met for the first time in Montreal with fellow anti-fascists from southern Massachusetts, organized under the Fall River Portuguese Committee for Democratic Action. About seventy-five participants agreed to form a united front against the Estado Novo. It is not clear if any of the CPDP's members were present at this meeting. We know, however, that Águas continued to fight the Estado Novo from the United States, since in April 1970 he co-organized a press conference for Mário Soares in New York.[45]

Opposition to Portugal's colonialism from American and Canadian radical organizations, as well as Protestant and Catholic clergymen, also intensified in this period.[46] Portuguese diplomatic offices in North America became the target of pickets and bomb threats. On 9 June 1970, undetonated bombs were found outside the Casa de Portugal, as well as outside the South African, Brazilian, and Haitian consulates in New York City. On the night of 29 August, a dynamite bomb exploded in front of the Portuguese embassy in Washington, causing significant property damage. Two days later, another undetonated device was found in an annex of the embassy, this one capable of destroying the entire building. The Revolutionary Action Party assumed responsibility for these and other explosives placed in the embassies of countries engaged in "the exploitation and oppression of African people around the world."[47] In 1973, Toronto's Portuguese consulate also received a bomb threat and had its telephone lines severed, while Boston's had its walls vandalized with graffiti reading: "Defeat Portuguese colonialism," "Viva FRELIMO," and "Blood of Africans." By April 1974, anti-colonial protests outside Portugal's foreign offices were a regular affair, generating a mixture of outrage and embarrassment among those immigrants and descendants who identified with their imperial heritage.[48]

A new significant demographic emerging in this period were newcomer seniors that followed their emigrant children to North America. This was an especially vulnerable group, given that their greater need for social and health services was often unmet, owing to their lack of language skills and overall unfamiliarity with their host societies, which led to alienation, isolation, depression, and subsequent health problems. As one group of seniors in Toronto explained in a letter to the federal government:

> We do not qualify for Canadian pensions, so most of us live by the generosity of our children for room and board ... Our children work hard, and our grandchildren are busy as all children are, so we are often lonely ... After full lives as farmers, fishermen and housewives in Portugal, Toronto is a huge and often fearful place.

Fortunately for them, the number of Portuguese interpreters and social workers in government and non-profit agencies increased in the 1970s, as was the case with Toronto's St Christopher's House, whose Older Adult Centre came to serve the Portuguese predominantly at this point. Many of the social workers assisting these seniors were young Portuguese Canadians, whose generation would bring about many significant changes in their communities.[49]

Generational Shifts: Young Activists and Their Political Uses of Race and Ethnicity

In the 1970s, a new generation of male and female social workers, journalists, teachers, and other civic professionals from various regions of Portugal emerged in North America's Portuguese communities. Some had migrated at a young age or been born in the host country, while others had only recently arrived. They were usually young, bilingual, generally better educated than their peers, and moved comfortably in both mainstream and immigrant contexts. These budding activists were well aware of the large social movements of the 1960s–70s and the deep social inequalities existing in their host countries, learning from personal experience and by observing their working-class immigrant neighbourhoods. While their activism developed at a time when interest in Old World politics was re-emerging among European descendants, the trajectory of these newcomers and second-generation immigrants was the inverse. Like the older anti-fascists, they too were "radical ethnic brokers," who mediated between immigrant and mainstream societies. But unlike their predecessors, these young progressives focused primarily on North American realities and strove to improve the everyday lives of immigrant workers, as opposed to addressing the political situation in the homeland. Nonetheless, they maintained deep connections with Portugal and followed its political developments with much interest. This was especially true after the 1974 revolution, which delivered a jolt of national pride and extensive political lessons to Portuguese democrats around the world. Many of these emerging community leaders were inspired by the revolutionary enthusiasm in Portugal and adopted its pervasive Marxist language and goals.

Among them were social workers influenced by the "community development" methods in vogue in the United States since the 1960s, which focused on empowering marginalized individuals by including them in the planning and management of social programs addressing systemic problems and promoting their self-determination. These community workers created their own secular social agencies, often clearly demarcated from the parishes' own services. Still, Catholicism remained an important element in the social consciousness of many of these activists, as was the case with the Micaelense João Medeiros and the mainlander Domingos Marques. Both men had studied for the priesthood in Portugal before moving to Canada and were deeply influenced by the reforms of Vatican II and the social doctrine of Liberation Theology. Medeiros, who had once hoped to become a missionary in Angola, became politicized while studying theology in the greater Lisbon area. In 1971, he joined his parents and siblings in Toronto and found a job with the YMCA as a Portuguese youth outreach worker. There, Medeiros recruited other young Portuguese volunteers (including Marques) and founded the Portuguese Communitarian Movement (MCP). In 1975, its newsletter, *Informações*, grew into the progressive newspaper *Comunidade*, thanks to a government grant.

Marques, who quit his seminary studies in 1968 to join his parents in Canada (his father having jumped ship in Newfoundland in 1957), later noted how priests were role models for young idealists like him, because of the vital social work they did in rural Portugal. Once in Toronto, Marques started working as a youth organizer at St Mary's church and as a reporter in Fr Cunha's *O Jornal Português*. He remembers becoming politically aware upon watching politicians "going after the ethnic vote" at community events and learning about the different factions in Portuguese and Canadian polities from Fr Cunha's power-mongering machinations. In 1970, Marques cut ties with St Mary's after the overbearing priest took over the parish's youth group. Before joining the MCP in 1972, he furthered his knowledge of social justice issues as a volunteer interpreter tasked with conveying to Canadian courts and bureaucrats

NOTÍCIAS DO Y.M.C.A.

PORTUGUESES ACTIVOS NO Y.M.C.A.

FRANCO SAVOIA
Director do West End YMCA

JOÃO MEDEIROS
Co-ordenador
do Departamento Português

ROSA MARQUES
Co-ordenadora do Clube
Recreativo dos Idosos
Portugueses

O Y.M.C.A., situado na College e Dovercourt, tem um Departamento Português no qual trabalham actualmente dez pessoas.
Os programas oferecidos aos portugueses neste momento são três: Aulas de Inglês nocturnas, Serviço Informação Útil e Clube Recreativo dos Idosos Portugueses.
Além destes programas especiais para portugueses, o Y.M.C.A. oferece programas de educação física, ginástica e natação para adultos e programas de recreio depois da escola para crianças. Além disso, o Y.M.C.A. mantém abertos todas as noites três centros para juventude em que se desenrolam diversas actividades desportivas na Bloor Collegiate, Parkdale Collegiate e Oakwood Collegiate. Em todos estes programas há portugueses a participar.
O Y.M.C.A. é uma organização não-governamental, não-lucrativo, existente em cerca de 80 países do mundo.
O Y.M.C.A. é uma organização aberta a todas as pessoas que desejam participar nas suas actividades. Se quiser participar em alguma actividade do Y.M.C.A. não hesite em falar com qualquer pessoa que ali trabalhe.
Veja o que o Y.M.C.A. tem para si e sua família.

JOSÉ GONÇALVES
Informação Útil
(Learning to Cope)

TERESA RODRIGUES
Informação Útil
(Learning to Cope)

DOMINGOS MARQUES
Co-ordenador de Informação
Útil (Learning to Cope)

ANA MERGULHÃO
Informação Útil
(Learning to Cope)

CARLOS PEREIRA
Informação Útil
(Learning to Cope)
Professor de Inglês

MARGARIDA AGUIAR
Professora de Inglês

ROBERTO MACHADO
Professor de Inglês

SÃO PEREIRA
Professora de Inglês

Este é o seu jornal

7.1 Clipping from the *Comunidade* issue of February 1977, introducing the YMCA's Portuguese workers, among them João Medeiros (top row, middle) and Domingos Marques (middle row, third from the left). CTASC, Domingos Marques fonds.

the various problems facing his fellow immigrants. This experience, along with his collaboration with Medeiros, furthered Marques's progressive views, which he disseminated through the *Comunidade*, first as a reporter and editor and later as director and owner.[50]

A self-avowed champion for the rights of immigrant workers, *Comunidade*, which had Azoreans and mainlanders among its collaborators, dedicated much of its content to advancing the labour movement, gender equality, and criticizing Canadian capitalism with blatant Marxist language. While promoting ethnic diversity and heritage-language instruction, the newspaper was also critical of specific multicultural programs and denounced the electoral patronage that came with government grants. Its support of Portugal's socialist revolutionaries was also well known to Canadian authorities, which placed the newspaper and its editors under surveillance. Medeiros, Marques, and other MCP/*Comunidade* collaborators were also involved with the NDP as local organizers and later as candidates. Despite its oppositional stance, *Comunidade* managed to stay in circulation for four years, thanks in large part to revenue from federal multicultural ads and provincial multilingual announcements. Still, these sources were hardly enough to cover its publication costs, already kept low by the volunteerism of its contributors. Shortly before closing, the newspaper tried to appeal to the growing Hispanic community in Toronto (and Kensington Market) by publishing content in Spanish. As the editors' saw it: "We are all latinos (honorably) and there is no sense in having a separationist spirit."[51] This attempt failed, however, and *Comunidade* published its last issue in November 1979.[52]

Another inter-ethnic progressive initiative in Toronto that involved Portuguese social workers was the Women's Community Employment Centre (later Working Women Community Centre, WWCC). Founded in June 1974, this organization started by providing employment counselling to newcomer women from Portugal, Africa, the Caribbean islands, and Latin America. Today, it is one of the leading organizations serving immigrant women in Toronto, providing a wide range of programs in twenty-five languages, in four locations, and backed by a multi-million dollar budget. One of its first board members was Marcelina "Marcie" Ponte, then a young social worker. Born in the Azorean island of Santa Maria, Marcelina moved to Canada in 1963, at age seven, with her mother and siblings to join her father, who had arrived in the 1950s as a "bulk order" migrant worker, sent to western Canada to build railway tracks. In 1972, after living in Vancouver, British Columbia, and Kingston, Ontario – where an anglophone teacher shortened her name to Marcie – her family moved to Toronto and settled in a middle-class WASP neighbourhood. However, her immigrant, working-class status was not lost on young Marcie, who regularly helped in her family's bakery-cleaning business or slept in the workers' truck while her family picked worms during school nights. In school, her teachers tried to convince her that, as the daughter of Portuguese immigrants, she was not made for the academic studies stream. She disagreed and eventually enrolled in college in a social work program. Its first placement consisted of doing door-to-door outreach work with the Portuguese community in Kensington Market, where she rediscovered her roots. "For the first time since being in Toronto I felt I could actually breathe, because it felt like home. It felt comfortable," she later recalled.

> [The 1970s] was my favourite time to work in the sector because of the energy that we felt ... everybody was organizing, for different reasons. There was less fear to be vocal. And I think there were enough of us in the Portuguese community who were encouraging that vocal voice ... There was a real sense that if women were going to do well they were going to have to fight for themselves. I found men a little bit more docile and not as willing to take charge and come out and be active.[53]

During the 1970s, Marcie joined the PCDA, the MCP/*Comunidade* team, helped unionize Portuguese women factory and cleaning workers, and became an NDP organizer. In 1999, Marcie became the executive director of the WWCC, where she reintroduced many of the community development methods that she had learned in the 1970s, and she continued advancing educational, political, youth, and other social causes in the Portuguese-Canadian community.

Montreal also saw the emergence of a group of secular social workers, many of them former members of Santa Cruz Mission's youth group and the St Vincent de Paul Society. In 1972, some of these young activists co-founded the Centre portugais de référence et promotion sociale (CPRPS),[54] which offered various settlement and social programs. After securing core funding from Ottawa the next year, the centre moved from the Santa Cruz's basement into its own office and its workers started receiving wages. Despite the Catholic mission's initial support, in the eyes of CPRPS staff members (interviewed by Domingos Marques years after 1974), the priests had delayed the immigrants' social "evolution," especially after pastor Fatela took over from the French-Canadian Leblanc. The MDP's participation in the CPRPS's founding prompted the Portuguese ambassador to request that Lisbon elevate the Montreal consulate to a higher diplomatic class, so it could hire more staff and deal with the growing threat of a united opposition.[55] Also in 1972, a small group of Canadian, American, and

Portuguese youth launched Radio Centre-Ville, a "pirate" station in Montreal's Mile End neighbourhood. Their goal was to become an outlet for the residents of their working-class neighbourhood to discuss local issues and other meaningful topics neglected by mainstream media, such as housing, unemployment, and intercultural relations. In a clear break with past practices, when the consuls were invited to deliver the inaugural addresses, these young radio hosts interviewed the MDP's Rui Viana in their first broadcast. After expanding its multilingual programming in 1975, with new shows targeting the Hispanic, Greek, and Haitian communities, the "pirate" station became CINQ-FM, the first multicultural community radio station in Quebec. While "multicultural," this station has strived to "offer information enabling citizens to turn towards community action in order to effect social, political and cultural change," among other social justice and pluralist goals.[56]

Progressive social justice organizations mushroomed in various Portuguese centres in North America, including the Cambridge Organization of Portuguese-Americans (COPA), Fall River's Portuguese Youth Cultural Organization, Somerville's Portuguese-American League, Gloucester's Portuguese Communities Activities Council, Toronto's Working Women Community Centre and Portuguese Interagency Network, to name just a few. All offered important services and outreach programs, produced needs assessment studies, and advocated on behalf of immigrant workers and their families on a variety of social issues. Like their predecessors, this generation of civic leaders understood there was power to be gained if Portuguese immigrants presented a united front when dealing with political officials, and took steps in that direction. In June 1973, COPA organized the "Portuguese National Convention" at Harvard University, bringing together 200 delegates from New England, New Jersey, New York, Pennsylvania, and California. For three days, the participants discussed how to address a range of socio-economic problems affecting the Portuguese and ways to raise their communities' cultural and political consciousness. The organizers had great ambitions for this gathering, which they believed would "mark a conscious and definite change in our way of acting and decision-making as a Community." They invited various American officials, including President Nixon, who declined. Notably missing from their guest list were Lisbon's diplomats and most of the priests, doctors, lawyers, professors, and other distinguished personalities of the Portuguese-American establishment. As reported to the ambassador by an infiltrated observer, most of the delegates were young, held political ambitions or aimed to become community leaders, and wished to move beyond the saudade of previous generations, even though some had only recently arrived from Portugal.[57]

The convention's organizers were admittedly inspired by African-American activism. In the words of COPA's director, Aurélio Torres: "A lot was being said about black awareness at the time – we wanted to raise Portuguese awareness."[58] They were prompted into action after the mayor of Cambridge, Alfred Vellucci, failed to secure federal funds to develop a Portuguese cultural district in that city. Hence, the main topic in the convention's agenda was the racial matrix used by government officials when allocating funds for underprivileged minorities, and their failure to recognize the Portuguese as a distinct "cultural entity." As the organizers saw it, despite Cambridge's Portuguese population being about twice that of blacks and four times that of Hispanics, their group received little federal funding because they were counted as part of the latter. But instead of resorting to the rising language of "white grievance" that turned civil rights politics on its head by attacking "black privilege" (supposedly provided by affirmative action), these young organizers tried to take advantage of their ethnic group's long-standing racial complexity and "not-*quite*-whiteness" in order to access government aid. In a 500-to-3 vote, the delegates at the Cambridge convention passed a resolution calling for all levels of government to recognize Portuguese Americans as a legal minority and urging its members to "preserve," "develop," and "exalt" their "ethnic values." A subsequent resolution clarified that Portuguese ethnicity, like that of Hispanics, included all who identified with that heritage, regardless of "race, creed, or sex."[59]

Ironically, the success of older ethnic leaders in asserting the whiteness of European Portuguese was now detrimental to the progressive goals of their successors, who saw other racial minorities gain access to employment, housing, and other welfare programs. Among the beneficiaries were those Cape Verdeans who assumed an African-American identity. Other racial and linguistic groups lobbied Washington to recognize their status as marginalized minorities deserving of equity programs. Still, the inclusion of American Indians, Asian Americans, Latinxs, and women under the Equal Employment Opportunity Commission's scope of action resulted less from their mass mobilization than from the legislators' perception of which groups were "analogous to blacks." Other equity programs launched in this period, targeting racial, ethnic, and linguistic minorities, always left out the Portuguese. The only exception was the 1972 Ethnic Heritage Studies Act, which introduced grants for developing elementary and secondary school programs; however, the funding allocated was modest.[60]

As reported in the *Cape Verdean* newspaper of Lynn, Massachusetts, the Cambridge convention's participants described it as a pivotal moment in Portuguese-American history, one that represented a clear shift away from the previous white assimilationist mentality that had marginalized Cape Verdeans towards the creation of a multiracial pan-Portuguese identity. Onésimo Almeida, one of the organizers, told the Cape Verdean publication: "no matter how [Lisbon] considers them ... the Portuguese here will be welcome – whether they're black or white – if they want to join us."[61] At this point, however, Cape Verdean Americans had begun organizing themselves as a distinct ethnic group. In 1972, its leaders founded the Cape Verdean American Federation in Rhode Island to promote "nation-wide participation of people of Capeverdean birth or descent and friends in projects that will benefit them in this country and their kinfolks abroad."[62] The next year, Governor Joseph Garrahy endorsed the federation's mission to increase awareness of Cape Verdean culture and history in his state by proclaiming a Cape Verdean heritage week in June. In February 1974, 800 Cape Verdeans from across the United States met in Providence for their federation's first national convention, where they discussed their homeland's political future and their identity as hyphenated Americans.

Support for the nationalist PAIGC also grew considerably in the 1970s, owing to the efforts of party organizers such as Black Power activist Salahudin Matteos (aka Milton X, aka Omowali). Born Milton Matthews in 1933, this son of Cape Verdean immigrants grew up in New Bedford and Boston, where he had a typical "inbetween" identity before encountering blatant racism for the first time as a US soldier in the Korean War. A spiritual man, Matteos had hoped to become a Catholic priest until a white pastor discouraged him, on account of his being "black." After this deterrence, Matteos's career as an activist began, first with the Nation of Islam, where he worked closely with Malcolm X in Philadelphia, then with the All-African People's Revolutionary Party and the Black Economic Development Conference. Starting in 1969, Matteos went on a two-year journey through Africa looking for Amílcar Cabral, who eluded him. During this time he fought alongside PAIGC militants in Guinea-Bissau. Ironically, after returning to the United States in 1972, Matteos finally met Cabral when he joined the Cape Verdean leader as he toured the country. This encounter inspired Matteos to return to Boston and spread Cabral's "universalist" message. That year he founded the PAIGC-USA Support Committee and began educating college and university students across the country about the anti-colonialist party and the Cape Verdean struggle.[63] The rising national and ethnic self-awareness of Cape Verdean Americans occurred amidst much internal debate between those who emphasized their Portuguese heritage, those who asserted a distinct Kriolu ethnicity, and those who saw themselves first and foremost as African-Americans. Another major discussion was whether their homeland should become an independent state or join Guinea-Bissau after the Colonial Wars. Whatever the case, most Cape Verdean immigrants and descendants no longer sought to be recognized as "Portuguese," which explains why so few rallied behind the call for multiracial unity coming from Cambridge.

Older Portuguese Americans also rejected the Cambridge reinterpretation of their racial identity. Having witnessed the subjugation of non-whites throughout their lives, they believed that striving for anything other than full whiteness was counter-productive. One of the most vocal critics of this minority status campaign was the distinguished Irish-Portuguese-American Harvard Professor Francis Rogers. The grandson of an Azorean whaler who arrived in Connecticut in 1853, whose family name was changed from "da Rosa" by an immigration officer, Rogers was a firm believer in assimilation and saw ethnic and racial identifiers as being divisive and fuelling "the fires of condescension and prejudice." Like his paternal forebears, Rogers saw his family's anglicization as a blessing that had enabled their social ascension within mainstream America. At the same time, his grandmother, an Irish famine immigrant, raised him to appreciate his Portuguese background, which he did, to the point of making a career of it as the most prominent Portuguese studies scholar in the United States and involved with various Portuguese-American cultural organizations. Together with other influential Portuguese Americans, Rogers contacted his connections in the Massachusetts congressional delegation and successfully convinced them to shun the Cambridge resolution, arguing that the Portuguese were indeed white, unlike Hispanics. However, some white Portuguese Americans who rejected this multiracial group reclassification were prepared to embrace a larger southern European identity and associate with Italians and Greeks.[64]

Not all senior Portuguese-American leaders opposed COPA's ethnic activism. In 1973, the media entrepreneur and PAF manager António Costa organized a gathering a few weeks after the Cambridge meeting titled the United Portuguese Community Convention, whose goal was to consolidate New Jersey's lusophone peoples under a single pan-ethnic linguistic group. As the owner, producer, and host of various lusophone media outlets, Costa was able to disseminate his message of unity while simultaneously berating his "ill intentioned" critics, dubbed as "losers" and "zeros," who saw their relevance in the community slipping away. Writing in Costa's *Portuguese Times*, Onésimo Almeida, who had arrived in the United States in 1972, joined him in lambasting the old elites: "There [were] no medals. Nor decorations. Nor sashes for knights of the nameless Order. Nor crosses of merit Tower and Sword. Little claps for you, little claps for me ... The Convention was work."[65] A similar rejection of the old guard was common among young community activists in Canada. For instance, in 1973, the CPRPS organized Montreal's Portugal Day celebrations, which they boasted had no "honorary tribunes," no "paternalism from the 'notables,'" or no "reserved seats"; instead, "the people reunited and made their own feast." Their communiqué added: "Portuguese workers know how to walk on their own feet, they don't need crutches! Down with the 'notables'!" Nonetheless, like the ethnic entrepreneurs they criticized, the CPRPS was committed to preserving Portuguese customs and traditions, but only "to the extent that they contribute to improving Canada's pluricultural (pluriethnic) society."[66]

The new generation of ethnic leaders also made repeated calls for the greater participation of Portuguese workers in the American and Canadian labour movements. However, their efforts to "arouse the consciousness" of immigrant workers, unionize their workplaces, and launch class action suits against exploitative employers, were met with resistance or apathy by their co-ethnics, who feared losing their jobs. Just a month before the April 25th revolution, Cambridge's *Harvard Crimson* asked COPA's directors and a few local political exiles to gauge their success in reaching the city's Portuguese. Though optimistic, they admitted their idealism had been shaken by their fellow immigrants' general unresponsiveness to their calls for political mobilization and unity. According to these activists, one of the reasons for this reluctance was the decreasing yet still strong assimilationist pressures of American society, which made immigrants hesitant about engaging in identity politics. A greater obstacle, they claimed, was "the heritage of oppression and forced non-involvement that the Portuguese bring with them from Portugal." This political alienation translated into low naturalization rates, which prevented community leaders from offering a cohesive voting bloc to politicians willing to take up their causes, resulting in the Portuguese being "ignored by the rest of the city."[67] That political disengagement would change after 25 April 1974.

Hope and Apprehension: Portuguese Communities during the PREC

On 9 June 1974, 200 people gathered in Toronto's Trinity-Bellwoods Park to celebrate the first Portugal Day since the fall of the Estado Novo and to cheer the Armed Forces Movement. Organized by a PCDA member, the event was attended by young and old immigrants and their Canadian friends, who sang revolutionary songs and listened to various speakers talk about the future of their homeland and of their own community. Among the speakers was a former chaplain in Angola, who noted: "We Portuguese, who did not desire to be simply seafarers and yearners of a past that is as epic as it is distant, are now starting to live the most essential of human rights – FREEDOM."[68] A young factory worker and an older "cleaning lady" spoke of their experiences in trying to unionize their workplaces, urging others to follow the revolutionary example of their brothers and sisters in Portugal by joining a union. The school board trustee Dan Leckie spoke of the discrimination that Portuguese children suffered in the Anglocentric public school system. Other speakers, such as the MCP's João Medeiros and the NDP city councillor Dan Heap, celebrated the revolution by drawing parallels with the immigrants' struggle in Canada.

In New York, Consul Mário Freitas organized a large reception at the International Institute of Education (across the street from the UN headquarters) to which he invited various influential people, including presidents of large corporations, bank managers, UN delegates, members of the American and foreign press, Portuguese-American civic and business leaders, and former political exiles. As reported by the *New York Post*, "the place was filled with Portuguese-Americans, several hundred of the 25,000 New Yorkers of Portuguese origin, people who had never before been sought out by the Portuguese diplomats here, much less invited to a party ... Portuguese diplomats around the world, said one official ... had received instructions from Lisbon to celebrate by forging links with the working-class Portuguese expatriate communities around them." The reporter interviewed the father of a Portuguese-language school student in Manhattan, who said the revolutionary Junta had promised to assist his daughter's school, "something the old one never did," he claimed. Also interviewed was the American Portuguese Cultural Society's president, an American businessman with investments in Portugal, who was used to "enjoying Portuguese official hospitality in the old days." The *Post*'s reporter noted the man's gold cigarette case as he commented on the odd mix of business people and immigrants of "very simple origin." Among the guests was the future president of Portugal, Jorge Sampaio (1996–2006), then "a young socialist lawyer" representing Lisbon's provisional government at the United Nations, along with the ambassadors for the Soviet Union, Tanzania, Algeria, and other African nations.[69] Alongside the lively crowd of well-dressed bourgeoisie, a group of short-sleeved immigrants played accordions, raised their fists in the air, and held signs with messages in Portuguese: "Hunt DGS ex-PIDE in the USA," "Let there be conditions in Portugal for the emigrants to return," and "We want voting rights for all emigrants."[70] Similar demands could be heard in other North American cities. In Toronto, the PCDA demonstrated outside the headquarters of Fr Alberto Cunha's newspaper, radio, and television shows, which they accused of spreading lies about the situation in Portugal.[71] In Swansea, Massachusetts, protesters demonstrated outside the restaurant – where then Foreign Affairs Minister Mário Soares dined with former CPDP members honouring the veteran republican Abílio Águas – demanding that the Portuguese ambassador in Washington be replaced, and that the identities of PIDE agents and informants in the United States be revealed.[72]

During his trip to North America in June 1974, where he attended a NATO summit in Ottawa, Soares had the opportunity to interact with Portuguese emigrants as the guest of honour at a community dinner attended by 500 people. Speaking to the Portuguese-Canadian media, Soares admitted that remittances were "very appreciated" but not the return of "4 million" emigrants, which would be "catastrophic." Upon returning to Lisbon, he would describe this event to a national newspaper as one of the most instructive parts of his trip, since he was able to hear about the emigrants' experiences, problems, and expectations directly from their mouths. He was particularly touched by a teary-eyed father who told him that, because of the revolution, his five-year-old son was no longer ashamed of calling himself Portuguese at school and was proud to see Soares on Canadian television. According to the former political exile turned minister, who confessed to not being previously aware of such a large emigrant community in Canada: "For the Portuguese, who are so used to being the subject of all kinds of international criticism and polemics, this is extremely interesting."[73]

Like Soares, other provisional government representatives visited North America shortly after the revolution. In Canada, they were usually hosted by the PCDA or the MDP, which organized information sessions where these visitors explained their political program and asked for the emigrants' support in building a democratic and socialist Portugal. In September 1974, Toronto and Montreal received an official delegation on a "goodwill tour of Portuguese communities," which included the "April Captain" Salgueiro Maia – who had led the MFA troops into Lisbon and forced Caetano to capitulate on the April 25th – and other government officials, including the new secretary of state for emigration, Pedro Coelho. They visited the community's clubs, schools, pool halls, and businesses, where they learned about the emigrants' views on the political shift in Portugal and what they expected from the new government. As a *Toronto Star* reporter noted: "There was none of the pomp that usually accompanies such visits by foreign government representatives within [Toronto] communities. About seventy-five people followed them around. But there were no large throngs to welcome them. There were no cheers, no noisy greeting."[74] The Portuguese delegation also met with Canadian external affairs officials to request Ottawa's help in easing the employment and housing crisis prompted by the return of former emigrant workers, demobilized soldiers, and eventually colonial settlers. Presumably informed by the "bulk order" migration agreement negotiated in the 1950s, Secretary Coelho proposed inaugurating a new movement of low- and high-skilled workers, including temporary farmhands. The Canadians showed no interest, alleging that the current legislation did not allow for special immigration provisions for individual countries, although such an arrangement is exactly what Ottawa had with its Jamaican counterpart under the Seasonal Agricultural Workers Program launched in 1966 and with Mexico starting in 1974. Perhaps a more truthful reason was the fact that bringing temporary workers from across the Atlantic was too costly.[75]

Visits from prominent political figures continued in the months and years following the revolution. In October, Toronto hosted the communist singer/songwriter José "Zeca" Afonso, another beloved anti-fascist, whose song *Grândola Vila Morena* was broadcast on the morning of the April 25th as a signal for the MFA's forces to advance and has since become the revolution's anthem. Together with the musician Rui Pato and the writer Urbano Tavares Rodrigues (a PCP militant), Afonso enlivened that year's 1910 Republican Revolution commemorations with two concerts that attracted over 1,700 people.[76] Curiously, two Portuguese banks in Toronto donated funds to help cover the costs of the event, co-organized by the PCDA, MDP, and the Fall River Democratic Movement. Over fifty new members joined the PCDA in the days following the concerts; another 150 had done so in the first six months of 1974. This success encouraged them to organize more shows with leftist artists from Portugal, which they did for years to come. Portuguese revolutionaries were also invited by Canadian socialists to talk at their events. For example, in October 1975, the Independent Socialists – the NDP's former radical wing known as "the Waffle" – invited a member of both the Portuguese Revolutionary Councils of Workers, Soldiers and Sailors and the Proletariat Revolutionary Party/Revolutionary Brigades, to speak at ten cities in North America.[77]

Political figures on the right also visited North America during the Ongoing Revolutionary Process (PREC). One of the most high-profile visitors was General António Spínola, the former president of the short-lived National Salvation Junta, who fled to Brazil after his failed right-wing coup on 11 March 1975. While in exile, Spínola became the leader of the far-right Democratic Movement for the Liberation of Portugal and the Portuguese Liberation Army. He held an information session at Toronto's St Lawrence Centre for the Arts on 23 November, two days before the far-left's own attempted coup in Portugal and the subsequent seizure of power by the centre-right. Spínola spoke for nearly three hours to a crowd of about 800 people "amid repeated cheers and thunderous applause." As reported in the *Globe and Mail*: "five medium-sized plastic garbage cans were passed around to the audience, and they quickly filled with $5 and $10 bills"; according to the *Comunidade*, the collection grossed a few thousand dollars. Outside, an even larger crowd tried to get in. Among them were over 200 protesters from the PCDA, NDP, League for Socialist Action, and other left-wing organizations, which condemned Spínola's efforts to organize a "fascist" coup in Portugal.[78]

The emigrants' initial cheers for the revolution's promise of democracy were gradually muted among the conservative majority as they saw the successive provisional governments veer farther to the left. The MFA's Revolution Council recognized that the emigrants' fear of losing their hard-earned savings and properties in Portugal could turn them into a strong reactionary force. To placate their growing anxieties, in April 1975, the council prohibited the occupation of vacant houses without consent from the overseeing "Residents Committee," which based its decision on the circumstances behind these properties' vacancy. Under their supervision, "the emigrant's property [was] sacred," as a visiting member of the Popular Socialist Front explained during a PCDA information session. But the MFA's priorities were also made clear. Their goal was to "end the exploitation of man by man, and whoever rejects this principle is being counter-revolutionary and will not be accepted in the country. If the [e]migrant doesn't like it ... he can pack up his bags and turn back."[79]

Fear of communism and what it could mean for the emigrants' relatives and investments at home was reinforced by North American mainstream and some ethnic media, such as Fr Cunha's new radio and television shows, which presented the political developments in Portugal through a Cold War prism. To challenge such "alarmist interpretations and lack of objectivity," the PCDA bought advertising space in the *Globe and Mail* (paid for with community donations) and published a statement of support for the MFA, signed by a long list of Portuguese immigrants and illustrious Canadian allies. The newly appointed consuls urged emigrants to seek information about Portugal

294   This Pilgrim Nation

7.2 Crowd gathered outside Toronto's St Lawrence Centre for the Arts while General António Spínola speaks inside, 23 November 1975. CTASC, Domingos Marques fonds.

from "reliable" sources, such as the Casa de Portugal's bulletin circulated by the consulates.[80] Nonetheless, the leading members of the PCDA and MDP clearly sided with the communists, which provoked tensions among its members; in fact, the MDP reportedly expelled moderate socialists and Trotskyists from its ranks at this point.[81]

Purging the Estado Novo's diplomats was a top priority for former political exiles immediately following the revolution. The Portuguese Democratic Action Congress of North America, founded in Montreal in 1973, sent a delegation to Portugal a few days after the revolution to meet with the provisional Junta and communicate their expectations, which included "liberating" the expatriate communities from "fascist" diplomats. In fact, the PCDA planned to occupy the Toronto consulate should the Junta fail to replace the consul. In this action, they were supported by the newly created federation of PS branches abroad, which made similar calls to remove officials with "undemocratic pasts" from Lisbon's foreign service and asked that social attachés be sent to countries with significant emigrant populations to renegotiate immigration agreements and issue ordinary passports to long-term expatriates. Expat delegates from Canada also urged the Junta government to stop subsidizing emigrant organizations previously funded by the dictatorship and to modernize community schools in order to prevent "individuals with no cultural training and committed to fascism from continuing to assume positions of responsibility in these institutions." The PCDA was able to present these views directly to the state secretary for emigration during the first emigration policy consultation meeting in Lisbon in August 1974.[82]

As requested, the old diplomats were replaced with new ones, who vowed never to subject the emigrants to the same neglect that they had supposedly suffered under the dictatorship. According to the new consul in Toronto, Ernesto Feu, the previous regime had regarded the emigrants simply as a source of remittances. By contrast, he proposed to turn his office into a social service agency dedicated to integrating Portuguese expats into Canadian society and to sponsor an "institute" dedicated to resolving the community's legal, educational, health, and work-related problems. Like his predecessors, Feu urged the city's Portuguese to project a "united face," so they could "be recognized as an important sector in Canada's multicultural society" and transmit to Canadians "those Portuguese cultural values that are among the oldest in History."[83] The old émigrés were now keen to collaborate with the new consuls and advise them on community matters, including which individuals and organizations they should stay away and withhold their patronage from. These activists bemoaned the persistent presence at consular events of community leaders who had previously supported the dictatorship and now claimed to have been democrats all along. These "Chameleons" with their "same old (snobbish) faces," as the *Voz* described them, tried to ingratiate themselves with the new homeland officials and were seen by the "anti-situationists" as an insidious threat to their communities' renovation. A more outward enemy was Fr Cunha, whom they accused of being the leader of the "fascist" reaction in Canada. At this point, the PCDA began investigating the source of Cunha's wealth and real estate with the help of city councillor Dan Heap, hoping to find something unlawful they could present to Catholic authorities and trigger his removal. Their attempts to unseat Cunha reached the highest level of diplomatic relations when Prime Minister Gonçalves brought it to the attention of Prime Minister Pierre Trudeau at a meeting in Brussels, in June 1974. The Canadian delegation was "puzzled" by the fact that this was the first item raised by Gonçalves. It must have been especially troubling given that, just a few weeks earlier, Trudeau had walked alongside Cunha and other community conservatives during St Mary's Santo Cristo procession.[84]

These anti-fascists were also eager to partner with the Portuguese consulates in educating emigrants about their citizenship rights and duties. However, at this point, some of them were opposed to granting external voting rights. They shared the communists' view on the issue, as expressed by the writer Urbano Rodrigues after a visit to Canada, where he concluded that it was "practically impossible" for Marxist candidates to campaign in countries "of a decidedly capitalist nature." For the PCDA's Jaime Monteiro, the problem was not only the context but also the intellectual character of most emigrants, whom he argued were "far removed, not only from Portuguese reality, but also from the political, economic and social changes taking place all over the world." Still, he blamed their host countries for doing "nothing to overcome the political retardation of their citizens, much less their immigrants." The ambivalent stance of these pro-democratic activists towards enfranchising expatriate citizens is exemplified by Monteiro's own actions, helping the consulate compile its voters list for the 1975 constitutive assembly elections despite opposing the immigrants' external voting rights.[85]

Portuguese postwar immigrants, the majority of whom had not yet become American or Canadian citizens, were given the chance to vote for the first time in 1975. Expats in the United States had the second-largest turnout (behind Germany) with 4,685 votes, most of them in Newark (2,565), followed by New York City (1,380), Boston (536), Washington, DC (147), and San Francisco (57). Canada registered the fourth-largest turnout (the third being France) with 2,142 votes, most of them in Toronto (1,720), then Montreal (212), Vancouver (125), and Ottawa (85). Considering the number of Portuguese citizens living in North America at this point, the turnout was extremely low. The numbers also point to greater voter participation among newcomer settlements with a higher portion of mainlanders.[86]

Two months after the constitutive elections, the *Correio Português* asked five immigrants in Toronto to offer their views on voting in homeland elections and on the revolution's impact in their community. One of them was Monteiro, who maintained that immigrants were not used to dealing with complicated political matters, although he was happy to see them "making an effort to overcome this handicap," even claiming that Toronto's Portuguese were the "most conscious of the need to move the [PREC] towards ... authentic socialism." Monteiro added that the immigrants' children would likely lose interest in homeland affairs, since they led "Canadian lives." Yet he believed it was possible for youth to develop a Portuguese identity in Canada that was neither "exclusivist nor nationalistic, but co-operative and positive." One such youth was the Goan-Portuguese-Canadian Fernando Costa, the son of the extinct PCC's conservative president. Interviewed by the *Correio*, Costa noted the community's growing political awareness, which he hoped would translate into greater engagement – ideally, he added, of a socialist kind. The young lawyer praised the revolution for improving attitudes towards women and was pleased to see several anti-racist campaigns emerging in Portugal. Another of the interviewees was the branch manager of Toronto's Fonsecas & Burnay Bank, who was pleased to see his fellow countrymen develop "a keen interest in day-to-day happenings in Portugal." In his opinion, Lisbon should enfranchise all emigrants, since "we live in a world where distances mean nothing and where we can follow what is happening in other countries day by day." The progressive conservative António Vaz had a different opinion. In his view, only citizens living in Portugal's national territory should have a say in running their government, as was the case in Canada. Curiously, Vaz, who had rallied behind Galvão and Delgado alongside the PCDA in 1961 and later became an ally of Fr Cunha and the consul, berated those pro-Estado Novo community "elites" who made an about-face on their political views after the revolution, calling them deceitful and self-interested. The former PCDA president, Firmino Oliveira, now a Socialist Party representative in Toronto, had hesitantly come around to supporting external voting rights. Like other leftists, he argued that immigrants' confusion about the political situation in Portugal resulted from their lack of political experience, geographic distance, and widespread misleading information.[87]

Canadian authorities monitored political debates in the Portuguese communities and were alarmed by the increasing socialist tendencies of many of their leaders. The Ethnic Press Analysis Service of the Secretary of State Department, which scrutinized the Portuguese-Canadian press, kept a closer eye during this time. According to this service, most Portuguese-Canadian periodicals shifted to the far left after the revolution, including former SNI-backed publications such as the *Correio Português* and *Voz de Portugal* and newer ones such as the *Comunidade* and *Tribuna Portuguesa* (launched in Montreal in 1972). Only Fr Cunha's *O Jornal Português*, which endorsed Spínola, remained "moderate." Besides the news, communiqués, and opinions from revolutionary Portugal, some newspapers published political glossaries introducing immigrants to the new pervasive lexicon, with words such as "fascism," "dictatorship," "democracy," and "class struggle." Of special concern to Canadian inspectors were the visits by political emissaries from different Portuguese political factions, especially those on the left. In one case, Joaquim Meirim, a popular football coach in Portugal and an outspoken communist, toured the immigrant communities of North America, stopping in Toronto in November 1977. Interviewed by the *Comunidade*, which was regularly monitored, owing to its "Marxist character," Meirim explained that his trip was motivated by a desire to see old friends and his curiosity about how the immigrants lived and organized. Ottawa's analyst interpreted this visit as an attempt by the PCDA to organize local football clubs as centres for communist youth indoctrination.[88]

Canadian officials also were alarmed by the growing tension between opposing political factions in Portuguese communities. This sentiment was shared by Lisbon's new ambassador to Ottawa, who understood "the danger" for international relations of allowing the transplanting of Portuguese political conflicts into Canada and asked for the assistance of Canadian intelligence services in monitoring these communities. Such concerns were legitimized by news of a reactionary coup being prepared in the expatriate communities, as reported in Toronto's *Correio*, where immigrants, with their "archaic, medieval ... ideologically bourgeois education," were supposedly vulnerable to reactionary propaganda disseminated by a transnational network of "fascist" exiles. The paper mentioned "a group of agitators" in Toronto who threatened to set fire to the PCDA's headquarters and attacked left-wing immigrants and their businesses, especially on the days when newspapers arrived from Lisbon. On 23 August 1975, about 200 right-wing demonstrators from cities across Ontario marched on Kensington Market to protest what they saw was a communist takeover in Portugal. The rally had been announced a few days earlier through an anonymous pamphlet circulated in the community calling for "death to communists," including those who had signed the PCDA's statement of solidarity to the MFA published in the *Globe and Mail*.[89]

Another right-wing movement with considerable impact in North America's Portuguese communities was the separatist Azorean Liberation Front (FLA).[90] Founded in London, on 8 April 1975, the FLA was led by the former União Nacional parliamentarian José de Almeida, and backed by the large landowners and economic elites of São Miguel, who feared losing their wealth and property to the agrarian reform and nationalization program carried out by the socialist Lisbon government. The FLA blended various political stripes from the centre left to the far right and framed its separatism as an anti-colonialist struggle against a metropolis that had exploited the islands for centuries. Its leaders appropriated the symbols of an earlier monarchist pro-autonomy movement, including the blue and white flag, along with traditional Azorean cultural references, such as the Feast of the Holy Ghost's hymn. But more than a political program, which was never fully articulated, it was the rejection of communism and its anti-clericalism plus a rapidly growing sense of Azorean ethnicity that united FLA militants and its supporters in the diaspora. In the summer of 1975, the FLA organized its first rally in Ponta Delgada, where its supporters announced their willingness to use violence as a means to achieve their goals. They confirmed this attitude by destroying the offices of the PCP and other socialist parties in São Miguel and Terceira; socialists in Toronto reacted by organizing a rally in solidarity with those "Azorean patriots expelled from their land by fascist terror."[91]

Azoreans in North American were a major source of funding and political support for the FLA. Many of them had embraced their host nation's capitalist ethos and Cold War mentality, and they urged their relatives back home to ward off communism and even separate from Portugal if necessary, assuring them the United States would come to their aid. Almeida tried repeatedly to obtain formal support from President Nixon and the United Nations, but with little success. However, he met a mainly positive response when touring the Azorean communities, where he spread his nationalist vision and raised funds for his movement. Almeida's supporters formed separatist committees in various North American cities, such as the Frente de Apoio à Independência dos Açores in Toronto or the Azorean Committee 75, the latter counting fifteen chapters across New England and California. They held information sessions, distributed political propaganda, launched petitions, and organized rallies, including those outside the UN headquarters and the White House, the latter drawing seventeen buses from Massachusetts and Rhode Island. Their views were also disseminated in the emerging Azorean ethnic press, such as Toronto's *Jornal Açoreano* (1975–85?), and among churchgoers in Azorean-dominated parishes.[92]

The Portuguese far left was convinced that the Azorean independence movement was backed by Washington out of fear of losing the Lajes Air Base. The Americans had recently been reminded of the strategic importance of the Terceira base, which they relied on for delivering support to the Israeli army during the Yom Kippur War of 1973. A 1978 story in the *Boston Magazine* furthered suspicion of Washington's involvement with the FLA. According to this publication, the FLA had links with the far-right French armed group Organisation armée secrète, whose operatives had been granted asylum in Portugal after 1963 and had since cooperated with the PIDE through the covert anti-communist "mercenary" agency Aginter Press. In April 1975, a secrète operative travelled to the United States to obtain financial and military support for the FLA from Republican Senators Strom Thurmond and Jesse Helms and to meet with President Gerald Ford's National Security Advisor Brent Scowcroft. The magazine maintained that the secrète arranged for the FLA and General Spínola to buy weapons through its contacts in Nicaragua, in Miami's Cuban community, and in New York's crime syndicates, in a deal brokered by two Americans, including an aide to Senator Thurmond. Almeida refused this deal, which depended on the Azores becoming a tax and gambling haven after independence.[93]

Former political exiles also suspected the presence of PIDE agents and other "fascists" among the colonial white retornados who began arriving in North America after 1975. The Lisbon government requested Canadian and American officials to ease restrictions and expedite immigration applications from its citizens escaping the civil war in Angola, which started shortly after that country's independence. However, Ottawa did not consider these former colonial settlers to be "refugees," since their Portuguese citizenship allowed them to return to Portugal unimpeded and without fear of persecution. This interpretation conflicted with the personal views of the former settlers, many of whom were born in the colonies and saw themselves primarily as "Angolans," "Mozambicans," or "people without a country" and who felt betrayed by or unwelcome in Portugal. Regardless of Ottawa's views, a significant number of them settled in North America, either sponsored by relatives or arriving as "visitors" and later applying for landed status or simply staying undocumented. Some communities organized support groups to help them settle in the new country and pressure host governments to regularize their status. The Toronto-based Portuguese Refugee Aid Committee mobilized secular and religious leaders across Ontario and discussed the plight of undocumented "refugees" from Angola and Mozambique with Canadian politicians. By April 1976, more than 1,200 Angolans had entered Canada as visitors, about half of them going to Toronto. According to the committee's chair: "They'll go into hiding. They'll get jobs and remain here illegally. They have nothing to look forward to in Portugal."[94] By June, the committee had raised and distributed over CA$13,000 among these "refugees." Their lobbying efforts also helped Lisbon officials reach an agreement with Ottawa on 22 March 1976, in which the latter agreed to prioritize applications from these post-imperial immigrants if sponsored by relatives in Canada. By February 1978, approximately 3,000 former colonial settlers were living in southern Ontario, the majority of them coming from Angola.[95] While more studies are needed before we can reach definitive conclusions about this migrant cohort, it seems that they integrated fairly well into Toronto's Portuguese community, where many of them assumed prominent positions. This was not the case everywhere, as Kimberly Holton noted about Newark, where most white colonial "refugees" (many of them African-born) preferred to socialize with lusophone Africans, Brazilians, African Americans, and Latinxs, rather than with white Portuguese Americans.[96]

The empire's collapse also had major repercussions for Cape Verdeans in the United States, who could now identify with an independent ancestral homeland, whose nascent democratic politics were heavily transnational. For instance, the Boston-based American Committee for Cape Verde, founded in January 1975 by Raymond Almeida (a third-generation immigrant descendant), was a leading advocate for Cape Verde's interests in the United States, lobbying Washington to offer aid to the new African nation and educating Americans about Kriolu culture through its popular newsletter *Tchuba*. That year, on 22–3 February, Roy Teixeira and a group of right-wing expatriate nationalists, who later founded the Democratic and Independent Cape Verdean Union party in 1977, met at Boston's Sheraton Hotel for the Juridical Congress of World Cape Verdean Communities, where they proclaimed Cape Verde's independence. Their attempt to overtake the political transition process and prevent Lisbon from transferring power to the socialist PAIGC and its proposed one-party system failed. Cape Verde's independence was officially declared on 5 July 1975, at its new capital city of Praia.[97]

Post-Imperial Epilogues: Change and Continuity under Portugal's New Democratic Era

The 1976 constitutional government elections marked the end of the revolutionary period and the beginning of a new democratic era. Afterwards, tensions de-escalated as political debates became institutionalized. That year, right-wing parties received most of the emigrant votes: the centre-right PPD (later PSD) elected a member of parliament in each electoral region; the conservative CDS elected one "Outside of Europe;" and the socialist PS (the national winner) another in "Europe." Curiously, the communist PCP received 100 times more votes within Europe (5,082) than outside (508). Toronto had the fourth-largest voter turnout after Dusseldorf, Johannesburg, and Rio de Janeiro.[98] Expatriate voters were now courted directly by candidates running in emigration districts, who campaigned in foreign neighbourhoods with the help of local party representatives selected from among old and new community leaders. This approach introduced yet another transnational layer to an already intricate political constituency.

In the eyes of Canadian officials, "overt politicking" from visiting politicians from Portugal was "disruptive to the Canadian integration and citizenship processes."[99] But as in the past, concerns for homeland politics did not preclude immigrant activists from engaging with their host nation's polity – quite the contrary. In Canada, the political profile of Portuguese communities increased in the latter half of the 1970s, as evinced by the growing number of candidates running in municipal elections.[100] Partially sustaining this increasing political clout were the growing numbers of community members involved in ethnic clubs and associations, such as the FPCC, which in 1976 had about 1,500 members and generated an annual turnover of CA$1 million.[101] The number of Portuguese workers involved in labour unions, including those in positions of leadership, also grew in this period. The wildcat strike at the Toronto Dominion Centre by the "cleaning ladies" and their unionization at the Ontario Legislature building in 1974–5 remain two of the most prominent cases of Portuguese labour activism in Canada.[102] In 1979, the Laborers' International Union of North America (LIUNA) Local 183, which represents workers in industrial, commercial, and residential construction in the Greater Toronto Area and whose membership at the time was about 50 per cent Italian and 35 per cent Portuguese, hired a team of Portuguese stewards to inform their co-ethnic members about their labour rights and convince them to become actively engaged in their union. In 2018, Local 183 is the largest construction local in North America, with over 53,000 members, about 70 per cent of whom are Portuguese immigrants or descendants, including much of its executive.[103]

One of the factors driving this rise in labour activism was the consciousness-raising impact of the April 25th revolution. Its cathartic effect ended the long-standing characterization and self-understanding of the Portuguese as a docile, conservative, and contented people. The images and sounds of smiling, hugging, singing, and marching revolutionaries, with their predominantly Marxist publications, songs, slogans, rallies, occupations, parties, and policies, opened a new, intensely political dimension in the psyche of Portuguese people everywhere. Another factor contributing to this labour activism was the existence of well-established community infrastructures, activists, and politicians with various resources that these ethnic workers could mobilize. For example, at an electronics factory in Boston, Portuguese workers, most of them women, were able to muster the support of civic leaders and hold meetings in their ethnic club halls in their efforts to unionize. In Toronto, downtown office cleaners involved in various labour actions recruited progressive Portuguese community agencies and a newspaper, along with Canadian social workers and politicians. In both cases, ethnicity was an important organizational factor for these immigrants, who were able to rely on a shared language, kinship, neighbourhoods, and other "ethno-cultural expressions of militancy and solidarity," which granted them "a cohesiveness as a group that most [mainstream] workers lacked."[104]

The rape and murder of the young Azorean "shoeshine boy," Emanuel Jaques, on Toronto's Yonge Street in the summer of 1977 is often hailed as the moment that awakened the Portuguese community's political consciousness, said to be silent and invisible until then.[105] Indeed, this event was a major turning point not only for the Portuguese but for most Torontonians, who were shocked to discover that their city did not correspond with their idealized peaceful and conservative "Toronto the Good." Various rallies occurred after Jaques's murder, demanding that the city "clean" its seedy downtown strip and calling for the death penalty to be reinstated. After gathering close to 4,000 mourners at St Agnes Church for Jaques's funeral a few days earlier, Portuguese organizers rallied nearly 15,000 demonstrators outside City Hall on 8 August.[106] It was the largest Portuguese political gathering in Toronto to date, but certainly was not the first. Portuguese immigrants had taken to the streets to express their political views many times before, including after the murder of Ângelo Nóbrega in 1969. Nonetheless, this display of numerical strength spiked the interest of Canadian politicians, who recognized the electoral potential of the Portuguese and began attending their events more diligently. The "shoeshine boy" rally also stirred immigrants with political ambitions into thinking they could win an election with their co-ethnic vote. The following year, five Portuguese-Canadians ran for city council for the first time, all in the same ward (Trinity-Bellwoods and Little Italy); one of them was the MCP/*Comunidade*'s João Medeiros. However, the political momentum generated by the rally did not carry over to the ballot box, since none of the candidates came close to challenging the incumbents. After 1978, the average number of Portuguese-Canadian candidates fell to about one per election. It would be another ten years before a Portuguese immigrant was elected into government – Martin Silva, a radio announcer and former *Comunidade* contributor, who became a Toronto city councillor in 1988 representing the leftist NDP.

Though temporarily reinvigorated by the revolution, the old anti-fascist committees lost their original raison d'être after 1976 and struggled to stay relevant as activist organizations. Some of their most dynamic leaders returned to Portugal and participated in the revolutionary transition process, such as the MDP's Rui Viana, who left Canada in 1975 and became the chief redactor of the newsletter of the Intersindical (later Confederação Geral dos Trabalhadores Portugueses), the largest trade union federation in Portugal. These political organizations continued to engage in progressive movements, promoting racial and gender equality, children's rights, pacifism and other causes, though never focusing on a specific platform. Local left-wing politicians still frequented their community halls and attended their functions, which were now primarily cultural or educational. While these organizations assumed many of the same characteristics as other ethnic clubs, their members liked to stress that their programs were more sophisticated and enriching than those of traditional ethnic organizations. More women became involved with the PCDA and MDP in the late 1970s, injecting new life into their tired memberships, which helps explain how they managed to stay active for decades after the revolution. Still, it was not until the 1980s that women started assuming positions of leadership in these and other ethnic organizations.

The Azorean and Madeira separatist movements also abated after 1976, when the new constitution enshrined the archipelagos' autonomous regional governments. What little hope the FLA had in Washington's supporting its cause disappeared after the Lisbon government consolidated democratic rule and confirmed its NATO alliance. Azorean nationalists continued to attract interest from private Americans, such as the Las Vegas real estate millionaire and capitalist libertarian Michael Oliver, whose Phoenix Foundation was dedicated to creating tax havens in small independent nations. Curiously, the only nations to ever endorse the FLA were Soviet-backed Algeria and Libya, whose officials highlighted the islands' "Africanness."[107] Although the political momentum of Azorean nationalism subsided, its symbolic expression continued to elevate the ethnic and civic pride of Azoreans at home and abroad, as reflected in the multiplication of blue and white flags with golden *açores* (northern goshawks), waving at community gatherings and emblazoned on T-shirts, bumper stickers, and tattoos.

The influence of Azorean public intellectuals also grew in the 1970s, with a new generation of scholars, writers, and artists, many of them based in the United States, such as Onésimo Almeida, Eduardo Mayonne Dias, Vamberto Freitas, and Rogério Silva, who followed in the footsteps of Vitorino Nemésio, the founder of *Açorianidade*, who died in February 1978. The autonomous government in Ponta Delgada also helped raise the islanders' diasporic consciousness by aiding their expat communities' growing civic activity, where more secular organizations began to emerge. Meanwhile, ethnic leaders still tried to consolidate their communities under a single Portuguese identity, as was the case in 1978, when the FPCC's president invited the Azorean-American Cardinal Medeiros to lead a religious ceremony in Toronto – where he had family – with the intention of bringing Azoreans and mainlanders

7.3 Portuguese, Canadian, and Azorean (FLA design) flags waving in Nathan Phillips Square during Toronto's Portugal Day celebrations of June 1979. CTASC, Domingos Marques fonds.

together. This event never came to fruition, since Toronto's archdiocese did not approve it, owing to scheduling conflicts.[108]

Support for Portuguese-language schools remained the most common request heard by homeland officials visiting the emigrant communities. The latter now had the chance to address their demands directly to their state secretaries and members of parliament in Lisbon, who were more receptive than the Estado Novo's officials. But while post-revolutionary governments liked to contrast their progressive diasporic commitments with the dictatorship's neglect and unreliability, they eventually pointed to a familiar constraint: "There is little money."[109] Still, in the late 1970s, Portuguese immigrants had more options when it came to enrolling their children in heritage-language classes, in both community and mainstream schools. In 1977, Ottawa followed Washington's example and implemented the Cultural Enrichment Program, which covered close to 10 per cent of the operating costs of heritage-language schools run by ethnic communities. Ontario and Quebec introduced their Heritage Languages Program and Programme d'enseignement des langues d'origine soon after, which allocated funding to public school boards that offered these classes. Portuguese became one of the most prominent languages in both cases, driven mostly by the children of mainland immigrants.[110] Immigrant education advocates, like those associated with Toronto's MCP and *Comunidade*, welcomed this curricular shift away from previous prejudicial emphasis on assimilation. That approval, however, did not stop them from criticizing the heritage languages programs for being poorly conceived, excessively bureaucratic, neglecting to engage immigrant parents, not consulting or collaborating with community educators, and failing to address the high student dropout rates.[111] Besides encouraging immigrant children to be proud of their cultural background, these classes also helped develop a wider lusophone identity in North America's heterogeneous "Portuguese" settlements. However, the pan-linguistic cohesion tended to downplay regional and national diversity in the lusophone world and legitimized the centrality of mainland Portugal as the referential source of "Portugueseness." This was especially the case in Canada, where the majority of Portuguese teachers still were mainlanders.[112]

Remittances grew to record heights after 1975 despite the sharp drop in emigration. Besides cementing relations between homeland and diaspora, this increase bolstered the emigrants' sense of entitlement and leverage when making demands of Lisbon, which was happy to offer them incentives to invest or deposit their savings in Portugal. In 1977, twenty-four Bank of Portugal representatives visited various diasporic communities in North America to advertise financial products and fiscal benefits available to emigrants. For the latter, these were not "privileges" but "act[s] of justice." Asked by the *Comunidade* if the Portuguese government was continuing a "Salazar-Caetano type of policy" where emigration was effectively stimulated for the sake of boosting remittances, the state secretary of emigration answered categorically that it was not, yet he acknowledged that "at first glance [both policies] might appear to be similar."[113]

The tourism industry kept pushing its brand of saudade in the diaspora, assisted by Portugal's National Tourism Office in Manhattan, which now also had an office on Toronto's Bay Street and Montreal's Place Bonaventure. By 1976, TAP flew to Lisbon via the Azores five times a week from cities in Canada and the northeastern United States. Like the Casa de Portugal earlier, TAP now sponsored visits to Portugal by ethnic media directors and travel agents. Its marketing in the ethnic press also echoed familiar messages of old, as in this 1977 ad:

> Father. Mother. Brothers and cousins, all will be delighted to be with you ... You're going to claim those long awaited feasts [and] take copious naps in that field where the old pine tree waits for you ... Come with us ... Aboard our people. Aboard your language. Aboard our friendliness. Come along, as this is your home.[114]

In the first seven months of that year, Portugal saw a 38 per cent increase in the total number of tourists: 65 per cent among Canadians and 76 per cent among Americans.[115]

Emigrants visiting Portugal now encountered a different reality from the one they had left, and in most cases they were positively impressed by the social and economic progress in their hometowns, leading some to question their decision to leave in the first place. In 1977, the *Comunidade* asked three immigrants recently returned from their holidays in mainland Portugal to share their impressions on its post-revolutionary society. The men mentioned the improvements in consumer power and quality of life and drew examples from their family and friends. One emigrant noted that his old pals now volunteered to pay for drinks at the bar, as opposed to expecting him to pick up the tab, as was customary in the past. Another man argued that the attitudes of those visiting Portugal had changed as well:

> There was a time when relations between the locals and the emigrants were not very good. The emigrant wanted to show himself, he was pompous ... Now the emigrant who goes [to Portugal] doesn't say that things [in Canada] are fantastic. Now he notices: "Ah, you have unemployment here? So do we" ... They've reached the conclusion that things aren't so different after all.[116]

Another interviewee added:

> While [people in Portugal] may not think, for instance, in buying a house, they can afford a car as I do, have their home as well equipped as mine, and go to restaurants, movies, the beach, or a night out. I don't do that here. Over there, socially, they are living better than me.[117]

Notwithstanding the substantial improvements in transportation and telecommunications, the gulf of personal experiences and collective memories between Portuguese emigrants and national residents expanded and became harder to straddle. The emigrants' "roots" in the adopted country deepened as their children grew up as hyphenated ethnics with little or no desire to "return" to Portugal. Their parents also began accepting the fact that they could never "return home," since the places they experienced in youth and romanticized in senior years had changed considerably. Never return in their lifetime, that is, because in death many mainland emigrants have chosen to send their remains to their hometowns in Portugal, so they can be buried with their ancestors. Azoreans, on the other hand, rarely send their dead back to the islands, reflecting greater family transplantation and less identification with the "homeland."[118]

For many postwar immigrants, the late 1970s was a time of retrospection, especially in Canada, where Portuguese migration memory was yet to be articulated. In fact, the first heritage campaign led by Portuguese immigrants in Canada began in December 1974, when a group of business and professional men from Quebec proposed to Canada Post that it create a stamp commemorating the Portuguese settler Pedro da Silva, who, they claimed, was the first mail courier in seventeenth-century New France; however, the stamp would not be issued until 2003.[119] Older and newer generations began preoccupying themselves with honouring the lives of those sojourner-turned-immigrant men (the "pioneers") who arrived in Canada in the 1950s. Their common stories of toil, isolation, discrimination, camaraderie, and triumph were first captured by the young social workers Domingos Marques and João Medeiros, who published them in 1978, on the occassion of the twenty-fifth anniversary of the *Saturnia*'s arrival in Halifax. Common to other European immigrant "bootstraps" narratives of the time,[120] tributes to the largely male "pioneers" have since centred on their hard-working ethic, personal sacrifice, and family dedication, which have been the mainstay of Portuguese immigration anniversaries in Canada. By embracing "triumph over adversity" tropes and the familiar Christian narrative of redemption, the injustices and indignities forced upon the immigrants by the capitalist and nativist societies that exploited their labour have been somewhat exonerated, as their communities' ongoing social, economic, educational, and health problems became metaphorical trials essential to their personal tales of overcoming and absolution. Moreover, by placing the male "pioneers" at the centre of the Portuguese-Canadian story, 13 May celebrations have framed that group's official public memory within a patriarchal and Portuguese-born interpretation of their past, where immigrant women and their Canadian-born children are either ancillary or incidental. That seems to have been the thinking behind the award given to the immigrant Maria Celeste Pereira for being the first Portuguese woman to give birth to a child in Canada, bestowed by the president of Madeira's regional government, Alberto J. Jardim, in Toronto during the twenty-fifth anniversary celebrations of the *Saturnia*'s arrival.[121]

Still, these "pioneer" stories were important in forming the cultural and social consciousness of Canadian-born or -raised Portuguese, who previously had lacked the historical context from which to make sense of their experiences, as was the case with Marcie Ponte:

> I remember when Domingos wrote his first book, it was really exciting to hear the stories of the first pioneers who came to Canada. And lo and behold, I had no idea that my father was part of that group. That started to change things for me and how I became more Portuguese than I was at that time ... The revolution in Portugal and the whole Salazar era, once I started learning ... about that whole history, for me it was really awe-inspiring ... I started to understand that there was more to this than just being Portuguese. There was a history that people walked away from ... And it shaped me, politically.[122]

The Day of Portugal, Camões and the Portuguese Communities, as it became known in 1977, interwove the immigrants' "bootstraps" narrative with the national discourses of home and host nations, and reinforced transnational bonds of "Portugueseness" between near and far diasporic communities. That year, Lisbon sent navy vessels to Brazil, France, the Netherlands, and the United States, where they released 500 bottles into the sea containing messages from the people of Portugal inviting the lucky recipients to visit the country, with their trip paid by the Portuguese government.[123] Portugal Day parades and surrounding festivities grew in size at this point, showcasing the civic strength and cultural diversity of the ethnic constituency. In Toronto, men, women, and children in traditional garments displayed their peasant and fishermen roots as they marched down Augusta Avenue onto Dundas Street West – mirroring the community's growth pattern – followed by an entourage of politicians, community leaders, diplomats, and other dignitaries. An estimated 80,000 people attended the 1977 festivities at Trinity-Bellwoods Park, where they enjoyed performances from homeland and local Portuguese artists, including amateur fado singers, such as Consul Ernesto Feu. The next year, Portugal Day celebrations were dedicated to commemorating the twenty-fifth anniversary of Portuguese mass migration to Canada. In Toronto's High Park, ethnic leaders erected a monument to their community in the form of a *padrão*,[124] alluding to their homeland's imperial history.[125]

Present at the unveiling were a group of successful "pioneers," Portuguese diplomats, Canadian politicians, and the visiting "April

7.4 Community leaders, the "April Captain" Vitor Alves, Alderman Art Eggleton, and Portuguese diplomats posing in front of the padrão monument to the immigrant "pioneers," June 1978. Courtesy of photographer Gilberto Prioste.

Captain" Vitor Alves, who had chaired Portugal's national holiday celebrations the year before. As in the past, host politicians at these multicultural events extolled the imperial heritage of the Portuguese and traced direct links between the seafaring explorers and the "persistent, hard working, disciplined, friendly" immigrants, who made "good citizens anywhere they settle," while Lisbon officials urged the emigrants to unite and flex their political muscle.[126]

The emigrants' scepticism or cynicism about their homeland's promised commitment to them continued to grow. Commentators such as Onésimo Almeida characterized the annual national-diasporic celebrations as nothing more than empty words:

> June 10 will be back in a few months ... More emotional speeches sending saudades and kisses to the emigrants, more officialized revelries here

and there, embassies of fado and football across this world, dilating that-nostalgic-weeping and that-leftover-empire. Portuguese people around the world will once again be messaged with the same dose of sentimental verbosity as the year before ... Promises of fidelity will be made, enduring and fecund love, care for their problems, contacts, and, in return, they will simply be asked to reciprocate that love ... by sending those very needed remittan$$es [sic] that shall help rebuild the Pátria.[127]

Adriano Moreira, who returned from exile in Brazil in 1977, noticed the echoes of his own diasporic project in Lisbon's post-imperial outreach to the emigrants, and he accused the new regime of appropriating his idea without acknowledging its past. He saw no harm in doing so, as long as those implementing his vision were competent, which he believed was not the case. According to Moreira, the new government had not yet understood "the transcending national importance" of emigration, which it approached with useless "uninspired folklore." The former colonial minister also lamented the redefinition of Portuguese nationality along blood (hence racial) lines in the 1975 Nationality Law, since it excluded the majority of non-white former colonials from obtaining citizenship. Included in this group were those Cape Verdean immigrants and their American-born descendants who still self-identified as Portuguese.[128]

After their country's independence, Cape Verdeans were freed from Lisbon's colonial bureaucracy and able to apply for emigration directly at the desired nation's diplomatic representations in Praia. This opportunity gave rise to a new mass exodus, primarily to New England, Portugal, and the Netherlands. The post-independence migrant cohorts introduced a more articulate and assertive Kriolu culture into the United States and amplified the ethnic distinctiveness of Cape Verdean Americans at a time when multiculturalism rewarded cultural diversity. In December 1975, after Cape Verdeans had petitioned the Massachusetts state legislature, Kriolu was officially recognized as "a living foreign language" distinct from Portuguese, which allowed its instructors to receive funds earmarked by Chapter 71A. At this point, Cape Verdean Americans became more aware of their national identity, now reinforced by their homeland government, which developed its own transnational citizenship and diasporic council.[129]

Conclusion

The 1970s were marked by various intersecting watershed moments that stretched the identities and solidarities of Portuguese communities in multiple new directions. In a decade rich with cultural, political, and economic transformations, three shifts were of special importance to the lives of Portuguese immigrants and descendants in North America: the rise of white ethnic politics and related multiculturalist legislation, the emergence of new progressive ethnic leaders, and the political regime change in Portugal. When studying the period before and after the April revolution, it is hard to miss the ironic and sometimes hypocritical role reversals of community leaders and homeland officials and how new political agents continued to employ old methods. Among other unexpected turns, this decade saw young activists criticize the old guard of self-appointed ethnic leaders while preaching ethnic unity to uncooperative immigrants; Portuguese Americans pleading to be recognized as "non-white," while Cape Verdeans became comfortable in their "in-between" skin; right-wing political exiles planning coups with their transnational networks; pro-democratic advocates opposing the political enfranchising of expat citizens. After 1974, the revolutionaries' interpretation of the "fascist" dictatorship became the dominant narrative of Portugal's recent political past. The new democratic government highlighted the many negative aspects of the Estado Novo's emigration policies and effaced those that laid the foundation for its diasporic project. While warranted in many aspects, criticism of the previous regime's neglect of emigrants was sometimes overly simplistic or even unfounded. Indeed, Salazar paid little attention to emigrants and his government largely ignored their requests or dealt with them in an ad hoc manner. Nonetheless, many Portuguese diplomats took a genuine interest in the affairs of emigrant communities and advanced their causes in Lisbon, where they occasionally found receptive ears. The fact that Estado Novo officials had ulterior motives should not take away from the intrinsic value of their diasporic contributions, even when compared with those of their democratic successors, who also had political agendas that included boosting trade and remittances. Moreover, while post-1974 diplomats paid greater attention to the emigrants' concerns and had a clearer vision of how to address them in a more democratic manner, they soon were confronted with the same lack of funds that had plagued their predecessors and forced them too to limit the scope of their actions. Such a disappointing realization added to the emigrants' frustration with the homeland and their growing scepticism about Lisbon's promises.

Another interesting irony was the fact that the fall of the dictatorship, which had largely been responsible for Portugal's mass exodus, contributed in many ways to further uproot emigrants from their homeland, despite the revolutionary governments' appeals for their return. The rapidly changing consciousness, identities, and lifestyles of Portuguese national residents; the growing Azorean separatist nationalism; and the displacement of former imperial settlers from their colonial homes all prompted a large number of "Portuguese" expatriates to distance themselves from their supposed "homeland." The diasporic discourses assumed by national and regional governments, with their claims that Portuguese people were "at home" everywhere, would eventually repair these ties. But in the process, the homeland became a symbolic function of the pluri-national diaspora as much as the diaspora reaffirmed the homeland's ethos as a global nation.

Public memory helped postwar immigrants come to terms with these transitions by framing their collective identity as a story of mobility and deterritorialized belonging, in a way that bridged the country they had left and the one their children called home. Their triumphalist "bootstraps" narratives validated their migrant choices for themselves, their families, and their host and home countries' societies, at a time when the quality of life in Portugal had improved dramatically. Theirs was hardly an "assimilation blues" or "ethnic revivalism," since they were, for the most part, first-generation immigrants discovering their ethnicity for the first time. Still, their memorialization efforts resonated with mainstream North American audiences, now drawn to the familiar "Ellis Island" immigrant story and its "Pier 21" Canadian equivalent. While efforts to transform the historical gateway in Halifax into a museum did not begin until the late 1980s, the enfranchising of all immigrants into the nation's official multiculturalist self-understanding favoured the creation of conciliatory immigrant mythologies (although it also opened the door to discussing past racist injustices). Those Portuguese "pioneers" with personal histories of upward mobility and economic success, who were usually the ones celebrating their life stories, tended to impress an apologetic or integrationist tone on their public memories of immigration. As Jacobson noted, such triumphalist immigrant narratives reinforced the hegemonic capitalist and colonialist ethos of their host societies by confirming "the possibility of upward mobility in an economy that rarely delivers on that promise," obscuring the nation's "less flattering 'foundings,'" and providing "a nationalist narrative of choiceworthiness." In this light, it may seem surprising that progressive ethnics took a personal interest in memorializing the "bootstraps" narrative of "self-congratulation and erasure." However, this approach was common to leftist multiculturalism, fond of ethnicity's anti-assimilation stance against North America's atomistic capitalist society, whose exploitation of migrant labour they denounced through the memories of hardship of the "pioneers." Still, narratives of European immigration on both ends of the political spectrum were about "downtroddenness ... never, ever, [about] *privilege*."[130]

The conservative shift in European ethnic revivalism and its pluralist "Ellis Island whiteness" in the 1970s reinforced the US racist hegemony by celebrating the supposed "self-reliance" of white ethnics over the "welfare dependency" of African Americans. Against this background, the efforts of progressive Portuguese-American activists to obtain official non-white, minority-group status in order to access affirmative action resources and counter the capitalist exploitation of immigrant workers are remarkable. They were not alone in their attempts to be recognized as a deserving ethnic "minority." As Skrentny noted, other white "ethnics" tried to join the "minority rights revolution" and failed, mainly because they were below the "threshold of perceived discrimination that legitimated claims of oppression or victimhood" and because their "multiplicity of identities further undermined the analogy with blacks, who were seen principally in terms of race."[131] While moved by anti-racist sentiments, the pan-linguistic identity proposed by progressive European Portuguese in North America was utilitarian in its attempt to benefit from legislation meant to redress historically marginalized racial groups. In doing so they exercised their white privilege by appropriating blackness and its rich culture of resistance without experiencing the full extent of "black pain."[132] Their proposed lusophone identity, based on Portugal's imperial heritage, was also poorly timed, as African nationalist forces were still fighting for independence from their Portuguese colonizers.

While European Portuguese were generally understood by Americans to be Latin in culture and character, the terms "Latinos" or "Hispanics" were seldom used to describe these northeastern communities prior to the 1960s; the situation might be different for Portuguese Americans in the west, where Spanish-speaking communities are much older and bigger. As the numbers of Latin-American immigrants grew in the United States after 1965 and in Canada after 1967, their cultural and linguistic affinity with European Portuguese allowed for these newcomer groups to live and work together, which in turn generated new bonds and group perceptions. The 1970s generation of Portuguese ethnic activists in Canada welcomed and in some cases sought this association with Latinidad. In the United States, where Latinx or Hispanic communities were of much greater size and visibility, Portuguese-American leaders were ambivalent about that correlation. On one hand, it lent them a useful "legal minority status" and increased their political leverage when pursuing common goals. On the other, it worked against local Portuguese-American interests, since it diluted their specific needs and made them invisible within the much larger Hispanic pan-ethnicity. The solution they found to access the government resources they needed was to use the terminology of the new multiculturalist era and advance an alternative pan-linguistic "minority" identity similar to that of "Hispanics," whose term gained official recognition in the United States only in the late 1960s.

In Canada, as Bloemraad argued, the fact that official multiculturalism was based more on ethnicity than on race explains why Portuguese-Canadian activists were more straightforward and more successful when obtaining government funds for their advocacy and social programs. According to leftist critics, such as Giles, immigrant activists working within the policy framework of state multiculturalism were "cornered into arguing on an ethnic (rather than a class, gender, and racialized) basis."[133] In other words, they were expected to be ethnic brokers, much like the old community leaders they hoped to replace. But while policymakers may have sought to homogenize the immigrants' "multiplicity of identities" and limit the range of issues they were able to advocate for, young "radical ethnic brokers" were smart enough to put government multiculturalist resources to more subversive uses.

Conclusion

How does a small peripheral government with few material resources assert itself as a geopolitical player in an era of rising global governance, when rival superpowers threaten the sovereignty of nation states and colonial empires? This was the question in the minds of Estado Novo officials when they were developing their foreign policies in the second half of the twentieth century and the one driving this study. For Salazar and his followers, the answer was to reinvent Portugal's imperial regime as a Western stronghold against international communism and the nation as a pluri-continental and multiracial haven whose contributions to Christian civilization were at the genesis of Western global dominance. When this imperial fantasy began to crumble in the face of the anti-colonialist "winds of history," the regime's propaganda continued to push its lusotropicalist fiction while drafting the nation's youth to kill and die in unfamiliar "overseas provinces." Meanwhile, a parallel offspring version of pluri-continental and multiracial nationhood gained traction in those ministries engaged in foreign and colonial affairs. Inspired imperialists like Adriano Moreira envisioned the unification of all Portuguese expatriates and descendants under one large diaspora loyal to the homeland and mobilized substantial resources and political support to make it so. Eventually, the Estado Novo's sovereignty-by-force strategy led to its own demise, along with the centuries-old empire that legitimized Portugal's claim to being a large country. Hovering above its debris remained the deterritorialized version of nationhood, where "being Portuguese" meant sharing in a national heritage that celebrated itinerancy and hybridity. Before securing its EEC membership and re-imagining itself as a modern European nation (of immigrants), the post-revolutionary government adopted this lingering lusotropicalist discourse to overcome its "crisis of national identity" and reassert itself on the international stage as a postmodern global nation (of emigrants), no longer legitimized by *overseas provinces* but by its *Portuguese communities.*

The "bottom up" response to these grand narratives differed according to the audiences and the agents that promoted, interpreted, or rejected them. Workers, entrepreneurs, exiles, activists, mainlanders, Azoreans, Cape Verdeans, men, and women – all pinpointed their "homeland" in different places and related to it in varied ways. Few consciously sought to create a diaspora; they were too busy worrying about their individual and family issues or were focused on organizing their local communities. Still, their remittances, religious exchanges, transatlantic charities, sports and arts tours, political networks, and other transnational engagements linked their expatriate organizations to their hometowns and to other Portuguese settlements in North America. These interactions reinforced regional and national bonds of solidarity that helped develop a sense of belonging to a larger diaspora. Over time, those agents tasked with advancing the Estado Novo's agenda in the emigrant communities, such as the diplomats, priests, newspapers editors, and other influential individuals who had the means and the will to articulate the larger picture, wove these loose transnational bonds into a national-imperial imagining.

Diplomats, the basic medium in international relations (between nations), often broke the rules and became agents of transnational relations (in spite of nations). Portuguese ambassadors and consuls recruited, coerced, and manipulated immigrant leaders and their institutions to do the homeland government's bidding, in direct contravention of non-interventionist diplomatic conventions. At the same time, diplomats were not mere instruments of the Estado Novo's foreign policy. Indeed, much of their organizational efforts abroad had little resonance in Lisbon and were inhibited by their superiors' lack of support or vision, especially before the mid-1960s. It was common for consuls and ambassadors to advocate on behalf of expatriate communities and even to take matters into their own hands when they failed to obtain a timely or satisfactory response from Lisbon. Foreign officers tended to have a more liberal world view than their domestic peers, given their cosmopolitan education and prolonged residence in democratic nations. Still, they carried out their missions with a great deal of cognitive dissonance and relativism, since they stimulated in the emigrant communities the very civic and political engagement that the dictatorship curbed at home. Moreover, despite objecting to the emigrants' cultural "backwardness" and parochialism, the diplomats' admiration for the expats' continued dedication to the homeland inspired them to go beyond their expected duties. The corresponding goals and community outreach efforts of diplomatic patrons and their local clients laid the organizational foundation for the diaspora-building policies, with their unifying federations and ethnonational celebrations.

The "bottom up" paradigm of earlier social historians downplayed the role of ethnic elites in shaping their communities, given the latter's aloofness from the everyday realities of common immigrants. This social disconnect did exist in many cases, but not in all. Many middle-class ethnic entrepreneurs shared social backgrounds and sojourning experiences similar to those of the immigrant workers they catered to. This was especially true in postwar settlements, like those in Canada, where the term "elites" is a less apt description for these upwardly mobile immigrants than it is for the established Portuguese-American bourgeoisie. To a large extent, the social ascension of immigrant intermediaries was tied to their transnational brokerage and the value of their patronage. Patrons themselves, although more highly placed in the "supply chain," diplomats provided ethnic entrepreneurs with resources, status, and influence (though not always wealth). These foreign officials empowered select community leaders in order to better manipulate them and increase Lisbon's leverage in their host societies. Their outreach efforts were more extensive in the United States, where Portuguese Americans were better organized, more numerous, and more powerful. Because their status and power did not derive entirely from the homeland's patronage and transnational relations, Portuguese-American elites were in a better position to resist or negotiate the diplomats' encroachment in their community affairs than their co-ethnics to the north, who had a more unilateral relation with Lisbon.

Middle- and upper-class community leaders, almost all of them men, had the most to say about the collective identity of Portuguese immigrants. As businessmen, journalists, and other tradesmen catering to the ethnic market, they also had the most to profit from reinforcing their shared cultural heritage. Simultaneously, by endorsing the Estado Novo's narrative about their homeland's contributions to Western civilization, Portuguese intelligentsia carved a space for themselves in the Eurocentric founding mythology of home and host countries, and asserted their full membership as bona fide (white) American and Canadian nationals. In their heritage celebrations, the agendas of ethnic leaders, host nation politicians, and homeland diplomats intersected in a relationship of convenience moved by mutual self-interest, where political differences were momentarily set aside, for they all reaped benefits from participating in such events. For community leaders, to be seen mingling with state dignitaries elevated their elite status and brokerage reputation. For American and Canadian politicians, it was important to be seen supporting a potentially useful ethnic constituency in increasingly multiculturalist polities. And for Portuguese diplomats, these were excellent opportunities to meet with influential people in less formal and more candid settings, survey the mood in their government agencies with respect to Portuguese interests, and try to curry their favour.

The most fervent champions of the Estado Novo's nationalist and imperialist (or "ecumenical") message in North America were the Catholic missionaries sent from Portugal to ward off the emigrants' cultural assimilation. Many of these clerics kept close ties with diplomats and other Lisbon officials as well as with other community leaders, with whom they created various lay and secular organizations. They were not "elites" in the classic sense of the term, since their religious vocation and social work demanded that they remain close to the lower-class emigrants they served. However, their role did not stop some from coveting wealth and power, to the point of becoming insubordinate and belligerent. Though usually pivotal allies of the dictatorship, these migrant priests could become serious nuisances to its diplomats, especially when they fell outside the jurisdiction of Portugal's episcopacy, which meant that Lisbon had little control over them. While keen to promote loyalty to the homeland and its empire, missionaries (including those from the mainland) were also eager to observe the "unsavory" rites and symbols of their mainly Azorean parishioners, which conflicted with the "respectable" spirituality of Irish-American, Irish-Canadian, French-Canadian, and sometimes mainland Portuguese Catholicism. Parish halls, lay associations, and religious festivals helped consolidate a distinct Azorean identity in North America that later grew into a separatist national and diasporic consciousness. The missionaries' receptiveness to this regional liturgy was in large part what earned them their parishioners' loyalty (the source of their worldly power), though it also made priests more dependent on the gratitude of their flocks.

In North America, where the Catholic Church was less powerful and centralized than in Portugal, the laity played a greater fundraising and administrative role in the parishes and thus had more leverage over its priests. Sometimes this fact led to tensions between parishioners and the more traditionalist priests from Portugal. It was especially the case in the United States, where most of the laity were Americanized immigrant descendants, who preserved homeland traditions selectively and assigned different meanings and purposes to the religious festivities imported by their ancestors. Their greater independence and adaptability allowed them to negotiate the terms of engagement with their priests and shun those who were uncooperative. Portuguese-American lay organizations also had greater means to coordinate nationwide charity and disaster relief campaigns to aid those in need in their hometowns. It was common for these expatriate benefactors to use transnational Church channels and avoid Lisbon's direct intervention. Together with their steady flow of remittances, the casual small charitable contributions of individual emigrants had a great impact on the lives of their impoverished beneficiaries and their local economies in Portugal.

Political exiles also relied on transnational networks extending across Europe, Africa, and the Americas to denounce the Estado Novo's human rights abuses and educate largely uninformed North American audiences about their authoritarian NATO ally. While professionals, skilled workers, and businessmen often led these exiled organizations, many of their members were labourers with humble social and educational backgrounds. They were able to circulate political literature, organize numerous public rallies, draw endorsements from influential Americans and Canadians, and capture the attention of mainstream media, thanks in large part to the logistic and financial support of fellow exiles around the world. As "radical ethnic brokers," their commitment to democracy in Portugal was matched by their active citizenship in Canada and the United States, where they urged other immigrants to engage with the politics of their host societies. Despite fighting for democracy, American and Canadian secret services spied on these anti-fascists and shared damning information about their activities and affiliations with the unaccountable PIDE. The sense of betrayal, disappointment, and exclusion felt by these activists was compounded by the widespread complacency and even hostility of their fellow immigrants, accused by the exiles of turning their backs on the misery and oppression of their kin in Portugal after improving their own economic situation. In their correspondence, newspapers, literature, music, and other communications, these political migrants articulated a distinct diasporic consciousness based on their self-understanding as outcasts of a nation that had failed them, but to which they remained committed and hoped one day to return.

Another alternative diaspora developing in North America was that of Cape Verdeans. After a long history of exclusion from "white" Portuguese-American spaces, Cape Verdeans started building their own separate institutions. Though originally not trying to assert a distinct ethnicity, their continued rejection by white ethnic and mainstream Americans and their own distancing from black or African Americans prompted Cape Verdeans to develop their hybrid Kriolu language and culture. Still, until the 1960s, most Cape Verdean immigrants saw themselves as citizens of Portugal's multiracial empire, which their organizations acted on by requesting aid from Lisbon for cultural initiatives. But by the time that Portuguese-American leaders had adopted a multiracial version of nationhood and began welcoming Cape Verdeans into their midst, the latter had already formed their own autonomous organizations and were moving away from a "Portuguese," "European," "white" identity. At this point, Cape Verdeans had multiple choices regarding their ethnicity and nationality, which were passionately debated between foreign- and American-born generations and fuelled by the Black Power and the PAIGC's anti-colonial movements. After their "African" nation's independence, their once reticent Kriolu culture became the dominant identity in Cape Verdean-American communities, now animated by the arrival of a new cohort of proud immigrants and a homeland government that sought to affirm its own national-diasporic identity. Also boosting Cape Verdean ethnic pride were the multiculturalist policies introduced in New England in the 1970s promoting the study and celebration of their distinct Kriolu culture. In contrast, Canada's official multiculturalism helped subsume the increasingly separatist identity of Azorean immigrants under a homogeneous Portuguese-Canadian identity, which was largely defined by those mainlanders who dominated the secular civic and cultural organizations of the country's largest and most heterogeneous Portuguese communities.

Ironically, both the civil rights movement and the rise of multiculturalism ideology suited the Estado Novo's lusotropicalist propaganda. Lisbon's foreign officials liked to contrast Portugal's supposedly peaceful multiracial empire with the United States's violent racial segregation and even to pay lip service to the liberation struggles of African Americans, at the same time as their government was killing African nationalists in the colonies. Concurrently, white ethnic revivalism and its liberal-conservative multiculturalism, which favoured the most picturesque and seemingly traditional elements of European cultural heritage, fit perfectly with the regime's engineering of Portuguese folk culture along with Salazar's ruralist ethos. The collectivist and anti-modernist appeal of multiculturalist ethnicity was an excellent platform for marketing Portugal's growing tourism industry, consumer products, and cultural exports, couched in Old World bucolic nostalgia.

The 1970s generation of "radical ethnic brokers" also adopted the discourses and resources of American and Canadian identity politics. While critical of the older generation's power-mongering tactics and their deference to homeland officials, these emerging progressive leaders also tried to instrumentalize their ethnicity to unite their immigrant communities and increase their leverage with host government officials.

Similar to those earlier Portuguese-American elites who redrew their group's ethnic boundaries along the multiracial lines of lusotropicalism, these young activists broadened their ethnic self-understanding to include other lusophones, and even Latinxs. Although their methods, ideologies, and goals were significantly different, both generations had ulterior political reasons for advancing a more inclusive Portuguese racial identity. The *lusotropicalists* were essentially liberal-conservative middle- and upper-class men who sought to elevate their ethnic group's cultural and political status within the limited latitude conceded by the white American society. To do so, they employed propagandistic resources provided by their homeland, which were tailored to fit both liberal (pluralist) and conservative (Western supremacist) tenets of American nationalism and Cold War mentality. The *lusophones*, on the other hand, were progressive, working- and lower-middle-class men and women, who dedicated much of their civic and professional careers to improving the lives of immigrant workers. They were inspired by the civil rights, Black Power, and other radical movements of the 1960s–70s, whose language of minority group rights they appropriated to access affirmative action and multiculturalist resources in order to battle the effects of and advocate against their countries' capitalist systems.

Diasporas are not partial to any one political ideology. In the same way that the fascist regime in Italy executed the diaspora-building plans of the previous liberal government,[1] Portuguese left-wing democrats continued the diasporic policies originally articulated by the conservative dictatorship. Before diasporic visions came to dominate Lisbon's post-1974 emigration policy, the Marxist revolutionary governments saw emigration as a tragic consequence of "capitalism" and "fascism," whose structural inequalities and political oppression had led to the massive exodus of Portugal's labour force. Like Caetano, leftist politicians believed that most emigrants would want to return and invest in their homeland, given the proper economic incentives. Indeed, remittances increased rapidly and many emigrants did return after 1974. However, some expatriates, such as the Azorean nationalists and many of those post-imperial refugees who chose to re-emigrate, cut ties with mainland Portugal at this point. Still others, arguably the majority, maintained a vague aspiration to return but knew that the places of their youth had changed dramatically with Portugal's modernization unfolding since the 1950s and more rapidly after the revolution. Those centrist governments that followed the PREC gradually recoiled from their interim predecessors' Marxist goals, and they resumed the diaspora-building project started during the dictatorship, to which they made various progressive changes. It was then that the emigrants were elevated to the status of "ambassadors" of the global nation, and references to its imperial past reappeared in official homeland addresses to the now lukewarm diasporic audiences. Still, Portuguese communities welcomed the resources provided by Lisbon to fulfil its diasporic vision. The fact that immigrants could now visit their families in Portugal more frequently, use instant long-distance communication technologies to speak with their loved ones on a regular basis, and eventually follow the daily occurrences in Portugal and other expatriate communities by tuning in to RTPi simultaneously reinforced their ties with the homeland and made their permanent return less necessary. Though still central to their national and ethnic identities, Portugal became not so much a *home* but a *nexus* of diasporic connections facilitated by the post-imperial state. As Noivo argued, Portuguese immigrants now inhabited "reconstructed locations" where their "diasporicity derives from stitching together experiences and contradictory emotional connections – including both a longing for home and a resentment of exclusion from it – grounding a complex collective imagination."[2]

The multiracial, pan-linguistic identity advanced by the 1970s generation preceded by a couple of decades the lusophone consciousness promoted by Lisbon since the 1990s, when it replaced the diaspora with language as the crux of its global national identity and cultural hybridity. Although it failed to capture the imagination of most emigrants when it was first proposed, this lusophone identity would gain greater currency after the fall of the empire, when more Angolan, Brazilian, Cape Verdean, and Mozambican immigrants began settling in North America's Portuguese neighbourhoods – although not without conflict.[3] In this, *Lusofonia* is similar to *Latinismo*, whose intellectual and political project never fully materialized in Latin America but found strong expression in North America.[4] It is too early to say whether the label "lusophone" will ever have the same public recognition as "Hispanic" in North America. For most Americans, the Portuguese remain a difficult group to categorize. This confusion is reflected in the world's most powerful Internet search algorithm. Typing the words "Are Portuguese" on Google, one is given the following top search suggestions (by ranking): "hispanic," "latino," "people white," "latin," and "black."[5] Popular culture has perpetuated this ambiguity by including Portuguese artists in the Latin Grammy Awards; in the creative and commercial exploits of high-profile luso-descendent musicians, such as Nelly Furtado, who has recorded and performed in Spanish; and in the recurrent casting of Portuguese immigrant and descendent actors/actresses to play Latinx roles. It is difficult to say how much the 1970s generation welcomed or resisted this Latinoization. Pursuing that question would take us beyond the historical period framing this study. But by any measure, it is hard to see how such a small and localized group of people could impact the widespread yet vague understandings that North Americans have of "Latinos" or "Hispanics," a much larger and more powerful pan-ethnicity, whose boundaries are fuzzy and situational by design. The two identities have been blurred by the facts that Brazil is the largest country in South America and the largest lusophone nation in the world; that both Latinxs and lusophones are multiracial groups; and that there is close proximity between Portuguese and Spanish history, language, culture, and geography. Their ongoing ethnic and racial ambiguity in the eyes of Americans has allowed the Portuguese some flexibility over their identities, which can be advantageous. For instance, Portuguese actors/actresses can find work playing Latinx and other ambiguous "ethnics" on screen.[6] On the other hand, this co-optation obscures Portuguese-specific representations, which remains an irritant among the communities' intelligentsia. I learned about this feeling at a conference in Rhode Island in 2011, when the audience uttered a collective groan after a Portuguese-American publisher relayed that a major television network was interested in adapting one of its novels, provided that the author agreed to change the ethnicity of its central characters from Portuguese to Mexican.

Debate about whether or not Portuguese Americans are a historically disadvantaged minority is very much alive today, the conclusion of which has significant material implications. Some US government agencies, such as the Department of Transportation and the Small Business Administration, include "persons with origins from Portugal" in their definition of "Hispanic Americans," who are "in the absence of evidence to the contrary ... presumed to be socially disadvantaged" and therefore eligible for equity programs.[7] In March 2018, a judge in the Suffolk County Superior Court disagreed with this view and ruled against granting Portuguese-owned businesses equity-seeking privileges when it came to securing construction contracts offered by the state of Massachusetts – by law, 10.4 per cent of that state's building contracts (except transportation infrastructure) must be granted to "minority-owned" businesses. Court documents revealed that, in 2015, over 61 per cent of all construction contracts were awarded to Portuguese-owned businesses under this equity rule. According to the ruling, it resulted from a civil servant having arbitrarily certified Portuguese-American businesses as "minority-owned" without "any evidence that persons of Portuguese origin have ever suffered discrimination in the construction industry in Massachusetts." The lawyer representing the plaintiff – a non-Portuguese female subcontractor – argued that Portuguese-American businessmen today no longer face discrimination, noting that their construction companies made more money than their non-Portuguese male competitors. Furthermore, she argued, a study commissioned by Massachussetts state bureaucrats had lumped together Portuguese and Brazilians in an effort to skew the results towards showing that anti-Portuguese discrimination still existed.[8]

As evinced by the growing identification with Portuguese heritage and by the instiutional viability of its diaspora in North America today, one can safely say that Portuguese ethnic leaders have succeeded in developing their communities regardless of Latinoization. Cultural identities, diasporic or otherwise, cannot stay fixed for long, even when they try or pretend to be. Noivo's observation above, published in 2002, might still hold true for some diasporic Portuguese today. But new ripples have since emerged in that complex canvas as new generations create their own relationships with the sophisticated, cosmopolitan, technologically advanced, largely progressive, and widely popular contemporary Portugal. An online survey in 2010 found that up to fourth-generation luso-descendants in Canada and the United States had significant rates of identification with the country of their ancestors, which they kept abreast of through conventional and social media and by travelling there.[9] These cultural ties have a significant material expression in the form of remittances. In 2016, the volume of remittances from the United States (€243,170) was the highest since 2003, despite the average number of official immigration from Portugal (847) remaining relatively low and stable since 2008.[10] Numerous anecdotes confirm the strengthening of transnational ties between the Portuguese in North America and their ancestral homeland in recent years, including the growing size and number of FLAD's educational, scientific, business, international development, and political exchange programs between the United States and Portugal; the 2011 opening of the Arte Institute in Manhattan, dedicated to promoting Portuguese contemporary arts and culture, and funded by FLAD, the Lisbon government, and major Portuguese corporations; the large street celebrations in various "Little Portugals" following the national football team's victory in the 2016 UEFA Euro Cup tournament; the still growing number of participants in Toronto's thirty-year old Portugal Day parade, despite the steadily low volume of official immigration into Canada; the US$200,000 donated by Portuguese Americans to the victims of the forest fires that devasted central Portugal in the summer of 2017; the protocol signed in November 2017 between Ontario's LIUNA

Local 183 and the União Geral dos Trabalhadores, the second largest trade union federation in Portugal; and the sizable number of American and Canadian music, film, television, and sports "celebrities" who are second- or third-generation descendants of Portuguese immigrants, and who now publicly affirm their cultural heritage and maintain personal connections with Portugal. The Portuguese in North America are yet another example of how cultural assimilation theories, which predict the inevitable effacing of homeland languages, customs, and identities after multiple generations, do not capture the complex ebbs and flows of ethnic or diasporic consciousness, especially in a world where transnational belongings are increasingly easier to maintain.

"Diasporas" and "nations" have in common the fact that they are both "imagined communities," yet they differ when it comes to geography, because "nations," unlike "diasporas," are traditionally limited by territory and political borders. However, as the Portuguese case reveals, national and diasporic consciousness can become intertwined and difficult to differentiate, especially when reinforced by imperial imaginings. The Portuguese nation, before and after the fall of its empire, may not have imagined itself to be "coterminous with mankind," but it certainly claimed a large part of Christian civilization as being of its own making. When Portugal's territorial borders shrank and it became a small peripheral country, its national imagination remained limitless, reaching every corner of the world where Portuguese emigrants had established communities, claiming them as outposts of the new diasporic nation. Such imaginings were not immaterial or inconsequential to the lives of Portuguese emigrants. Though dealing in symbols, cultural references, and historical narratives, these official discourses legitimized the homeland state's encroachment on the affairs of immigrant communities and vice versa. They justified the diplomats' clandestine interventions in the domestic affairs of foreign countries; the immigrants' expectations that Lisbon would provide for their well-being and help them build their institutions abroad; the PIDE's prerogative to request intelligence on expatriate "subversives" from foreign governments willing to incriminate their naturalized citizens; the extension of voting rights and parliamentary representation for expatriate citizens; and the creation of a diasporic council to advise the homeland government on emigration and foreign policy matters. These transnational exchanges contradicted the immigrants' "bootstraps" myth of willing self-reliance, since they followed from their leaders' persistent requests (and later demands) for various kinds of government aid from Lisbon. This is not to say that Portuguese immigrants had little agency, ingenuity, or mutualist spirit, or even that their communities ultimately depended on their homeland's assistance, but simply that they developed them with significant even if insufficient help from the Portuguese government.

In sum, the formation of diasporic identities is a messy process, full of juxtapositions, contradictions, and situational strategies. The making of Portuguese diasporic communities in North America, with their complex ethnic, racial, national, and regional identities, was paradoxical, as they simultaneously challenged and reproduced hegemonic notions of nationhood while pursuing inclusion in both home and host nations. Though often seen as benign and empowering, hybrid diasporic identities can perpetuate asymmetrical power relations within their constructed "ancestral" memories of homeland and mobility. As the Portuguese case shows, diasporas and nations can be co-dependent, as one sometimes validates the other. However, the mirror on which they are reflected is slanted – in this case, with an imperialist bend. The revolution and the fall of the empire broke this mirror into several fragments. While not uniform, some parts remain more central than others whenever they are reassembled in a lusophone frame. We must take these reflections into account if we are to understand the resilience of nation states and the legacies of imperialism in our era of transnational belonging and global citizenship.

Notes

Introduction

1 Voting from Abroad Database, International Institute for Democracy and Electoral Assistance, http://www.idea.int/elections/vfa/search.cfm (last accessed 23 October 2016).
2 Michael Hogan, "Turkish Minister Accuses Germany of Political Pressure on Turks," *Reuters*, 7 March 2017, https://www.reuters.com/article/us-turkey-referendum-germany-rally/turkish-minister-accuses-germany-of-political-pressure-on-turks-idUSKBN16E2IT; Stefan Wagstyl, "Merkel Threatens to Bar Campaigns by Turkish Politicians," *Financial Times*, 15 March 2017, https://www.ft.com/content/001b0482-0967-11e7-97d1-5e720a26771b (accessed 8 May 2019).
3 Lili Bayer, "Vikto Órban Courts Voters beyond 'Fortress Hungary,'" *Politico*, 22 August 2017, https://www.politico.eu/article/viktor-orban-courts-voters-in-transylvania-romania-hungarian-election-2018/ (accessed 8 May 2019).
4 Russel Newlove, "Why Expat Americans Are Giving Up Their Passports," 9 February 2016, *BBC News*, https://www.bbc.com/news/35383435; Gover Norquist and Patrick Gleason, "American Expats Are Left High and Dry by Trump's Tax Reform," *NBC News*, 17 January 2018, https://www.nbcnews.com/think/opinion/american-expats-are-left-high-dry-trump-s-tax-reform-ncna838006 (accessed 8 May 2019).
5 For more on this topic see Gilberto Fernandes, "On Guard for Canadian Parochialism," Parts 1–3, 8–22 September 2015, ActiveHistory.ca.
6 Michael Collyer, "Introduction," in *Emigration Nations: Policies and Ideologies of Emigrant Engagement*, ed. Collyer (New York: Palgrave Macmillan, 2013), 14.
7 Adriano Moreira's speech, 9 May 1964 (my translation), in *Congregação Geral das Comunidades Portuguesas*, conference proceedings (Sociedade de Geografia de Lisboa, 1964), 20.

8 Speech by President António R. Eanes, cited in *Comunidade*, June 1977, 5 (my translation).
9 The philosopher Eduardo Lourenço best articulated Portugal's postimperial "crisis of national identity" and its solutions: "Our problem has never been one of *identity*, but the excessive way in which we live, in short, our *hyper-identity*, which has been historically derived not only from our intense [territorial, linguistic, and political] singularity, but also from the supplement we aggregated when we took ourselves to be 'lords of conquest in Guinea, Ethiopia, etc.' ... After a brief hesitation, we changed from colonizer people par excellence, multispatial and racial, to a nation that creates nations. Thus, the Salazarist mythology of ourselves, refuted in practice, triumphed on the symbolic plane. We can continue to be the same while being something else. Once more, the simple manipulation of discourse spared us from an examination of our conscience that could be devastating, as identity crises often are" ("Crise de Identidade ou Ressaca Imperial?" *Prelo* 1 [October–December 1983]: 17, 20 [my translation]).
10 The western regions of Canada and the United States also have sizable Portuguese populations, but their characteristics and histories are significantly different from their eastern peers and deserve their own separate study.
11 John Bodnar, *The Transplanted: A History of Immigrants in Urban America* (Bloomington: Indiana University Press, 1985); Robert Harney, "Commerce of Migration," *Canadian Ethnic Studies* 9, no. 1 (1977): 42–53.
12 Carmela Patrias, *Patriots and Proletarians: Politicizing Hungarian Immigrants in Interwar Canada* (Montreal and Kingston: McGill-Queen's University Press, 1994).
13 Ulf Hanerz, *Cultural Complexity: Studies in the Social Organization of Meaning* (New York: Columbia University Press, 1993), 116.
14 Ann Hua, "Diaspora and Cultural Memory," in *Diaspora, Memory, and Identity: A Search for Home*, ed. Vijay Agnew (Toronto: University of Toronto Press, 2005), 195
15 Donna Gabaccia, *Italy's Many Diasporas* (London and New York: Routledge, 2000), 8.
16 For more on this topic see Yossi Shain, *Kinship and Diasporas in International Affairs* (Ann Arbor: University of Michigan Press, 2007); Terrence Lyons and Peter Mandaville, eds, *Politics from Afar: Transnational Diasporas and Networks* (London: Hurst, 2012).
17 Jonathan Wagner, *Brothers beyond the Sea: National Socialism in Canada* (Waterloo, ON: Wilfrid Laurier University Press, 1982); Roberto Perin, "Making Good Fascists and Good Canadians: Consular Propaganda and the Italian Community in Montreal in the 1930s," in *Minorities and Mother Country Imagery*, ed. Gerald L. Gold (St John's: Institute of Social and

Economic Research, Memorial University of Newfoundland, 1984); Luigi G. Pennachio, "Exporting Fascism to Canada: Toronto's Little Italy," in *Enemies Within: Italian and Other Internees in Canada and Abroad*, ed. Franca Iacovetta, Roberto Perin, and Angelo Principe (Toronto: University of Toronto Press, 2000); Mark I. Choate, *Emigrant Nation: The Making of Italy Abroad* (Cambridge, MA: Harvard University Press, 2008); Patrias, *Patriots and Proletarians*.

18 Jeffrey Lesser, *Negotiating Identity: National Identity, Immigrants, Minorities, and the Struggle for Ethnicity in Brazil* (Durham, NC: Duke University Press, 1999); Anne-Marie Fortier, "Bringing It All (Back) Home: Italian-Canadians' Remaking of Canadian History," in *Communities across Borders: New Immigrants and Transnational Cultures*, ed. Paul Kennedy and Victor Roudometof (London and New York: Routledge, 2002); Daphne Winland, *We Are Now a Nation: Croats between "Home" and "Homeland"* (Toronto: University of Toronto Press, 2007); Laurie Brand, *Citizens Abroad: Emigration and the State in the Middle East and North Africa* (Cambridge: Cambridge University Press, 2008); Collyer, *Emigration Nations*.

19 Benedict Anderson, *Imagined Communities: Reflections on the Origin and Spread of Nationalism* (New York: Verso, [1983] 2006), 6–7.

20 See for instance, Homi Bhabha, "The Third Space: Interview with Homi Bhabha," and Stuart Hall, "Cultural Identity and Diaspora," in *Identity: Community, Culture, Difference*, ed. Jonathan Rutherford (London: Lawrence & Wishart, 1990); Paul Gilroy, *The Black Atlantic: Modernity and Double Consciousness* (Cambridge, MA: Harvard University Press, 1993).

21 Robin Cohen, *Global Diasporas: An Introduction* (Seattle: University of Washington, 1997); Gabaccia, *Italy's Many Diasporas*; Rogers Brubaker, "The 'Diaspora' Diaspora," *Ethnic and Racial Studies* 28, no. 1 (2005): 1–19; Martin Sökefeld, "Mobilizing in Transnational Space: a Social Movement Approach to the Formation of Diaspora," *Global Networks* 6, no. 3 (2006): 265–84.

22 Bhabha, "The Third Space."

23 Vijay Agnew, "Introduction," in *Diaspora, Memory, and Identity*, 12–13.

24 Edite Noivo, "Towards a Cartography of Portugueseness: Challenging the Hegemonic Center," *Diaspora: A Journal of Transnational Studies* 11, no. 2 (Fall 2002): 258.

25 The term "emigrant colonies" was also used by Italian officials from the nineteenth century until the end of the fascist regime, during which time Italy tried to "make itself abroad" (Choate, *Emigrant Nation*).

26 Victor Pereira, *A Ditadura de Salazar e a Emigração. O Estado Português e os seus emigrantes em França (1957–1974)* (Lisbon: Círculo de Leitores, 2012), 15 (my translation).

27 The Holy See created Caritas Internationalis in 1951 as a confederation of Roman Catholic humanitarian relief and social service organizations

of the same name, operating in various Western countries, including Portugal, the United States, and Canada.
28 The Society of St Vincent de Paul is an international lay Catholic charity dedicated to providing alms for the poor. Founded in 1833 in Paris, it quickly expanded to other parts of the world, including the United States in 1845, Canada in 1846, and Portugal in 1859.
29 Junta da Acção Social, *Guia Prático da Previdência* 17, Biblioteca Social e Corporativa, "Formação Social" collection, 1961, cited in Victor Pereira, "Emigração e Desenvolvimento da Previdência Social em Portugal," *Análise Social* 54, no. 192 (2009): 474.
30 The Azorean archipelago is made up of nine islands in the North Atlantic Ocean, the largest being São Miguel, followed by Pico, Terceira, São Jorge, Faial, Flores, Santa Maria, Graciosa, and Corvo.
31 Victor Rosa and Salvato Trigo, *Azorean Emigration: A Preliminary Overview* (Porto: Fernando Pessoa University Press, 1994), 66–7.
32 Pelouro Cultural da FNAT (1944), cited in Daniel Melo, *Salazarismo e Cultura Popular (1933–1958)* (Lisbon: Imprensa de Ciências Sociais, 2001), 70 (my translation).
33 In 1945, the Portuguese empire included Angola, Mozambique, Guinea-Bissau (then Portuguese Guinea), Cape Verde, and São Tomé and Principe in Africa; Dadra, Nagar Haveli, Goa, Daman and Diu in India; Macau and East Timor in East Asia.
34 "Colonial Act," Art. 2, 8 July 1930, cited in Valentim Alexandre, "The Colonial Period," in *Modern Portugal*, ed. António C. Pinto (Palo Alto, CA: SPOSS, 1998), 48–9.
35 *50 Anos de Estatísticas da Educação*, Vol. 1 (Instituto Nacional de Estatística, 2009), 17.
36 Pereira, *A Ditadura*, 48.
37 Matthew F. Jacobson, *Roots Too: White Ethnic Revival in Post-Civil Rights America* (Cambridge, MA: Harvard University Press, 2006), 7–9, 35.
38 Ibid., 8–9, 65.

1 Portuguese Migration

1 Cited in Bela Feldman-Bianco, "Multiple Layers of Time and Space: The Constructions of Class, Ethnicity, and Nationalism among Portuguese Immigrants," in *Community, Culture and the Making of Identity: Portuguese-Americans along the Eastern Seaboard*, ed. Kimberly DaCosta Holton and Andrea Klimt (Dartmouth: University of Massachusetts Press, 2009), 56 (henceforth *Community, Culture*).
2 For a general history of Portuguese emigration see Malyn Newitt, *Emigration and the Sea: An Alternative History of Portugal and the Portuguese* (New York: Oxford University Press, 2015).

3 Miriam H. Pereira, "A Política de Emigração Portuguesa (1850–1930)," in *A Historiografia Portuguesa, Hoje*, ed. José Tengarrinha (São Paulo: Hucitec, 1999), 184 (my translation).
4 Joel Serrão, *A Emigração Portuguesa* (Lisbon: Livros Horizonte, [1972] 1982), 38.
5 Oliveira Martins, "A Emigração Portuguesa" (1891), cited in Joel Serrão, "Notas sobre a emigração e mudança social no Portugal Contemporâneo," *Análise Social* 21, nos 87–9 (1985): 996 (my translation).
6 Based on the concept of *saudade* (an expressive longing, nostalgia, or melancholy), this was a spiritual, literary, artistic, and political doctrine founded on mystic and messianic beliefs that called for the national regeneration of Portugal through its past.
7 Serrão, *A Emigração*, 180.
8 Fernando Silva, *Emigração Portuguesa* (Lisbon: Tipografia Universal, 1917), cited in ibid., 175 (my translation).
9 Leo Pap, *The Portuguese Americans* (Boston: Twayne, 1981), 83; Dorothy Ann Gilbert, *Recent Portuguese Immigrants to Fall River: An Analysis of Relative Economic Success* (New York: AMS Press, 1989), 63; Bela Feldman-Bianco and James MacDonald, "Portuguese," in *American Immigrant Cultures – Builders of a Nation (Encyclopedia)*, comps David Levinson and Melvin Ember (New York: Macmillan, 1997).
10 Alberto Pena-Rodríguez, "Manipulaciones del fascismo português: diplomacia, censura y propaganda salazarista en la comunidade lusa de Estados Unidos," *Revista Brasileira de História da Mídia* 7, no. 1 (January–June 2018): 31–51.
11 Jerry Williams, *In Pursuit of Their Dreams: A History of Azorean Immigration to the United States* (Dartmouth: University of Massachusetts Press, 2007), 58, 108.
12 Feldman-Bianco, "Multiple Layers"; Pena-Rodríguez, "Manipulaciones"; Heloísa Paulo, *"Aqui também é Portugal": A Colónia Portuguesa do Brasil e o Salazarismo* (Coimbra: Quarteto, 2000); Rui Correia, "Salazar in New Bedford: History of the *Diário de Notícias*, New Bedford's Portuguese Newspapers," in *Community, Culture*.
13 Maria Baganha, "Portuguese Emigration after World War II," in Pinto, *Modern Portugal*, 5, 8; "Report on Portuguese Community in France" (Institute of International Social Cooperation, 2011), 11; Pereira, *A Ditadura*, 48.
14 Pereira, *A Ditadura*, 49–55.
15 Collyer, *Emigration Nations*.
16 Pereira, *A Ditadura*, 64, 67 (my translation).
17 Maria Baganha, "Social Marginalization, Government Policies, and Emigrants' Remittances, Portugal, 1870–1930," in *Estudos e Ensaios em Homenagem a Vitorino Magalhães Godinho*, ed. Joaquim Magalhães and Luís Albuquerque (Lisbon: Livraria Sá da Costa Editora, 1988).

18 Maria Baganha, "As Correntes Emigratórias Portuguesas no Século XX e o seu Impacto na Economia Nacional," *Análise Social* 29, no. 128 (4) (1994): 959–80; Pereira, *A Ditadura*, 78–88.
19 Art. 40, Decree 47 478, 31 December 1966, cited in Pereira, *A Ditadura*, 320–1 (my translation).
20 Pereira, *A Ditadura*, 41–7, 305–7, 313–20.
21 Ibid., 113.
22 Pereira, "Emigração e Desenvolvimento," 493–4.
23 Vanda Santos, *Discurso Oficial do Estado Sobre a Emigração dos Anos 60 a 80 e Imigração dos Anos 90 à Actualidade* (Lisbon: Alto Comissariado para a Imigração e Minorias Étnicas, 2004), 72.
24 Marcello Caetano's speech, 27 September 1972, cited in ibid., 40; Pereira, *A Ditadura*, 70, 122–7.
25 Interview with Minister Baltasar Rebelo Sousa, 9 April 1975, cited in *Comunidades Portuguesas*, 6, no. 24 (October 1971): 75–6.
26 Maria Baganha, "From Closed to Open Doors: Portuguese Emigration under the Corporatist Regime," *e-Journal of Portuguese History* 1, no. 1 (Summer 2003): 1–16.
27 This section is a truncated version of my article "Moving the 'Less Desirable': Portuguese Mass Migration to Canada, 1953–74," *Canadian Historical Review* 96, no. 3 (September 2015): 339–74.
28 Grace Anderson and David Higgs, *A Future to Inherit: The Portuguese Communities of Canada* (Toronto: McClelland & Stewart, 1976), 13.
29 Edite Noivo, *Inside Ethnic Families. Three Generations of Portuguese Canadians* (Montreal and Kingston: McGill-Queen's University Press, 1999); Susana Miranda, "Not Ashamed or Afraid: Portuguese Immigrant Women in Toronto's Cleaning Industry, 1950–1995" (PhD diss., York University, 2010).
30 Library and Archives Canada (henceforth LAC), 540-6-613, Vol. 772, pt 3, RG 76, letter, DCI's Ross Fitzpatrick to MPP Perry Ryan, 10 December 1965.
31 Historical-Diplomatic Archives of the Portuguese Ministry of Foreign Affairs (henceforth HDA), 2P M446 A6, report by Consul José Taveira (22 October 1957) and various correspondence (October–November 1957); 2P M557 A7, letter, Emigration Junta's António Baptista to various Civil Governors, 21 October 1958 (my translation).
32 LAC, 540-6-613, Vol. 722, pt 3, RG 76, letter, Citizenship and Immigration Minister René Tremblay to Finance Minister Walter Gordon, 14 July 1964.
33 Ninette Kelley and Michael Trebilcock, *The Making of the Mosaic: A History of Canadian Immigration Policy* (Toronto: University of Toronto Press, 1998), 370–1.
34 1981 Census of Canada, Vol. 2, Provincial Series: population: language, ethnic origin, religion, place of birth, schooling, Ottawa, 1984.

35 HDA, PEA M181, letter, Embassy Counselor João Affra to Portuguese-American Civic League of Massachusetts's Bertha Johnson, 22 April 1955.
36 Sec. 2 (a) Refugee Relief Act of 1953.
37 In 1953–6, Fernandes was the Portuguese ambassador to both the United States and Canada.
38 HDA, 2P M446 A6, PMFA service information, Luis Nunes, 2 January 1957.
39 Frederico Machado, Willard Parsons, Adrian Richards, John Mulford, "Capelinhos Eruption of Faial Volcano, Azores, 1957–1958," *Journal of Geophysical Research* 67, no. 9 (August 1962): 3519–29.
40 Decree 41679, 16 June 1958.
41 On 7 October 1958, twenty-five families left Horta for Mozambique's Limpopo Colonate, their passages paid by the Portuguese government (HDA, 2P M558, memo, PMFA's Caldeira Coelho, 16 October 1958).
42 Public-Law 85–892, US House of Representatives, Office of the Law Revision Counsel, United States Code.
43 HDA, 2P M558, letter, Embassy Counselor Castro Abreu to PMFA, 28 October 1958; HDA, PEA M307, "Portugal Pays Tribute to Monsignor Furtado," *Standard Times*, 24 May 1964.
44 HDA, 2P M558, memos, Caldeira Coelho (16 October), António Baptista (21 October), 1958.
45 Williams, *In Pursuit*, 112.
46 Erika Lee, "American Gatekeeping: Race and Immigration Law in the Twentieth Century," in *Not Just Black and White: Historical and Contemporary Perspectives on Immigration, Race, and Ethnicity in the United States*, ed. Nancy Foner and George Fredrickson (New York: Sage, 2004), 128–9.
47 Jorge Arroteia, *A Emigração Portuguesa – suas origens e distribuição* (Lisbon: Instituto de Cultura e Língua Portuguesa, Ministério da Educação, 1983), 35; *Yearbook of Immigration Statistics: 2013* (Washington, DC: US Department of Homeland Security, Office of Immigration Statistics, 2014).
48 "The Portuguese Archipelago" includes New Bedford, Fall River, Mansfield, Attleboro, Norton, Seekonk, Rehoboth, Dighton, Taunton, Berkley, Swansea, Somerset, Freetown, Westport, Dartmouth, Acushnet, Rochester, Fairhaven, Mattapoisett, and Marion (Maria Sá and David Borges, "Context or Culture? Portuguese-Americans and Social Mobility," in *Community, Culture*, 268–9).
49 Baganha, "Portuguese Emigration," 8.
50 Stephen Lubkemann, "The Moral Economy of Portuguese Postcolonial Return," *Diaspora* 11, no. 2 (Fall 2002): 191, 199–203.
51 Caroline Brettell, "The Emigrant, the Nation, and the State in Nineteenth- and Twentieth-Century Portugal: An Anthropological

Approach," *Portuguese Studies Review* 2 (1993): 54; Pereira, "Emigração e Desenvolvimento," 478.
52 Victor Pereira, "Os Exiliados Políticos Portugueses en Francia entre 1958 e 1974," *Estudios Migratorios* 15–16 (2003): 126.
53 RTP Arquivo online, "Emigrantes: Vieram para Ver" (broadcast 22 August 1974), 25m. Centro de Documentação 25 de Abril, University of Coimbra (henceforth CD25A), Manuel de Lima, "Emigrante: A Revolução Precisa de Ti," *O Século Ilustrado*, 21 June 1975 (my translation); LAC, RG6-F-2, b127, f3260-P2-2, Portuguese press report, December 1974.
54 Comissão Nacional de Eleições, Resultados Eleitorais website, http://eleicoes.cne.pt/.
55 Law 74/77, 28 September 1977; Santos, *Discurso Oficial*, 75–6.
56 Interview with Secretary of State for Emigration João Lima, *Comunidade*, 31 March 1977, 13 (my translation).
57 Brettell, "The Emigrant," 60.
58 Eanes, speech (1977).
59 Portugal's national holiday has been celebrated on 10 June since 1911. The secular holiday was introduced by the First Republic as part of its project to reduce the Church's influence in Portuguese society. The date marks the death of sixteenth-century poet Luis Vaz de Camões, the author of the national epic *Os Lusíadas* (*The Lusiads*). Previously called the Day of Portugal (1910–43), the holiday was rebranded by the Estado Novo as the Day of Portugal, Camões, and the Portuguese Race (1943–77). It was not until the regime appropriated the holiday and turned it into a militaristic propaganda feast (especially after 1963) that it became a prominent national and diasporic celebration.
60 "Sá Machado aos Emigrantes," *Correio Português*, 30 March 1978, 5.
61 The term *Açorianidade* was coined by the writer Vitorino Nemésio in 1932, referring to what he believed was the Azoreans' ethnic consciousness as islanders with a deep spiritual connection to the soil, sea, and shifting volcanic bedrock of their homeland.
62 "Sá Carneiro aos Emigrantes," *Povo Livre*, 27 August 1980, 6.
63 Values not adjusted to inflation. In 1974–89, the median inflation rate was close to 20 per cent, with a tendency to drop over time, which increased the relative value of these remittances even further (Trading Economics, www.tradingeconomics.com).
64 Baganha, "Portuguese Emigration," 15.
65 Interview with Maria Manuela Aguiar, *Lusopresse*, Montreal, 1 December 2006 (my translation), http://www.lusopresse.com/2006/150/noticia.aspx?Ser%20Mulher%20Em%20Portugal%20E%20Na%20Emigracao.htm (accessed 8 May 2019).

66 Decree 373/80, 12 September 1980 (my translation).
67 Canada and the United States each were given four seats at the CPC for "community associations" representatives and one for media representatives. Brazil sent the most delegates (fourteen), followed by France (eleven), and South Africa (eight). Other countries with one or two representatives included West Germany, Venezuela, Spain, England, Luxembourg, Belgium, Netherlands, Switzerland, the "Nordic countries," Angola, Mozambique, Cape Verde, Guinea-Bissau, São Tomé and Príncipe, and Argentina.
68 Maria M. Aguiar, "O Conselho das Comunidades Portuguesas e a Representação dos Emigrates," *Revista Migrações – Número Temático Migrações entre Portugal e América Latina* 5 (Fall 2009): 257–62.
69 The most outspoken delegates came from Europe and Canada, particularly Montreal and Winnipeg (LAC, Multiculturalism Directorate, f3217-202-P2 pt 1, b20).
70 "History and Mission," Luso-American Development Foundation website, http://www.flad.pt/en/history-and-mission/ (accessed 21 December 2017).
71 Sá Carneiro's speech, Fermentelos, Aveiro, 23–4 August 1980, cited in "Sá Carneiro aos Emigrantes."
72 Between 1960 and 1981, Portugal's foreign-born population grew from 0.33 per cent to 1.24 per cent. In the 1990s, the number of documented immigrants increased 113 per cent (Carlota Solé, "Portugal and Spain: From Exporters to Importers of Labour," in *The Cambridge Survey of World Migration*, ed. Robin Cohen [Cambridge: Cambridge University Press, 1995]; Conselho Superior de Estatística, "Estatísticas dos Movimentos Migratórios," March 2006, 26).
73 Timothy Sieber, "Composing Lusophonia: Multiculturalism and National Identity in Lisbon's 1998 Music Scene," *Diaspora* 11, no. 2 (Fall 2002): 163–88.
74 Interview with José Barroso, *Prelo* 17 (October–December 1987): 39 (my translation).
75 The CPLP's founding members were Angola, Brazil, Cape Verde, Guinea-Bissau, Mozambique, Portugal, and São Tomé and Principe. East Timor joined in 2002 after gaining independence from Indonesia. In 2014, Equatorial Guinea joined the CPLP despite Lisbon's opposition, given that country's terrible human rights record.
76 Sieber "Composing Lusophonia," 184; Lubkemann, "The Moral Economy," 208.
77 The Migration Integration Policy Index is a triennial study launched in 2004 by a range of international institutions; it evaluates national

immigration policies promoting labour market mobility, family reunion, long-term residence, anti-discrimination, political participation, access to citizenship, and education. In 2007 and 2010, Portugal ranked second, behind Sweden. For more details, see www.mipex.eu/

78 The actual estimation proposed in 1999 was 4,806,353 Portuguese living abroad.

79 For more on my work with RTPi see https://pchp-phlc.ca/2018/01/13/farewell-adeus-hora-dos-portugueses-thank-you-obrigado/

80 See, for instance, Erika Vasconcelos, *My Darling Dead Ones* (Toronto: Knopf Canada, 1997); Charles Felix, *Through a Portagee Gate* (Dartmouth, MA: Tagus Press, 2004); Anthony de Sa, *Barnacle Love* (Toronto: Penguin Random House Canada, 2008) and *Kicking the Sky* (Toronto: Penguin Random House Canada, 2013); Anthony Barcellos, *Land of Milk and Honey* (Dartmouth, MA: Tagus Press, 2012); and Brian Sousa, *Almost Gone* (Dartmouth, MA: Tagus Press, 2013).

81 Soft Power Survey 2018/19, *Monocle*, https://monocle.com/film/affairs/soft-power-survey-2018-19/ (accessed 8 May 2019).

82 "Passos Coelho sugere a emigração a professores desempregados," *Público*, 18 December 2011, https://www.publico.pt/2011/12/18/politica/noticia/passos-coelho-sugere-aos-professores-desempregados-que-emigrem-1525528 (accessed 8 May 2019).

83 Ana Pereira, "A (re)construção da figura do emigrante," *Público*, 4 March 2017, https://www.publico.pt/2017/03/04/sociedade/noticia/a-re-construcao-da-figura-do-emigrante-1763881 (accessed 8 May 2019).

84 São José Almeida, "Governo anuncia 50 milhões de euros para empresários regressados da Venezuela," *Público*, 11 October 2018, https://www.publico.pt/2018/10/11/politica/noticia/governo-anuncia-50-milhoes-de-euros-para-empresarios-regressados-da-venezuela-1847024 (accessed 8 May 2019); "CDS quer Governo a apoiar e pagar regresso de portugueses da Venezuela," *Diário de Notícias*, 24 September 2018, https://www.dn.pt/mundo/interior/venezuela-cds-quer-governo-a-apoiar-e-pagar-regresso-de-portugueses-9901780.html (accessed 8 May 2019).

85 "Museu da Diáspora e da Língua Portuguesa de Matosinhos será projectado por Sousa de Moura," *Público*, 11 March 2016, https://www.publico.pt/2016/03/11/culturaipsilon/noticia/souto-de-moura-projecta-museu-em-matosinhos-1725872 (accessed 8 May 2019).

86 Fernandes, "Moving the 'Less Desirable.'"

87 Guido Tintori, "Italy: The Continuing History of Emigrant Relations," in Collyer, *Emigration Nations*, 134.

88 Victor Pereira, "Os Exiliados Políticos Portugueses en Francia entre 1958 e 1974," *Estudios Migratorios* 15–16 (2003): 126.

2 Making Diasporic Souls

1 Cited in Maria Rocha-Trindade and Eugénia Quaresma, *A Igreja Face ao Fenómeno Migratório* (Lisbon: O Planeta da Escrita, 2012), 49.
2 As John Zucchi explained: "A national parish differs from the more common territorial parish in that membership is based on ethnicity rather than place of residence. National parishes were introduced in North America to meet the needs of immigrants who spoke a language foreign to the host diocese. Under normal circumstances a Roman Catholic is obliged to belong to the parish in which he resides. However, if he belongs to a particular ethnic group which has a national parish in the diocese, then he can belong to the national parish ... If there is more than one national parish for a particular ethnic group in the diocese, then each is given a geographic territory, and the Catholic must belong to the appropriate parish"; *Italians in Toronto: Development of a National Identity, 1875–1935* (Montreal and Kingston: McGill-Queen's Univerity Press, 1988), 120.
3 Caroline Brettell, "Ethnicity and Entrepreneurs: Portuguese Immigrants in a Canadian City," in *Ethnic Encounters: Identities and Contexts*, ed. George Hicks and Philip Leis (Duxbury, MA: Duxbury Press, 1977), 177.
4 For an anthropologic analysis of some of the religious festivals discussed in this chapter see João Leal, *Azorean Identity in Brazil and the United States: Arguments about History, Culture, and Transnational Connections*, trans. Wendy Graça (Dartmouth, MA: Tagus Press, 2011); and Stephen Cabral, *Tradition and Transformation: Portuguese Feasting in New Bedford* (New York: AMS Press, 1989).
5 António C. Pinto, *O Salazarismo e o Fascismo Europeu: Problemas de Interpretação nas Ciências Sociais* (Lisbon: Estampa, 1992), 60.
6 On 13 May 1917, three young shepherds (Lúcia, Francisco, and Jacinta) claimed to have been visited by the Virgin Mary at Cova da Iria, in Portugal's mainland town of Fátima. After regular monthly apparitions, a large crowd claimed to have witnessed the sun move in strange motions. In 1930, the Vatican recognized this event as a bona fide miracle. Along with a message of daily penitence and prayer centred on the rosary, the shepherds were said to have been given three prophetic visions, kept secret for decades. According to Rome's official interpretation, the first and second secrets, made public in 1941, predicted the end of the First World War and the start of the Second; it also asked for the apostate Soviet Russia to consecrate itself to the Immaculate Heart of Mary. The third secret, made public in 2000, predicted the attempted assassination of Pope John Paul II on 13 May 1981. Since 1917, Cova da Iria became a pilgrimage site attracting large crowds of believers and tourists.

Construction of the Sanctuary of Our Lady of Fátima on the site of the apparitions started in 1928, with support from the Estado Novo.
7 Adriano Moreira, *O Novíssimo Príncipe. Análise da Revolução* (Braga-Lisbon: Edição Intervenção, 1977), 166, cited in Manuel Martins, *O Estado Novo e a Oposição* (Sintra: P. Ferreira, 2000).
8 Bishop Giovanni Scalabrini founded the Missionaries of St Charles Borromeo in Italy in 1887. Reporting to the cardinals in Rome on the difficult material and spiritual conditions that Italian immigrants faced in the United States, Scalabrini argued that most of their problems stemmed from their cultural and linguistic distinctiveness, which were linked to their religiosity. He then recommended the creation of "national parishes," equipped with schools and social agencies dedicated to assisting immigrants in their native language and directed by trained missionaries.
9 Rocha-Trindade and Quaresma, *A Igreja*, 106 (my translation).
10 Letter, Bishop José Neves, 13 December 1962 (my translation), cited in ibid., 49.
11 These missions were located in Nelson and Vancouver (BC), Kingston, Hamilton, and Toronto (ON), and Montreal (QC).
12 Pereira, *A Ditadura*, 329.
13 Aurélio Escudeiro, 1974, cited in Rocha-Trindade and Quaresma, *A Igreja*, 51.
14 According to the Dillingham Commission, the largest cohort among the 212 Portuguese professionals who arrived in the United States in 1899–1910 were clergymen; Robert Harney, "'Portygees' and Other Caucasians: Portuguese Migrants and the Racialism of the English-Speaking World," in *Portuguese Migration in Global Perspective*, ed. David Higgs (Toronto: Multicultural History Society of Ontario, 1990), 126.
15 Leo Pap, *The Portuguese Americans* (Boston: Twayne, 1981), 179.
16 Rocha-Trindade and Quaresma, *A Igreja*, 147.
17 Timothy Meagher, *Inventing Irish America: Generation, Class, and Ethnic Identity in a New England City, 1880–1928* (Notre Dame, IN: University of Notre Dame Press, 2000); James Barrett and David Roediger, "The Irish and the 'Americanization' of the 'New Immigrants' in the Streets and in the Churches of the Urban United States, 1900–1930," *Journal of American Ethnic History* 24, no. 4 (Summer 2005): 3–33.
18 HDA, PEA M307, correspondence, PMFA and Ambassador Fernandes, 18 February and 28 March 1955; clipping, *Novidades*, 30 April 1957.
19 HDA, M182, correspondence, Ambassador Fernandes, Archbishop Thomas Walsh, Manuel Rocha, Consul M.9N. Silva, and PMFA, 9 July 1951 to 4 February 1954 (my translation).
20 There were non-Portuguese Catholic organizations in the United States dedicated to spreading the cult of Fátima, the largest being the Blue Army of Our Lady of Fatima, founded in New Jersey by the

Irish-American priest Harold Colgan in 1947. Despite its rapid international growth, this anti-communist organization had little interaction with Portuguese-American parishes.
21 It is not clear if the 1952 Warner Brothers Pictures film *The Miracle of Our Lady of Fatima* follows from Rocha's proposition. Still, the movie's anti-communist overtones matched the Estado Novo's own Cold War propaganda and its reviling of the previous anti-clerical Republicans, portrayed in this movie as socialist heathens.
22 HDA, PEA M405, Consul Jorge Freitas's speech transcript (1970) in *Fatima Review*, 1973.
23 HDA, PEA M251, letter, Manuel Rocha to Senator John F. Kennedy, October 1960; clippings, "Expression of Amity for Portugal Asked?" May 1961; Rocha, "Cartas da América," *Novidades*, 9 May 1961; letter, Ambassador Fernandes to PMFA, 15 June 1961.
24 An apostolic vicariate is a provisional Catholic jurisdiction commonly established in missionary regions where there are no dioceses. The vicariate is directly administered by the Holy See through a titular bishop (vicar) or a priest (administrator). Some non-Roman Catholic immigrant communities, such as Ukrainian Orthodox, had their own apostolic vicariates in North America.
25 HDA, PEA M405, correspondence, Manuel Rocha, Consul Jorge Freitas, Ambassador João Themido, 1–3 November 1972.
26 HDA, PEA M609, PEA 251-A, PEA M334, correspondence, Manuel Rocha, Ambassador Fernandes, Ambassador Vasco Garin, Consul Jorge Freitas, PMFA, 1958–69.
27 This Lisbon-based charitable foundation was created in 1956 with the massive wealth and art collection of Armenian oil magnate Calouste Gulbenkian and is dedicated to promoting the arts, education, and science in Portugal. Ambassador Pedro Teotónio Pereira, who helped convince the Armenian exile to settle in Portugal, later became one of the foundation's administrators.
28 HDA, PEA 251-A, letter, Manuel Rocha to Cardinal Joseph Ritter, 10 August 1964; PEA 251-A, "NY Foundation Assists Ludlow Portuguese Center," *Fatima Review*, 1964; PEA M609, clipping, *New York Herald Tribune*, (?) 1964; PEA M334, letter, Lusitania Institute's Executive Director Howard Rodenhizer to Gulbenkian Foundation's (New York) Kathleen Channing, 29 December 1966.
29 HDA, PEA M609, correspondence, Ambassador Garin to PMFA, 9 March 1964; PEA M334, Consul Jorge Freitas to PMFA, 7 April 1969; Manuel Rocha to Ambassador Garin, 30 October 1970.
30 "For God and Country: From Brownsville to Boston," *Herald of Freedom* 9, no. 11 (2 October 1970): 1–3. "The Successor to Cardinal Cushing. Humberto Sousa Medeiros," *New York Times*, 9 September 1970, 38.

31 J. Anthony Lukas, *Common Ground: A Turbulent Decade in the Lives of Three American Families* (New York: Knopf Doubleday, 1985), 372–404.
32 HDA, PEA M656, telegram, Consul Jorge Freitas, Boston, to PMFA, 15 September 1970; PEA M735, telegram, Ambassador Themido to PMFA, 16 February 1972.
33 HDA, PEA M253, *Portuguese-American Federation Quarterly* 13 (Fall 1973): 2; PEA M405, "Cardinal's Trip Filmed by Ch. 4," *Boston Globe*, 30 August 1973, 65; "Jubilant Azoreans Acclaim the Return of Cardinal Medeiros," *The Pilot*, 31 August 1973, 1, 13; Vice-Consul Carlos Nunes, Boston, to PMFA, 31 August 1973.
34 "O Agradecimento do Cardeal Medeiros," *Diário dos Açores*, 20 August 1973, 1 (my translation).
35 For more see Noivo, *Inside Ethnic*; Fernando Nunes, "Portuguese-Canadian Youth and Their Academic Underachievement: A Literature Review," *Portuguese Studies Review* 11, no. 2 (Winter-Spring 2003): 41–87; Miranda, "Not Ashamed."
36 Franca Iacovetta, *Gatekeepers: Reshaping Immigrant Lives in Cold War Canada* (Toronto: Between the Lines, 2006); Miranda, "Not Ashamed."
37 Fr Manuel Almeida combined his job as vice-consul in Montreal with being a priest in the Diocese of São Paulo, Brazil. In 1953, the bishop of São Paulo ordered Almeida to return to his pastoral duties, but he refused. Consequently, the archbishop of Montreal stripped Almeida of his right to say mass and threatened him with further penalties should he fail to comply. Lisbon was not aware of Almeida's problematic situation until they were pressured by the papal nuncio in Ottawa to exonerate him, which they did in 1954 (HDA, PEA 194, memo, PMFA's Amândio Pinto, 7 July 1953; 2P A55 M66, telegram, Caldeira Coelho, Ottawa, to PMFA, 17 November 1954; letter, Vice-Consul Manuel Almeida, Montreal, to PMFA, 30 June 1954).
38 HDA, 2P M190, correspondence, Consul Vital Gomes, Montreal, to PMFA, 7 May 1955 (my translation); 2P M446 A6, Consul Gomes to PMFA, 28 May 1957.
39 José M. Coelho, *Small Stories, Great People: Portuguese Pioneers in Canada* (Toronto: Creative 7, 2004), 30–1, 53, 103–5, 187–8.
40 According to Portuguese diplomats, the immigration services of the Montreal, Ottawa, Kingston, and London dioceses were competent, unlike those of Toronto and Hamilton (HDA, 2P M190, correspondence, PMFA and Emigration Junta, April-May 1955).
41 Ibid. correspondence, Consul Vital Gomes, Montreal, to PMFA, 17 May 1955; Emigration Junta's António Baptista to PMFA, 7 July 1955.
42 LAC, RG6-F-2, b128, f3260-P2-190 L39, Foreign Language Press Review Service, DCI, Canadian Citizenship Branch, report on *Luso-Canadiano* issues of 29 September and 30 November 1962.

43 "Portuguese with Problems Ask This Girl to Solve Them," *Toronto Daily Star*, 2 March 1970, 23.
44 Archives of the Roman Catholic Archdiocese of Toronto (henceforth ARCAT), Portuguese Congregation 1958–1972, Parish collection, letter, Alfredo Camacho to Society of St Vincent de Paul's J.B. Conacher, Toronto, 27 September 1958.
45 HDA, PEA M401, letter, Ambassador Alexandre Veiga to PMFA, 28 March 1968. ARCAT, Portuguese Congregation 1958–1972, Parish collection, correspondence, Feldman & Weisbrot Barristers & Solicitors and Coadjutor Archbishop of Toronto Philip Pocock, 1–9 March 1965. York University, Clara Thomas Archives and Special Collections (henceforth CTASC), David Higgs fonds, Maria Ribeiro, *O Canadá e a Presença Portuguesa*, 1990.
46 Frank Luce, "Confronting the *Estado Novo*: Canadian Missionaries and a Polemic Entitled *Angola Awake*," *Portuguese Studies Review* 23, no. 2 (2015): 147–89.
47 HDA, PEA M533, PIDE report, Luanda, 5 October 1966; letter, Ambassador Eduardo Brazão to PMFA, 17 November 1966; Loren Lind, "Tale of Portuguese Brutality in Angola," *Globe and Mail*, 9 March 1968, T16.
48 HDA, EEA 400, letter, Manuel Leite, Toronto, to PMFA, 23 November 1965 (my translation).
49 Ibid., correspondence, Manuel Leite, Ambassador Brazão, Minister João Themido, 23 November 1965 to 1 January 1966.
50 Pereira, *A Ditadura*, 336.
51 HDA, PEA 400, correspondence, PMFA and Ambassador Brazão, 13–19 January 1966 (my translation).
52 Leite returned to Portugal, while Lourenço moved back to Ludlow to teach at the Lusitania Institute (HDA, PEA M401, letter, Ambassador Alfredo Veiga, to PMFA, 28 March 1968).
53 HDA, PEA M400, telegram, Ambassador Brazão to PMFA, 11 March 1963; letter, Emigration Junta's António Baptista to PMFA, 20 May 1963 (my translation).
54 In his self-published memoir, *Um Passado Recente* (2007), Jaime Monteiro, a self-exiled communist, claimed that Cunha sent "goons" to assault him at his furniture store in Toronto. A local Portuguese radio worker was caught in the fracas and taken to hospital. According to Monteiro, one of the assailants was caught by the police and later tried. Monteiro laid charges against Cunha but the priest was acquitted. In 1995, the *Toronto Star* published an exposé of Cunha's alleged criminal activities throughout his life, including extortion, embezzlement, and tax evasion (Dale Brazão and Kevin Donovan, "Non-profit Projects a Holy Mess," *Toronto Star*, 27 May 1995, A1).
55 HDA, PEA M400, telegram, Ambassador Brazão to PMFA, 16 March 1966 (my translation); PEA M401, letters, PMFA's Nunes Freitas to Salazar,

10 September 1968; Ambassador Veiga to PMFA, 28 March 1968; memo, Consul Luis Martins, Toronto, 31 October 1968.
56 LAC, RG6-F-2, b127, f3260-P2-2, Solomon Nigosian, "The Portuguese Community in Metropolitan Toronto," DCI, Citizenship Branch, June 1971.
57 HDA, PEA M656, correspondence, António Ribeiro to Ambassador Veiga, February 25, 1970; and Ambassador Veiga to PMFA, 5 May 1970 (my translation). The records pertaining to Alberto Cunha at the ARCAT were not fully accessible at the time of my research.
58 Nigosian, "The Portuguese"; Anderson and Higgs, *A Future*, 145; Domingos Marques and John Medeiros, *Portuguese Immigrants: 25 Years in Canada* (Toronto: Marquis Printers, 1980).
59 HDA, 2P M558, letter, Consul Artur Nogueira, Montreal, to PMFA, 21 October 1958 (my translation).
60 HDA, PEA M400, report, Consul Artur Nogueira, Montreal, 18 February 1961.
61 HDA, PEA M194, correspondence, Consul Nogueira, Manuel Teixeira, PMFA, 9 December 1958 to 11 April 1959 (my translation). Coelho, *Small Stories*, 304–6.
62 HDA, PEA 400, letter, Domingos Vieira to Consul Fernando Marques, Montreal, 4 June 1961 (my translation).
63 Ibid. correspondence, Vice-Consul Camilo Melo, Montreal, to Chargé d'Affaires Luis Oliveira, Ottawa, 20 August 1961; António Janeiro, New Bedford, to PMFA, 3 October 1961.
64 HDA, PEA 400, letter, Consul Marques, Montreal, to Ambassador Brazão, 31 December 1964.
65 A 1964 pamphlet signed by the Portuguese Liberation Committee and circulated in Montreal claimed that Leblanc had rejected CA$1,255 from the Portuguese consul to his parish centre because he did not want to collaborate with PIDE (HDA, PEA M13B).
66 HDA, EEA M140, correspondence, Ambassador Brazão to PMFA, 1 April 1963, and 21 January 1965.
67 HDA, PEA 400, correspondence, PMFA to Cardinal-Patriarch of Lisbon's Secretary, 27 January 1965 (my translation) and 8 March 1965.
68 António Araújo, *25o Aniversário da Igreja Santa Cruz 1986–2011* (Outremont, QC: Les éditions du passage, 2011), 82.
69 Cabral, *Tradition and Transformation*, 35.
70 *Toronto Star*, "Big Day for Portuguese: 55,000 Attend Festival," 28 May 1973, 25, and "Portuguese Honor Santo Cristo," 20 May 1974, B11. Anderson and Higgs, *A Future*, 144; HDA, PEA M656, correspondence, António Ribeiro to Ambassador Veiga, 25 February 1970; Ambassador Veiga to PMFA, 5 May 1970.

71 The word used by Veiga was *penoso*, which can also mean "penitent" or "contrite." In this case, he seemed to refer to the fervent displays of piety that typically occurred in the procession as cause for embarrassment.
72 Similarly, in 1955, close to 5,000 White Fleet fishermen in St John's, Newfoundland, carried a Virgin Mary statuette that they had brought from Portugal, from the harbour to the hilltop Basilica of St John the Baptist, as a thank you gift for the city's hospitality.
73 Cabral, *Tradition and Transformation*, 138.
74 HDA, PEA M182, letter, Manuel Rocha to Ambassador Fernandes, (?) November 1959 (my translation).
75 Cabral, *Tradition and Transformation*, 47, 50, 117.
76 There were a few all-female Portuguese-American mutual aid societies. The largest and most prestigious was the Portuguese Society of Queen Saint Elizabeth. Founded in 1901, in Oakland, California, it grew to about 14,000 members and 158 lodges by 1960 (Pap, *The Portuguese Americans*, 172).
77 Not to be confused with the 1 July holiday celebrated by the Madeiran autonomous government since 1976.
78 HDA, PEA M171, "Dia Madeirense," *Jornal Português*, Oakland, (?) September 1951.
79 HDA, PEA M183, Madeiran Day booklets, 1951, 1953, 1955–8.
80 Letter, Armando Medeiros to Salazar, 11 February 1953, cited in Filipe Meneses, *Salazar: A Political Biography* (New York: Enigma, 2009), 346.
81 Torre do Tombo National Archives (henceforth TTNA), Arquivo Salazar, PC-1D cx. 572, pt 40, letter, PMFA's António Lucerna to Salazar, 20 August 1958. HDA, PEA M251, letter, Consul M. Silva, San Francisco, to Ambassador Garin, 13 January 1965. "Atingiram $2,802, os Donativos Angariados em R.I.... ," *Diário de Notícias*, 28 August 1958.
82 HDA, M51, correspondence, Consul Alexandre Veiga, New York, to Ambassador o Garin, 3 January 1968. LAC, MG28-I270, Canadian Flood Relief for Portugal's Alberto Cunha, Toronto, to Oxfam Canada, (?) May 1968.
83 João Santos, *O Canadá é o Meu País, Portugal a Minha Pátria* (Toronto: Santos, 2012), 111–12.
84 The *Cristo-Rei* monument is a large-scale replica of Rio de Janeiro's colossal Christ the Redeemer statue. It stands on the southern shore of the Tagus river, overlooking Lisbon. Construction began in 1959 and finished in 1969. The Catholic Church in Portugal built the statue with the Estado Novo's support, as a gift to God for having spared the country the devastation of the Second World War.
85 TTNA, AOS/CO/?PC-69, pt 3, 1964–6 Angariação de Fundos pelo Cabrilho, letter, Director Manuel Freitas, "Cabrilho" Portuguese Radio Programs (San Jose), to Salazar, 2 April 1964. HDA, PEA M251, letter, Consul Ribeiro Silva, San Francisco, to Ambassador Garin, 13 January 1965.

3 Making Ethnic Civil Societies

1 LAC, RG25-A-3-c, Vol. 11081, f20-18-1-14, Portuguese Canadian Ethnic Press Analysis, November 1973 (translated by Jane Touzel of the Department of External Affairs).
2 Robert Paine (1971), cited in Brettell, "Ethnicity and Entrepreneurs," 169–70.
3 Mendes was eventually granted asylum in Poland (Penn Reeve, "Portuguese Labor Activism in Southeastern Massachusetts," in *Community, Culture*, 353).
4 In 1969, Fall River had the second-lowest median annual household income in Massachusetts, with US$8,289 (US$2,546 less than in the rest of the state). In 1971, 10.8 per cent of all Fall River families earned an income below the poverty line (Gilbert, *Recent Portuguese*, 93).
5 In 1958, the population of New Bedford-Fall River had the lowest median number of school years of any American city with over 10,000 people (ibid., 95). In Massachusetts and Rhode Island, 60 per cent of Portuguese-born residents over twenty-five years old who immigrated between 1970 and 1980 had five years of schooling or less (Maria Sá Pereira, *A Posição Socioeconómica dos Imigrantes Portugueses e seus Descendentes nos Estados de Massachusetts e Rhode Island (USA)* [Lisbon: Secretaria de Estado da Emigração, 1985, 34]).
6 Grace Anderson, *Networks of Contact: The Portuguese and Toronto* (Waterloo, ON: Wilfrid Laurier University Press, 1974); Miranda, "Not Ashamed"; Duarte Lopes, *Peregrinação: uma História das Comunidades Portuguesas do Quebeque (1953–1999)* (Ponta Delgada: Governo da Região Autónoma dos Açores, 2000), 142.
7 For more on this topic see the website, oral history videos, and documentary series in my public history project "City Builders: A History of Immigrant Construction Workers in Postwar Toronto," https://toronto-city-builders.org/.
8 Miranda, "Not Ashamed."
9 While present in the Azores and Madeira, mutual aid societies were most popular in the mainland, where they sometimes comprised thousands of members, spanning various towns. In 1933, when the Estado Novo effectively banned the freedom of association, close to 570,000 Portuguese belonged to a mutual aid society (Pap, *The Portuguese Americans*, 166–7).
10 HDA, M45, PCU's annual report, 1971; PEA M181, letter, PCU's Aníbal Branco to Ambassador Luis Fernandes, 17 October 1957.
11 HDA, PEA 159, various correspondence and news clippings, 1950 (my translation).
12 HDA, PEA M181, PEA M333, M45, PCU's annual reports, 1955, 1965–72.

13 HDA, PEA M425, letter, Consul of Portugal (?), San Francisco, to PMFA.
14 Francis Rogers, *Americans of Portuguese Descent: A Lesson in Differentiation* (Beverly Hills, CA: Sage, 1974).
15 For more see Fernandes, "Moving the 'Less Desirable,'" 368.
16 HDA, 2P M55 A7, letter, Consul Artur Nogueira, Montreal, to PMFA, 7 April 1958.
17 HDA, 2P M55 A7, correspondence, PMFA's Director-General of Internal and Political Affairs to Internal Economy, 25 February 1958; PEA M194, Consul Artur Nogueira, Montreal, to PMFA, 28 March 1959 (my translation). TTNA, PIDE/DGS, Jornal "O Luso Canadiano," SC CI (2) pr. 5552, u.i. 7397, Vice-consul (?) Montreal to PMFA, 25 June 1960.
18 The short-lived Portuguese-Canadian Association was founded on 14 November 1956 by a group of Azoreans who splintered from the FPCC (Coelho, *Small Stories*, 180, 187).
19 LAC, RG6-F-2, b128, f3260-P2-190 p133, FPCC incorporation application, 2 May 1964.
20 Not to be mistaken for the daily newspaper of the same name published in Lisbon since 1864.
21 Manuela Marujo, Carlos Teixeira, and Domingos Marques, *Portuguese Canadian Press in a Multicultural Society*, exhibit catalogue, University of Toronto, 7–30 June 1995.
22 Letter, Ambassador João Bianchi to Salazar, 10 June 1936, cited in Pena-Rodríguez, "Manipulaciones," 38.
23 Pena-Rodríguez, "Manipulaciones," 38.
24 Pap, *The Portuguese Americans*, 174.
25 Not to be confused with the daily radio show with the same name hosted by Fr Alberto Cunha in 1973 on Toronto's CHIN radio.
26 Francisco Grelo interviewed by the author for the RTPi show *Hora dos Portugueses* on 1 June 2016.
27 Lori Baptista, "Images of the Virgin in Portuguese Art at the Newark Museum," in *Community, Culture*, 178.
28 Raymond Breton defined "institutional completeness" as the degree to which an "ethnic community could perform all the services required by its members" ("Institutional Completeness of Ethnic Communities and the Personal Relations of Immigrants," *American Journal of Sociology* 70, no. 2 [September 1964]: 194).
29 Lopes, *Peregrinação*, 91–5.
30 CTASC, transcript of interview with António Sousa, 1978 (?), Domingos Marques fonds 2010–019/001 (10).
31 "Nazaré e o seu porto de abrigo," *Correio Português*, 15 April 1978.
32 Here is a list of "first businesses" opened by Portuguese in Toronto: restaurant, boarding house, barber shop, grocery store (1956); travel

agency, driving school, bakery, goods importing firm (1958); auto shop and gas station (1959); photo studio (1960); fish store, butcher shop (1961); newspaper, clothing store (1963); bookstore, typography (1965); children's store, movie theatre, radio and TV equipment store; music record store (1969) (Ribeiro, *O Canadá*).

33 Brettell, "Ethnicity and Entrepreneurs," 173.

34 Between 1945 and 1979, Rhode Island elected nine Portuguese-American state senators, twenty house representatives, and many more city councillors (Elmer Cornwell Jr, "Ethnic Group Representation: The Case of the Portuguese," *Polity* 13, no. 1 [Autumn 1980]: 5–20).

35 Luso-American Elected Officials History Project, Institute for Portuguese Lusophone World Studies, Rhode Island College, url: http://vimeo.com/18097330.

36 HDA, PEA M424, letter, Consul Fernando Figueirinhas to Ambassador Garin, 5 June 1964 (my translation).

37 HDA, M181, correspondence, Ambassador Fernandes to PMFA, 11 May 1959; M253, Consul Jorge Freitas, Boston, to Ambassador Hall Themido, 30 November 1972.

38 According to the former secretary of state for emigration, Manuela Aguiar, the idea for the CPC was first proposed to her by Ribeiro.

39 "The Seven Who Are Trying to Unite Metro's 50,000 Portuguese Immigrants," *Toronto Star*, 15 July 1972, 19.

40 Letter to the editor, Eurico Nunes, *Toronto Star*, 19 August 1972, 9.

41 Pena-Rodríguez, "Manipulaciones."

42 Editorial, *Diário de Notícias*, 11 November 1953, 1; HDA, M182, letter, Ambassador Fernandes to PMFA, 14 November 1953.

43 HDA, PEA 159, letter, Ambassador Fernandes to PMFA, 30 September 1950; PEA M307, correspondence, Ambassador Fernandes to PMFA, 24 May and 1 August 1955. "Comentário do Dia," *Diário de Notícias*, 26 July 1955, 1.

44 HDA, M182, letter, Ambassador Fernandes to PMFA, 22 September 1953 (my translation).

45 HDA, PEA 159, letter, PCU's Aníbal Branco to Embassy's Councillor Manuel Rocheta, 17 October 1950 (my translation).

46 HDA, M181, letter, José Mota, Feast of the Blessed Sacrament's Executive Committee, to "Veiga Beirão" school's Director Álvaro Gomes, Lisbon, 20 October 1955.

47 "Foi carinhosamente homenageado ... o 'ardina' Johnny Furtado," *Diário de Notícias*, 9 January 1950, 1.

48 HDA, PEA 181, Correspondence Manuel Almada, Ambassador Fernandes, John Furtado, 18 November 1952.

49 Similar elitist preferences when endorsing community leaders were expressed by the Portuguese consul in Paris at around the same time as Pinto's recommendations (Pereira, *A Ditadura*, 337–40).

50 HDA, PEA M424, correspondence, Casa de Portugal's Director Ramiro Valadão to Ambassador Garin, 6 April 1966; M45, Consul Pedro Pinto, New York City, to PMFA, 30 July 1965 (my translation).
51 The consul in Paris also asked a local wealthy Portuguese banker to become the first president of the National Association of Portuguese in France, created in December 1965; letter, Consul Pinto, 30 July 1965; Pereira, *A Ditadura*, 340).
52 HDA, PEA M332, report, PAF's First Annual Congress, 18 September 1966; M45, Supreme Secretary Francisco Mendonça, PCU's *Annual Report*, 1972.
53 Archives of Ontario (henceforth AO), RG 8-5 Box 233, B229091, PCC by-laws, 26 September 1969.
54 For more on Ângelo Nóbrega's death and the community's response see the Portuguese Canadian History Project's (henceforth PCHP) online exhibits, http://archives.library.yorku.ca/exhibits/show/pchp/galleries.
55 "Importante Reunião de Todas as Organizações Portuguesas de Toronto," *Luso-Canadiano*, 25 July 1969; "Ministros num Jantar do Congresso," *Correio Português*, 15 April 1970 (my translation); AO, RG 8-5 Box 233, B229091, letter, FPCC's Cândido Guerreiro to Premier John P. Robarts, 5 January 1970; letter to the editor, Domingos Gomes, *O Jornal Português*, 9 January 1970. LAC, RG25-A-3-c, Vol. 11081, f20-18-1-14, internal memo, Secretary of State for External Affairs, Ottawa, 8 September 1969.
56 AO, RG 8-5 Box 233, B229091, letter, Fernando Costa to Minister of Education Robert Welch, 15 December 1970; memos, D. Russ Colombo, February-March, 1971. LAC, Multiculturalism Directorate, Ban 2003-01367-9, box 128, File 3260-P2-190/P15, notes for the minister.
57 HDA, PEA M307, letter, Casa de Portugal's Director J. Freire d'Andrade to SNI, 10 December 1956.
58 *Diário de Notícias*, 19 June 1958, 3 (my translation).
59 HDA, M607, letter, Consul Manuel Carvalho, Providence, to PMFA, 10 June 1969.
60 HDA, PEA M425, letter, Consul Alexandre Veiga, New York, to Ambassador Garin, 21 July 1967 (my translation).
61 CD2A-CPDP, correspondence, Abílio Águas to Eduardo Covas, 9 June and 26 July 1964; HDA, PEA M656, clipping, *Luso-Americano*, 4 June 1970; CTASC, PCDA fonds, 2009–022/002 (10) ... /004 (14) ... /005 (4), "Manifesto de Antifascistas Portugueses Emigrados e Exilados no Canadá à Tripulação da Fragata *Almirante Pereira da Silva*," 1967; F. Piteira Santos, FPLN, to PCDA, 21 June 1967; communiqué, MDP, June 1970 (my translation and emphasis).
62 ARCAT, Portuguese congregation, 1858–1972, parish collection, letter, Alberto Cunha to Coadjutor Archbishop of Toronto Philip Pocock, 1 June 1967.

63 AO, Department of the Provincial Secretary and Citizenship, RG 8–5 Box 233, B229091, memo, John Gallucci and D.R. Colombo to Donald Martyn, 27 April 1971; CTASC, PCDA fonds, 2009–022/001 (13), José Henriques, "Ainda a Semana Portuguesa," *O Boletim* 9 (June–July 1971): 3–4; "Clubs, Churches Hoe Own Rows: Portuguese Unity Hard to Achieve," *Globe and Mail*, 27 August 1971, 5.

64 William J. Smyth, *Toronto, the Belfast of Canada: The Orange Order and the Shaping of Municipal Culture* (Toronto: University of Toronto Press, 2015), 253.

65 CTASC, PCDA fonds, 2009–022/001 (13), Manuel Sanches, "Carta Aberta ao 'Novo Mundo,'" *O Boletim* 9 (June–July 1971): 4–5.

66 A question mark is handwritten beside this sentence, presumably by the letter's recipient. Another staff member noted: "We are a little puzzled as to how the [PCDA] could be considered to have left-wing or communist leanings ... I assume there could be a tendency for the Portuguese Government to consider them subversive and to attach a left-wing or communist label to the group. However, there is nothing that we could discover in the program of the Association, or the attitudes of its members, that would support such a statement"; AO, RG 8–5 Box 233, B229091, letter, D.R. Colombo to D.R. Martyn, 5 May 1971).

4 Making Ethnic Culture

1 The Rancho of the Provinces and Islands of Portugal is a folk dance troupe based in Hamilton, Ontario, founded in the early 1980s (my translation).

2 Sökefeld, "Mobilizing," 265–8.

3 Jacobson, *Roots Too*, 23.

4 Canadian statistics from the 1970s onward have consistently ranked Portuguese near the top in heritage-language retention; Rema Helms-Park, "Two Decades of Heritage Language Education," in *The Portuguese in Canada: From Sea to the City*, ed. Carlos Teixeira and Victor da Rosa (Toronto: University of Toronto Press, 2000).

5 Emanuel da Silva, "Sociolinguistic (Re)constructions of Diaspora Portugueseness: Portuguese-Canadian Youth in Toronto" (PhD diss., University of Toronto, 2011), 105.

6 While often thought to be common across the archipelago, the "Azorean" accent is specific to the island of São Miguel. Other islands have their own accents, though none as distant from the "standard" Portuguese as Micaelense. This distinctive accent is said to result from the island's mixed colonization by Portuguese settlers from southern mainland regions (which have their own distinct accents) and France.

7 Eric Hobsbawm, "Introduction: Inventing Traditions," in *The Invention of Tradition*, ed. E. Hobsbawm and Terence Ranger (Cambridge: Cambridge

University Press, 1983), 1–2; Kathleen Conzen, David Gerber, Ewa Morawska, George Pozzetta, and Rudolph Vecoli, "The Invention of Ethnicity: A Perspective from the USA," *Journal of American Ethnic History* 12, no. 1 (Fall 1992): 3–41.
8 António Salazar's speech, 11 May 1935 (my translation), cited in Melo, *Salazarismo e Cultura*, 53.
9 David Corkill and José Almeida, "Commemoration and Propaganda in Salazar's Portugal: The *Mundo Português* Exposition of 1940," *Journal of Contemporary History* 44, no. 3 (2009): 393–4.
10 Melo, *Salazarismo e Cultura*, 375.
11 Pena-Rodríguez, "Manipulaciones," 44–7.
12 Pereira, *A Ditadura*, 195–6.
13 António Salazar interview with António Ferro, *Diário de Notícias* (Lisbon), 16 October 1938 (my translation), cited in Melo, *Salazarismo e Cultura*, 53.
14 Kimberly Holton, *Performing Folklore: Ranchos Folclóricos from Lisbon to Newark* (Bloomington: Indiana University Press, 2009).
15 Iacovetta, *Gatekeepers*, 60, 96.
16 HDA, PEA M400, correspondence, Consul Fernando Marques, Montreal, to PMFA, 12 May 1962 (my translation); Consul Jorge Ritto, Toronto, to Ambassador Brazão, 13 May 1964 (my translation).
17 Raphael Costa "The 'Great Façade of Nationality': Some Considerations on Portuguese Tourism and Multiple Meanings of *Estado Novo* Portugal in Travel Literature," *Journal of Tourism History* 5, no. 1 (2013): 50–72.
18 Pedro Oliveira, "O corpo diplomático e o regime autoritário (1926–1974)," *Análise Social* 41, no. 178 (2006): 145–66.
19 HDA, PEA M297, correspondence, Consul Artur Nogueira, Montreal, to PMFA, 26 March 1958 (my translation); Consul José Fragoso, New York City, to PMFA, 21 July 1960 (my translation).
20 TTNA, Actividade da Casa de Portugal, 1964 [1965], AOS/CO/PC-81B, pt 10, Annual Report 1964.
21 "Fala a este jornal ... Dr. Esteves Fernandes," *Diário de Notícias*, 2 April 1954, 1 (my translation).
22 *Diário de Notícias*, 4 August 1961, 6 (my translation).
23 *Correio Português*, 24 October 1963, 4; HDA, PEA M405, *Fatima Review*, 1973.
24 "Fala a este jornal ..."; "Os Portugueses dos Estados Unidos e a Mãe Pátria," *Diário de Notícias*, 11 January 1955, 1; HDA, PEA M181, Wedemann & Godknecht advertisement in the Portuguese-American Progressive Association's 11th Anniversary booklet, 1954; M557 A7, APC's *Bulletin* 5 (December 1957):5.
25 "O Dr. Moreira Baptista Fala da Sua Visita aos E. Unidos," *Diário de Notícias*, 23 November 1960, 6 (my translation).

26 "Mesa Redonda com Victor Ricardo Barbosa Horta," *Correio Português*, 15 August 1971. *Casa de Portugal* annual report 1964. José Mendes, "Relações Económicas entre Portugal e as Comunidades Portuguesas no Estrangeiro," in *Congregação Geral*; Ribeiro, *O Canadá*.
27 HDA, PEA M400, letter, Consul Fernando Marques, Montreal, to PMFA, 2 February 1964; PEA M297, correspondence Consul Artur Nogueira and various government agencies in Lisbon; "A Prova dos Vinhos Portugueses," *Correio Português*, 27 February 1964.
28 Coelho, *Small Stories*, 113–15, 127–8, 251–4, 258–60.
29 Internet Archives, Smithsonian Libraries, 1970 Festival of American Folklife (Washington DC: Smithsonian Institution, 1970).
30 Mendes, "Relações Económicas"; António A. Costa, "A Música Portuguesa nos Estados Unidos," *Diário de Notícias*, 18 April 1953, 4.
31 "D. Maria Leonor ... no Canadá a convite da Canadian Pacific," *Correio Português*, 24 October 1963, 1–4.
32 *Correio Português*, 30 August 1969.
33 António Ribeiro, editorial, *Correio Português*, 15 April 1969 (my translation).
34 See Ricardo Serrado, *O Estado Novo e o Futebol* (Lisbon: Prime Books, 2012).
35 Jaime Monteiro, *Um Passado Recente*; Manuel de Almeida Moura and Imitério Soares, *Pionniers: L'avant-garde de l'immigration portugaise, Canada 1953* (Montreal: Private pub., 2003), 141.
36 *Diário de Notícias*: "Rocky Marciano na Sessão da Continental," 22 June 1953, 1; "Para a História dos Portugueses dos E.U. da América," 24 May 1965, 3; Michael Bamberger, "From the Portuguese: A Passion for Soccer a New England Community in Flux," *Philadelphia Inquirer*, 26 July 1995.
37 Victor Pereira, "Os futebolistas invisíveis: os portugueses e França e o futebol," *Etnográfica* 16, no. 1 (February 2012): 110–13. For more on this topic see Manuel A. Oliveira and Carlos Teixeira, *Jovens Portuguese e Luso-Descendentes no Canadá* (Oeiras: Celta Editora, 2004), and Miguel Moniz, "Adaptive Transnational Identity and the Selling of *Soccer*: The New England Revolution and Lusophone Migrant Populations," in *Globalised Football: Nations and Migration, the City and the Dream*, ed. Nina Tiesler and João Coelho (London and New York: Routledge, 2008), 20–38.
38 *Correio Português*, 2 July 1964.
39 Santos, *O Canadá*, 123–4.
40 HDA, PEA M182, letter, Counselor João Affra, Washington, to Manuel Rocha, 21 May 1955 (my translation); CD25A, CPDP fonds, SC: Correspondência, 1960–1 (henceforth CD25A-CPDP) letter, Eduardo Covas to Abílio Águas, 14 July 1962.
41 The son of a Portuguese father and German mother, John Philip Sousa, composed "Stars and Stripes Forever," "Semper Fidelis," and other classics of the genre; he also invented the Sousaphone.

42 Bandas Filarmónicas website, http://www.bandasfilarmonicas.com/bandas/.
43 Maestro Miguel Domingos, Sagrado Coração de Jesus Band, interviewed by the author for the RTPi show *Hora dos Portugueses* on 10 January 2016.
44 Noivo, *Inside Ethnic*; Miranda, "Not Ashamed."
45 Statistics Canada, 1971 Census of Canada, Vol. 1, pt 4, Population: Cross-classifications of characteristics, 1975; 1981 Census of Canada, Vol. 2, Provincial series, 1984. The 1971 census did not include the option "Portuguese" when asking about the respondent's national origins.
46 Campbell Gibson and Emily Lennon, *Historical Census Statistics on the Foreign-Born Population of the United States: 1850 to 1990* (Washington, DC: US Bureau of the Census, 1999).
47 HDA, PEA M159, PCU's Annual Report 1950.
48 "Escola Oficial Portuguesa de New Bedford," *Diário de Notícias*, 3 and 27 February 1940, 2.
49 HDA, PEA M251, letter, Consul José Fragoso, New York City, to Ambassador Luis Fernandes, 16 May 1960.
50 TTNA, SNI Censura cx. 733, Jornal "Diário de Notícias" em New Bedford (1948–54); *Diário de Notícias*, 24 October 1950, 1–4 (my translation).
51 HDA, PEA M171, letter, Ambassador Luis Fernandes to PMFA, 1 May 1951.
52 Laurinda Andrade, *The Open Door* (New Bedford: Reynolds-DeWalt, 1968).
53 "É Recomendado o Ensino da Língua Portuguesa nas Escolas dos E.U.," *Diário de Notícias*, 23 October 1950.
54 "Eisenhower Recomenda o Estudo de Português," *Diário de Notícias*, 9 March 1960. Letter, Consul Fragoso to Ambassador Fernandes, 16 May 1960.
55 Luso-American Life Insurance Society, "Luso-American Education Foundation: history," http://www.luso-american.org/laef/.
56 HDA, PEA M307, correspondence, IAC's A. Medeiros-Gouvêa to PMFA, 14 November 1958; M20, Consul José Fragoso, New York, to IAC's secretary, 21 January 1960, and Consul F. Esteves, New York, to Medeiros-Gouvêa, 17 March 1966; PEA M334, Consul N. Cordeiro, Newark, to Ambassador Vasco Garin, 13 June 1970.
57 HDA, PEA M251, letter, Ambassador Pedro Pereira to PMFA, 27 March 1963.
58 CTASC, David Higgs fonds, 2020–018/001, Humberto Ferreira, *Escola do "First Portuguese." 25 Anos de História*, 1989. LAC, RG-F-4, file CB 9-402-1, letter, Débora Raposo, FPCC school director, to MP Charles Caccia, Ottawa, 5 December 1970.
59 HDA, PEA M251, various correspondence, 1963–5 (my translation); PEA M334, letter, Ambassador Vasco Garin to IAC's A. Medeiros-Gouvêa,

5 December 1967; letter, Consul Vasco Vilela to Ambassador Garin, 22 October 1968 (my translation).
60 Pereira, *A Ditadura*, 345–8.
61 HDA, PEA M251, correspondence, Ambassador Pedro Pereira to PMFA, 12 February 1963; IAC's Medeiros-Gouvêa to Ambassador Pereira, 6 March 1963; PEA M332, PMFA to Ambassador Vasco Garin, 2 January 1967.
62 "Nove mil jovens americanos aprendem, presentemente, a língua portuguesa,", *Diário de Notícias*, 17 January 1968, 1, 6; Fernando Matos, "Ensino da Língua Portuguesa nos Estados Unidos, Inglaterra e Canadá," *I Simpósio Luso-Brasileiro Sobre a Língua Portuguesa Contemporânea* (Coimbra: Instituto de Alta Cultura, 1968).
63 In *Voz* newspaper, 31 March 1969 (my translation), cited in Santos, *Discurso Oficial*, 74.
64 Pereira, *A Ditadura*, 334.
65 HDA, PEA M333, APCS' Mission Statement, 1966; PEA M253, meeting report, APCS's Executive VP William Weissel, 30 September 1971.
66 Fernanda Viveiros, ed., *Memória: An Anthology of Portuguese Canadian Writers* (Bellingham, WA: Fidalgo Books, 2013).
67 Robert Moser and António Tosta, eds, *Luso-American Literature: Writings by Portuguese-Speaking Authors in North America* (New Brunswick, NJ: Rutgers University Press, 2011).
68 HDA, PEA M425, notes, PMFA's Caldeira Coelho, 30 April 1968.
69 CTASC, PCDA fonds, 2009–022/003 (4), letter, PCDA's F. Ciriaco Cunha to José Neves (São Paulo), 8 May 1960; CD25A-CPDP, letter, Eduardo Covas, Newark, to João Pimentel, São Paulo, 4 June 1961.
70 Sökefeld, "Mobilizing," 266.

5 Making Imperial Citizens

Parts of this chapter were first published in Gilberto Fernandes, "'Oh Famous Race!' Imperial Heritage and Diasporic Memory in the Portuguese American Narrative of North America," *Public Historian* 38, no. 1 (February 2016): 18–48.

1 Moreira speech, 9 May 1964, 20.
2 James Barrett and David Roediger, "Inbetween Peoples: Race, Nationality, and the 'New Immigrant' Working Class," *Journal of American Ethnic History* 16, no. 3 (Spring 1997): 3–34.
3 Thomas Guglielmo, *White on Arrival: Italians, Race, Color, and Power in Chicago, 1890–1945* (New York: Oxford University Press, 2003), 6.
4 Harney, "Portygees"; Marilyn Halter, *Between Race and Ethnicity: Cape Verdean American Immigrants, 1860–1965* (Champaign: University of Illinois Press, 1993), 16; Noel Ignatiev, *How the Irish Became White* (London: Routledge, 1995).

5 See, for instance, Agnew, *Diaspora*.
6 Gilberto Freyre, *The Masters and the Slaves: A Study in the Development of Brazilian Civilization* (New York: Knopf, 1946); Gerald Bender, *Angola under the Portuguese: The Myth and the Reality* (Berkeley; University of California Press,1978), 3–4.
7 The 15 March death toll reported in the press at the time varied from 164 to 6,000, while the immediate backlash unleashed by white settlers was reported to have killed up to 30,000 Africans. As historians have argued, knowing the exact number of victims in that hinterland region, for which there are no reliable statistics, is impossible; Hugh Kay, *Salazar and Modern Portugal* (London: Eyre & Spottiswoode, 1970), 222; Douglas Wheeler and René Pélissier, *Angola* (New York: Praeger, 1971), 179.
8 Canada had sold these jet fighters to Germany, which later resold them to Portugal. As Lewis revealed, after having publicly forbidden the resale to Portugal in 1965, Ottawa later allowed that deal to proceed through backroom channels (CTASC, PCDA fonds, 2009–022/005 (8), Stephen Lewis, speech to the United Church of Canada's Board of World Mission, (?) March 1971).
9 Donald Taft, "Two Portuguese Communities in New England" (PhD diss., New York: Columbia University, 1923).
10 Reinaldo Silva, *Representations of the Portuguese in American Literature* (Dartmouth: Centre for Portuguese Studies and Culture, University of Massachusetts Dartmouth, 2008).
11 Canadian immigration officials in the 1950s characterized the Portuguese as "religious, patriarchal, honest, kind, courteous, courageous, disciplined, hard working, happily disposed, with limited initiative but intelligence within their own confines" (LAC, 568-3-23, Vol. 690, RG 76, memo, O. Cormer, Paris, to Director [Att. Operations], Ottawa, 13 March 1954).
12 Non-white colonial "Portuguese" had no such luck in Canada. In 1955, Minister Cunha asked Canadian immigration officials if they were willing to include Goans in their labour migration agreement, to which Prime Minister Pearson replied that, despite being Portuguese citizens, Goans were still Asian, and were therefore excluded by Canada's immigration laws (LAC, 3-33-27, Vol. 130, RG 26, letter, Under-Secretary of State for External Affairs to Deputy Minister Laval Fortier, 16 December 1955).
13 Miguel Moniz, "The Shadow Minority: An Ethnohistory of Portuguese and Lusophone Racial and Ethnic Identity in New England," in *Community, Culture*, 418.
14 Robert Mason, "A Precarious Whiteness: Exploring Australian Cultural Diversity through the Legacies of the Portuguese Empire," in *Intersecting Diaspora Boundaries: Portuguese Contexts*, ed. Irene M.F. Blayer and Dulce M. Scott (New York: Peter Lang, 2016), 55–70.

15 Manuel E. Costa Sr, *The Making of the Cape Verdean*, ed. Jeanne Costa (Bloomington, IN: AuthorHouse, 2011), 85–92.
16 HDA, M20, Letter, Consul José Fragoso, New York, to PMFA, 21 July 1960 (my translation).
17 "Century-Old Stigma Remains: 'Portuguese' Youngsters Segregated in Carolina," *Virginian-Pilot* and *Portsmouth Star*, 26 January 1958, 4; "A Situação Dificil da Colónia 'Portuguesa' de Northampton," *Diário de Notícias* (Lisbon), 4 February 1958, 1; "Só a ignorância que ainda se vive nalguns pontos da Carolina justifica a denominada 'segregação' dos portugueses," *Diário da Manhã*, 24 February 1958; "A Denominação 'Portugueses' Está a Ser Utilizada de Maneira Pejorativa ou Degradante por Legisladores dos E.U.A.," *Diário Ilustrado*, 4 March 1958.
18 João Rocha, "Comentário do Dia," *Diário de Notícias*, 14 February 1958, 1 (my translation).
19 "Ainda o caso das famílias 'Portuguesas' segregadas ... Carolina do Norte," *Diário de Notícias*, 24 February 1958, 1.
20 Jacobson, *Roots Too*, 2.
21 *Diário de Notícias*: "Não São Portuguesas as Dezasseis Famílias que Vivem Segregadas nos Estados Unidos," 25 February 1958, 1; "O Embaixador de Portugal protestou junto do Governo dos Estados Unidos," 17 March 1958, 1–4.
22 HDA, PEA 71, letter, Ambassador Luis Fernandes to PMFA, 4 March 1958.
23 In his self-published *The Forgotten Portuguese* (2001), the businessman and amateur historian Manuel Mira argued that a group of mixed-race people known as the Melungeons, who settled in the Appalachian Mountains in the sixteenth century, were descendants of Portuguese shipwrecked sailors who arrived in North America before the Spanish and the British. According to Mira, the "Portuguese" of Gaston were descendants of this group, as was Abraham Lincoln, which explained his "Portuguese features."
24 HDA, PEA 71, Bernardo Teixeira's report, March 1958.
25 HDA, PEA 71, correspondence, Ambassador Luis Fernandes to PMFA, 3 April and 11 March 1958; Luis Norton de Mattos to Ambassador Fernandes, 11 April 1959.
26 Rogers, *Americans of Portuguese Descent*.
27 Peter A. Landry, "The Portuguese: A Heritage of Oppression, A Search for Identity," *Harvard Crimson*, 25 March 1974, https://www.thecrimson.com/article/1974/3/25/the-portuguese-a-heritage-of-oppression/ (accessed 9 May 2019).
28 For centuries, the Dighton Rock has been the subject of speculation by archaeology aficionados, who have submitted it as flagrant evidence to a range of historical theories regarding the arrival of the

first Europeans to North America. The boulder, originally located in the riverbank of the Taunton River in Berkley, is remarkable for the petroglyphs covering its surface. In 1912, Professor Edmund Delabarre claimed to have discovered the Portuguese coat of arms on the surface of the Rock, along with a Latin inscription, which translates as "Miguel Corte Real, by the will of God, here chief of the indians, 1511." In 1963, Silva convinced Massachusetts state officials to remove the rock from the water and build a state park and museum dedicated to the history of Portuguese maritime explorations; Fernandes, "'Oh Famous Race!'"; Douglas Hunter, *The Place of Stone and the Erasure of America's Indigenous Past* (Chapel Hill: University of North Carolina Press, 2017).

29 *Diário de Notícias*, 17 October 1966, 1; HDA, PEA M333, transcript, Manuel Silva on *A Voz dos Açores* radio show, Middletown, RI, 5 April 1970.

30 HDA, PEA M400, Ambassador Eduardo Brazão's speech, Newfoundland, 30 May 1963.

31 "Homenagem da Terra Nova aos Pescadores Portugueses," *Diário de Notícias*, 13 September 1965, 1, 6.

32 The Cabrillo Day was launched in California in 1935 and promoted by the Cabrilho Civic Clubs, a nexus of Portuguese-American organizations in that state. This organization convinced Lisbon to donate the Cabrillo National Monument to the city of San Diego, which unveiled it in 1942, in Point Loma (Fernandes, "'Oh Famous Race!'").

33 HDA, PEA M609-A, letter, Ambassador Vasco Garin to Minister Franco Nogueira, 18 September 1964.

34 *Diário de Notícias*: "Celebrações Henriquinas em Greater Boston," 10 October 1960, 1; "Foi Luzido o Cortejo em Fall River," 14 November 1960, 1, 4.

35 HDA, PEA M425, *Novos Rumos*, 1 July 1967, 149 (my translation).

36 *Diário de Notícias*, 10 July 1967, 6 (my translation).

37 HDA, PEA M181, Joseph Warner's address at Taunton High School Auditorium (10 June 1951), in *Portuguese World*, December 1951 (my translation).

38 California Legislature, Resolution 62, re: Cabrillo Festival, 24 February 1969.

39 HDA, PEA M334, letter, Governor Ronald Reagan to Admiral Sarmento Rodrigues, 27 May 1970.

40 In 1968, Governor Reagan confided to Ambassador Garin that he thought it "inexplicable that anyone could consider Angola a colony, where [the Portuguese have been] for over 500 years" (cited in HDA, PEA M425, letter from Ambassador Vasco Garin to Minister Franco Nogueira, Lisbon, 5 January 1968).

41 Halter, *Between Race*, 9, 164.
42 *Diário de Notícias*, 26 October 1960, 1.
43 HDA, M20, correspondence, Consul José Fragoso, Consul Henrique Martins, Ambassador Luis Fernandes, Overseas Ministry Carlos Freitas, PMFA, 21 July 1960 to 28 July 1962; PEA M332, *Casa de Portugal*'s Ramiro Valadão to SPPH's José Monte, 4 July 1967.
44 "For Brilhante a Festa de Debutantes da Associação Beneficiente Caboverdeana," *Diário de Notícias*, 29 May 1967, 1, 6.
45 HDA, PEA M251, letter, Consul Fernando Figueirinhas, Boston, to Ambassador Garin, 30 June 1964.
46 "Activities of Nondiplomatic Representatives of Foreign Principals in the United States," Senate Committee on Foreign Relations: United States Senate (Washington, DC: US Government Printing Office, 1963), 1183–5 (henceforth SCFR).
47 Fundação Mário Soares (henceforth FMS), Amílcar Cabral Archives, 04614.070.080, letter, Roy Teixeira to José Mendes, Jersey City, 1 February 1963.
48 CD25A-CPDP, correspondence, Abílio Águas and Eduardo Covas, 11 August 1961 to 12 August 1964. HDA, PEA M333, letter, PCU President A. Pereira and Secretary-General F. Mendonça to Ambassador Vasco Garin, 12 November 1970.
49 HDA, M181, Aníbal Branco, PCU Executive Report, 1955.
50 "Mass. Mixed-Bloods Reject Negro Heritage," *Washington Post*, 1 December 1968.
51 HDA, Relações Bilaterais Portugal-E.U. Atentado à Bomba ... telegrams, Consul Nuno Cordeiro to PMFA, 24 November 1970; Ambassador Vasco Garin to PMFA, 4 December 1970.
52 "Os Portugueses Newark Insurgem-se Contra os Insultos de que Foram Alvo," *Luso-Americano*, 3 December 1970. HDA, PEA M334, Don Prial, *Newark Evening News*, (?) December 1970.
53 Jama Lazerow, "'A Rebel All His Life': The Unexpected Story of Frank 'Parky' Grace," in *In Search of the Black Panther Party: New Perspectives on a Revolutionary Movement*, ed. J. Lazerow and Yohuru Williams (Durham, NC: Duke University Press, 2006).
54 "Os distúrbios de New Bedford atribuidos às autoridades municipais," *Diário de Notícias*, 19 August 1970, 1.
55 "New Bedford, Quiet but Tense, Still Faces Its Problems," *Harvard Crimson*, 4 August 1970, https://www.thecrimson.com/article/1970/8/4/new-bedford-quiet-but-tense-still/ (accessed 9 May 2019).
56 "Repetiram-se em New Bedford os Tumultos e Incêndios," *Diário de Notícias*, 30 July 1970, 1; HDA, PEA M656, correspondence, Minister Rui Patrício to Consul Jorge Freitas, (?) September 1970.

57 "Comicio de Apoio aos Portuguese de Goa," *Diário de Notícias*, 24 April 1950, 1, 4; "O Caso de Goa e os Portugueses de Rhode Island," *Diário de Notícias*, 13 May 1950, 1, 3; "Deputado Martin secunda os protestos dos luso-americanos no caso de Goa," *Diário de Notícias*, 24 May 1950, 1; HDA, PEA M159, letter, Madeiran Day Director Carlos Morais to Chargé d'Affairs Manuel Rocheta, Portuguese Embassy, 1 June 1950.
58 US Department of Justice, Foreign Agents Registration Act website, www.fara.gov/, "Report[s] of the Attorney General to the Congress of the United States on the Administration of the Foreign Agents Registration Act of 1938," 1942–78 (henceforth FARA Reports).
59 "Terminaram domingo em New Bedford as celebrações do Ano Henriquino," *Diário de Notícias*, 8 November 1960, 4.
60 Basil Brewer's bio, Pickler Memorial Library, Truman State University website, http://library.truman.edu/archives/biographies/brewer.asp.
61 "O Sr. Basil Brewer, esteve ontem presente á recepção em honra do dr. Paulo Cunha," *Diário de Notícias*, 28 September 1951, 1; CD25A-CPDP, letter, Abílio Águas to American Commitee on Africa's George Houser, 19 April 1962.
62 Letter, Consul Figueirinhas to Ambassador Garin, 5 June 1964.
63 TTNA, SNI Censura cx. 733, Jornal "Diário de Notícias" em New Bedford (1948–1954), letter, Censorship Services Director to Presidency Ministry, Lisbon, 8 March 1952.
64 Ibid., correspondence between various government officials, 31 May 1948 to 21 August 1951; "É Violada a Mala do Correio em Portugal?" *Diário de Notícias*, 9 August 1951, 1.
65 HDA, PEA M307, correspondence, Ambassador Luis Fernandes to PMFA, 31 December 1953 to 25 February 1954; PEA M251-A, Consul (?), Boston, to Ambassador Pedro Pereira, 20 September 1961.
66 Initially the ban was lifted only in the mainland, until the governor of Ponta Delgada requested that it be extended to the Azores, to not upset its large emigrant community in New Bedford (TTNA, SNI Censura cx. 733, Jornal "Diário de Notícias" em New Bedford [1948–54], letter, Governor Aniceto Santos to the Interior Ministry's chief of staff, 16 June 1954).
67 TTNA, PIDE/DGS, João Rodrigues Rocha, SC SR 2886/57 nt. 2815, correspondence, PIDE's Agostinho Lourenço, PIDE's Manuel Brás, Consul Vasco Vilela, 28 December 1957 and 14 April 1958; João Rocha, "O Dr. Oliveira Salazar Manifestou Interesse pelos Portugueses da America," *Diário de Notícias*, 2 May 1958, 1.
68 HDA, PEA M400, Consul Artur Nogueira's report, 18 February 1961.
69 HDA, M20, correspondence, Consul José Fragoso, New York, to SNI Director César Baptista, 8 February 1961; PEA M251-A, correspondence,

Embassy Counselor Menezes Rosa to José Capote, 5 June 1962; César Baptista and Ambassador Vasco Garin, 9 October and 5 November 1964; "Cerejas de Santa Comba" and "Salada de Frutas," (*Correio de Vouga*) *Novos Rumos*, 1 August 1964.
70 Stone also used the pseudonyms Paul Dickson and João Prado.
71 TTNA, PIDE/DGS, Gil Stone, SC SR. 551/ 45 np. 2465, correspondence, Gil Stone (Red Bank, New Jersey), Henrique Medina (Lisbon), PIDE's Álvaro Carvalho, July–October, 1963.
72 According to FARA Reports, out of the close to 240 registrants, Selvage & Lee was the ninth-largest recipient of funds from a foreign principal in 1961–3. The 1964 report does not provide funding amounts.
73 SCFR, 900–8, 917, 1006; HDA, PEA M424, letter, Consul Figueirinhas to Ambassador Garin, 5 June 1964.
74 SCFR, 910, 912–15, 928, 946, 948–9, 951–2, 1001, 1048, 1192; HDA, PEA M253, "The Communists and Angola," pamphlet, PACFA, 9 October 1961.
75 HDA, PEA M253, PACFA press releases, 16 November 1961 and 10 December 1962; letters, Martin Camacho to Martins Cabral, 4 and 5 May 1964; SCFR, 937, 939, 950–7, 1032, 1035–6, 1142–5.
76 Portuguese-American Fund ads, *Diário de Notícias*, 27 September 1961, 4, and 19 January 1962, 5; HDA, PEA M400, telegram, Ambassador Eduardo Brazão to PMFA, 13 May 1964.
77 HDA, PEA M251-A, correspondence, Consul C. Carvalho, Boston, and Ambassador Pedro Pereira, 27 October and 6 November 1961.
78 Correspondence, Pereira to Salazar, 26 October 1961 and 5 July 1962, cited in João Almeida, *António Oliveira Salazar, Pedro Teotónio Pereira: Correspondência Política, 1945–1968* (Braga: IHN, Círculo de Leitores, Temas e Debates, 2008), 676, 690; Luís Rodrigues, *Salazar-Kennedy: A Crise de Uma Aliança* (Editorial Notícias, 2002), 203. SCFR, 984.
79 SCFR, 866–9, 1010.
80 SCFR, 837–8, 853, 857, 865–6, 1040–4, 1053, 1088, 1179–80.
81 For a more detailed account and analysis of this Portuguese public relations campaign and its aftermath, see my forthcoming article "Breaking the News: American Public Relations, Portuguese Colonialist Lobbying, and the Foreign Agents Registration Act Amendments of 1966."
82 Casa de Portugal annual report, 1964 (my translation).
83 HDA, PEA M424, letter, Casa de Portugal's Ramiro Valadão to Ambassador Vasco Garin, 6 April 1966.
84 HDA, PEA M332, correspondence between Portuguese-American organizations and individuals in California, New York, and New Jersey, the UN

Security Council, and Prime Minister Marcello Caetano, 11 March to 19 November 1968.
85 Luis C. Pina, *O Dever de Portugal para com as Comunidades Lusíadas da América do Norte* (Lisbon: Ateliers Gráficos Bertrand, 1945), 64–73 (my translation).
86 HDA, PEA M307, letter, Overseas Minister Sarmento Rodrigues to PMFA, 4 January 1955 (my translation).
87 Moreira, *Congregação Geral*, 13, 21 (my translation).
88 Ibid. (my translation), 22.
89 *Diário de Notícias*, "Visita do Prof. Adriano Moreira às Comunidade Portuguesas de Connecticut," 27 August 1964, 1; *Luso-Americano*, 27 August 1964; *Standard Times*, 28 August 1964; HDA, PEA M609-A, Adriano Moreira's speech at Sacramento's Cabrilho Day celebrations, 12 September 1964.
90 Pereira, *A Ditadura*, 107.
91 José Magalhães' communication, *Congregação Geral*.
92 Communications by Anibal Branco and Mário Figueiredo, *Congregação Geral*; "Congresso das Comunidades," *Diário da Manhã*, 25 December 1964, 27 (my translation).
93 Communications by Lopo Abreu and Manuel Cruz, *Congregação Geral*.
94 "Statutes of the Union of Portuguese Cultural Communities, 17 December 1964," *Congregação Geral* (my translation).
95 HDA, PEA M332, letter, PAF Establishment Committee's Joseph Fernandes to Ambassador Vasco Garin, 25 March 1966.
96 Communication by Manuel Leal, *Congregação Geral*; HDA, PEA M251, letter, Consul Fernando Figueirinhas to PMFA, 12 January 1965.
97 "Mozambique Parley Seeking to Preserve Portuguese Culture," *New York Times*, 20 August 1967, 11.
98 Communications by Sérgio Cruz and Armando Pereira, *II Congresso das Comunidades de Cultura Portuguesa*, conference proceedings, Vol. 2 (Lisbon: Sociedade de Geografia de Lisboa, 1967).
99 António Costa, "A Imagem do Emigrante," *Comunidades Portuguesas* 7, no. 25 (January 1972): 65.
100 Guglielmo, *White on Arrival*, 125–6.
101 Nadia Venturri, "'Over the Years People Don't Know': Italian Americans and African Americans in Harlem in the 1930s," in *Italian Workers of the World: Labour Migration and the Formation of Multiethnic States*, ed. Donna Gabaccia and Fraser Ottanelli, trans. Michael Rocke (Chicago: University of Illinois Press, 2001), 206.
102 Fortier, "Bringing It," 41–2.
103 Ignatiev, *How the Irish Became White*.
104 Barrett and Roediger, "Inbetween Peoples," 28–33.

6 The Radicals' Diaspora

1 CTASC, PCDA fonds, 2009–022/004 (17), pamphlet distributed by MDP members to the crewmen of the Portuguese frigate *Almirante Pereira da Silva* during its visit to Montreal in 1967.
2 Distinguishing "political" from "economic" migrants is not always possible given that both motivations sometimes coexisted in the same individual. As Pereira (2003) noted, for those in France the term "exiles" was usually reserved for middle- and upper-class politicians and intellectuals. Politically motivated lower-class emigrants have typically not been characterized as "exiles" because they did not frequent the same circles as these elite few. That is not the case in this study, where I use the term "exile" to describe migrants of any social class, whose political beliefs or defiant acts against the established order in Portugal were the main reason for their exodus and/or who later engaged in political activities against the Portuguese government and its colonial empire while abroad.
3 Bodnar, *The Transplanted*, 161.
4 Robert Perin, "Writing about Ethnicity," in *Writing about Canada: A Handbook for Modern Canadian History*, ed. John Schultz (Scarborough, ON: Prentice-Hall Canada, 1990), 220–1.
5 Patrias, *Patriots and Proletarians*, 230.
6 Elisabetta Vezzosi, "Radical Ethnic Brokers: Immigrant Socialist Leaders in the United States between Ethnic Community and the Larger Society," in Gabaccia and Ottanelli, *Italian Workers*, 121.
7 David Raby, *Facism and Resistance in Portugal: Communists, Liberals, and Military Dissidents in the Opposition to Salazar, 1941–1974* (Manchester: Manchester University Press 1988), 197.
8 Fernando Rosas, *História de Portugal*, Vol. 7: *O Estado Novo* (Lisbon: Editorial Estampa, 1993), 532 (my translation).
9 CTASC, PCDA fonds, 2009–022/003 (1), correspondence, Comissão Inter-Ligação's João Pimentel and Manuel Sertório (São Paulo) to PCDA, 29 March 1961; Unidade Democrática Portuguesa (São Paulo) to the Anti-Salazarist Internal Front, 20 January 1962.
10 David Raby, "Portuguese Exile Politics: The 'Frente Patriótica de Libertação Nacional,' 1962–1973," *Luso-Brazilian Review* 31, no. 1 (Summer 1994): 84.
11 João Camoesas was Portugal's Minister of National Instruction in 1923–5. He promised to reform Portugal's education system along Frederik Taylor's scientific organization ideas and the American school system. In 1928 he was deported to Angola, and from there he moved to the United States two years later, settling in Taunton, Massachusetts.
12 Joaquim Alves Correia, or Father Larguezas, was a Catholic priest from the mainland who authored various works on Catholic social doctrine

and wrote for influential opposition publications. In 1946, shortly after joining a prominent pro-democratic organization, Correia was sent to San Diego to serve that city's Portuguese congregation. Before he died in 1951, he became a sociology professor at Duquesne University in Pittsburgh, Pennsylvania.

13 CD25A, Committee Pro-Democracy in Portugal finding aid; TTNA, PIDE/DGS, SC CI (2) 478 np. 7012, [Abilio Águas], "Um Português Ilustre nos E. Unidos," *República*, 29 August 1960; letter, Abílio Águas to Sociedade Agrícola e Comercial da Boaventura's Monteiro Macedo, Praia, Cape Verde, 20 August 1961.

14 TTNA, PIDE/DGS, Eduardo Covas, SUF, 768/50, nt. 647.

15 The Portuguese-American Commitee for Democracy, founded by Camoesas, Miguéis, and Águas in 1945, was defunct at this point. Pena-Rodríguez, "Manipulaciones," 39–42.

16 CD25A-CPDP, correspondence, Eduardo Covas, António Dias, Abílio Águas (Newark), Silvério Letra and João Pimentel (São Paulo), 23 May 1960 to 29 July 1961. TTNA, PIDE/DGS, Eduardo Covas, SC, CI (2) 3972, nt. 7309, correspondence, US Embassy in Paris's Norman Philcox, PIDE's Director Silva Pais, PIDE; FBI agent, 4 March to 30 April 1964.

17 CD25A-CPDP, correspondence, Águas and Covas, 17 May 1961 to 21 February 1962; Águas to Amândio Silva (Rio de Janeiro), 18 August 1962.

18 CD25A-CPDP, correspondence, Águas and Covas, 9 June and 26 July 1961.

19 TTNA, PIDE/DGS, [CPDP] SC, CI (2), pr. 3926, u.i. 7307, "Comunicado," *Diário de Notícias*, 31 May 1961, sent by PMFA to PIDE's Director Homero Matos, 18 July 1961.

20 CD25A-CPDP, correspondence, Águas to Covas, 20 June 1961 to 9 June 1964.

21 TTNA, PIDE/DGS, [CPDP] SC, CI (2), pr. 3926, u.i. 7307, letter, Henrique Galvão (São Paulo), sent through António Almeida (Newark) to José Campos (Lisbon), and intercepted by PIDE, 31 August 1961; FBI Report (unsigned), 1 November 1961.

22 CD25A-CPDP, correspondence, between Águas, Galvão, and Covas, 30 April to 20 June 1962.

23 CD25A-CPDP, communiqué, Humberto Delgado (Rio de Janeiro), 5 November 1962; TTNA, PIDE/DGS, [CPDP] SC, CI (2), pr. 3926, u.i. 7307, letter, Movimento Nacional Independente's Arajaryr Campos to Eduardo Covas, 17 July 1963.

24 Among them were Roger Baldwin, founder of the American Civil Liberties Union and the International League for the Rights of Man, George Houser of the American Committee on Africa, and US

congressmen (CD25A-CPDP, letter, Eduardo Covas to Manuel Serqueira, Montreal, 26 March 1962; Águas to Houser, 19 April 1962).
25 CD25A-CPDP, correspondence, Águas to Covas, 27 August and 21 October 1964.
26 CD25A-CPDP, correspondence, Águas to Covas, 28 July 1964.
27 At the time of my research, the CPDP's records at the CD25A pertaining to 1966–84 were not yet available for consultation.
28 The PCDA's original structure included a Feminine Relations subcommittee, apparently constituted by the members' wives. There is no mention of their activities in the records. Only in the 1980s did women begin joining the PCDA in larger numbers and assuming more prominent roles.
29 CTASC, PCDA fonds, 2009–022/003 (4), Ciriaco Cunha's open letter to Salazar, October 1959 (my translation).
30 CTASC, PCDA fonds, 2009–022/003 (1 & 4) & ... /002 (1), letter to the editor, Ciriaco Cunha, *Globe and Mail*, 2 February 1962; correspondence, Cunha to *Portugal Democrático*'s João Neves (São Paulo), 4 December 1959; Galvão, 5 March 1960. LAC, Ethnic Organizations, Portuguese Canadian Democratic Association, RG6-F-2, b128, f3260-P2-190/P136, letter, Fernando C. Cunha to DCI, Citizenship Branch; DCI report by C.L. Grant to G.P. Allen, 14 December 1959.
31 CTASC, PCDA fonds, 2009–022/002 (1) ... /003 (1 & 5), PCDA membership list; correspondence, Ciriaco Cunha to Galvão (Caracas), 31 March and 21 June 1960 (my translation); Suzana Torres (Tangier) to Cunha, 7 April 1960; Cunha to Casa dos Portugueses, Montreal, 23 January 1962; Firmino Oliveira to José Reis (São Paulo), 4 April 1963.
32 CTASC, PCDA fonds, 2009–022/003 (1 & 3), correspondence, Ciriaco Cunha, Américo Marques, João Neves, Guilherme Manaças, 2 February, 11 April, and 25 June 1960.
33 HDA, PEA M400, Consul Artur Nogueira's report, 18 February 1961.
34 Lopes, *Peregrinação*, 87.
35 After the failed takeover of Beja's military barracks, Maximino Rosa Serra – his brother, Manuel Serra, was one of the leaders of the assault – and his comrade Mavilio Mendes fled to the coastal village of Santa Cruz, where they stole a light aircraft from a local flight club and flew to the Algarve. There they refuelled and continued on to Tangier, where they were granted political asylum. They later moved to Montreal with UN passports (TTNA, PIDE/DGS, Maximino Rosa Serra, SC, E/GT 144, n.t. 1436, investigation notes, 21 October 1963).
36 TTNA, PIDE/DGS, [MDP], SC, CI (2), pr. 4779, u.i. 7370, letter from "the Agent" (illegible signature) to PIDE, 18 November 1965.
37 *Toronto Daily Star*: "In Trinidad Everybody Has a Theory," 25 January 1961, 3, and "Star Man Sees Her First," 28 January 1961, 1.

38 "Police-Victim Says: 'Good Luck to Pirates,'" *Toronto Telegram*, 26 January 1961.
39 *Toronto Daily Star*: "Pirate Chief Claims Followers in Canada," 25 January 1961, 3; "Message Sent to *The Star* by Gen. Delgado. It's Blow for Freedom Says Rebel General," and "Told Pirate Secret. I'm Not Telling Where She Is Bound," 27 January 1961, 1, 21."Ship Capture Seed Fuse of Revolt," *Toronto Telegram*, 26 January 1961, 13.
40 "Only 15 of 5,000 Portuguese Here Demonstrated – Consul," *Montreal Gazette*, 3 February 1961; HDA, PEA M400, *La Presse*, letters to the editor, Artur Ribeiro, 2 February 1961, and Manuel Teixeira, 8 February 1961.
41 "1,000 Portuguese Riot on Bay Street," *Toronto Daily Star*, 30 January 1960, 25; "Portuguese Stage Riot on Bay St.," *Globe and Mail*, 30 January 1960, 1; "Portuguese in Bay St. Battle," *Toronto Telegram*, 29 January 1961.
42 *Toronto Daily Star*: "Portuguese in Bay St.," 29 January 1961, "Bay St. Riot Claim: 'I Recognized Salazar Gestapo,'" 31 January 1961, 23; HDA, PEA M3, correspondence, Consul Augusto Patrício, Ambassador Emílio Patrício, and PMFA, 14 March to 28 April 1961.
43 "Claimed Outsiders Aided Portuguese Bay St. Riot," *Toronto Daily Star*, 1 February 1961, 9; CTASC, PCDA fonds, 2009–022/003 (1 & 3), correspondence, Ciriaco Cunha to Américo Marques, 2 February 1960; and DCI Charity Grant liaison officer, 23 February 1960.
44 CTASC, PCDA fonds, 2009–022/003 (2), correspondence, Henrique Bello to Ciriaco Cunha, 4 July and 8 August 1961.
45 CTASC, PCDA fonds, 2009–022/003 (2 & 5), correspondence, Bello and Ciriaco Cunha, 1 October and 25 December 1961.
46 CD25A-CPDP, correspondence, Covas and Mário Sequeira (Montreal), 11–20 January 1962; CTASC, PCDA fonds, 2009–022/003 (1 & 17), correspondence, Silvério Letra (São Paulo) to Ciriaco Cunha, 29 November 1960; Bello to Cunha, 28 February 1962; "Eduino Martins e A Voz de Portugal, Mordomos de Santa Cruz de 2016," *Espírito Santo: Santa Cruz 2016, Voz de Portugal* (supplement), 2016, 46–7; Armando Barqueiro's obituary, Alfred Dallaire's Memoria, http://www.memoria.ca/95-grand-disparu-barqueiro-armando.html.
47 HDA, PEA M400, correspondence, Ambassador Brazão and PMFA, 25 February to 13 March 1963; Consul Fernando Marques, Montreal, to Ambassador Brazão, 4 March 1963. Maria Ribeiro, "Pórtico," *Correio Português*, 30 January 1964, 1. CTASC, PCDA fonds, 2009–022/001 (9), "À Custa da Fome em Portugal," *A Verdade* 7 (April 1965): 6. TTNA, PIDE/DGS, Gil Stone, 1965, SC SR. 551/ 45 np. 2465, *Luso-Canadiano*, 30 April.
48 HDA, PEA M140, letter, Consul Augusto Patrício, Toronto, to PMFA, 15 May 1961.

49 CTASC, PCDA fonds, 2009–022/003 (5 & 15), correspondence, Firmino Oliveira to Consul Jorge Ritto, Toronto, (?) November 1962; to *Portugal Democrático*, 14 January 1963, and to PCDA, 9 July 1964. TTNA, PIDE/DGS, [Xavier], SC, SR pr. 1759/73, ui. 4084, "Xavier's" testimonial to PIDE agents Álvaro Carvalho and Álvaro Melo, 13 January 1968.
50 CTASC, PCDA fonds, 2009–022/001 (9& 10), *A Verdade* 5; "A Canadian Socialist Viewpoint on Portugal," *The Truth* 4 (May 1965): 7–8.
51 CTASC, PCDA fonds, 2009–022/003 (5), letter, Firmino Oliveira to Humberto Delgado, ? 1963. CD25A-CPDP, correspondence, Águas to Galvão, 25 February 1964; António José (Taunton) and Águas, 28–31 March 1964.
52 CTASC, PCDA fonds, 2009–022/001 (9), "Carta Aberta a Um Portugês dos Açores," *A Verdade* 4 (December 1964): 11–12 (my translation).
53 CTASC, PCDA fonds, 2009–022/001 (9 & 10), *A Verdade*: "Vozes de Asno Não Chegam ao Céu," 3 (November 1964): 5 (my translation), "... Ex-Candidato a Agente da PIDE," 5 (January 1965): 3–7; "Uma Referência Justa," 10 (July 1965), 4; TTNA, PIDE/DGS, [PCDA] SC, CI (2), pr. 1913, u.i. 7685, "Carta Aberta ao Presidente do [PCDA]."
54 CTASC, PCDA fonds, 2009–022/002 (6) ... 003 (8), correspondence, Guilherme Santos and Humberto Delgado, 8 December 1964 to 20 January 1965; Santos to Frente Portuguesa de Libertação Nacional (Rabat), 29 March 1965; Santos to Henrique Cerqueira, 15 March–3 April 1965; and Santos to FPLN-JRN, 20 April 1965.
55 CTASC, PCDA fonds, 2009–022/001 (9), *A Verdade*: "Reafirmação," 7 (April 1965): 15, and (May 1965): 7–8.
56 For reasons apparently related to Cerqueira's conspiracy theories surrounding Delgado's death, four people were expelled from the PCDA after clashing with other members. Two of them (Mavílio Mendes and José Vale) had come from Morocco, where they met Cerqueira; another claimed to know of a PIDE infiltrator in the PCDA, but failed to provide evidence; and another got into a minor scuffle with Guilherme Santos. The latter was also the target of defamatory letters circulated in the community (CTASC, PCDA fonds, 2009–022/003 (8 & 14) ... 005 (7), PCDA's communiqué, 28 May 1965; Luis Vasconcelos, open letter (Scarborough), [?] 1965; F0579).
57 CTASC, PCDA fonds, 2009–022/001 (9 & 10) ... /003 (7 & 8), *A Verdade*: "Acções a Favor da Libertação do General Humberto Delgado," 7 (April 1965): 10, 15; "O Representante da FPLN no Canadá," 9 (June 1965): 14; "Uma Intrusão Condenável," 10 (July 1965): 3–4; Guilherme Santos, "Os Pigmeus da Oposição Portuguesa," 12 (December 1965): 15–17; and correspondence, G. Santos and Piteira Santos, 28 May–20 November 1965 (my translation).

58 CTASC, PCDA fonds, 2009–022/002 (10), ... /003 (8), ... /004 (17), correspondence, Guilherme Santos to FPLN-JRN, 31 July–16 December 1965; Piteira Santos to PCDA, 11 March and 9 May 1966; and Neves Rodrigues to PCDA, 18 July 1966.

59 Two decades later, Joaquim Alves (Santos's vice-president) recalled that Santos was expelled after being found to be a "PIDE agent." I found no evidence corroborating Alves's statement. However, it is clear there were other reasons for his "removal" besides the reported minor disagreement over by-laws, which the new executive was careful not to mention in their correspondence, other than saying that details were best discussed in person ("Origens da Portuguese Can. Democratic Association," *Aliança Community Newspaper*, 30 April 1988; CTASC, PCDA fonds, 2009–022/004 (9), letter, Júlio Félix to Bello, 8 August 1966).

60 TTNA, PIDE/DGS, Guilherme Antunes Santos, Registo Geral de Presos, liv. 141, 28053, PIDE/E/010/141/28053, personal file. CTASC, PCDA fonds, 2009–022/004 (31), letter, PCDA to FPLN, 17 November 1968; ... 002(10), letter, Piteira Santos to PCDA, 11 March 1966.

61 Luce, "Confronting the *Estado Novo*."

62 HDA, PEA M533, telegram, Ambassador Brazão to PMFA, 25 October 1966; LAC, RG25-A-3-c, Vol. 9345, file 20-PRTGAL-16-8, correspondence between the Secretary of State for External Affairs, Ottawa, and the Canadian embassy in Lisbon, December 1966–May 1967.

63 CTASC, PCDA fonds, 2009–022/001 (12), editorial, *A Verdade* 15 (8 August 1966), 1–5 (my translation).

64 CTASC, PCDA fonds, 2009–022/002 (10), ... /004 (9, 10, 19), ... /005 (2), correspondence, George Kimball to prospective sponsors, 5 May 1966; PCDA to FPLN, 7 May 1966; Silas Cerqueira to PCDA, 25 August 1966; Júlio Félix to Comissão de Apoio à FPLN c/o Port. Democrático (São Paulo), 7 October 1966; Águas to PCDA, 17 October 1966; Eduardo Covas to PCDA, 14 November 1966. CD25A-CPDP, correspondence, Águas to Covas, 16 February and 27 March 1962; and Águas to Bello, 13 June 1962.

65 CTASC, PCDA fonds, 2009–022/001 (12), *A Verdade* 14 (June–July 1966), and 16 (October–November 1966): 6–8.

66 The four prisoners selected for amnesty were José Bernardino, Sofia Ferreira, Captain Varela Gomes, and Manuel Serra (the last two involved in the Beja assault). The labour leader José Vitoriano, incarcerated for sixteen years with an expired sentence, was on the conference organizers' original list before being released in August 1966.

67 CTASC, PCDA fonds, 2009–022/004 (3 & 7), conference proceedings, 28–30 October 1966; CCAP Newsletter, 29 November 1966. HDA, PEA M533, letter, Andrew Brewin and David MacDonald to Ambassador Brazão, Ottawa, 31 October 1966; telegrams, Ambassador Brazão to

PMFA, 2 November, and Consul Pedro Pinto, Montreal, to PMFA, 24 November 1966.
68 HDA, PEA M533, correspondence, Ambassador Brazão to PMFA, 25–31 October and 17 November 1966; António Vaz to Prime Minister Pearson, 13 November 1966. TTNA, PIDE/DGS, SC, CL (2) 6747, nt. 7459, Andrew Brewin and David MacDonald files.
69 CTASC, PCDA fonds, 2009–022/004 (4) & ... /005 (13), fundraising records, 1966, 1973; letter, Manuel Oliveira (Griffith) to PCDA, 13 October 1966 (my translation; I tried to replicate the grammar mistakes in the original Portuguese version).
70 TTNA, PIDE/DGS, [MDP] n. 34. SC, CI (2), pr. 4779, u.i. 7370, "Uma Nova Fase na Vida do Movimento Democrático Português," *Luso-Canadiano*, 15 September 1967.
71 TTNA, PIDE/DGS, [PCDA], SC, CI (2), pr. 1913, u.i. 7685, transcript of *Rádio Voz da Liberdade* broadcast, 17 November 1968; [Rui Cunha Viana], n. 13, SC, CL (2), pr. 3419, u.i. 7264, "O [MDP] sugere reunião magna da oposição," *Portugal Democrático*, 13 December.
72 CTASC, PCDA fonds, 2009–022/003 (2), letter, Bello to Minister Fairclough, 1 November 1961.
73 Pereira, *A Ditadura*, 365–418.
74 The PIDE's archival collection at the Portuguese national archives has significant gaps, especially its correspondence with foreign intelligence agencies, which were reportedly destroyed on 25 April 1974 as the revolutionaries advanced on its headquarters (see ibid., 372).
75 Irene Pimentel, *A História da PIDE* (Lisbon: Circulo de Leitores, 2007), 103, 105, 325.
76 Reg Whitaker, *Double Standard: The Secret History of Canadian Immigration* (Toronto: Lester & Orpen Dennys, 1987), 48.
77 Reg Whitaker, Gregory Kealey, and Andrew Parnaby, *Secret Service: Political Policing in Canada: From the Fenians to Fortress America* (Toronto: University of Toronto Press, 2012), 532.
78 HDA, PEA M314, correspondence, Foreign Affairs Minister Paulo Cunha, PIDE Director Agostinho Lourenço, and Canadian consul in Lisbon, 21 May–8 August 1951; 2P A52 M67, letter, PMFA to Lourenço, 19 February 1953.
79 Donald Avery, *"Dangerous Foreigners": European Immigrant Workers and Labour Radicalism in Canada, 1896–1932* (Toronto: McClelland & Stewart, 1979).
80 CTASC, PCDA fonds, 2009–022/003 (1 & 5) & ... /004 (?), correspondence, Casa dos Portugueses's Alberto Araújo to PCDA, 26 December 1961; Firmino Oliveira and Citizenship and Immigration Minister Richard Bell, 12 September and 7 November 1962; Oliveira to

William Miller (Montreal), 9 October 1963; and Piteira Santos (Algiers) to PCDA, 13 May and 25 October 1969.
81 TTNA, PIDE/DGS, Serviços Canadianos – José Luis da Ponte Rebelo, SC, SR pr. 1056/48, ui. 2628, memo, Portuguese consulate, Montreal, 9 November 1961. CTASC, PCDA fonds, 2009–022/003 (2) correspondence, Ciriaco Cunha to Minister Fairclough, 21 October 1961; Bello to Cunha, 27 October 1961; Humberto Correia (Quebec) to Cunha, 31 October 1961.
82 LAC, RG76, Vol. 690, f568-3-23, pt. 3, clipping, A.S. Murray, "Political Refugees," *Globe and Mail*, 25 May 1967; memo to minister, Tom Kent, Deputy Minister of Immigration, Ottawa, 25 May 1967.
83 "Told to Return, Immigrant Jumps to Death," *Globe and Mail*, 15 December 1967, 2; TTNA, PIDE/DGS, [MDP] SC, CI (2), pr. 4779, u.i. 7370, *Portugal Democrático*, February 1968, 126. CTASC, PCDA fonds, 2009–022/004 (17), letter from "The Portuguese organizations of Montreal" to Minister Jean Marchand, 14 December 1967.
84 In his memoir, Monteiro referred to "Minister of Immigration Nicholson," although John Nicholson no longer occupied that office in 1967 (Monteiro, *Um Passado Recente*, 31–2).
85 CTASC, PCDA fonds, 2009–022/005 (4), "Manifest of the Antifascist Portuguese Emigrants and Exiles in Canada," distributed to the crew of the *Gago Coutinho* frigate, 27 July 1970 (my translation).
86 Eduardo M. Dias, "Palma Inácio, revolucionário e aventureiro," *Portuguese Times*, 11 June 2008; "Foi Preso em Conn. Um Conspirador Contra Salazar," *Diário de Notícias*, 25 March 1954, 1–2; TTNA, PIDE/DGS, [CPDP] SC, CI (2), pr. 3926, u.i. 7307, letter, Águas to Galvão, 9 March 1965.
87 HDA, PEA M549, correspondence, PIDE Director Homero Matos, Consul Silva Martins, Consul Manuel Carvalho (Providence), Consul C. Carvalho (Boston), Portuguese consul in São Paulo, and PMFA, 19 June 1961 to 3 March 1962.
88 TTNA, PIDE/DGS, [PCDA] SC, CI (2), pr. 1913, u.i. 7685; [MDP] pr. 4779, u.i. 7370.
89 *Toronto Daily Star*: "Bay St. Riot Claim: 'I Recognized Salazar Gestapo,'" 31 January 1961, 9; "Claimed Outsiders Aided Portuguese Bay St. Riot," 1 February 1961, 23; "Charges Portuguese Secret Police Here," 21 November 1961. LAC, RG6-F-2, b128, f3260-P2-190/P136, Foreign Language Press Review Service, DCI, report on the 11 November 1963 issue of *Luso-Canadiano*.
90 LAC, RG25-A-3-c, Vol. 11081, f20-18-1-14, various correspondence from and to the Secretary of State for External Affairs, 6 July to 15 September 1970; CTASC, PCDA fonds, 2009–022/005 (4) correspondence, PCDA's José Henriques to FPLN (Algiers), 24 August and 21 September 1970.

91 Pereira, *A Ditadura*, 378, 411.
92 TTNA, PIDE/DGS, Andrew Brewin and David MacDonald, SC, CL (2) 6747, nt. 7459, memo, PIDE's Orlando Pinto, 18 January 1967.
93 TTNA, PIDE/DGS, Gil Stone, SR. 551/ 45 np. 2465, correspondence, Gil Stone to PIDE's Álvaro Carvalho, 22 August 1963 to 29 December 1967; Stone to Henrique Medina (Lisbon), 15 August 1963; PIDE's Director Silva Pais to PMFA's Chargé d'Affaires, 24 October 1963. HDA, PEA M552, letter, SNI's Ramiro Valadão to PMFA's Chargé d'Affaires, 7 August 1964; and telegrams, Ambassador Vasco Garin to PMFA, 8 October and 10 December 1964.
94 HDA, PEA M554, letter, George Peabody to SNI's César Baptista, 28 March 1963.
95 Lopes, *Peregrinação*, 86 (my translation).
96 TTNA, PIDE/DGS, [Xavier], SC, SR pr. 1759/73, ui. 4084, letter, Consul José Jacinto, Madrid, to PIDE's Director Silva Pais, 4 November 1967; various documents, November–December 1967. HDA, PEA M549, correspondence, [Xavier] to Consul José Silva, 26 November 1967; and Ambassador Brazão to PMFA, 19 December 1967.
97 Whitaker, Kealey, and Parnaby, *Secret Service*.
98 TTNA, PIDE/DGS, [CPDP] SC, CI (2), pr. 3926, u.i. 7307, correspondence, PMFA to PIDE's Director Homero Matos, 8 November 1961; FBI reports, 1 and 27 November 1961 and 19 June 1964; [PCDA] SC, CI (2), pr. 1913, u.i. 7685, letter RCMP's William Higgitt to PIDE's Agostinho Cardoso, 21 September 1967.
99 LAC, RG25-A-3-c, Vol. 11081, f20-18-1-14, internal memos from the Secretary of State for External Affairs, Ottawa, 1 and 21 February 1968.
100 Galvão initially signed as "Cynthia Frocks," under which Águas set up a post office box in Segregansett, Massachusetts. In 1963, he changed the name to "Kathleen Smith," after the PIDE confiscated the address book of one of his Lisbon contacts (CD25A-CPDP, correspondence, Abílio Águas to Henrique Galvão, 24 March 1964; Águas to Covas, 28 March 1964).
101 In April 1963, a DDS leader was arrested shortly after meeting with a CPDP member in Lisbon carrying a message from Águas. I found no evidence linking the two events (CD25A-CPDP, letter, Águas to Galvão, 22 March and 1 May 1963; and Águas to Covas, 24 May1963. TTNA, PIDE/DGS, [Eduardo Covas] SC CI (2) 3972, nt. 7309, FBI reports, 30 March 1964; and PIDE's António Ribeiro's notes, 29 July 1964 and 24 November 1965).
102 TTNA, PIDE/DGS, [MDP] SC, CI (2), pr. 4779, u.i. 7370, letter, Bello to *República*'s Carvalhão Duarte (Lisbon), 16 February 1967; transcript of *Rádio Voz de Portugal* broadcast, 16 July 1967. CTASC, PCDA fonds, 2009–022/003 (1 & 5) correspondence, Ciriaco Cunha to João Neves, 12 March 1960, and to Montreal's Casa dos Portugueses, 23 January 1962.

103 TTNA, PIDE/DGS, [CPDP] SC, CI (2), pr. 3926, u.i. 7307, correspondence, Abílio Águas to DDS' Moreira Campos, 27 March–14 October 1965; [Eduardo Covas] SC CI (2) 3972, nt. 7309, correspondence, PIDE's Director Silva Pais and his agents, June 1963 to July 1968. CD25A-CPDP, letter, Águas to Covas, 11 November 1962.
104 RG6-F-2, b128, f3260-P2-190/P136, DCI report by C.L. Grant to G.P. Allen, 14 December 1959.
105 CD25A-CPDP, correspondence, António Almeida to US State Department, 16 May 1960; Abílio Águas to Eduardo Covas, 11 November 1962. TTNA, PIDE/DGS, [Eduardo Covas] SC, CI (2) 3972, nt. 7309, letter, US Embassy in Paris's Norman Philcox PIDE's Director Silva Pais, 4 March 1964; [CPDP] SC, CI (2), pr. 3926, u.i. 7307, letter, Águas to Galvão, 26 November 1964 and 9 March 1965.
106 TTNA, PIDE/DGS, [Abilio Águas] SC, CI (2), 478 np. 7012, correspondence, Covas, Águas, Moreira Campos, and the US Department of Justice, 7 January to 16 June 1965.
107 Cornwell, "Ethnic Group Representation"; Bloemraad, *Becoming a Citizen*; Gilberto Fernandes, "Beyond the 'Politics of Toil': Collective Mobilization and Individual Activism in Toronto's Portuguese Community, 1950s–1990s," *Urban History Review* 39, no. 1 (2010): 59–72.
108 Patrias, *Patriots and Proletarians*, 232.
109 Donna Gabaccia, "Class, Exile, and Nationalism at Home and Abroad: The Italian Risorgimento," in Gabaccia and Ottanelli, *Italian Workers*, 23.
110 Pereira, *A Ditadura*, 385.
111 Harold Troper and Morton Weinfeld, *Old Wounds: Jews, Ukrainians, and the Hunt for Nazi War Criminals in Canada* (Toronto: Viking, 1988), 107.

7 New Beginnings, Old Journeys

1 "Eu Vim de Longe ..." (1982) is one of Branco's most famous songs. Its lyrics express the initial jubilation, followed by disappointment and sense of betrayal felt by Branco and other communists after the 1974 revolution and the ensuing transition to a social-democratic/liberal political order in Portugal.
2 Wenona Giles, *Portuguese Women in Toronto: Gender, Immigration, and Nationalism* (Toronto: University of Toronto Press, 2002); Bloemraad, *Becoming a Citizen*.
3 David Colburn and George Pozzetta, "Race, Ethnicity, and the Evolution of Political Legitimacy," in *Sixties: From Memory to History*, ed. David Farber (Chapel Hill: University of North Carolina Press, 1994), 140.
4 John Skrentny, *Minority Rights Revolution* (Cambridge, MA: Belknap Press, 2002), 277.

5 "Exploring the Cultural Pleasures of Newark," in *New York Times*, 26 March 1982.
6 Kay Anderson, *Vancouver's Chinatown: Racial Discourse in Canada, 1875–1980* (Montreal and Kingston: McGill-Queen's University Press, 1995).
7 Lopes, *Peregrinação*, 51; Gilbert, *Recent Portuguese*, 51, 71; Maria Sá Pereira, *A Posição Socioeconómica dos Imigrantes Portugueses e seus Descendentes nos Estados de Massachusetts e Rhode Island (USA)* (Lisbon: Secretaria de Estado da Emigração, 1985), 34.
8 Grace Anderson, *Networks of Contact: The Portuguese and Toronto* (Waterloo, ON: Wilfrid Laurier University Press, 1974); Pap, *The Portuguese Americans*; Noivo, *Inside Ethnic*; Giles, *Portuguese Women*; Miranda, "Not Ashamed."
9 See City Builders website for more, https://toronto-city-builders.org
10 In the 1980s, Sá Pereira found that Portuguese newcomers who landed in Massachusetts and Rhode Island after 1970 with more higher education and English-speaking skills earned less income than lower-educated non-anglophone labourers. Similar observations were made about Portuguese immigrants in Canada. In 1964, Edith Ferguson found that the average length of schooling among Portuguese immigrants in Toronto was 3.7 years for men and 2.8 years for women. Meanwhile, the proportion of Portuguese workers earning CA$10,000 or more (66.6 per cent) was higher than other immigrant groups with similar or higher educational levels who arrived in 1967–77. While Toronto provided greater opportunities for educational and occupational advancement than Fall River and New Bedford, the academic achievements of young Portuguese males has remained one of the lowest in that Canadian city. A possible explanation for this is Toronto's booming construction industry, driven by the city's ever-expanding downtown and suburban residential development (Edith Ferguson, *Newcomers in Transition* [Toronto: International Institute of Metropolitan Toronto, 1964]; Sá Pereira, *A Posição*, 55, 59–61; Gilbert, *Recent Portuguese*, 49, 120–1; Miranda, "Not Ashamed," 96).
11 Nunes, "Portuguese-Canadian Youth"; Gilbert, *Recent Portuguese*, 122–37; and Sá and Borges, "Context or Culture?"
12 Sections 901 & 902, Title IX, Ethnic Heritage Program, Elementary and Secondary Education Act, May 1972.
13 Jacobson, *Roots Too*, 54; Skrentny, *Minority Rights*, 276–7, 304.
14 Joaquim Eusébio, *Falando Português em Montreal: Escola Santa Cruz e Escola Secundária Lusitana Passado, Presente e Futuro* (Montreal: Escola Santa Cruz e Escola Secundária Lusitana, 2001), 20, 22.
15 Nigosian, "The Portuguese"; letter, Débora Raposo, 5 December 1970.
16 "Cartas ao Director," *Correio Português*, 15 August 1971; "Escola Oficial dos First Portuguese Canadian Club," *Comunidade*, 3 March 1976; Ferreira, *Escola do "First"*; Eusébio, *Falando Português*, 35–6, 58, 114–23.

17 In the first trimester of 1974, there were 375 Portuguese classes in France and 78 in Germany for students between the ages of six and twelve (Pereira, *A Ditadura*, 335).
18 HDA, M969, letter, WGCY Radio's António Costa to Consul Jorge Freitas, Boston, 30 January 1971.
19 "Português na Harbord", *Comunidade*, 11 July 1975 (my translation).
20 Coelho, *Small Stories*, 65–6, 95–6, 146–7.
21 Marujo, Teixeira, and Marques, *Portuguese Canadian Press*.
22 In December 1964, the Lisbon government approved funding for a newspaper called *Correio de Portugal*, with the subtitle *The Newspaper of the Portuguese Communities in the World*. It is not clear if this newspaper was ever published (TTNA, AOS/CO, Correspondência ... "Correio de Portugal," PC-57, Pt 33).
23 TTNA, Censura cx. 403 & 738, SNI-DSC/ 9/ 2004, correspondence, January 1970 to July 1973; Henrique Medeiros, "Carta dos Estados Unidos 3. A Naturalização é uma Necessidade," *O Emigrante*, 31 January 1973 (my translation).
24 Henrique Medeiros, "Que Nos deram em Troca?" *O Emigrante*, 3 May 1973 (my translation).
25 HDA, PEA M405, letter, Committee Feast of the Blessed Sacrament's President David Correia to Ambassador João Hall Themido, 4 April 1973.
26 HDA, M45, PCU Annual Report 1971.
27 "Êxito sem precedentes do Rancho da Casa do Povo de Maiorca nos E. Unidos," *Diário de Notícias*, 18 August 1971, 1.
28 HDA, PEA M333, flyer, 1969; Eurico Mendes, "So long, Natércia," *Portuguese Times*, 21 October 2009. Avelino Teixeira, "Dina Maria," *Milénio Stadium*, 27 April 2012.
29 Coelho, *Small Stories*, 300–1.
30 HDA, PEA M656, flyers and clippings, June–July 1970; PEA M761, letter, Consul Luis Silva, Montreal, to PMFA, 23 October 1970; LAC, RG25-A-3-c, Vol. 11081, f20-18-1-14, Portuguese Canadian Ethnic Press Analysis, June 1973.
31 "Diplomat in Newark. Portuguese Official Visits," *Sunday Star-Ledger*, 15 November 1970; *Correio Português*, 30 April 1971.
32 *Correio Português*: "Mesa Redonda ...," "O Ministro Allan Grossman ... de visita a Lisboa," and "Cartas ao Director," 15 August 1971; HDA, M45, letter, TAP delegate Mário Félix to Consul Mário Freitas, New York, 5 December 1971; CTASC, David Higgs fonds, 2010–018/002, David Higgs's research notes; Pereira, *A Ditadura*, 88–91.
33 TTNA, PIDE/DGS, [PCDA] SC, CI (2), pr. 1913, u.i. 7685, MDP's communiqué, 5 October 1971. CTASC, PCDA fonds, 2009–022/005 (3), PCDA's 1970 annual report.

34 CTASC, PCDA fonds, 2009–022/005 (4), MDP's communiqué, 20 December 1970.
35 On 22–4 October 1971, Spanish exiles in Toronto organized their own pro-amnesty conference, which had many of the same sponsors as the PCDA's 1966 conference, including Rev. Kimball, Andrew Brewin, David MacDonald, Pierre Berton, and others (CTASC, PCDA fonds, 2009–022/005 [4 & 8], correspondence, PCDA's Secretary Tony Godinho to ?, 5 February 1970; flyer, Conference for Amnesty in Spain).
36 Besides being an influential Marxist thinker, arrested many times by Brazil's dictatorship, Fernandes was also the main critic of Freyre's lusotropicalist thesis (CTASC, PCDA fonds, 2009–022/004 (14), correspondence, *Portugal Democrático* (São Paulo) to PCDA, 22 September 1969; and PCDA's Tony Godinho to Florestan Fernandes, 3 November 1969).
37 CTASC, PCDA fonds, 2009–022/005 (4), letter, Rui Viana to PCDA, 10 September 1970.
38 TTNA, PIDE/DGS, [PCDA], SC, CI (2), pr. 1913, u.i. 7685, letter, PMFA's Caldeira Coelho to PIDE's Director Silva Pais, 15 November 1972; CTASC, PCDA fonds, 2009–022/001 (10 & 13), "Eleições Gerais no Canadá," *A Verdade* 11 (October 1965): 16; José Henriques, "Ainda a Semana Portuguesa" *O Boletim* 9–10 (June–July 1971): 3–4; and "Ainda as Eleições," *O Boletim* 12 (September 1971): 12, 14.
39 Lopes, *Peregrinação*, 87–8, 103–5, 183.
40 PCDA's 1970 annual report.
41 CTASC, PCDA fonds, 2009–022/001 (9), "Uma Ideia em Marcha," *A Verdade*, 5 (January 1965): 11; David Higgs fonds, 2010–018/004 (5), Jaime Monteiro, "A PCDA Afunda-se Por Culpa de Quem?" *Luso-Canadiano*, 15 February 1971.
42 Lopes, *Peregrinação*, 87; Moura and Soares, *Pionniers*, 146.
43 CTASC, PCDA fonds, 2009–022/004 (17), letter, MDP's Rui Viana and Amadeu Moura to PCDA, 21 July 1969 (my translation); LAC, RG6-F-2, b128, f3260-P2-190/P136, Foreign Language Press Review Service, DCI, report on the *Luso-Canadiano* issue of 17 February 1967.
44 Pereira, "Os Exiliados," 139.
45 "Portuguese Opposition Abroad," *The Torch*, 19 October 1973, 6; FMS, Mário Soares Archive, 00034.001.018, Mário Soares's statement at New York's Overseas Press Club, 1 April 1970.2
46 "Priest Says Portuguese Crush Africans Like Animals," *Toronto Star*, 26 June 1971.
47 HDA, Relações Bilaterais ... Estados Unidos, telegrams, Portuguese UN delegate Vaz Pinto to PMFA, 9 June 1970; Portuguese embassy's Cabrita Matias to PMFA, 30–1 August 1970; "Police Find New Bomb near Portuguese Embassy,"*Washington Post*, 31 August 1970.

48 HDA, PEA M761, telegram, Consul Mello Gouveia, Toronto, to PMFA, 9 April 1973; telegrams, Ambassador Hall Themido to PMFA, 27 September and 2 November 1973.
49 LAC, RG6-F-2, b127, f3260-P2-2, letter, St Christopher House's Older Adult Centre to unknown recipient, New Horizons program, Ottawa, 23 July 1973.
50 Domingos Marques interview, 16 April 2011, in PCHP online exhibit, *Comunidade Newspaper, 1975–1979*, http://archives.library.yorku.ca/exhibits/show/pchp.
51 "Introduction to the Polyglot," *Comunidade*, 31 August 1979, 3.
52 For a comprehensive history of the *Comunidade* and the MCP, see the PCHP's online exhibit *Comunidade Newspaper, 1975–1979*.
53 Marcie Ponte interviewed by the author for the RTPi show *Hora dos Portugueses* on 31 March 2017.
54 In 1994, the CPRPS changed its name to Centre d'action socio-communautaire de Montréal.
55 Lopes, *Peregrinação*, 73–4; CTASC, Domingos Marques fonds, 2010–019/001, transcript of interview with CPRPS staff, 1978 (?); HDA, PEA M761, telegram, Ambassador Sampayo Garrido to PMFA, 5 July 1973.
56 Radio Centre-Ville website: http://radiocentreville.com/wp/en/information/the-mandate/.
57 "Conference Seeks Recognition of Portuguese Minority Status," *Harvard Crimson*, 4 June 1973; HDA, PEA M253, letter, Vice-Consul Carlos Nunes, Boston, to Ambassador Hall Themido, 30 April 1973; Portuguese National Convention's program, June 1–3; report for Ambassador Themido (author unknown), June 1973; Portuguese National Convention steering committee's communiqué, 10 June 1973; António Cirurgião, "A Propósito do Primeiro Congresso Português na América," *Portuguese Times*, 28 June 1973 (my translation).
58 Landry, "A Heritage of Oppression."
59 HDA, PEA M253, Portuguese National Convention's circular, 3 March 1973; letter, Consul Jorge Freitas, Boston, to Chargé d'Affaires António Matias, Washington, 9 August 1973; Moniz, "The Shadow Minority," 410.
60 Skrentny, *Minority Rights*, 90, 304.
61 HDA, PEA M253, 73C24, Portuguese National Convention resolutions; "City Suggested for Next Parley. Portuguese Seek Minority Benefits," *Standard-Times*, 4 June 1973; HDA, PEA M253, 73C23, " Portuguese Demand Status of Recognized Minority," *Cape Verdean*, June–July 1973, 12.
62 HDA, PEA M253, M253, 73C23, 3, 20, "Acting Governor of Rhode Island Proclaims Cape Verdean Week upon Inauguration of Headquarters for Cape Verdean-American Federation," *Portuguese Times*, 19 July 1973.

63 "A Spiritual Journey," *South Coast Today*, 13 February 2001; "The Cape Verdeans and the PAIGC Struggle for National Liberation: An Interview with Salahudin Omowale Matteos," *Ufahamu* 3 (Winter 1973): 43–8.
64 Sheila Ackerlind, ed., *Internationalism and the Three Portugals: The Memoirs of Francis Millet Rogers* (New York: Lind, 1992); Moniz, "The Shadow Minority," 410, 422–3
65 HDA, PEA M253, 73C24, "A convenção," *Luso-Americano*, and "Os que teimam na desunião," *Portuguese Times*, 7 June 1973; "Convenção da United Portuguese Community," and "Harvard – Congresso dos Portugueses na América," *Portuguese Times*, 14 June 1973 (my translation).
66 CTASC, David Higgs fonds, 2010–018/002, CPRPS flyer, 1974 (my translation); Domingos Marques fonds, 2010–019/001, transcript of interview with CPRPS staff, (?) 1978; CPRPS report 1975–6, (my translation).
67 *Harvard Crimson*: Peter Landry, "Cambridge's Forgotten Minority," and "A Heritage of Oppression," 22 March 1974.
68 CTASC, PCDA fonds, 2009–022/006 (4), "O que foi o Dia de Portugal," *Informações*, 22 June 1974 (my translation).
69 Invitations, Consul Mário Freitas, March 1974; "City's Portuguese – A New Pride," *New York Post*, 11 June 1974.
70 HDA, M45, photo contact sheet.
71 Monteiro, *Um Passado Recente*, 39–41.
72 Eurico Mendes, "Rosa Casaco," *Portuguese Times*, 23 April 2008.
73 "Mário Soares – Regresso a Lisboa," *Diário de Notícias* (Lisbon), (?) 1974; LAC, RG25-A-3-c, Vol. 11081, f20-18-1-14, Ethnic Press Analysis, July 1974.
74 "Hero of Portuguese Coup Says Democracy Thriving at Home," *Toronto Star*, 24 September 1974.
75 LAC, RG25-A-3-c, Vol. 11081, f20-18-1-14, meeting notes (confidential), 24 September 1974.
76 CTASC, PCDA fonds, 2009–022/006 (2), ledger, minutes for 16 October 1974.
77 CTASC, PCDA fonds, 2009–022/006 (3, 4 & 6), PCDA's general assembly report, June 1974; letters to PCDA from Pinto & Sotto Mayer Bank's and Fonsecas & Burnay Bank's managers, Toronto, 3–4 October 1974; "Revolucionário Português," *Comunidade*, October 1975, 6.
78 "Exiled Former President Promises to Liberate Portugal," *Globe and Mail*, 24 November 1975; *Comunidade*, December 1975, 8.
79 "Representantes da F.S. em Toronto," *Comunidade*, 8 August 1975, 5.
80 CTASC, PCDA fonds, 2009–022/006 (4 & 7), letter, PCDA's Tony Godinho to *Portugal Hoje* (Lisbon), 27 May 1975; *News and Facts* bulletin; "Solidarity with Portugal," *Globe and Mail*, 24 May 1975, 12.
81 Lopes, *Peregrinação*, 89.

82 LAC, RG25-A-3-c, Vol. 11081, f20-18-1-14, Ethnic Press Analysis, *Mensageiro*, Vancouver, 28 June 1974; CTASC, PCDA fonds, 2009–022/006 (3–4), letter, Manuel Sanches (Bachstrab, Germany), 26 April 1974; Portuguese Democratic Action Congress of North America's communiqué, 21 May 1974.

83 "Immigrants Neglected, Need Help to Integrate, Portuguese Consul Says," *Globe and Mail*, 22 January 1975, 5; Ernesto Feu, communiqué, *Comunidade*, 8 August 1975, 5 (my translation).

84 CTASC, PCDA fonds, 2009-022/006 (2-4, 7), ledger, minutes for 1, 17 July and 14, 21 August 1974; letter, PCDA's Didimo Godinho to Minister Mário Soares (unknown date). LAC, RG25-A-3-c, Vol. 11081, f20-18-1-14, Ethnic Press Analysis, June 1974; confidential memo, E.P. Black, 11 June 1975.

85 Urbano Rodrigues, "Meu Canadá Português," *Diário de Notícias* (Lisbon), 16 October 1976; LAC, 3217-202-P2 pt 1, b20 & b127, Portuguese press report, June 1975.

86 António Bandeira, "As Eleições em Portugal," cited in *Comunidade*, 8 August 1975, 7.

87 LAC, Portuguese press report, January 1975.

88 "Entrevista com Joaquim Meirim," *Comunidade*, November–December 1977, 15; LAC, RG6-F-2, b127 f3260-P2-2 & b20 3217-202-P2 pt 1, Portuguese press reports October–November 1974 and December 1977; RG25-A-3-c, Vol. 11081, f20-18-1-14, Ethnic Press Analysis, 1974.

89 LAC, RG25-A-3-c, Vol. 11081, f20-18-1-14, confidential memo, E.P. Black, Bureau of European Affairs, 11 June 1975; CTASC, David Higgs's research notes; "Estranha Manifestação," *Comunidade*, September 1975, 1, 8.

90 A similar separatist movement existed in Madeira, led by the Frente de Libertação do Arquipélago da Madeira, or FLAMA. This movement had little expression in North America given the small size of its emigrant population.

91 Martim Maya and Cândido Forjaz, *Açores: Autonomia ou Indepêndencia?* (self-published, 1985); Duarte Figueiredo, "A Crise nos Açores. O que é a FLA?" *O Século Ilustrado*, 9 August 1975; "Comício de Solidariedade," *Comunidade*, November 1975, 8.

92 "Toronto's Portuguese Flock to Hear Rebel," *Globe and Mail*, 5 September 1975; William Hamilton, "Azores Freedom Spirit Builds in New Bedford," *Boston Globe*, 5 October 1975, 29–30; "Incidentes na sessão da F.A.I.A.," *Comunidade*, 11 July 1975, 1, 3; Tony Amaral, "Opinião," *Comunidade*, 8 August 1975, 7.

93 Fred Strasser and Brian McTigue, "The Fall River conspiracy ..., " *Boston Magazine*, November 1978, cited in José Ferreira, *História de Portugal*, Vol. 8: *Portugal em Transe* (Lisbon: Editorial Estampa, 1993), 185–7.

94 Joe Serge, "Angolans Must Quit Canada 'Might Go Underground,'" *Toronto Star*, 2 April 1976, A5.
95 *Comunidade*: "Pedido de Auxílio ao Canadá para Angolanos," 8 January 1976, 4; "Retornados de Angola," 25 March 1976, 1, 5; "Refugiados do Ex-Ultramar," 15 April 1976, 4; "Portuguese Refugee Aid Committee," 30 June 1976, 4; "Embondeiro. Associação dos Portuguese do Ex-Ultramar," 28 February 1978, 4.
96 Kimberly Holton, "Angola Dreaming: Memories of Africa among Portuguese Retornados in Newark, NJ," in *Community, Culture*, 501.
97 Raymond Almeida, "Chronological References: Cabo Verde/Cape Verdean American," UMASS, http://www.noeasyvictories.org/research/almeida1997.php; Pedro Cruz, "Ideologias Políticas: Direita e esquerda em Cabo Verde, de 1975 a 2010" (MA thesis, Universidade Técnica de Lisboa, 2012).
98 "Resultados eleitorais no estrangeiro," *Comunidade*, 10 June 1976, 8.
99 Briefing notes for Minister James Fleming.
100 Fernandes, "Beyond 'the Politics,'" 65.
101 LAC, RG6-F-2, b128, f3260-P2-190 p133, report, April 1976.
102 Miranda, "Not Ashamed."
103 "Local 183 tenta interessar os sócios portugueses," *Comunidade*, 31 January 1979, 1, 6–7. Jack Oliveira, Business Manager, LIUNA Local 183, interviewed by the author for the RTPi show *Hora dos Portugueses* on 13 June 2017.
104 Ann Bookman, "Unionization in an Electronics Factory: The Interplay of Gender, Ethnicity, and Class," in *Community, Culture*, 402; Miranda, "Not Ashamed," 324.
105 Bill Moniz, *The Shoeshine Boy*, documentary, 95 min. (Vista-Global Productions, 2006).
106 *Toronto Star*: "4,000 Mourn Slain Shoeshine Boy," 4 August 1977, A3; "Angry Crowd Seeks Revenge for Emanuel," 9 August 1977, B1. This episode has re-emerged in Toronto's public memory through Anthony De Sa's 2013 novel *Kicking the Sky*.
107 *Correio Português*: "FLA quer transformar Açores num 'Paraiso Fiscal,'" 30 January 1978, 7; "Organização Holandesa disposta a apoiar separatismo açoreano," 15 April 1978, 2. Ferreira, *História de Portugal*, 188.
108 Santos, *O Canadá*, 118–20.
109 *Comunidade*: "São as comunidades que devem tomar iniciativas ...," 31 March 1977, 13, and "Esclarecimento do Banco de Portugal para os Imigrantes," June 1977, 1. "Entrevista a João Lima," *Correio Português*, 28 February 1978, 5.
110 Helms-Park, "Two Decades," 131; Lopes, *Peregrinação*, 80.

111 "Education, Heritage Language and Multiculturalism," *Comunidade Newspaper, 1975–1979*, online exhibit, PCHP website, http://archives.library.yorku.ca/exhibits/show/pchp/comunidade_records/education_multiculturalism.
112 C.B. Paulston, "Educational Language Policies in Utopia," in *The Development of Second Language Proficiency*, ed. B. Harley et al. (Cambridge: Cambridge University Press), 187–97; Da Silva, "Sociolinguistic (Re)constructions," 118.
113 Interview with João Lima, *Comunidade*, 31 March 1977, 13 (my translation).
114 TAP advertisement, *Comunidade*, 31 March 1977, 6 (my translation).
115 *Comunidade*: "Desenvolvimento turístico nos Açores," 15 April 1976, 1; TAP advertisement, 5 May 1976, 5; "Centro de Turismo de Portugal no Canadá," September 1977, 8.
116 "A situação em Portugal vista por alguns de nós," *Comunidade*, September 1977, 4–9 (my translation).
117 Ibid.
118 Fr Fernando Couto, St Mary's Church, and Eduíno Martins, *Voz de Portugal* and Memória Funeral Home, interviewed by the author for the RTPi show *Hora dos Portugueses* on 21 April and 10 May 2016.
119 LAC, RG6-F-2, b127, f3260-P2-2, Portuguese press report, December 1974.
120 Colburn and Pozzetta, "Race, Ethnicity," 135.
121 Coelho, *Small Stories*, 225.
122 Interview with Marcie Ponte.
123 "10 de Junho – Dias das Comunidades," *25 de Abril* 18 (April/May 1977): 17.
124 A padrão is a tall stone post with the Portuguese coat of arms and a cross on top. Explorers placed these markers in the lands they "discovered" as a symbolic way of claiming them for the Portuguese crown, much like the modern-day flag planting. Today the padrão is one of the most recognizable symbols of Portugal's explorations, a recurrent element in national monuments, and a common marker of Portuguese presence in the world.
125 Another padrão was unveiled in Montreal in 1973 to mark the twentieth anniversary of Portuguese mass migration to Canada (Araújo, *25o Aniversário*, 173).
126 Briefing notes for Minister James Fleming; *Correio Português*, 1978: "O embaixador de Portugal em Toronto,"15 April; "Crónica da quinzena," 15 June.
127 Onésimo Almeida, "É pouco o que chega às comunidades," *Correio Português*, 30 March 1978, 3 (my translation).

128 Adriano Moreira interviewed by *O Diabo*, in *Correio Português*, 30 January 1978, 1 (my translation).
129 Marilyn Halter, "Diasporic Generations: Distinctions of Race, Nationality, and Identity in the Cape Verdean Community, Past and Present," in *Community, Culture*, 525–53.
130 Jacobson, *Roots Too*, 67, 147, 243–4 (emphasis original).
131 Skrentny, *Minority Rights*, 264–5.
132 bell hooks, *Black Looks: Race and Representation* (Boston: South End Press, 1992), cited in Jacobson, *Roots Too*, 373.
133 Giles, *Portuguese Women*, 96.

Conclusion

1 Tintori, "Italy," 138.
2 Edite Noivo, "Towards a Cartography," 271.
3 Ana Ramoz-Zayas, "Stereotypes of the Tropics in 'Portuguese Newark': Brazilian Women, Urban Erotics, and the Phantom of Blackness," in *Community, Culture*, 431–59.
4 José Itzigsohn, "The Formation of Latino and Latina Panethnic Identities," in Foner and Fredrickson, *Not Just Black and White*, 197.
5 Search made on 23 December 2017.
6 Interviews with Paulino Nunes, Tamara Duarte, and Jess Salgueiro produced by the author for the RTPi show *Hora dos Portugueses* on 17 March 2016, 22 June and 9 October 2017.
7 Disadvantage Business Enterprise, Federal Highway Administration, US Department of Transportation, 9 January 2010, in Internet Archives, https://web.archive.org/web/20100109165512/http://www.fhwa.gov/civilrights/faq.htm; Small Business Act, 8(a) Business Development Program: Definition of Socially and Economically Disadvantaged Individuals, http://www.sbda.com/sba_8%28a%29.htm (accessed 10 May 2019).
8 Jennette Barnes, "Court Rules in Portuguese Business Case, but Fight Isn't Over Yet," *South Coast Today*, 2 March 2018, https://www.southcoasttoday.com/news/20180302/court-rules-in-portuguese-business-case-but-fight-isnt-over (accessed 10 May 2019).
9 Irene M.F. Blayer and Dulce M. Scott, "The 'Diaspora,'" in Blayer and Scott, *Intersecting*, 18.
10 Table A.6 Remessas, 2000–2016, Observatório da Emigração, http://observatorioemigracao.pt/np4/paises.html?id=230; (accessed 1 January 2018).

Index

Page numbers in *italics* refer to images or figures.

A Bola (Lisbon), 161
A Luta (New York City), 120, 210
Acheson, Dean, 206
Açorianidade. *See* Azoreans: Azorean ethnicity
Acushnet, MA, 275
affirmative action, 17, 267, 286, 314, 322
Afonso, José "Zeca," 292
African Americans: anti-colonialism, 223; Black Panthers, 87, 205; Black Power, 18, 87, 287, 321, 322; Cape Verdeans (*see* Cape Verdeans); civil rights (*see* civil rights movement); conservatives, 211; cultural nationalism, 196, 222; Estado Novo, 187, 321; Portuguese Americans, 222–3, 286, 301; white supremacy, 314
African Asian bloc. *See* United Nations: anti-colonialism
African Party for the Independence of Guinea and Cape Verde. *See* Cape Verdeans: independence
Agência de Notícias e Informação, 207
Aginter Press, 299

Agnew, Vijay, 9
Águas, Abilio Oliveira: American officials, 231, 233, 256, 261–2, 264; Canada, 247, 249; Cape Verdeans, 203, 230, 232; colonialism, 203, 232, 264; community relations, 231–2, 234, 264; CPDP, 231–4, 249, 260–2, 291; Delgado, Humberto, 233; Dighton Rock, 230; FPLN, 232; Galvão, Henrique, 232–4, 260, 370n100; Inácio, Palma, 256; republican opposition, 230, 363n16; Soares, Mário, 234, 279, 291
Aguiar, Maria Manuela, 63–4, 348n38
Aica, José, 279
Algeria: Azores, 304; exiles, 122, 224, 229, 246–7, 249; United Nations, 234, 290
Aliança Liberal Portuguesa, 230
All-African People's Revolutionary Party, 287
Almeida, José de, 298–300
Almeida, Manuel, 90, 342n37
Almeida, Onésimo, 279, 287–8, 304, 310

Almeida, Raymond, 301
Alves, Vitor, *310*
ambassadors: Bianchi, João António, 121, 130, 169; Brazão, Eduardo (*see* Brazão, Eduardo); Fernandes, Luis (*see* Fernandes, Luis); Garin, Vasco V., 85–6, 173, 199, 357n40; Pereira, Pedro T. (*see* Pereira, Pedro Teotónio); Themido, João Hall, 87, 274, 285, 291; Veiga, Alfredo, 96–7, 103, 284 345n71
American Committee for Cape Verde, 301
American Communist Party, 113
American Portuguese Cultural Society (APCS), 176, 290
American Portuguese Loyalty Association, 130–1
Amnesty International, 246
Anderson, Benedict, 8
Anderson, George W., Jr, 176
Andrade, Celestino, 123
Andrade, Laurinda, 170
Angola: anti-colonialism, 93, 186–7; Canadian government response, 189; civil war, 58, 300; colonial government, 17, 228, 243, 332n33, 337n67; Colonial Wars, 17, 186, 187, 189, 212, 217; corporations, 210; immigrants, 323; lusophonie, 337n75; massacre, 186–7; missionaries, 93, 246, 281; Portuguese opposition, 228, 232, 237, 290, 362n11; Reagan, Ronald, 357n40; retornados, 57–8, 300; UPA, 186; US government response, 189, 203
APC. *See* Association portugaise du Canada
apostolic vicariate. *See* Catholic Church: apostolic vicariate

April 25th. *See* Revolution of the Carnations
"April in Portugal." *See* fado
Araujo, George, 161
Argentina, 27, 217, 337n67
Argue, Hazen, 241
Armed Forces Movement. *See* Revolution of the Carnations: Movimento das Forças Armadas
Armenian, 8, 341n27
Associação Democrática Portuguesa. *See* Portuguese Canadian Democratic Association
Association portugaise du Canada (APC): Estado Novo, 118–19, 242; football, 161; membership, 118–19; rivalries, 199, 241; school, 172; trade, 154
Auriol, Vincent, 247
Australia, 37, *37*, 192, 204, 217
auxiliary committees. *See* women: auxiliary committees
Azorean Committee, 75, 299
Azorean Liberation Front. *See* Frente de Libertação dos Açores
Azoreans: air flights, 153, 306; Azorean ethnicity, 62, 70, 299, 304, 319, 336n61; Azorean Refugee Acts, 53–4, 196; Capelinhos volcano, 53–4; Catholic churches, priests, and laymen, 91, 97, 99, 101, 167 (*see also* Medeiros, Humberto; Rocha, Manuel); civil society, 75, 116–19, 123, 125, 127–9, 177, 182, 272, 281, 283, 299, 346n9, 347n18; diaspora, 23, 51, 61–2, 67, 77, 275, 279, 299, 317; education, 170, 172, 174–5, 245, 271; exiles, 238, 244–5; imperial heritage, 183, 197; intelligentsia, 178, 279, 288, 304; islands, 12, 15, 28, 44, 88–9, 183, 275, 278, 298–9, 332n30;

Lajes Air Base (*see* Lajes Air Base); language, 146, 166–7, 174–5, 271, 350n6; marching bands, 164–5, 182; migration and settlement, 27–8, 38, 44–5, 47, 50–2, 53–6, 119, 272, 308; musicians, 69–70, 158, 275; nationality, 193, 198, 244–5; post-revolutionary period, 62, 66–7, 298–300, 304, 306; ranchos folclóricos, 144; religious celebrations, 103, 105, 319 (*see also* Festa do Divino Espírito Santo; Senhor Santo Cristo dos Milagres); remittances and charity, 41, *41*, 107–8; separatism, 7, 298–300, 304–5, 312, 321–2; unions, 113; workers, 28, 45, *45*, 47, 113, 115

Balsemão, Pinto, 62
banks, emigrant branches, 271, 276–7, 292, 297, 306
Bannon, Steve, 10
Baptista, António, 39
Baraka, Imamu A., 204–5
Barqueiro, Armando, 242
Barrett, James, 183, 222
Barroso, José M., 67
Basto, Alexandre P., 217
Belenenses, Os. *See* football: Belenenses
Belgium, 134, 229, 235, 337n67
Bello, Henrique Tavares: APC, 119; death, 252–3; *Luso-Canadiano*, 119, 241–3, *252*, 253; MDP, 236, 238; NDP, 241; PIDE, 253; *Santa Maria*, 242
Bender, Gerald, 185
Bermudans, 92, 103
Berton, Pierre, 249, *250*, 374n35
Bhabha, Homi, 9
Bianchi, João António. *See* ambassadors

Bishop, Mariano, 113
Black Panthers, 87, 205
Black Power movement. *See* African Americans: Black Power
Blessing of the Fleet, 104, 131
Bloemraad, Irene, 266–7, 315
Bodnar, John, 6, 224–5
Boland, Thomas (archbishop), 81–2
bootstraps narrative, 18–19, 65, 308–9, 313, 326
Boston: air flights, 160; Cape Verdeans, 287, 301; Catholic Church, 80, 87–9, 104; celebrations, 199–200, 211; consulate (*see* consulates: Boston); diaspora, 296; immigrants, 28, 267; mutual aid societies, 116, 134; political districts, 213, 296; radio and television, 88, 122; workers, 28, 302
Boston Magazine, 299
Botelho, David, 92
Bourassa, Robert, 275
Branco, Aníbal, 116, 131, 218–19
Branco, José Mário, 266, 371n1
Brazão, Eduardo: Canadian government, 250–1; Catholic priests, 94, 96, 100–1; Corte-Real, Gaspar, 198–9; ethnic press, 94, 242–3; exiles, 242–3, 259; patriotism, 213; SNI/SEIT, 147
Brazil: anti-colonialism, 186; clandestine emigration, 47, 50; cod, 48; diaspora, Portuguese, 217, 220, 337n67, 337n75; diplomats, 127, 279; economy, 170; education, 170, 175; emigrants, Brazilian, 66, 301, 323; Estado Novo, 186; exiles, Brazilian, 277, 374n36; exiles, Portuguese, 30, 179, 187, 224, 227–9, 230, 233–5, 237, 251, 256, 258, 260, 293, 311; Hispanidad,

218; immigrants, Portuguese, 25, 27, 30, 34, 37, 57, 78, 256, 342n37; language, 85, 170, 175; Latinxs, 324; lusophonie, 170, 175, 324, 325; lusotropicalism (*see* Freyre, Gilberto); missionaries, Brazilian, 97–8; missionaries, North American, 93, 196; music, 160; race, 185; remittances, 34

Brettell, Caroline, 61, 112, 124

Brewer, Basil, 206–7

Brewin, Andrew, 249–51, 257, 374n35

Bridgeport, CT, 55, 82, 202

Britain. *See* Great Britain

British Columbia, 50–1, 69, 151, 251, 283

bulk order migration. *See* Canada, federal Department of Citizenship and Immigration

Cabral, Amílcar, 202–3, 287

Cabral, Olga, 178

Cabral, Stephen, 101

Cabrilho, João Rodrigues. *See* imperial heritage: Cabrilho, João Rodrigues

Cacella, José, 210

Caetano, Marcello: anti-Caetano opposition, 140, 253; Carnations Revolution, 20, 189, 291; Colonial Wars, 20, 189; emigration, 43, 73, 306, 322; liberal wing, 62; Ministry of the Presidency, 85, 188; Portuguese Americans, 215; reforms, 13, 19, 148, 175, 189; right-wing opposition, 20

Caisse d'économie des Portugais, 123

California: Azorean separatism, 299; Cabrillo Day, 199, 201, 357n32; charity, 106–7; congressmen, 213; diaspora, Portuguese, 217; Estado Novo, 156, 201, 212, 217; exiles, 256; mutual aid societies, 116–17, 171, 345n76; Portugal Day, 136; Portuguese Americans, 80, 103, 173, 178, 212, 214–15, 217, 273, 285; Portuguese immigration, 28–9, 51, 55

Camacho, Alfredo, 92, 98

Camacho, Martin T., 211–14, 261

Cambridge, MA, 82, 114, 116, 197, 285–6, 288–9

Cambridge Organization of Portuguese-Americans (COPA), 285–6, 288–9

Camoesas, João, 230, 362n11

Canada, federal Department of Citizenship and Immigration (DCI): bulk order migration, 44–7, 56, 72, 91, 96, 283, 292; exiles, 235, 240–1, 243; Montreal, 100; Toronto, 271

Canada, federal government: Adjustment of Status Program, 51; arms sales, 186, 189, 260, 355n8; Department of External Affairs, 250; employment equity legislation, 267; Ethnic Press Analysis Service, 297; Immigration Appeal Board, 50–1; immigration legislation, 47, 50–1; ministries of immigration, 253, 255–6, 271; multiculturalism (*see* multiculturalism: Canadian government); RCMP (*see* Polícia Internacional e de Defesa do Estado: RCMP)

Canadian Broadcasting Corporation (CBC), 97, 99, 257

Canadian Committee for Amnesty in Portugal (CCAP), 249–51, 260

Canadian Pacific Air Lines, 153, 159

Capelinhos volcano, 53–4

Cape Verdean American
   Federation, 287
Cape Verdean Beneficent
   Association, 202–3
Cape Verdeans: affirmative action,
   286; Black Power, 205, 287, 321;
   Catholic Church, 190, 192, 204, 287;
   colonial state, 58, 190–1, 198, 230;
   diaspora, 311, 317, 321, 337n67;
   employment, 28, 191; identity,
   African, 58, 192, 201–5, 287–8, 232,
   286, 320–1; identity, Portuguese, 33,
   33, 183–4, 190–2, 202–5, 219, 232,
   286–8, 311, 320–1; independence,
   7, 202–3, 232, 287, 301, 311, 321;
   islands, 28, 332n33; Kriolu, 24,
   192, 202, 287, 301, 311–12, 320–1;
   leaders, 128, 202–5, 232, 287, 301,
   321; lusophonie, 190, 323, 337n75;
   media, 286–7, 301; migration and
   settlement, 28, 33, 58, 191, 230;
   secular organizations, 116–17, 161,
   192, 202–4, 232, 287, 320
Capote, José, 82, 210, 214
Cardoso, Agostinho Barbieri, 260
Cardozo, António, 203
Caritas, 12, 54, 80, 108, 331n27
Carlos, Roberto, 160
Carmona, Óscar, 11
Carneiro, Francisco Sá, 62–3, 65
Carvalho, Eduardo de, 25
Carvalho, Humberto, 129
Casa de Portugal: annual
   expenditures (1942–63), 207;
   anti-colonialism, 205, 279; ethnic
   media, 153–6, 207–8, 210, 242–3;
   popular culture, 147, 247; Portugal
   Day, 136, 139; post-revolution,
   294, 304; public relations, 178, 214;
   SNI/SEIT, 147, 156, 224; staff and
   operations, 207–8, 210; tourism
   and trade, 15, 147, 153–6

Casas do Povo, 11–12
Cassidy, James (bishop), 167
Catholic Centre d'Assistance aux
   Immigrants de Bon-Conseil, 90
Catholic Church: apostolic vicariate,
   84, 341n24; Brazilians (see Brazil:
   missionaries, Brazilian); Cape
   Verdeans (see Cape Verdeans:
   Catholic Church); charity and
   humanitarian relief, 12, 80, 87,
   103, 105–8, 110, 320, 331n27,
   332n28; Day of the Emigrant,
   78; ecumenical diaspora, 4,
   22–3, 62, 76–7, 79, 109–10, 216,
   319: education and schools, 13,
   84–6, 109, 151, 167–8, 172, 175,
   190, 271, 278; empire, 76, 78–9,
   85, 88, 96–7, 109–10, 190, 278, 319;
   Estado Novo, 12–13, 76–8,
   80–91, 94, 96–7, 100–1, 103, 108–9,
   214–16, 319, 345n84; Fátima (see
   Fátima); feasts and processions,
   96–7, 101–7, 110, 118, 158, 295, 319;
   French Canadians, 76, 81, 97–101,
   108–9, 278, 319; Higher Council
   for Emigration, 78; International
   Catholic Migration Commission,
   54; Irish, 76, 81, 84, 87–9, 102, 104,
   108–9, 167, 319, 340n20; Jocist
   movement, 82; laymen; 22–3, 54,
   78, 97–100, 103–5, 107–10, 319;
   national identity, 42, 88, 108, 110,
   132, 190, 192, 204; OCPM (see
   Portuguese Catholic Organization
   for Migrations); parishes, 54, 80–4,
   86, 92–4, 96–7, 100, 103–5, 109–10,
   118, 167–8, 205, 210, 271, 281, 284,
   295, 303, 319, 339n2; popes, 77–8,
   87; Portuguese Catholic Action,
   77, 82; prelates, American, 80–9,
   109, 167, 214; prelates, Canadian,
   93–4, 98–101, 109, 295; prelates,

386 Index

Portuguese, 75, 77–80, 96, 98, 101, 104, 108; priests, 5, 22, 75–6, 78–88, 90, 92–104, 108–10, 167, 210, 214–15, 230, 281, 284, 287, 295, 319, 362n12; progressives, 20, 43, 78, 86–9, 210, 214, 230, 247, 279, 362n12; Salazar, António (*see* Salazar, António); social doctrine and work, 11, 13, 42, 53, 78, 90–4, 97, 100, 107–8, 281, 284, 331n27, 332n28, 362n12; Vatican, 13, 42, 76–9, 81–3, 85–6, 96, 281, 331n27, 341n24, 339n6, 340n8
Catholic Pro-Aliis Club, 90
Catholic Welfare Conference, 53
CBC. *See* Canadian Broadcasting Corporation
CCAP. *See* Canadian Committee for Amnesty in Portugal
CDS. *See* Centro Democrata Social
censorship and propaganda: Cape Verdeans, 202; censorship, 13, 42, 149, 178, 209, 218, 241, 359n66; ethnic media, 93, 121, 207, 210, 273, 297, 241–3; Ferro, António, 147, 153, 181; imperial (*see* lusotropicalism); National Secretariat of Propaganda, 13, 178; opposition, 220, 241, 247, 261, 299; politics of the spirit, 147, 181; popular culture and ethnicity, 13, 23, 145–6, 149, 152, 161, 164, 180, 182; Portugal Day (*see* Portugal Day); public relations, 147, 153, 203, 206–7, 210, 212–16, 258, 360n81; religious (*see* Fátima); SNI/SEIT, 13, 35, 92, 94, 147, 297, 149, 152–3, 156–7, 159, 161, 171, 180, 202, 206–7, 209–10, 217, 242–3, 244, 258; trade and tourism, 153–4, 156–7, 159, 244
Central Intelligence Agency (CIA), 187, 254

Centre portugais de référence et promotion sociale (CPRPS), 284, 289, 375n54
Centro Democrata Social (CDS), 301, 1n84
Cerejeira, Manuel G. (cardinal), 77, 80, 85, 101, 104, 215
Cerqueira, Henrique, 229, 245–6, 366n56
Cerqueira, Silas, 247, 249
charity. *See* Catholic Church: charity and humanitarian relief
Chavez, César, 86–7
children and youth: activism, 87, 133, 284–5, 296; assimilation, 34, 166, 179, 202, 269, 308; black youth, 18, 201; businesses, 348n32; church, 105, 109, 140, 247, 281, 284; criminality, 90; education, 60, 66, 85, 92, 109, 148, 168–9, 171–2, 175, 192, 195–6, 269–70, 290, 305–6; ethnic traditions, 149, 309; football, 70, 162, 298; household economy, 29, 269; language, 145, 149, 166–7, 172, 179, 270–1, 306; memory, 154, 273, 308; migration and settlement, 42–3, 46, 53, 56, *56*, 74, 90, 169, 235, 271, 280, 313, 322; military draft, 17, 247, 316; Moçidade Portuguesa (*see* Moçidade Portuguesa); nationality, 39, 65; romance, 200; segregation, 192, 195–6; social and cultural programs, 90, 97, 100, 278, 281, 284, 304
CIA. *See* Central Intelligence Agency
Cília, Luis, 278
civil rights movement: activism, 89, 204, 266–7; Cape Verdeans, 204; Estado Novo, 199, 321; immigration, 55; legislation,

17–18, 199; Portuguese Americans, 184, 204, 267, 289, 322
cleaning workers, 114–15, 284, 290, 302
Clube Madeirense S.S. Sacramento, 105
Clube Republicano Português, 230
cod fishing. *See* White Fleet
Coelho, Pedro, 291–2
Coelho, Pedro Passos (prime minister), 70
Colburn, David, 267
Cold War: mentality, 51, 90, 199, 293, 299, 322; military, 15; propaganda, 341n21; superpowers, 5, 14–15; surveillance, 225, 259, 263
Collyer, Michael, 4
Colonial Wars: armed conflict and casualties, 17, 20, 187, 189, 273, 316; empire's end, 5, 20, 288; massacre, 186; opposition, 40, 189, 205, 227, 249; remittances, 40, 277; war resisters, 17, 40, 43, 73, 139, 229, 236, 255–6, 265, 277, 279
Committee Pro-Democracy in Portugal (CPDP): Brazil, 231–2; Canada, 247, 249, 279; community relations, 231–2, 234, 264; Delgado, Humberto, 233, 258; FPLN, 232, 234; Galvão, Henrique, 232–5, 258, 261; leaders (*see* Águas, Abílio Oliveira; Covas, Eduardo); membership, 139, 231–2, 261–2, 264; post-revolutionary period, 291; surveillance, 235, 256, 258, 260–2, 370n101
Communist Party of Canada, 277
Community of Portuguese Language Countries, 68, 337n75
Comunidade (Toronto), 281–4, *282*, 293, 297–8, 303, 306–7

Conceição, Natércia, 275
Congress of the Portuguese Communities, 133, 215, 217–20, 234
Connolly, James (bishop), 81
Conséil supérieur des Français de l'étranger, 63
construction industry: anti-fascists, 245; businesses, 129, 324–5; immigration, 45, 47, 114, 160; mainlanders, 115; unions, 115, 270, 302; workers, 45, 47, 114–15, 120, 160, 245, 269–70, 302, 372n10
consulates, Portuguese: Boston, 15, 87, 116, 205, 209, 218, 279; Fall River, 15; Montreal, 16, 45, 48, 50, 90–1, 98–100, 118–19, 151–2, 210, 238, 242–3, 255, 271, 284, 296; New Bedford, 15, 173, 206; New York City, 15, 132–3, 152, 169, 178, 202, 256, 260, 290; Newark, 15, 81, 138–9, 171, 205, 210; Paris, 80, 349n51; Providence, 15, 230; Toronto, 16, 91, 97, 134, 139–40, 172, 238–40, 243–5, 247, 250–1, *250*, 271, 276–7, 279, 294–5, 309; Vancouver, 16; Waterbury, 15, 133, 271
consuls: Carvalho, Eduardo de, 25; Feu, Ernesto, 295, 309; Figueirinhas, Fernando, 127; Fragoso, José, 152, 171, 210; Freitas, Jorge, 84, 206; Freitas, Mário, 290; Gomes, Vital, 90–1, 118–19; Marques, Fernando, 151, 242–3; Martins, Silva, 369; Nogueira, Artur, 98–9, 119, 152, 210, 236; Patrício, Augusto, 238–9, 243; Pinto, Pedro Corte-Real, 132–3, 136, 147, 348n49; Ritto, Jorge, 243–4; Veiga, Alexandre, 138; Vilela, Vasco, 173, 209

COPA. *See* Cambridge Organization of Portuguese-Americans
Correia, Joaquim, 230, 362–3n12
Correio Português (Toronto): advertisement, 162; circulation, 121; elites, 157; entertainment, 160; Estado Novo, 94, 96, 243, 297; post-revolutionary period, 296–8; publishers, 94, 96, 127; rivalries, 96, 243
Corte-Real brothers. *See* imperial heritage: Corte-Real brothers
Costa, António (prime minister), 71
Costa, António Alberto (entrepreneur), 272, 288
Costa, Fernando, Jr, 296–7
Costa, Fernando, Sr, 135–6, 140–1
Costa, Manuel, 204
Council of Portuguese Communities (CPC), 63–5, 217, 337n67, 348n38
Council of the Portuguese Diaspora, 71
Covas, Eduardo: CPDP, 139, 232, 260–2; exile, 231; Portugal Day, 139; surveillance, 260–1
CPC. *See* Council of Portuguese Communities
CPDP. *See* Committee Pro-Democracy in Portugal
CPLP. *See* Community of Portuguese Language Countries
CPRPS. *See* Centre portugais de référence et promotion sociale
crisis of national identity, 4, 316, 330n9
Cruz, Francisco X., 202
Cunha, Alberto: Azoreans, 96–7, 102–3; Canadian officials, 103, 140–1, 295; Estado Novo, 96–7, 297; leadership style, 96–7, 135, 141, 281, 343n54; newspaper (*see Jornal Português, O*); Nóbrega,

Ângelo, 95, 134–5; parish work, 94; Portugal Day, 139–40; post-revolutionary period, 291, 293, 295, 297; prelates, 96; rivalries, 96–7, 124, 134–5, 140–1, 241, 271, 291, 295, 343n54
Cunha, Fernando Ciriaco da, 235–9, *238*, 241, 243, 256–7, 259, 261
Cunhal, Álvaro, 57, 228–9
Cushing, Richard (archbishop), 80, 87

Day of Portugal. *See* Portugal Day
Day of the Emigrant. *See* Catholic Church
DCI. *See* Canada, federal Department of Citizenship and Immigration
DDS. *See* Directório Democrato-Social
Delabarre, Edmund, 230, 357n28
Delgado, Humberto: death, 229, 246, 249, 260, 366n56; early career, 226–7; external font, 226–9, 233, 236–7, 244–6, 256, 258; Galvão, Henrique, 227–8, 233; presidential campaign, 16, 226–7, 232; *Santa Maria*, 187, 227, 237, 239; supporters, 179, 227, 235–7, 243–5, 256, 258, 297
Democratic and Independent Cape Verdean Union, 301
Democratic Movement for the Liberation of Portugal, 293
Democratic Party, 84, 125, 231
Dennison, William, 140, 249
Diário de Notícias (New Bedford), 120; advertising, 154, *155*, 214, 273; Cape Verdeans, 205; censorship, 169, 208–9; circulation, 120–1, 242; democratic opposition, 121, 208–9, 230, 256; Estado Novo, 121, 154,

156, 169, 208–9, 214; language, 169, 177, 208; lusotropicalism, 193; PCU, 208; Portugal Day, 136; propaganda, 207, 213; publisher, 208–9; race, 193, 205; *Sagres*, 200; staff, 208, 210
Diário dos Açores, 88
Dias, António, 231
Dias, Eduardo Mayonne, 304
Diefenbaker, John G., 240, 249
Dighton Rock. *See* imperial heritage: Dighton Rock
Dinis, Edmund, 127–8, *128*
Directório Democrato-Social (DDS), 226, 234, 260–1, 370n101
Dos Passos, John, 178
Downs & Roosevelt, 214
draft dodgers. *See* Colonial Wars: war resisters
Drapeau, Jean, 276

Eanes, Ramalho, 4, 25, 61
East Providence, RI, 118, 121, 125, 161, 206, 279
ecumenism. *See* Catholic Church: ecumenical diaspora
EEC. *See* European Economic Community
EFTA. *See* European Free Trade Association
Eggleton, Art, *310*
Eisenhower, Dwight D., 52–3, 171, 186, 226
Elbrick, Charles, 196
Ellis Island, 18, 55, 313–14
Emigrante, O (Lisbon), 273
Emigration Junta: Canada, 46, 50, 91, 96; colonial settlers, 79; operations, 38–9, 43, 148; views on emigration, 39–40
England. *See* Great Britain
English as a Second Language, 166

Estado Novo: Catholic Church (*see* Catholic Church: Estado Novo; Fátima); Cold War, 14–16; colonial empire, 14, 16, 35 (*see also* Colonial Wars; lusotropicalism); corporatist ideology, 11–12, 146; cultural policies (*see* censorship and propaganda; Instituto de Alta Cultura; ranchos folclóricos); diaspora building, 4–5, 23, 33–4, 39, 112, 116, 118, 127, 130–4, 142–3, 146, 217; dictators (*see* Caetano, Marcello; Salazar, António); education policies, 13, 77, 148, 245; elections, 16, 226–7; emigration, 25, 33–4, 38–47, 50–2, 72–3, 306, 322 (*see also* Emigration Junta); football (*see* football: Estado Novo); industrialization, 16, 27, 39–40, 145, 181; Ministerial Council, 11, 42–3, 174; Ministry of Corporations and Social Welfare, 13, 39, 43; Ministry of Finance, 10–11, 85; Ministry of Foreign Affairs (*see* Portugal, Ministry of Foreign Affairs); Ministry of the Interior, 38, 40, 42, 208–9; Ministry of National Defense, 137, 187; Ministry of National Education, 85, 147; Ministry of Overseas, 4, 85, 179, 188, 212, 216–17; Ministry of the Presidency, 85, 147; National Assembly, 11, 20, 107, 174, 219, 228, 251, 257; National Secretariat of Emigration, 43, 175, 220; nationality laws, 39, 58, 64–5, 311; origins, 10–11; political repression (*see* Polícia Internacional e de Defesa do Estado; Tarrafal); reforms, 13, 16, 19, 148, 175, 185, 188–9; SNI/SEIT (*see* censorship and propaganda);

social and economic policies, 12–13, 16; United Nations (*see* United Nations: Estado Novo)
ethnic entrepreneurs: businesses, 120, 124, 180, 127, 268; concept, 112; Estado Novo, 180, 318; language, 165; social status, 120, 125, 141, 208, 289, 318
European Economic Community (EEC), 15, 65, 67, 316
European Free Trade Association (EFTA), 15, 276
Eusébio, 163
Exsul Familia, 78, 82
external voting: Canada 4; Portugal, 59–60, *60*, 63, 66, 296–7, 301; world, 3

fado: "April in Portugal," 157–8; Estado Novo, 157, 160, 164, 182; mainstream, 157–9, 268; performers, 157–9, 257, 275, 309
Fairclough, Ellen, 253, 255
Fall River, MA: businesses, 87; Cape Verdeans, 202; Catholic Church, 81, 86, 103, 167; celebrations and rallies, 200, 206; consulate (*see* consulates: Fall River); education, 167, 175, 270; ethnic culture, 159; exiles, 279, 292; football, 163; marching bands, 164–5; migration and settlement, 28, 55, 86, 269; political representatives, 52, 130, 206; radio and television, 122; secular organizations, 130, 161, 279, 285, 292; unions, 113; workers, 28, 34, 113–14, 346n4, 372n10
Fall River Democratic Movement, 292
Farage, Nigel, 10
Faria, Lourdes, 275
Fatela, Frederico, 93, 101, 271, 284

Fátima: apparitions, 77, 139, 339n6; churches (*see* Our Lady of Fatima, Catholic churches); emigration, 79; Estado Novo, 77, 79–80, 84, 160; Hollywood, 82, 341n21; Marian cult, 77, 340n20; pilgrimages, 154; sanctuary, 80, 97, 100
FBI (Federal Bureau of Investigation). *See* Polícia Internacional e de Defesa do Estado: FBI
Feast of the Blessed Sacrament, 104–6, 131, 205, 274
Feast of the Holy Ghost. *See* Festa do Divino Espírito Santo
Félix, Júlio, 246
Félix, Valentina, 275
Fernandes, Florestan, 277, 374n36
Fernandes, Joseph, 125, 133
Fernandes, Luis: American officials, 52, 193, 196; Catholic priests, 81, 83–4; community relations, 116, 130–2, 163–4; consuls, 131; ethnic press, 154, 156, 209
Ferro, António. *See* censorship and propaganda: Ferro, António
Festa do Divino Espírito Santo, 103–5, 118, 298
Feteira, Lúcio, 256
Figo, Luis, 70
First Portuguese Canadian Club (FPCC): anti-fascists, 237, 244; Azoreans, 119, 304, 347n18; Canadian officials, 276; charity, 108; football, 120, 162–3, *163*; founders, 118–19, 124, 159; post-revolutionary period, 302, 304; school, 172, 271
First Republic: anti-clericalism, 10, 13, 148, 341n21; conservative, 11; emigration, 30; exiles, 34–5, 178, 226, 230–1, 234, 260, 291; First

Index 391

Republic, 10, 13, 77, 147–9, 336n59; opposition, internal, 227, 234, 256; revolution, 10, 231, 292
FLA. *See* Frente de Libertação dos Açores
FLAD. *See* Luso-American Development Foundation
Fonseca, Manuel da, 179
Fonseca, Mary L., 127
football: Belenenses, 163–4; diaspora, 182, 311, 325; Estado Novo, 160–1, 164–5, 274; France, 162; Montreal, 161; New Bedford, 162; Portugal national team, 69–70, 325; Sport Lisbon Benfica, 161–3; Sporting Club of Portugal, 163; Toronto, 120, 139, 158, 161–3, 297–8; US national team, 161
Ford, Gerald (president), 299
Foreign Affairs Ministry, Portugal. *See* Portugal, Ministry of Foreign Affairs
FPCC. *See* First Portuguese Canadian Club
FPLN. *See* Frente Patriótica de Libertação Nacional
France: Azorean, 350n7; bidonvilles, 37, *37*, 42; diaspora, 217, 337n67; Estado Novo, 43, 80, 175, 186, 217, 309, 337n67, 349n51; exiles, 58, 224, 229, 247, 255, 258, 278, 362n2; external voting, 296; football, 162; immigrants, Portuguese, 37–8, 42–3, 56–7, 66, 122, 174–5, 277, 296, 349n51; Portugal Day, 309; remittances, 277; schools, 174–5, 272, 373n17
Francisco, Peter, 193
Franco, Francisco, 7, 216
Freitas, Vamberto, 304
Frente de Libertação dos Açores (FLA), 298–300, 304–5

Frente Patriótica de Libertação Nacional (FPLN): CPDP, 232, 249; external front, 229, 253, 265; MDP, 256, 264, 277; membership, 234, 258; PCDA, 244, 246–7, 249–51, 264, 277
Freyre, Gilberto, 185, 220, 374n36
Furtado, Augusto, 53, 82
Furtado, Johnny, 131–2
Furtado, Nelly, 69, 323

Gabaccia, Donna, 6, 263
Gagnon, Raoul, 97–9
Galt, ON, 212, 239
Galvão, Henrique: Brazil, 227–8, 234, 256; colonialism, 203, 228, 232–4; CPDP, 203, 232–5, 258, 260–1; Delgado, Humberto, 227–8; PCDA, 236–7, 244; *Santa Maria*, 187, 209–11, 227, 230, 232, 237–43, 251, 260; Social-Democratic Action, 234, 261; surveillance, 258, 260, 370n101; United Nations deputation, 233–5, 261
Garin, Vasco V. *See* ambassadors
Garrahy, Joseph, 287
Gaston, North Carolina, 192–6, 222
Germany: collaborative neutrality, 186; external voting, 3; jet fighters, 355n8; Portuguese emigrants, 37, 42, 57, 175, 272, 296, 337n67, 373n17
Gilbert, Dorothy, 270
Giles, Wenona, 265, 267, 315
Giraud, Yvette, 157
Globe and Mail, 237, 239, 251, 293, 298
Gloucester, MA, 104, 131, 285
Goans, 135, 188, 296, 332n33, 355n12
Gomes, Domingos Costa, 134–5, 237
Gomes, Francisco, 159
Gomes, Luis, 208
Gomes, Ruy, 253

Gomes, Varela, 367
Gonçalves, Adelino Billy, 161
Gonçalves, Lourenço "Rodrigues,"
    172, 177
Gonçalves, Vasco, 21, 295
Grace, Frank "Parky," 205
Great Britain: diaspora, Portuguese,
    311, 337n67; emigration to
    Canada, 47, 55, 73; exiles, 229;
    Portugal, relations, 13, 15–16, 27,
    153, 186–7, 199, 237
Greece: exiles, 277; homeland, 156;
    immigration to the United States,
    55, 270; Portuguese Americans,
    204, 288; Portuguese Canadians,
    277, 285
Grossman, Allan, 276
Guinea Bissau: colonial empire,
    201, 330n9, 332n33, 337n67;
    Colonial Wars, 17, 186, 186, 217;
    lusophonie, 337n75; PAIGC, 202,
    287, 288
Gulbenkian Foundation:
    Gulbenkian, Calouste, 341n27;
    high culture, 176; libraries, 179,
    202; Lusitania Institute, 85–6;
    propaganda, 217; schools, 172

Haiti, 277, 279, 285
Halter, Marilyn, 202
Hamilton, ON, 96, 134, 239, 340n11,
    342n40, 350n1
Harbord Collegiate Institute
    (Toronto), 272
Hargis, Billy, 212
Harney, Robert, 6
Harper, Stephen (prime minister), 4
Hartford, CT, 33, 82, *150*
Harvard Crimson (Cambridge, MA),
    197, 205, 289
Hawaii, 27–9, 212, 217
Heap, Dan, 290, 295

Helms, Jesse, 299
Henry the Navigator. *See*
    imperial heritage: Prince Henry
    quincentennial
Herculano, Alexandre, 30
Heyward Associates, 206
HGBB. *See* Holy Ghost Beneficial
    Brotherhood
Higgitt, William, 260
Higher Council for Emigration. *See*
    Catholic Church
Hispanic: activism, 270; community,
    283, 285–6, 314; Hispanidad, 216,
    218; pan-ethnicity, 286, 314–15,
    323–4; race, 288; studies, 170
Hitler, Adolf, 7, 11, 235, 237
Holton, Kimberly, 300
Holy Christ of Miracles. *See* Senhor
    Santo Cristo dos Milagres
Holy Ghost Beneficial Brotherhood
    (HGBB), 118, 125, 161
Holy See. *See* Catholic Church:
    Vatican
honorific titles: Catholic prelates, 81,
    87, 167; critics, 289; newsmen, 207,
    214; worker, 131–2
Horthy, Nicholas, 7
Hua, Ann, 6
Huddleston, Trevor (bishop), 249
humanitarian relief. *See* Catholic
    Church: charity and humanitarian
    relief
Hungarians, 3, 225

IAC. *See* Instituto de Alta Cultura
Iacovetta, Franca, 150
ICEM. *See* Intergovernmental
    Committee for European
    Migration
imagined transnational
    communities, 6, 8–9, 145, 184, 223,
    326

Immigrant Aid Society, 91
imperial heritage: advocates, 127, 197, 222, 230–1, 234, 263–4, 279, *310*, 314, 318; Dighton Rock, 197, 201, 230, 234, 356–7n28; Prince Henry quincentennial, 152, 199–202, 207, 211
Inácio, Hermínio Palma, 228, 256
India, 186, 188, 200, 206, 220, 332n33
Indigenous peoples: American, 188, 212, 222, 251, 357n28; African, 186, 221, 286
Institute of Hispanic Culture. *See* Hispanic: Hispanidad
Instituto de Alta Cultura (IAC): high culture, 176; language, 175; libraries, 179–80, 219; mandate, 149; schools, 168–9, 171–4, 180, 219, 271
Intergovernmental Committee for European Migration (ICEM), 54
Interior Ministry. *See* Estado Novo: Ministry of the Interior
International Catholic Migration Commission. *See* Catholic Church
International Committee for European Migration, 54
International Institute of Metropolitan Toronto, 90, 240–1, 243
Intersindical, 20, 303
Ireland: Catholics (*see* Catholic Church: Irish); diaspora, 7–8; Kennedy, John F., 18, 88–9; music, 158; prelates (*see* Catholic Church: prelates, Irish); Rogers, Francis, 288
Ironbound. *See* Newark: Ironbound
Italy: Catholic Church, 93, 97, 340n8; diaspora, 156, 322, 331n25; empire, 221; fascism, 7, 221, 235; immigrants, 53, 55; music, 158; neighbourhoods, 204, 268, 303; prominenti, 221; race, 183, 288; radicals, 263; sports, 161; unions, 302

Jacobson, Matthew, 18, 145, 313
Janeiro, António, 99–100
Jaques, Emanuel, 303
Jardim, Alberto João, 309
Jehovah's Witnesses, 247
Jewish exiles and refugees, 8, 52; gymnasium, 100
JFK. *See* Kennedy, John F.
Jocists. *See* Catholic Church: Jocist movement
Jodoin, Claude, 241
John XXIII (pope), 78
Johnson, Lyndon B. (president), 55, 175, 189, 220
Jones, LeRoi. *See* Baraka, Imamu A.
Jornal Açoreano (Toronto), 299
Jornal Português, O (Toronto), 96, 121, 281, 297

Keith, Hastings, 189, 207
Kennedy, John F. (president): anti-colonialism, 84, 186–9, 203, 211, 213; Azorean Refugee Acts, 53; Catholic Church, 84, 87; Estado Novo, 187–9, 233; immigration policy, 55; Irish roots, 18, 88–9; Peace Corps, 85; Portuguese Americans, 53, 84, 127–8, 203, 211–13
Kennedy, Ted (senator), 211
Kensington Market. *See* Toronto, ON: Kensington Market
Kimball, George, 93, 247, 373n35
Kriolu. *See* Cape Verdeans: Kriolu

Laborers' International Union of North America Local 183, 302, 326

Ladeira, Ernesto, 200
Lajes Air Base, 15, 124, 187–9, 233, 261, 299
Latin, European, 7, 46, 131, 314, 323, 357n28
Latinoization, 324, 325
Latinx(s) (Latinos, Latinas): activism, 87; immigration, 55, 283, 314; *Latinismo*, 323; legal minority status, 286, 314; Portuguese, 7, 283, 301, 314, 322–5
laymen. *See* Catholic Church: laymen
LCA. *See* Luso Canadian Association
League for Socialist Action, 259, 293
Leblanc, Thomas, 100–1, 284, 344n65
Leckie, Dan, 290
Léger, Paul-Émile (cardinal), 97, 100
Leite, Manuel de Freitas, 93–4, 343n52
Leo XIII (pope), 77
Lévesque, René (premier), 278
Lewis, Stephen, 189
Leza, B. *See* Cruz, Francisco X
Liberal Party of Canada, 47, 127, 250
liberation theology. *See* Catholic Church: social doctrine
Lima, João, 60
Lima, Lester, 205
Lisbon Geographic Society, 183, 188, 193, 209, 216–17, 219
LIUNA Local 183. *See* Laborers' International Union of North America Local 183
Lourenço, Eduardo, 330n9
Lourenço, Joaquim, 85, 93–4, 343n52
Ludlow: Catholic church (*see* Our Lady of Fatima, Catholic churches: Ludlow); Estado Novo, 84, 212; football, 163–4; Lusitania Institute (*see* Rocha, Manuel: Lusitania Institute)

Luís de Camões School. *See* schools, Portuguese language: Newark
Lusitania Institute. *See* Rocha, Manuel
Lusitano, O (Montreal), 121, 242
Luso-American Development Foundation (FLAD), 65, 325
Luso-American Education Foundation, 171
Luso-American Fraternal Federation / United National Life Insurance, 117, 171
Luso-Americano (Newark), 120, 214, 242
Luso Canadian Association (LCA), 92, 119–20, 124
Luso-Canadiano (Montreal), 241–3, 251, *252*; APC, 119, 241; circulation, 120, 241; Estado Novo, 210, 242–3; MDP, 242, 252–3; PCDA, 246–7, 257; rivalries, 119, 242
lusophonie, 67–9, 74, 118, 288, 306, 314, 322–4
lusotropicalism: diaspora, 218, 223, 316; Estado Novo, 24, 186, 218, 221, 316, 321; imperial heritage, 218; Portuguese Americans, 193, 197, 204, 223, 322; thesis, 185
Luxembourg, 42–3, 337n67
Luz, Maria, 173

MacDonald, David, 249–51, 257, 374n35
MacGuigan, Mark, 250
Macmillan, Harold, 186
Madeira Club of Toronto, 162
Madeiran Day, 105–7, *106*, 206
Madeirans: activism, 206; diaspora, 62; exiles, 236; football, 161–2; immigrants and descendants, 91, 134, 173, 178, 211, 236;

imports, 155; Madeira Field, 105; nationality, 193, 198; post-revolutionary period, 62, 304, 309; priests, 92; ranchos folclóricos, 144, 274; secular organizations, 116–17, 119, 128, 162, 346n9; separatism, 304, 377n90
Maia, Salgueiro, 291
mainlanders: businesses, 160; civil society, 92, 108, 110, 113, 116–17, 119, 128–9, 134, 142, 167, 182, 236, 281, 321; education, 120, 177, 272, 306; ethnic media, 121, 242, 283; exiles, 134, 236, 279; external voting, 296; language, 146, 182, 306; migration, 45, 55, 166; regional rivalries, 132, 146, 304; religious celebrations, 94, 105, 304; women, 272; workers, 115
Maison des Portugais. *See* Mouvement démocratique portugais
Manitoba, 51, 151, 236
Marchand, Jean, 256
marching bands, 101, 164–5, *165*, 182, 199, 272
Maria, Dina, 275
Maria I (queen), 29
Marino, Roberto, 97
Marques, Domingos, 281–4, 308
Martin, Joseph W., 52–3, 130, 189, 200, 206
Martins, Oliveira, 30
Marxists: Brazil, 374n36; Portugal 20–1, 302, 322; Toronto, 243–4, 281, 283, 296, 298
Mascarenhas, Rui, 158
Matateu, 120
Matos, Norton de, 116, 123
Matteos, Salahudin, 287
Matthews, Milton. *See* Matteos, Salahudin

McCormack, John W., 189
McGuigan, James (cardinal), 93–4
MCP. *See* Movimento Comunitário Português
MDP. *See* Mouvement démocratique portugais
Medeiros, Armando, 107
Medeiros, Humberto, 86–9, 304
Medeiros, João, 281–3, 290, 303, 308
Medina, Henrique, 258
Meirim, Joaquim, 297–8
Melo, Antero de, 93, 97
Melville, Herman, 190
Mendes, Eula, 113, 346n3
Mendes, Ferreira, 121
Mendes, Mavílio, 236, 364n35, 366n56
Mendes, Shawn, 69–70
Mexican American Youth Organization, 87
MFA. *See* Revolution of the Carnations: Movimento das Forças Armadas
Micaelense. *See* Azoreans: language
Miguéis, José Rodrigues, 178, 230
Mile End. *See* Montreal: Mile End
Ministerial Council. *See* Estado Novo
Ministry of Corporations and Social Welfare. *See* Estado Novo
Mira, Manuel, 125, 135, 356n23
missionaries. *See* Catholic Church: priests
Mississauga, ON, 51, 124, 272
Mocidade Portuguesa, 11, 82, 235, 276
Moniz, Carolina, 173
Moniz, Júlio Botelho, 187, 228
Moniz, Marcelino, 91
Monteiro, Jaime, 161, 237, 256, 296, 343n54, 369n84

Montreal, QC: air flights, 160; anti-fascists (*see* Mouvement démocratique portugais); businesses, 48, 123–4, 278; churches and religious feasts, 97–101, 103–4, 271, 284; city, 114, 135, 153, 160; consulate (*see* consulates: Montreal); education and schools, 172, 271; entertainment, 160, 275, 278; ethnic leaders, 45, 99, 118, 123, 127, 129, 289 (*see also* Bello, Henrique Tavares; Teixeira, Manuel; Viana, Rui Cunha); ethnic media, 121–2, 179, 273, 285, 297 (see also *Luso-Canadiano*; *Voz de Portugal*); external voting, 296; football, 161; immigration and settlement, 46, 48, *48*, 50–1, 90, 124, 224, 254–6; Mile End, 111, 285; Plateau Mont-Royal, 269, 276; Portugal Day, 139, 275–6, 289; ranchos folclóricos, 151–2; secular organizations, 123, 129, 284, 289, 375n54 (*see also* Association portugaise du Canada); visits by homeland officials, 291

Morais, Carlos, 206

Moreira, Adriano: Lusitania Institute, 85; Minister of Overseas, 188, 212; pilgrim nation, 4, 183, 216–17, 220, 234, 265, 273, 311, 317

Morocco, 228–9, 236, 246, 256, 366n56

Moura, Amadeu, 278

Mouvement démocratique portugais (MDP): anti-torture, 277; CPRPS, 284; cultural programming, 278; FPLN, 247, 256, 258, 264, 277; Maison des Portugais, 119, 236, 242; membership, 236, 246, 253, 258, 264; PCDA, 245–7, 253–5, 264, 277, 279, 291–2, 294; post-revolutionary period, 291–2, 294, 303; protests, 245; Quebec separatism, 277–8; surveillance, 256, 258, 260; war resisters, 236, 254–6; women's role, 304

Movimento Comunitário Português (MCP), 281, 283–4, 290, 303, 306

Movimento das Forças Armadas (MFA). *See* Revolution of the Carnations: Movimento das Forças Armadas

Mozambique: civil war, 58; colonial government, 17, 20, 220, 230, 332n33, 335n41, 337n67; Colonial Wars, 17, 186, 189; corporations, 210; football, 120, 163; immigrants, 323; lusophonie, 337n75; Mondlane, Eduardo, 187; retornados, 58, 300

multiculturalism: Canadian government, 19, 143, 146, 167, 267, 305–6, 315; Cape Verdeans, 311, 321; critics, 150–1, 180, 267, 315; Estado Novo, 180, 321; folklore, 145, 150–1, 180, 264, 321; homeland politics, 140, 263; host nation politics, 266–7, 315, 313; lusophone, 67–8, neighbourhoods, 268; New England programs, 19, 270, 311, 321; Ontario programs, 306; proto-multiculturalism, 23, 112, 150; Quebec programs, 309; US government, 19, 270

Mundo Português. See *Emigrante, O* (Lisbon)

Murray, A.S., 255

Museum of Diaspora and Portuguese Language, 71

Mussolini, Benito, 7, 221, 235 welfare state, 116, 274; women's role, 345n76

Namora, Fernando, 177
Nation of Islam, 287
national parishes. *See* Catholic Church
National Secretariat of Emigration (SNI). *See* Estado Novo: National Secretariat of Emigration
National Secretariat of Propaganda. *See* censorship and propaganda
nations of immigrants, 4, 18–19, 55, 88
natives. *See* Indigenous peoples
NATO. *See* North Atlantic Treaty Organization
Navarro, Modesto, 59
NDP. *See* New Democratic Party
Nehru, Jawaharlal, 188, 206
Nemésio, Vitorino, 304
Neves, José Maria (bishop), 75, 79
New Bedford, MA: assimilation, 34, 36; business, 87; Cape Verdeans, 203–5, 287; education, 168–70, 172–5, 270, 346; ethnic media, 120, 122, 209, 272–3; football, 161–3; migration and settlement, 28, 55; political representatives, 52, 207, 272; priests, 100; public celebrations and rallies, 200, 206–7; religious celebrations, 101, 105, 203; republican opposition, 35; unions, 113; workers, 28, 34, 113–14, 131–2, 270
New Democratic Party (NDP): antifascists, 241, 250, 277; Colonial Wars, 189; FPLN, 250; post-revolutionary period, 290, 292–3; progressive generation, 283–4, 290, 303; RCMP, 259
New Haven, CT, 33
New York City, NY: air flights, 160; Azorean separatism, 300; Cape Verdeans, 192, 202; Catholic Church, 80, 210; education, 167, 169, 290; ethnic media, 120, 210, 258; exiles, 35, 178, 224, 231, 249, 264, 279; external voting, 296; football, 163–4; language, 85, 167, 174; migration and settlement, 5, 28, 32, 55, 81; mutual aid societies, 116, 133; post-revolutionary period, 220, 325; propaganda, 147, 206; public celebrations and rallies, 136, 152, 199–200, 212, 220; ranchos folclóricos, 274; secular organizations, 178, 192, 202, 285, 290; United Nations, 233, 235, 249–50, 261; workers, 28, 32, 178
New York Times, 220, 268
Newark, NJ: Cape Verdeans, 204; Catholic Church, 81–2; education, 168, 171; ethnic media, 120, 170, 200, 210, 214, 242; external voting, 296; football, 163; Ironbound district, 114, 268, 276; migration and settlement, 32, 55, 300; protests, 204–5; public celebrations and rallies, 137, 139, 200; ranchos folclóricos, 275; workers, 114
Newfoundland, 44, 49, 198–9, 281, 345n72
Nixon, Richard M., 19, 88, 176, 189, 285, 299
Nóbrega, Ângelo, 95, 134–5, 303
Noivo, Edite, 9, 323, 325
Nogueira, Cândido, 94
Nogueira, Franco, 187, 213
North Atlantic Treaty Organization (NATO): allies, 15–16, 21, 139, 187, 189, 213, 224, 246, 254, 320; arms sales, 186, 188–9, 249; Portuguese government, 15–16, 67, 213, 249, 291, 304
North Easton, MA, 133
Notre-Dame Basilica, 97–8, *98*

Novo Mundo (Toronto), 111, 177
Novos Rumos (Newark), 120, 200, 210, 214
Nunes, Eurico, 129, 257–8

O Desterrado (*The Uprooted*) (Reis), 30, *31*, 32
Obra Católica Portuguesa de Migrações. *See* Portuguese Catholic Organization for Migrations
OCPM. *See* Portuguese Catholic Organization for Migrations
OECD. *See* Organisation for Economic Co-operation and Development
OEEC. *See* Organisation for European Economic Cooperation
O'Leary, Thomas (bishop), 83
Oliveira, Firmino, 243–4, 257, 297
Oliver, Michael, 304
Omowali. *See* Matteos, Salahudin
O'Neill, Thomas "Tip," Jr, 189, 213
Ongoing Revolutionary Process. *See* Revolution of the Carnations: revolutionary transition
Órban, Viktor, 3
Order of Christ, title. *See* honorific titles
Organisation for Economic Co-operation and Development (OECD), 50
Organisation for European Economic Cooperation (OEEC), 15
Ottawa. *See* Canada, federal government
Our Lady of Fatima, Catholic churches: Bridgeport, 82; Cumberland, 82; Elizabeth, 82; Hartford, 82; Ludlow, 83–4, *83*, 104; Newark, 82, 205; Peabody, 82

Our Lady of Good Voyage of Gloucester, Catholic church, 104
Our Lady of Immaculate Conception of New Bedford, Catholic church, 104
Our Lady of Mount Carmel, Catholic churches: New Bedford, 167–8; Toronto, 92–3, 97
Overseas Companies of Portugal, 210, 212–14, 217
Oxfam, 108

PACFA. *See* Camacho, Martin T.
padrão, 309, *310*, 379n124, 379n125
PAF. *See* Portuguese American Federation
PAIGC. *See* Cape Verdeans: independence
Partido Social Democrata (PSD): emigration 3, 62, 64, 301; post-revolutionary period, 62, 70; revolutionary transition period, 21, 301
Partido Socialista (PS): exile, 57; external voting, 59, 297, 301; post-revoutionary period, 60–1, 73; revolutionary transition period, 21
Pascoaes, Teixeira de, 32
Pastore, John, 53
Pato, Rui, 292
Patrias, Carmela, 225, 262
Patrício, Rui, 176, 276
Paul VI (pope), 86
PCC. *See* Portuguese Canadian Congress
PCDA. *See* Portuguese Canadian Democratic Association
PCP. *See* Portuguese Communist Party
PCU. *See* Portuguese Continental Union
Peabody, George, 206, 209, 258

Peabody, MA, 82
Pearson, Lester B. (prime minister), 151, 240, 250–1, 260, 355n12
Pennsylvania: Estado Novo, 212; ethnic federations, 285; exiles, 363n12; immigration, 196; mutual aid societies, 116, 274; Portugal Day, 136; rancho folclórico, 274
Pereira, Maria Celeste, 308
Pereira, Pedro Teotónio: Catholic priests, 83; ethnic press, 209; Gulbenkian Foundation, 341n27; language schools, 172; propaganda, 212–14; *Sagres*, 137; Salazar's successor, 188; SNI/SEIT, 147
Pereira, Victor, 37, 39, 162, 362n2
Perin, Roberto, 225
Perry, Joseph, 53
PIDE. *See* Polícia Internacional e de Defesa do Estado
Pier 21, 45, 313
pilgrim nation. *See* Moreira, Adriano
Pimenta, Ida, 211
Pimentel, António, 54
Pina, Luis Câmara, 215–17
Pinilla, Rojas, 235
Pius XI (pope), 77
Pius XII (pope), 78
Plateau Mont-Royal. *See* Montreal
Polícia Internacional e de Defesa do Estado (PIDE): assassination, 229, 249, 260; emigration, 38, 40, 43, 254–5; FBI, 235, 260–1, 265; fear of, 14, 123, 225, 227, 229, 231, 243, 253, 255, 300; political prisoners, 16, 20, 134, 188, 228, 244, 246–51, 257, 260, 277, 367n66; political repression, internal, 14, 16, 123, 179, 227, 229, 243; post-revolutionary period, 291, 299–300; RCMP, 254, 259–61; security measures, 16, 246, 249;

surveillance, 209, 231, 253–4, 256–61, 320, 326, 367n59, 368n74; torture, 16, 228, 257
Polish immigrants to the United States, 55
Polish-Canadian White Eagles football club, *163*
politics of the spirit. *See* censorship and propaganda: politics of the spirit
Ponte, Marcelina "Marcie," 283–4, 309
Portugal, Ministry of Foreign Affairs: ambassadors (*see* ambassadors); APCS, 176; Casa de Portugal, 147; Catholic Church, 81, 85, 93, 100–1; diaspora, 42, 71, 217; embassies (*see* embassies, Portugal); emigration, 39, 91; empire, 187, 213; exiles, 223; language, 85; Portuguese Americans, 34, 131, 206, 209, 258, 276, 291; post-revolutionary period, 67, 71; Salazar, António, 34; United Nations, 233
Portugal Day: Brazil, 71; Montreal, 139, 275–6, 289; New York City, 136; Newark, 137, 139; origins, 336n59; Pawtucket, 136; post-revolutionary period, 61–2, 71, 309; Providence, 137; San Francisco, 171; Toronto, 136, 139–41, 289, *305*, 309, 325; Vancouver, 275; Washington, 211
Portugal Democrático (São Paulo), 179, 231–2, 241
Portugal Investment Corporation, 278
Portugal Republicano (São Paulo), 231
Portuguese American Athletic Club, 161

Portuguese American Civic Leagues: of Massachusetts, 126–7, 211; of Rhode Island, 126, 198, 230
Portuguese-American Committee on Foreign Affairs (PACFA). *See* Camacho, Martin T.
Portuguese American Federation (PAF), 133, 219, 288
Portuguese-American League, 285
Portuguese Archipelago, 55, 114, 335n48
Portuguese Benefit Association, 117, 171
Portuguese Canadian Congress (PCC), 134–6, 140–1
Portuguese Canadian Democratic Association (PCDA): amnesty conference, 246–51, 374n35; Azoreans, 244–5; community relations, 129, 136, 140–1, 236, 244–5, 247, 277, 295, 298; Delgado, Humberto, 237, 239, 245; FPLN, 244, 246–7, 249–51, 264, 277; Galvão, Henrique, 236, 239; literature, 179, 244–5; mainstream media, 237, 239–40, 251, 293; MDP, 241, 245–7, 253–5, 264, 277, 279, 291–2, 294, 298; membership, 159, 235–7, 243–6, 257, 259, 264, 277–8, 284, 291, 304, 366n56, 367n59; post-revolutionary period, 291, 293–8; programs, 172, 243, 291; protests, 238–41, 243, 291, 293–4; *Santa Maria*, 237–41, 243; surveillance, 256–61, 298, 350n66; war resisters, 254–6; women in, 304, 364n28
Portuguese Catholic Action. *See* Catholic Church
Portuguese Catholic Organization for Migrations (OCPM), 75, 79–80, 96, 98
Portuguese Club of Mississauga, 272
Portuguese Communist Party (PCP): censorship, 179; emigration, 58; exiles, 57, 161, 229, 236–7, 246–7, 253, 278–9, 292; opposition, internal, 13–14, 20, 226–8; post-revolution, 301; revolutionary transition, 21–2, 299; surveillance, 254
Portuguese Communitarian Movement. *See* Movimento Comunitário Português
Portuguese Communities Activities Council, 285
Portuguese Continental Union (PCU): Azoreans, 116; Cape Verdeans, 116, 204; education, 171; Estado Novo, 116, 130–2; language, 167; mainlanders, 116; membership, 116–17, 133, 204; sports, 161
Portuguese Democratic Movement. *See* Mouvement démocratique portugais
Portuguese Educational Society of New Bedford, 170
Portuguese "foreign stock" by state, 29
Portuguese Guinea. *See* Guinea Bissau
Portuguese Interagency Network, 285
Portuguese Liberation Army, 293
Portuguese Official School of New Bedford. *See* schools, Portuguese language: New Bedford
Portuguese Refugee Aid Committee, 300
Portuguese Socialist Action, 234
Portuguese Times (New Bedford), 288
Portuguese United of New Bedford, 162

Portuguese Workers Club, 178
Portuguese Youth Cultural
  Organization, 285
Pozzetta, George, 267
PREC. *See* Revolution of the
  Carnations: revolutionary
  transition
Prince Henry the Navigator. *See*
  imperial heritage: Prince Henry
  quincentennial
Pro-Culture Society, 129
Progressive Conservative Party, 46,
  127, 129, 135, 241, 250
Protestants: assimilation, 76, 108;
  Catholics, 102; missionaries, 91,
  93, 190, 209, 246; opposition,
  93–4, 236, 246–7, 279; Portuguese
  congregation, 93, 236; social
  workers, 76, 90–1, 108
Provincetown, MA, *126*
PS. *See* Partido Socialista
PSD. *See* Partido Social Democrata

Quadros, Jânio, 186, 227
Queiroz, António Eça, 178
Quiet Revolution, 114

radical ethnic brokers, 225, 263, 280, 315, 320–1
radio: Emissora Nacional, 207;
  Estado Novo, 147, 157, 207,
  214–15; exiles, 122, 236, 257, 285;
  language, 93, 177; personalities,
  121, 124, 158–9, 272, 275, 291,
  293, 303, 343n54; propaganda,
  210–11, 214; stations and shows,
  92, 120–2, 124, 127, 133, 160,
  214–15, 236, 285, 291, 293,
  347n25
Rádio Televisão Portuguesa
  internacional (RTPi), 68–9, 323
Rafael, José, 124

ranchos folclóricos: Azoreans,
  164; Connecticut, *150*; Estado
  Novo, 148–9, 151–2, 156, 160–1,
  181–2, 274; Hamilton, 144, 350n1;
  invented tradition, 149, 181;
  Montreal, 151; multiculturalism,
  149–51; New Bedford, 274;
  Newark, 275; rurality, 149;
  Toronto, 124, 151, 199
RCMP. *See* Polícia Internacional e de
  Defesa do Estado: RCMP
Reagan, Ronald (president), 88, 201,
  357n40
Régio, José, 179
Rego, Mariano, 158–9, *159*
Reis, Soares dos, 30–2, *31*
remittances: banks, 277; Brazil, 32,
  34; Colonial Wars, 17, 40; credit
  unions, 123; diaspora, 317, 325;
  economic impact, 40–1, 320;
  emigration policy, 39–40, 42;
  France, 277; opposition, 58, 277,
  295; post-revolutionary period,
  58–9, 63–4, 291, 306, 311–12, 322,
  336n63; Salazar, António, 34, 73
Republican Party: congressmen, 52,
  189, 206, 213, 299; lobbying, 211,
  213; Portuguese Americans, 125
republicans, Portugal. *See* First
  Republic
retornados, 56, *56*, 57–8, 71, 73, 80, 300
Revolution of the Carnations:
  April 25th, 4, 20, 43, 55, 289, 290,
  292, 309; Movimento das Forças
  Armadas, 20–1, 59, 291–3, 298;
  post-revolutionary period, 24, 51,
  57, 66, 80, 281, 301–7, 312, 316, 327;
  revolutionary transition period,
  5, 20–1, 25, 59, 73, 266, 283, 291–7,
  322
Revolutionary Action Party, 279
Ribeiro, António, 94, 96

Ribeiro, Artur, 238, 242
Ribeiro, Maria Alice, 92, 94, 127, 243, 348n38
Riley, Thomas J. (bishop), 199
Robarts, John P. (premier), 134
Roberto, Holden, 186–7
Rocha, João: Estado Novo, 154, 156, 208–9, 214; lusotropicalism, 193; propaganda, 154, 156, 213–14; publisher, 208–9
Rocha, Manuel: Americanization, 104; Estado Novo, 83–6; Fátima, 82–4, 341n21; Ludlow, 82–3; Lusitania Institute, 85–6, 343n52
Rodrigues, Amália, 157, 275
Rodrigues, António (bishop), 79
Rodrigues, José Neves, 242–3, 246, 278
Rodrigues, Sarmento, 201
Rodrigues, Urbano Tavares, 292, 296
Roediger, David, 183, 222
Rogers, Francis M., 196–7, 205, 288
Rogers, George, 205
Ronaldo, Cristiano, 70
Roosevelt, Franklin D. (president), 113
Rosa, Gomes, 255–6
Royal Canadian Mounted Police. *See* Polícia Internacional e de Defesa do Estado: RCMP
RTPi. *See* Rádio Televisão Portuguesa internacional
Rural Settlement Society of Canada, 91
Rusk, Dean, 213, 233
Russell, Bertrand, 247, 249

Sagres, 137–8, *138*, 200, 232, 234
Salazar, António: Catholic faith, 12, 77–8, 99; corporatist ideology, 12, 146; diaspora, 33–4, 39, 217; education, 13, 77, 148, 245; elections, 226; emigration and remittances, 33–4, 40, 42–3, 73, 107, 148, 217, 254, 306, 312; empire and lusotropicalism, 16, 35, 185–6, 188, 217, 316, 330n9; football, 161; foreign affairs, 15–16, 54, 107, 186–9, 199, 207, 213, 233; industrialization, 39–40; memory, 309; minister of finance, 10–11; PIDE, 14, 254; Portuguese Americans, 121, 184, 206, 208–10; Portuguese Canadians, 99, 238–40; propaganda, 10, 145–7, 153, 161, 206, 209, 213, 321; reforms, 16, 185, 188; successors, 13, 19; traditionalism, 12, 145–6, 161, 181, 321
Salvini, Matteo, 10
Sampaio, Jorge, 290
Santa Cruz Mission, 100, 271, 284
Santa Maria. *See* Galvão, Henrique: *Santa Maria*
Santos, Fernando Piteira, 229, 246
Santos, Guilherme Antunes, 243–4, 246, 259, 366n56, 367n59
Saturnia, 45, 123, 159, 254, 308–9
saudade: emigrants, 42; fado, 157; Portuguese Americans, 200, 285, 310; propaganda, 147; *saudosismo* movement, 32, 333n5; tourism, 154, 157, 306
Scalabrinians, 78–9, 340n8
schools, Portuguese language: Azoreans, 167, 172, 175, 182, 271–2; Estado Novo, 43, 169, 172–5, 180, 215, 219, 271; Fall River, 167, 175; Gaston, *194*; heritage language programs, 270, 272, 286, 306; IAC (*see* Instituto de Alta Cultura); Lusitania Institute (*see* Rocha, Manuel: Lusitania Institute); Montreal , 99, 101, 172,

271; New Bedford, 167–70, *168*, 172–3, 175; New Jersey, 169; New York, 169; Newark, 168, 172, 171–2; newcomers, 19, 169, 271; post-revolutionary, 60, 290–1, 295, 305; Providence, 175; Toronto, 92–3, 120, 172–3, 271–2
Scowcroft, Brent, 299
SCP. *See* Sport Club Portuguese
Second Vatican Council. *See* Catholic Church: social doctrine
Secretariado de Estado de Informação e Turismo (SEIT). *See* censorship and propaganda: SNI/SEIT
Secretariado Nacional de Informação, Cultural Popular e Turismo (SNI). *See* censorship and propaganda: SNI/SEIT
SEIT. *See* censorship and propaganda: SNI/SEIT
Selvage & Lee, 203, 210–14, 360n72
Sena, Jorge de, 178
Senhor da Pedra feast, 105
Senhor Santo Cristo dos Milagres, 96–7, *98*, 101–3, 158, 164, 295, 345n71
seniors, 12, 280
Serra, Maximino Rosa, 236, 364n35
Serrão, Joel, 32
Service d'Acceuil aux Voyageurs et aux Immigrants, 90
Silva, Cavaco, 71
Silva, Emanuel da, 145–6
Silva, Fernando, 32
Silva, José (bishop), 78–9, 98
Silva, Manuel Luciano da, 197–8, 357n28
Silva, Martin, 303
Silva, Pedro da, 308
Silva, Rogério, 304
Skrentny, John, 270, 314

Smallwood, Joseph (premier), 198–9
SNE. *See* Estado Novo: National Secretariat of Emigration
SNI. *See* censorship and propaganda: SNI/SEIT
Soares, Mário: exile, 58, 234, 279; president, 65; prime minister, 59, 73; revolutionary transition period, 57, 291
soccer. *See* football
Social Democratic Party. *See* Partido Social Democrata (PSD)
Social-Democratic Action, 234, 261
Socialist Party. *See* Partido Socialista (PS)
Society for the Perpetuation of Portuguese Heritage, 192, 202
Society of St Vincent de Paul: Montreal, 100, 284; Portugal, 12, 107, 332n28; Toronto, 92, 172
Sökefeld, Martin, 9, 223
Somerville, MA, 114, 285
Sousa, António, 123–4, 254, *310*
Sousa, Charles, 124
Sousa, John Philip, 164, 193, 352n41
Sousa, Marcelo R. de, 71
South Africa, 37, 37, 185, 217, 279, 337n67
Soviet Union: African liberation movements, 186, 203, 212, 234; Azores, 304; Cold War, 14–15; Fátima, 339n6; Portuguese Communist Party, 20, 226; revolution, Portugal, 21, 290
Spain: Delgado, 229, 245; diaspora, 132, 156, 216, 218; diplomats, 245; exiles, 187, 238, 245, 277, 374n35; language, 171, 270, 283, 314, 323–4; migrants, 37, 37, 178; music, 158; Portugal, relations, 153, 186, 217, 337n67; seafaring, 356
Spanish. *See* Hispanic

Spellman, Francis (cardinal), 80, 85
Spínola, António: Colonial Wars, 20; exile, 293, 300; revolutionary transition, 21; Toronto, 293–4, *294*, 297
Sport Club Portuguese (SPC), 168, 172
Sport Lisbon Benfica. *See* football
Sporting Club of Portugal. *See* football
St Agnes of Toronto, Catholic church, 97, 303
St Anthony's Mission of New York, 210
St Christopher House, 90, 280
St Elizabeth's of Bristol, Catholic church, 84
St Francis Xavier of East Providence, Catholic church, 118
St Helen's of Toronto, Catholic church, 97
St John of God of Somerset, Catholic church, 54
St John's Night feast, 105
St Mary's of Toronto, Catholic church: charity (*see* Society of St Vincent de Paul); marching band, 164; Portuguese service, 92–4; school, 271; social services, 96; youth, 281
St Michael's of Fall River, Catholic church, 86
St Vincent de Paul Society. *See* Society of St Vincent de Paul
State Department. *See* United States, federal government
Steinbeck, John, 190
Stone, Gil, 210, 258, 360n70
Switzerland, 229, 337n67

Tabico, António Câmara, 275
TAP. *See* Transportes Aéreos Portugueses

Tarrafal, 16, 188, 228, 249
Tchuba (New Bedford), 301
Teixeira, Bernardo, 193–6, *194*, 214
Teixeira, Manuel, 97–9, *98*
Teixeira, Roy F., 203, 232–3, 301
television: Estado Novo, 207, 214; exiles, 251; language, 273; mainstream, 151, 158, 207, 214, 251, 291, 324, 326; personalities, 159, 291, 293; propaganda, 210, 214; RTPi (*see* Rádio Televisão Portuguesa internacional); stations and shows, 121, 273, 291, 293
textile workers, 28, 32, 34, 86, 113
Themido, João Hall. *See* ambassadors
Thurmond, Strom (senator), 299–300
Torga, Miguel, 179
Toronto, ON: air flights, 159; antifascists (*see* Portuguese Canadian Democratic Association); businesses, 123–4, 156, 160; Canadian Conference for Amnesty in Portugal, *248*; churches (*see* Our Lady of Mount Carmel, Catholic churches: Toronto; St Agnes of Toronto, Catholic church; St Helen's of Toronto, Catholic church; St Mary's of Toronto, Catholic church); consulate (*see* consulates: Toronto); demonstrations, *135*, *240*, *250*; diaspora, 9; education and schools, 172–3, 271–2, 306; entertainment, 158–60, 275, 292, 309; ethnic leaders, 45, 124, 127, 129, 134–5, 241, 281–4, 303 (*see also* Cunha, Alberto; Ribeiro, Maria Alice); ethnic media, 121–2, 161, 177, 179, 273, 297 (see also *Comunidade*; *Correio Português*; *Jornal Português, O*);

external voting, 296, 301; football, 161–3, 297; immigration and settlement, 46, 51, 90, 123, 224, 240–1, 267, 280, 283–4, 296, 300, 309; Kensington Market, 111, 122, 124, 162, 236, 268, 276, 283–4, 298; marching bands, 164; municipal government, 114, 140, 153; padrão monument, 310; ranchos folclóricos, 151, 199; religious celebrations (*see* Senhor Santo Cristo dos Milagres); Scarborough, 236; secular organizations, 92, 129, 162, 272, 284, 298–9 (*see also* First Portuguese Canadian Club; Movimento Comunitário Português; Portuguese Canadian Congress); visits by homeland officials, 61, 212–13, 291–2, 309; workers and unions, 115, 267, 269, 302, 325–6

Toronto Star (*Toronto Daily Star* pre-1971), 103, 129, 256, 292, 343n54

Toronto Telegram, 237

Torres, Aurélio, 286

tourism: advertisement, 154, 156–7, 208; clandestine migration, 48, *48*, 50; economic impact, 149, 153, 307; multiculturalism, 104, 180, 268, 321; propaganda, 153; religious, 154, 339n6; saudade, 154, 202, 306–7; SEIT/SNI (*see* censorship and propaganda)

Transportes Aéreos Portugueses (TAP), 159, 176, 228, 274, 306–7

travel agencies: Casa de Portugal, 153; clandestine migration, 48, *48*, 50, 119; ethnic entrepreneurs, 112, 120, 124, 242, 244; organized trips, 154, 278; SNI/SEIT, 156, 244; social services, 92, 94; TAP, 307

Tribuna Portuguesa (Montreal), 297

Troper, Harold, 263

Trudeau, Pierre E. (prime minister), 19, 50, 263, 295

Truman, Harry S. (president), 51–2, 231

Trump, Donald (president), 3

Turkey, 3, 217, 257

UCP. *See* Union Catholique Portugaise

União Nacional, 11, 85, 215, 235, 298

Union Catholique Portugaise (UCP), 97–100

Union of Peoples of Angola, 186

Union of Portuguese Cultural Communities, 219–20

United Church of Canada (UCC), 90, 91, 93, 247

United Kingdom. *See* Great Britain

United Nations (UN): anti-colonialism, 14, 16, 185–7, 203, 234; Azorean liberation, 299; Estado Novo, 15–16, 185–8, 203; exiles, 233, 249, 250, 256–7; lobbying, 211; Portuguese Americans, 210, 215; refugees, 54; revolution 290

United States, federal government: Central Intelligence Agency (CIA), 187, 254; Civil Rights Act (*see* civil rights movement); Department of Justice, 211, 235, 261–2; education legislation, 170, 175; employment equity legislation, 267; FBI (*see* Polícia Internacional e de Defesa do Estado: FBI); Foreign Agents Registration Act, 211, 261; Foreign Intelligence Advisory Board, 176; House of Representatives, 52, 213–14, 348n34; immigration legislation, 51–2, 54, 113; Library of Congress, 170; Refugee Relief Act, 52; State Department, 53, 171, 193, 196, 209, 214, 233, 261

University of Coimbra, 157–8, 171, 175, 177, 228, 246
UPCC. *See* Union of Portuguese Cultural Communities
Uruguay, 217, 229

Valério, Frederico, 158
Vatican. *See* Catholic Church: Vatican
Vatican II. *See* Catholic Church: social doctrine
Vargas, Eugénio, 236, 246
Vaz, Amadeu, 160
Vaz, António, 241, 251, 297
Veiga, Alfredo. *See* ambassadors
Vellucci, Alfred, 286
Venezuela: clandestine migrants, 50; diaspora, 217, 337n67; Estado Novo 217; exiles, 227, 229, 236; immigration, Portuguese, 37; re-emigrants, 47; returnees, 71
Verdade, A (The Truth). *See* Portuguese Canadian Democratic Association: literature
Vezzosi, Elizabetta, 225
Viana, Rui Cunha, 237, 278–9, 285, 303
Vieira, António, 167
Vieira, Arlindo, 278
Vieira, Domingos, 99
Vietnam War, 87, 89, 189, 205
Voz de Portugal (Montreal): Azorean, 177; Estado Novo, 119–20, 210, 238, 242–3, 255, 276; post-revolutionary period, 295, 297; priests, 100

Walsh, Thomas (archbishop), 81
war resisters. *See* Colonial Wars: war resisters
Warner, Joseph E., 201
Washington. *See* United States, federal government

Waterbury, CT, 15, 82, 271
Weinfeld, Morton, 263
whaling, 27–8, 137, 288
White Fleet, 44, 47–9, 104, 199, 281, 345n72
women: auxiliary committees, 6, 105–7, 118, 126–8, 364; cleaning workers (*see* cleaning workers); construction, 325; diaspora, 6, 217, 317; domestic workers, 46; education, 13, 17, 173, 269, 272; employment equity, 267, 286; entertainers, 157–8, 160, 275; exclusion, 6, 63, 103, 105, 118, 127–8, 217, 364; factory workers, 28–9, 114, 269, 284, 302; heritage, 200, 288, 309; household economy, 29; marriage, 39–40, 46, 166; memory, 308; migration and settlement, 28–9, 40, 46, 90, 166, 267, 283; motherhood, 36, 39, 65, 196, 200, 203, 239, 283, 288, 307–9; nationality, 39, 65; prominent, 63, 92, 94, 113, 127, 157–8, 170, 243, 275, 283–4; queens, 30, 103–5, 203, 345n76; religion, 103, 105–7, 247; secular organizations, 92, 106, 126–8, 304, 345n76; social work, 269, 280, 283; unions, 113, 302, 269, 284–5, 302; women's rights, 63, 297
Working Women Community Centre, 283, 284–5
Wynne, Kathleen (premier), 124

X, Malcolm, 201, 287
X, Milton. *See* Matteos, Salahudin

Yaremko, John, 136, 141
Young Christian Workers. *See* Catholic Church: Jocist movement

www.ingramcontent.com/pod-product-compliance
Lightning Source LLC
Chambersburg PA
CBHW020349080526
44584CB00014B/945